THE PORTABLE
NORTH AMERICAN
INDIAN READER

The Portable
NORTH AMERICAN
INDIAN READER

Edited and with an Introduction by

FREDERICK W. TURNER III

THE VIKING PRESS • NEW YORK

First published in the United States in 1974 by
The Viking Press, 40 West 23rd Street, New York,
New York 10010

Portable is a registered trademark of Viking Penguin, Inc.

Printed and Bound in the United States of America

Library of Congress Cataloging-in-Publication Data

The Portable North American Indian reader.

Bibliography: p.
1. Indians of North America.   2. Indian literature.
3. American literature—Indian authors.   I. Turner,
Frederick W., 1937–
[E77.P79   1986]   810'.8'03520397   86-13266
ISBN 0-517-61888-5
h g f e d c b a

In honor of the memory of
Jennie Spotted Elk
April 30, 1951–December 14, 1968

Acknowledgments

Assembling a collection of this sort is inevitably a humbling task as it becomes progressively clear how terribly incomplete one's knowledge of the North American Indian must be. In acknowledging the debts I owe to the following persons I, of course, do not make them parties to whatever errors I may have committed.

To my teachers, then—Roy Harvey Pearce and Anthony F. C. Wallace—for introducing me years ago to various aspects of American Indian studies; to Thomas Berger, whose superb novel, *Little Big Man,* rekindled my interest in the Indian and showed that it was possible to present the Indian as he was and find him all the more admirable; to Peter Farb, whose criticism of these contents I have tried to meet; to Joseph Langland, Paul Mariani, and William Preston for advice and criticism; a very special debt to Lionel Williams whose contacts with young Indian writers made possible their representation here; to John Seelye for first suggesting to the publishers that I undertake this task; and finally, to Barbara Burn, whose editorial advice and patient understanding made this all completely pleasurable.

FREDERICK W. TURNER III
Amherst, Massachusetts

Contents

III | CULTURE CONTACT

IV | IMAGE AND ANTI-IMAGE

Introduction

1

My purpose in assembling this reader is both simple and ambitious. It is to introduce the general American reader to the traditions and the historical realities of the North American Indian. The story of the South American Indian is equally important, but it is another story—and perhaps another book—and there are several good reasons why North Americans need to know first some of the root realities and truths of the land that is now theirs. Such a purpose has of itself defined the scope of this book, in which I have sought to include as many aspects of American Indian traditions and history as is possible within two covers.

We begin at the beginning of Indian time with a sampling of myths and tales drawn from various groups. These are perhaps as near as we can now get to a sense of the way the world seemed, the way it looked and felt and smelled to the original inhabitors of these lands before the white man began his irresistible intrusion. These narratives range from the poetic to the ribald; from the creations of mighty confederacies to those of obscure wanderers; from the woods of the Northeast to the merciless stretches of the Southwest and to the northern shores of the Pacific, where the smell of fish mingles wonderfully with shape-shifting monsters who not surprisingly often take the forms of the creatures these Indian knew and hunted. So strange and strangely compelling are these narratives—for all timeless stories must seem to us both strange and strangely familiar—that the temptation is great simply to make up the whole out of these and let the reader find the other materials as he will. I have resisted this temptation, however, because it seems to me that what is crucially needed is the fullest and most accurate portrait of the Indian that we can possibly construct from the remains of the past and the realities of the present. Nevertheless, the opening section, Myths and Tales, is intended as a historical and referential base for all that follows, something the reader should always have at the back of his mind as he encounters other sorts of records and to which he can turn to remind himself of primary orientations and modes of perception, of the differences between the Indian's image of himself and the ways others have seen him, and of the important distinctions to be made between kinds of truth and between cultural systems.

The section Poetry and Oratory is really an extension of this first section since it presents us with additional examples of Indian artistry. There is a difference, however, for in the speeches we find the intrusive figure of the white man, and their poetry is the poetry of saddened dignity, of defeat, and of resignation. These are qualities largely foreign to the myths and tales and to the poems per se, and so this section should serve as a marker or a kind of burial mound to remind us of all that beauty and human vitality that had to be destroyed, as William Carlos Williams has written, "because of the names men give their emptiness."

The hovering presence of which the Indian orators speak takes its own voice in the section Culture Contact. If the reader has already experienced the first two sections of this collection before he listens to the voices of the white explorers and settlers, he will be able to sense something of that feeling of outrage which is so evident in the words of the dispossessed Indian. For these white voices speak as if they were describing a cultural and historical vacuum, as if nothing in America had actuality before their own intrusions. Neither Bernal Diaz at the beginning of the whole process nor Lewis and Clark at its logical conclusion gives us any real sense of people with equal rights to existence and self-determination; nowhere in their accounts can we imagine the possibilities of myths, tales, poetry, all the rich creations which were there for sympathetic eyes to see. The truth is that in describing the Indian and his lands the white man was describing himself, his own drives and consuming desires.

The effects of such tunnel vision should be altogether too familiar to present-day Americans, and yet the truth of ethnocentrism and its consequences remains for most of us either a theory or wholly fictional. That it *is* truth—that the attitudes of Diaz and of Lewis and Clark have disastrous even tragic consequences—can be understood by reading the narratives of the Winnebago brother and sister which conclude this section. *Here* are the consequences in that most immediate of translations—personal experience—and in that most ancient of human tongues—agony.

The collection's final section, Image and Anti-Image, brings us full circle, a form in itself particularly appropriate to a book about the Indian. We begin here with the conflicting popular images of the Indian in white literature and subliterature, pass to contemporary re-evaluations of these old images, but end up in the hands of the subject himself: after hundreds of years of being written about the Indian writes back. It is an echo twisted in the canyon of time and circumstance into a refutation of much that has gone before, flinging back into white faces the challenge that has been there all along. Nowhere has it been better expressed than in the heavy words of the defeated old war chief Black Hawk when he first met President Andrew Jackson: "I am a man, and you are another."

2

If we think about it for a moment, it will appear odd that after more than four centuries on this continent it should seem necessary to introduce anyone to what must have been the first and most engaging fact of the New World itself: the people who lived here. And yet, to judge from the evidence of American history past and present, this is precisely our need. The American government is still pursuing an Indian policy that alternates between brutal neglect and racist paternalism; private enterprise and state and local governments are still raping the natives' remaining natural resources; at the broadest levels of our popular culture we still find redactions of that most cherished myth of how we won the country from the skulking savages; and deep in the hearts of too many of us there resides the notion that all that is significant in American culture has been the achievement of the Anglo-Saxon white. What all this points to, of course, is our ignorance concerning the North American Indian and the part he has played in the shaping of the American experience. Nor is this an isolated phenomenon, but rather another illustration of our general refusal to face up to our past and its meanings. Here as in so many other instances the majority of Americans have refused to confront the continuing, fundamental challenge and contradiction which the American Indian is and represents to our republican democracy. Our strategies of avoidance have ranged from attempted genocide to the creation of various racist stereotypes, but even after two hundred years of this the challenge, the contradiction remain. After two hundred years of sovereignty the newer Americans still have neither understood the original ones nor solved the predicament presented by the existence of a people with a prior claim to territory and the dignity and endurance to voice that claim through all the intervening years of defeat, diseases, blasphemous treaties, and the building up around them of an enormously complicated and impersonal federal bureaucracy. Yet the voices of the tribes are heard, however faintly, disturbing us like the dripping of a broken faucet in a far-away room.

It is our sense of this coupled with our inability to initiate reformative changes that makes so many of our collective responses oddly poignant. We seem rather like some benign, blinded Polyphemus who gropes in utter darkness toward expressions of good will. And let none mistake this: American good will is a reality, whatever the rest of the world may call it, whatever we ourselves may call it—racism, genocide, callous economic opportunism. These are the ghastly blunders of the giant doomed to commit them out of historical ignorance and fear. This is indeed tragic, for the truth is that the average white American, whether Newark hardhat or California grape-grower, genuinely wants everybody to be happy in this sprawling country; wants, for example, the Indian to have his share of the national pie—except that there is the way the country developed, the way Western Europeans first came to it, what they did here, the very names by which we know ourselves. All this militates constantly, silently, against everything that in our hearts we want for all men. And all this the average American either knows nothing about or avoids.

Once, on a dusty back country road in Wyoming I met this agonized condition of my country in the muzzle of a gun held in the glare of a pickup truck's headlights: our car's generator had gone out, and I was guiding us by flashlight when I was confronted by a motorized cowboy, his finger on the trigger of a pistol, a shotgun racked up behind him and a canister of Mace on the seat. It seems we had passed through a portion of his spread, and the dim spot of my flashlight had awakened his sense of territory and individualism. Just weeks before thieves had taken off with a pair of his skis, and so now he was ready to confront this potential marauder. In that little moment which he has undoubtedly forgotten, something larger than both of us was abroad in the country darkness; it was something of the past with all its gnarled realities—call it cultural history if you like—a powerful, subterranean force whose existence he would have vehemently denied. Like too many of us the cowboy had no real belief in the past and its ability to shape actions and events in the present. More precisely, his sense of the past was rigorously selective and thus almost wholly fictional.

Somewhat later I learned in conversation with the cowboy that he was a decent and essentially well-intentioned man. Yet in that summer night in a territory barely wrested from the first dwellers I had been transmogrified by ignorance into the Indian as these men had been taught to see him—a ruthless and casual depredator who threatened what good men had put together. In the darkness of our antihistorical civilization the cowboy had only been acting out his second nature. As were those other cowboys who a few days later in nearby Casper captured a roving hippie and pulled his long hair out by the roots.

In view of these situations one is forced to the conclusion that many of the actions that have made up the American experience have been misguided and uninformed.

We could begin, for convenience, with Columbus, who, as Albert Murray reminds us, "set out for destinations east on compass bearings west." Driving toward the fabulous riches of the Indies, Columbus found a tropical island, the original name of which was never even recorded before it was rechristened San Salvador. The name of the first tribe to greet this white man in unsuspecting amazement was the Arawak, but little else remains of them or their history, so quickly and completely were they engulfed by the events that followed in the wake of the Spanish ships. But because Columbus was a man with a dream, a dream that had haunted men of his world for centuries, the tribe became . . . just Indians, a generic designation which prevented the whites from ever *seeing* them for what they truly were.

This was only the second mistake. Others followed with the rapidity which only the loosing of long-pent-up desires can bring: Mexico became New Spain, the Southwest became the locale of the Seven Cities of Gold, the southeastern peninsula became Florida, the Island of Flowers, and somewhere in its recesses nestled the Fountain of Youth. And all the while the tribes were losing their several identities and becoming just Indians. They still are, and the misnomer should serve as a continual reminder to us of how ignorant we remain of the realities of this land we live in.

The consequences of this ignorance are so vast and tangled that to attempt to explore them is to become another De Soto, lost and sweating in a jungle of lianas and palmetto groves. Still, if we are to free ourselves, if we are to find ourselves and so escape the heavy oppression that ignorance always entails, we must begin somewhere and what better place than with the original inhabitants themselves? But here at the very outset of our exploration one meets with a consequence of our ignorance and of the mad haste and greed with which we swarmed over the continent: the aboriginal past of the American tribes in something of its full and accurate detail is forever lost to us. No whites in those early days thought it worth the effort to record the histories, traditions, customs of nonliterate and often hostile "savages." What we now have is what archaeologists and anthropologists have been able to piece together; the spare, bleak accounts of some old soldiers and explorers; fragmentary tribal legends all but obliterated by the destruction of the tribal cultures. The picture we have of the tribes in the first moments of contact is thus like some ruined hieroglyphic, legible only in parts and then only to specialists, with other areas a mute and unforgiving blankness. Nor can we escape the blame for this great loss by reminding ourselves that the social sciences, which would have made possible the preservation of all this precious material, had not even been invented, for what does it say about a civilization that it can develop the science and the technology to get to distant lands but not the intellectual equipment to understand these lands and their peoples when it does arrive? I say nothing here of the justifications for colonization or of the spiritual equipment necessary for such tasks.

And so there are these gaps, these blanknesses, and they are there because they are in us as well, in the civilization we have made. What, for example, were the conditions of the tribes of the interior in 1600? What was the culture of the Pequots like before King Philip's War? What of the Cherokee before 1830? We can supply fragmentary answers at best but the worst is that so few Americans still can care whether these questions might have answers. They will only see and lament our present-day condition—a divided and deeply troubled nation, streaked with racial, sectional, and class antagonisms, uncertain of its global position, morally enfeebled. The roots of all this lie buried in our past, and despite the disheartening losses of which I speak, it is our first imperative to try to trace what we can.

3

Lately, it has seemed that efforts have been made in this direction. The very existence of a collection such as this one indicates that a demand now exists for Indian materials. In recent years a swelling stream of books and films has had the effect of bringing the Indian to the attention of the general public and in so doing altering the older stereotype of the red man as a stone-faced, monosyllabic horseman of the Plains. Actually, this process has been under way for some time, since people like Natalie Curtis, Frances Densmore, Oliver La Farge, and John Niehardt caught between the covers of books the last whispers of ancient tribal ways. But this earlier work went largely unnoticed, and it has remained for Americans of the late 1960s and early '70s to discover such classics as *The Indians' Book, Laughing Boy,* and *Black Elk Speaks* in shiny new paperback format. We are always being surprised by our history, and here it seems surprising that such works could have done little more than gather dust in the interval between then and now.

If I could think of one book that forcefully turned national attention toward the Indian it would be Peter Farb's *Man's Rise to Civilization* (1968). Farb, a naturalist-anthropologist, presented a fact-filled, cross-cultural survey of the Indians of the Americas in a style available to the nonspecialist. There were, of course, other works surrounding this one, but *Man's Rise to Civilization* seemed to catch a development and carry it to a trend. Other books have followed, many of them not as responsible as Farb's, in what has now become almost a publishing flood: collections of materials on the Indian problem such as Jack D. Forbes' *The Indian in America's Past* and Wilcomb Washburn's *The Indian and the White Man;* reprintings of older Indian books long out of print such as Thomas Marquis' *Wooden Leg,* the aforementioned *Black Elk Speaks,* and Geronimo's autobiography; Vine Deloria, Jr.'s Indian manifestoes, *Custer Died for Your Sins* and *We Talk, You Listen;* books on the Red Power movement such as Stan Steiner's *The New Indians;* books about the use of hallucinogens in Indian cultures such as Carlos Castaneda's accounts of the Yaqui sorcerer, Don Juan—*The Teachings of Don Juan, A Separate Reality,* and *Journey to Ixtlan;* collections of Indian poetry such as William Brandon's *The Magic World* and John Bierhorst's *In the Trail of the Wind.* Most recently Dee Brown's immensely successful *Bury My Heart at Wounded Knee* has capitalized on this trend and is probably now *the* book most Americans would know in this connection.

And, of course, on college campuses, at rock festivals, on city streets and summer beaches vestiges of the Indian are to be seen in the forms of headbands, body painting, feathers, beads, fringed leatherwear, and moccasins. Posters showing blown-up images of Geronimo, Sitting Bull, and Chief Joseph can be had at head shops and record stores everywhere. The Indian has become a national fad.

In the process white Americans are succeeding once again in avoiding a knowledge of the complex truths of their collective history and are perpetuating the past's old mistakes which condemn them to ignorant actions at home and around the world.

In this latest instance it becomes clearer yet that Americans seem to find it necessary to indulge in some kind of moral fad, some crusade to occupy their attention. Such galvanic situations were provided by World Wars I and II and by the ensuing battle to Stop Communism. When this last effort began to show signs of losing its credibility Americans cast about and discovered in the shadows of their own moldering cities the Blacks. Here indeed was a problem which could call forth all of the good will and best wishes of natural democrats. Only it has turned out that this is not a moral fad which can be turned on and off; it cannot be merchandised and commercialized into obsolescence (though with the deluge of articles, films, and books it now appears that, like boxing and pro football, this issue has suffered from overexposure). No, this is not a crusade, but a genuine problem so fundamental and pervasive that it will be with us until we solve it, whether we choose to think about it or not. And because we would rather not think about it any longer, since thinking must lead to action in the nature of massive socio-economic reform, we now turn away from the Blacks and toward the Indian.

The situation here is much better. For one thing, there are so few of them left. And for another, they seem so far away from the centers of population. For these reasons the occasionally annoying militancy of their younger spokesmen can easily be countenanced. Finally, since we won the country from them we are in the altogether comfortable position of enjoying the fruits of our success while we lament the "plight" of the losers. Not that we are prepared to do anything to alleviate the plight, but the Indian *is* a convenient symbol as well as a suitably removed repository for the self-lacerating national guilt which white

Americans curiously prefer to constructive action. Now, scant years after the repopularization of the Indian, we can discern the new stereotypic image that we have made for him:

1. The Indian was the original ecologist, killing only what he needed, caring for the natural world through which he moved.

2. The Indian was the original communist with a small "c"; he lived in a highly communal atmosphere in which not only material goods and services were shared but also love and affection.

3. The Indian, although a superb fighter, did not wage aggressive warfare, fought only when attacked, and even then rarely pressed tactical advantages to the utter defeat of his enemies.

4. The Indian was a natural democrat, easily tolerating differences between individuals within the tribe and between the tribes themselves.

5. The Indian was noncompetitive, preferring the advancement of the whole group to his own.

6. The Indian, because he was prescientific, had a profound wisdom about the workings of the world and the universe; he divined essential rhythms which allowed him to live a happy, harmonious existence destroyed forever by the coming of the white man.

Two things are true of all stereotypes. One is that they fulfill some needs of the makers; and the other is that they are partially correct. It is obvious from the foregoing one that we have made the Indian over into an image that represents all that we are not but wish we might have been. Ecology; communal living; nonaggressiveness; equal opportunity; natural, non-Western wisdom—these are the catchwords and -phrases of our time, now all brought together in the New Indian. So now when the cavalry splashes through a shallow ford, spurs, sabers, and bits clinking, riding against a band of painted warriors (and their families) there are more boos than cheers, the latter response being reserved for the Indians, as in Arthur Penn's film version of *Little Big Man* or in *Soldier Blue*.

But history is never simple, its truths are not so easily come by, its lessons often painful. Least of all could this be the case when one tries to understand the realities of the North

American Indian, where one is dealing with hundreds of tribes speaking perhaps as many as a thousand mutually unintelligible tongues, and differing in cultures from sedentary agriculturalists to nomadic hunters, from tribal confederacies to wandering bands, from nations as large as twenty thousand to ones hardly more than a hundred.

We cannot afford to deal in such stereotypes any longer, for not only do they provide us with grossly inaccurate bases for action, but they are a way of avoiding action. In the end they have a way of turning into the hideous warrants for state racism. Let us try to refine this one just a bit, recognizing that generalizations about such diverse groups as make up the American Indian are open to numerous objections and qualifications.

The Indian *was* to a remarkable extent aware of and sensitive to his physical environment. He had to be because the level of his science and technology had not yet imposed a buffer between him and his land, and so he could never forget how inextricably connected he was with his particular physical world. In the Indian materials reprinted here nothing is more striking than this deep feeling for terrain and climate, particularly, I think, in the section Myths and Tales. In most cases the idea of waste was simply not a possible mental occurrence to the Indian, since tribal existence was often at little more than a subsistence level and was occasionally less than that. Many tribes, such as those of the upper Midwest, suffered severe seasonal deprivations. Yet it is also true that when the Plains tribes acquired the horse and the gun from the whites their killing of game began gradually to exceed their needs. There is also evidence, though this is in dispute, that even before the horse and the gun these tribes slaughtered more game in their surrounds and drives than could be used. In light of these facts and from what we know about ourselves it seems admissible to suggest that although the Indian did have that admirable (and now so clearly necessary) trait of reverence for the natural world, had his technology developed along other lines he might in time have arrived at that state of arrogance and contempt which characterizes all the technologically advanced nations of the world. It seems arguable at the very least that as soon as man can by his ingenuity free himself from the immediate grip of his environment his attitude toward it will undergo a corresponding alteration in the direction of carelessness.

There can be no doubt either that the communal life-style of the Indian cultures was one of their most attractive and compelling features, and it must seem particularly so to us in this day when the family as we have known it is under such continuous attack by those who are persuaded that the alternative of the extended family offers such manifold psycho-social benefits. These benefits seem to have been actual in many Indian cultures, but here once again the stereotype ignores significant contradictory evidence. The extended family living arrangement often brought with it the brutal treatment of elderly members of the group, while on the other end of the age spectrum it may well have resulted in certain fundamental identity problems for preadolescents (interested readers should consult George Devereux's *Reality and Dream: Psychotherapy of a Plains Indian* and the chapter "Hunters Across the Prairie" in Erik Erikson's *Childhood and Society*).

As to the amount and direction of aggression in Indian cultures nothing in a study of these emerges more clearly than the fact that a considerable degree of stress was placed on success in warfare and related activities by groups as diverse as the Iroquois and the Apache. I do not know of a single Indian tribe that did not practice warfare, did not bestow honors on those skilled in war, did not celebrate the defeat of enemies. There may indeed have been such groups, but they are far outnumbered by those for whom warfare was an essential part of tribal life. The great amount of violence in the myths, tales, and songs provides a key here. Nor was it just retaliatory warfare against the whites. Every bit of evidence we have suggests that intertribal warfare was a condition of aboriginal life before the coming of the Europeans, though there is no doubt that this was greatly exacerbated by the intrusion of the hairy men from the East.

We might even go a step further here and venture that in some cases the most attractive and remarkable achievements of certain tribal cultures were made possible in part by the existence of culturally sanctioned outer-directed aggression. Such a case, I think, might well be made for the Iroquois, who waged such cruel and terrible war against their neighbors while they were developing a form of government that inspired the admiration and emulation of America's founding fathers and a theory of psychoanalysis that anticipated many of the major discoveries of Sigmund Freud.

Here again, a larger question presents itself, a question that cannot even be discerned by those who persist in hiding behind stereotypes of their own creation: is man inherently aggressive and must this drive find its outlet against strangers if the home culture is to survive and flower? And if this be so in a nuclear world, then what?

In the matter of tolerance, perhaps the highest of communal virtues, it must be said that the Indian seems to have possessed it in unusual degree—but that it existed side by side with the weapon and the fear of ridicule. Deviations from the tribal norm seem to have been countenanced for those who could consistently carry off their idiosyncratic life-styles, berdaches and holy men, for example. But woe to those who might accidentally or in a fit of pique or passion fall away from traditional ways. Here the cruel ridiculing of the aberrant was often almost worse than death itself, and suicide among Indians was sometimes the result of just such situations. In the Myths and Tales section the Sioux tale called "High Horse's Courting" illustrates the feelings of panic and desperation that a social aberrant might feel. As a melancholy postscript to this aspect of Indian cultures let it be recorded here that certain Indian groups picketed showings of the film version of *Little Big Man* because they said it portrayed the Cheyenne as accepting transvestism. It did, and they did, which redounds to the credit of the old Cheyenne way as it does to the discredit of a sexually fearful white culture that has succeeded here as elsewhere in making the Indian ashamed of one of his great virtues.

The image of Indian cultures as dominated by the ideal of communal service rather than that of individual advancement is once again an exaggeration of a truth and an avoiding of crucial evidence. The value of sharing was certainly an important one in a great many tribes, as their traditions so clearly indicate, but modern ethnographic studies have shown (principally those collected by Margaret Mead in *Cooperation and Competition Among Primitive Peoples*) that competition, rivalry, and intense individualism were also aspects of tribal cultures, even among those groups generally characterized as cooperative. We must consider here too the male ideals of individual excellence in hunting and warfare, gambling and horse racing, and talk of noncompetitiveness surely would have made less sense to a young Sioux or Cheyenne than to a late-twentieth-century white American youth; such talk would have made even less sense to the chiefs of some Northwest Coast tribes or to the household heads from the same area who engaged in an unending struggle with their peers for rank and prestige.

The final aspect of the new stereotype is perhaps more important than any of the others and it is less easy to handle. How does one, after all, compare the wisdom and contentment of prescientific groups with those of a civilization which over the last five hundred years has come to pray to science as the tribes once prayed to their gods? What shall be our gauge here? Success in warfare? Invention and proliferation of people conveniences? Individual and collective accumulations of wealth and territory? Survival itself? Measured so, only the foolish or the willfully ignorant could say that the Indian's wisdom was greater, his happiness more complete, than those of his scientifically oriented counterpart, and it was Cortés, as shown in the section Culture Contact, who first saw how the technological disparity created by white science might become a psychological weapon more powerful in conquest than the actual mechanical instruments themselves. Time and again in the four-hundred-year history of this conquest we find the tribes baffled and terrorized by the scientific knowledge and technological ingenuity of their adversaries until at length this was the very thing which broke the spiritual vertebrae of the cultures, caused them to forsake their traditions and gods, and to seek new ones. The last episode in this aspect of the process was the Ghost Dance movement of the late 1880s which culminated in the slaughter at Wounded Knee. In this movement we find an admission by the tribes that the power of traditional wisdom was inferior to the knowledge of the antitraditional whites, and so they sought a new type of vision, the spiritual equivalent of an atom bomb, which would utterly wipe out these unfathomable tyrants. In this clash between visions and Hotchkiss guns the latter won.

But if one could talk precisely about the *quality* of life, then on this last point of relative wisdom and happiness, it might be possible to discover more than wishful thinking in the stereotype. In the myths and tales, in the poetry and oratory, we find a wisdom rooted so deeply in things that it goes quite through them and beneath them to what we are compelled by our own ancient memories and feelings to consider some kind of ultimate truth, an entrance into elusive contentment. And it is just here that what the Indian was merges with what he has always represented to his conquerors: the Indian lived a life saturated with violence, pocked by acts of cruelty to enemies, characterized in good measure by ethnocentrism, male chauvinism, and severe deprivation; he fought, tortured, owned slaves, lusted after glory and recognition, died; *but he never lost sight of the fact that all this was distinctively, essentially, radically human, that he was human and thus part of the universal community of the living.* Perhaps this is as good a definition of wisdom and earthly happiness as any. And this is the great and wonderful possibility which he represents for us. To talk of the Indian's humanity is to talk of nothing more or less than just this. Standing as we do on this side of the scientifically guaranteed technological barrier which we have raised for ourselves, we peer back over its glittering metallic edge toward a figure who looks to us for this very reason more human and who seems more fully sensitive to place and surroundings.

This, then, is the great lesson which the history of the American Indian has for us: the knowledge *and* the acceptance of what it is to be human in a world with many forms of life, but it is a lesson obscured by a lazy and craven subscription to a stereotype which in essence *denies* the Indian this most precious knowledge by making him over into something other than mortal. In denying him this we deny it for ourselves and so fail once again here (and how many more chances will there be?) to learn from our history. Still ensnarled in South-east Asia, with similar commitments made in other areas of the world, and with a bulging stockpile of ultimate weapons, Americans may need to learn this lesson more than any other people on earth.

4

I hope it is sufficiently clear from the foregoing paragraphs that I think the average American greatly needs a proper intro-duction to the American Indian and the part he has played in the American past. What part he may play in our future may depend in some small way, I suppose, on what a reader chooses to make of his experiences with the materials herein. Any book is potentially a manual for action, and I would hope that this one would not end by simply becoming yet another trickle in that literary torrent I have mentioned above.

The materials themselves have been culled from a wide variety of sources. Chief among these are the collections of government agencies such as the Bureau of Ethnology and scholarly organizations such as the American Folklore Society. Were it not for the dedicated and too-little-recognized work of the men and women of these groups much if not most of the Indian's traditions would have been irretrievably lost. Other sources include old books long out of general circulation as well as newer anthologies that resuscitate much that was hidden and forgotten. Throughout, my major preoccupation has been that of authenticity. When able to choose between versions of a tale, myth, or episode I have chosen that which strikes me as closest to the bone in spirit and intent—except in one or two instances where I have deliberately chosen a version that is warped by the intrusion of an alien culture. Since I am not a linguist, it is impossible for me to say whether the versions I have used in any ways violate the exact letters of the originals. This is an unavoidable problem in the presen-tation of Indian materials, for language, while it might not shape thought to the extent the metalinguists have claimed, yet is a powerful determinant of content. I do not mean blithely to dismiss here the linguistic barrier; I only claim that the potential gains to be realized in printing such a collection far outweigh the valid objections that specialists may raise. It is quite simply one of the many ambiguous conditions of the American experience that the original American for centuries has been unable to speak to us in his own tongue but has had to rely upon the interpretations of his conquerors.

I have no doubt that there will be many who find even these translations obscure and opaque to the point of uselessness. Particularly might this be the case in the opening selections of myths and tales. To these readers I suggest that they begin someplace where they are slightly at home, say with the folklore of the Sioux or the Blackfeet, or perhaps with Hyemeyohsts Storm's magnificent explication of a Northern Cheyenne tale in the final section. Having established some footing, they will then be able to work back to some of the more unfamiliar materials. If even this fails, take the book outdoors into whatever natural or seminatural setting can be found, and try to establish some mutual context for the words and the world around. Indian literature, after all, is literature inspired primarily by the outdoors. In any case, it will be necessary for the reader to make a sincere effort to divest himself of his strong, unconsciously held expectations as to what a myth or tale should be like, wha should happen in these, what the world looks like, what lives, and what is inanimate. Only by making such an effort can he hope to gain entrance to a world other than his own. And this is one of the supreme benefits which can come from a consideration of alien cultures, for it is, as Walter Goldschmidt has so beautifully remarked, in the gap between our own culturally conditioned view of the world and that of another with a radically different orientation that we may catch a glimpse of the way the world really is. That hope should be sufficient to keep us all exploring.

Finally, I have hoped, more by the selections included than by what I have struggled to articulate in this Introduction, to present the American Indian to other Americans as a human being in all his variety and not just as an image, a symbol, or a convenient stereotype. There are indeed selections here that do lend themselves to image-making, particularly those from white literature about the Indian, but otherwise I have deliberately sought to render the Indian "with the bark on," to show

I
MYTHS AND TALES

The reader uninitiated in the oral traditions of the American Indian stands now on the threshold of a strange and wonderful world. Like all significant passages, this one is not without its difficulties, and the alteration of perception may prove annoying to those who come to literature wanting only their prejudices confirmed, their expectations granted. To those who come in a spirit of genuine inquiry this world may well be a disturbing, even frightening one at first, in which, beset by strange shapes and bizarre occurrences, he searches in vain for old landmarks. If this reader, however, is not routed by his unease but instead remains to be instructed by it, he will at last have succeeded in making an entrance into the Indian's world insofar as words can take him there.

Almost all the difficulties to be encountered here are the results of the assumptions, values, and modes of perception which are our heritage from Western civilization. Whatever prior experiences we may have had with folk literatures are likely to be with those still within this large cultural context: we can all read and to a certain extent appreciate a translation of a German or French folk tale as well as tales from Italian or even Russian folklore. But American Indian lore is another matter, though it may be of some comfort that its themes and motifs are quite often those with which we are familiar.

To begin with, it is generally the case that the narrator of a myth (a narrative recognized by the teller as ancient and probably sacred) or a tale (a more contemporary narrative whether "actual" or completely imaginary) will supply in words only the bare skeleton of his story. This skeleton is made up largely of a recitation of external actions with a minimum (and sometimes a complete absence) of scene setting, description, or analysis of the characters' feelings. It is this more than anything else that gives the uninitiated reader the sense that he has been dropped into the middle of a dark forest with only a flickering match to guide him. He must remember, however, that he is reading *oral* literature and that the narrator is supplying supplementary information to his audience with his voice, his gestures, his facial expressions. Moreover, the audience that listens to him is so homogeneous and so familiar with the narrative or a similar version of it that it has no difficulty in filling whatever gaps might remain. Help for us as outsiders comes from the fact that it is these actions themselves which contain the meaning of the narrative or which suggest the symbolic application, just as they do in European folklore. So the reader can, with some trust, concentrate his attention on the actions and feel that he is on the right path, even if some of the cultural nuances inevitably escape him.

Another difficulty that the more literal-minded reader may encounter is that of the continual shape-shifting that characterizes almost every one of these narratives. Transformations, however, were not simply an artistic device for the Indian but an article of belief, even if this is safely removed to an older time when "such things were possible." Perhaps all that need be said here is that the Indian's sense of the range of phenomenal possibilities was far wider than ours today, though there lurks in the folklore of the Old World a vestige of this wider range. One must simply accept it here.

Then there is the matter of multiple worlds as in the wonderful Navaho evolutionary narrative of creation in which the reader is led by the hand as befits an initiate upward through four strange and beautiful worlds into the fifth in which we live. Here, as elsewhere, contemporary readers are probably better prepared to accept and understand the existence of these multiple worlds than any Westerners have been in the last two hundred years: the great coming together of Freudian/Jungian psychoanalytic theory, Eastern mysticism, space and sea explorations, and the popularization of mind-expanding drugs has opened many to the possibility that ours may

not be the only world there is. Here in these narratives
it is clear that the Indian lived in a very real and physi-
cally grounded world but that for him this was only
one of several. To have kept that strong and secure
sense of physical locale side by side with a belief in
other spheres must strike us as one of his great psychological achievements. Finally, in this connection it should
be noted that passage back and forth between worlds
was relatively easy in mythic times before the entrances
became blocked by man's mistakes, the gods' discretion,
or simply the light of modern history.

Most of the more familiar Old World folk tales have
morals either imbedded in them or lamely appended.
Most of the myths from the classical worlds of Greece
and Rome are in some way etiological. Indian folklore
shares these traits with the traditions of white Westerners
in the sense that even the most seemingly innocuous or
obscene tale contains value standards and prohibitions,
while many of the myths explicitly state their expla-
nations of natural phenomena or tribal customs. What
may not be so clear is that just as often the real moral
of these narratives is just that they are history itself, the
oral repositories of the records of the past. For a people
without writing this was more than sufficient reason to
keep them current—as it should be for us to read them.

Melville Jacobs once stated in his superb analysis of
Clackamas Chinook myths and tales that Indian folklore
should not be printed without a full accompanying description of the socio-cultural context within which the
materials originally existed. This, I take it, was advice
to specialists, and Jacobs surely had in mind also a
somewhat restricted audience, though it is equally certain
that the general reader whom I have in mind could profit
as much or more by such supporting material. But in this
case such additions would require a separate volume
altogether. Such volumes, in fact, already do exist and
interested readers (or perhaps perplexed ones) should
consult these where appropriate. I have made occasional
suggestions in the headnotes to the various selections,

Penobscot

A Maine tribe of the Abnaki confederation. The beliefs and lore of the Penobscot have been seriously eroded through almost four centuries of contact with whites. These narratives were collected in 1907 by Frank Speck from those few who recalled the ancient stories. Said one of these to Speck, " 'My friend, we ought to have all night to get to the bottom of that story.' "

The Origin of Corn and Tobacco

A famine came upon the people and the streams and lakes dried up. No one knew what to do to make it different. At length a maid of great beauty appeared and one of the young men married her. But she soon became sad and retiring and spent much time in a secret place. Her husband followed her one day and discovered that she went to the forest and met a snake, her lover. He was sad, but he did not accuse her; he loved her so much he did not wish to hurt her feelings. He followed her, however, and she wept when she was discovered. Clinging to her ankle was a long green blade of a plant resembling grass. She then declared that she had a mission to perform and that he must promise to follow her instructions; if so, he would obtain a blessing that would comfort his mind in sorrow and nourish his body in want, and bless the people in time to come. She told him to kill her with a stone axe, and to drag her body seven times among the stumps of a clearing in the forest until the flesh was stripped from the bones, and finally to bury the bones in the center of the clearing. He was told to return to his wigwam and wait seven days before going again to the spot. During this period she promised to visit him in a dream and instruct him what to do afterward. He obeyed her. In his dream she told him that she was the mother of corn and

From "Penobscot Tales and Religious Beliefs," *Journal of American Folklore* 48 (January-March 1935), 1-107.

tobacco and gave him instructions how to prepare these plants to be eaten and smoked. After seven days he went to the clearing and found the corn plant rising above the ground and the leaves of the tobacco plant coming forth. When the corn had born fruit and the silk of the corn ear had turned yellow he recognized in it the resemblance to his dead wife. Thus originated the cultivation of corn and tobacco. These plants have nourished the bodies of the Indians ever since and comforted their minds in trouble.

Turn Over, the Origin of Medicines

There was once a young girl who lived with her mother at the village. She used to like to go into the woods gathering medicinal plants. One time she wandered into the woods above the village at Indian Island, and gathered a quantity of roots. While she was strolling along a party of Mohawk, who were hovering near watching for a chance to attack the village, saw her and captured her. Then they turned back to their country and took her along. The last thing the girl did before being led away was to hide one of the roots of her stock in the bosom of her dress. On the road back to the Mohawk country they began to torture her. One time they made her hold her fingers in the blaze of the fire until the ends of her fingers were scorched. Then they named her Pa'kwa'ekasiasit, Arrowhead Finger. She stood the pain without crying. At last they arrived at the Mohawk village and all the people came to meet the warriors with yells to see if they had captives. So the young Penobscot girl was brought in and kept until they could decide what to do with her. They held council several days and finally the chiefs decided that she should be burned to death. And they appointed a day. But some of the Mohawk objected because the young girl was so brave and the day was put off. On the day chosen for her to be burned, the women of the village were sent into the woods to gather stumps for the fire, and the young girl went with them helping to bring in a load of wood for her own fire. They thought this very brave and so put the day off. At last the girl bore a son. He was a small, undersized baby and grew old very fast. In a few weeks he could talk as well as any of the people and was the same as a full grown man only he was small. This son was the piece of medicine root that the girl had put in her bosom. She had not had any husband, it was a magic medicine son. At last the girl was adopted by an old man and woman who had no children left. Their sons had all been killed in the wars with the eastern Indians. So they adopted the girl and her baby as their own and so she was in no danger of being burned again. She was very good to the old people and they came to love her as their own child. So they lived for some time until the chiefs said that some captives must be burned and they decided upon the young girl. Now the old man and woman begged the girl to run away before the day set for her death. "You escape and we will take care of your son," they said. But she refused, saying that she would stay. They talked with her for several nights until at last she consented. The Mohawk did not keep watch over the girl because they saw she did not want to go. She went every day into the woods to gather firewood. So the old woman said, "Start the next time you go for wood. Now you run all day on the path that runs eastward. The first day you will come to an open place in the forest where there are a lot of bones. As you go through do not look behind you, no matter what you hear. That night, hide in an old cabin you will see. The next day keep on and you will rest that night. The next day you will come to a lake. There you will be met by a young man in a canoe. He will take you to a camp and then you will be among your own people, the Penobscot, and they will send you home." So she started off as the old woman told her.

The Mohawk did not learn of her escape for a while so she had a good start. She was very sorry to leave her son but they urged her to go. The first day she came past the place of bones, and there lay the skulls all grinning and clacking as she passed. But she did not look back even though she could hear them right behind her. Later she came to an old cabin all fallen in, and crept beneath it into a hole, and there she slept. The next morning she heard horses' hoofs on the trail and lay low in the hole. Then she saw ten Mohawk each

on a horse come by single file and they hurried past down
the trail looking for her. But she lay still until she heard them
coming back. She counted them until ten had passed, then
she knew her path was clear and she started on again. The
next day she came to the lake and there was a young man in
a canoe waiting for her. Without speaking to her he paddled
her across to an island where an old woman was waiting in
a wigwam. "Kwe, grandchild, you have come at last," said the
old woman, as though she had been waiting. The girl rested
there, as this old woman was a Penobscot, and from there she
was escorted back to Indian Island, where her people had
given her up as dead. They rejoiced greatly to see her back
again. And there she lived with her people.

As to her son left behind in the Mohawk village, when his
mother left he would not leave the wigwam, nor would he
eat. He just sat by the fire. So things went on, until one morning
one of the babies in the Mohawk village died and no one could
tell what caused its death. The next morning another died and
the next morning another. This went on until the chiefs took
council to try to find out what was the cause. "If we do not
stop this, all of our people will be dead and we will die out."
All this time the little boy never ate nor left his place. Then
they set a watch on him. During the night the watcher saw him
get up and go outside, and soon come back carrying a liver.
This he held before the fire until it was roasted and then ate it.
Then he went to sleep. The next morning a little baby was
found dead and they discovered that its liver was taken out.
So they found out that the medicine-boy was causing the death
of the children. So the chiefs held a council what to do. They
said, "If we try to kill him, he is stronger in magic than we
and he may kill us all. Let us go around and ask him what
he wants to let us be." So they sent some chiefs to him and
said, "We are sorry that we abused your mother. We know that
you are killing our children and you are very strong. We do
not want you to kill us all. So we will make you our head chief,
so we will all be your people and you will spare us." But the
medicine-boy said, "You are right. I have been killing the people and I would keep on until all were dead. Now I do not
want to be your chief. But I will lie in this wigwam on my

one side for one year and then J will turn over. Underneath where I have been lying, when you turn me over, you will find medicine plants growing that will cure your children. I will live forever. My name will be Gwélǝb'hot, Turn Over. Whenever you need medicine, turn me over and you will find the cure beneath me. I will be the father of all the Indians. I will give medicine to all the tribes for all diseases." And they agreed. Gwélǝb'hot is living in that village somewhere yet and every year they turn him over and the new medicine herbs grow up. He is the father of medicine. It all comes from him.

The Magic Flight

A shaman was once pursuing a man whom he wanted to kill. When the chase started the man was given a whetstone, some soap, some punk fungus, and an awl to help him in his flight. When the shaman gained on the man he threw down his soap and it became a bed of quaking mud. The shaman could hardly get through this but at last succeeded and began gaining on the victim again. This time the man threw down his whetstone and this became a wall of rock which stopped the shaman until he got an army of woodpeckers to pick it to pieces for him. Then he went on again, and soon gained on the man. Then the man threw down his punk. This turned into a burning tract. The shaman could hardly live getting through this place but at last he succeeded, and began gaining on the man again. Lastly the man threw down his awl. This became a thicket of thorns which entangled the shaman. In spite of his efforts he could not free himself and there he stuck. The man then escaped and got home.

Why the Negro Is Black

There was once a boy who laughed constantly at his parents. Every time they said anything he would laugh till he was black in the face. So he became black and the father of the Negro race. They are always laughing and showing their teeth.

Micmac

This once-numerous and important Algonquian tribe occupied Nova Scotia, Cape Breton, Prince Edward Island, and the south and western portions of Newfoundland. They may have encountered whites as early as 1497, when the Cabots touched the continent—the first time since the Norse that whites had done so.

In the tale "Taken-From Guts" the minor character Gluskap is the Micmac version of the trickster, possibly the most important single figure in North American Indian lore. Cf. the Winnebago trickster cycle on pp. 106-24 of this section.

Taken-from-Guts (*Muspusye′ gɛnan*)

There were two wigwams in which they were camping, an old man and his son. These two were giant man-eaters (*kogwe′-sk*). After a while the young man got married, and a boy was born by his wife. When this boy was about six years old, another was about to be born; and the young giant, knowing his wife was pregnant, went to his father and said, "I'll give you my wife. You can kill and eat her." So the next day the old man took his walking-stick and went to his son's camp. When he entered the wigwam, he told his daughter-in-law to bend her head down; and having put the end of his stick into the fire, when it was red-hot, he poked it into her heart and killed her. The little boy, her first son, was watching his grandfather, and saw what he did. Then the old man took a knife and cut out the mother's bowels, and left them lying near the spring where they got water. Her carcass he took home with him. So the poor little boy was left alone, as his father was away hunting. Every day, as he went to the spring where

From Frank G. Speck, "Some Micmac Tales from Cape Breton Island," *Journal of American Folklore* 28 (1915), 59-69.

his mother's bowels were, he saw a tiny boy. He tried to catch him, but failed every time. Nevertheless he saw the tiny creature smile at him. At last one day he did catch him, and he took him home. This little fellow had now grown larger and stronger. He had a little bow and arrow, and a bladder full of oil, and the old man wondered what it was. The elder brother asked him to make him another bow and arrow, and he asked what he wanted to do with them. "Give them to another little fellow," he answered. So another bow and arrow were made, and the elder boy gave them to the small one. One day while they were playing and shooting, they hit the bladder of oil and spilled it. Every night, after playing together about the camp, the small boy would return to the spring before the old man came home; but one day he came early and watched them playing. Then he ran and closed the wigwam, so that the little fellow could not escape. The little boy cried and begged to be freed, but the old man gave the little fellow some bluejay feathers to coax him to stop crying. At last the little fellow got tame and stopped crying. After this he grew fast, and soon was bigger than his elder brother. This little fellow's name was Taken-from-Guts (Muspusye' gɛnan) because he was born from his mother's bowels after they had been cut out by the old giant her father-in-law.

Now, one day Taken-from-Guts asked his elder brother, "Where is mother?" Then the brother told him, "Our father got grandfather to kill mother." So Taken-from-Guts said, "We'll kill the old fellow." Then they built a big strong wigwam, getting lots of bark and hanging two or three dry trees inside, so that it would burn well. Then they invited their father inside; and as he was tired and sleepy, they made a big fire inside, and soon he fell asleep. Then they got ready and set fire to both ends of the camp at the same time, went out, and closed the door. Then their father began crying inside, but he soon burned to death. When there was nothing left but bones and ashes, the boys gathered the bones; and Taken-from-Guts took them, crushed them into powder in his hand, and blew them into the air. "You will become mosquitoes to torment and eat the people," he said. And so the giant was turned into the mosquitoes who now try to kill people by sucking their blood.

Next Taken-from-Guts asked his elder brother, "Where is our grandfather?" When he told him, they went to their grandfather's camp. On the way they killed a moose. When they reached their grandfather's wigwam, the old people were glad, because they expected to eat the two boys. But they said, "We have killed a moose. Tomorrow we will go back and get the carcass." So they went back to the moose and cut up the meat. When they got back to where the moose was, their grandfather, who went with them, was tired and sleepy. When he fell asleep, they warmed the fat from the moose's guts, and held it on top of the old man until in a short time he was dead. Then they cut out his heart and took it back to the wigwam, where their grandmother was waiting. They gave it to her to cook, telling her it was a piece of the moose's heart. She roasted it; and as soon as she ate it, she knew what it was, and said, "He had a very sweet heart." Then Taken-from-Guts took a tomahawk and killed the old woman.

Now they started on, and Taken-from-Guts asked his brother where they were going. Said he, "We are going to kill all the rest of the giants." Soon they reached where Marten and his grandmother were camping. When they entered the camp, Taken-from-Guts asked Marten for a drink of water, as he was thirsty. Marten's grandmother answered, "We can't get any water around here. Unless you have a good-looking daughter, it is impossible." Taken-from-Guts asked, "Why?" She said, "A creature named Bull-Frog (Ablege′mu) has taken all the water, and you can't get any." Then Taken-from-Guts asked Marten again for a drink, and Marten went and brought him some rill water; but when Taken-from-Guts saw it, he threw it away. He was so thirsty that he licked his fingers for the moisture. Then Taken-from-Guts went to see Bull-Frog, and beheld in his camp thousands of bladders all full of water. When he entered, Bull-Frog looked up, and Taken-from-Guts hit and killed him with his tomahawk. Then he sent home all the girls that Bull-Frog had taken from the people in payment for drinking-water. Then he went out and broke all the bladders of water, and rivers and lakes appeared everywhere.

The next day the boys built a canoe to travel on the river. Then they went down the river and stopped at the place where

Porcupine had his den. It was all full of rocks. Porcupine's wife was at home; and when they went in, she built up a fire so hot that Taken-from-Gut's brother soon died. Nevertheless Taken-from-Guts said, "I'm very cold," and he wrapped a bear-skin about him. Soon Porcupine-Woman could not stand it any longer. Then Taken-from-Guts revived his brother, and they started on in the canoe until they came to where the giants had built a trap. It was a place where steep rocks crushed everybody who tried to go by. Taken-from-Guts saw the trap ahead, and said to his brother, "Look out! there is a trap ahead. Strike with your paddle!" So Taken-from-Guts broke it away with his paddle, and they passed through.

Soon they came to a pond where there were lots of wild geese, that looked up as they came in sight, and were about to screech. These geese belonged to Gluskap, who lived across the pond. They were his watch-birds, and informed Gluskap when any one approached, by screeching. Then Taken-from-Guts held up his hand and told the geese to keep quiet. The geese kept quiet. Then they landed and went into Gluskap's camp, and quickly put up their wigwam. When Gluskap came out, he saw it, and wondered at such a powerful man. But toward evening he went and visited Taken-from-Guts, and talked with the boys. Taken-from-Guts gave Gluskap a pipe to smoke. Gluskap drew on it once and smoked it dry. Then he gave Taken-from-Guts a pipe, and said, "Fill this." And Taken-from-Guts smoked it dry. Twice he did this. When Gluskap went out, Taken-from-Guts said to his brother, "It's going to be a cold night tonight, I can see it by the clouds." That night was indeed so cold that when he put his pot to boil, one side of it boiled while the other side froze. The next morning it was fine and warm, and Taken-from-Guts went to wake his brother, who said, "I'm frozen to death." At evening Taken-from-Guts said, "It's going to be windy today by the looks of the clouds," and he told it to Gluskap, who thought, "I had better fix up my camp, for this is a very powerful man." So he put weights all around his wigwam. That night it blew a gale so hard that he could just about keep his camp up. It nearly blew down. The next day was fine, so the brothers left Gluskap and started on. When they left, Gluskap gave Taken-from-Guts a piece of fur for a present, one skin. Taken-from-Guts handed it to his brother to carry. As they went along, it grew bigger and heavier, until at last he could not carry it any farther. So Taken-from-Guts carried it; but soon he stopped, and said to his brother, "You stay here and start a fur business with this skin. I can't carry it any longer." His brother then remained.

Taken-from-Guts, however, kept on, and at last came to two camps where old woman Skunk lived. She had some daughters. When he entered, she said, "Come in the back of the wigwam, my son-in-law!" The next day she said, "We'll go to the island and get some eggs." So they did go; and when they reached the island, the old woman told him that there were more eggs farther in from the shore. "I want you to get them," she said. So he went farther in, and she paddled off in the canoe and left him there. When he came back to the shore, she was gone and he was alone. The Gulls came by where he stood, and he asked them to carry him to the mainland. The Gulls did so, and he reached the camp ahead of the old woman. At this she was very much astonished. When night came, she told him, "I shall have to sleep with you tonight. That's the rule."—"All right," said he. That night she covered him up with fur and skins and lay down with him, intending to stifle him with her odor when he was asleep; but Taken-from-Guts made a hole through the coverings with his knife. Through this hole he could breathe. She tried very hard to kill him with her smell; but he breathed through the hole, and the next morning got up all right. The next day she had another test for him. She had a deep hole where she threw her other sons-in-law to kill them, and into this she threw Taken-from-Guts. When he reached the bottom, he found an old Turtle sitting there waiting for his prey. Turtle looked about for his knife to kill Taken-from-Guts; but while he was looking, Taken-from-Guts climbed out safely. They could not kill him.

Panther Loses His Member

Panther was going along by the river. On the opposite shore he saw some good-looking women washing and pounding their clothes on the stones on the beach. He desired to copulate with them. So he took off his penis and fixed it upon the end of a stick and pushed the stick under water across the stream. But before he got it across a chub swimming by took and swallowed the bait. Thereupon Panther got a canoe and fish spear and went spearing fish to recover his member. Said he to his friend who handled the spear in the bow, "When you see the fish, be sure and strike just so, on the head." When they came up to the fish Panther's friend struck the fish but missed his head and hit him in the middle. Panther rejoiced to recover his member but when he put it on again he got it on upside down and thus it has remained upon the panther family until now. I left then!

Iroquois

Measured by power, sphere of influence, and cultural achievement, perhaps the greatest of the North American Indian groups, with the possible exception of the Cherokee. Actually a federation of six nations (Cayuga, Mohawk, Seneca, Oneida, Onondaga, and, later, Tuscarora), the Iroquois at the height of their power controlled a vast territory from what is now western Massachusetts all the way west to Ohio; from southern Canada to perhaps northern Kentucky. There is abundant literature on them, as for example Cadwallader Colden's early *The History of the Five Indian Nations,* Joseph Mitchell and Edmund Wilson's *Apologies to the Iroquois,* and Anthony F. C. Wallace's *The Death and Rebirth of the Seneca.*

The Creation

The Council Tree

In the faraway days of this floating island there grew one stately tree that branched beyond the range of vision. Perpetually laden with fruit and blossoms, the air was fragrant with its perfume, and the people gathered to its shade where councils were held.

One day the Great Ruler said to his people: "We will make a new place where another people may grow. Under our council tree is a great cloud sea which calls for our help. It is lonesome. It knows no rest and calls for light. We will talk to it. The roots of our council tree point to it and will show the way."

Having commanded that the tree be uprooted, the Great Ruler peered into the depths where the roots had guided, and summoning Ata-en-sic, who was with child, bade her look

From Harriet Maxwell Converse, "Myths and Legends of the New York State Iroquois," *New York State Museum Bulletin 125,* edited by Arthur C. Parker (Albany, 1908), 5-195.

down. Ata-en-sic saw nothing, but the Great Ruler knew that the sea voice was calling, and bidding her carry its life, wrapped around her a great ray of light and sent her down to the cloud sea.

Hah-nu-nah, the Turtle

Dazzled by the descending light enveloping Ata-en-sic, there was great consternation among the animals and birds inhabiting the cloud sea, and they counseled in alarm.

"If it falls it may destroy us," they cried.

"Where can it rest?" asked the Duck.

"Only the oeh-da (earth) can hold it," said the Beaver, "the oeh-da which lies at the bottom of our waters, and I will bring it." The Beaver went down but never returned. Then the Duck ventured, but soon its dead body floated to the surface.

Many of the divers had tried and failed when the Muskrat, knowing the way, volunteered to obtain it and soon returned bearing a small portion in his paw. "But it is heavy," said he, "and will grow fast. Who will bear it?"

The Turtle was willing, and the oeh-da was placed on his hard shell.

Having received a resting place for the light, the water birds, guided by its glow, flew upward, and receiving the woman on their widespread wings, bore her down to the Turtle's back.

And Hah-nu-nah, the Turtle, became the Earth Bearer. When he stirs, the seas rise in great waves, and when restless and violent, earthquakes yawn and devour.

Ata-en-sic, the Sky Woman

The *oeh-da* grew rapidly and had become an island when Ata-en-sic, hearing voices under her heart, one soft and soothing, the other loud and contentious, knew that her mission to people the island was nearing.

To her solitude two lives were coming, one peaceful and patient, the other restless and vicious. The latter, discovering light under his mother's arm, thrust himself through, to contentions and strife, the right born entered life for freedom and peace.

These were the Do-ya-da-no, the twin brothers, Spirits of Good and Evil. Foreknowing their powers, each claimed dominion, and a struggle between them began, Hah-gweh-di-yu claiming the right to beautify the island, while Hah-gweh-da-ĕt-gäh determined to destroy. Each went his way, and where peace had reigned discord and strife prevailed.

The Sun, Moon, and Stars

At the birth of Hah-gweh-di-yu his Sky Mother, Ata-en-sic, had died, and the island was still dim in the dawn of its new life when, grieving at his mother's death, he shaped the sky with the palm of his hand, and creating the Sun from her face, lifted it there, saying, "You shall rule here where your face will shine forever." But Hah-gweh-da-ĕt-gäh set Darkness in the west sky, to drive the Sun down behind it.

Hah-gweh-di-yu then drew forth from the breast of his Mother, the Moon and the Stars, and led them to the Sun as his sisters who would guard his night sky. He gave to the Earth her body, its Great Mother, from whom was to spring all life.

All over the land Hah-gweh-di-yu planted towering mountains, and in the valleys set high hills to protect the straight rivers as they ran to the sea. But Hah-gweh-da-ĕt-gäh wrathfully sundered the mountains, hurling them far apart, and drove the high hills into the wavering valleys, bending the rivers as he hunted them down.

Hah-gweh-di-yu set forests on the high hills, and on the low plains fruit-bearing trees and vines to wing their seeds to the scattering winds. But Hah-gweh-da-ĕt-gäh gnarled the forests besetting the earth, and led monsters to dwell in the sea, and herded hurricanes in the sky which frowned with mad tempests that chased the Sun and the Stars.

The Animals and Birds

Hah-gweh-di-yu went across a great sea where he met a Being who told him he was his father. Said the Being, "How high can you reach?" Hah-gweh-di-yu touched the sky. Again he asked, "How much can you lift?" and Hah-gweh-di-yu grasped a stone mountain and tossed it far into space. Then said the Being, "You are worthy to be my son"; and lashing upon his back two burdens, bade him return to the earth.

Hah-gweh-di-yu swam for many days, and the Sun did not leave the sky until he had neared the earth. The burdens had grown heavy but Hah-gweh-di-yu was strong, and when he reached the shore they fell apart and opened.

From one of the burdens flew an eagle guiding the birds which followed, filling the skies with their song to the Sun as they winged to the forest. From the other there came animals led by the deer, and they sped quickly to the mountains. But Hah-gweh-da-ĕt-găh followed with wild beasts that devour, and grim flying creatures that steal life without sign, and creeping reptiles to poison the way.

Duel of Hah-gweh-di-yu and Hah-gweh-da-ĕt-găh

When the earth was completed and Hah-gweh-di-yu had bestowed a protecting Spirit upon each of his creation, he besought Hah-gweh-da-ĕt-găh to reconcile his vicious existence to the peacefulness of his own, but Hah-gweh-da-ĕt-găh refused, and challenged Hah-gweh-di-yu to combat, the victor to become the ruler of the earth.

Hah-gweh-da-ĕt-găh proposed weapons which he could control, poisonous roots strong as flint, monsters' teeth, and fangs of serpents. But these Hah-gweh-di-yu refused, selecting the thorns of the giant crab-apple tree, which were arrow pointed and strong.

With the thorns they fought. The battle continued many days, ending in the overthrow of Hah-gweh-da-ĕt-găh.

Hah-gweh-di-yu, having now become the ruler, banished his brother to a pit under the earth, whence he cannot return. But he still retains Servers, half human and half beasts, whom he sends to continue his destructive work. These Servers can assume any form Hah-gweh-da-ĕt-găh may command, and they wander all over the earth.

Hah-gweh-di-yu, faithful to the prophesy of the Great Ruler of the floating island, that the earth should be peopled, is continually creating and protecting.

Ga-oh, Spirit of the Winds

Though of giant proportions, Ga-oh, who governs the winds, is confined in the broad north sky. Were Ga-oh free, he would tear the heavens into fragments.

In the ages of his solitary confinement, he does not forget his strength, and punishes the winds to subjection when they suddenly rear for flight.

At the entrance of his abode and reined to his hands are four watchers: the Bear (north wind), Panther (west wind), Moose (east wind), and Fawn (south wind).

When Ga-oh unbinds Bear, it leads its hurricane winter winds to Earth; when he loosens Panther, its stealthy west winds creep down and follow Earth with their snarling blasts; when Moose is released, its east wind meets the Sun and its misty breath floats over the Sun's path blinding it with rains; and when Ga-oh unlocks his reins from Fawn, its soothing south winds whisper to Earth and she summons her Spring, who comes planting the seeds for the summer sunglow.

Though in his subjugation of the winds it is Ga-oh's duty to pacify them, frequently they are influenced by his varying moods. When Ga-oh is contented and happy, gentle and invigorating breezes fan Earth; when he is irritated by his confinement and restless, strong winds agitate the waters and bend the forest trees; and when, frenzied to mighty throes, Ga-oh becomes vehement, ugly blasts go forth, uprooting trees, dashing the streams into leaping furies, lifting the sea waters to mountainous waves, and devastating the earth.

Notwithstanding these outbursts, Ga-oh is faithful in disciplining the winds to their proper seasons, and guarding Earth from the rage of the elements.

When the north wind blows strong, the Iroquois say, "The Bear is prowling in the sky"; if the west wind is violent, "The Panther is whining." When the east wind chills with its rain, "The Moose is spreading his breath"; and when the south wind wafts soft breezes, "The Fawn is returning to its Doe."

Naming the Winds

When, in the creation of the earth, Hah-gweh-di-yu limited

the duties of the powerful Ga-oh to the sky, assigning to him the governing of the tempests, he blew a strong blast that shook the whole earth to trembling, and summoned his assistants to a council.

Ga-oh chose his aides from the terrestrial because of their knowledge of the earth; and when his reverberating call had ceased its thunderous echoes, he opened his north gate wide across the sky and called Ya-o-gah, the Bear.

Lumbering over the mountains as he pushed them from his path, Ya-o-gah, the bulky bear, who had battled the boisterous winds as he came, took his place at Ga-oh's gate and waited the mission of his call. Said Ga-oh, "Ya-o-gah, you are strong, you can freeze the waters with your cold breath; in your broad arms you can carry the wild tempest, and clasp the whole earth when I bid you destroy. I will place you in my far north, there to watch the herd of my winter winds when I loose them in the sky. You shall be North Wind. Enter your home." And the bear lowered his head for the leash with which Ga-oh bound him, and submissively took his place in the north sky.

In a gentler voice Ga-oh called Ne-o-ga, the Fawn, and a soft breeze as of the summer crept over the sky; the air grew fragrant with the odor of flowers, and there were voices as of babbling brooks telling the secrets of the summer to the tune of birds, as Ne-o-ga came proudly lifting her head.

Said Ga-oh, "You walk with the summer sun, and know all its paths; you are gentle, and kind as the sunbeam, and will rule my flock of the summer winds in peace. You shall be the South Wind. Bend your head while I leash you to the sky, for you are swift, and might return from me to the earth." And the gentle fawn followed Ga-oh to his great gate which opens the south sky.

Again Ga-oh trumpeted a shrill blast, and all the sky seemed threatening; an ugly darkness crept into the clouds that sent them whirling in circles of confusion; a quarrelsome, shrieking voice snarled through the air, and with a sound as of great claws tearing the heavens into rifts, Da-jo-ji, the Panther. sprang to the gate.

Said Ga-oh, "You are ugly, and fierce, and can fight the

strong storms; you can climb the high mountains, and tear down the forests; you can carry the whirlwind on your strong back, and toss the great sea waves high in the air, and snarl at the tempests if they stray from my gate. You shall be the West Wind. Go to the west sky, where even the Sun will hurry to hide when you howl your warning to the night." And Da-jo-ji, dragging his leash as he stealthily crept along, followed Ga-oh to the farthermost west sky.

Yet Ga-oh rested not. The earth was flat, and in each of its four corners he must have an assistant. One corner yet remained, and again Ga-oh's strong blast shook the earth. And there arose a moan like the calling of a lost mate, the sky shivered in a cold rain, the whole earth clouded in mist, a crackling sound as of great horns crashing through the forest trees dinned the air, and O-yan-do-ne, the Moose, stood stamping his hoofs at the gate.

Said Ga-oh, as he strung a strong leash around his neck, "Your breath blows the mist, and can lead the cold rains; your horns spread wide, and can push back the forests to widen the path for my storms as with your swift hoofs you race with my winds. You shall be the East Wind, and blow your breath to chill the young clouds as they float through the sky." And, said Ga-oh, as he led him to the east sky, "Here you shall dwell forevermore."

Thus, with his assistants, does Ga-oh control his storms. And although he must ever remain in his sky lodge, his will is supreme, and his faithful assistants will obey!

Ga-Nus-Quah and Go-Gon-Sa, the Stone Giants and False Faces

Tall, fierce and hostile, they were a powerful tribe, the Stone Giants!

They invaded the country of the Iroquois during the early days of the Confederation of the Five Nations, the Mohawks, Onondagas, Oneidas, Cayugas, and Senecas, who had sent their warriors against them only to be defeated, and they threatened the annihilation of the Confederacy.

They were feared, not because of their prodigious size, but because they were cannibals as well, and would devour men, women, and children.

The Shawnees have a legend of these Giants which describes them as at one time living in a peaceful state, and although powerful, gentle and hospitable in their intercourse with the neighboring tribes; but from some disturbing cause they became restless, abandoned their home, and migrated to the far north-west snow fields, where the extreme cold of the winters "froze away their humanity," and they became "men of icy hearts."

Unable to withstand the severity of the climate, or provide themselves with sufficient food, they were again controlled by the spirit of restlessness and they became wanderers, enduring all the discomforts and hardships of a nomadic life; and sub-sisting on raw meat and fish, they finally drifted into canniba-lism, reveling in human flesh.

In the summer they would roll in the sand to harden their flesh, and their bodies became covered with scales which re-sisted the arrows of an enemy. For generations they had devas-tated nations before they swept down upon the Iroquois. There they found caves wherein they concealed themselves, and would sally forth, destroying some village and feasting on the people.

The Iroquois were being rapidly depleted in their numbers, when Ta-ha-hia-wa-gon, Upholder of the Heavens, who had bestowed upon them their hunting grounds and fisheries, beholding their distress, determined to relieve them of the merciless invaders, and transforming himself to a stone giant, came down to the earth and united with their tribe.

Wonderstruck at his marvelous display of power, they made him their chief; and he brandished his club high in the air, saying, "Now we will destroy the Iroquois, make a great feast of them, and invite all the Stone Giants of the sky." In pretense of this intention, the Sky Holder led them to a strong fort of the Onondagas where he bade them hide in a deep hollow in the valley and await the sunrise, when they would attack and destroy the unsuspecting people. But before day, he scaled a high place above them and overwhelmed them with a great mass of rocks. Only one escaped, who fled to the Allegheny mountains. There he secreted himself in a cave, where he remained and grew in huge strength, when he was transformed to the myth Giant, Ga-nus-quah.

Ga-nus-quah, the Depredator

He was vulnerable only on the bottom of his foot. No one could hope to destroy him without wounding the spot on his foot, and this was not in the power of a mortal to do; and thus secure, the whole earth was his path.

No human being had ever seen him. To look upon his face would be instant death. His trail could be traced in the forests by the fallen trees he had uprooted when they obstructed his way. His footprints were seen impressed on the rocks where in his travels he had leaped. If a river opposed his going, he would swoop it up with his huge hands and turn it from its course, and so cross on the dry land. Should a mountain impede his way, with his strong fists he would push a gorge through it, the more quickly to reach the other side. In the tumult of storms, his voice could be heard warning the Thunderers away from his cave, this Ga-nus-quah, the last of the Stone Giants!

It was once the fate of a young hunter to meet this fear-inspiring creature. During a terrific storm, the young hunter, a chief, blinded and bruised by the hail which fell like sharp flints, and having lost the trail, sought shelter within the hollow of a great rock.

Night with its darkness deepened the shadows, and the young hunter prepared for night's sleep, when suddenly the rock began to move, and from a far recess a strange sound approached him. At one moment, the tone was brisk as the gurgling stream, at the next, gentle as the lullaby of a singing brook, again to burst forth like the moan of a tumbling cataract or the wail of a mad torrent, then dying away as tenderly as the soft summer breeze.

During a pause in the weird harmony, the marveling young hunter heard a voice addressing him in a stentorian strain, saying: "Young warrior, beware! You are in the cave of the Stone Giant, Ga-nus-quah! Close your eyes. No human being has ever looked upon me. I kill with one glance. Many have wandered into this cave; no one lives to leave it. You did not come to hunt me; you came here for shelter; I will not turn you away. I will spare your life, which now is mine, but henceforth you must obey my commands. I will be unseen, but you will hear my voice. I will be unknown, yet will I aid you. From here you will go forth, free to live with the animals, the birds, and the fish. All these were your ancestors before you were human, and hereafter it will be your task to dedicate your life to their honoring!

"Whichever of these you meet on your way, do not pass until you have felled a strong tree and carved its image in the wood grain. When you first strike the tree, if it speaks, it will be my voice urging you and you must go on with your task. When the trees were first set in their earth mold, each was given a voice. These voices you must learn, and the language of the entire forest. Now, go on your way; I am watching and guiding you. Go, now, and teach the mankind people kindness, the brother goodness of all dumb things, and so win your way to live forever!"

When the young hunter opened his eyes, he was standing beside a basswood tree which gradually transformed to a great mask; and related to him its power.

The Go-gon-sa (Mask)

It could see behind the stars. It could create storms, and summon the sunshine. It empowered battles or weakened the forces at will. It knew the remedy for each disease, and could overpower Death. It knew all the poison roots and could repel their strong evils. Its power was life, its peace the *o-yank-wah*, the tobacco which drowsed to rest. The venomous reptiles knew its threat and crept from its path. It would lead the young hunter back to his people when the Stone Giant directed. It said: "My tree, the basswood, is soft, and will transform for the molder. My tree wood is porous, and the sunlight can enter its darkness. The wind voice can whisper to its silence and it will hear. My tree wood is the life of the Go-gon-sa. Of all in the forest there is none other."

With this knowledge, the young hunter started on his way carving go-gon-sa-so-oh (false faces). From the basswood he hewed them. By the voice of the Stone Giant he was guided to choose; and well he learned the voices of all the forest trees before he completed his task.

In his travels he met many strange animals and birds, which he detained until he had carved them in the basswood; and inviting them to tarry, learned their language and habits; and though fearing the Giant's reproval, for he constantly heard his voice encouraging or blaming, he learned to love these descendants of his ancestors, and was loath to leave them when compelled to return to his home.

Many years had passed in the laborious task, and he who entered the cave a youth had become a bent old man when, burdened with the go-gon-sas he had carved, he set out on his return to his people. Year after year his burden had grown heavier, but his back broadened in strength, and he had become a giant in stature when he reached his home and related his story.

Gau-wi-di-ne and Go-hay, Winter and Spring

The snow mountain lifted its head close to the sky; the clouds wrapped around it their floating drifts which held the winter's hail and snowfalls, and with scorn it defied the sunlight which crept over its height, slow and shivering on its way to the valleys.

Close at the foot of the mountain, an old man had built him a lodge "for a time," said he, as he packed it around with great blocks of ice. Within he stored piles of wood and corn and dried meat and fish. No person, animal, or bird could enter this lodge, only North Wind, the only friend the old man had. Whenever strong and lusty North Wind passed the lodge he would scream "ugh-e-e-e, ugh-e-e-e, ugh-e-e-e," as with a blast of his blustering breath he blew open the door, and entering, would light his pipe and sit close by the old man's fire and rest from his wanderings over the earth.

But North Wind came only seldom to the lodge. He was too busy searching the corners of the earth and driving the snows and the hail, but when he had wandered far and was in need of advice, he would visit the lodge to smoke and counsel with the old man about the next snowfall, before journeying to his home in the north sky; and they would sit by the fire which blazed and glowed yet could not warm them.

The old man's bushy whiskers were heavy with the icicles which clung to them, and when the blazing fire flared its lights, illuminating them with the warm hues of the summer sunset, he would rave as he struck them down, and glare with rage as they fell snapping and crackling at his feet.

One night, as together they sat smoking and dozing before the fire, a strange feeling of fear came over them, the air seemed to be growing warmer and the ice began to melt. Said North Wind: "I wonder what warm thing is coming, the snow seems vanishing and sinking lower in the earth." But the old man cared not, and was silent. He knew his lodge was strong, and he chuckled with scorn as he bade North Wind abandon his fears and depart for his home. But North Wind went drifting the fast falling snow higher on the mountain until it groaned under its heavy burden, and scolding and blasting, his voice gradually died away. Still the old man remained silent and moved not, but lost in thought sat looking into the fire when there came a loud knock at his door. "Some foolish breath of North Wind is wandering," thought he, and he heeded it not.

Again came the rapping, but swifter and louder, and a pleading voice begged to come in.

Still the old man remained silent, and drawing nearer to the fire quieted himself for sleep; but the rapping continued, louder, fiercer, and increased his anger. "Who dares approach the door of my lodge?" he shrieked. "You are not North Wind, who alone can enter here. Begone! no refuge here for trifling winds, go back to your home in the sky." But as he spoke, the strong bar securing the door fell from its fastening, the door swung open and a stalwart young warrior stood before him shaking the snow from his shoulders as he noiselessly closed the door.

Safe within the lodge, the warrior heeded not the old man's anger, but with a cheerful greeting drew close to the fire, extending his hands to its ruddy blaze, when a glow as of summer illumined the lodge. But the kindly greeting and the glowing light served only to incense the old man, and rising in rage he ordered the warrior to depart.

"Go!" he exclaimed. "I know you not. You have entered my lodge and you bring a strange light. Why have you forced my lodge door? You are young, and youth has no need of my fire. When I enter my lodge, all the earth sleeps. You are strong, with the glow of sunshine on your face. Long ago I buried the sunshine beneath the snowdrifts. Go! you have no place here.

"Your eyes bear the gleam of the summer stars, North Wind blew out the summer starlights moons ago. Your eyes dazzle my lodge, your breath does not smoke in chill vapors, but comes from your lips soft and warm, it will melt my lodge, you have no place here.

"Your hair so soft and fine, streaming back like the night shades, will weave my lodge into tangles. You have no place here.

"Your shoulders are bare and white as the snowdrifts. You have no furs to cover them; depart from my lodge. See, as you sit by my fire, how it draws away from you. Depart, I say, from my lodge!"

But the young warrior only smiled, and asked that he might remain to fill his pipe; and they sat down by the fire when the old man became garrulous and began to boast of his great powers.

"I am powerful and strong," said he. "I send North Wind to blow all over the earth and its waters stop to listen to his voice as he freezes them fast asleep. When I touch the sky, the snow hurries down and the hunters hide by their lodge fires; the birds fly scared, and the animals creep to their caves. When I lay my hand on the land, I harden it still as the rocks; nothing can forbid me or loosen my fetters. You, young warrior, though you shine like the Sun, you have no power. Go! I give you a chance to escape me, but I could blow my breath and fold around you a mist which would turn you to ice, forever!

"I am not a friend to the Sun, who grows pale and cold and flees to the south land when I come; yet I see his glance in your face, where no winter shadows hide. My North Wind will soon return; he hates the summer and will bind fast its hands. You fear me not, and smile because you know me not. Young man, listen. I am Gau-wi-di-ne, Winter! Now fear me and depart. Pass from my lodge and go out to the wind."

But the young warrior moved not, only smiled as he refilled the pipe for the trembling old man, saying, "Here, take your pipe, it will soothe you and make you stronger for a little while longer"; and he packed the *o-yan-kwa* (Indian tobacco) deep and hard in the pipe.

Said the warrior, "Now you must smoke for me, smoke for youth and Spring! I fear not your boasting; you are aged and slow while I am young and strong. I hear the voice of South Wind. Your North Wind hears, and Ga-oh is hurrying him back to his home. Wrap you up warm while yet the snowdrifts cover the earth path, and flee to your lodge in the north sky. I am here now, and you shall know me. I, too, am powerful!

"When I lift my hand, the sky opens wide and I waken the sleeping Sun, which follows me warm and glad. I touch the earth and it grows soft and gentle, and breathes strong and swift as my South Wind ploughs under the snows to loosen your grasp. The trees in the forest welcome my voice and send out their buds to my hand. When my breezes blow my long hair to the clouds, they send down gentle showers that whisper the grasses to grow.

"I came not to tarry long in my peace talk with you, but to smoke with you and warn you that the Sun is waiting for me to open its door. You and North Wind have built your lodge strong, but each wind, the North, and the East, and the West, and the South, has its time for the earth. Now South Wind is calling me; return you to your big lodge in the sky. Travel quick on your way that you may not fall in the path of the Sun. See! it is now sending down its arrows broad and strong!"

The old man saw and trembled. He seemed fading smaller, and grown too weak to speak, could only whisper, "Young warrior, who are you?"

In a voice that breathed soft as the breath of wild blossoms, he answered: "I am Go-hay, Spring! I have come to rule, and my lodge now covers the earth! I have talked to your mountain and it has heard; I have called the South Wind and it is near;

the Sun is awake from its winter sleep and summons me quick and loud. Your North Wind has fled to his north sky; you are late in following. You have lingered too long over your peace pipe and its smoke now floats far away. Haste while yet there is time that you may lose not your trail."

And Go-hay began singing the Sun song as he opened the door of the lodge. Hovering above it was a great bird whose wings seemed blown by a strong wind, and while Go-hay continued to sing, it flew down to the lodge and folding Gau-wi-di-ne to its breast, slowly winged away to the north, and when the Sun lifted its head in the east, it beheld the bird disappearing behind the faraway sky. The Sun glanced down where Gau-wi-di-ne had built his lodge, whose fire had burned but could not warm, and a bed of young blossoms lifted their heads to the touch of its beams. Where the wood and the corn and the dried meat and fish had been heaped, a young tree was leafing, and a bluebird was trying its wings for a nest. And the great ice mountain had melted to a swift running river which sped through the valley bearing its message of the springtime.

Gau-wi-di-ne had passed his time, and Go-hay reigned over the earth!

De'hodyǎ'tgā'ewĕⁿˋ (*He Whose Body Is Divided in Twain*)

A Traditional Journal of an Expedition to the Skyland

This is a saga concerning the First People—the Ancient People—the People of the Beginnings—who live now and who lived also when the Earth was new, and, therefore, was young.

In the land of the Sunrise, at a place called Diyo'hnyowā'nĕⁿˋ (i.e., There at the Great Lowland Cape), there was situated a village of these First People, when the Earth was young.

There came a day when one of the young men, De'haĕⁿ-'hyō'wĕⁿˋs (i.e., He-Who-Cleaves-the-Sky-in-Twain), dwelling

From J. N. B. Hewitt, "Iroquoian Cosmology," *43rd Annual Report of the Bureau of American Ethnology, 1925-26* (Washington, 1928),pp. 449-891.

in the village at Diyoʻhnyowäʹnĕnᶜ resolved to form an expedition to make a raid westward into the distant regions through which passes the daily path of the Sun.

So to promote his design Deʻhaĕnʻhyōʹwĕnᶜs induced his friends to prepare a great war feast, to which he invited all the First People of that village. It being the custom of the country, he announced to the public assembled there his purpose of leading a troop of warriors far into the west, following the path of the Sun and going beyond the end of the earth to slaughter unknown men and to obtain the scalps of alien peoples as tokens of their prowess and their courage in warfare.

The feast having been prepared and the people having received the notched sticks of invitation—white for the children and the general public, green for the young warriors and Women Chiefs, and red for the Chiefs, Sorcerers, Elder Men, and the Elder Chiefs—all then assembled in the Long-lodge of public assembly. While the guests were enjoying the good things provided for their entertainment, their host, Deʻhaĕnʻhyōʹwĕnᶜs, arose in his place and in a set speech announced his purpose to lead an expedition of a war party into the west, even through the regions over which the Sun follows his path, for the purpose of destroying and scalping all the alien peoples whom they might find on their way thither.

In his address he urged the young men to volunteer to accompany him and to share with him the hardships of his enterprise; but he asked only for young men who had reached manhood's estate, just after maturing from the age of puberty. He further informed those who would volunteer as members of his party that they would have to renounce their kith and kin, and even their lives; and that they must also agree to observe strict adherence to a unanimity of purpose, and also that they must agree to continue on the journey forward no matter what the nature of forbidding obstacles in the way might be; and that his own brother, Gaĕnʻhyăkdoñʹdye' (i.e., Along-the-Edge-of-the-Sky, or The Horizon), had already volunteered to accompany him, and that in the capacity of war chiefs, they two would lead the party, should such a war party be formed to go.

In response to this appeal twenty-eight young virile men

besides the two brothers volunteered to be members of the war party of the two ambitious adventurers.

Having set a date for starting and a rendezvous for the assembling of the troop, De'haĕⁿ'hyō'wĕⁿ's earnestly urged all the volunteers to be ready to depart at the designated time.

The time for departure having arrived, De'haĕⁿ'hyō'wĕⁿ's, by messenger, notified all the volunteers that the time had come for starting. Eagerly did the volunteers present themselves at the rendezvous and having completed all other preparations they set out, directing their course toward the Place of Sunset.

The minds of the two leaders were fixed on the place where the Sun habitually sinks from view, so thither did they wend their way.

As these warriors traveled on they finally reached a place in which they found the habitations of a people whom they did not know, but these unoffending persons they ruthlessly killed and scalped. After this bloody exploit they journeyed westward.

Having gone a short distance farther they suddenly came upon the village of another people. At the dawn of day they attacked these people, slaying all the males who did not escape in the darkness, and having scalped the slain they passed on, following the course of the Sun.

Having gone a day's journey farther they came to the dwelling place of a third people. At night these people also were attacked, killed, and scalped; all the males who did not escape them in the darkness were massacred. In the morning the war party passed on. These bloody exploits were repeated wherever they found a village of people dwelling on the line of their march. This bloody work continued for many moons.

It is said that after pursuing this course of conduct during a long period of time the packs of scalps which they carried on their backs grew so heavy as to hamper their movements. In their several encounters a number of the band had been killed on their way. So there came a time when many of those who remained alive complained that the weight of the packs of scalps was becoming too great to be borne.

These said, "It seems advisable now that we should store

our packs of scalps here in some secret place for safekeeping until our return." Finally, De'haĕⁿ'hyō'wĕⁿ's said, "It is probable also that we may now soon see what we seek; namely, the scalp of all scalps. That we might use to cover all those which we have. Moreover, this kind of thing which we bear with us does not readily spoil."

About this time they fell in with a person, a male Man Being, whose towering stature reached one-half the height of the tallest trees.

Then it was that Gaĕⁿ'hyăkdoñ'dye' (Along-the-Edge-of-the-Sky, i.e., The Horizon) said, "Now, then, speaking inferentially, our good fortune has brought about the fulfillment of the purpose of our expedition, upon which we had agreed, namely, that we should see in our hands a large quantity of scalps. Again, speaking inferentially, I think that the next move to be made is to decide to kill this Man Being whom we have met in this place. We shall then be possessed of the large scalp about which my brother has already prophesied. So let us attack him at once."

So deploying they at once began to assault him by shooting their arrows at him, and by striking him with their war clubs and with their stone hatchets; but they could not make any impression on him; they failed to harm him in the least.

At last the strange Man Being said to them, kindly, "What is it that you desire to do? Do you imagine that you can kill me?" Then they answered, "That is, indeed, our purpose, as it has been our design in making our journey hither to kill all persons who might fall in our way, no matter who they might be."

To this frank admission of their purpose to kill him, this strange Man Being replied, "The purpose for which you are banded together is not good. And from this time forward you must utterly renounce it and strictly desist from carrying it out. It is quite impossible for you to kill me. And I came to meet you here for the purpose of giving you this counsel.

"I watched you on your way to this place, and I saw with grief that you killed many people. I want wou to know that the reason why I came to meet you is that you have now committed wrongs enough on innocent people. And I want you to know that if you will not cease from committing these wrongs you yourselves also shall perish."

Then De'haĕⁿ'hyō'wĕⁿ's replied, saying, "We are very thankful to you for this good counsel, and we will try to abide by it. We will pass beyond this point, as we have bound ourselves by a vow to attempt to reach the place where the Sun habitually sinks from view—to the spot where the Sun goes to and fro." Then the strange Man Being merely replied, "Do you then start on your journey." And while they listened to him with bowed heads he vanished from them; they did not know or see whither he went.

Then realizing that they were again alone they departed. They traveled on for a long time, finally coming to a very large lake which barred further progress ahead.

When seeing that there was apparently no means of crossing the lake De'haĕⁿ'hyō'wĕⁿ's said, "What thing is it that we should do to cross over this lake?" Thereupon, one of the band who seldom uttered a word declared, "We have indeed made an agreement, bound with a vow, that no matter what the circumstances or the obstacles might be in our path, we would nevertheless advance through them, as we have overcome what is past. Indeed, the time has now come to fulfill our agreement."

De'haĕⁿ'hyō'wĕⁿ's then answered, saying, "Verily, it is even as you have said. Come then, it is thou who must now take the lead."

At once the man addressed took the lead. Alone he now went upon the surface of the lake, walking upon the water. Thither he went unflinchingly. Then, each in turn, the others in the band followed in his wake. They crossed the lake safely.

Upon reaching the dry land on the farther shore of the lake, they stood still, looking around and examining the new country. They were surprised at seeing the visible sky rise and fall again, at regular intervals. In their estimation it rose to the height of the tallest pine tree known to them, before falling back. They saw, too, that the place from which it rebounded was so smooth that it glistened.

While watching the rising and falling of the Sky, they beheld a large number of pigeons flying out from the other side of the

Sky, and which after flying around for some time returned whence they had come.

Then De'haĕⁿ'hyō'wĕⁿ's said, "What manner of thing shall we now do? To be sure, here seems to be, indeed, the end of the earth. It is evident, indeed, that there is another country lying beyond this sky-barrier which is thus continually rising and falling."

Again that member of the band who was never in the habit of speaking much said, "You are, of course, well aware of the requirement of the agreement by which we bound ourselves together before starting from home; did we not agree that no matter what might be taking place, or what might be the obstacles in our way, nevertheless we should not recoil from going forward?

"Besides, you know, too, that those of us who still live number five. Only five of our original number are still alive. Furthermore, the opportunity now presents itself for us to perform our vow which we made; its fulfillment is now required of us; it is for us now to act to redeem our mutual pledges."

Then De'haĕⁿ'hyō'wĕⁿ's said, "Come, then, let us now secretly store our burden of scalps here for safekeeping until our return."

So, each man carefully concealed his bundle of scalps in such wise that he could find it, should he ever be given the opportunity of repassing that point.

When the packs of scalps were carefully secreted then De'haĕⁿ'hyō'wĕⁿ's, addressing himself to the last speaker, said, "Now, then, it is thou who must lead us in passing this obstacle that seemingly bars our path. For our way, indeed, leads directly into that farther country; we must pass so quickly under the sky as it rises that we shall not be caught by it when it falls back."

Then the man who had been addressed, reassuring himself, selected a favorable starting point for his dash under the rising sky. Carefully timing the rising and falling of the sky he dashed forward as swiftly as possible. His friends watched him rush onward until he had disappeared on the farther side of the obstacle.

As the sky kept rising and falling the second man, making

like dispositions, dashed forward, clearing the barrier as the first man had, and disappeared on the other side. The third man and the fourth man had like success in clearing this obstacle. The sky, however, did not cease from rising and falling back onto its bed.

It was now the turn of the fifth and last man to tempt the peril of attempting to pass under the sky. His four companions anxiously watched him making ready to clear the danger which they had safely passed.

The quartet did not see him start, but as the sky arose they saw him running still far from the passage. But, just as he leaped, the sky fell back, crushing him to death. He had miscalculated the time and distance he had to run, and his career ended in that place.

Then De'haĕⁿ'hyō'wĕⁿ's said, "Let us be thankful that we have been fortunate enough to pass this danger safely. We now number only four. Only four of us have been spared to reach this land. We are without our arms or other means of defense. We know not whether we shall require them or not. So, now, verily, I believe that we must at all events go forward. And, verily, it is easily seen that we are now in a land which is quite different from the other known to us.

"We see that the light of this land is unequaled in its brightness; it is verily true, that the daylight of the land whence we started is such that it is like the light of a starlight night as compared with that of this land. And now, then, let us depart hence. We will seek to find other human beings, if such there be, who may have a settlement here."

Now, without further parleying they set forward. As they traveled on they saw that the standing trees of all kinds were very large, tall, and fine looking, and that they severally were in full bloom; and that these trees were of surpassing beauty. The travelers were greatly surprised to learn that the flowers of these trees were the sole source of the light of that world. They also noted the fact that all the beasts and animals and birds possessed exceptionally fine bodies and attractive presence. They remarked, too, that they had seen nothing, during their journey thither, so wonderful and so strange.

They saw with astonishment the exuberance of the growing

grasses and plants, and among these they beheld in rich profusion the fruited stalks of the strawberry plants, which were
just as tall as the grasses among which they grew. During their
entire journey thither they had not seen such large luscious
berries growing.

Having gone some distance into the new country they were
surprised at seeing in the distance a great multitude of Man
Beings who were assembled on the heath, the playground
of that people; they appeared to the travelers to be at games
of amusement.

Then De'haĕⁿ'hyō'wĕⁿ's said, "What is to be done now, my
friends, seeing that we have now arrived at the dwelling place
of strange Man Beings, and that we have now no arms with
which to defend ourselves should these people living here
attempt to do us harm?"

Thereupon Gaĕⁿ'hyăkdoñ'dye' spoke, saying, "We have,
indeed, made an agreement, as you know, that we would forsake our kindred and our lives to accomplish the purpose of
this expedition. You know that each of us volunteered by
'notching the rod' to carry out that agreement. And now, if
we are to die here, we can do nothing to avoid such an end;
we must not break our resolution and compact to follow the
path of the Sun to its end. Nevertheless, the only thing that is
certain, in the case of our death, is that our careers would
end here."

Then his brother, De'haĕⁿ'hyō'wĕⁿ's, replied to him, saying,
"The matter stands even as you have stated it, so, then, let
us go forward to meet this people." They then started, going
thither to the place where they saw the people assembled.

In a very short time they arrived at the place where the great
multitude was assembled. There, not far from the others, the
anxious travelers came to a standstill. Looking around them
they saw that the inhabitants of the village were in readiness
to see a game of lacrosse ball-play, and that the players were
even then standing in their accustomed places.

In a short time the game commenced, and the vast multitude
drew near to be spectators of it. As soon as the game was fairly
under way there arose a great tumult; there was shouting and
loud cries of excitement and approbation caused by the varying

fortunes of favorite players. The great multitude rejoiced, and the new arrivals were greatly delighted with what they saw.

At this time one of the players exhibited great rudeness in his manner of playing, for he struck right and left with his netted club without regard to the other players who might be injured by his recklessness. Then a person from the multitude went up to that player and said to him, "Do thou cease from acting so rudely; thy manner is too violent, because one who rejoices does not act in this manner. So do not act thus again."

The players at once resumed the game, playing as they never had played before. In a short time, however, the player who had been cautioned to be more mild in his methods of play again exhibited his violence toward his playmates.

Then the man who had reprimanded him before went up to him again and said, "Assuredly, I forbade you acting so rude as you have; I told you not to act thus violently again. Yet, thou hast disregarded my request. And so, now you shall, moreover, rest for a time. You are too unkind and headstrong."

Thereupon, seizing the ball player by the nape of the neck and by the legs and lifting him up bodily he bore him from the field. Not far therefrom stood a very large tree. Thither the man carried the ball player, and having arrived beside the tree, and still carrying the ball player, he cast the body headlong against the trunk of the tree. Head foremost the body penetrated the tree trunk, the head coming part way out on the opposite side of the tree, while his feet still protruded on the other. Then the man quietly returned to the ball ground, and the game was resumed; it was continued until one of the sides had scored the requisite number of points to win the game, and then the players again commingled with the multitude.

Then the man who had imprisoned the rude player in the tree trunk went to that tree and released the prisoner and set him free with an admonition to be more mild in his method of play in the future. Upon his return to the multitude, he told them that it was time for them to return to their several homes, and they dispersed.

It was then that this man, who appeared to be one of the chief men of the settlement, came to the place where stood the traveling company of Deʻhaĕⁿʻhyŏ′wĕⁿ's. As soon as he came up to them he asked familiarly, "So you have arrived, have you?"

Replying, De'haĕⁿ'hyō'wĕⁿ's said, "We have now arrived."

It was then that the man said, "Assuredly, the reason that you have arrived safely in this land is that one of your number began at the very time of your departure from home to think, repeatedly soliloquizing, 'O Thou Master of Life, Thou shouldst have pity on us, so that we may pass through all the dangers which beset the accomplishment of the purpose of our solemn agreement. But, if it so be that we shall die on this earth, grant that we may also arrive in that other land that is extant, where Thou Thyself abidest, Thou Master of Life.' Every day, every night also, such was his mind and prayer.

"It was that attitude of mind which was able to bring your persons safely into this land—this elder country.

"So now, moreover, you have fully accomplished what I promised you when I met you on your way hither.

"So now, let me ask you, who among you is individually willing that I should restore his life—i.e., refit his being?"

Then one of the four travelers answered, saying, "I am just the one that is willing; do you begin on me." Then this Man Being, going forward to the place where stood a tree not far distant, reached the tree and, raising his arm to its full length, seized the standing tree and bent it down to the earth, and stripped the bark in one entire piece from the trunk of the tree. Then placing this piece of bark on the ground, he said to the volunteer, "Now, do thou come hither to me."

Then the man who had consented to have his body and being refitted, went forward to him, while his three companions intently watched their host in what he was doing to their companion; and they saw him begin his work. Then the host placed the man on the outspread piece of bark. He took apart the flesh body of their companion; he, too, unjointed severally all the joints of his skeleton, laying each several bone aside. And then he took each of the bones, and every one of the joints of the bones, and wiped it very carefully. He soon completed his task of washing and cleaning them.

He then began to join together all the bones and all the portions of flesh in their proper relations. And as soon as he had completed his task he said to his guests, "Now, I have refinished this work. What is solely of the other world has been removed. For what is of 'the earth earthy' is out of place here. Now, my friend, do thou arise again."

Then the man whose body and being had been remodeled arose, standing erect and casting his eyes around him. Then his host said to him, "Like unto what is your life, as you now feel it? Do you feel different from what you did before I remodeled your body and being?"

To which the renewed man replied, "Its condition is indeed such that it feels immeasurably more delightful, and I am happier than before the change."

Then his host said to him, "If this be, indeed, true, attempt to seize that deer standing yonder. If it so be that thou canst overtake it, do thou seize it, also."

So looking in the distance the deer was seen standing there. Then when the remodeled man ran toward it, the deer at once fled in terror. The man sped swiftly in pursuit of it. It had not gone very far before he overtook it and seized it. He brought it back to the place where his host stood, who said to him, "Now, assuredly, thy life has become a new thing—you have acquired the life of this country."

While they two were yet speaking another man of the troop of Deʻhaĕⁿhyŏ′wĕⁿ's said, "I, too, desire to have the same thing performed on my body and life; thou must remake my life, and I want it done now."

His host directed him to lie down on the piece of bark as did the other man; at once he proceeded in a manner similar to that followed in the case of the first patient. It was not long before he was ready to ask him to arise, having remade or refitted his life with new life forces. Now the two men who had had their lives renewed felt that they had acquired new life and that they were immeasurably more delightful to have, and that the joy of living was refined.

Now the remaining two men, seeing how desirable was the change brought about in the bodies and lives of the other two men by having them remodeled, said, "We, too, wish to have the same thing performed on our lives that was wrought in the bodies and lives of our two companions. So we ask you that this be done for us, too."

Then the host of the troop of De'haĕⁿ'hyō'wĕⁿ's proceeded to renew and remodel the bodies and the lives of these two men. When he had finished this task, he said to them, "Now, I have reformed all your lives; I have finished everything that concerns and fits them for this country. So we will now go to the lodge where you shall remain as in your home while you are in this country."

So the troop of De'haĕⁿ'hyō'wĕⁿ's and their host started. They walked leisurely along, noting the many strange things which attracted their attention on every side. They had not gone very far, however, before they reached a very large lodge, into which their host led the party; therein they saw a very old woman, a Man Being, who presided over it. Upon entering the lodge the host of De'haĕⁿ'hyō'wĕⁿ's and his friends said to the old woman, "Now, it is this matter. I have brought here those persons whom, I said, would take up their abode here when they arrived in this country. So now they shall remain with you under your care and keep."

Then the aged woman who was the mistress of the lodge replied, saying, "It shall be even as you have said it. These, my grandchildren, shall be one with me in this lodge."

Then, the Man Being who had brought the visitors there said, "Now furthermore, as to myself I will go forth. Make yourselves at home," and he at once left the lodge to attend to his other affairs.

Then the mistress of the lodge, who was very old, said to her guests to make them feel more at home, "I am now quite alone, you perceive, in caring for the lodge, which is very large, as you see. The male persons who dwell here are absent hunting; they will soon return for the night. I will now prepare something for you to eat," and she at once set before them what was ready cooked in the lodge.

When they first entered the lodge the band of De'haĕⁿ'hyō'-wĕⁿ's noticed that the old woman was busily at work; they saw that she was engaged in making a mantle for herself; at intervals she held the work up at arm's length to note the effect of her labor. The visitors also discovered the fact that human hair was the material out of which the old woman was weaving her mantle.

They also saw that their aged hostess possessed a dwarf dog, which reposed nearby on her couch. They were astonished also, when the old woman left her work for a few moments, to see the dwarf dog quickly arise and go over to the place where the old woman had left her hair-work and begin to unravel quickly but stealthily all the work that the old woman had in the meanwhile done on her mantle. But when the dwarf dog had nearly unraveled all the work, the old woman returned to take it up again and to continue her task.

While the visitors were eating what the old woman had set before them the male members of the old woman's household returned, each bearing a bundle. Upon entering the lodge they said to the old woman, "Now, we have returned. We were fortunate throughout the entire expedition in the killing of much game."

Then the mistress of the lodge said to the returned hunters, "Verily, be it known, that a short time ago, De'haĕⁿ'hyāwă''gi' brought to this lodge the human beings, oñ'gwe', whom he said were coming to this country and whom he said would abide in this lodge when they would arrive. So they have arrived; these men here are they. So talk with them and become acquainted with them."

So the men who had just returned to their lodge drew near to the visitors and conversed with them, saying, "We are, indeed, thankful that you have safely arrived here. It is now a long time that we have kept watching you on your way hither. Moreover, be it known, that we have now seen one another, and so we are greatly rejoiced." Then it was that they severally and mutually stroked the bodies of one another, as was the custom on such occasions, and they greatly rejoiced to become acquainted one with another.

Then the old woman began to prepare food for the returned hunters. When the food was cooked, she called the men to eat, saying, "Now, of course, you will eat the food which I have prepared for you." And the men began to take their nourishment.

But the method they adopted for taking their sustenance was most singular to the companions of Deʻhaĕⁿʻhyō′wĕⁿʻs. So they intently watched the hunters eat, for they did not eat the food set before them; they merely absorbed the exhalations from the food, and it was the odor or effluvium of the food that satisfied their hunger. When they had finished their meal, the old woman said to them, "It is now time, perhaps, that you should go out to hunt game which our human guests can eat, for you know that they do not eat the same kind of things that you do."

So the hunters started out of the lodge to seek for game for their guests. As soon as the men were gone the old woman put her hands to the headrest of her couch and took therefrom a single grain of corn and a single squash seed. Then she went to the end of the fireplace and there she prepared in the ashes two small hills or beds, in one of which she placed the grain of corn and in the other the squash seed, and carefully covered them with rich dirt.

In a very short while the visitors looked and were greatly surprised to see that the seeds had sprouted and had shot out of the ground small plantlets, which were growing rapidly. Not very long after this they saw the cornstalk put forth ears of corn and the squash vine squashes, so in the short space of a few hours these plants had supplied the old woman with ears of corn and squashes. These she prepared and cooked.

Then the men who were out hunting returned to the lodge, bringing with them the fine carcass of a deer which they had killed. At once they set to work to skin it and to dress it. As soon as they had finished this task the old woman set the venison, the corn, and the squashes over the fire to cook. She set her kettles over the fire on stone supports and promoted the cooking by putting hot stones into them.

When these things were cooked she placed them on fine bowls of bark and set these bowls before the visitors and bade them eat heartily. So Deʻhaĕⁿʻhyō′wĕⁿʻs and his friends ate their fill.

This now came to pass. The aged woman now, verily, said, "It is now time, you will agree, I think, for you to go again to hunt." This remark she made to the male members of her family.

Then the visitors saw something very strange. They saw the old woman take from under her couch a large quantity of corn husks. She then went to what appeared to be an added lodge, or separate room, and there pushed aside the door flap. In that room the visitors saw what seemed to them a lake, which was round in figure. The old woman, making a circuit of the lake, then heaped the corn husks around its edges.

When this task was finished she set the corn husks on fire and they quickly burst into flames and the flames took up all the water of the lake. Then she said to the men of her household, "Now, I have again completed the preparations. Moreover, do you start now. And this shall also take place. You must be careful. In the course of your excursion you must not injure any person." These words she addressed to the men of her lodge. They then departed on their usual trip over the land.

And it was so, that the companions of De'haĕⁿ'hyō'wĕⁿ's remained in the lodge of the old woman during the entire time that they were in that country.

Furthermore, it happened that when they took a stroll in the country while the men of the lodge were absent, they came upon a spring of water which formed a large pool. So one of the party taking his bow and using it as a cane thrust it into the pool of water to see whether he could find any living thing in it; but he saw nothing to attract his attention. And so when they had returned to the lodge they again stood their bows in the customary place in a corner of the room.

When the men of the lodge had returned home from their excursion into the country, one of them said, "There is something in this lodge that has the smell of game (i.e., something to be killed)," and he at once began looking around from place to place.

Then the others after sniffing the air exclaimed, "It is true; there is something in here that smells like a game animal," and one went over to the place where the bows belonging to the companions of De'haĕⁿ'hyō'wĕⁿ's were standing. Taking one of the bows in his hand he said, "It is, indeed, this bow that has the scent," and turning to De'haĕⁿ'hyō'wĕⁿ's said, "To what place have you been? What is the place like where you touched something with this bow?"

In answering De'haĕⁿ'hyō'wĕⁿ's said, "Yonder, not far away, you know, there is a cliff, and on the farther side of it there is a spring of water, forming a deep pool."

Thereupon the men of the lodge exclaimed, "Let us all go to that place right away," and all started out of the lodge and they ran swiftly to the spring. When they arrived there De'haĕⁿ-'hyō'wĕⁿ's said to his companions, "There, in this spring and pool of water, I thrust my bow to rouse whatever might dwell in this pool."

Then one of the men of the country said, "It is assuredly certain that some mysterious creature abides herein. We shall see what it is. Furthermore, do you, our friends, stand yonder, a little aloof, and then you shall see the thing done, how we will kill it."

Heeding this admonition, the companions of De'haĕⁿ'hyō'-wĕⁿ's drew back a short distance and watched the men of the country make their dispositions to make the attack. They did not wait long to see a wonderful phenomenon. For the man of the country at once began their task. One touched with a rod the bottom of the pool, whence flowed the spring of water. And now, too, there began to be heard loud sounds, even such as are heard when the voicings of Thunder fill the air with a deafening din. Such was the tumult and confusion at this time that the now thoroughly frightened human beings ran fleeing from the spot to seek safety. Then, also, there were flashes of lightning followed by loud crashes and deep rumblings of the thunder. This uproar continued for some time when suddenly it ceased and one of the hosts of De'haĕⁿ'hyō'wĕⁿ's said, calling his guests back, "Oh, come back. We have now killed this creature."

Thereupon, when they had again assembled they departed, going back to their lodge. When they reached the lodge they said to the old woman, "We have now killed that uncanny creature, that otkon. Indeed, we do not know in what possible way it happened that this creature took up its abode so very near this lodge. We had never before noticed it. Perhaps it has been there a long time, since it had become so large in size. We have, perhaps, barely escaped some great misfortune." The old woman replied, saying gratefully, "What a very re-

markable matter it is, in which our visitors have been of assistance to us." And then in a moment she asked, "What is the
otkon? What is the figure and kind of thing you have so fortunately killed?" The men answered, "It is, indeed, the Great
Blue Lizard, which we have destroyed." So they rested for
the night.

Then next morning the old woman said to the men of her
lodge, "For myself, I am thinking that it is time, the exact time
of the year, when you should again make mellow and dampen
all the things that grow on the earth. What do you say?"

Thereupon, one of the men replied, "It would seem well,
perhaps, that you should ask Him who is the principal one to
be consulted in regard to our duties in this matter. It is possible
that He may say, 'It is now the proper time of the year in
which you should again make mellow and dampen all the
things that severally grow on the earth.' " And he ceased from
talking with her.

Then the aged woman arose from her seat and, gently pushing aside the door flap hanging at the doorway leading to the
adjoining room, said, "Do you not think that it is now, perhaps,
the proper time that the men should again make damp and
mellow the things that grow on the earth and the soil as well?"

Then the person addressed answered, saying, "For myself,
I, too, think that it is time, perhaps, for doing that about which
you have asked me. So let it be done as you wish."

Then, allowing the door flap to fall back the old woman
withdrew to her own location in the lodge. And in order to
make the needed preparations for carrying out the purpose of
her request she gathered a quantity of corn husks and again
entered the place in which the lake of water was and she again
heaped the corn husks along the edge or shore of the lake. When
she had placed the corn husks along the entire circuit of the
lake she set them on fire.

When the fire had become brisk and bright the old woman
turned to the men of the lodge and said to them, "I have now,
again, made the necessary preparations for the performance
of your accustomed task. And now, moreover, you had better
start on your journey to make all things that grow on the earth
damp and mellow, and the soil as well. And this also shall be

done; they who are visiting us shall accompany you wherever you may go; and you must carefully keep them from harm; and you must show them all things of interest along your journey."

Then, taking up their implements and weapons the men of the lodge and their guests departed. During the course of their long journey one of the hosts of De'haĕⁿ'hyō'wĕⁿ's and his men said, "You shall now see the things over which we have charge. He whom you are wont to call Hawĕññī'yo' (He the Ruler) is the person who has charged us with all these matters; and we shall continue to have the care of them as long as the earth endures— as long as it lasts. We shall tend all those things which he has planted on the earth; we shall habitually cause moisture (water) to fall on them, and we shall also keep all the water in the several rivers on the earth fresh at all times; and we shall also water all those things upon which you and your people live, so that all things which he has made to be shall live and shall not perish for the need of water. And you, you human beings, shall then live in health and contentment. Such are our duties from day to day."

Then it was that De'haĕⁿ'hyō'wĕⁿ's and his party looking down beneath saw another earth far below them. As they proceeded they heard loud sounds; they were like the voicings of Thunder when he approaches on earth; and now too there began to be bright flashes of lightning, and then there began to be rain; and then they, the raindrops, fell to the lower earth.

As they moved onward they saw a huge serpent which had formidable horns protruding from its head. Then one of the hosts of De'haĕⁿ'hyō'wĕⁿ's and his friends said, "Look at that thing, moving along swiftly yonder. It is known that were it to emerge permanently from the interior of the earth it would bring great misfortune to the things that dwell on the earth. In fact, it would bring to an end the days of a large multitude of you human beings. And that it never come forth permanently out of the ground is one of the duties with which we are strictly charged." Then, in a moment, the speaker continued, "Now, also, you shall see what will take place when we kill it."

Having their attention thus called to it, the party of De'haĕⁿ-'hyō'wĕⁿ's looking down saw on the lower earth a huge serpent having formidable horns protruding from its head; it moved swiftly along the ground. As they watched their hosts began to pursue it, and the voice of the Thunder was exceedingly loud and the flashes of lightning amazingly vivid.

Finally, the huge serpent was hit by its pursuers and it began to flee from them; it sought unsuccessfully to hide beneath standing trees, but these trees were struck and riven into splinters; and then it fled to the mountains, seeking to conceal itself beneath their shelter; but this was in vain, for it was repeatedly hit by the men of Thunder, and finally, it was killed.

As an explanation of this phenomenon, the hosts of De'haĕⁿ'-hyŏ'wĕⁿ's and his friends said, "It is verily true that beneath the surface of the ground whatever is otkon (i.e., malign by nature) moves to and fro from place to place. It would, indeed, be most unfortunate for us all should this species of being be permitted to travel from place to place upon the earth. And so they are doomed to abide beneath the surface of the ground in the interior of the earth.

"And now concerning the origin of these beings; it was he whom we call O'hä'ä' (The Ice-clad) that formed their bodies; and so too it came to pass that he whom you call Hawĕñnī'yo' (i.e., the Disposer, or Ruler) decided that so long as the earth endures these beings shall abide under the surface of the earth. And, furthermore, we will say that we ourselves believe that He who charged us with the performance of this task of keeping them beneath the surface of the earth will cause it to come to pass, perhaps when the earth is nearing its ending, then, and not until then, that these beings shall be permitted to come forth upon the earth. So is it, indeed, to come to pass that when the event is not distant—the ending of the earth—He will bring to an ending the duties with which we are severally charged to be performed for the benefit of the things that live upon the earth.

"And not until then shall the waters which are held in their several places become polluted; all other things shall likewise become old and decayed upon the earth; and all things that grow out of the ground too shall grow old and sear; indeed, all things shall become withered and decayed. So, now let us turn back homeward."

Then turning homeward the party retraced their steps. Upon

re-entering their lodge the spokesman of the party said to the old woman who presided over the lodgehold (household), "We have now completed the task of making damp and mellow all things that grow upon the face of the earth."

Then, the aged matron of the lodge arising from her seat went into the adjoining room of the lodge and said to the Person who occupied that room, "Now, they have, indeed, returned." Then the old woman withdrew and resumed her accustomed seat.

In a short time the door flap separating the adjoining room was pushed aside and the Person—a Man Being (Hĕñ'gwe')—thrust his head through the doorway and asked the returned men, "Have you now, indeed, completed the work? Have you made damp and mellow all things that grow on the earth that is beneath this one?"

Then the men replied in unison, "We have indeed accomplished our task as we were charged to do." And the Person from the adjoining room said, "Now, moreover, you must rest until there shall be another day; and then you shall again recommence the performance of the duties with which you are severally charged."

This conversation supplied the opportunity of seeing the Person to De'haĕⁿ'hyŏ'wĕⁿ's and his party. They were convinced that he too was Man; that he was, in fact, a Hĕñ'gwe'. But they were surprised, and even amazed, to see that one half of the body of this strange Person was in all respects like that of a human being but that the other half of his body was, in substance, crystal ice. They too, at this moment, felt a breeze that was chilling strike them from out of that doorway; but at this moment, this strange Man Being withdrew, and the door flap concealed the room from their further gaze.

Then, the aged matron of the lodge, addressing her guests, said, "That Person whom you have just seen is, in fact, the Foremost One, the Principal One, of all those who are charged with duties to perform in the economy of the earth. And he is called by us De'hodyă'tgă'ewĕⁿ' (i.e., He-Whose-Body-Is-Cleft-in-Twain); and He is also named Owi'soñ'dyoñ' (i.e., It Casts Ice, or It Hails); and it is this that you saw when He showed his face at the doorway, that there at once came forth from Him a cold breeze. And so that act will immediately cause the prospective days and the prospective nights on the earth below to become cold and wintry. Moreover, when the day again dawns (i.e., Next Year) He will again show His face but the other side of his body, and immediately there will blow hither a warming breeze."

Then the members of the lodge said one to another, "We now have paused in our labors in order to rest. Moreover, tomorrow it will come to pass that we shall take you back to the place whence you departed, for you have been here now many days. And this is, of course, what you human beings call Springtime."

Then all the members of the lodge fell asleep in their several places. When morning came the door flap separating the room from the adjoining one was again thrust aside, and the strange Man Being, De'hodyă'tgā'ewĕⁿ', again showed his face and the other half (the flesh side) of his body at the doorway, and He called out aloud, "Now then, all you people, awake and arise; it is now time to do so." Then all the sleepers awoke. And as they awoke from sleep they severally outstretched their arms and bodies, loudly yawning and uttering loud vociferations, as is the case on earth, when the voice of Thunder is heard. There arose, too, a warm breeze of wind, and then the men of the lodge went out.

It was but a short time after this that they re-entered the lodge and said to their guests, "You should accompany us on our intended journey, so that you may see an otkon (a daimon) which inhabits certain trees standing hard by the place whence we returned. It is, indeed, now a long time that we have been making attempts to kill and destroy this Being, for it is possessed of very powerful orenda, or magic power."

Thereupon, De'haĕⁿ'hyō'wĕⁿ's replied, "It is, of course, perhaps true, that that should come to pass, that we accompany you to learn what manner of being that may be."

So, all the men of the lodge started on their journey, and went directly to the place where the being, the otkon, had its lair. Having gone a long distance, the men of Thunder finally said to their guests, "There, indeed, is the place where we have kept saying, 'An otkon abides.' You must stand in yonder place, quite safely removed from any danger from this being. And then you shall see it as we shall cause it to come forth from its lair."

Thereupon the party of De'haën'hyō'wĕn's withdrew to the designated position. Then they saw one of their hosts go forward and strike one of the trees several sharp blows with his club; then they saw the being come forth from its lair, and they concluded that it was what they themselves called a squirrel. But the Being, or Squirrel, in turn, thrust its body only partly out of its hiding place; at once the Men of Thunder hurled their shots at it; there were loud thunderings and the lightning flashes were vivid, and there arose a great tumult and a terrific hurricane of wind.

But, in a short time, the Men of Thunder ceased for a moment, having failed to hit the Being. At once the Squirrel, or Being, quickly descended the tree on which it then was, and running to another tree climbed it in an effort to escape its tormentors. But, in a very short time, the Men of Thunder shivered this tree, and the Squirrel fled back to the tree in which was its lair and it swiftly climbed back into it. And the Men of Thunder said, "Now, indeed, you have seen what we call otkon (daimon). And the time is now, indeed, long since we have been making vain efforts to destroy this Being, this great Otkon."

In replying De'haën'hyō'wĕn's said, "It is now our turn; we will now attempt to kill the Otkon." But the Men of Thunder answered, "We fear that the attempt will not result favorably; you may be injured, for, indeed, this is an Otkon endued with power beyond measure."

But De'haën'hyō'wĕn's assuringly replied, "We know that we ourselves can do this task." Then the Men of Thunder replied, "If you are determined to make the attempt, we will assist you, should you fail in your attempt."

At once one of the party of De'haën'hyō'wĕn's went up to the tree in which the Squirrel had its lair and tapped on it with his club. As soon as he began to tap on the tree the Squirrel again thrust out its head and half its body and gazed at the men. Then De'haën'hyō'wĕn's, taking a knob-headed arrow from his quiver, shot at it, hitting it fair in the head, and then the body of the Squirrel came tumbling to the ground.

Thereupon the Men of Thunder took up the body of the Squirrel to carry back with them and then with their guests they started for their home. When they reached their lodge the Men of Thunder said to the old woman, "Now, in fact, our visitors, for their part, have killed it—they have, indeed, killed the Otkon, which for a very long time we have failed to kill."

Answering this statement of the men of her lodge, the old woman said, "I am indeed very thankful to receive this news. This then shall be done; the skin of this Otkon shall belong to me, seeing that it is so precious, and it shall be the robe of my couch."

And so De'haĕⁿ'hyō'wĕⁿ's set to work and carefully skinned the Squirrel; and then he neatly prepared it and then he spread it on a suitable frame to dry. When it had thoroughly dried De'haĕⁿ'hyō'wĕⁿ's presented it to the old woman, assuring her that that was the method his people employed in preserving the skins of animals. The old woman received the skin with many thanks, for she felt that she had come into possession of a skin which was very precious to her.

Then, addressing the men of her lodge she said, "They who are our visitors are the ones who have accomplished this matter for us. So in token of this the following shall come to pass; and that is, that one of these persons, our visitors, shall remain here as one of us; he shall become a coworker with you, for the reason that he and his kindred were able to accomplish that which you yourselves were unable to do."

In giving assent to this proposition the men replied, "Let that, too, be done; let Him who is foremost among us speak it, and it shall be done." The old woman replied, "That is even so; His consent is all that is required to accomplish this desirable thing." And she at once arose from her seat, and going thence to the doorway leading to the adjoining room, and pushing aside the door flap she said, "Behold. Will you confirm the proposition that one of the men visiting us shall remain here as one of us, while his companions shall return hence to their own homes? And the reason for this is, that he was able to kill the Squirrel—the Otkon—and since the men who live in this lodge had for so long a time failed to do it; I desire further that he shall at all times assist them and that he shall be a coworker with them."

Answering the old woman, De'hodyă'tgā'ewĕnᶜ said, "I willingly confirm this proposition, if it so be, that he himself is freely willing, and, of course, that he will, perhaps, volunteer to have his life pounded (in a mortar). It will then, as you know, be possible for him to help them continually." And He ceased speaking.

Then the old woman returned to the group comprising the party of De'haĕnᶜhyō'wĕnᶜs and said to elect man, "Hatch′kwĭᶜ (Behold), wilt thou confirm the proposition that thou shalt remain here alone, while your companions return to their own homes? If thou wilt be willing to agree to this proposition, I will, furthermore, give thee a new name, and this shall be the name by which they shall hereafter habitually call thee, namely, Dăgā′ĕnᶜdă′ (i.e., The Thaw, or the Warm Spring Wind)."

Thereupon, this member of the party of De'haĕnᶜhyō'wĕnᶜs replied, "I willingly agree to this proposal; I am quite willing to be an assistant to them in their work." And the old woman answering, said, "I am much pleased that the matter is now settled. We, indeed, have become of one opinion, having one purpose in view."

At this time De'hodyă'tgā'ewĕnᶜ interrupted by saying, "Now, then, do bring his person (body) into this room, and let him at once be prepared for his duties."

Then, the old woman addressing the visitor, who had consented to remain, said, "Come. The time has now arrived for doing what you have agreed to do for us, for doing what you require to fit yourself for your new duties."

Then the man who had consented to remain entered the room in which abode De'hodyă'tgā'ewĕnᶜ. As soon as he had entered the room De'hodyă'tgā'ewĕnᶜ said to him, "Here stands the mortar. Thou must place thyself in it. Now, verily, thou shalt change thyself, thy person, as to the kind of its flesh and thy life." Obeying his instructor, the man at once placed himself in the mortar, that is, in the hollowed end of the mortar wherein the grain was usually pounded, and then De'hodyă'tgā'ewĕnᶜ drew near and taking up the pestle pounded him in the manner in which corn is pounded, striking three several blows, and he then said to the visitor, "Thy flesh has now changed in kind. The task is now accomplished. So now you may sing to try your voice."

The transformed man began to sing, and De'haĕⁿ'hyŏ'wĕⁿ's and his one remaining friend heard the singing, which sounded to them exactly like the voice of approaching Thunder, only that its volume was somewhat less, as they heard it. And they said, one to the other, "Now, it is known that he, Dăgă'ĕⁿ'dă', is approaching," and, shortly, their transformed friend re-entered the room.

In a short time thereafter the old woman said to the men of the lodge, now including the newly transformed person, "Furthermore, you shall now start on your journey, and you shall now begin again to make mellow and wet anew all the things that are earth-products, growing on the earth beneath. And this, moreover, shall be done. Dăgă'ĕⁿdă' shall take the lead. And so it shall be he whom they who dwell on the earth below shall name first in the Spring of the year. Of course the human beings will say, 'Now, the Warm Wind of Spring has come down; now the hot spring wind blows again. And so now the spring season will come upon us.' And it shall continue thus, moreover, so long as the earth shall stand, that it shall be customary when the Spring season arrives for the human beings to name him first, who came from the earth beneath. And it shall be customary for them to say, 'Now, the Warm Wind of Spring has descended—the Spring Wind.' And, verily, they shall never forget, indeed, each several time it arrives— the interchange on the earth—the line of demarcation between the snowtime and the summertime, for Dăgă'ĕⁿ'dă' shall continue to change the prospective days and the prospective nights of the future time. Now, you men must start to accompany a part of the way homeward those who have been visiting us for so many days." But before they got started she resumed her discourse, saying, "Now I will tell you who are human beings of the earth that it is even I whom you call the 'Nocturnal Light-Orb' (the Moon). And He it is whom you and your ancestors have called De'hăĕⁿ'hyawă"gi', and some-times Hawĕññi'yo' (the Master or Ruler), who has commis-

sioned me. And this is what He has commissioned me to do:
When it becomes dark on the earth, then it is I who shall
cause it to be measurably light and to be warm on the earth,
so that it become not too cold nor too dark; so that all the
things that should grow, may grow unharmed on the earth,
and also all those things on which you, human beings, live,
dwelling as you do on the earth beneath. Until the time that
the earth shall stand no more He has commissioned me to
act and to do my duty. It is thus with us all. He has commissioned us only for the time during which the earth beneath
shall stand, or endure. Moreover, I will now impart to you
the following information, so that you oñ'gwe' (human beings),
living on the earth, shall know that they who abide here in
this place are, as you know, those whom you call 'Hadi-
wĕññoda'dye's' (They Whose Voices Stand Out from Place
to Place), the Thunderers; and so that you shall know that
He who established this world is One whom you call De'haĕⁿ'-
hyawä''gi' and also Hawĕññni'yo', or the Ruler, or the Disposer.

"It was He who decreed that these men shall customarily
appear to the lower world from a certain direction, and that
is, from the west, and that they shall move in the direction
of the east.

"And so let this be a sign to you who dwell on the lower
earth, that when it so comes to pass that these Men of Thunder
shall come from the east, you shall know at once its meaning,
and shall say one to another, 'Now, it seems that the time is
coming near at hand in which He will take to pieces the earth
as it stands.' Verily, such is the strict manner in which He has
commissioned us, charging us with definite duties. It is well
known that the Diurnal Light-Orb (the Sun) customarily comes
from one certain direction; in like manner, it is also true of me,
for I too must appear to the lower world from one certain
direction. And this obligation on our part is fixed; and our
coming shall never occur in a different manner as long as the
earth endures—at least until that day in the future when He
himself whom you call sometimes Hawĕññni'yo' shall change
and transform what He himself has established.

"So now, moreover, the time has arrived for you to start for
your home; but, first, before you depart, you must stroll about

this upper world to see everything that may be beneficial to you and to your people in the days to come; and by the time you will return from this tour of inspection, I will have made ready what you shall take with you, when you shall go again to make mellow and wet the earth beneath. And this, too, upon which I am at work is something about which I must tell you something. I am engaged in making myself a mantle, and the material out of which I am weaving it is, indeed, truly what you think it is—for it is human hair with which I am working. And you have observed as well, that each time I lay my work aside for a moment, my small dwarf dog often undoes quite all that I have done. I will now tell you by what means I obtain the human hair with which I am making myself a mantle.

"It is a fact, that when some human being dies on the earth below, one hair from his or her head detaches itself and departs thence, coming directly to me. And it is these hairs that I am using in making my mantle.

"And this too serves as a sign to me that one has ceased to be on the earth below, and that that person is traveling hither. And this too shall endure as long as the earth beneath shall endure and have form. Moreover, mark this well, that when He will cause the expiring of human beings on the earth below to cease, it shall just then and not before be possible for me to finish the mantle upon which I am working; and that (the number of hairs in the mantle) shall then bear witness to the number of persons who have visited the earth below while it lasted. So now you may take a stroll."

Then the men of the lodge and the entire party of Deꞌhaĕⁿ-ꞌhyŏ'wĕⁿ's started out to view the notable things in the vicinity of the lodge. They first went to that place where for the first time during their visit they saw the beauty and pleasantness of that upper world; they admired the strawberry plants, growing there and bearing luscious berries, that were as tall as the high grasses among which they grew; and they were also in bloom, for their bearing season was continuous; and they saw too the growing trees full of rich blossoms; never before had they seen such beautiful flowers, which supplied the light of that upper world; and they saw the plants and the shrubs and bushes full of fruits of all kinds, all growing luxuriantly; and never before had they seen such fine paths leading in various directions; and they saw along these paths the trees whose overhanging boughs and lower branches loaded with blossoms made them seem like long bowers of flowers, freighted with all manner of fragrance.

They also saw figures of human beings—oñ'gwe'—promenading along the paths from place to place, but they realized that their faces were sights (or visions), and so it was not possible for them to hold any conversation with them.

Farther along in their ramble they came to a village which was inhabited, there being many lodges standing in different places in the manner of a village of human beings.

In passing through the village one of the hosts, addressing De'haĕⁿ'hyō'wĕⁿ's, said, "In this lodge, standing here apart, thy mother dwells. She was still on the earth below when you and your party departed on this journey; but she started for this country soon after you had departed therefrom. Here, also, dwell your relations—all those who were able to observe the customs of their ancestors during the time they dwelt on the earth below."

It was then that they returned to the place where the old woman awaited their return, and on entering the lodge they said to her, "We have now returned from our ramble." And the old woman answered, "I have quite completed my preparations. And now, moreover, you must start on your journey homeward and the men of the lodge will accompany you a part of the way home. In going home, you must go around by the place where abides the Light-Orb (the Sun) that travels by day. Let them see him too. And may your dreams foreshadow your safe arrival home."

Thereupon they departed from the lodge of the old woman. Not far distant from the home of their hosts there stood a lodge. One of their hosts told De'haĕⁿ'hyō'wĕⁿ's and his friend that that was the lodge of the Sun. They said, "Thence, he starts to give light to the world beneath this one."

Having reached the lodge, they entered it and they saw the Sun engaged in cooking chestnut meal mush. And then one of the men of Thunder said, "We are now on our journey, accompanying these human beings a part of their way home.

We are taking these men back to the earth below this one. And the reason that we have come around this way is that we desired to have you and them see one another."

Then the Master of the lodge raised his voice and said to his vistors, "It is I, indeed, who has met with you and it is I whom you habitually call in your ceremonies, 'Ho'sgĕⁿ'äge''-dăgōnă', He-the-Great-War-Chief, and our Elder Brother, the Diurnal Orb of Light.' And I have just completed my usual preparations for my journey upon which I am about to start. Furthermore, just as soon as you will depart hence, I will start on my journey to make the earth below light and warm again."

And, in a short time, the visitors, having seen all that was interesting in the lodge, said, "Let us now, moreover, go hence on our journey," and they at once resumed their own course.

They had not gone very far when the Men of Thunder said, "It is now time for us to begin. And, moreover, it shall be Dăgă'ĕⁿdă' who shall be the first one to act."

Then Dăgă'ĕⁿ'dă', the former member of the party of De'ha-ĕⁿ'hyō'wĕⁿ's, began to sing in a loud voice and thus set his orenda (mystic power) to work out his function. And then the two human beings who were to return to the earth below saw it in the distance beneath them, and they heard, too, the people dwelling on the earth say, "Now the beginning of the Spring Season has come upon us. Indeed, the Spring Wind is blowing warm and hot, and now, too, the Thunders are singing thence, in the distance."

Then the party moved on; and they looked down on the earth below from above the sky and the clouds, and they saw the effect of the singing of the Thunder Men. At this time, the voices of the Thunder Men who were singing sounded loud and angry, as it were, as they moved along the sky, and on the earth below fell torrents of rain with great force, and they, too, saw the creeks and rivers swell and overflow their banks.

They had not, seemingly, to the human beings of the party, gone very far, when they were startled by their alighting on the earth below. And then one of the Thunder Men said to them, "Now, indeed, you are again at your homes. Indeed you departed hence, and so now we have fully discharged our obligation to bring you safely back to your homes. So, moreover, we will now tell you something regarding another matter. It is now a long time since the former inhabitants of this country have withdrawn from here and have gone to another settlement. You will, indeed, find them in the place where they are now living."

Having conducted them some distance on the ground, one of the Men of Thunder said, "Moreover, we will now separate one from another. And, in the future, this, too, shall come to pass. And that is, that you must keep us in remembrance. And, moreover, for this purpose, you shall employ the Native Tobacco (i.e., Gayĕⁿʻgwănōwĕⁿsgwă˝gōñă'), making an offering thereby in words and in act. And this shall be quite sufficient for the purpose, for we will hear the thanksgiving and will accept the offering at once; and in like manner shall it be done to all those, and only to those, who are charged by Him with duties and important functions. If you should think of Him or of Them, that is the chief and essential thing—the employment of Native Tobacco by you in this important matter habitually. Such is the method which you who still live on the earth here below must customarily employ in forming your messages of thanksgiving. Verily, such is the regulation and decree ordained and promulgated by Him whom you call Dehaĕⁿʻhyāwă˝gi', and familiarly as Hawĕññi'yo' (He, the Master). And these are the words which we thought it necessary for you to hear before we separated one from another. So may you have good dreams (i.e., good luck)."

Then the two parties separated, the one from the other. And the Men of Thunder departed from the earth, going back into cloudland, and so back to their own lodge.

In their turn, Deʻhaĕⁿʻhyō'wĕⁿ's and his lone companion started from the place where they had been left. They were not long in finding the traces of the former home of their friends, and they found that the place had become overgrown with trees which had grown large and which stood thick; and one who was unacquainted with the facts would be in doubt whether or not any person had ever lived in that place before that time.

Then Deʻhaĕⁿʻhyō'wĕⁿ's said to his companion, "Verily, it

seems that now we must depend on ourselves to find our people. We must, therefore, now go to seek the place where they now dwell." And they started, directing their course eastward, toward the sunrise, as they had been instructed.

At no great distance they saw the smoke from a village, and they made their way to it. So, on entering the first lodge they reached, De'haĕⁿ'hyō'wĕⁿ's said, "We have now returned home." In reply, the master of the lodge said, "Whither did you go? And who are you? As to myself, I do not know you."

Answering him, De'haĕⁿ'hyō'wĕⁿ's said, "Have you not at any time heard a tradition, that a number of men, thirty in all, started on a journey following the path of the Sun?—a party formed by De'haĕⁿ'hyō'wĕⁿ's and Gaĕⁿ'hyăkdoñ'dye', two famous war chiefs, of men who had thoroughly habituated themselves to warlike exercises? They undertook while going toward the sunsetting to kill and scalp all the people whom they might encounter on their way."

Then the master of the lodge said to them in reply, "I myself know nothing of the matter about which you are speaking. When such a thing may have taken place I do not know. It may be that the old woman, living in yonder lodge, may, perhaps, for her part, know about this matter. You should go over to consult her about it."

Then De'haĕⁿ'hyō'wĕⁿ's and his companion passed on, going to the lodge pointed out to them. So entering the lodge in which the old woman designated lived, De'haĕⁿ'hyō'wĕⁿ's again said, "Do you know the circumstance in the history of your people that, in the long ago, some men—warriors, three times ten in number—went on an expedition, from which they never returned; the party was formed by two war chiefs, De'haĕⁿ'hyō'wĕⁿ's and Gaĕⁿ'hyăkdoñ'dye'? They went toward the sunsetting, following the path of the Sun."

Answering these questions the old woman said, "It is indeed true that such an event took place. I have heard my deceased grandmother customarily say that when she was still a child men to the number of thirty started out on an expedition, but that they never returned to their homes." And then after some moments of thinking she added, "Probably the man who dwells yonder in that lodge, not far away from here, remembers the whole matter, for he has been living during an exceedingly long life; and so he probably is familiar with the tradition about which you speak. So you had better visit him and seek for further information from him."

So De'haĕⁿ'hyō'wĕⁿ's and his companion again started on their quest for someone who might know them. Reaching their new destination they found the very old man, of whom the old woman had spoken, and they asked him, "Do you remember an affair which took place hitherto many years ago, in which warriors to the number of thirty departed hence, going on an expedition along the path of the Sun?"

After a few moments of reflection the old man replied, "I remember the matter full well. This is what took place: There lived a people yonder, at some distance from here; and there is where this affair took place; there were a number of young men who had grown up together, and they were all about sixteen years of age; and thirty of these young men organized themselves into a war party, binding themselves together by means of an oath, or vow.

"And when they had fully organized their troop, they caused the people of the entire community to assemble at the Long-lodge of public gatherings. And when the people were assembled in the Long-lodge De'haĕⁿ'hyō'wĕⁿ's arose and said, 'Now then, it shall be made known to you who have assembled here that we have indeed completed our preparations. We, young men, who are three tens in number, have enlisted by notching the stick to go out on an expedition along the path of the Sun. We made the agreement strong, for we commingled together our minds into unity; and so now it is as if we had only a single head, only a single body of flesh, only a single life, and we shall bleed as one person. Moreover, we now renounce our kindred, and we also forswear our lives.

" 'Moreover, we will now depart from here. We will direct our course toward the sunsetting, for we desire to make an excursion to the place of sunsetting—to the place where the Diurnal Light-Orb customarily promenades to and fro. Our band have appointed me and my dear brother to be their chiefs to lead them. We, too, have made a solemn vow that no matter what the situation confronting us, no matter what will be transpiring ahead of us, we will nevertheless pass onward in our journey.

" 'We have indeed enlisted in this matter seriously by notching the stick, and this is of course, as you well know, the pledge that each one of us will do what we have agreed to do one with another.' Then they departed from us, and they have never returned."

Then, De'haĕⁿ'hyō'wĕⁿ's replying to the old man said, "How long ago may it be since that event took place?" The old man answered, "It is now three generations ago; that is, three generations have passed away since that time." And then De'haĕⁿ'hyō'wĕⁿ's asked, "Who were the chiefs of those who departed?" And the old man said, "De'haĕⁿ'hyō'wĕⁿ's and his brother, Gaĕⁿ'hyakdoñ'dye'. These two persons were chosen as the chiefs of the party."

To which De'haĕⁿ'hyō'wĕⁿ's replied, "Verily, Grandsire, we are the remaining members of that party—my brother, Gaĕⁿ-'hyăkdoñ'dye', our friend, Dagā'dye', and I. So many of the number have now returned home. It was, verily, our party that departed from the place where your and my people formerly dwelt, at that place yonder not far away."

But the old man, still doubting what he had heard, said, "It is probably not you who went away, because it appears from your youthful aspect that you have just reached manhood, and that event occurred a very long time ago."

De'haĕⁿ'hyō'wĕⁿ's, however, answered, saying, "Nevertheless, we are the very persons who started, those of us who still are left alive. We have now arrived home again." And the old man said, "If possible, then, do tell me the name of the chief of our people when you departed."

De'haĕⁿ'hyō'wĕⁿ's quickly answered, "Dăgä'hidoñ'dye' was the name of the chief of our people at that time." Now convinced of what he had doubted, the old man answered, "That statement is, indeed, also true. The fact that he was my grandfather is the reason why I am so fully acquainted with that matter. And now I submit that I am convinced that it is indeed you and your friends who departed so many years ago, and that it is you who have returned home. And as it is meet so to do, our present chief shall now be made cognizant of this matter. So remain here in this lodge, and I will now send him word of your return to await his pleasure."

So the chief was made acquainted with the matter. He at once sent out runners, giving notice to all the people to assemble immediately in the Long-lodge of public meetings to hear something that was most startling and important; he set the following day for the assembling of the people.

So, when the morning of the next day dawned, all the people made the necessary preparations to attend the great council and hurriedly made their several ways to the assembly hall. De'haĕⁿ'hyō'wĕⁿ's and his two companions also went there in company with their host, the old man, whose grandfather was a former chief of his people.

The assemblage was large, for everyone who could possibly leave home attended in person.

When all were seated, the chief arose, and, ceremoniously greeting the newly arrived men, said, "We have learned only a hint of what occurred during your expedition, and we desire fervently to know more of the events through which you have passed while you have been absent. And so now we shall listen to the whole account. And we will now listen to the leader of the party, De'haĕⁿ'hyō'wĕⁿ's."

De'haĕⁿ'hyō'wĕⁿ's then arose amidst great silence and spoke only as follows: "There were thirty of us who started on the expedition along the path of the sun; but there are only three of us who have returned. It is I who bear the name De'haĕⁿ'hyō'wĕⁿ's. On this hand sits my brother, Gaĕⁿ'hyakdoñ'dye', for such is the name that he bears; and on this hand sits our friend, Dăga'dye', for such is the name that he bears; so many only are we who survive.

"And this, too, came to pass during the time of our expedition along the path of the Sun, to the skyland. One of our number remains there as an assistant to the people in that faraway land. It is, moreover, quite impossible for him to return to this earth to live again."

And then De'haĕⁿ'hyō'wĕⁿ's related at great length all that had occurred to him and his party from the time they had left their homes until their return. He told of all things that had transpired and all things that they had seen during their absence; these things were recited in detail, completing the recital with their return home. Then De'haĕⁿ'hyō'wĕⁿ's resumed his seat.

The chief then said, "It was in fact a marvelous thing that was done by this party. It is a very long time ago since you departed from your homes. But, now, you have returned to them, numbering only three persons. Of course, one of the most essential things about this matter to be remembered is that Dc'haĕⁿ'hyawă"gi', sometimes called Hawĕñni'yo', forewilled that you, and only you, should be enabled to return home safely.

"Furthermore, preparations have been made so that we may now mutually and severally exchange greetings. And, further, then, this shall be done. You, the surviving ones of the party, three in number, will take a suitable position, and then I will take the lead in a ceremonial greeting to you; for I of course stand in the stead of the one who was the chief of the people when you departed; my name is, indeed, Dagä'hidoñ'dye'; and then we will do this: we will mutually and severally stroke one another's body in greeting. This ceremony shall be for all persons, including our children—we will all greet one another in this ceremonial manner; for such was the custom of our fathers on such occasions."

So De'haĕⁿ'hyō'wĕⁿ's and his two friends arose and took suitable positions to receive the greetings of the people. And the people with the chief in the lead came forward and cordially stroked their bodies according to the custom. All the men, all the women, and all the children arose and greeted them.

When the ceremony was over the chief said, "This, too, shall be done. We will do, in the future, all the things that we have today learned should be done. And this, too, you shall know— you who have just returned home—that you and we shall be equal in the enjoyment and disposition of the things that we possess; so that our minds and yours shall think in peace. Here, you know, dwell the people, and now of course we again shall commingle and associate together. So now, too, everything is ready for us to rejoice and be happy, seeing that you have returned home in safety and health.

"And the first thing to be done is to make merry by a game.

They whose bodies are strong will play at a game of lacrosse ball; and thus shall they amuse your and our minds, that you may rejoice. When that shall have passed, then we shall dance, beginning with the Song of the Pigeons.

"And when that is passed, it will be time for us to disperse to our homes." Thereupon, De'haĕⁿ'hyŏ'wĕⁿ's arose and said, "It is indeed a marvelous matter to know that we have been absent from our people during three generations. And that, too, that we are rejoicing that we have, though much decreased in number, returned to our homes. We are indeed very happy that we are again one people with you."

Then the young men went to the public gaming grounds and there engaged in an exciting game of lacrosse ball. And when this game was over, the people assembled in the Long-lodge of public meetings and there they performed the ceremony of the Song of the Pigeons. They danced all the songs of this ceremony, which is quite long and exciting. Even the children danced to show their pleasure at seeing the returned men. (This is the end of the story.)

Cherokee

Before smallpox, wars, and removal the Cherokee numbered upward of twenty thousand people ranged through a vast and sprawling territory which covered essentially the entire Allegheny region—about forty thousand square miles. Their proper tribal name is Yûñ′ wiyă′, signifying the "real people," and the fall of this empire is one of the darkest blots on our national escutcheon, for the Cherokee made every attempt to accommodate themselves to the white life-style that surrounded them. They built schools, libraries, mills; they farmed and owned livestock. It was not enough; their land was too valuable, and Andrew Jackson sent them west with the other tribes. These myths and stories, however, were gathered on the old home grounds of the tribe in North Carolina where a few of them still live, separated by several hundred miles from their brothers and sisters in Oklahoma. There are several excellent studies of Cherokee culture and history, the most recent of which is Thurman Wilkins' *Cherokee Tragedy*.

How the World Was Made

The earth is a great island floating in a sea of water, and suspended at each of the four cardinal points by a cord hanging down from the sky vault, which is of solid rock. When the world grows old and worn out, the people will die and the cords will break and let the earth sink down into the ocean, and all will be water again. The Indians are afraid of this.

When all was water, the animals were above in Gălûñ′lătĭ, beyond the arch; but it was very much crowded, and they were wanting more room. They wondered what was below the water,

From James Mooney, *Myths of the Cherokee, 19th Annual Report of the Bureau of American Ethnology, 1897-98*, Part I (Washington, 1900).

and at last Dâyuni'sĭ, "Beaver's Grandchild," the little Water-beetle, offered to go and see if it could learn. It darted in every direction over the surface of the water, but could find no firm place to rest. Then it dived to the bottom and came up with some soft mud, which began to grow and spread on every side until it became the island which we call the earth. It was after-ward fastened to the sky with four cords, but no one remembers who did this.

At first the earth was flat and very soft and wet. The animals were anxious to get down, and sent out different birds to see if it was yet dry, but they found no place to alight and came back again to Gălûñ'lătĭ. At last it seemed to be time, and they sent out the Buzzard and told him to go and make ready for them. This was the Great Buzzard, the father of all the buzzards we see now. He flew all over the earth, low down near the ground, and it was still soft. When he reached the Cherokee country, he was very tired, and his wings began to flap and strike the ground, and wherever they struck the earth there was a valley, and where they turned up again there was a mountain. When the animals above saw this, they were afraid that the whole world would be mountains, so they called him back, but the Cherokee country remains full of mountains to this day.

When the earth was dry and the animals came down, it was still dark, so they got the sun and set it in a track to go every day across the island from east to west, just overhead. It was too hot this way, and Tsiska'gĭlĭ', the Red Crawfish, had his shell scorched a bright red, so that his meat was spoiled; and the Cherokee do not eat it. The conjurers put the sun another handbreadth higher in the air, but it was still too hot. They raised it another time, and another, until it was seven hand-breadths high and just under the sky arch. Then it was right, and they left it so. This is why the conjurers call the highest place Gûlkwâ'gine Di'gălûñ'lătiyûñ', "the seventh height," be-cause it is seven handbreadths above the earth. Every day the sun goes along under this arch, and returns at night on the upper side to the starting place.

There is another world under this, and it is like ours in everything—animals, plants, and people—save that the seasons are different. The streams that come down from the mountains are the trails by which we reach this underworld, and the springs at their heads are the doorways by which we enter it, but to do this one must fast and go to water and have one of the underground people for a guide. We know that the seasons in the underworld are different from ours, because the water in the springs is always warmer in winter and cooler in summer than the outer air.

When the animals and plants were first made—we do not know by whom—they were told to watch and keep awake for seven nights, just as young men now fast and keep awake when they pray to their medicine. They tried to do this, and nearly all were awake through the first night, but the next night several dropped off to sleep, and the third night others were asleep, and then others, until, on the seventh night, of all the animals only the owl, the panther, and one or two more were still awake. To these were given the power to see and to go about in the dark, and to make prey of the birds and animals which must sleep at night. Of the trees only the cedar, the pine, the spruce, the holly, and the laurel were awake to the end, and to them it was given to be always green and to be greatest for medicine, but to the others it was said: "Because you have not endured to the end you shall lose your hair every winter."

Men came after the animals and plants. At first there were only a brother and sister until he struck her with a fish and told her to multiply, and so it was. In seven days a child was born to her, and thereafter every seven days another, and they increased very fast until there was danger that the world could not keep them. Then it was made that a woman should have only one child in a year, and it has been so ever since.

The First Fire

In the beginning there was no fire, and the world was cold, until the Thunders (Ani′-Hyûñ′tĭkwălâ′skĭ), who lived up in Gălûñ′lătĭ, sent their lightning and put fire into the bottom of a hollow sycamore tree which grew on an island. The animals knew it was there, because they could see the smoke coming out at the top, but they could not get to it on account of the water, so they held a council to decide what to do. This was a long time ago.

Every animal that could fly or swim was anxious to go after the fire. The Raven offered, and because he was so large and strong they thought he could surely do the work, so he was sent first. He flew high and far across the water and alighted on the sycamore tree, but while he was wondering what to do next, the heat had scorched all his feathers black, and he was frightened and came back without the fire. The little Screech-owl (Wa'huhu') volunteered to go, and reached the place safely, but while he was looking down into the hollow tree a blast of hot air came up and nearly burned out his eyes. He managed to fly home as best he could, but it was a long time before he could see well, and his eyes are red to this day. Then the Hooting Owl (U'guku') and the Horned Owl (Tskĭlĭ') went, but by the time they got to the hollow tree the fire was burning so fiercely that the smoke nearly blinded them, and the ashes carried up by the wind made white rings about their eyes. They had to come home again without the fire, but with all their rubbing they were never able to get rid of the white rings.

Now no more of the birds would venture, and so the little Uksu'hĭ snake, the black racer, said he would go through the water and bring back some fire. He swam across to the island and crawled through the grass to the tree, and went in by a small hole at the bottom. The heat and smoke were too much for him, too, and after dodging about blindly over the hot ashes until he was almost on fire himself he managed by good luck to get out again at the same hole, but his body had been scorched black, and he has ever since had the habit of darting and doubling on his track as if trying to escape from close quarters. He came back, and the great blacksnake, Gûle'gĭ, "The Climber," offered to go for fire. He swam over to the island and climbed up the tree on the outside, as the blacksnake always does, but when he put his head down into the hole the smoke choked him so that he fell into the burning stump, and before he could climb out again he was as black as the Uksu'hĭ.

Now they held another council, for still there was no fire, and the world was cold, but birds, snakes, and four-footed animals all had some excuse for not going, because they were all afraid to venture near the burning sycamore, until at last Kănăne'skĭ Amai'yĕhĭ (the Water Spider) said she would go.

This is not the water spider that looks like a mosquito, but the other one, with black downy hair and red stripes on her body. She can run on top of the water or dive to the bottom, so there would be no trouble to get over to the island, but the question was, How could she bring back the fire? "I'll manage that," said the Water Spider; so she spun a thread from her body and wove it into a *tusti* bowl, which she fastened on her back. Then she crossed over to the island and through the grass to where the fire was still burning. She put one little coal of fire into her bowl, and came back with it, and ever since we have had fire, and the Water Spider still keeps her *tusti* bowl.

Origin of Disease and Medicine

In the old days the beasts, birds, fishes, insects, and plants could all talk, and they and the people lived together in peace and friendship. But as time went on the people increased so rapidly that their settlements spread over the whole earth, and the poor animals found themselves beginning to be cramped for room. This was bad enough, but to make it worse Man invented bows, knives, blowguns, spears, and hooks, and began to slaughter the larger animals, birds, and fishes for their flesh or their skins, while the smaller creatures, such as the frogs and worms, were crushed and trodden upon without thought, out of pure carelessness or contempt. So the animals resolved to consult upon measures for their common safety.

The Bears were the first to meet in council in their townhouse under Kuwâ'hĭ mountain, the "Mulberry Place," and the old White Bear chief presided. After each in turn had complained of the way in which Man killed their friends, ate their flesh, and used their skins for his own purposes, it was decided to begin war at once against him. Someone asked what weapons Man used to destroy them. "Bows and arrows, of course," cried all the Bears in chorus. "And what are they made of?" was the next question. "The bow of wood, and the string of our entrails," replied one of the Bears. It was then proposed that they make a bow and some arrows and see if they could not use the same weapons against Man himself. So one Bear got a nice piece of locust wood and another sacrificed himself for the good of the rest in order to furnish a piece of his entrails for the string. But when everything was ready and the first Bear stepped up to make the trial, it was found that in letting the arrow fly after drawing back the bow, his long claws caught the string and spoiled the shot. This was annoying, but someone suggested that they might trim his claws, which was accordingly done, and on a second trial it was found that the arrow went straight to the mark. But here the chief, the old White Bear, objected, saying it was necessary that they should have long claws in order to be able to climb trees. "One of us has already died to furnish the bowstring, and if we now cut off our claws we must all starve together. It is better to trust to the teeth and claws that nature gave us, for it is plain that Man's weapons were not intended for us."

No one could think of any better plan, so the old chief dismissed the council and the Bears dispersed to the woods and thickets without having concerted any way to prevent the increase of the human race. Had the result of the council been otherwise, we should now be at war with the Bears, but as it is, the hunter does not even ask the Bear's pardon when he kills one.

The Deer next held a council under their chief, the Little Deer, and after some talk decided to send rheumatism to every hunter who should kill one of them unless he took care to ask their pardon for the offense. They sent notice of their decision to the nearest settlement of Indians and told them at the same time what to do when necessity forced them to kill one of the Deer tribe. Now, whenever the hunter shoots a Deer, the Little Deer, who is swift as the wind and cannot be wounded, runs quickly up to the spot and, bending over the bloodstains, asks the spirit of the Deer if it has heard the prayer of the hunter for pardon. If the reply be "Yes," all is well, and the Little Deer goes on his way; But if the reply be "No," he follows on the trail of the hunter, guided by the drops of blood on the ground, until he arrives at his cabin in the settlement, when the Little Deer enters invisibly and strikes the hunter with rheumatism, so that he becomes at once a helpless cripple. No hunter who has regard for his health ever fails to ask pardon of the Deer for killing it, although some hunters who have not learned the prayer may try to turn aside the Little Deer from his pursuit by building a fire behind them in the trail.

Next came the Fishes and Reptiles, who had their own complaints against Man. They held their council together and determined to make their victims dream of snakes twining about them in slimy folds and blowing foul breath in their faces, or to make them dream of eating raw or decaying fish, so that they would lose appetite, sicken, and die. This is why people dream about snakes and fish.

Finally the Birds, Insects, and smaller animals came together for the same purpose, and the Grubworm was chief of the council. It was decided that each in turn should give an opinion, and then they would vote on the question as to whether or not Man was guilty. Seven votes should be enough to condemn him. One after another denounced Man's cruelty and injustice toward the other animals and voted in favor of his death. The Frog spoke first, saying: "We must do something to check the increase of the race, or people will become so numerous that we shall be crowded from off the earth. See how they have kicked me about because I'm ugly, as they say, until my back is covered with sores"; and here he showed the spots on his skin. Next came the Bird—no one remembers now which one it was—who condemned Man "because he burns my feet off," meaning the way in which the hunter barbecues birds by impaling them on a stick set over the fire, so that their feathers and tender feet are singed off. Others followed in the same strain. The Ground-squirrel alone ventured to say a good word for Man, who seldom hurt him because he was so small, but this made the others so angry that they fell upon the Ground-squirrel and tore him with their claws, and the stripes are on his back to this day.

They began then to devise and name so many new diseases, one after another, that had not their invention at last failed them, no one of the human race would have been able to survive. The Grubworm grew constantly more pleased as the name of each disease was called off, until at last they reached the end of the list, when someone proposed to make menstruation sometimes fatal to women. On this he rose up in his place and cried: "Wadâñ'! [Thanks!] I'm glad some more of them

will die, for they are getting so thick that they tread on me."
The thought fairly made him shake with joy, so that he fell over
backward and could not get on his feet again, but had to wriggle
off on his back, as the Grubworm has done ever since.

When the Plants, who were friendly to Man, heard what had
been done by the animals, they determined to defeat the latters'
evil designs. Each Tree, Shrub, and Herb, down even to the
Grasses and Mosses, agreed to furnish a cure for some one of
the diseases named, and each said: "I shall appear to help Man
when he calls upon me in his need." Thus came medicine; and
the plants, every one of which has its use if we only knew it,
furnish the remedy to counteract the evil wrought by the re-
vengeful animals. Even weeds were made for some good
purpose, which we must find out for ourselves. When the doctor
does not know what medicine to use for a sick man the spirit
of the plant tells him.

How the Rabbit Stole the Otter's Coat

The animals were of different sizes and wore coats of various
colors and pattern. Some wore long fur and others wore short.
Some had rings on their tails, and some had no tails at all. Some
had coats of brown, others of black or yellow. They were
always disputing about their good looks, so at last they agreed
to hold a council to decide who had the finest coat.

They had heard a great deal about the Otter, who lived so
far up the creek that he seldom came down to visit the other
animals. It was said that he had the finest coat of all, but no
one knew just what it was like, because it was a long time since
anyone had seen him. They did not even know exactly where
he lived—only the general direction; but they knew he would
come to the council when the word got out.

Now the Rabbit wanted the verdict for himself, so when it
began to look as if it might go to the Otter he studied up a plan
to cheat him out of it. He asked a few sly questions until he
learned what trail the Otter would take to get to the council
place. Then, without saying anything, he went on ahead and
after four days' travel he met the Otter and knew him at once
by his beautiful coat of soft dark-brown fur. The Otter was

glad to see him and asked him where he was going. "Oh," said the Rabbit, "the animals sent me to bring you to the council; because you live so far away they were afraid you mightn't know the road." The Otter thanked him, and they went on together.

They traveled all day toward the council ground, and at night the Rabbit selected the camping place, because the Otter was a stranger in that part of the country, and cut down bushes for beds and fixed everything in good shape. The next morning they started on again. In the afternoon the Rabbit began to pick up wood and bark as they went along and to load it on his back. When the Otter asked what this was for the Rabbit said it was that they might be warm and comfortable at night. After a while, when it was near sunset, they stopped and made their camp.

When supper was over the Rabbit got a stick and shaved it down to a paddle. The Otter wondered and asked again what that was for.

"I have good dreams when I sleep with a paddle under my head," said the Rabbit.

When the paddle was finished the Rabbit began to cut away the bushes so as to make a clean trail down to the river. The Otter wondered more and more and wanted to know what this meant.

Said the Rabbit, "This place is called Di'tatlâski'yĭ (The Place Where It Rains Fire). Sometimes it rains fire here, and the sky looks a little that way tonight. You go to sleep and I'll sit up and watch, and if the fire does come, as soon as you hear me shout, you run and jump into the river. Better hang your coat on a limb over there, so it won't get burned."

The Otter did as he was told, and they both doubled up to go to sleep, but the Rabbit kept awake. After a while the fire burned down to red coals. The Rabbit called, but the Otter was fast asleep and made no answer. In a little while he called again, but the Otter never stirred. Then the Rabbit filled the paddle with hot coals and threw them up into the air and shouted, 'It's raining fire! It's raining fire!'

The hot coals fell all around the Otter and he jumped up.

"To the water!" cried the Rabbit, and the Otter ran and jumped into the river, and he has lived in the water ever since.

The Rabbit took the Otter's coat and put it on, leaving his own instead, and went on to the council. All the animals were there, every one looking out for the Otter. At last they saw him in the distance, and they said one to the other, "The Otter is coming!" and sent one of the small animals to show him the best seat. They were all glad to see him and went up in turn to welcome him, but the Otter kept his head down, with one paw over his face. They wondered that he was so bashful, until the Bear came up and pulled the paw away, and there was the Rabbit with his split nose. He sprang up and started to run, when the Bear struck at him and pulled his tail off, but the Rabbit was too quick for them and got away.

How the Deer Got His Horns

In the beginning the Deer had no horns, but his head was smooth just like a doe's. He was a great runner and the Rabbit was a great jumper, and the animals were all curious to know which could go farther in the same time. They talked about it a good deal, and at last arranged a match between the two, and made a nice large pair of antlers for a prize to the winner. They were to start together from one side of a thicket and go through it, then turn and come back, and the one who came out first was to get the horns.

On the day fixed all the animals were there, with the antlers put down on the ground at the edge of the thicket to mark the starting point. While everybody was admiring the horns the Rabbit said: "I don't know this part of the country; I want to take a look through the bushes where I am to run." They thought that all right, so the Rabbit went into the thicket, but he was gone so long that at last the animals suspected he must be up to one of his tricks. They sent a messenger to look for him, and away in the middle of the thicket he found the Rabbit gnawing down the bushes and pulling them away until he had a road cleared nearly to the other side.

The messenger turned around quietly and came back and

told the other animals. When the Rabbit came out at last they accused him of cheating, but he denied it until they went into the thicket and found the cleared road. They agreed that such a trickster had no right to enter the race at all, so they gave the horns to the Deer, who was admitted to be the best runner, and he has worn them ever since. They told the Rabbit that as he was so fond of cutting down bushes he might do that for a living hereafter, and so he does to this day.

Ûñtsaiyĭ′, the Gambler

Thunder lives in the west, or a little to the south of west, near the place where the sun goes down behind the water. In the old times he sometimes made a journey to the east, and once after he had come back from one of these journeys a child was born in the east who, the people said, was his son. As the boy grew up it was found that he had scrofula sores all over his body, so one day his mother said to him, "Your father, Thunder, is a great doctor. He lives far in the west, but if you can find him he can cure you."

So the boy set out to find his father and be cured. He traveled long toward the west, asking of everyone he met where Thunder lived, until at last they began to tell him that it was only a little way ahead. He went on and came to Ûñtiguhĭ′, or Tennessee, where lived Ûñtsaiyĭ′, "Brass." Now Ûñtsaiyĭ′ was a great gambler, and made his living that way. It was he who invented the gatayûstĭ game that we play with a stone wheel and a stick. He lived on the south side of the river, and everybody who came that way he challenged to play against him. The large flat rock, with the lines and grooves where they used to roll the wheel, is still there, with the wheels themselves and the stick turned to stone. He won almost every time, because he was so tricky, so that he had his house filled with all kinds of fine things. Sometimes he would lose, and then he would bet all that he had, even to his own life, but the winner got nothing for his trouble, for Ûñtsaiyĭ′ knew how to take on different shapes, so that he always got away.

As soon as Ûñtsaiyĭ′ saw him he asked him to stop and play a while, but the boy said he was looking for his father, Thunder, and had no time to wait. "Well," said Ûñtsaiyĭ', "he lives in the next house; you can hear him grumbling over there all the time"—he meant the Thunder—"so we may as well have a game or two before you go on." The boy said he had nothing to bet. "That's all right," said the gambler, "we'll play for your pretty spots." He said this to make the boy angry so that he would play, but still the boy said he must go first and find his father, and would come back afterward.

He went on, and soon the news came to Thunder that a boy was looking for him who claimed to be his son. Said Thunder, "I have traveled in many lands and have many children. Bring him here and we shall soon know." So they brought in the boy, and Thunder showed him a seat and told him to sit down. Under the blanket on the seat were long, sharp thorns of the honey locust, with the points all sticking up, but when the boy sat down they did not hurt him, and then Thunder knew that it was his son. He asked the boy why he had come. "I have sores all over my body, and my mother told me you were my father and a great doctor, and if I came here you would cure me." "Yes," said his father, "I am a great doctor, and I'll soon fix you."

There was a large pot in the corner and he told his wife to fill it with water and put it over the fire. When it was boiling, he put in some roots, then took the boy and put him in with them. He let it boil a long time until one would have thought that the flesh was boiled from the poor boy's bones, and then told his wife to take the pot and throw it into the river, boy and all. She did as she was told, and threw it into the water, and ever since there is an eddy there that we call Ûñ'tiguhĭ', "Pot-in-the-water." A service tree and a calico bush grew on the bank above. A great cloud of steam came up and made streaks and blotches on their bark, and it has been so to this day. When the steam cleared away she looked over and saw the boy clinging to the roots of the service tree where they hung down into the water, but now his skin was all clean. She helped him up the bank, and they went back to the house. On the way she told him, "When we go in, your father will put a new dress on you, but when he opens his box and tells you to pick out your ornaments be sure to take them from the bottom. Then he

will send for his other sons to play ball against you. There is a
honey locust tree in front of the house, and as soon as you
begin to get tired strike at that and your father will stop the
play, because he does not want to lose the tree."

When they went into the house, the old man was pleased to
see the boy looking so clean, and said, " I knew I could soon
cure those spots. Now we must dress you." He brought out a
fine suit of buckskin, with belt and headdress, and had the boy
put them on. Then he opened a box and said, "Now pick out
your necklace and bracelets." The boy looked, and the box was
full of all kinds of snakes gliding over each other with their
heads up. He was not afraid, but remembered what the woman
had told him, and plunged his hand to the bottom and drew
out a great rattlesnake and put it around his neck for a necklace. He put down his hand again four times and drew up four
copperheads and twisted them around his wrists and ankles.
Then his father gave him a war club and said, "Now you must
play a ball game with your two elder brothers. They live beyond
here in the Darkening Land, and I have sent for them." He
said a ball game, but he meant that the boy must fight for his
life. The young men came, and they were both older and
stronger than the boy, but he was not afraid and fought against
them. The thunder rolled and the lightning flashed at every
stroke, for they were the young Thunders, and the boy himself
was Lightning. At last he was tired from defending himself
alone against two, and pretended to aim a blow at the honey
locust tree. Then his father stopped the fight, because he was
afraid the lightning would split the tree, and he saw that the
boy was brave and strong.

The boy told his father how Ûñtsaiyĭ′ had dared him to
play, and had even offered to play for the spots on his skin.
"Yes," said Thunder, "he is a great gambler and makes his
living that way, but I will see that you win." He brought a
small cymling gourd with a hole bored through the neck, and
tied it on the boy's wrist. Inside the gourd there was a string
of beads, and one end hung out from a hole in the top, but
there was no end to the string inside. "Now," said his father,
"go back the way you came, and as soon as he sees you he
will want to play for the beads. He is very hard to beat, but

this time he will lose every game. When he cries out for a drink, you will know he is getting discouraged, and then strike the rock with your war club and water will come, so that you can play on without stopping. At last he will bet his life, and lose. Then send at once for your brothers to kill him, or he will get away, he is so tricky."

The boy took the gourd and his war club and started east along the road by which he had come. As soon as Ûñtsaiyï' saw him he called to him, and when he saw the gourd with the bead string hanging out he wanted to play for it. The boy drew out the string, but there seemed to be no end to it, and he kept on pulling until enough had come out to make a circle all around the playground. "I will play one game for this much against your stake," said the boy, "and when that is over we can have another game."

They began the game with the wheel and stick and the boy won. Ûñtsaiyï' did not know what to think of it, but he put up another stake and called for a second game. The boy won again, and so they played on until noon, when Ûñtsaiyï' had lost nearly everything he had and was about discouraged. It was very hot, and he said, "I am thirsty," and wanted to stop long enough to get a drink. "No," said the boy, and struck the rock with his club so that water came out, and they had a drink. They played on until Ûñtsaiyï' had lost all his buckskins and beaded work, his eagle feathers and ornaments, and at last offered to bet his wife. They played and the boy won her. Then Ûñtsaiyï' was desperate and offered to stake his life. "If I win I kill you, but if you win you may kill me." They played and the boy won.

"Let me go and tell my wife," said Ûñtsaiyï', "so that she will receive her new husband, and then you may kill me." He went into the house, but it had two doors, and although the boy waited long Ûñtsaiyï' did not come back. When at last he went to look for him he found that the gambler had gone out the back way and was nearly out of sight going east.

The boy ran to his father's house and got his brothers to help him. They brought their dog—the Horned Green Beetle —and hurried after the gambler. He ran fast and was soon out of sight, and they followed as fast as they could. After a while they met an old woman making pottery and asked her if she had seen Û͏ñtsaiyĭ' and she said she had not. "He came this way," said the brothers. "Then he must have passed in the night," said the old woman, "for I have been here all day." They were about to take another road when the Beetle, which had been circling about in the air above the old woman, made a dart at her and struck her on the forehead, and it rang like brass—*ûñtsaiyĭ'!* Then they knew it was Brass and sprang at him, but he jumped up in his right shape and was off, running so fast that he was soon out of sight again. The Beetle had struck so hard that some of the brass rubbed off, and we can see it on the beetle's forehead yet.

They followed and came to an old man sitting by the trail, carving a stone pipe. They asked him if he had seen Brass pass that way and he said no, but again the Beetle—which could know Brass under any shape—struck him on the forehead so that it rang like metal, and the gambler jumped up in his right form and was off again before they could hold him. He ran east until he came to the great water; then he ran north until he came to the edge of the world, and had to turn again to the west. He took every shape to throw them off the track, but the Green Beetle always knew him, and the brothers pressed him so hard that at last he could go no more and they caught him just as he reached the edge of the great water where the sun goes down.

They tied his hands and feet with a grapevine and drove a long stake through his breast, and planted it far out in the deep water. They set two crows on the end of the pole to guard it and called the place Kâgûñ'yĭ, "Crow Place." But Brass never died, and cannot die until the end of the world, but lies there always with his face up. Sometimes he struggles under the water to get free, and sometimes the beavers, who are his friends, come and gnaw at the grapevine to release him. Then the pole shakes and the crows at the top cry *Ka! Ka! Ka!* and scare the beavers away.

Nûñ'yunu'wĭ, the Stone Man

This is what the old men told me when I was a boy.

Once when all the people of the settlement were out in the mountains on a great hunt one man who had gone on ahead climbed to the top of a high ridge and found a large river on the other side. While he was looking across he saw an old man walking about on the opposite ridge, with a cane that seemed to be made of some bright, shining rock. The hunter watched and saw that every little while the old man would point his cane in a certain direction, then draw it back and smell the end of it. At last he pointed it in the direction of the hunting camp on the other side of the mountain, and this time when he drew back the staff he sniffed it several times as if it smelled very good, and then started along the ridge straight for the camp. He moved very slowly, with the help of the cane, until he reached the end of the ridge, when he threw the cane out into the air and it became a bridge of shining rock stretching across the river. After he had crossed over upon the bridge it became a cane again, and the old man picked it up and started over the mountain toward the camp.

The hunter was frightened, and felt sure that it meant mischief, so he hurried on down the mountain and took the shortest trail back to the camp to get there before the old man. When he got there and told his story the medicine man said the old man was a wicked cannibal monster called Nûñ′yunu′wĭ, "Dressed in Stone," who lived in that part of the country, and was always going about the mountains looking for some hunter to kill and eat. It was very hard to escape from him, because his stick guided him like a dog, and it was nearly as hard to kill him, because his whole body was covered with a skin of solid rock. If he came he would kill and eat them all, and there was only one way to save themselves. He could not bear to look upon a menstrual woman, and if they could find seven menstrual women to stand in the path as he came along the sight would kill him.

So they asked among all the women, and found seven who were sick in that way, and with one of them it had just begun. By the order of the medicine man they stripped themselves and stood along the path where the old man would come. Soon they heard Nûñ′yunu′wĭ coming through the woods, feeling his way with his stone cane. He came along the trail to where the first woman was standing, and as soon as he saw her he started and cried out: "Yu! my grandchild; you are in a very bad state!" He hurried past her, but in a moment he met the next woman, and cried out again: "Yu! my child; you are in a terrible way," and hurried past her, but now he was vomiting blood. He hurried on and met the third and the fourth and the fifth woman, but with each one that he saw his step grew weaker until when he came to the last one, with whom the sickness had just begun, the blood poured from his mouth and he fell down on the trail.

Then the medicine man drove seven sourwood stakes through his body and pinned him to the ground, and when night came they piled great logs over him and set fire to them, and all the people gathered around to see. Nûñ'yunu'wĭ was a great ada'wehĭ and knew many secrets, and now as the fire came close to him he began to talk, and told them the medicine for all kinds of sickness. At midnight he began to sing, and sang the hunting songs for calling up the bear and the deer and all the animals of the woods and mountains. As the blaze grew hotter his voice sank low and lower, until at last when daylight came, the logs were a heap of white ashes and the voice was still.

Then the medicine man told them to rake off the ashes, and where the body had lain they found only a large lump of red wâ'dĭ paint and a magic u'lûñsû'ti stone. He kept the stone for himself, and calling the people around him he painted them, on face and breast, with the red wâ'dĭ, and whatever each person prayed for while the painting was being done— whether for hunting success, for working skill, or for a long life—that gift was his.

The Bear Man

A man went hunting in the mountains and came across a black bear, which he wounded with an arrow. The bear turned and started to run the other way, and the hunter followed, shooting one arrow after another into it without bringing it down. Now, this was a medicine bear, and could talk or read the thoughts of people without their saying a word. At last he stopped and pulled the arrows out of his side and gave them to the man, saying, "It is of no use for you to shoot at me, for you cannot kill me. Come to my house and let us live together." The hunter thought to himself, "He may kill me," but the bear read his thoughts and said, "No, I won't hurt you." The man thought again, "How can I get anything to eat?" But the bear knew his thoughts, and said, "There shall be plenty." So the hunter went with the bear.

They went on together until they came to a hole in the side of the mountain, and the bear said, "This is not where I live, but there is going to be a council here and we will see what they do." They went in, and the hole widened as they went, until they came to a large cave like a townhouse. It was full of bears—old bears, young bears, and cubs, white bears, black bears, and brown bears—and a large white bear was the chief. They sat down in a corner, but soon the bears scented the hunter and began to ask, "What is it that smells bad?" The chief said, "Don't talk so; it is only a stranger come to see us. Let him alone." Food was getting scarce in the mountains, and the council was to decide what to do about it. They had sent out messengers all over, and while they were talking two bears came in and reported that they had found a country in the low grounds where there were so many chestnuts and acorns that mast was knee deep. Then they were all pleased, and got ready for a dance, and the dance leader was the one the Indians call Kalâs'-gûnăhi'ta, "Long Hams," a great black bear that is always lean. After the dance the bears noticed the hunter's bow and arrows, and one said, "This is what men use to kill us. Let us see if we can manage them, and maybe we can fight man with his own weapons." So they took the bow and arrows from the hunter to try them. They fitted the arrow and drew back the string, but when they let go it caught in their long claws and the arrows dropped to the ground. They saw that they could not use the bow and arrows and gave them back to the man. When the dance and the council were over, they began to go home, excepting the White Bear chief, who lived there, and at last the hunter and the bear went out together.

They went on until they came to another hole in the side of the mountain, when the bear said, "This is where I live," and they went in. By this time the hunter was very hungry and was wondering how he could get something to eat. The other knew his thoughts, and sitting up on his hind legs he rubbed his stomach with his forepaws—*so*—and at once he had both paws full of chestnuts and gave them to the man. He rubbed his stomach again—*so*—and had his paws full of huckleberries, and gave them to the man. He rubbed again—*so*—and gave the man both paws full of blackberries. He rubbed again—*so* —and had his paws full of acorns, but the man said that he could not eat them, and that he had enough already.

The hunter lived in the cave with the bear all winter, until long hair like that of a bear began to grow all over his body and he began to act like a bear; but he still walked like a man. One day in early spring the bear said to him, "Your people down in the settlement are getting ready for a grand hunt in these mountains, and they will come to this cave and kill me and take these clothes from me"—he meant his skin—"but they will not hurt you and will take you home with them." The bear knew what the people were doing down in the settlement just as he always knew what the man was thinking about. Some days passed and the bear said again, "This is the day when the Topknots will come to kill me, but the Split-noses will come first and find us. When they have killed me they will drag me outside the cave and take off my clothes and cut me in pieces. You must cover the blood with leaves, and when they are taking you away look back after you have gone a piece and you will see something."

Soon they heard the hunters coming up the mountain, and then the dogs found the cave and began to bark. The hunters came and looked inside and saw the bear and killed him with their arrows. Then they dragged him outside the cave and skinned the body and cut it in quarters to carry home. The dogs kept on barking until the hunters thought there must be another bear in the cave. They looked in again and saw the man away at the farther end. At first they thought it was another bear on account of his long hair, but they soon saw it was the hunter who had been lost the year before, so they went in and brought him out. Then each hunter took a load of the bear meat and they started home again, bringing the man and the skin with them. Before they left the man piled leaves over the spot where they had cut up the bear, and when they had gone a little way he looked behind and saw the bear rise up out of the leaves, shake himself, and go back into the woods.

When they came near the settlement the man told the hunters that he must be shut up where no one could see him, without anything to eat or drink for seven days and nights, until the bear nature had left him and he became like a man again. So they shut him up alone in a house and tried to keep very still about it, but the news got out and his wife heard of it. She came for her husband, but the people would not let her near him; but she came every day and begged so hard that at last after four or five days they let her have him. She took him home with her, but in a short time he died, because he still had a bear's nature and could not live like a man. If they had kept him shut up and fasting until the end of the seven days he would have become a man again and would have lived.

Winnebago

This Upper Midwest tribe is one of the most thoroughly researched in North America, largely because of the efforts of one individual—the great Paul Radin. Since their culture and its heartbreaking disintegration is so fully described in the autobiographies in the section Culture Contact, it will be sufficient here to say that these excerpts from the Winnebago trickster cycle illustrate this pre-eminent figure in all his bewildering yet wonderful complexity. And here we also see what his function might have been for all the tribes in whose traditions he so prominently figures: he may represent the individual psyche growing from undifferentiated ignorance through self-awareness to constructive social action. I include Radin's synopsis of the entire cycle.

The Winnebago Trickster Cycle

1. Trickster cohabits with woman before war party.
2. Trickster wishes to go on warpath alone.
3. Trickster discourages his followers from accompanying him on warpath.
4. Trickster kills buffalo.
5. Trickster makes his right arm fight his left.
6. Trickster borrows two children from his younger brother.
7. Children die because Trickster breaks rules.
8. Father of children pursues Trickster.
9. Trickster swims in ocean inquiring where shore is.
10. Trickster chases fish.
11. Trickster mimics man pointing.
12. Dancing ducks and talking anus.

From Paul Radin, *The Trickster: A Study in American Indian Mythology* by Paul Radin. Philosophical Library (1956) and Routledge & Keegan Paul Ltd.

13. Foxes eat roasted ducks.
14. Trickster burns anus and eats his own intestines.
15. Penis placed in box.
16. Penis sent across water.
17. Trickster carried by giant bird.
18. Women rescue Trickster.
19. Trickster and companions decide where to live.
20. Changed into woman, Trickster marries chief's son.
21. Last child of union cries and is pacified.
22. Trickster visits wife and son.
23. Trickster and the laxative bulb.
24. Trickster falls in his own excrement.
25. Trees mislead Trickster in finding water.
26. Trickster mistakes plums reflected in water for plums on tree.
27. Mothers seek plums while Trickster eats children.
28. Skunk persuaded by Trickster to dig hole through hill.
29. Mothers lured in hole by Trickster and eaten.
30. Tree teases Trickster, who gets held fast in fork.
31. Wolves come and eat Trickster's food under tree.
32. Flies in elk's skull lure Trickster, who gets caught in elk's skull.
33. People split elk's skull off.
34. Trickster changes self into deer to take revenge on hawk.
35. Bear lured to his death by Trickster.
36. Mink outwits Trickster and gets bear meat.
37. Trickster pursues mink in vain.
38. Chipmunk causes Trickster to lose part of his penis.
39. Discarded pieces of penis thrown into lake and turn into plants.
40. Coyote leads Trickster to village.
41. Trickster imitates muskrat who turns ice into lily-of-the-valley roots.
42. Trickster imitates snipe's method of fishing.
43. Trickster imitates woodpecker's way of getting bear.
44. Trickster imitates pole-cat in getting deer.
45. Mink soils chief's daughter as Trickster planned.
46. Coyote is duped into being tied to horse's tail.

11

Again he wandered aimlessly about the world. On one occasion he came in sight of the shore of a lake. To his surprise, he noticed that, right near the edge of the lake, a person was standing. So he walked rapidly in that direction to see who it was. It was someone with a black shirt on. When Trickster came nearer to the lake, he saw that this individual was on the other side of the lake and that he was pointing at him. He called to him, "Say, my younger brother, what are you pointing at?" But he received no answer. Then, for the second time, he called, "Say, my younger brother, what is it you are pointing at?" Again he received no answer. Then, for the third time, he addressed him, again receiving no answer. There across the lake the man still stood, pointing. "Well, if that's the way it's going to be, I, too, shall do that. I, too, can stand pointing just as long as he does. I too, can put a black shirt on." Thus Trickster spoke.

Then he put on his black shirt and stepped quickly in the direction of this individual and pointed his finger at him just as the other one was doing. A long time he stood there. After a while Trickster's arm got tired so he addressed the other person and said, "My younger brother, let us stop this." Still there was no answer. Then, for the second time, when he was hardly able to endure it any longer, he spoke, "Younger brother, let us stop this. My arm is very tired." Again he received no answer. Then, again he spoke, "Younger brother, I am hungry! Let us eat now and then we can begin again afterward. I will kill a fine animal for you, the very kind you like best, that kind I will kill for you. So let us stop." But still he received no answer. "Well, why am I saying all this? That man has no heart at all. I am just doing what he is doing." Then he walked away and when he looked around, to his astonishment, he saw a tree-stump from which a branch was protruding. This is what he had taken for a man pointing at him. "Indeed, it is on this account that the people call me the Foolish One. They are right." Then he walked away.

12

As he was walking along suddenly he came to a lake, and there in the lake he saw numerous ducks. Immediately he ran back quietly before they could see him and sought out a spot where there was a swamp. From it he gathered a large quantity of reed-grass and made himself a big pack. This he put on his back and carried it to the lake. He walked along the shore of the lake carrying it ostentatiously. Soon the ducks saw him and said, "Look, that is Trickster walking over there. I wonder what he is doing? Let us call and ask him." So they called to him, "Trickster, what are you carrying?" Thus they shouted at him, but he did not answer. Then, again they called to him. But it was only after the fourth call that he replied and said, "Well, are you calling me?" "What are you carrying on your back?" they asked. "My younger brothers, surely you do not know what it is you are asking. What am I carrying? Why, I am carrying songs. My stomach is full of bad songs. Some of these my stomach could not hold and that is why I am carrying them on my back. It is a long time since I sang any of them. Just now there are a large number in me. I have met no people on my journey who would dance for me and let me sing some for them. And I have, in consequence, not sung any for a long time." Then the ducks spoke to each other and said, "Come, what if we ask him to sing? Then we could dance, couldn't we?" So one of them called out, "Well, let it be so. I enjoy dancing very much and it has been a very long time since I last danced."

So they spoke to Trickster, "Older brother, yes, if you will sing to us we will dance. We have been yearning to dance for some time but could not do so because we had no songs." Thus spoke the ducks. "My younger brothers," replied Trickster, "you have spoken well and you shall have your desire granted. First, however, I will erect a dancing-lodge." In this they helped him and soon they had put up a dancing-lodge, a grass-lodge. Then they made a drum. When this was finished he invited them all to come in and they did so. When he was ready to sing he said, "My younger brothers, this is the way in which you must act. When I sing, when I have people dance for me, the dancers must, from the very beginning, never open their eyes." "Good," they answered. Then when he began to sing he said, "Now remember, younger brothers, you are not to open your eyes. If you do they will become red." So, as soon as he began to sing, the ducks closed their eyes and danced.

After a while one of the ducks was heard to flap his wings as he came back to the entrance of the lodge, and cry, "Quack!" Again and again this happened. Sometimes it sounded as if the particular duck had somehow tightened its throat. Whenever any of the ducks cried out then Trickster would tell the other ducks to dance faster and faster. Finally a duck whose name was Little-Red-Eyed-Duck secretly opened its eyes, just the least little bit it opened them. To its surprise, Trickster was wringing the necks of his fellows ducks! He would also bite them as he twisted their necks. It was while he was doing this that the noise which sounded like the tightening of the throat was heard. In this fashion Trickster killed as many as he could reach.

Little-Red-Eyed-Duck shouted, "Alas! He is killing us! Let those who can save themselves." He himself flew out quickly through the opening above. All the others likewise crowded toward this opening. They struck Trickster with their wings and scratched him with their feet. He went among them with his eyes closed and stuck out his hands to grab them. He grabbed one in each hand and choked them to death. His eyes were closed tightly. Then suddenly all of them escaped except the two he had in his grasp.

When he looked at these, to his annoyance, he was holding in each hand a scabby-mouthed duck. In no way perturbed, however, he shouted, "Ha, ha, this is the way a man acts! Indeed these ducks will make fine soup to drink!" Then he made a fire and cut some sharp-pointed sticks with which to roast them. Some he roasted in this manner, while others he roasted by covering them with ashes. "I will wait for them to be cooked," he said to himself. "I had, however, better go to sleep now. By the time I awake they will unquestionably be thoroughly done. Now, you, my younger brother, must keep watch for me while I go sleep. If you notice any people, drive them off." He was talking to his anus. Then, turning his anus toward the fire, he went to sleep.

13

When he was sleeping some small foxes approached and, as they ran along, they scented something that seemed like fire. "Well, there must be something around here," they said. So they turned their noses toward the wind and looked and, after a while, truly enough, they saw the smoke of a fire. So they peered around carefully and soon noticed many sharp-pointed sticks arranged around a fire with meat on them. Stealthily they approached nearer and nearer and, scrutinizing everything carefully, they noticed someone asleep there. "It is Trickster and he is asleep! Let us eat this meat. But we must be very careful not to wake him up. Come, let us eat," they said to one another. When they came close, much to their surprise, however, gas was expelled from somewhere. "Pooh!" Such was the sound made. "Be careful! He must be awake." So they ran back. After a while one of them said, "Well, I guess he is asleep now. That was only a bluff. He is always up to some tricks." So again they approached the fire. Again gas was expelled and again they ran back. Three times this happened. When they approached the fourth time gas was again expelled. However, they did not run away. So Trickster's anus, in rapid succession, began to expel more and more gas. Still they did not run away. Once, twice, three times, it expelled gas in rapid succession. "Pooh! Pooh!" Such was the sound it made. Yet they did not run away. Then louder, still louder, was the sound of the gas expelled. "Pooh! Pooh! Pooh!" Yet they did not run away. On the contrary, they now began to eat the roasted pieces of duck. As they were eating, the Trickster's anus continued its "Pooh" incessantly. There the foxes stayed until they had eaten up all the pieces of duck roasted on sticks. Then they came to those pieces that were being roasted under ashes and, in spite of the fact that the anus was expelling gas, "Pooh! Pooh! Pooh! Pooh!" continuously, they ate these all up too. Then they replaced the pieces with the meat eaten off, nicely under the ashes. Only after that did they go away.

14

After a while Trickster awoke. "My, oh my!" he exclaimed joyfully, "the things I had put on to roast must be cooked crisp by now." So he went over, felt around, and pulled out a leg. To his dismay it was but a bare bone, completely devoid of meat. "How terrible! But this is the way they generally are when they are cooked too much!" So he felt around again and pulled out another one. But this leg also had nothing on it. "How terrible! These, likewise, must have been roasted too much! However, I told my younger brother, anus, to watch the meat roasting. He is a good cook indeed!" He pulled out one piece after the other. They were all the same. Finally he sat up and looked around. To his astonishment, the pieces of meat on the roasting sticks were gone! "Ah, ha, now I understand! It must have been those covetous friends of mine who have done me this injury!" he exclaimed. Then he poked around the fire again and again but found only bones. "Alas! Alas! They have caused my appetite to be disappointed, those covetous fellows! And you, too, you despicable object, what about your behavior? Did I not tell you to watch this fire? You shall remember this! As a punishment for your remissness, I will burn your mouth so that you will not be able to use it!"

Thereupon he took a burning piece of wood and burned the mouth of his anus. He was, of course, burning himself and, as he applied the fire, he exclaimed, "Ouch! Ouch! This is too much! I have made my skin smart. Is it not for such things that they call me Trickster? They have indeed talked me into doing this just as if I had been doing something wrong!"

Trickster had burned his anus. He had applied a burning piece of wood to it. Then he went away.

As he walked along the road he felt certain that someone must have passed along it before for he was on what appeared to be a trail. Indeed, suddenly, he came upon a piece of fat that must have come from someone's body. "Someone has been packing an animal he had killed," he thought to himself. Then he picked up a piece of fat and ate it. It had a delicious taste. "My, my, how delicious it is to eat this!" As he proceeded however, much to his surprise, he discovered that it was a part of himself, part of his own intestines, that he was eating. After burning his anus, his intestines had contracted and fallen off, piece by piece, and these pieces were the things he was picking up. "My, my! Correctly, indeed, am I named Foolish One,

Trickster! By their calling me thus, they have at last actually turned me into a Foolish One, a Trickster!" Then he tied his intestines together. A large part, however, had been lost. In tying it, he pulled it together so that wrinkles and ridges were formed. That is the reason why the anus of human beings has its present shape.

15

On Trickster proceeded. As he walked along, he came to a lovely piece of land. There he sat down and soon fell asleep. After a while he woke up and found himself lying on his back without a blanket. He looked up above him and saw to his astonishment something floating there. "Aha, aha! The chiefs have unfurled their banner! The people must be having a great feast for this is always the case when the chief's banner is unfurled." With this he sat up and then first realized that his blanket was gone. It was his blanket he saw floating above. His penis had become stiff and the blanket had been forced up. "That's always happening to me," he said. "My younger brother, you will lose the blanket, so bring it back." Thus he spoke to his penis. Then he took hold of it and, as he handled it, it got softer and the blanket finally fell down. Then he coiled up his penis and put it in a box. And only when he came to the end of his penis did he find his blanket. The box with the penis he carried on his back.

16

After that he walked down a slope and finally came to a lake. On the opposite side he saw a number of women swimming, the chief's daughter and her friends. "Now," exclaimed Trickster, "is the opportune time: now I am going to have intercourse." Thereupon he took his penis out of the box and addressed it, "My younger brother, you are going after the chief's daughter. Pass her friends, but see that you lodge squarely in her, the chief's daughter." Thus speaking he dispatched it. It went sliding on the surface of the water. "Younger brother, come back, come back! You will scare them away if you approach in that manner!" So he pulled the penis back, tied a stone around its neck, and sent it out again. This time it dropped to the bottom of the lake. Again he pulled it back, took another stone, smaller in size, and attached it to its neck. Soon he sent it forth again. It slid along the water, creating waves as it passed along. "Brother, come back, come back! You will drive the women away if you create waves like that!" So he tried a fourth time. This time he got a stone, just the right size and just the right weight, and attached it to its neck. When he dispatched it, this time it went directly toward the designated place. It passed and just barely touched the friends of the chief's daughter. They saw it and cried out, "Come out of the water, quick!" The chief's daughter was the last one on the bank and could not get away, so the penis lodged squarely in her. Her friends came back and tried to pull it out, but all to no avail. They could do absolutely nothing. Then the men who had the reputation for being strong were called and tried it but they, too, could not move it. Finally they all gave up. Then one of them said, "There is an old woman around here who knows many things. Let us go and get her." So they went and got her and brought her to the place where this was happening. When she came there she recognized immediately what was taking place. "Why, this is First-born, Trickster. The chief's daughter is having intercourse and you are all just annoying her." Thereupon she went out, got an awl and strad-dling the penis, worked the awl into it a number of times, singing as she did so:

"First-born, if it is you, pull it out! Pull it out!"

Thus she sang. Suddenly in the midst of her singing, the penis was jerked out and the old woman was thrown a great distance. As she stood there bewildered, Trickster, from across the lake, laughed loudly at her. "That old naughty woman! Why is she doing this when I am trying to have intercourse? Now, she has spoiled all the pleasure."

17

Again Trickster started out walking along aimlessly. After a while, as he went along, he heard something shrieking in the air. He listened and there to his great amazement was a very large bird flying above him. It was coming straight toward him. Then the thought suddenly struck him that it would be nice to be like this bird. So, when the bird, a turkey-buzzard, came close, Trickster spoke to it, "My, my, my, younger brother! You certainly are a lucky one to have such a fine time! I wish I could be able to do what you are doing." Thus he addressed it. Then, again, he spoke, "Younger brother, you can carry me on your back if you want to, for I like your ways very much." "All right," said the bird. So he got on the bird's back. The bird exerted himself to fly and, after a while, succeeded. They were now high in the air and Trickster chattered contentedly, "My younger brother, it is very pleasant. This is indeed a pleasant time we are having." Then the turkey-buzzard began to fly sideways and Trickster, uneasy, appealed to him in a loud tone of voice, saying, "Be very careful, younger brother, be very careful, for you might drop me." So the bird continued to carry Trickster around properly, and the latter was enjoying himself hugely. The turkey-buzzard, however, was busily looking for a hollow tree. He wanted to play a trick on Trickster. After searching for a while he saw a hollow tree, one entirely without branches. He flew rather close to it and then dropped Trickster right down into it. That is exactly what happened. "Alas! That horrible thing! He is indeed a very wicked being. He has turned the tables on me." Thus Trickster spoke.

20

Trickster now took an elk's liver and made a vulva from it. Then he took some elk's kidneys and made breasts from them. Finally he put on a woman's dress. In this dress his friends enclosed him very firmly. The dresses he was using were those that the women who had taken him for a raccoon had given him. He now stood there transformed into a very pretty woman indeed. Then he let the fox have intercourse with him and make him pregnant, then the jaybird and, finally, the nit. After that he proceeded toward the village.

Now, at the end of the village, lived an old woman and she immediately addressed him, saying, "My granddaughter, what is your purpose in traveling around like this? Certainly it is with some object in view that you are traveling!" Then the old woman went outside and shouted, "Ho! Ho! There is someone

here who has come to court the chief's son." This, at least, is
what the old woman seemed to be saying. Then the chief said
to his daughters, "Ho! This clearly is what this woman wants
and is the reason for her coming; so, my daughters, go and
bring your sister-in-law here." Then they went after her. She
certainly was a very handsome woman. The chief's son liked
her very much. Immediately they prepared dried corn for her
and they boiled slit bear-ribs. That was why Trickster was getting married, of course. When this food was ready they put it
in a dish, cooled it, and placed it in front of Trickster. He
devoured it at once. There she (Trickster) remained.

Not long after Trickster became pregnant. The chief's son
was very happy about the fact that he was to become a father.
Not long after that Trickster gave birth to a boy. Then again he
became pregnant and gave birth to another boy. Finally for the
third time he became pregnant and gave birth to a third boy.

21

The last child cried as soon as it was born and nothing could
stop it. The crying became very serious and so it was decided
to send for an old woman who had the reputation for being
able to pacify children. She came, but she, likewise, could not
pacify him. Finally the little child cried out and sang:

"If I only could play with a little piece of white cloud!"

They went in search of a shaman, for it was the chief's son
who was asking for this and, consequently, no matter what the
cost, it had to be obtained. He had asked for a piece of white
cloud, and a piece of white cloud, accordingly, they tried to
obtain. But how could they obtain a piece of white cloud? All
tried very hard and, finally, they made it snow. Then, when the
snow was quite deep, they gave him a piece of snow to play
with and he stopped crying.

After a while he again cried out and sang:

"If I could only play with a piece of blue sky!"

Then they tried to obtain a piece of blue sky for him. Very
hard they tried, but were not able to obtain any. In the spring
of the year, however, they gave him a piece of blue grass and
he stopped crying.

After a while he began to cry again. This time he asked for

some blue (green) leaves. Then the fourth time he asked for some roasting ears. They gave him green leaves and roasting ears of corn and he stopped crying.

One day later, as they were steaming corn, the chief's wife teased her sister-in-law. She chased her around the pit where they were steaming corn. Finally, the chief's son's wife (Trickster) jumped over the pit and she dropped something very rotten. The people shouted at her, "It is Trickster!" The men were all ashamed, especially the chief's son. The animals who had been with Trickster, the fox, the jaybird, and the nit, all of them now ran away.

22

Trickster also ran away. Suddenly he said to himself, "Well, why am I doing all this? It is about time that I went back to the woman to whom I am really married. Kunu must be a pretty big boy by this time." Thus spoke Trickster. Then he went across the lake to the woman to whom he was really married. When he got here he found, much to his surprise, that the boy that had been born to him was indeed quite grown up. The chief was very happy when Trickster came home. "My son-in-law has come home," he ejaculated. He was very happy indeed. Trickster hunted game for his child and killed very many animals. There he stayed a long time until his child had become a grown-up man. Then, when he saw that his child was able to take care of himself, he said, "Well, it is about time for me to start traveling again for my boy is quite grown up now. I will go around the earth and visit people for I am tired of staying here. I used to wander around the world in peace. Here I am just giving myself a lot of trouble."

23

As he went wandering around aimlessly he suddenly heard someone speaking. He listened very carefully and it seemed to say, "He who chews me will defecate; he will defecate!" That was what it was saying. "Well, why is this person talking in this manner?" said Trickster. So he walked in the direction from which he had heard the speaking and again he heard, quite near him, someone saying: "He who chews me, he will defecate; he will defecate!" This is what was said. "Well, why does this person talk in such fashion?" said Trickster. Then he walked to the other side. So he continued walking along. Then right at his very side, a voice seemed to say, "He who chews me, he will defecate; he will defecate!" "Well, I wonder who it is who is speaking. I know very well that if I chew it, I will not defecate." But he kept looking around for the speaker and finally discovered, much to his astonishment, that it was a bulb on a bush. The bulb it was that was speaking. So he seized it, put it in his mouth, chewed it, and then swallowed it. He did just this and then went on.

"Well, where is the bulb gone that talked so much? Why, indeed, should I defecate? When I feel like defecating, then I shall defectate, no sooner. How could such an object make me defecate!" Thus spoke Trickster. Even as he spoke, however, he began to break wind. "Well this, I suppose, is what it meant. Yet the bulb said I would defecate, and I am merely expelling gas. In any case I am a great man even if I do expel a little gas!" Thus he spoke. As he was talking he again broke wind. This time it was really quite strong. "Well, what a foolish one I am. This is why I am called Foolish One, Trickster." Now he began to break wind again and again. "So this is why the bulb spoke as it did, I suppose." Once more he broke wind. This time it was very loud and his rectum began to smart. "Well, it surely is a great thing!" Then he broke wind again, this time with so much force that he was propelled forward. "Well, well, it may even make me give another push, but it won't make me defecate," so he exclaimed defiantly. The next time he broke wind, the hind part of his body was raised up by the force of the explosion and he landed on his knees and hands. "Well, go ahead and do it again! Go ahead and do it again!" Then, again, he broke wind. This time the force of the expulsion sent him far up in the air and he landed on the ground, on his stomach. The next time he broke wind, he had to hang onto a log, so high was he thrown. However, he raised himself up and, after a while, landed on the ground, the log on top of him. He was almost killed by the fall. The next time he broke wind, he had to hold on to a tree that stood near by. It was a poplar and he held on with all his might yet, nevertheless, even then, his feet flopped up in the air. Again, and for the second time, he held on to it when he broke wind and yet he pulled the tree up by the roots. To protect himself, the next time, he went on until he came to a large tree, a large oak tree. Around this he put both his arms. Yet, when he broke wind, he was swung up and his toes struck against the tree. However, he held on.

After that he ran to a place where people were living. When he got there, he shouted, "Say, hurry up and take your lodge down, for a big war party is upon you and you will surely be killed! Come let us get away!" He scared them all so much that they quickly took down their lodge, piled it on Trickster, and then got on him themselves. They likewise placed all the little dogs they had on top of Trickster. Just then he began to break wind again and the force of the expulsion scattered the things on top of him in all directions. They fell far apart from one another. Separated, the people were standing about and shouting to one another; and the dogs, scattered here and there, howled at one another. There stood Trickster laughing at them till he ached.

Now he proceeded onward. He seemed to have gotten over his troubles. "Well, this bulb did a lot of talking," he said to himself, "yet it could not make me defecate." But even as he spoke he began to have the desire to defecate, just a very little. "Well, I suppose this is what it meant. It certainly bragged a good deal, however." As he spoke he defecated again. "Well, what a braggart it was! I suppose this is why it said this." As he spoke these last words, he began to defecate a good deal. After a while, as he was sitting down, his body would touch the excrement. Thereupon he got on top of a log and sat down there but, even then, he touched the excrement. Finally, he climbed up a log that was leaning against a tree. However, his body still touched the excrement, so he went up higher. Even then, however, he touched it so he climbed still higher up. Higher and higher he had to go. Nor was he able to stop defecating. Now he was on top of the tree. It was small and quite uncomfortable. Moreover, the excrement began to come up to him.

24

Even on the limb on which he was sitting he began to defecate. So he tried a different position. Since the limb, however, was very slippery he fell right down into the excrement. Down he fell, down into the dung. In fact he disappeared in it, and it was only with very great difficulty that he was able to get out of it. His raccoon-skin blanket was covered with filth, and he came out dragging it after him. The pack he was carrying on his back was covered with dung, as was also the box containing his penis. The box he emptied and then placed it on his back again.

25

Then, still blinded by the filth, he started to run. He could not see anything. As he ran he knocked against a tree. The old man cried out in pain. He reached out and felt the tree and sang:

"Tree, what kind of a tree are you? Tell me something about yourself!"

And the tree answered, "What kind of a tree do you think I am? I am an oak tree. I am the forked oak tree that used to stand in the middle of the valley. I am that one," it said. "Oh, my, is it possible that there might be some water around here?" Trickster asked. The tree answered, "Go straight on." This is what it told him. As he went along he bumped up against another tree. He was knocked backward by the collision. Again he sang:

"Tree, what kind of a tree are you? Tell me something about yourself!"

"What kind of a tree do you think I am? The red oak tree that used to stand at the edge of the valley, I am that one." "Oh, my, is it possible that there is water around here?" asked Trickster. Then the tree answered and said, "Keep straight on," and so he went again. Soon he knocked against another tree. He spoke to the tree and sang:

"Tree, what kind of a tree are you? Tell me something about yourself!"

"What kind of a tree do you think I am? The slippery elm tree that used to stand in the midst of the others, I am that one." Then Trickster asked, "Oh, my, is it possible that there would be some water near here?" And the tree answered and said, "Keep right on." On he went and soon he bumped into another tree and he touched it and sang:

"Tree, what kind of a tree are you? Tell me something about yourself!"

"What kind of a tree do you think I am? I am the basswood tree that used to stand on the edge of the water. That is the one I am." "Oh, my, it is good," said Trickster. So there in the water he jumped and lay. He washed himself thoroughly.

It is said that the old man almost died that time, for it was only with the greatest difficulty that he found the water. If the trees had not spoken to him he certainly would have died. Finally, after a long time and only after great exertions, did he clean himself, for the dung had been on him a long time and had dried. After he had cleansed himself he washed his raccoon-skin blanket and his box.

26

As he was engaged in this cleansing he happened to look in the water and much to his surprise he saw many plums there. He surveyed them very carefully and then he dived down into the water to get some. But only small stones did he bring back in his hands. Again he dived into the water. But this time he knocked himself unconscious against a rock at the bottom. After a while he floated up and gradually came to. He was lying on the water, flat on his back, when he came to and, as he opened his eyes, there on the top of the bank he saw many plums. What he had seen in the water was only the reflection. Then he realized what he had done. "Oh, my, what a stupid fellow I must be! I should have recognized this. Here I have caused myself a great deal of pain."

46

In the village in which they were staying the people owned two horses. The coyote had married into the village. Trickster was very desirous of revenging himself on him and coyote, on his side, had the desire of playing a trick on Trickster. However, Trickster discovered what coyote intended to do and did not like it. "Many times he has done me wrong and I let it pass, but this time I am not going to overlook it. This time I intend to play a trick on him," said Trickster.

Then he went into the wilderness, to the place where the horses belonging to the village generally stayed. He found one of them and put it to sleep. When he was quite certain that the horse was asleep he went after mouse and said, "Say, there is an animal dead here. Go to coyote and tell him, 'My grandson, there is an animal dead over there and I was unable to move him. It is over there near the village. Pull it to one side and then we will be able to have it to ourselves.'" Mouse was quite willing and ran over to coyote and said, "Grandson, I know you are very strong and therefore I wish to tell you that there is an animal over there near the village, lying dead. If you will push it aside, it will be good. I wanted to do it myself but I was unable to pull it and that is why I have come over here to tell you, for I have compassion upon you." Coyote was very much delighted and went to the place. Trickster at the same moment ran back to the village and waited for them. The mouse and the coyote soon arrived and the mouse tied the horse's tail to the coyote. Tightly she tied the two together. Then the coyote said, "I am very strong and I know that I can pull this animal. The animal that I am about to pull is called an elk or a deer." "Well, everything is ready, you may pull it now," said the mouse. "All right," said the coyote and tried to pull it. He woke the horse up and it got scared. Up it jumped and finding an animal tied to its tail it got even more frightened and began racing at full speed. Coyote was pulled along looking as though he were a branch being dragged. The horse ran to the village and Trickster shouted at the top of his voice, "Just look at him, our son-in-law, coyote! He is doing something very disgraceful. Look at him!" Then all the people ran out and there, unexpectedly, they saw coyote tied to the horse's tail bouncing up and down. The horse finally went to its master and there it was caught. They untied the coyote and his mouth just twitched as he sat up. He was very much ashamed. He did not even go back to his lodge. He left the village and was not more seen. He had a wife and many children but those too he left. From that time on he has not lived among people. If a person sees him anywhere he is ashamed of himself and when one gets very close to him his mouth twitches. He is still ashamed of what happened to him long ago.

47

Trickster stayed at that village for a long time and raised many children. One day he said, "Well, this is about as long as I will stay here. I have been here a long time. Now I am going to go around the earth again and visit different people for my children are all grown up. I was not created for what I am doing here."

Then he went around the earth. He started at the end of the Mississippi river and went down to the stream. The Mississippi is a spirit-village and the river is its main road. He knew that the river was going to be inhabited by Indians and that is why he traveled down it. Whatever he thought might be a hindrance to the Indians he changed. He suddenly recollected the purpose for which he had been sent to the earth by Earthmaker. That is why he removed all these obstacles along the river.

As he went along he killed and ate all those beings that were molesting the people. The waterspirits had their roads only at a short distance below the surface of the earth so he pushed these farther in. These waterspirit-roads are holes in the rivers. Many rivers have eddies which it would be impossible for a boat to pass through and these he pushed farther down into the ground.

48

He went all over the earth, and one day he came to a place where he found a large waterfall. It was very high. Then he said to the waterfall, "Remove yourself to some other location for the people are going to inhabit this place and you will annoy them." Then the waterfall said, "I will not go away. I chose this place and I am going to stay here." "I tell you, you are going to some other place," said Trickster. The waterfall, however, refused to do it. "I am telling you that the earth was made for man to live on and you will annoy him if you stay here. I came to this earth to rearrange it. If you don't do what I tell you, I will not use you very gently." Then the waterfall said, "I told you when I first spoke to you that I would not move and I am not going to." Then Trickster cut a stick for himself and shot it into the falls and pushed the falls onto the land.

49

Finally he made a stone kettle and said, "Now for the last time I will eat a meal on earth." There he boiled his food and when it was cooked he put it in a big dish. He had made a stone dish for himself. There he sat and ate. He sat on top of a rock and his seat is visible to the present day. There, too, can be seen the kettle and the dish and even the imprint of his buttocks. Even the imprint of his testicles can be seen there. This meal he ate at a short distance from the place where the Missouri enters the Mississippi. Then he left and went first into the ocean and then up to the heavens.

Under the world where Earthmaker lives, there is another world just like it and of this world, he, Trickster, is in charge. Turtle is in charge of the third world and Hare is in charge of the world in which we live.

Sioux

Perhaps no single group has so symbolized the American Indian as have the Sioux. The faces of Red Cloud, Sitting Bull, Gall, and other great leaders, their legendary fierceness in battle, their equestrian skill, all have combined to engrave them on the national memory. Yet, as these selections clearly show, this was a various people with a great many more dimensions than those popularized by the pulps and movies. There is, naturally, a rich literature on this far-flung confederacy, but the reader could get some bearings from George Hyde's *Red Cloud's Folk,* Amos Bad Heart Bull and Helen Blish's *A Pictographic History of the Oglala Sioux,* and Gordon Macgregor's *Warriors without Weapons.*

Sioux Genesis

... Our legends tell us that it was hundreds and perhaps thousands of years ago since the first man sprang from the soil in the midst of the great plains. The story says that one morning long ago a lone man awoke, face to the sun, emerging from the soil. Only his head was visible, the rest of his body not yet being fashioned. The man looked about, but saw no mountains, no rivers, no forests. There was nothing but soft and quaking mud, for the earth itself was still young. Up and up the man drew himself until he freed his body from the clinging soil. At last he stood upon the earth, but it was not solid, and his first few steps were slow and halting. But the sun shone and ever the man kept his face turned toward it. In time the rays of the sun hardened the face of the earth and strengthened the man and he bounded and leaped about, a

From Chief Luther Standing Bear, *Land of the Spotted Eagle* (Boston and New York: Houghton Mifflin Company, 1933; reprint Ann Arbor: University Microfilms, 1969).

free and joyous creature. From this man sprang the Lakota nation and, so far as we know, our people have been born and have died upon this plain; and no people have shared it with us until the coming of the European. So this land of the great plains is claimed by the Lakotas as their very own. We are of the soil and the soil is of us.

The Younger Brother

Once a man lived with his two wives and brother. One day the brother went out to hunt, and as he was coming back he shot an owl, which he brought home with him. As he was coming up toward the brother's tepee, his sister-in-law met him and asked for the owl. The brother refused to give it to her. Then she cried. She took a sharp stone, scratched her face and thighs, and came before her husband in that condition. She related that her brother-in-law had inflicted these wounds trying to lie with her. This made her husband very angry. So he sent for a friend, and directed him to take his brother out to an island and leave him there. The friend did this, and when he returned received the woman who caused the trouble for his wife.

The brother lived alone on the island. He could find nothing to eat but rose berries. He soon ate all of these, but was still very hungry. One day, while he was sleeping, he heard a noise near him, and, looking down, saw three wild turnips pushing up from the ground. He took these and they supplied him with food for several days. But at last they were eaten, and he became very hungry again. One day, while he was sleeping, he heard a noise, and, looking around, saw a small animal. He caught this animal, took out his paint bag, and painted him, praying to him for some kind of power to get to the mainland. Then he released the animal. It at once plunged into the lake, disappeared under the water, and presently there arose in its place a very large animal with large horns. This monster addressed the brother, directed him to climb upon his back and take hold of his horns. "Now," said the monster, "I shall

From Clark Wissler, "Some Dakota Myths," *Journal of American Folklore* 20 (January-March 1907), 195-206.

take you to the shore, but you must watch the sky, and if you see a cloud you must tell me." So they started out, the man holding the monster's horns. When they were near the shore, the brother saw a cloud. Now the brother was afraid that if he told the monster about the cloud, the monster would dive into the water and he would be drowned. So he kept still and said nothing about the cloud. Just as they reached the shore, and the brother sprang off on dry land, the thunder came down from the cloud and killed the monster.

As the brother walked on he heard some women cry. They said, "Our grandfather is killed! Our grandfather is killed!" Looking around, the brother finally made out that the noise came from a buffalo skull lying on the ground. Looking inside, he saw a great many mice. "What are you doing in here?" he said. Then he took them out and killed all of them.

Then the brother went on his way, and presently came to a lodge where an old woman lived. As soon as the old woman saw him she cried out, "Oh! my son, my lost son!" She called the young man inside and cooked some meat for him. Now the brother was very sleepy, but was suspicious of the woman, so he lay quietly and watched. After a while the woman took some paint and began to rub it on one of her legs. As she did so, the leg became exceedingly large. This was the way the old woman killed people. While she was doing this, the brother sprang upon her and stabbed her with a crane's bill which he always carried with him. The old woman screamed, and the brother sprang out of the lodge as quickly as possible. Presently he came back, and, peeping in, saw the body of the old woman lying in the fire. Then he gathered together much wood and threw into the fire. In this way he burned up, not only the body of the old woman, but the entire lodge. If he had not done this, women would still have the power to increase the size and the strength of their legs to such an extent that they could kill men with them.

After this he went on his journey and came to another lodge. Looking in, he saw a woman. When she saw him, she invited him to come in, and began to cook some meat for him. As he sat watching her, he saw that she had a hole in the top of her head. As she cooked she took out some of her brains and mixed them with the meat in the pot. Now the brother called up his friend the gopher. This was the animal that helped him to get away from the island. The brother directed the gopher to watch the woman at her cooking, and if the food was dangerous to gnaw a hole in the bottom of the pot, so that the soup might run down into the ground. Then the brother lay down as if to sleep. The gopher gnawed a hole in the bottom of the pot so that the food all ran down into his hole in the ground. Then the brother pretended to eat from the pot. Then he lay down on his bed as if in deep sleep. This is the way this woman killed people. She mixed poisonous soup for them, and after they had eaten they became unconscious and died. Now the brother watched the woman, and when she lay down to sleep he arose, and taking a hot stone from the fire, dropped it into the hole in her head. The woman sprang up, the hot stone sputtered and sizzled. The woman reeled, screamed, and fell down dead. Then the brother threw the body into the fire and burned it up, together with all her belongings. If he had not done this, women would still mix the poison of their brains with the food they cook.

As the brother went on again he came to another lodge. An old woman was looking out, and he heard her say, "There comes a man." A voice from the inside said, "I have seen such a thing before." The old woman invited him to enter. Fine food was set before him. There were two beautiful girls there. Each had a bed on opposite sides of the lodge. When night came each invited the brother to bed. As he did not move, the girls fell to disputing as to which he would choose. At last the brother settled the argument by going to one of the beds. Now these girls had teeth in the vagina, and when they were in erethism the teeth could be heard grating upon each other. The brother heard the noise. He took his crane's bill, thrust it into the vagina and upward, killing the girl. Then he went over to the other bed and did the same. Soon he went on his way. If he had not done this to these girls, all women would be dangerous to their lovers.

Then he continued his journey, and presently saw a cloud on the top of a hill. As he came on, he turned about and saw many animals following him. They were of all kinds, and he was afraid. Then he saw there was a woman with them. He threw away his clothes, painted his body with mud, and, taking a cane, walked along bent over like an old person. Then the woman called all the animals back saying, "You must not hurt such an old man." Then the woman spoke to the brother and told him that he would find some old weak animals in the rear that would serve him as food. When the man went to look for them, he found nothing but skunks, porcupines, and badgers. He killed some of them, however, and ate them. This is the way that people came to eat the flesh of animals.

As he went on he came to another lodge. He saw a poor woman going out for water. When he came up to her, he saw that she was his sister. She told him that her husband was very cruel to her and always beat her when he came home. Now the brother told her to go in to her husband as before and say nothing. The brother stood outside. When the man began to beat the woman he sprang into the lodge and struck down the cruel husband. Because he did this it has come to pass that cruel husbands are punished by their wife's relatives.

As he continued on his way, he came at last to the camp of his people. His brothers lived here and also his father, who was now very old. They were all glad to see their long-lost brother, and the father was so glad that he died from the excitement. One day the young man went out to hunt and killed a great many buffalo. He killed so many that when the meat was piled up it looked like a hill. Then he returned to the camp, told his people to take their horses and go out for the meat. When they came to the place they found that birds and animals in great numbers had come from every direction to eat the meat. When the people came up the animals fell upon them, and all the people were destroyed. This is why animals now eat the flesh of men.

High Horse's Courting

You know, in the old days, it was not so very easy to get a girl when you wanted to be married. Sometimes it was hard

From John G. Neihardt, *Black Elk Speaks* (Lincoln, 1932, 1961), pp. 67-76.

work for a young man and he had to stand a great deal. Say I am a young man and I have seen a young girl who looks so beautiful to me that I feel all sick when I think about her. I cannot just go and tell her about it and then get married if she is willing. I have to be a very sneaky fellow to talk to her at all, and after I have managed to talk to her, that is only the beginning.

Probably for a long time I have been feeling sick about a certain girl because I love her so much, but she will not even look at me, and her parents keep a good watch over her. But I keep feeling worse and worse all the time; so maybe I sneak up to her tepee in the dark and wait until she comes out. Maybe I just wait there all night and don't get any sleep at all and she does not come out. Then I feel sicker than ever about her.

Maybe I hide in the brush by a spring where she sometimes goes to get water, and when she comes by, if nobody is looking, then I jump out and hold her and just make her listen to me. If she likes me too, I can tell that from the way she acts, for she is very bashful and maybe will not say a word or even look at me the first time. So I let her go, and then maybe I sneak around until I can see her father alone, and I tell him how many horses I can give him for his beautiful girl, and by now I am feeling so sick that maybe I would give him all the horses in the world if I had them.

Well, this young man I am telling about was called High Horse, and there was a girl in the village who looked so beautiful to him that he was just sick all over from thinking about her so much and he was getting sicker all the time. The girl was very shy, and her parents thought a great deal of her because they were not young any more and this was the only child they had. So they watched her all day long, and they fixed it so that she would be safe at night too when they were asleep. They thought so much of her that they had made a rawhide bed for her to sleep in, and after they knew that High Horse was sneaking around after her, they took rawhide thongs and tied the girl in bed at night so that nobody could steal her when they were asleep, for they were not sure but that their girl might really want to be stolen.

Well, after High Horse had been sneaking around a good

while and hiding and waiting for the girl and getting sicker all
the time, he finally caught her alone and made her talk to him.
Then he found out that she liked him maybe a little. Of course
this did not make him feel well. It made him sicker than ever,
but now he felt as brave as a bison bull, and so he went right
to her father and said he loved the girl so much that he would
give two good horses for her—one of them young and the
other one not so very old.

But the old man just waved his hand, meaning for High
Horse to go away and quit talking foolishness like that.

High Horse was feeling sicker than ever about it; but there
was another young fellow who said he would loan High Horse
two ponies and when he got some more horses, why, he could
just give them back for the ones he had borrowed.

Then High Horse went back to the old man and said he
would give four horses for the girl—two of them young and
the other two not hardly old at all. But the old man just waved
his hand and would not say anything.

So High Horse sneaked around until he could talk to the
girl again, and he asked her to run away with him. He told
her he thought he would just fall over and die if she did not.
But she said she would not do that; she wanted to be bought
like a fine woman. You see she thought a great deal of herself too.

That made High Horse feel so very sick that he could not
eat a bite, and he went around with his head hanging down
as though he might just fall down and die any time.

Red Deer was another young fellow, and he and High Horse
were great comrades, always doing things together. Red Deer
saw how High Horse was acting, and he said, "Cousin, what is
the matter? Are you sick in the belly? You look as though you
were going to die."

Then High Horse told Red Deer how it was, and said he
thought he could not stay alive much longer if he could not
marry the girl pretty quick.

Red Deer thought awhile about it, and then he said, "Cousin,
I have a plan, and if you are man enough to do as I tell you,
then everything will be all right. She will not run away with
you; her old man will not take four horses; and four horses

are all you can get. You must steal her and run away with her. Then after a while you can come back and the old man cannot do anything because she will be your woman. Probably she wants you to steal her anyway."

So they planned what High Horse had to do, and he said he loved the girl so much that he was man enough to do anything Red Deer or anybody else could think up.

So this is what they did.

That night late they sneaked up to the girl's tepee and waited until it sounded inside as though the old man and the old woman and the girl were sound asleep. Then High Horse crawled under the tepee with a knife. He had to cut the rawhide thongs first, and then Red Deer, who was pulling up the stakes around that side of the tepee, was going to help drag the girl outside and gag her. After that, High Horse could put her across his pony in front of him and hurry out of there and be happy all the rest of his life.

When High Horse had crawled inside, he felt so nervous that he could hear his heart drumming, and it seemed so loud he felt sure it would waken the old folks. But it did not, and after a while he began cutting the thongs. Every time he cut one it made a pop and nearly scared him to death. But he was getting along all right and all the thongs were cut down as far as the girl's thighs, when he became so nervous that his knife slipped and stuck the girl. She gave a big, loud yell. Then the old folks jumped up and yelled too. By this time High Horse was outside, and he and Red Deer were running away like antelope. The old man and some other people chased the young men but they got away in the dark and nobody knew who it was.

Well, if you ever wanted a beautiful girl you will know how sick High Horse was now. It was very bad the way he felt, and it looked as though he would starve even if he did not drop over dead sometime.

Red Deer kept thinking about this, and after a few days he went to High Horse and said, "Cousin, take courage! I have another plan, and I am sure, if you are man enough, we can steal her this time." And High Horse said, "I am man enough to do anything anybody can think up, if I can only get that girl."

So this is what they did.

They went away from the village alone, and Red Deer made High Horse strip naked. Then he painted High Horse solid white all over, and after that he painted black stripes all over the white and put black rings around High Horse's eyes. High Horse looked terrible. He looked so terrible that when Red Deer was through painting and took a good look at what he had done, he said it scared even him a little.

"Now," Red Deer said, "if you get caught again, everybody will be so scared they will think you are a bad spirit and will be afraid to chase you."

So when the night was getting old and everybody was sound asleep, they sneaked back to the girl's tepee. High Horse crawled in with his knife, as before, and Red Deer waited outside, ready to drag the girl out and gag her when High Horse had all the thongs cut.

High Horse crept up by the girl's bed and began cutting at the thongs. But he kept thinking, "If they see me they will shoot me because I look so terrible." The girl was restless and kept squirming around in bed, and when a thong was cut, it popped. So High Horse worked very slowly and carefully.

But he must have made some noise, for suddenly the old woman awoke and said to her old man, "Old Man, wake up! There is somebody in this tepee!" But the old man was sleepy and didn't want to be bothered. He said, "Of course there is somebody in this tepee. Go to sleep and don't bother me." Then he snored some more.

But High Horse was so scared by now that he lay very still and as flat to the ground as he could. Now, you see, he had not been sleeping very well for a long time because he was so sick about the girl. And while he was lying there waiting for the old woman to snore, he just forgot everything, even how beautiful the girl was. Red Deer who was lying outside ready to do his part, wondered and wondered what had happened in there, but he did not dare call out to High Horse.

After a while the day began to break and Red Deer had to

leave with the two ponies he had staked there for his comrade and girl, or somebody would see him.

So he left.

Now when it was getting light in the tepee, the girl awoke and the first thing she saw was a terrible animal, all white with black stripes on it, lying asleep beside her bed. So she screamed, and then the old woman screamed and the old man yelled. High Horse jumped up, scared almost to death, and he nearly knocked the tepee down getting out of there.

People were coming running from all over the village with guns and bows and axes, and everybody was yelling.

By now High Horse was running so fast that he hardly touched the ground at all, and he looked so terrible that the people fled from him and let him run. Some braves wanted to shoot at him, but the others said he might be some sacred being and it would bring bad trouble to kill him.

High Horse made for the river that was near, and in among the brush he found a hollow tree and dived into it. After a while some braves came there and he could hear them saying that it was some bad spirit that had come out of the water and gone back in again.

That morning the people were ordered to break camp and move away from there. So they did, while High Horse was hiding in his hollow tree.

Now Red Deer had been watching all this from his own tepee and trying to look as though he were as much surprised and scared as all the others. So when the camp moved, he sneaked back to where he had seen his comrade disappear. When he was down there in the brush, he called, and High Horse answered, because he knew his friend's voice. They washed off the paint from High Horse and sat down on the river bank to talk about their troubles.

High Horse said he never would go back to the village as long as he lived and he did not care what happened to him now. He said he was going to go on the warpath all by himself. Red Deer said, "No, cousin, you are not going on the warpath alone, because I am going with you."

So Red Deer got everything ready, and at night they started out on the warpath all alone. After several days they came to a Crow camp just about sundown, and when it was dark they sneaked up to where the Crow horses were grazing, killed the horse guard, who was not thinking about enemies because he thought all the Lakotas were far away, and drove off about a hunderd horses.

They got a big start because all the Crow horses stampeded and it was probably morning before the Crow warriors could catch any horses to ride. Red Deer and High Horse fled with their herd three days and nights before they reached the village of their people. Then they drove the whole herd right into the village and up in front of the girl's tepee. The old man was there, and High Horse called out to him and asked if he thought maybe that would be enough horses for his girl. The old man did not wave him away that time. It was not the horses that he wanted. What he wanted was a son who was a real man and good for something.

So High Horse got his girl after all, and I think he deserved her.

Ben Kindle's Winter Count

A Teton Sioux proverb says that "A people without history is like wind on the buffalo grass." As we are beginning to realize, there are various kinds of history, and not all of the most meaningful of these are written. This one is an oral calendar of events which marked the winters of the Oglala Sioux from 1759 to the year before it was taken down from the lips of Ben Kindle, who got it in his turn from his grandfather, Afraid-of-Soldier. The actual Oglala words are usually mnemonic devices or keys to call to memory the skeleton of an incident which is then further elaborated. As poetry and as history this gives remarkable insight into the life of a people.

From Martha Warren Beckwith, "Mythology of the Oglala Sioux," *Journal of American Folklore* 43 (October-December 1930), 339-442.

1759 Wic'a'b.lecahą Wani× yetu
They are broken apart / year.
> When the tribes scattered.

1760 Hok'u'wa Wic'a'ktepi
Fishermen / they are killed. (While engaged in fishing, they are killed.)
> Two Sioux boys went fishing in the creek and the enemy killed them.

1761 Wąb.li'k'uwa Wic'a'ktepi
Eagle-trappers / they are killed.
> Two Shoshone were trapping eagles and some Sioux killed them.

1762 Pte A'nųwąpi
Buffalo / they swim out for them.
> Hunters chased buffaloes into the Missouri river and killed them there, then dragged them to land.

1763 T'uki' mi'layapi
Shell / they use for knives.
> The Indians had no knives, hence they brought shells from the Missouri and Platt rivers to use as knives.

1764 T'ażu'śkala kte'pi
"Little ant" / they kill him.
> A Sioux called "Little Ant" was killed.

1765 Wazi'k'ute ahi'ktepi
"He shoots at the pine" / coming they kill him.
> The Sioux Indians attack the Crow and a Sioux named Shooting-Pine is killed.

1766 Wale'ġala kte'pi
"Pouch" (made out of the rough lining of the first stomach) / he is killed.
> A Sioux called "Pouch" is killed.

1767 Anųk' op iya'yapi
Both sides / in company with / they go off.
> The Crow Indians are at peace with the Sioux and the two live together, also the Sioux are at peace with the Pawnee and they live together. When the Crow and

Pawnee fight together, they find that there are Sioux on both sides and so they make peace.

1768 Iye'ska kic'i'zapi

White or clear speakers (those whose language is understandable, i.e., those in the same tribe) / they fight against each other.

The first civil war among the Sioux Indians: the Standing Rock Indians and the Cheyenne fight against the Oglala and Rosebud.

1769 Ite'hakit'ula kte'pi

"He (little one) wears a mask" / they kill him (or, he is killed).

A Sioux named "Mask-On" is killed. The mask is made out of buckskin fastened to a willow hoop with eyes cut for a mask.

1770 Wak'ą't'ąka ihą×b.la wįyą wą g.naśkį'yą

God / to see in vision, or dream of in sleep / woman / a / she goes crazy.

A woman has been accustomed to go to lonely places for visions and then come back and tell the people where to go for buffalo and when the enemy is coming. One morning she cannot speak, she does not know anything and soon she dies.

1771 Miwa'tani oǧu'wic'ayapi

Mandans / they are burned out.

Hostile Indian dig a trench down by the creek and the Sioux are unable to drive them away. So they build fires all about the trench and the enemy have to escape in the night.

1772 C'ąk'į' ya'm.ni ahi'wic'aktepi

Carriers of wood on the back / three / coming to them they kill them. (Ahi'wic'aktepi always means that an enemy coming there from a great distance commits the deed. It implies the killer journeying there to do it.)

The Sioux make a new camp and the Crows hide in the timber and kill three old women sent after

wood as they are returning with the wood on their
backs.

1773 Sų'ka k'o išta' niyą'pi

Dogs / even / eyes / they are inflamed.

Even the dogs got snow-blindness this winter because
there was a heavy fall of snow and they had to move
camp constantly to escape attack by hostile Indians.

1774 Heyo'k'akağa wą kte'pi

Clown / a / he is killed.

The Sioux camp in a circle and the clowns put on
their masks, come to the circle and then go down to
the creek and back to pray for the thunder. When they
go back to the creek, hostile Indians in hiding kill them.

1775 Paha'ta i num wic'a'ktepi

To the top of the hill / they went / two / they are killed.
(Two individuals who had gone up to the hill were
killed.)

About forty or fifty young people of the Sioux start out
on a war party. They are concealed in the heavy
timber down by the big creek. Two scouts on the hill
look about and see the enemy coming down the creek,
about seventy or eighty of them on foot with two Crow
ahead. The Sioux mount their horses and kill the two
Crow.

1776 Kig.lela hi

[This word may be K'ig.le'la — He goes back home
(little one); or K'įg.le'la — He goes home carrying on
his back (little one); or it may be a corruption of the
white man's name[1]] / he arrives.

A half-breed joins the Sioux.

1777 Ho'he ahi'

Assiniboines / they arrive.

The Assiniboines make peace with the Sioux.

1778 Cąna'k'sa yuha' kte'pi

"Stick broken with the foot / he carries" / he is killed.

---

[1] "La" after a man's name does not always mean little; it is more apt to
indicate that it is his joking or nickname, not his serious name.

They were playing a game and the braves got to fighting and this man was killed.

1779 Tuktel′ wani′t′i t′ąi̦′śni awe′tupi

What place / winter camp / it is not clear / spring comes on them.

During the winter the people generally camp by the creek with an abundance of hay and wood and move in the spring, but this year there was no feed so they had to move often throughout the winter.

1780 Slukela haka′ iwo′to

(A proper name, but unidentified) / spearlike stick used in the game / he bumps into it.

Two men were playing haka′ų′ pi, or Shooting-the-Spear. They hit the umpire through the thigh with the stick so that later he died.

1781 Sųknu′ni o′ta ahi′

Stray horses / many / they come.

This year while they were in camp with their ponies in the center of the circle, many wild horses came down from the hills and joined their ponies; so they divided up the wild horses.

1782 Nawi′c′aśli

They break out with a rash.

The first epidemic of measles.

1783 Śina′lutai̦ wą kte′pi

Wearer of a red blanket / a / he is killed.

The man with a red blanket was killed in war.

1784 Aki′c′ita o′ta c′uwi′tat′api

Soldiers / many / they freeze to death.

White soldiers were encamped by the creek and Indians came down the creek and shot them and ran away. It was so cold that all the white men were frozen to death.

1785 Og.la′la hate′ icu′pi

Og.lalas / cedar / they took.

The Sioux came west after cedar to use as medicine. " 'Fraid for the Thunder" is the name of cedar smoke because if men have passed through its smoke, the lightning will not strike them in a thunderstorm. They also burn cedar for the sick.

1786 Pʻeicu'ya zuya' g.li

"He goes to take scalps" / on warpath / he returns home.

A man vowed to go down to the Crow Indians by himself after a scalp. He stayed away for a week and then came back pretending to bring back a scalp, but it was only buffalo hair. He came into the tent carrying the scalp on a stick and singing, "I killed a Crow Indian." At first they believed him, but the brother-in-law saw the pretended scalp and recognized the fraud.

1787 O'hazi atku'ku kte'pi

"Shade" / his father / they kill.

The father of a boy named "Shade" is killed in a quarrel over whose arrow shot the buffalo.

1788 Heyo'kʻakaġa num wicʻa'ktepi

Clowns / two / they are killed. ("Make," in this sense, always means to act the part of.)

Two clowns are killed. The Sioux have three camps by the river. The clowns circle the camps and when they come down to the last one, the Shoshone hiding in the timber kill the two clowns.

1789 Kʻaġi' o'ta cʻuwi'tatʻapi

Crows / many / they freeze to death.

Many crows die of the cold. These are not the summer crows but a bigger crow that stays in the winter.

1790 Miwa'tani num cʻahcʻo'ka wicʻa'ktepi

Mandans / two / out on the ice / they are killed.

Two hostile Indians came down to the Sioux camp on the ice and, when the Sioux pursued, they killed them on the ice.

1791 Wo'wapi makʻo'kawįh ahi'yayapi

Flag / around the earth / they carry it along.

The American flag is carried to all the Indian tribes all around the state.

1792 Wį'ya wą ska wąya'kapi
Woman / a / white / they see.

Once three Indians had gone after buffalo and were returning with the meat tied to the saddles. They looked up toward a hill just at sunset and saw a woman in white looking toward the sun. They ran back to camp and before dawn twelve young men went out to investigate and saw the woman in white at sunrise looking toward the sun. They believed this to be a spirit warning them of the approach of an enemy and they moved camp.

1793 Miwa'tani awi'c'at'ipi
Mandans / they camp close to. (They, the Sioux, camp close to the Mandans to crowd them off by making the proximity unpleasant.)

Sioux Indians camp close to hostile Indians and the two fight every day.

1794 Ite' ci'k'a wą kte'pi
Face / small / a / they kill (a small-faced enemy).

The Ponca Indians are large men with little faces, hence called "Small-Face." Three Poncas lie in hiding near the Sioux camp and try to steal horses, and the Sioux kill one "Small-Face."

1795 P'ehį' hą'skaska wą kte'pi
Hair / long (reduplication indicates each hair is long) / a / they kill him.

They killed a Sioux Indian with long hair.

1796 M.ni'yaye yuha' wą kte'pi
Water container / carried / a / they killed.

A Sioux woman going after water before sunrise with a buffalo-paunch bucket on her back is killed by a hostile Indian in hiding near the camp.

1797 Wap'a'hakit'ų wą kte'pi
Wearer of a war bonnet / a / he is killed.

A Sioux warrior kills a Blackfoot who wears a war bonnet and thus gets possession of his war bonnet. This event marks the introduction of the war bonnet as well as of the buffalo horn headdress among the Sioux.

1798 Wak'ą't'ąkawįyą wą iye'yapi
   Great Spirit woman / a / she is found.

> This year, three young men went hunting. It was in the spring and very misty. They camped across the creek. At midnight came a woman, but where she entered they could not say, for the enclosure was walled with logs like a stockade. There she stood by the fire. She gave them three words of advice: "Grow many and you will live" — "Pack up and run away for two big gangs of the enemy will come after you" — "Go in that direction and I will bring many buffalo." Then she vanished they knew not where—up, down, or where. The young men cried and prayed.

1799 Wii'g.luš'aka o'ta t'a'pi
   Pregnant women / many / they die.

> Many pregnant women died.

1800 T'ac'ą'ta Yu'tešni wae'c'ų
   "Ruminant's heart / He eats not" / does a deed.

> A man named "Never-eats-buffalo-heart" made a feast for all the people. This was the first feast among the Sioux.

1801 Nawi'c'ašli
   They break out with a rash.

> The second epidemic of measles.

1802 Waši'cu wą wašte' hi
   White man / a / good / he arrives.

> The first white preacher came to the Sioux.

1803 Šake'maza o'ta awi'c'ag.lipi
   Horseshoes / many / they bring home. (They brought home many shoed horses.)

> The Sioux Indians were going to steal horses and for the first time saw horseshoes on them.

1804 Šųkġu'gula o'ta awi'c'ag.lipi
   Horses burned all over / many / they brought home (curly-haired horses).

> The Sioux stole horses from the Blackfoot, many of them curly-haired.

1805 T'así'ta ų aki'c'ilowąpi

Horsetail / with (as instrument) / they sang over each other. (This generally means the "Hųka'" Ceremony when the candidates are made huká by the songs sung over them by the officiating priest who at the same time waves a wand with pendant horsehair.. T'a- means any ruminant; the more usual word for horsehair is śųksį'ta, but people call it t'así'ta, too.)

They first introduce the custom of adopting a member of another family by swinging the horsetail over the person thus adopted.

1806 Śag.lo'gą ahi'wic'aktepi

Eight / arriving here they kill them. (The enemy came here or near here and killed seven men.)

Nine Sioux went to war against the Crow. One of their number was posted as scout on a hill with a telescope. The Crow hid in the tent with bows drawn and when the Sioux approached they killed all but the scout, who ran two nights and a day before he reached the Sioux camp about dinnertime.

1807 Wąb.li'k'uwa eya' wic'a'ktepi

Eagle trappers / some / they are killed (i.e. away from home: indicates that the Sioux went off somewhere and killed some eagle trappers of another tribe).

The Sioux killed some Arapaho eagle-trappers.

1808 O'g.leluta ų wą itkop' heyo'k'a ahi'ktepi

Red Shirt / he wears / a / meeting / in an anti-natural manner / he is killèd by those arriving. (A fighter who is an anti-natural, does the opposite to what the others on his side are doing, and so confuses the fighters that his own side, not realizing, of course, kill him.)

The Crow Indians are fighting the Sioux and the clown, wearing no mask but in a red shirt, runs toward the Crow and shoots at the Sioux, and the Crow kill him.

1809 Śina't'o atku'ku P'ala'ni ahi'ktepi

Blue-blanket / his father / Pawnee / arriving they kill.

Pawnee Indians kill Blue-Blanket's father.

1810 C'a'pa Ci'k'ala tii'le
Beaver / Little / has his house burn down. (Of itself, i.e.,
without anyone planning it on purpose.)
  A white man set up a store and collected beaver-skin.
  The Indians called him "Little Beaver." His camp
  burned.[2]

1811 Sį'te wa'k'šupi o'ta awi'c'ag.lipi
Tail / decorated / many / they are brought home.
  They steal horses with feathers on their tails.

1812 P'ala'ni top wic'a'ktepi
Pawnees / four / they are killed.
  They kill four Pawnee.

1813 C'aku't'ą×ka atku'ku P'ala'ni kte'pi
"Road-Big" / his father / Pawnees / they kill him.
  Big-Road's father is killed by Pawnees.

1814 Witapahata ų wą kahu'hugapi
Dweller at Island Butte / a / they break (kahu'ga means
to break something with a hard shell, like an egg, a skull,
a turtle's back, etc.).
  A Mandan came down to the Sioux camp and talked
  with his hand, telling them not to kill him. A Sioux
  whose brother had been killed (by a Mandan) came
  up to him with a concealed ax and chopped off his
  head.

1815 Ita'zipc'o t'it'a'ka ot'i'pi
Sans-arcs / big house / they live in.
  The No-Bow (Sans-arc) build the first log house.

1816 Ną ak'e' ot'i'pi
And / again / they live in.
  The house is used for a second year.

1817 C'ąše'ca ų t'ika'gapi
Dead wood / with (as material) / they build house.
  They build houses of dry wood.

---

[2] Kindle said, "They burned his camp," but in this case it should read
C'a' pa ci'k'al a t'i ki ile' yapi, or oi'leyapi.

1818 Nawi'c'ašli
>They break out with rash.
>The third epidemic of measles.

1819 Sic'ą'ġu c'ąpų'pų ų t'ica'ġapi
>Burnt-Thighs / rotten wood / with / they build house.
>Rosebud Indians build houses of rotten wood.

1820 Wą Nų'p.lala iwi'c'icaške ki'caġapi
>"Arrow / Only two" / ? / they make for him.
>Two-Arrow, who made the Crow dance as a vow for brave men, himself ran away when they went out to fight.

1821 Wic'a'hpi wą hot'ų' hiya'ya
>Star / a / with voice / it went by.
>A shooting star flew from east to west with a noise like thunder.

1822 Wasku'la hu špą
>"He pares with a knife" (such things as pumpkin, potatoes, apples, wild turnips, etc.). This is a nickname, indicated by the la; hu, leg, / špa, burn, or better, cook.[3]
>Man with burned legs came to camp.
>He-pares-with-knife's legs got frostbitten.

1823 Wag.me'za o'ta ši'ce.
>Corn / much / it is bad.
>Much corn spoiled. White men camped and the Indians took their sacks of corn to be ground and it got wet and moldy because they did not know how to keep it.

1824 Yeye'la hmųh kte'pi
>"Unstable" / by bewitching / they kill. (Yeye'la, shaky and unsteady, like a table, a limb of a tree, if it is liable to break when climbed, etc., hmųh, to position by supernatural means.)
>"Swing-gently" was killed.

---

[8] This would mean generally that a man named Wasku 'la had his legs frozen. If it happened with fire, they would in nine times out of ten indicate *how* it happened. Peta u, they would say (by fire). But when the means is not indicated, it means by frostbite. One would more accurately say ġu, instead of špa, if it meant by fire.

1825 M.ni wic'a't'e

Water / they die. (They drown.)

In March the people camped across the Missouri River. One morning before sunrise someone called them to wake because the water was coming. One heard the voice, but no one would listen. The banks did overflow and some of the old men and old women were drowned, while the able-bodied had to swim in the broken ice to reach high land. The horses were tied and could not get away, so they were all drowned.

1826 Ką i wą agl.it'e

Aged / he went / a / returning died.

An aged Sioux was scalped by the Crow Indians and he returned to camp and died.

1827 P'sa ohą'pi

Reed or rush / they wear on their feet.

The Sioux Indians first made snowshoes out of kinnikinnick and willows.

1828 Miwa'tani o'ta wic'a'ktepi

Mandans / many / they are killed.

They kill many enemies.

1829 Ite' g.le'ġa wia'k'siże

"Face / striped" / retains or keeps in his possession, a woman.

An old man named "Spotted-face" forces a young girl to be his wife and her father cannot get her away.

1830 Ptesą' o'ta wic'a'opi

White buffalo / leg / it is broken. Ptesą', white buffalo.

They kill many white buffaloes.

1831 Ptesą' hu kawe'ġe

White buffalo / leg / it is broken. Ptesą', white buffalo. (Now and then, very rarely, a light-colored buffalo was found in the herd. They were priceless because they were rare, and some put a supernatural power to them. Hence Ptesą' is a fine name for man or woman.)

White-Buffalo broke his leg.

1832 He Wążi'ca hu kawe'ġe
"Horn / only one" / it is broken.
One-Horn broke his leg.

1833 Wic'a'hpi ok'i'cam.na
Stars / they go in all directions (crossing each other's
path. Icam.na means "it snows." The way the stars
seemed to fly in every way looked like snow coming
down. Ok'i'cam.na is used to express confusion, especially among a crowd, when everyone runs hither and
yon).
Stars change places, i.e., there are many shooting stars
seen in the heavens.

1834 Šahi'yela t'ig.le' wą kte'pi
Cheyenne / established in his home / a / they kill.
A Cheyenne of good family is killed by another Chey-
enne because he is so rich in horses.

1835 T'at'ą'ka wą c'e'pa o'pi
Buffalo-bull / a / it is fat / they shoot with an arrow.
They kill a fat buffalo bull.

1836 C'ąha'ka ų aki'c'ilowąpi
Branched stick / with / they sing over each other.
(C'ąha'ka is a part of a bough with several branches or
forks left on, like an elk-horn. This of course means such
a part of the tree was used in place of the usual horsehair
switch referred to in 1805.)
A man about to give the sign of adoption saw some
buffalo coming and thought they were soldiers. In his
haste he waved a stick instead of the horsetail over
the adopted person.

1837 Ite'hepi Sapki'ya t'ia'paktepi
"Lower half of the face / he blackens his" / they kill him
and his household right in their tepee.
Black-face, who painted half his face black from the
nose down, camped away from the circle and was
killed by the Crow, he and his whole family.

1838 Šųkg.na'škįyą c'įcąwą kte'pi
"Crazy Wolf" / his son / a / they kill.
Crazy-Dog's son is killed by the Crow.

1839 Wic'a'akih'ą wat'a'kpe ai'
　　　Famine-striken / for offensive warfare / they go.
　　　　　During this year of famine they attacked a steamboat
　　　　　on the river, but without success.

1840 Wakį'yą ci'k'ala sųka'ku num wic'a'ktepi
　　　"Thunder / Little" / his younger brothers / two / they
　　　are killed.
　　　　　Little-Thunder has two brothers who go to battle with
　　　　　the Crow Indians and are killed.

1841 Sųkna'kpoġi o'ta t'ewi'c'ayapi
　　　Brown-eared horses / many / they were caused to die.
　　　　　Many white horses with brown ears (a color much
　　　　　admired by the Sioux) are killed in quarrels over their
　　　　　possession.

1842 Wi'yaka Owį' sųkyu'ha na'zį wą kte
　　　"Feather / Earring" / holding horse / he stands / a / he
　　　kills.
　　　　　The Sioux called "Feather-Earrings" attacks and kills
　　　　　a Crow Indian who is guarding a herd, and takes the
　　　　　horses.

1843 Waya'ka ag.li'pi
　　　Captives / they bring home.
　　　　　The Sioux Indians take Crow slaves.

1844 K'ągi'b.loka× ahi'ktepi
　　　"Male-crow" / coming they kill him.
　　　　　He-Crow is killed by the Crow.

1845 Nawi'c'aśli
　　　They break out with a rash.
　　　　　The fourth epidemic of measles.

1846 Susu' ska wą kte'pi
　　　Testicles / white / a / they kill.
　　　　　White-Testicles is killed.

1847 K'ągi'wąb.li× c'ap'a'pi
　　　Crow-eagle / he is stabbed.
　　　　　Crow-Eagle is knifed.

1848 Wį'kte wą kte'pi
　　　Hermaphrodite / a / they kill.

A hermaphrodite of the Crow dressed like a woman is killed.

1849 Nawi'c'at'ipa
They cramp.
There is an epidemic of cramp.[4]

1850 Wic'a'ḣaḣą
They have sores (smallpox).
The first smallpox epidemic.

1851 Wakpa'm.nipi t'ą×ka
They pass things around / big. (Giving out of annuities on a grand scale.)
For the first time rations were distributed to the Indians.

1852 Wani'yetu wašmą×
Winter / deep snow.
A year of deep snow.

1853 Mat'o' wą wišą' manų'hi
Bear / a / "mons veneris" / he came to steal.[5]
A man shot a bear in his tent. He woke suddenly from sleep and looked over at the horses. They were

---

[4] Called in other counts Na-wi'-c 'a-k' še-ca, to double up. Such spasms are said to have been prevalent until one man on the march in his spasmodic movements fell into a stream and immediately recovered. After that any such attack was cured by throwing the victim into water.

[5] Wiša Manu. To steal contact with a woman. It is said that in the old days a man could claim a woman if he overpowered her and touched her vagina. Or if he saw her naked, while in swimming perhaps, she could no longer claim to be a virgin. Women had to be extremely careful of their persons, for if they were careless enough to let these things happen, the man could claim them. They had to be careful in their conversation with men, also, for if they answered "yes" to a simple question the man might say, "Now you have yielded to me, for although I asked you a simple question with my lips, I had another in my head and that you have consented to." Young women used to be bound and tied from the hips down by their grandmothers, mothers or aunts before they slept and were usually placed to sleep near the fire and away from the edge of the tent, because a man of low character might pull up the tentpins at night, crawl in and attempt to touch the part while the girl slept, in which case she was obliged to consent to marry him. Such an act on his part was held in derision because he had no power to charm the girl and had to resort to stealing her. The bear in the "count" is jestingly said to have entered the tent for a similar purpose.

snorting. He saw a black object right under the tent. He took his gun and said, "What you doing over here?" No answer. The bear said, "Whi-h-u-u!" It had pulled up two pickets of the tent and got inside.

1854 Mat'o' Wayu'hi kte'pi
"Bear / he causes confusion" / they kill.
Mat'o' Wayu'hi was killed.

1855 Wic'a'yažipa waa'k'šiža
"Wasp" / he refuses to have them go.
Wasp, who is a poor man, suggests after the sun-dance that "We have a good time here; let us stay three or four months more."

1856 K'ągi'wic'aša ok'i'yapi
Crow Indian / they confer with.
The Sioux make peace with the Crow.

1857 K'ągi'wic'aša wik'ce'm.na wic'a'ktepi
Crow Indians / ten / they are killed.
The Sioux kill ten Crow Indians.

1858 T'aši'na Ġi P'sa'loka kte'pi
"His robe / Brow" / Crows / they kill him.
Big-Blanket is killed by Crow Indians.

1859 K'ągi' T'ą×ka ahi'ktepi.
"Crow / Big" / coming they kill.
Big-Crow is killed by the Crow.

1860 ......

1861 Hokšic'ala hohpa'sotapi
Children / by a cough they are wiped out.
An epidemic of whooping cough among the babies and many died.

1862 Hokši'la wą wašpa'pi
Boy / a / they scalp him.
A Sioux boy crossed the creek from camp and as he was coming back about nine or ten o'clock some Shoshone Indians scalped him.

1863 Og.la'la šag.lo'ġą ahi'wic'aktepi
Oglalas / eight / coming they kill them.
The Crow killed eight Oglala Sioux.

1864 P'sa top wic'a'ktepi
Crow / four / they are killed.
The Oglala killed four Crow.

1865 Šųkso'tapi
Horses are wiped out, die off.
A winter of heavy snow and most of the horses died.

1866 Waši'cu opa'wįǧe wic'a'ktepi
Whites / hundred / they are killed.
The Sioux kill a hundred whites.

1867 Šų'šųla t'ihi' wą kte'pi
Shoshone / come right into camp / a / they kill.
A Shoshone came into the Sioux camp to steal and was killed.

1868 Wakį'yą Het'ų' e'ihpeyapi
"Thunder / has horns" / they take him off and leave him there.
Horned-Thunder went with a war party of Sioux to fight the Ute. His feet swelled, so they left him behind with food and wood close by the creek and went on to the war, but Horned-Thunder never came back.

1869 Winų'hcala wą c'ąka't'a
Old woman / a / she is killed by a tree.
And old woman who camped under a tree was killed by the wind blowing the tree over.

1870 C'ąku' Wąka'tuya ahi'ktepi
"Road / High" / coming they kill him.
A very brave man named "High-Road" is killed by the Crow.

1871 C'ąha'hake t'ąį'šni
"Spinal column" / disappears.
Back-Bone is lost when out hunting.

1872 Nata'hlo'ka k'ąǧi'wic'aša e'wic'akte
"Head with a hole in it" / Crow Indians / going he killed them.
Hollow-Head was sleeping up on a hill with a telescope,

gun, and arrows. He saw two Crow Indians and shot them both without any aid.

1873 Oma'ha num wic'a'ktepi
Omahas / two / they are killed.
The Sioux kill two Omaha Indians.

1874 Eha'ke k'owa'katą ai'
For the last time / across the River / they went.
The Sioux cross the Missouri for the last time.

1875 Wa'g.luhe śako'wį ahi'wic'aktepi
Camp-followers / seven / coming they kill them.
Seven Sioux Indians from Loafer Camp go visiting to Big Horn River and are attacked by Crow Indians and killed.

1876 Mahpi'ya Lu'ta śųkk'i'pi
"Cloud / Red" / they take his horses from him. (The white soldiers demanded all the horses from his tribe. This was to prevent another uprising.)
The white soldiers take his horses from Red Cloud, the Oglala chief (Custer massacre).

1877 T'aśų'ke Witko× kte'pi
"His horse / crazy" / they kill.
The Oglala chief Crazy Horse, who has harried the settlers in the Black Hills as they came through with oxen, is killed this year.

1878 Śahi'yela Wak'a⁶ kte'pi
Cheyenne / Holy / they kill him. (Had it been a Cheyenne medicine man, it would have been "Sahiyela wak'ą× wą kte'pi.")
Cheyenne Holy Man was killed this year. He was a Sioux medicine man and at a gathering at the agency he claimed to be invulnerable. So they shot at him and killed him. (This is the year of the opening of the agency at Pine Ridge.)

1879 Sųkma'nitu G.leśka' kte'pi
"Wolf / Spotted" / he is killed.
Spotted-Wolf is killed by a Sioux.

---

⁶ Probably a proper name, Śahi'yela Wak'ą'.

1880 Susu′ G.leṡka′ kte′pi
"Testicles / Spotted" / they kill.
Spotted-Testicles is killed by a Sioux.

1881 Sįte′g.leṡka kte′pi
Spotted Tail / they kill.
Spotted-Tail (chief at Rosebud) is killed.

1882 C‛ą′c‛eġa k‛į′la c‛įca′ wą ic‛i′kte
"Drum / he carries on his back (nickname)" / his son /
a / he kills himself.
Drum-on-the-back's son shoots himself.

1883 Ite′c‛ągu×ġu t‛ahu′ pawe′ġe
"Face-blackened with wood charcoal" / his neck / it is
broken.
Black-paint-on-the-face broke his neck chasing the
steers at the old slaughter house at Pine Ridge.

1884 T‛at‛ą′ka Ska t‛awi′cu kikte′
"Buffalo-bull / White" / his wife / he kills his own.
White-Bull killed his wife.

1885 P‛e′tawic‛aṡa e′iḣpeyapi
Fire-man (Man of fire) / they take him far and leave
him.
Fire-Man went to visit the Arapaho and died there.

1886 Yuptą′yą wanu′ktepi
"Turn it over" / is accidentally killed.
Turn-them-over was killed.

1887 Wak‛ą′ wanų′ktepi
"Holy" / is accidentally killed.
Holy was killed.

1888 Wo′p‛aḣta yuble′capi
"Bundles" / they are opened and exposed.
Policemen stopped the traffic in "medicine."

1889 O′g.le Ṡa t‛ąk‛ṡi′tku wą ic‛i′kte
"Shirt / Red" / his younger sister / a / she hanged her-
self.
Red-Shirt's sister hanged herself.

1890 Si T'ą′ka kte′pi
　　　"Big / foot" / they kill.
　　　　Chief Big-Foot came to the Ghost Dance at Oglala. The
　　　　Agency stopped the dance and at Brennan the soldiers
　　　　attacked them and killed the chief and many others.

1891 Maka′ ma′niakic'ita wic'a′kaǵapi
　　　Ground / walking soldiers (Infantry) / they are made.
　　　　The Indian are taken to Omaha and Fort Mink and
　　　　put into the army.

1892 C'ą Num Yuha′ pteyu′ha wic'a′kte
　　　"Sticks / two / he has" / cattle-owners / he kills them.
　　　　Some cowboys down by White River are troubling the
　　　　cattle and Two-Sticks and his son go down and kill the
　　　　cowboys.

1893 Owa′yawat'ąka ile′ (Pine Ridge Agency)
　　　Big school / it burns.
　　　　The first boarding school is burned at the Pine Ridge
　　　　Agency.

1894 C'ą Num Yuha′ p'a′nak'seyapi
　　　"Sticks / two / he has" / they behead him.
　　　　They hang Two-Sticks for killing the cowboys.

1895 Og.la′la om.ni′ciye t'ą′ka ka′ǵapi
　　　Oglalas / gathering / great / they make.
　　　　(Om.niciye T'ą′nka is the general term among all the
　　　　Indians for religious gatherings. It is probable this was the
　　　　first Episcopal Convocation on the Oglala reserve.)
　　　　They call the first meeting of the big Oglala council.

1896 Zikta′la Ska Waya′su t'a
　　　"Bird / White" / judge / he dies.
　　　　White-Bird, the judge, died at the agency.

1897 T'alo′t'ipi wą ile′yapi; Mak'a′ṡa el
　　　Beef-house / a / they burn it; / Mak'a′ṡa / at.
　　　　The slaughterhouse was burned by incendiaries who did
　　　　not want it there.

1898 Og.la′la t'oka′ c'ų′kaṡke ka′ǵapi
　　　Oglalas / first time / fences / they make.
　　　　A fence is built all around the Oglala reservation.

1899 P'eta'ǵa t'a
　　"Live coal" / he dies.
　　　Fire (an old man who worked at the reservation)
　　　died.

1900 Wo'kpam.ni nat'a'kapi
　　Annuities (of goods) / they lock or close or bar.
　　　Rations are not given out.

1901 Wic'a'hąhą
　　Smallpox.
　　　Second smallpox epidemic.

1902 Winų'hcala wą t'ąį'śni
　　Old woman / a / she disappears.
　　　An old man and an old woman came drunk from
　　　Chadron and the old woman disappeared.

1903 T'a'hcak'ute wic'a'ktepi
　　Antelope-hunters / they are killed.
　　　The Sioux went down to Wyoming to hunt antelope
　　　and the policemen went after them and killed four. The
　　　Sioux killed one policeman from Newcastle.

1904 T'oka' mak'i'yu't'api
　　First time / they surveyed the land.
　　　For the first time land was allotted in the reservation.

1905 Wap'a'ha Ho'ta c'įca' kat'i'ye'kiya
　　"War-bonnet / Gray" / his son / he kills his own by
　　shooting.
　　　Gray-war-bonnet killed his son when he was drunk.

1906 Sa'pawic'aśa owi'cayuspapi
　　Black-men (Utes) / they are captured.
　　　Some Ute Indians camped within the Cheyenne River
　　　agency were transferred to the Ute reservation.

1907 Mak'i'yu't'a wo×kazuzu icu'pi
　　Land survey / payment / they receive.
　　　The first payment was made for the allotment benefit.

1908 Waśi'cu T'aśu×ke t'a
　　"White man / His horse" / he dies.
　　　Chief American-Horse died.

1909 Mi'wak'ą Yuha' t'a
"Sword / he has" / he dies.
  Chief Sword died.

1910 Mahpi'ya Lu'ta t'a
"Cloud / Red" / he dies.
  Chief Red Cloud died.

1911 Mat'o' K'oki'p'api t'a
"Bear / they fear him" / he dies.
  Afraid-of-Bear died.

1912 Wo'wapi Wąkal' a'yapi
Flag / upward / they raise it.
  Flag-raising at the agency. "The Indians and white men
  held the ropes. My father had one and another old
  Indian had another. One spoke and said, 'Always
  where this flag is you must fight for it; you don't want
  this flag down.' "

1913 Wa'ta wą m.nit'a'
Ship / a / it drowns.
  The sinking of the *Titanic.*

1914 Iya' Si'ca t'oka' oki'c'ize
Speech / Bad[7] / first / there is war.
  War declared with Germany.

1915 Waśi'cuik'ceka oki'c'ize
Common whites (French) / there is war.
  France at war with Germany.

1916 United States wa'ta nap'o'pyapi
United States / ship / they explode it.
  A United States ship sunk (*the Lusitania*).

1917 President Wilson oki'c'iżekta c'ażo'ic'iwa
President Wilson / there shall be war / he signs his name.
  President Wilson wants men to enlist in the army.

1918 United States oki'c'ize ohi'yapi; Flu ewi'c'ac'eca
United States / war / they win it; / Flu / they get it.
  The United States has peace from the war; flu epidemic.

---

[7] Because German speech is considered particularly unintelligible.

1919 Iye′c′įka ig.lu′ha wic′a′yuśtąpi
Of their own accord / to keep themselves / they are made.
> Some Sioux Indians become citizens.

1920 M.nitą′ t′ą×ka wą wak′a′heża k′o m.nit′a′pi
Flood / great / a / children / too / they die by drowning.
> White Clay creek is flooded in June and horses, cattle and dogs are drowned. One house "drew away" with everything in it and two children died.

1921 July ośka′te yub.le′capi
July / celebration / they break it into parts.
> There is a fourth of July celebration at each station.

1922 Aki′c′itahokśila ahi′
Soldier-boys / they arrive.
> Soldiers get recruits for the army.

1923 President Wilson t′a
President Wilson / dies.
> President Wilson died.[8]

1924 Ate′yapi Tidwell wic′a′k′ute
Agent / Tidwell / he shoots at them.
> Agent Tidwell shot at Indians boys who had escaped from jail.

1925 Agent Jermark wo′żuok′olakic′iye ka′ġa
Agent Jermark / farming society / he makes.
> Agent Jermark makes a farming chapter.

[8] Wilson died in 1924.

Blackfeet

A three-tribe confederacy of the northern Plains taking its name from the principal tribe, the *Siksika* (Blackfeet); the others were the Bloods and the Piegans. Originally these people held an enormous stretch of mostly Canadian hunting grounds but seem to have been gradually drifting southward onto the Great Plains. Here they acquired the horse and the gun and became with the Sioux, Cheyenne, and Crow the archetypal Indian. George Bird Grinnell, who collected so much valuable Plains lore just as it was about to fall into utter decay, salvaged a handful of wonderful myths and tales from these people in his *Blackfoot Lodge Tales*, selections from which are reprinted here. The reader who wishes additional material on this tribe should see John C. Ewers' definitive *The Blackfeet* and James W. Schultz's *Blackfeet and Buffalo*.

The Blackfoot Genesis

All animals of the Plains at one time heard and knew him, and all birds of the air heard and knew him. All things that he had made understood him, when he spoke to them—the birds, the animals, and the people.

Old Man was traveling about, south of here, making the people. He came from the south, traveling north, making animals and birds as he passed along. He made the mountains, prairies, timber, and brush first. So he went along, traveling northward, making things as he went, putting rivers here and there, and falls on them, putting red paint here and there in the ground— fixing up the world as we see it today. He made the Milk River (the Teton) and crossed it, and, being tired, went up on a little

From *Blackfoot Lodge Tales* by George B. Grinnell. Reprinted by permission of the University of Nebraska Press.

hill and lay down to rest. As he lay on his back, stretched out on the ground, with arms extended, he marked himself out with stones—the shape of his body, head, legs, arms, and everything. There you can see those rocks today. After he had rested, he went on northward, and stumbled over a knoll and fell down on his knees. Then he said, "You are a bad thing to be stumbling against"; so he raised up two large buttes there, and named them the Knees, and they are called so to this day. He went on farther north, and with some of the rocks he carried with him he built the Sweet Grass Hills.

Old Man covered the plains with grass for the animals to feed on. He marked off a piece of ground, and in it he made to grow all kinds of roots and berries—camas, wild carrots, wild turnips, sweet-root, bitter-root, sarvis berries, bull berries, cherries, plums, and rosebuds. He put trees in the ground. He put all kinds of animals on the ground. When he made the bighorn with its big head and horns, he made it out on the prairie. It did not seem to travel easily on the prairie; it was awkward and could not go fast. So he took it by one of its horns, and led it up into the mountains, and turned it loose; and it skipped about among the rocks, and went up fearful places with ease. So he said, "This is the place that suits you; this is what you are fitted for, the rocks and the mountains." While he was in the mountains, he made the antelope out of dirt, and turned it loose, to see how it would go. It ran so fast that it fell over some rocks and hurt itself. He saw that this would not do, and took the antelope down on the prairie, and turned it loose; and it ran away fast and gracefully, and he said, "This is what you are suited to."

One day Old Man determined that he would make a woman and a child; so he formed them both—the woman and the child, her son—of clay. After he had molded the clay in human shape, he said to the clay, "You must be people," and then he covered it up and left it, and went away. The next morning he went to the place and took the covering off, and saw that the clay shapes had changed a little. The second morning there was still more change, and the third still more. The fourth morning he went to the place, took the covering off, looked at the images, and told them to rise and walk; and they did so. They walked down to the river with their Maker, and then he told them that his name was Na'pi, Old Man.

As they were standing by the river, the woman said to him, "How is it? Will we always live, will there be no end to it?" He said: "I have never thought of that. We will have to decide it. I will take this buffalo chip and throw it in the river. If it floats, when people die, in four days they will become alive again; they will die for only four days. But if it sinks, there will be an end to them." He threw the chip into the river, and it floated. The woman turned and picked up a stone, and said: "No, I will throw this stone in the river; if it floats we will always live, if it sinks people must die, that they may always be sorry for each other." The woman threw the stone into the water, and it sank. "There," said Old Man, "you have chosen. There will be an end to them."

It was not many nights after that the woman's child died, and she cried a great deal for it. She said to Old Man: "Let us change this. The law that you first made, let that be a law." He said: "Not so. What is made law must be law. We will undo nothing that we have done. The child is dead, but it cannot be changed. People will have to die."

That is how we came to be people. It is he who made us.

The first people were poor and naked, and did not know how to get a living. Old Man showed them the roots and berries, and told them that they could eat them; that in a certain month of the year they could peel the bark off some trees and eat it, that it was good. He told the people that the animals should be their food, and gave them to the people, saying, "These are your herds." He said: "All these little animals that live in the ground—rats, squirrels, skunks, beavers—are good to eat. You need not fear to eat of their flesh." He made all the birds that fly, and told the people that there was no harm in their flesh, that it could be eaten. The first people that he created he used to take about through the timber and swamps and over the prairies, and show them the different plants. Of a certain plant he would say, "The root of this plant, if gathered in a certain month of the year, is good for a certain sickness." So they learned the power of all herbs.

In those days there were buffalo. Now the people had no arms, but those black animals with long beards were armed; and once, as the people were moving about, the buffalo saw them, and ran after them, and hooked them, and killed and ate them. One day, as the Maker of the people was traveling over the country, he saw some of his children, that he had made, lying dead, torn to pieces and partly eaten by the buffalo. When he saw this he was very sad. He said: "This will not do. I will change this. The people shall eat the buffalo."

He went to some of the people who were left, and said to them, "How is it that you people do nothing to these animals that are killing you?" The people said, "What can we do? We have no way to kill these animals, while they are armed and can kill us." Then said the Maker: "That is not hard. I will make you a weapon that will kill these animals." So he went out, and cut some sarvis berry shoots, and brought them in, and peeled the bark off them. He took a larger piece of wood, and flattened it, and tied a string to it, and made a bow. Now, as he was the master of all birds and could do with them as he wished, he went out and caught one, and took feathers from its wing, and split them, and tied them to the shaft of wood. He tied four feathers along the shaft, and tried the arrow at a mark, and found that it did not fly well. He took these feathers off, and put on three; and when he tried it again, he found that it was good. He went out and began to break sharp pieces off the stones. He tried them, and found that the black flint stones made the best arrow joints, and some white flints. Then he taught the people how to use these things.

Then he said: "The next time you go out, take these things with you, and use them as I tell you, and do not run from these animals. When they run at you, as soon as they get pretty close, shoot the arrows at them, as I have taught you; and you will see that they will run from you or will run in a circle around you."

Now, as people became plenty, one day three men went out on to the plain to see the buffalo, but they had no arms. They saw the animals, but when the buffalo saw the men, they ran after them and killed two of them, but one got away. One day after this, the people went on a little hill to look about, and the buffalo saw them, and said, "Saiyah, there is some more of our food," and they rushed on them. This time the people did not run. They began to shoot at the buffalo with the bows and arrows Na'pi had given them, and the buffalo began to fall; but in the fight a person was killed.

At this time these people had flint knives given them, and they cut up the bodies of the dead buffalo. It is not healthful to eat the meat raw, so Old Man gathered soft dry rotten driftwood and made punk of it, and then got a piece of hard wood, and drilled a hole in it with an arrow point, and gave them a pointed piece of hard wood, and taught them how to make a fire with fire sticks, and to cook the flesh of these animals and eat it.

They got a kind of stone that was in the land, and then took another harder stone and worked one upon the other, and hollowed out the softer one, and made a kettle of it. This was the fashion of their dishes.

Also Old Man said to the people: "Now, if you are overcome, you may go and sleep, and get power. Something will come to you in your dream that will help you. Whatever these animals tell you to do, you must obey them, as they appear to you in your sleep. Be guided by them. If anybody wants help, if you are alone and traveling, and cry aloud for help, your prayer will be answered. It may be by the eagles, perhaps by the buffalo, or by the bears. Whatever animal answers your prayer, you must listen to him."

That was how the first people got through the world, by the power of their dreams.

After this, Old Man kept on, traveling north. Many of the animals that he had made followed him as he went. The animals understood him when he spoke to them, and he used them as his servants. When he got to the north point of the Porcupine Mountains, there he made some more mud images of people, and blew breath upon them, and they became people. He made men and women. They asked him, "What are we to eat?" He made many images of clay, in the form of buffalo. Then he blew breath on these, and they stood up; and when he made signs to them, they started to run. Then he said to the people, "Those are your food." They said to him, "Well, now, we have those animals; how are we to kill them?" "I will show you," he said. He took them to the cliff, and made them build rock piles like this, > ; and he made the people hide behind these piles of rock, and said, "When I lead the buffalo this way, as I bring them opposite to you, rise up."

After he had told them how to act, he started on toward a herd of buffalo. He began to call them, and the buffalo started to run toward him, and they followed him until they were inside the lines. Then he dropped back; and as the people rose up, the buffalo ran in a straight line and jumped over the cliff. He told the people to go and take the flesh of those animals. They tried to tear the limbs apart, but they could not. They tried to bite pieces out, and could not. So Old Man went to the edge of the cliff, and broke some pieces of stone with sharp edges, and told them to cut the flesh with these. When they had taken the skins from these animals, they set up some poles and put the hides on them, and so made a shelter to sleep under. There were some of these buffalo that went over the cliff that were not dead. Their legs were broken, but they were still alive. The people cut strips of green hide, and tied stones in the middle, and made large mauls, and broke in the skulls of the buffalo, and killed them.

After he had taught those people these things, he started off again, traveling north, until he came to where Bow and Elbow rivers meet. There he made some more people, and taught them the same things. From here he again went on northward. When he had come nearly to the Red Deer's River, he reached the hill where the Old Man sleeps. There he lay down and rested himself. The form of his body is to be seen there yet.

When he awoke from his sleep, he traveled farther northward and came to a fine high hill. He climbed to the top of it, and there sat down to rest. He looked over the country below him, and it pleased him. Before him the hill was steep, and he said to himself, "Well, this is a fine place for sliding; I will have some fun," and he began to slide down the hill. The marks where he slid down are to be seen yet, and the place is known to all people as the "Old Man's Sliding Ground."

This is as far as the Blackfeet followed Old Man. The Crees know what he did farther north.

In later times once, Na'pi said, "Here I will mark you off a piece of ground," and he did so. Then he said: "There is your land, and it is full of all kinds of animals, and many things grow in this land. Let no other people come into it. This is for you five tribes (Blackfeet, Bloods, Piegans, Gros Ventres, Sarcees). When people come to cross the line, take your bows and arrows, your lances and your battle axes, and give them battle and keep them out. If they gain a footing, trouble will come to you."

Our forefathers gave battle to all people who came to cross these lines, and kept them out. Of late years we have let our friends, the white people, come in, and you know the result. We, his children, have failed to obey his laws.

The Theft from the Sun

Once Old Man was traveling around, when he came to the Sun's lodge, and the Sun asked him to stay a while. Old Man was very glad to do so.

One day the meat was all gone, and the Sun said, "Kyi! Old Man, what say you if we go and kill some deer?"

"You speak well," replied Old Man. "I like deer meat."

The Sun took down a bag and pulled out a beautiful pair of leggings. They were embroidered with porcupine quills and bright feathers. "These," said the Sun, "are my hunting leggings. They are great medicine. All I have to do is to put them on and walk around a patch of brush, when the leggings set it on fire and drive the deer out so that I can shoot them."

"Hai-yah!" exclaimed Old Man. "How wonderful!" He made up his mind he would have those leggings, if he had to steal them.

They went out to hunt, and the first patch of brush they came to, the Sun set on fire with his hunting leggings. A lot of white-tail deer ran out, and they each shot one.

That night, when they went to bed, the Sun pulled off his leggings and placed them to one side. Old Man saw where he put them, and in the middle of the night, when everyone was asleep, he stole them and went off. He traveled a long time, until he had gone far and was very tired, and then, making a pillow of the leggings, lay down and slept. In the morning, he heard someone talking. The Sun was saying, "Old Man, why are my leggings under your head?" He looked around, and saw he was in the Sun's lodge, and thought he must have wandered around and got lost, and returned there. Again the Sun spoke and said, "What are you doing with my leggings?" "Oh," replied Old Man, "I couldn't find anything for a pillow, so I just put these under my head."

Night came again, and again Old Man stole the leggings and ran off. This time he did not walk at all; he just kept running until pretty near morning, and then lay down and slept. You see what a fool he was. He did not know that the whole world is the Sun's lodge. He did not know that, no matter how far he ran, he could not get out of the Sun's sight. When morning came, he found himself still in the Sun's lodge. But this time the Sun said: "Old Man, since you like my leggings so much, I will give them to you. Keep them." Then Old Man was very glad and went away.

One day his food was all gone, so he put on the medicine leggings and set fire to a piece of brush. He was just going to kill some deer that were running out, when he saw that the fire was getting close to him. He ran away as fast as he could, but the fire gained on him and began to burn his legs. His leggings were all on fire. He came to a river and jumped in, and pulled off the leggings as soon as he could. They were burned to pieces.

Perhaps the Sun did this to him because he tried to steal the leggings.

Scarface

Origin of the Medicine Lodge

I

In the earliest times there was no war. All the tribes were at peace. In those days there was a man who had a daughter, a very beautiful girl. Many young men wanted to marry her, but every time she was asked, she only shook her head and said she did not want a husband.

"How is this?" asked her father. "Some of these young men are rich, handsome, and brave."

"Why should I marry?" replied the girl. "I have a rich father and mother. Our lodge is good. The parfleches are never empty. There are plenty of tanned robes and soft furs for winter. Why worry me, then?"

The Raven Bearers held a dance; they all dressed carefully and wore their ornaments, and each one tried to dance the best. Afterward some of them asked for this girl, but still she said no. Then the Bulls, the Kit-foxes, and others of the I-kun-uh'-kah-tsi held their dances, and all those who were rich, many great warriors, asked this man for his daughter, but to every one of them she said no. Then her father was angry, and said: "Why, now, this way? All the best men have asked for you, and still you say no. I believe you have a secret lover."

"Ah!" said her mother. "What shame for us should a child be born and our daughter still unmarried!" "Father! Mother!" replied the girl, "pity me. I have no secret lover, but now hear the truth. That Above Person, the Sun, told me, 'Do not marry any of those men, for you are mine; thus you shall be happy, and live to great age'; and again he said, 'Take heed. You must not marry. You are mine.' "

"Ah!" replied her father. "It must always be as he says." And they talked no more about it.

There was a poor young man, very poor. His father, mother, all his relations, had gone to the Sand Hills. He had no lodge, no wife to tan his robes or sew his moccasins. He stopped in one lodge today, and tomorrow he ate and slept in another; thus he lived. He was a good-looking young man, except that on his cheek he had a scar, and his clothes were always old and poor.

After those dances some of the young men met this poor Scarface, and they laughed at him, and said: "Why don't you ask that girl to marry you? You are so rich and handsome!" Scarface did not laugh; he replied: "Ah! I will do as you say. I will go and ask her." All the young men thought this was funny. They laughed a great deal. But Scarface went down by the river. He waited by the river, where the women came to get water, and by and by the girl came along. "Girl," he said, "wait. I want to speak with you. Not as a designing person do I ask you, but openly where the Sun looks down, and all may see."

"Speak then," said the girl.

"I have seen the days," continued the young man. "You have refused those who are young, and rich, and brave. Now, today, they laughed and said to me, 'Why do you not ask her?' I am poor, very poor. I have no lodge, no food, no clothes, no robes and warm furs. I have no relations; all have gone to the Sand Hills; yet, now, today, I ask you, take pity, be my wife."

The girl hid her face in her robe and brushed the ground with the point of her moccasin, back and forth, back and forth; for she was thinking. After a time she said, "True. I have refused all those rich young men, yet now the poor one asks me, and I am glad. I will be your wife, and my people will be happy. You are poor, but it does not matter. My father will give you dogs. My mother will make us a lodge. My people will give us robes and furs. You will be poor no longer."

Then the young man was happy, and he started to kiss her, but she held him back, and said: "Wait! The Sun has spoken to me. He says I may not marry; that I belong to him. He says if I listen to him, I shall live to great age. But now I say: Go to the Sun. Tell him, 'She whom you spoke with heeds your words. She has never done wrong, but now she wants to marry. I want her for my wife.' Ask him to take that scar from your face. That will be his sign. I will know he is pleased. But if he refuses, or if you fail to find his lodge, then do not return to me."

"Oh!" cried the young man, "at first your words were good. I was glad. But now it is dark. My heart is dead. Where is that far-off lodge? where the trail, which no one yet has traveled?"

"Take courage, take courage!" said the girl; and she went to her lodge.

2

Scarface was very sad. He sat down and covered his head with his robe and tried to think what to do. After a while he got up, and went to an old woman who had been kind to him. "Pity me," he said. "I am very poor. I am going away now on a long journey. Make me some moccasins."

"Where are you going?" asked the old woman. "There is no war; we are very peaceful here."

"I do not know where I shall go," replied Scarface. "I am in trouble, but I cannot tell you now what it is."

So the old woman made him some moccasins, seven pairs, with parfleche soles, and also she gave him a sack of food— pemmican of berries, pounded meat, and dried back fat; for this old woman had a good heart. She liked the young man.

All alone, and with a sad heart, he climbed the bluffs and stopped to take a last look at the camp. He wondered if he would ever see his sweetheart and the people again. "Hai′-yu! Pity me, O Sun," he prayed, and turning, he started to find the trail.

For many days he traveled on, over great prairies, along timbered rivers and among the mountains, and every day his sack of food grew lighter; but he saved it as much as he could, and ate berries, and roots, and sometimes he killed an animal of some kind. One night he stopped by the home of a wolf. "Hai-yah" said that one; "what is my brother doing so far from home?"

"Ah!" replied Scarface, "I seek the place where the Sun lives; I am sent to speak with him."

"I have traveled far," said the wolf. "I know all the prairies, the valleys, and the mountains, but I have never seen the Sun's home. Wait; I know one who is very wise. Ask the bear. He may tell you."

The next day the man traveled on again, stopping now and then to pick a few berries, and when night came he arrived at the bear's lodge.

"Where is your home?" asked the bear. "Why are you traveling alone, my brother?"

"Help me! Pity me!" replied the young man; "because of her words I seek the Sun. I go to ask him for her."

"I know not where he stops," replied the bear. "I have traveled by many rivers, and I know the mountains, yet I have never seen his lodge. There is some one beyond, that striped-face, who is very smart. Go and ask him."

The badger was in his hole. Stooping over, the young man shouted: "Oh, cunning striped-face! Oh, generous animal! I wish to speak with you."

"What do you want?" said the badger, poking his head out of the hole.

"I want to find the Sun's home," replied Scarface. "I want to speak with him."

"I do not know where he lives," replied the badger. "I never travel very far. Over there in the timber is a wolverine. He is always traveling around, and is of much knowledge. Maybe he can tell you."

Then Scarface went to the woods and looked all around for the wolverine, but could not find him. So he sat down to rest. "Haí'-yu! Haí'-yu!" he cried. "Wolverine, take pity on me. My food is gone, my moccasins worn out. Now I must die."

"What is it, my brother?" he heard, and looking around, he saw the animal sitting near.

"She whom I would marry," said Scarface, "belongs to the Sun; I am trying to find where he lives, to ask him for her."

"Ah!" said the wolverine. "I know where he lives. Wait; it is nearly night. Tomorrow I will show you the trail to the big water. He lives on the other side of it."

Early in the morning, the wolverine showed him the trail, and Scarface followed it until he came to the water's edge. He looked out over it, and his heart almost stopped. Never before had any one seen such a big water. The other side could not be seen, and there was no end to it. Scarface sat down on the shore. His food was all gone, his moccasins worn out. His heart was sick. "I cannot cross this big water," he said. "I cannot return to the people. Here, by this water, I shall die."

Not so. His Helpers were there. Two swans came swimming up to the shore. "Why have you come here?" they asked him. "What are you doing? It is very far to the place where your people live."

"I am here," replied Scarface, "to die. Far away, in my country, is a beautiful girl. I want to marry her, but she belongs to the Sun. So I started to find him and ask for her. I have traveled

many days. My food is gone. I cannot go back. I cannot cross
this big water, so I am going to die."

"No," said the swans; "it shall not be so. Across this water
is the home of that Above Person. Get on our backs, and we
will take you there."

Scarface quickly arose. He felt strong again. He waded out
into the water and lay down on the swans' backs, and they
started off. Very deep and black is that fearful water. Strange
people live there, mighty animals which often seize and drown
a person. The swans carried him safely, and took him to the
other side. Here was a broad hard trail leading back from the
water's edge.

"Kyi," said the swans. "You are now close to the Sun's lodge.
Follow that trail, and you will soon see it."

3

Scarface started up the trail, and pretty soon he came to
some beautiful things, lying in it. There was a war shirt, a
shield, and a bow and arrows. He had never seen such pretty
weapons; but he did not touch them. He walked carefully
around them, and traveled on. A little way farther on, he met
a young man, the handsomest person he had ever seen. His
hair was very long, and he wore clothing made of strange
skins. His moccasins were sewn with bright-colored feathers.
The young man said to him, "Did you see some weapons lying
on the trail?"

"Yes," replied Scarface; "I saw them."

"But did you not touch them?" asked the young man.

"No; I thought someone had left them there, so I did not
take them."

"You are not a thief," said the young man. "What is your
name?"

"Scarface."

"Where are you going?"

"To the Sun."

"My name," said the young man, "is A-pi-su'-ahts (Morning
Star). The Sun is my father; come, I will take you to our lodge.
My father is not now at home, but he will come in at night."

Soon they came to the lodge. It was very large and handsome; strange medicine animals were painted on it. Behind, on a tripod, were strange weapons and beautiful clothes—the Sun's. Scarface was ashamed to go in, but Morning Star said, "Do not be afraid, my friend; we are glad you have come."

They entered. One person was sitting there, Ko-ko-mik'-e-is (the Moon), the Sun's wife, Morning Star's mother. She spoke to Scarface kindly, and gave him something to eat. "Why have you come so far from your people?" she asked.

Then Scarface told her about the beautiful girl he wanted to marry. "She belongs to the Sun," he said. "I have come to ask him for her."

When it was time for the Sun to come home, the Moon hid Scarface under a pile of robes. As soon as the Sun got to the doorway, he stopped, and said, "I smell a person."

"Yes, Father," said Morning Star; "a good young man has come to see you. I know he is good for he found some of my things on the trail and did not touch them."

Then Scarface came out from under the robes, and the Sun entered and sat down. "I am glad you have come to our lodge," he said. "Stay with us as long as you think best. My son is lonesome sometimes; be his friend."

The next day the Moon called Scarface out of the lodge, and said to him: "Go with Morning Star where you please, but never hunt near that big water; do not let him go there. It is the home of great birds which have long sharp bills; they kill people. I have had many sons, but these birds have killed them all. Morning Star is the only one left."

So Scarface stayed there a long time and hunted with Morning Star. One day they came near the water, and saw the big birds.

"Come," said Morning Star; "let us go and kill those birds."

"No, no!" replied Scarface; "we must not go there. Those are very terrible birds; they will kill us."

Morning Star would not listen. He ran toward the water, and Scarface followed. He knew that he must kill the birds and save the boy. If not, the Sun would be angry and might kill him. He ran ahead and met the birds, which were coming toward him to fight, and killed every one of them with his spear: not one was left. Then the young men cut off their heads, and carried them home. Morning Star's mother was glad when they told her what they had done, and showed her the birds' heads. She cried, and called Scarface "my son." When the Sun came home at night, she told him about it, and he too was glad. "My son," he said to Scarface, "I will not forget what you have this day done for me. Tell me now, what can I do for you?"

"Hai'-yu," replied Scarface. "Hai'-yu, pity me. I am here to ask you for that girl. I want to marry her. I asked her, and she was glad; but she says you own her, that you told her not to marry."

"What you say is true," said the Sun. "I have watched the days, so I know it. Now, then, I give her to you; she is yours. I am glad she has been wise. I know she has never done wrong. The Sun pities good women. They shall live a long time. So shall their husbands and children. Now you will soon go home. Let me tell you something. Be wise and listen: I am the only chief. Everything is mine. I made the earth, the mountains, prairies, rivers, and forests. I made the people and all the animals. This is why I say I alone am the chief. I can never die. True, the winter makes me old and weak, but every summer I grow young again."

Then said the Sun: "What one of all animals is smartest? The raven is, for he always finds food. He is never hungry. Which one of all the animals is most Nat-o'-ye (having sun power, sacred)? The buffalo is. Of all animals, I like him best. He is for the people. He is your food and your shelter. What part of his body is sacred? The tongue is. That is mine. What else is sacred? Berries are. They are mine too. Come with me and see the world." He took Scarface to the edge of the sky, and they looked down and saw it. It is round and flat, and all around the edge is the jumping-off place (or walls straight down). Then said the Sun: "When any man is sick or in danger, his wife may promise to build me a lodge, if he recovers. If the woman is pure and true, then I will be pleased and help the man. But if she is bad, if she lies, then I will be angry. You shall build the lodge like the world, round, with walls, but first you must build a sweat house of a hundred sticks. It shall be like the sky (a hemisphere), and half of it shall be painted red. That is me. The other half you will paint black. That is the night."

Further said the Sun: "Which is the best, the heart or the brain? The brain is. The heart often lies, the brain never." Then he told Scarface everything about making the Medicine Lodge, and when he had finished, he rubbed a powerful medicine on his face, and the scar disappeared. Then he gave him two raven feathers, saying: "These are the sign for the girl, that I give her to you. They must always be worn by the husband of the woman who builds a Medicine Lodge."

The young man was now ready to return home. Morning Star and the Sun gave him many beautiful presents. The Moon cried and kissed him, and called him "my son." Then the Sun showed him the short trail. It was the Wolf Road (Milky Way). He followed it, and soon reached the ground.

4

It was a very hot day. All the lodge skins were raised, and the people sat in the shade. There was a chief, a very generous man, and all day long people kept coming to his lodge to feast and smoke with him. Early in the morning the chief saw a person sitting out on a butte near by, close wrapped in his robe. The chief's friends came and went, the sun reached the middle, and passed on, down toward the mountains. Still this person did not move. When it was almost night, the chief said: "Why does that person sit there so long? The heat has been strong, but he has never eaten nor drunk. He may be a stranger; go and ask him in."

So some young men went up to him, and said: "Why do you sit here in the great heat all day? Come to the shade of the lodges. The chief asks you to feast with him."

Then the person arose and threw off his robe, and they were surprised. He wore beautiful clothes. His bow, shield, and other weapons were of strange make. But they knew his face, although the scar was gone, and they ran ahead, shouting, "The scarface poor young man has come. He is poor no longer. The scar on his face is gone."

All the people rushed out to see him. "Where have you been?" they asked. "Where did you get all these pretty things?"

He did not answer. There in the crowd stood that young woman; and taking the two raven feathers from his head, he gave them to her, and said: "The trail was very long, and I nearly died, but by those Helpers, I found his lodge. He is glad. He sends these feathers to you. They are the sign."

Great was her gladness then. They were married, and made the first Medicine Lodge, as the Sun had said. The Sun was glad. He gave them great age. They were never sick. When they were very old, one morning, their children said: "Awake! Rise and eat." They did not move. In the night, in sleep, without pain, their shadows had departed for the Sand Hills.

Navaho

The version of the Navaho creation myth reprinted below was told to Aileen O'Bryan in late November 1928 by Sandoval, Hastin Tlo'tsi hee (Old Man Buffalo Grass), a principal Navaho chief. "You look at me," he said to the editor, "and you see only an ugly old man, but within I am filled with great beauty. I sit as on a mountaintop and I look into the future. I see my people and your people living together. In time to come my people will have forgotten their early way of life unless they learn it from white men's books. So you must write down what I tell you; and you must have it made into a book that coming generations may know this truth." I have retained the notes to this myth because of the unusually complicated cosmogony.

The Creation or Age of Beginning

The First World

These stories were told to Sandoval, Hastin Tlo'tsi hee, by his grandmother, Esdzan Hosh kige. Her ancestor was Esdzan at a', the medicine woman who had the Calendar Stone in her keeping. Here are the stories of the Four Worlds that had no sun, and of the Fifth, the world we live in, which some call the Changeable World.

The First World, Ni'hodilqil,[1] was black as black wool. It

From Aileen O'Bryan, "The Díné: Origin Myths of the Navaho Indians," *Bureau of American Ethnology*, Bulletin 163 (Washington, 1956).

[1] Informant's note : Five names were given to this First World in its relation to First Man. It was called Dark Earth, Ni'hodilqil; Red Earth, Ni'halchi; One Speech, Sada hat lai; Floating Land, Ni'ta na elth; and One Tree, De east'da eith. Washington Matthews, *Navaho Legends*. Collected and translated (New York and Boston, 1897), p. 65: The First World was red. Franciscan Fathers, *A Vocabulary of the Navaho Language*, 2 vols. (Saint Michaels, Arizona, 1912), p. 140: ni, the world or earth; ni'halchil; ni'hodilqil, the dark or lowest of the underworlds; (p. 111) lai, one or first. Franciscan Fathers, *An Ethnologic Dictionary of the Navaho Language* (Saint Michaels, Arizona, 1910), p. 81: said, a word, a language; Sad lai, First Speech.

had four corners, and over these appeared four clouds. These four clouds contained within themselves the elements of the First World. They were in color, black, white, blue, and yellow.

The Black Cloud represented the Female Being or Substance. For as a child sleeps when being nursed, so life slept in the darkness of the Female Being. The White Cloud represented the Male Being or Substance. He was the Dawn, the Light-Which-Awakens, of the First World.

In the East, at the place where the Black Cloud and the White Cloud met, First Man, Atse'hastqin[2] was formed; and with him was formed the white corn, perfect in shape, with kernels covering the whole ear. Dohonot i'ni is the name of this first seed corn,[3] and it is also the name of the place where the Black Cloud and the White Cloud met.

The First World was small in size, a floating island in mist or water. On it there grew one tree, a pine tree, which was later brought to the present world for firewood.

Man was not, however, in his present form. The conception was of a male and a female being who were to become man and woman. The creatures of the First World are thought of as the Mist People; they had no definite form, but were to change to men, beasts, birds, and reptiles of this world.[4]

Now on the western side of the First World, in a place that later was to become the Land of Sunset, there appeared the Blue Cloud, and opposite it there appeared the Yellow Cloud. Where they came together First Woman was formed, and with her the yellow corn. This ear of corn was also perfect. With First Woman there came the white shell and the turquoise and the yucca.[5]

First Man stood on the eastern side of the First World. He represented the Dawn and was the Life Giver. First Woman

[2] Franciscan Fathers (1912, p. 93): Aste'hastqin, First Man.

[3] Informant's note: Where much corn is raised one or two ears are found perfect. These are always kept for seed corn.

[4] Informant's note: The Navaho people have always believed in evolution.

[5] Informant's note: Five names were given also to the First World in its relation to First Woman: White Bead Standing, Yolgai'naziha; Turquoise Standing, Dolt i'zhi na ziha; White Bead Floating Place, Yolgai'dana elth gai; Turquoise Floating Place, Dolt i'zhi na elth gai; and Yucca Standing, Tasas y ah gai. Yucca represents cleanliness and things ceremonial.

stood opposite in the West. She represented Darkness and Death.

First Man burned a crystal for a fire. The crystal belonged to the male and was the symbol of the mind and of clear seeing. When First Man burned it, it was the mind's awakening. First Woman burned her turquoise for a fire. They saw each other's lights in the distance. When the Black Cloud and the White Cloud rose higher in the sky First Man set out to find the turquoise light. He went twice without success, and again a third time; then he broke a forked branch from his tree, and, looking through the fork, he marked the place where the light burned. And the fourth time he walked to it and found smoke coming from a home.

"Here is the home I could not find," First Man said.

First Woman answered: "Oh, it is you. I saw you walking around and I wondered why you did not come."

Again the same thing happened when the Blue Cloud and the Yellow Cloud rose higher in the sky. First Woman saw a light and she went out to find it. Three times she was unsuccessful, but the fourth time she saw the smoke and she found the home of First Man.

"I wondered what this thing could be," she said.

"I saw you walking and I wondered why you did not come to me," First Man answered.

First Woman saw that First Man had a crystal for a fire, and she saw that it was stronger than her turquoise fire. And as she was thinking, First Man spoke to her. "Why do you not come with your fire and we will live together." The woman agreed to this. So instead of the man going to the woman, as is the custom now, the woman went to the man.

About this time there came another person, The-Great-Coyote-Who-Was-Formed-in-the-Water,[6] and he was in the form of a male being. He told the two that he had been hatched from an egg. He knew all that was under the water and all that was in the skies. First Man placed this person ahead of himself in all things. The three began to plan what was to come

---

[6] Informant's note: The-Great-Coyote-Who-Was-Formed-in-the-Water, Mai tqo y elth chili. Franciscan Fathers (1912, p. 117): ma'itso, wolf (big roamer); and ma'ists o'si, coyote (slender roamer).

to pass; and while they were thus occupied another being came
to them. He also had the form of a man, but he wore a hairy
coat, lined with white fur, that fell to his knees and was belted
in at the waist. His name was Atse'hashke', First Angry or
Coyote.[7] He said to the three: "You believe that you were
the first persons. You are mistaken. I was living when you
were formed."

Then four beings came together. They were yellow in color
and were called the *tsts' na* or wasp people. They knew the
secret of shooting evil and could harm others. They were very
powerful.

This made eight people.

Four more beings came. They were small in size and wore
red shirts and had little black eyes. They were the *naazó zi* or
spider ants. They knew how to sting, and were a great people.

After these came a whole crowd of beings. Dark colored
they were, with thick lips and dark, protruding eyes. They were
the wolazhi'ni, the black ants. They also knew the secret of
shooting evil and were powerful; but they killed each other
steadily.

By this time there were many people. Then came a multitude
of little creatures. They were peaceful and harmless, but the
odor from them was unpleasant. They were called the wolazhi'ni nlchu nigi, meaning that which emits an odor.[8]

And after the wasps and the different ant people there came
the beetles, dragonflies, bat people, the Spider Man and Woman, and the Salt Man and Woman,[9] and others that rightfully
had no definite form but were among those people who peopled

---

[7] Informant's note: Some medicine men claim that witchcraft came with
First Man and First Woman, others insist that devil conception or witchcraft originated with the Coyote called First Angry.

[8] Informant's note: No English name given this insect. Ants cause
trouble, as also do wasps and other insects, if their homes are harmed.

Franciscan Fathers (1910, p. 346): Much evil, disease and bodily injury is
due also to secret agents of evil, in consequence of which the belief...
shooting of evil (sting) is widely spread.

[9] Informant's note: Beetle, ntlsa'go; Dragonfly, tqanil ai'; Bat people, ja
aba'ni; Spider Man, nashjei hastqin; Spider Woman, nashjei esdza; Salt
Man, ashi hastqin; Salt Woman; ashi esdza.

the First World. And this world, being small in size, became crowded, and the people quarreled and fought among themselves, and in all ways made living very unhappy.

The Second World

Because of the strife in the First World, First Man, First Woman, The-Great-Coyote-Who-Was-Formed-in-the-Water, and the Coyote called First Angry, followed by all the others, climbed up from the World of Darkness and Dampness to the Second or Blue World.[10]

They found a number of people already living there: bluebirds, blue hawks, bluejays, blue herons, and all the blue-feathered beings.[11] The powerful swallow people[12] lived there also, and these people made the Second World unpleasant for those who had come from the First World. There was fighting and Killing.

The First Four found an opening in the World of Blue Haze; and they climbed through this and led the people up into the Third or Yellow world.

The Third World

The bluebird was the first to reach the Third or Yellow World. After him came the First Four and all the others.

A great river crossed this land from north to south. It was the Female River. There was another river crossing it from east to west, it was the Male River. This Male River flowed through the Female River and on;[13] and the name of this place is tqo alna'osdli, the Crossing of the Waters.[14]

[10] Informant's note: The Second World was the Blue World, Ni'hodotl'ish.

[11] Informant's note: The names of the blue birds are: bluebird, do'le; blue hawk, gi'ni tso dolt ish; blue jay, jozh ghae' gi; and blue heron tqualtl a'gaale.

[12] Informant's note: The swallow is called tqash ji'zhi.

Matthews (1897, pp. 65-66): the swallow people, hast sosidine. Franciscan Fathers (1910, p. 349): The Blue World.

[13] Informant's note: The introduction of generation.

[14] Matthews (1897, p. 63): To'bil haski'di, Place Where the Waters Crossed.

There were six mountains in the Third World.[15] In the East was Sis ná jin, the Standing Black Sash. Its ceremonial name is Yol gai'dzil, the Dawn or White Shell Mountain. In the South stood Tso'dzil, the Great Mountain, also called Mountain Tongue. Its ceremonial name is Yodolt i'zhi dzil, the Blue Bead or Turquoise Mountain. In the West stood Dook'oslid, and the meaning of this name is forgotten. Its ceremonial name is Dichi'li dzil, the Abalone Shell Mountain. In the North stood Debe'ntsa, Many Sheep Mountain. Its ceremonial name is Bash'zhini dzil, Obsidian Mountain. Then there was Dzil na'odili, the Upper Mountain. It was very sacred; and its name means also the Center Place, and the people moved around it. Its ceremonial name is Ntl'is dzil, Precious Stone or Banded Rock Mountain. There was still another mountain called Chol'i'i or Dzil na'odili choli, and it was also a sacred mountain.

There was no sun in this land, only the two rivers and the six mountains. And these rivers and mountains were not in their present form, but rather the substance of mountains and rivers as were First Man, First Woman, and the others.

Now beyond Sis na' jin, in the east, there lived the Turquoise Hermaphrodite, Ashon nutli'.[16] He was also known as the Turquoise Boy. And near this person grew the male reed. Beyond, still farther in the east, there lived a people called the Hadahuneya'nigi,[17] the Mirage or Agate People. Still farther in the east there lived twelve beings called the Naaskiddi.[18]

[15] Informant's note: Sis na'jin, Mount Baldy near Alamos, Colorado; Tso' dzil, Mount Taylor, New Mexico; Dook'oslid, San Francisco Mountain, Arizona; Debe'ntsa, San Juan Mountains, Colorado; Dzil na'odili, El Huerfano Peak, New Mexico; and Choli, also given as El Huerfano or El Huerfanito Peak, New Mexico. These mountains of the Third World were not in their true form, but rather the substance of the mountains.

Matthews (1897, p. 71): The Third World, the mountains. The four mountains named by the First Man: Tsisnadzi'ne, East; Tso'tsil, South; Do koslid, West; Debe'ntsa, North.

[16] Informant's note: Ashon nutli', the Turquoise Hermaphrodite, later became masculine and was known as the Sun Bearer, Jo hona'ai.

[17] Informant's note: The Hadahuneya' nigi are the Stone People who live where there is a mirage on the desert.

[18] Informant's note: The Naaskiddi or Gha'askidi are the hunchback figures connected with seeds, fertility, and phallus worship. They are said to have come from the mountain called Chol'i'i.

And beyond the home of these beings there lived four others —the Holy Man, the Holy Woman, the Holy Boy, and the Holy Girl.

In the West there lived the White Shell Hermaphrodite[19] or Girl, and with her was the big female reed which grew at the water's edge. It had no tassel. Beyond her in the West there lived another stone people called the Hadahunes'tqin, the Ground Heat People. Still farther on there lived another twelve beings, but these were all females.[20] And again, in the Far West, there lived four Holy Ones.

Within this land there lived the Kisa'ni, the ancients of the Pueblo People. On the six mountains there lived the Cave Dwellers or Great Swallow People.[21] On the mountains lived also the light and dark squirrels, chipmunks, mice, rats, the turkey people, the deer and cat people, the spider people, and the lizards and snakes. The beaver people lived along the rivers, and the frogs and the turtles and all the underwater people in the water. So far all the people were similar. They had no definite form, but they had been given different names because of different characteristics.

Now the plan was to plant.

First Man called the people together. He brought forth the white corn which had been formed with him. First Woman brought the yellow corn. They laid the perfect ears side by side; then they asked one person from among the many to come and help them. The Turkey stepped forward. They asked him where he had come from, and he said that he had come from the Grey Mountain.[22] He danced back and forth four

---

[19] Informant's note: The White Shell Hermaphrodite or Girl later entered the Moon and became the Moon Bearer. She is connected with Esdzanadle, the Woman Who Changes, or Yolgai esdzan the White Shell Woman.

[20] Informant's note: The Corn Maidens are deities of fertility.

[21] Informant's note: The Great Swallow People, Tqashji'zhi ndilk'si, lived in rough houses of mud and sticks. They entered them from holes in the roof.

[22] Informant's note: The Gray Mountain is the home of the Gray Yei, Hasch el'ba'i, whose other name is Water Sprinkler. The turkey is connected with water and rain. Interpreter's note: Gray Mountain is San Francisco Mountain, Arizona. Tqo neinili, the Water Sprinkler, whose color is gray, lives there. He is also called the Gray God, Hasch e'lbai, and the Clown whose call is "do do," and whose name is Hasch e'dodi.

times, then he shook his feather coat and there dropped from his clothing four kernels of corn, one gray, one blue, one black, and one red. Another person was asked to help in the plan of the planting. The Big Snake came forward. He likewise brought forth four seeds, the pumpkin, the watermelon, the cantaloupe, and the muskmelon. His plants all crawl on the ground.

They planted the seeds, and their harvest was great.

After the harvest the Turquoise Boy from the East came and visited First Woman. When First Man returned to his home he found his wife with this boy. First Woman told her husband that Ashon nutli' was of her flesh and not of his flesh.[23] She said that she had used her own fire, the turquoise, and had ground her own yellow corn into meal. This corn she had planted and cared for herself.

Now at that time there were four chiefs: Big Snake, Mountain Lion, Otter, and Bear.[24] And it was the custom when the Black Cloud rose in the morning[25] for First Man to come out of his dwelling and speak to the people. After First Man had spoken the four chiefs told them what they should do that day. They also spoke of the past and of the future. But after First Man found his wife with another he would not come out to speak to the people. The Black Cloud rose higher, but First Man would not leave his dwelling; neither would he eat or drink. No one spoke to the people for four days. All during this time First Man remained silent, and would not touch food or water. Four times the White Cloud rose. Then the four chiefs went to First Man and demanded to know why he would not speak to the people. The chiefs asked this question three times, and a fourth, before First Man would answer them.

[23] Informant's note: First Woman and the Turquoise Hermaphrodite represented the female principle. Later he said: There is confusion among medicine men regarding this. Some say that the Turquoise Boy was Ashon nutli'; some say the Mirage Man, some contend that "it" was another "Turquoise Boy."

[24] Informant's note: Some medicine men call them the chiefs of the Four Directions.

[25] Informant's note: These are not the Black and White Clouds of the First World. As there was no sun, and no true division of night and day, time was counted by the black cloud rising and the white cloud rising.

He told them to bring him an emetic.[26] This he took and purified himself. First Man then asked them to send the hermaphrodite to him. When he came First Man asked him if the metate and brush[27] were his. He said that they were. First Man asked him if he could cook and prepare food like a woman, if he could weave, and brush the hair. And when he had assured First Man that he could do all manner of woman's work, First Man said: "Go and prepare food and bring it to me." After he had eaten, First Man told the four chiefs what he had seen, and what his wife had said.

At this time The-Great-Coyote-Who-Was-Formed-in-the-Water came to First Man and told him to cross the river. They made a big raft and crossed at the place where the Male River followed through the Female River. And all the male beings left the female beings on the river bank; and as they rowed across the river they looked back and saw that First Woman and the female beings were laughing. They were also behaving very wickedly.

In the beginning the women did not mind being alone. They cleared and planted a small field. On the other side of the river First Man and the chiefs hunted and planted their seeds. They had a good harvest. Nadle[28] ground the corn and cooked the food. Four seasons passed. The men continued to have plenty and were happy; but the women became lazy, and only weeds grew on their land. The women wanted fresh meat. Some of them tried to join the men and were drowned in the river.

First Woman made a plan. As the women had no way to satisfy their passions, some fashioned long narrow rocks, some used the feathers of the turkey, and some used strange plants (cactus). First Woman told them to use these things. One woman brought forth a big stone. This stone-child was later the

[26] Informant's note (with recorder's): The emetic was believed to be either *Babia woodhousei* Gray, of the thistle family, or the root of the wild cherry. In either case, after a hot brew is drunk, copious vomiting ensues.

[27] Informant's note: The metate and brush are symbolic of woman's implements.

[28] Informant's note: Nadle means that which changes. Ashon nutli', or nadle, the Turquoise Hermaphrodite, was the first man to change, or become, as a woman.

Great Stone that rolled over the earth killing men. Another woman brought forth the Big Birds of Tsa bida'hi; and others gave birth to the giants and monsters who later destroyed many people.

On the opposite side of the river the same condition existed. The men, wishing to satisfy their passions, killed the females of mountain sheep, lion, and antelope. Lightning struck these men. When First Man learned of this he warned his men that they would all be killed. He told them that they were indulging in a dangerous practice. Then the second chief spoke: he said that life was hard and that it was a pity to see women drowned. He asked why they should not bring the women across the river and all live together again.

"Now we can see for ourselves what comes from our wrong doing," he said. "We will know how to act in the future." The three other chiefs of the animals agreed with him, so First Man told them to go and bring the women.

After the women had been brought over the river First Man spoke: "We must be purified," he said. "Everyone must bathe. The men must dry themselves with white corn meal, and the women, with yellow."

This they did, living apart for four days. After the fourth day First Woman came and threw her right arm around her husband. She spoke to the others and said that she could see her mistakes, but with her husband's help she would henceforth lead a good life. Then all the male and female beings came and lived with each other again.

The people moved to different parts of the land. Some time passed; then First Woman became troubled by the monotony of life. She made a plan. She went to Atse'hashke', the Coyote called First Angry, and giving him the rainbow she said: "I have suffered greatly in the past. I have suffered from want of meat and corn and clothing. Many of my maidens have died. I have suffered many things. Take the rainbow and go to the place where the rivers cross. Bring me the two pretty children of Tqo holt sodi, the Water Buffalo,[29] a boy and a girl."

The Coyote agreed to do this. He walked over the rainbow.

---

[29] Franciscan Fathers (1910, p. 157): Tqo holt sodi, water buffalo, water ox, or water monster.

He entered the home of the Water Buffalo and stole the two children; and these he hid in his big skin coat with the white fur lining. And when he returned he refused to take off his coat, but pulled it around himself and looked very wise.

After this happened the people saw white light in the East and in the South and West and North. One of the deer people ran to the East, and returning, said that the white light was a great sheet of water. The sparrow hawk flew to the South, the great hawk to the West, and the kingfisher to the North. They returned and said that a flood was coming. The kingfisher said that the water was greater in the North, and that it was near.

The flood was coming and the Earth was sinking. And all this happened because the Coyote had stolen the two children of the Water Buffalo, and only First Woman and the Coyote knew the truth.

When First Man learned of the coming of the water he sent word to all the people, and he told them to come to the mountain called Sis na'jin. He told them to bring with them all of the seeds of the plants used for food. All living beings were to gather on the top of Sis na'jin. First Man traveled to the six sacred mountains, and, gathering earth from them, he put it in his medicine bag.[30]

The water rose steadily.

When all the people were halfway up Sis na'jin, First Man discovered that he had forgotten his medicine bag. Now this bag contained not only the earth from the six sacred mountains, but his magic, the medicine he used to call the rain down upon the earth and to make things grow. He could not live without his medicine bag, and he wished to jump into the rising water; but the others begged him not to do this. They went to the kingfisher and asked him to dive into the water and recover the bag. This the bird did. When First Man had his medicine bag again in his possession he breathed on it four times and thanked his people.

When they had all arrived it was found that the Turquoise

[30] Informant's note: Here, and following, magic is associated with First Man.

Recorder's note: The magic of First Man was considered white magic, reason, logos.

Boy had brought with him the big Male Reed;[31] and the White Shell Girl had brought with her the big Female Reed.[32] Another person brought poison ivy; and another, cotton, which was later used for cloth. This person was the spider. First Man had with him his spruce tree[33] which he planted on the top of Sis na'jin. He used his fox medicine[34] to make it grow; but the spruce tree began to send out branches and to taper at the top, so First Man planted the big Male Reed. All the people blew on it, and it grew and grew until it reached the canopy of the sky. They tried to blow inside the reed, but it was solid. They asked the woodpecker to drill out the hard heart. Soon they were able to peek through the opening, but they had to blow and blow before it was large enough to climb through. They climbed up inside the big male reed, and after them the water continued to rise.[35]

The Fourth World

When the people reached the Fourth World they saw that it was not a very large place. Some say that it was called the White World; but not all medicine men agree that this is so.

The last person to crawl through the reed was the Turkey from Gray Mountain. His feather coat was flecked with foam, for after him came the water. And with the water came the female Water Buffalo who pushed her head through the opening in the reed. She had a great quantity of curly hair which floated on the water, and she had two horns, half black and half yellow. From the tips of the horns the lightning flashed.

First Man asked the Water Buffalo why she had come and why she had sent the flood. She said nothing. Then the Coyote

[31] Informant's note: The big male reed is called luka'tso. It grows near Santo Domingo Pueblo, not far from the home of the Turquoise Boy, the little turquoise mountain south of Santa Fe, New Mexico.

[32] Informant's note: The big female reed is thought to be the joint cane which grows along the Colorado River. This was near the home of the White Shell Girl.

[33] Recorder's note: That the tree is here called a spruce and previously a pine is not explained.

[34] First Man's name, Aste'hastqin, corresponds to the sacred name of the kit fox.

[35] The Third or Yellow World: Matthews (1897, p. 66).

drew the two babies from his coat and said that it was, perhaps, because of them.

The Turquoise Boy took a basket and filled it with turquoise. On top of the turquoise he placed the blue pollen, tha'di'thee do tlij, from the blue flowers,[36] and the yellow pollen from the corn; and on top of these he placed the pollen from the water flags, tquel aqa'di din; and again on top of these he placed the crystal, which is river pollen. This basket he gave to the Coyote who put it between the horns of the Water Buffalo. The Coyote said that with this sacred offering he would give back the male child. He said that the male child would be known as the Black Cloud or Male Rain, and that he would bring the thunder and lightning. The female child he would keep. She would be known as the Blue, Yellow, and White Clouds or Female Rain. She would be the gentle rain that would moisten the earth and help them to live. So he kept the female child, and he placed the male child on the sacred basket between the horns of the Water Buffalo. And the Water Buffalo disappeared, and the waters with her.

After the water sank there appeared another person. They did not know him, and they asked him where he had come from. He told them that he was the badger, nahashch'id, and that he had been formed where the Yellow Cloud had touched the Earth. Afterward this Yellow Cloud turned out to be a sunbeam.[37]

The Fifth World

First Man was not satisfied with the Fourth World. It was a small, barren land; and the great water had soaked the earth and made the sowing of seeds impossible. He planted the big Female Reed and it grew up to the vaulted roof of this Fourth World. First Man sent the newcomer, the badger,

---

[36] Recorder's note: This blue pollen, tha'di'thee do tlij, is thought to be *Delphinium scaposum* Green.

[37] Informant's and interpreter's note: The Four Worlds were really twelve worlds, or stages of development; but different medicine men divide them differently according to the ceremony held. For the narrative they call them the Four Dark Worlds, and the Fifth World, the one we live in. An old medicine man explained that the Sixth World would be that of the spirit; and that the one above that would be "cosmic," melting into one.

up inside the reed, but before he reached the upper world water began to drip, so he returned and said that he was frightened.

At this time there came another strange being. First Man asked him where he had been formed, and he told him that he had come from the Earth itself. This was the locust.[38] He said that it was now his turn to do something, and he offered to climb up the reed.

The locust made a headband of a little reed, and on his forehead he crossed two arrows. These arrows were dressed with yellow tail feathers. With this sacred headdress and the help of all the Holy Beings the locust climbed up to the Fifth World. He dug his way through the reed as he digs in the earth now. He then pushed through mud until he came to water. When he emerged he saw a black water bird[39] swimming toward him. He had arrows[40] crossed on the back of his head and big eyes.

The bird said: "What are you doing here? This is not your country." And continuing, he told the locust that unless he could make magic he would not allow him to remain.

The black water bird drew an arrow from back of his head, and shoving it into his mouth drew it out his nether extremity. He inserted it underneath his body and drew it out of his mouth.

"That is nothing," said the locust. He took the arrows from his headband and pulled them both ways through his body, between his shell and his heart. The bird believed that the locust possessed great medicine, and he swam away to the East, taking the water with him.

Then came the blue water bird from the South, and the yellow water bird from the West, and the white water bird from the North, and everything happened as before. The locust per-

[38] Informant's note: The name of the locust was not given.

Franciscan Fathers (1912, p. 123): locust, nahacha'gi. This also means grasshopper, cicada.

[39] Informant's note: The water birds were grebes.

[40] Recorder's note: The arrows crossed on the back of the bird's head. See both Navaho and Zuni Arrow Ceremony.

formed the magic with his arrows; and when the last water bird had gone he found himself sitting on land.

The locust returned to the lower world and told the people that the beings above had strong medicine, and that he had great difficulty getting the best of them.

Now two dark clouds and two white clouds rose, and this meant that two nights and two days had passed, for there was still no sun. First Man again sent the badger to the upper world, and he returned covered with mud, terrible mud. First Man gathered chips of turquoise which he offered to the five Chiefs of the Winds who[41] lived in the uppermost world of all. They were pleased with the gift, and they sent down the winds and dried the Fifth World.

First Man and his people saw four dark clouds and four white clouds pass, and then they sent the badger up the reed. This time when the badger returned he said that he had come out on solid earth. So First Man and First Woman led the people to the Fifth World, which some call the Many-Colored Earth and some the Changeable Earth. They emerged through a lake surrounded by four mountains. The water bubbles in this lake when anyone goes near.[42]

Now after all the people had emerged from the lower worlds First Man and First Woman dressed the Mountain Lion with yellow, black, white, and grayish corn and placed him on one side. They dressed the Wolf with white tail feathers and placed him on the other side. They divided the people into two groups. The first group was told to choose whichever chief they wished. They made their choice, and, although they thought they had chosen the Mountain Lion, they found that they had taken the Wolf for their chief. The Mountain Lion was the chief for the other side. And these people who had the Mountain Lion for

[41] The First Chief, Nichi ntla′ie, the Left Course Wind; the Second Chief, Nichi lichi, the Red Wind; the Third Chief, Nichi shada ji na′laghali, the Wind Turning from the Sun; the Fourth Chief, Nichi qa′hashchi, the Wind with Many Points; the Fifth Chief, Nichi che do et siedee, the Wind with the Fiery Temper.

[42] Informant's note: The place of emergence is said to be near Pagosa Springs, Colorado. The white people have put a wire fence around our Sacred Lake.

their chief turned out to be the people of the Earth. They were
to plant seeds and harvest corn. The followers of the Wolf chief
became the animals and birds; they turned into all the creatures
that fly and crawl and run and swim.

And after all the beings were divided, and each had his own
form, they went their ways.

This is the story of the Four Dark Worlds and the Fifth, the
World we live in. Some medicine men tell us that there are two
worlds above us, the first is the World of the Spirits of Living
Things, the second is the Place of Melting into One.

The Order of Things, or the Age of
Animal Heroes

The First Hogan[48]

First Man planned to build a home.

He dug a shallow pit in the earth and raised the poles. For
the main poles First Man used the Black Bow, which is called
Altqin dilqil.[44] There were two parts of this Black Bow, and
two other parts, one cut from the Male Reed and one from the
Female Reed.[45] The other poles were those at hand. Then the
whole structure was covered with earth and grass, and the first
dwelling was built. First Woman ground white corn into meal,
and they powdered the poles with the meal, and they sprinkled
it inside the dwelling from East to West.

First Man said as he sprinkled the cornmeal: "May my home
be sacred and beautiful, and may the days be beautiful and
plenty."

Today there is a hogan ceremony, and a song is sung as the
poles are raised.

Now after the first hogan was built and they had seen four
dark and four light clouds rising First Man said that they were

---

[48] Informant's note: The first hogan was not like the hogans of today.

[44] Informant's note: The Dark or Black Bow is symbolic of the Slayers of
the Enemies. It is a symbol of the overthrow of evil.

[45] Informant's note: The Male and the Female Reeds are the symbols of
the male and female principles.

tired and that they must rest. He asked if anyone had brought the river stones. The badger said that he had five. First Man said that he would heat four and leave one. He had a plan to build two sweat houses out of the remaining poles.[46]

There are four parts of a chant sung at this time. It is the Sweat House Chant. One part is like this:

> He made it. He made it. He made it.
> At the place where the people emerged from the
>   underworld,
> Near the Lake of Emergence, he made it.
> He made it with the female wood and the male wood.
> He made it with the Black Mesa rock.
> He made it with the hard river rock.
> He made it with the help of The-Most-High-Power-
>   Whose-Ways-Are-Fearful.

Many chants are sung during this ceremony—the Horned Toad Chant, the Twin Brothers Chant, the Bear Chant, and the Mirage Stone Chant.[47]

The Creation of the Sun and Moon[48]

After the hogan was finished everyone rested.

The dwelling was occupied by Atse'hastqin, First Man, and Atse'esdza, First Woman. All their belongings were piled inside. The woman lay with her feet to the West, and the man lay with his feet to the East. Their heads crossed and their thoughts mingled, and these thoughts were sacred.

Now in the hogan there were also two other persons: Atse'-ashki, First Boy, and Atse'ataed, First Girl. They were not the children of First Man and First Woman, but the Turquoise Boy and the White Shell Girl who had come with the others from the underworld. Now First Boy lay to the south side of the hogan, and First Girl to the north. They lay down when they

---

[46] Informant's note: The building of the sweat house is very special; details will be given later.

[47] Recorder's note: The hogan faces the East. Hebrews of antiquity fronted their edifices to the East.

[48] Informant's note: Some medicine men say that the Turquoise Boy was without sex, or a hermaphrodite.

saw the period of darkness descending, and they listened. First Man and First Woman whispered together, but First Boy could not distinguish the words one from another. Each time the Dark Cloud covered them the four lay down, and First Man and First Woman whispered.

This happened four times, then First Boy stood and said: "What is this secret thing that you plan? We have lost our sleep through four dark spaces."

"It is not an unwise thing that we plan," said First Man. "We plan for the time which is to come, how we shall live, and how the people will live upon this earth. It is nothing but that, my child." And First Woman repeated what her husband had said. When First Boy heard this he agreed that it was better that the two should continue their planning.

First Man and First Woman whispered together during many nights. They planned with the help of the All-Wise-Coyote-Who-Was-Formed-in-the-Water. The three devised a scheme that would meet the problems that would later come to pass. They planned that there should be a sun, and day and night.[49] They said that the Coyote called First Angry had brought unhappiness and spoiled their life down below, and that he was not the proper person to have with them at this time. He should be kept away.

They spread a beautiful buckskin on the ground. This was the skin of a deer not killed by a weapon.[50] On the buckskin they placed a perfect turquoise, round like the sun. It was as large as the height of an average man if he stretched his arm upward. They stood twelve tail feathers from the eagle around it, and also twelve tail feathers from the flicker. On the great turquoise they marked a mouth and nose and eyes. They made a yellow streak below the mouth on top of the chin.

Now, although they had stationed four guards to be on the lookout for the Coyote, Atse'hashke', he came and asked them

---

[49] Franciscan Fathers (1912, p. 36): The Black Yei or Fire God, Hash'ch esh'zhini.

[50] Interpreter's note: Medicine men prize highly the skin of a deer not killed by a weapon. A deer struck by a car in the winter of 1935 brought the Navaho who found it two cows in exchange.

what they were doing. They told him: "Nothing whatsoever." He said: "So I see," and went away.

After that they visited the different places where there was fire under the earth. In one of these places they found Hashch'esh'zhini, the Black Yei, who is also called the Fire God. He was asked to use fire to heat the great turquoise which they had planned to use as their sun.

They placed a perfect white shell on the buckskin below the turquoise that was to become the sun. This great, perfect, white shell was to become the moon. First Man planned to heat it with the first crystal that he had used for his fire.

By this time they had posted two circles of guards around the place where they were planning; but even with this precaution the Coyote came to them. He appeared in their midst and said: "This must be something that you are planning." But they assured him that he saw nothing; they said that they were just sitting there. And again the Coyote left them. First Man called the guards together and asked them why they had let the one whose name was Atse'hashke' pass. They said that they had not seen the Coyote. First Man then placed three circles of guards around the sacred buckskin.

The Holy Ones asked the Turquoise Boy to enter the great, perfect turquoise that was to become the sun; and they asked the White Shell Girl to enter the great, perfect, white shell that was to become the moon. The Turquoise Boy was to carry a whistle made from the Male Reed. This whistle had twelve holes in it, and each time that the Turquoise Boy would blow on his whistle the earth would move one month in time. The White Shell Girl was also to carry a whistle. It was made from the Female Reed, and with it she should move the tides of the sea.

Just as this was planned the Coyote came among them and said: "Well, my cousins, there is something that you are planning. What is it?"

First Man answered: "We are planning nothing at all. We are just sitting here."

"Very well," said the Coyote, "I wanted to know, that was all." And he went away.

After he had gone they planned the twelve months of the year.[51]

The Twelve Months of the Year

October is the first month of the year and of winter, which is called qai. October's name is Gah'ji, meaning Back-to-Back, or the Parting-of-the-Seasons. It is the time when the deer come, the time to hunt. Nalashi, the Tarantula, is its feather or head-dress. Nlchi achi, Little Cold, is its heart. The blue hanging haze is over this month. Women shell corn, thrash, and store food for the winter. It is the month when mountain sheep breed.

November is the second month. It is called Nlchi'tso'si, the month or Time of Slender Winds. Its heart is Nlchi'tso'si, Slender Wind. Its feather is Hastin sakai (Orion), the Old Man with Legs Spread. It is also a month for hunting. The women gather certain grass and plant seeds on warm days,[52] which later they dry and grind into flour for the different bread cakes eaten in winter. The antelope breed.

The third month of the year is December. It is called Nlchi'-tso', the Great Wind. Its heart is also the Great Wind. Its feather is Atse'etso, the Big First One.[53] Digging sticks are prepared in this month. They are made with the stone ax; and the wood is dried in the dwellings so that when the planting time comes the sticks will be smooth and well seasoned. The women make moccasins, and they tan the hides from the hunting season. It is the time to begin to tell the sacred stories. The deer breed.

January is the fourth month. Its name is Zas'ntl'tis, Crusted Snow. Its heart is Tqin, Ice. Akaisda'hi, Which-Awaits-the-

[51] Recorder's note: The drawing of the Calendar Stone was checked by Sam Ahkeah and Gerald Nailor.

Informant's and interpreter's note: First Man made the marks on the buckskin. Later the people of Blue House had the Calendar Stone in their keeping. A medicine woman guarded it. The story of the sun and the moon and the twelve months were upon it. Hastin Tlo'tsi hee's (Sandoval's) ancestress, Esdzan at'a', the Hopi woman, was the guardian of this stone. Later it was hidden near the Carriso Mountains.

[52] Recorder's note: Edible seeds known to the Navaho. (Any of the genus Chenopodium.)

[53] Recorder's note: Atseet so, the Big First One; part of Scorpio.

Dawn, is its feather. This is the Milky Way. The young men hear the sacred stories and learn to become hatqa'li, singers or shamans. This is the time when preparations are made for the coming growing season. There are many ceremonies. The women cook the food and take part in certain rituals. The coyotes breed.

February, the fifth month, is called Atsa'biyazh, Baby Eagle. Nol'i, the Hail, is its heart. Its feather is Gahat'ei, the Rabbit Tracks (star cluster in Canis Major). It is the month of the changeable winds. The First Chief of the Winds shakes the earth and awakens the sleeping plants, the bear, the lizards and the snakes. The first plants start to come up. After this month the sacred stories must not be told to the young people. The rabbits breed.

The sixth month, March, is called Wozhchid.[54] It is the month when eaglets chirp in the shell and the antlers of the deer drop. Its heart is Becha na'chil,[55] Sudden Spring Storms. Its feather is Dede'nii, the Mountain Sheep Bird.[56] When you see these birds in the canyons it is spring. The mountain sheep drop their young. Nlchi'dotlish, the Blue Wind, moves over the earth and the first leaves come forth. Ceremonies are held to bless the fields before the seeds are planted.

April, the seventh month and the beginning of Shiji, summer, is called Da'chil, the month of little leaves. Its heart is Niyol, Wind-in-Action. Bit'aa, meaning Little Leaves, is its feather. Rabbits have their young. Nlchi'dilqil, the Black Wind, shakes the earth and it thunders. The leaves grow bigger and darker in color; and the people make ready for the planting.

May is the eighth month. It is called Dotso after the All-Wise Fly in the sacred legends. Its heart is Ayei'ne'denaiyote, meaning a mixture of rain and spring snow. Nlchi'dilqil, the Black Wind, is its feather. The grass becomes a darkish green. The antelope drop their young. Nlchi'litsui, the Yellow Wind, shakes the earth and it thunders. The flowers come forth and plants open their leaves. It is the time to plant. The early part of this month is called the planting time.

---

[54] Informant's note: The meaning is not known.

[55] Recorder's note: The spelling of this word is not certain.

[56] Informant's note: Dede'nii, the Mountain Sheep Bird, is the phoebe.

The ninth month, June, is called Yaish jash'chili, When-Few Seeds-Ripen. Its heart is Hado'yazhe, Little Heat. Jadi'yazhe, Little Antelope, is its feather. The women gather the first edible seeds, and they are used as the first fruits of the season. They gather the cactus fruit. This is the month of the first rain ceremonies.

July, the tenth month, is called Jas'tso, the Great Seed Ripening. Big Heat, Hado'tso, is its heart. Nltsa'najin, Dark Streaks of Rain, is its feather. It is the time when people gather many seeds and guard their fields. The deer drop their young. Dilye'he, the Pleiades, are seen in the early morning; and the fawns have their pattern on their rumps.

The eleventh month, August, is called Binint A'tso'si, Little Ripening. Its heart is A'tso'si, Light Ripening. Nltsa'bakha', the Male Rain, is its feather. The ears form on the corn and everything ripens. It is the time when wild fruits are gathered—the sourberry, the chokecherry, and yucca fruit.

The last month of the year and of summer is September.[57] It is called Binint a'tso, the Harvest Time. Binint a'tso, Great Ripening, is its heart. Nltsa'baad, the Female Rain, is its feather. Nuts are gathered. The corn is harvested and taken to the dwellings. The first foodstuffs are stored for the winter. And the Ceremony of All Blessings is held in thanksgiving.

When everything was in readiness they called Hashche'zhini from Heavy Rock where he lived. He came to heat the turquoise that was to become the sun. The Turquoise Boy stepped into the sun with his whistle, which was made from the Male Reed. This whistle had twelve holes in it; and each time he blew on it the earth would move one space or month. First Man heated with his crystal the Great White Shell that was to become the moon. The White Shell Girl stepped into the moon. She carried her whistle, made from the Female Reed, which also had twelve holes in it. And whenever she blew upon it she would help move the earth and the tides. These two Holy Beings were to form the seasons and the months and the days.

The Turquoise Boy asked to have one hundred and two trails; and the White Shell Girl asked to have one hundred trails.

---

[57] Informant's note: Some medicine men believe the original plan was for thirteen months.

They were to cross in the months of March and September. The Sun was to turn back in June, and again in December.

The Turquoise Boy said: "Everything is right so far, but I will not travel for nothing. I will travel if I am paid with the lives of the people of the earth, all the human beings, the animals which have four legs, the birds and insects of the air, the fishes and all the people of the underwater." And then the White Shell Girl repeated the same thing. She also wanted to be paid with the lives of the living.[58]

After everything was finished and four circles made around the whole, the Coyote, Atse'hashke', went to the Great Yei, Hasjelti, and demanded to know why he had not been allowed to have a part in the planning. He said that the others had tried to keep it a secret, but that he had known all that had happened. This made Hasjelti very angry, and seeing this, the Coyote ran away. He ran straight to the place where the others were planning and appeared in their midst. He asked First Man why he had kept everything a secret. He turned to First Woman and asked her why she had kept this thing from him. Then he told them everything that they had planned. He said that they had even set the month when he should visit his woman. He warned them that he had come for the purpose of spoiling their plan.

Atse'hashke' drew five lines over other marks he had made in the sand. He told the people that unless they could guess their proper meanings they would suffer greatly. Now the little Breeze whispered in First Man's ear and told him what to say. The first line was made of turquoise and it represented the green leaves. The second line drawn was of white shell. First Man said that he thought of ripe leaves and falling leaves. The third mark was made of jet; and he said that it stood for the dark, black mountains after the leaves had fallen. The fourth line was made of white bead. First Man said that it was the snow on the mountains. The fifth mark was of crystal, and its meaning was of snow and ice on the frozen rivers and lakes.

The Coyote spoke, "All right, everything you have guessed correctly. I thought of all those things as I made the five marks. By your guessing you have made the summer months six, and

[58] Recorder's note: The Arctic Highlanders say: "Will ye have eternal darkness and eternal life, or light and death?"

the winter months six; and you expect to count by the changes of the moon. But I will put in some extra days so that the months will not be even. Sometimes frost will come early, and sometimes it will remain late. First plants will sometimes freeze, and so also will animals. Sometimes the full moon will come before the end of the month; and at the end of the year you will find that you have thirteen moon periods instead of twelve." The Coyote continued. "You have in your minds that it was I who spoiled your way of living down in the underworlds. It was not my plan."

Then he addressed First Woman. "Why did you keep this sacred thing from me? When you asked me to steal the Water Buffalo's babies you said that you had suffered many things because of your husband's plan. Everything was well when I did as you wished. I have kept the female Water Buffalo baby; and by keeping her I am able to call the male rain and the female rain and all the different clouds and vapors. It is well. I followed your desires so that the people might have the seasons and the flowers and all that grows from the earth during the different times of the year. Your plan was for the benefit of those to come. But now I will place the female child back into the River. Whenever you wish rain you will have to go for the Water Buffalo's girl baby; and after you have used her power you will have to return her to the River again." He told them where they would find her; and he said that they would know when they should use her. "Now go ahead with your plans, Brothers,"[59] he said, and with that he left them.

After the Coyote had departed the others spread the blue sky above the earth. In the East they placed a black pole to hold up the eastern end of the sky. A blue one was planted in the South, a yellow one in the West, and a white one in the North. A hole was placed in the sky and sealed with water. Around the outer edge of the sky was placed a white ring, a yellow ring, a blue ring, and a black ring. They formed the border. They were placed there for the purpose of protecting the sky so that it would remain solid forever. No power on the earth or above

[59] Informant's note: The Coyote used the word "brother" first and last in all speeches after this.

the earth should harm it. And around the four posts they placed the same colors.

After all was finished they placed the sun in the sky, and also, they placed the moon there. And they placed Dilye' he, the Pleiades, there; and Atse'etso, the Big First One; and the Coyote's Feather, Atse'etso'si, which is also called the Slender One; and Baalchini, the children of Dilye'ha and Atse'etso'si; and Hastin sakai, The-Old-Man-with-Feet-Apart; and the Rabbit Tracks, Gahat'ei; and Akaisda'hi, Moving-toward-the-Dawn; and Nahokhos bokho, The-Main-Pole-which-Holds-All; and Nahokhos bakhai, The-Revolving-Male-Warrior-with-His-Bow-and-Arrows; and his wife, Nahokhos baadi, Who-Carries-the-Fire-in-Her-Basket.[60]

The Sun's Path

Above the mountain called Tso dzil[61] there is a square hole in the sky. And this hole in the sky is mirrored in a lake which

[60] Informant's note (checked with interpreter): Yaya ni'sin is the name of the corner or sky posts. Dilye'he, the Pleiades. Atse'etso, the forepart of Scorpio. Atse'etso'si, the belt and sword of Orion. Baalchini, the central double stars in the lower part of the Hyades. Hastin sakai, Orion. The left foot is Rigel and the right foot is Betelgeuse. Gahat'ei, the star cluster under Canis Major, Akaisda'hi, the Milky Way. Nahokos bokho, the North Star. Nahokos bakhai, Ursa Major, the Big Dipper. Nahokos baadi, Cassiopea, but some medicine men say Ursa Minor.

Robert H. Lowie, "The Test-Theme in North American Mythology," *Journal of American Folklore* 21 (1908), 123: "According to the naturalistic theory, constellations are apperceived by primitive man as objects or persons according to the characteristics that appear to him, and an explanatory tale is added"; e.g. The Pleiades—"the Shoshone tale of Coyote and his daughters"; the "Plains' legend of the girl who turns into a bear, and, after killing the tribesmen, pursues her brothers, who ascend to become a constellation" (the Dipper) (p. 126).

Interpreter's notes: 1. The Coyote added his own star, Mai'bizo, which is sometimes called So dondizidi, the No-Month Star. This is identified as Canopus. 2. The Coyote Man was thrown into the sky, and is known as Atse'etso'si. The Baalchini are his children by the woman Dilye'he, the Pleiades. Those who know of the Coyote cult and its weird rites understand incestuous relationship. 3. Dilye'he, the Pleiades, is sometimes represented as the mother-in-law who must not meet her son-in-law, Aste'etso'si, but must continually run from him. The myth of the Coyote Man is the origin of the mother-in-law taboo.

[61] Informant's note: Tso dzil is Mount Taylor.

lies between the two highest peaks of the mountain. There were three names given to the hole in the sky: the first is called Tse'an an hi'habetine, the Place Where the Most High Power Came Up; the second is Sash yota'betine, the Bear's Upper Sky Path; and the third name is Hojon yota'betine, Whose Ways Are Beautiful's Path. It is said that the Sun stops at this place at midday and eats his lunch; and the place where he stops and eats is called Nitsi ya'hatsis, The Place Where the Sun Man Has His Lunch and His Horse Eats Out of a Basket.

The Sky and the Earth

Then came the Earth Woman, Nahosdzan'esdza'. First Man told her that she was to be the wife of the Sky. She would face the East, and her husband over her, would face the West. And whenever the Fog covered the Earth they would know that the Sky had visited Nahosdzan'esdza'.

After that they set the corner posts and stretched the Sky in the four directions.

About twenty chants were sung at this time, and after the first ten sections of the first chant, the Sun Chant, the Sun began to move away. The next chant was for the Moon, and after a little time, it also began to move away.

Today different medicine men use different chants and prayers for this ceremony; but the chants of the Sun and Moon and Earth are always sung. Some say that black magic and evil entered the plan at this time, but others hold that it was not until later.

Now after the Sun rose in the sky the Dark Cloud that covered the earlier worlds during half periods became the night. The White Cloud was the dawn, and the sun's light became our day. And along the far horizons where the first ones used to see the blue and yellow clouds, there appeared the twilight and the false dawn.

The first day-period that the sun was raised in the sky the heat was unbearable. So the Holy Ones stretched out the four corners of the sky and this raised the sun still higher in the heavens. After they had done this four times it was like it is today. There was room on the earth for everyone, and the sun's

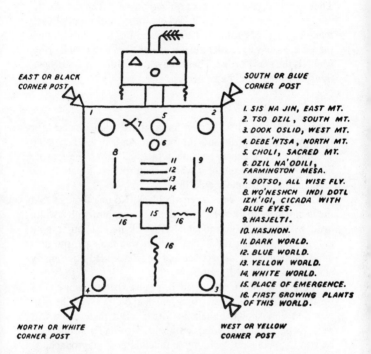

EAST OR BLACK CORNER POST

SOUTH OR BLUE CORNER POST

NORTH OR WHITE CORNER POST

WEST OR YELLOW CORNER POST

1. SIS NA JIN, EAST MT.
2. TSO DZIL, SOUTH MT.
3. DOOK OSLID, WEST MT.
4. DEBE'NTSA, NORTH MT.
5. CHOLI, SACRED MT.
6. DZIL NA'ODILI, FARMINGTON MESA.
7. DOTSO, ALL WISE FLY.
8. WO'NESHCH INDI DOTL IZH'IGI, CICADA WITH BLUE EYES.
9. HASJELTI.
10. HASJHON.
11. DARK WORLD.
12. BLUE WORLD.
13. YELLOW WORLD.
14. WHITE WORLD.
15. PLACE OF EMERGENCE.
16. FIRST GROWING PLANTS OF THIS WORLD.

Sand Painting of the Earth. (The plan of the Earth.) From the top of the mask projects a breath feather, tied with a white cotton string, the spider's gift. Coral and turquoise ear pendants are indicated. The body is dark gray. Borders, mask, neck, etc. The two arms and two legs are kos ischin, triangles set upon one another and symbolizing forming clouds or cloud terraces. (Sam Ahkead and Gerald Nailor got this from medicine men at Shiprock.)

warmth was right for the growing plants and the animals and the people.

Now it was the same with the earth as it was with the sky. They planned just how the earth should be.[62] They made the face of the earth white, with eyes and nose and mouth. They made earrings of turquoise for the ears; and for a border they placed a black ring, a blue ring, a yellow ring, and a white ring, which is the earth's edge. These rings are for the earth's protection; no power shall harm her. . . .

Old Age and Illness

First Man and First Woman had planned what was best for the sky and the earth and the people. And in the beginning whatever they planned became a fact; but after the Coyote interfered there were others who wished to have a part in the scheme of how people should live.

The people's hair was to remain black. No one thought that the beings were to grow old. But there came a bird with a white head who said: "My grandchildren, look here, I am turning gray; I am growing old." This person was tsish'gai, the nuthatch; and after he had spoken old age descended upon many and their hair turned gray.

The people of the earth had been given strong white corn for teeth. They were made strong, solid, and clean; and the plan was that they should remain so forever. But there came Old Man Gopher, Hastin Naazisi, with his face badly swollen for he was in great pain. "Oh, my grandchildren," he groaned, "I have a toothache. Pull my bad teeth for me." So they pulled the bad teeth, and only two remained that were really good. After that time it became a fact that people suffered from toothache, that teeth became old and worn.

So far there had been no babies born as they are now born. This was the plan. But a small bird with a red breast came and said: "My grandchildren, look at the blood that comes from me." It was a monthly occurrence after that, and it came to all female beings. The bird was chishgahi, the robin.

[62] Informant's note: The Sand Painting of the Earth and the description.

The Plan, or Order of Things

There was a plan from the stars down. The woman's strength was not to be as great as the man's strength. They could not attend to the planting and harvesting as the men could, therefore men would be worth more than women. And the plan was that women would propose marriage to men; but the Coyote came and said: "Brothers, listen, I have just married a woman." Again he spoiled their plan. Men propose marriage to women; but because of the older plan there are still cases where women go after men. Then not long after that, that which the bird, chishgahi, said came true; but they still thought it unwise to have babies born in the new way. Just then the Coyote came and said: "Brothers, I have a little baby."

Then they planned how a husband and a wife should feel toward each other, and how jealousy should affect both sexes. They got the yucca and the yucca fruit, and water from the sacred springs, and dew from all the plants, corn, trees, and flowers. These they gathered, and they called them tqo alchin, sacred waters. They rubbed the yucca and the sacred waters over the woman's heart and over the man's heart. This was done so they would love each other; but at the same time there arose jealousy between the man and the woman, his wife.

After that they planned how each sex would have its feeling of passion. A medicine was made and it was given to the man and to the woman. This medicine was for the organs of sex. The organ of the man would whistle; and then the organ of the woman would whistle. When they heard this each organ gave a long, clear whistle. After that they came together and the sound of the whistle was different. That is why the voices of the young boy and maiden are different; and it is why their voices change.

They planned that the rainbow should be used for a path whenever there was a deep canyon to cross; and it was to be thrown over a river and used as a bridge.

The gopher was told to remain hidden from the sun because he had caused toothache. That is why he stays down in the earth and seldom ventures out during the daytime.

First Man called the birds to him and said: "You who have

wings, go to the mountains for your food and good living."
So they went to the mountains. To each bird was given a name,
and to each was given the directions of his way of living.

Then all the different types of lizards came. They were sent
to the cliffs and told to make their homes among the rocks; and
to every type of lizard was given a name.

First Man called the beavers and the otters and the underwater animals; and they were given their names and sent to
the rivers and waters that would become their homes.

First Man and First Woman called the chiefs. First they
called the wolf. They told him that, although he was a chief,
he had done wrong, he had stolen. They told him that he should
be called ma'itso, the big wanderer. "You shall travel far and
wide over the face of the earth," they said.

The snake was called. They told him that because he could
not travel the year round he would be given a bag of medicine,
and, as he had no place to which he could tie it, they put it
in his mouth. First Man gave this to him and told him that
should the snake wish to harm someone he should swell this
poison and cast it out. But for its possession he must pay by
traveling but six months of the year.

Then First Man called another chief. "Come here, old man,"
he said. When this being came, First Man said that he should
be named ma'i, the coyote.[63] But the coyote got angry and said:
"Such a name!" And he declared that he would not have it;
and that he would leave; but First Man called him back and
told him that he would also be known as Atse'hashke', First
Angry. After that the coyote felt better. He thought that he had
a great name given him, and he went happily away, for he was
told that he would know all the happenings on the face of
the earth.

The bear was the next chief to be called. He was given a
name but he was not satisfied. He became so angry that First
Man used the word shash to quiet him. The bear repeated it
four times, and he said that it had a strange sound, and when

---

[63] Recorder's note: Ma'i, the Coyote, is not to be confused with the Great
Coyote or Wolf. This is the Coyote called First Angry or the Scolder, and
appears in Zuni and other myths.

one said it aloud one had an awesome feeling. So he went off well content that shash should be his name.

Up to this time all beings were people and could remove their coat forms at will;[64] but because of wrongdoing they were made to keep their coats; and they were made to keep to their kind and to live among themselves in different parts of the earth.

When all the birds and animals had started out on their way, First Man called one little gray bird back. It was tse na'olch'oshi, the little canyon wren, who had carried the cliff rock up from the Yellow World. First Man told him that, since he had been responsible for the cliffs he should make his home among the cliff rocks. And should anyone ever harm him he would have the power of getting even with him. That is why falling rocks sometimes harm people or animals.

All the people that First Man and First Woman named and sent forth now live on the earth. This is the way they planned the order of things.

[64] This is the same in Zuni myths, etc.

Hopi

The name "Hopi" is a contraction of Hopitu, meaning "peaceful one" or of Hopitu-shinumu, "peaceful all people." Such significations express a strong cultural value of these Pueblo Indians, and observers from Ruth Benedict on have commented on their strong, orderly, outwardly pacific nature. Others, however, have seen something behind this dominant attitude and have suggested that it is maintained only at the price of strong interpersonal antagonisms and barely suppressed aggression. Whatever the case, the Hopi have survived better than many other tribes and still remain approximately where they were when lost and dazed Coronado encountered them in 1540. A. M. Stephen's recording of the origin of the Snake Order introduces us to what is perhaps the most familiar and sensational aspect of Hopi culture, the Snake Order itself and its ritual dance. Relevant works on this tribe include Benedict's path-breaking *Patterns of Culture*, Laura Thompson and Alice Joseph's *The Hopi Way*, and Frank Waters' *The Book of the Hopi*.

Legend of the Snake Order of the Moquis, as Told by Outsiders

Many years ago, when the people were greatly scattered over the land, there lived in a house seven brothers, who were said to be the best of all men then living, for they did not of nights interfere with others, nor did they dwell with women. They were named Red-Corn, Blue-Corn, Yellow-Corn, White-Corn, Green-Corn, Spotted-Corn, and Black-Corn. None of them married until the youngest, Black-Corn, had attained the age of manhood. He was then told by his older brothers to take a wife. This displeased him, for among all the women of his

From A. M. Stephen, "Legend of the Snake Order of the Moquis, as Told by Outsiders," *Journal of American Folklore* 1 (April-June 1888), 109–14.

tribe there was none he liked. He grew sad, and said he would go away, and not return until after he had found a wife. He started upon his journey, taking with him only four plume-sticks and a bag of sacred meal. After journeying many days, until nearly dead with hunger and thirst, he came to a large lake which lay to the west of his own house. He did not drink from this lake, but from a stream of water which issued from a hill at a little distance from the lake. Next day, when he awoke, he went down to the side of the water, and said to Daw-wa, the sun-chief: "Oh, Daw-wa! father! I have been sent from my home, and my heart is heavy. I am weary, father; give me rest, give me a home, where my heart will once more be filled with the joyous song of the lark, and not with the sad song of the dove."

Daw-wa heard his prayer, and told him to tie his four sticks together and place them on the water, which done the sticks became great logs and the feathers a shade (after the manner of an umbrella). He was then directed to gather certain roots, after eating which he would not be hungry for a long while. He was told that in four days he was to sail away upon this raft, and after he started he was not to land until asked to come ashore by a snake, whose name was Wapa Tcua (Big Rattlesnake). On the fourth morning, before sunrise, he was awakened by the rocking motion of his raft, and after the sun had risen he looked around, but could see no land. He was afraid, but Oman comforted him, assuring him of safety. At sunset, one evening, after his voyage had continued several days, a buzzard came and told him that in two or three days he would see land, and cautioned him not to be frightened at anything he should see or hear. At the end of three days land came in view. He sailed two days in sight of land, and at sunset on the fourth day the raft was thrown upon the shore. It began to grow small, compelling him to get ashore. In the morning, Daw-wa told him to pick up his plume-sticks, which had now assumed their natural size. Daw-wa then directed him to travel to the south and west, telling him that he would be met by an old man, who would guide him to a running stream where the Big Snake kept watch, to whom he should give the plume-sticks and pouch of meal. He began his journey at noon, and night came on while he was climbing a mountain. He continued his journey in the early morning as soon as the star rose, and when the sun rose a very old man, leaning on a stick, came from behind a rock. This old man had eyes and ears, but had neither mouth nor nose; he could not speak, but with his stick, which was shaped like a crook, he seized the young man by the neck, and led him along, stopping at intervals to let his companion rest, for the old man almost ran, so fast was his gait. At sunset he stopped, and by signs told the young man that on the morrow his part of the journey would be done; that he had been a long time awaiting the young man's arrival. The old man said he was glad of his arrival, for now he (the old man) could go home and die in peace. While the old man was making signs, he was struck by a flash of lightning and rendered unconscious.

The young man's name was Kwe-teat-ri-yi, White-Corn.[1] White-Corn was afraid, and started to run away, but the old man opened his eyes, and called him by name, telling him to get a piece of black rock, lying near, and with it cut the skin on his (the old man's) face, beginning at a point between the eyes, and cutting downward the length of one of the plume-sticks, then cutting across the face the same distance. White-Corn did as he was directed, and immediately the old man became a young man. In the morning they resumed their journey in high glee, singing and telling each other of their homes. At noon they stopped to rest, and the young old man dug a hole in the sand, and, placing one of White-Corn's plume-sticks in it, he began to sing and dance, and the hole filled with water, from which they drank, and then resumed their journey. At sunset they came to the top of a hill, from which White-Corn saw the long-expected stream; so, when he spoke of it, he turned to look at his companion, but the latter had vanished. During the night White-Corn was afraid. At daylight he resumed his march, and got to the stream before sunrise. He sprinkled meal upon the water, and, hearing a peculiar sound in the grass, he turned round and saw a tremendous snake coming toward him, with head raised several feet above ground, its skin shining like beautiful rocks [gems?]. The snake halted

[1] The name changes without explanation.

at a little distance from him, and began to talk, making inquiry as to where he came from and where he was going, but especially questioning to ascertain whether he was trustworthy. By the direction of the snake, he again threw his remaining plume-sticks into the stream, and, as before, they immediately became a raft. He was directed to get upon the raft, and remain until noon of the fourth day. After this four days' voyage he would reach a hill, which he was to climb, and would then receive further instructions. He accordingly got upon the raft, and it at once began to move rapidly off, much faster than a horse could run; he was frightened, and longed to jump off upon the river bank, but he feared injury: so he sat still and gazed in wonder until night, when he watched the stars. In this way he continued until noon of the fourth day.

He was startled on the fourth day by seeing an immense rock in front, blocking up the entire passage of the river. While he was yet thinking how he could save himself, his raft was suddenly lifted by the roaring water, and he and it were thrown high up on the hill, beside the rock. He lay there, bruised and trembling, for a long while, and pondering over what course to pursue, until he fell asleep. When he awoke in the morning the sun was well up, and he hastened to climb the hill, the summit of which he reached at sunset. He stood looking at a rock partly buried in the sand, and as he continued to observe it a snake's head protruded from beneath. He sprinkled sacred meal, and placed his plume-sticks before the snake, which coiled around them, and breathed upon each separate feather. The snake then returned beneath the rock, and directed him to proceed with certain ceremonies. As directed, White-Corn placed the plume-sticks in front of the snake, then sprinkled corn-meal in such a manner as to describe a circle, then in the area of this circle he sprinkled meal in three straight lines. These three lines he named the points whence the rain and winds come.

The snake was well pleased with this conduct, and he concluded not to wait for morning, but to take White-Corn at once into the presence of the great snake-chief, and let him see what the young man did. The rock was suddenly lifted up, and a large opening was exposed. The snake told him to follow quickly, as it was growing dark and cold, and that, although the path was short, it was very rough, and in the dark would be attended by many falls. White-Corn immediately followed the snake, and in a little while after getting into this cavern a mighty noise like thunder was heard. The snake told him not to fear, as the noise was caused by rocks falling down to close up the entrance through which they had just come. This was to prevent anyone gaining entrance except those selected, and to prevent the escape of those who had entered. They went on until they heard the sound of falling water and beautiful music, filling the heart full of dreams of beautiful women bathing in streams of liquid light. Suddenly his eyes were dazzled by a great light, which disclosed, standing against the sides of a spacious cavern, men and women, clad on their right with sunbeams, and on their left with moonbeams. In the center were many maidens, dancing and tying each other with ribbons of fleecy clouds; these were clothed with the stolen rays of the stars and the spray of dashing waters. In the midst of the throng sat an old man, looking angrily at White-Corn.

While enjoying the scene, he was suddenly interrupted, and all of his happy thoughts spread like snow before the gale. The old man addressed him, saying that for many days he and his children had been watching in the east for the approach of him who was to break apart the rocks which held them from the sight of the sun and the beautiful world; for the approach of him who was to impart to them a new life, but who was to go through the ordeal of the Snake Order before being released or releasing others from the dark and lonely life. After many things had been told him, he was led by a snake up to the falling water; the snake then directed him to cast his clothing aside and bathe in it. After bathing, he was moving off from the water, but his foot was drawn back; then he noticed for the first time that all the others had a peculiar skin, like a snake's skin, and that he himself was being enveloped with a similar covering. He was then brought before the old man again, and told to get something to eat, and to choose a maiden for a sweetheart. He was unable to make a choice, and asked the old man to select one for him. The old man, reaching back, took hold of a cloudy substance, and began pulling, when there emerged from it a beautiful girl called "Bright Eyes," who was given to White-Corn for his wife. As directed, he followed her and got food. It is unknown how long he stayed in this house, but it was long enough for him to learn all the songs and ceremonials pertaining to the Snake Order.

One day, while all the people were present before the old man, White-Corn told them that he had been with them for a long while, and the time had now come for him to return to his own people; that his people were calling for him; that, while he was enjoying plenty, his brothers were doubtless suffering: hence he proposed to take his wife and start for his home. The people all laughed at him, but he said, "Never mind; the same god that brought me will show me the return path." All the inhabitants of the cave were sad except White-Corn and the old man, who were together oftener than formerly, and were in very secret confidences. One day (how they distinguished day from night is not told) White-Corn was seen to take a bunch of feathers from a long rope hanging from the ceiling. He tied the feathers to a short stick. From a peg in the wall he took a stick with two feathers fastened to it. He gave the bunch of feathers to his wife. He bade good-bye to all the people, and the old man took him by a secret path to the earth's surface. The old man, wishing White-Corn a speedy journey, returned to his cave. White-Corn asked his wife if she could tell him the direction in which his home lay; she said that when the sun came up she would be able to tell, as one of the Fits-ki, or rays, pointed directly to the home of his people. Next day, at sunrise, she pointed to a large mound, and said that from the top of it the mountains that were near his home could be seen. He ran to the top of this mound, so glad was he to get away from the constant glare of the magical light, and to think that in a few days he would again see his brothers and friends. They traveled fast for four days; on the fifth day the road led through such rough hills they were forced to turn toward the south. They found a well-traveled trail leading to water, around which were houses and places to keep sheep or horses—peculiar houses, too, almost round and very high, in which were found many strange vessels and other utensils made of clay and horn; also funnel-shaped baskets, designed to be carried on the back. They made but a short halt in these places, fearing that the people who built them might return and harm or kill them. So they kept going, until one morning, after they ascended a very high mountain, they saw the smoke of fires in the valley. Telling his wife to keep a little way behind, White-Corn went toward the fires, the first of which he reached at sunset. He found there his uncle and cousin, who had been searching for him, but, deeming him lost forever, were now on their return home. White-Corn told his adventures, and brought his wife to them. After a few day's travel they all reached home.

At this time there was a great drought prevailing, and it was observed that whenever Tcua-wuti (White-Corn's wife) came before the altar and sprinkled meal rain was sure to follow. So they called upon her husband to give them soup, whereby they, too, might invoke the rain-god of his wife's country. But she said No: but not until a son was born to her could the altar of her rain-god be raised in a strange land. After there had been a severe storm, it was observed that Tcua-wuti was with child, and this caused great rejoicing among the people, for they wished her to bear a boy who would become their rainchief. When the time came for her to bear her child, White-Corn went away with her to a high mesa on the west of the village. After an absence of seven days they returned to the village, bringing with them her offspring, consisting of five snakes. This enraged the people so that they would have killed them all, but an old man, who was standing by, said, "No, I will be their father; come and live with me." He took them to his home, and that night the people were startled by loud and strange cries coming from this old man's house; a great smoke issued from the doorway and other rents, where people on the outside could look in. No one but the old man, his wife, and one son, beside White-Corn, knew what took place in that house during the night, for the next day the old man went off to the valley. In three days, Tcua-wuti took her snake children and the old man, and went into the valley. In the afternoon the old man came back alone but Tcua-wuti has never been seen again.

Tlingit

Inhabitants of the southernmost portions of the coast and islands of Alaska and the westernmost tip of what is now British Columbia. The tribal name means "People." These narratives were recorded in English at Sitka and at Wrangell, Alaska, during the late winter of 1904. For materials on the rich artistic heritage and general culture of the Tlingit and the related tribes of the Pacific Northwest and Alaska see Polly and Leon Miller, *Lost Heritage of Alaska;* Frederica De Laguna, *The Story of a Tlingit Community;* and Philip Drucker, *Cultures of the North Pacific Coast.*

The Wolf-Chief's Son

Famine visited a certain town, and many people died of starvation. There was a young boy there who always went around with bow and arrows. One day, as he was hunting about, he came across a little animal that looked like a dog and put it under his blanket. He brought it to his mother, and his mother washed it for him. Then he took the red paint left by his dead uncles, spit upon the dog and threw paint on so that it would stick to its hair and face. When he took the dog into the woods, it would bring him all kinds of birds, such as grouse, which he carried home to his family. They cooked these in a basket pot. Afterward he brought the animal down, washed it, and put more paint upon its legs and head. This enabled him to trace it when he was out hunting.

One day after he had traced it for some distance, he found it had killed a small mountain sheep, and, when he came down, he gave it the fat part. With the meat so obtained he began to take good care of his mother and his friends. He had not yet found out whether the animal was really a dog.

From John R. Swanton, "Tlingit Myths and Texts," *Bureau of American Ethnology*, Bulletin 39 (Washington, 1909).

The next time they went hunting they came across a large flock of sheep, and he sent the dog right up to them. It killed all of them, and he cut the best one open for it. Then he took down the rest of the sheep and dressed them. What the animal was killing was keeping some of his friends alive.

One time the husband of a sister came to him and said, "I wish to borrow your animal. It is doing great things in this place." So he brought the little dog from the house he had made for it, painted its face and feet, and said to his brother-in-law, "When you kill the first one cut it open quickly and let him have it. That is the way I always do." Then this brother-in-law took up the little dog, and, when they came to a flock of sheep, it went straight among them, killing them and throwing them down one after another. But, after he had cut one open, he took out the entrails, threw them into the dog's face, and said, "Dogs always eat the insides of animals, not the good part." The dog, however, instead of eating it, ran straight up between the mountains, yelping.

Now when his brother-in-law brought the sheep down, the man asked him, "Where is the little dog?" And he said, "It ran away from me." That was the report he brought down. Then the owner of the dog called his sister to him and said, "Tell me truly what he did with the little dog. I did not want to let it go at first because I knew people would do that thing to it." His sister said, "He threw the entrails to it to eat. That is why it ran off."

Then the youth felt very sad on account of his little animal and prepared to follow it. His brother-in-law showed him the place between the mountains where the dog had gone up, and he went up in that direction until he came to its footprints and saw the red paint he had put upon it. This animal was really the wolf-chief's son who had been sent to help him, and, because the man put red upon its head and feet, a wolf can now be told by the red on its feet and around its mouth.

After he had followed the trail for a long distance he came to a lake with a long town on the opposite side. There he heard a great noise made by people playing. It was a very large lake, so he thought, "I wonder how I can get over there." Just then he saw smoke coming out from under his feet. Then a door swung open, and he was told to enter. An old woman lived there called Woman-always-wondering (Lūwat-uwadjī′gî-cānʌ′k!ᵘ), who said to him, "Grandchild, why are you here?" He answered, "I came across a young dog which helped me, but it is lost, and I come to find where it went." Then the woman answered, "Its people live right across there. It is a wolf-chief's son. That is its father's town over there where they are making a noise." So the old woman instructed him.

Then he wondered and said to himself, "How can I get across?" But the old woman spoke out, saying, "My little canoe is just below here." He said to himself, "It might turn over with me." Then the old woman answered, "Take it down. Before you get in shake it and it will become large." Then she continued: "Get inside of the boat and stretch yourself on the bottom, but do not paddle it. Instead wish continually to come in front of that place."

He did as she directed and landed upon the other side. Then he got out, made the canoe small and put it into his pocket, after which he went up among the boys who were playing about, and watched them. They were playing with a round, twisted thing called gîtcxʌnagā′t (rainbow). Then some one directed him to the wolf-chief's house at the farther end of the village. An evening fire, such as people used to make in olden times, was burning there, and, creeping in behind the other people, the man saw his little wolf playing about near it in front of his father.

Then the wolf-chief said, "There is some human being looking in here. Clear away from before his face." Upon this the little wolf ran right up to him, smelled him, and knew him at once. The wolf-chief said, "I feel well disposed toward you. I let my son live among you because your uncles and friends were starving, and now I am very much pleased that you have come here after him." By and by he said, " I think I will not let him go back with you, but I will do something else to help you." He was happy at the way the man had painted up his son. Now he did not appear like a wolf but like a human being. The chief said, "Take out the fish-hawk's quill that is hanging on the wall and give it to him in place of my son." Then he was instructed how to use it. "Whenever a bear meets you," he said, "hold the quill straight toward it and it will fly out of your hand." He also took out a thing that was tied up like a blanket and gave it to him, at the same time giving him instructions. "One side," he said, "is for sickness. If you put this on a sick person it will make him well. If anyone hates you, put the other side on him and it will kill him. After they have agreed to pay you for treating him put the other side on to cure him."

Then the chief said, "You see that thing that the boys are playing with? That belongs to me. Whenever one sees it in the evening it means bad weather; whenever one sees it in the morning it means good weather." So he spoke to him.

Then they put something else into his mouth and said to him, "Take this, for you have a long journey to make." He was gone up there probably two years, but he thought it was only two nights.

At the time when he came within sight of his town he met a bear. He held the quill out toward it as he had been instructed and suddenly let it go. It hit the bear in the heart. Still closer to his town he came upon a flock of sheep on the mountain, and sent his quill at them. When he reached them, he found all dead, and, after he had cut them all open, he found the quill stuck into the heart of the last. He took a little meat for his own use and covered up the rest.

Coming to the town, he found no one in it. All had been destroyed. Then he felt very sad, and, taking his blanket out, laid the side of it that would save people upon their bodies, and they all came to life. After that he asked all of them to go hunting with him, but he kept the quill hidden away so that they would not bother him as they had before. When they came to a big flock of mountain sheep, he let his quill go at them so quickly that they could not see it. Then he went up, looked the dead sheep over, and immediately cut out the quill. All his friends were surprised at what had happened. After they had gotten down, those who were not his close friends came to him and gave payment for the meat.

The people he restored to life after they had been dead for very many years had very deep set eyes and did not get well at once.

After that he went to a town where the people were all well

and killed some of them with his blanket. Then he went to the other people in that place and said, "How are your friends? Are they dead?" "Yes." "Well, I know a way of making them well." He went up to them again with his blanket and brought them back to life. They were perfectly well.

This man went around everywhere doing the same thing and became very famous. Whenever one was sick in any place they came after him and offered him a certain amount for his services, so that he became the richest man of his time.

The Woman Taken Away by the Frog People

There was a large town in the Yakutat country not very far back of which lay a big lake very full of frogs. In the middle of the lake was a swampy patch on which many frogs used to sit.

One day the town-chief's daughter talked badly to the frogs. She took one up and made fun of it, saying, "There are so many of these creatures, I wonder if they do things like human beings. I wonder if men and women cohabit among them."

When she went out of doors that night, a young man came to her and said, "May I marry you?" She had rejected very many men, but she wanted to marry this one right away. Pointing toward the lake he said, "My father's house is right up here," and the girl replied, "How fine it looks!" When they went up to it, it seemed as though a door was opened for them, but in reality the edge of the lake had been raised. They walked under. So many young people were there that she did not think of home again.

Meanwhile her friends missed her and hunted for her everywhere. Finally they gave her up, and her father had the drums beaten for a death feast. They cut their hair and blackened their faces.

Next spring a man who was about to go hunting came to the lake to bathe himself with urine. When he was done, he threw the urine among a number of frogs sitting there and they jumped into the water. When he was bathing next day he saw all the frogs sitting together in the middle of the lake with the missing woman among them. He dressed as quickly as possible, ran home to the girl's father and said, "I saw your daughter sitting in the middle of the pond in company with a lot of frogs." So her father and mother went up that evening with a number of other people, saw, and recognized her.

After that they took all kinds of things to make the frog tribe feel good so that they would let the woman return to her parents, but in vain. By and by her father determined upon a plan and called all of his friends together. Then he told them to dig trenches out from the lake in order to drain it. From the lake the frog chief could see how the people had determined, and he told his tribe all about it. The frog people call the mud around a lake their laid-up food.

After the people had worked away for some time, the trench was completed and the lake began draining away fast. The frogs asked the woman to tell her people to have pity on them and not destroy all, but the people killed none because they wanted only the girl. Then the water flowed out, carrying numbers of frogs which scattered in every direction. All the frog tribe then talked poorly about themselves, and the frog chief, who had talked of letting her go before, now had her dressed up and their own odor, which they called "sweet perfumery," was put upon her. After a while she came down the trench half out of water with her frog husband beside her. They pulled her out and let the frog go.

When anyone spoke to this woman, she made a popping noise "Hu," such as a frog makes, but after some time she came to her senses. She explained, "It was the Kîkca′ (i.e., Kîksa′dî women) that floated down with me," meaning that all the frog women and men had drifted away. The woman could not eat at all, though they tried everything. After a while they hung her over a pole, and the black mud she had eaten when she was among the frogs came out of her, but, as soon as it was all out, she died. Because this woman was taken away by the frog tribe at that place, the frogs there can understand human beings very well when they talk to them. It was a Kîksa′dî woman who was taken off by the frogs, and so those people can almost understand them. They also have songs from the frogs, frog personal names, and the frog emblem. All the people know about them.

Little Felon

A certain man had a felon (*kwêq*) on his finger and suffered terribly, so that he could get no sleep. He did not know what to do for it. One day somebody said to him, "Hold it under the smoke hole of the house and get some one to poke it with something very sharp through the smoke hole. You will find that it will get well." He did so, and the two eyes of the felon came right out. Then he wrapped them up and put them away. Late in the evening he looked at it and saw a little man there about an inch long. It was the disease from his finger. He took very good care of this little man and he grew rapidly, soon becoming large enough to run about. He called the little man Little Felon (Kwêqk!ᵘ).

Little Felon was a very industrious little fellow, always at work, and he knew how to carve, make canoes, paint, and do other similar things. When he was working his master could not keep from working himself. He simply had to work. They thought it was because he had come from the hand. Little Felon was also a good shot with bow and arrows, and he was a very fast runner, running races with all the different animals. Finally he started to run a race with the heron, and everybody said the heron would prove too much for him. They raced all the way round Prince of Wales island, and, when they were through, Little Felon said to the heron, "I have been way back among the mountains of this island, and there are thirty-three lakes." The heron answered, "I have been all along the creeks, and there are fifty creeks."

By and by a youth said to Little Felon, "There is a girl living with a certain old woman. She is a very pretty girl and wants to marry, but she hasn't seen anybody she likes. Her grandmother has the dried skin of an animal and she has been making all the young fellows guess the name of it. Those that guess wrong are put to death. You ought to try for her." But Little Felon said to the boy, "I don't care to marry, and I don't want to guess, because I know. You tell her that it is the skin of a louse. It was crawling upon the woman, and she put it into a box and fed it until it grew large. Then she killed and skinned it. You will get her if you tell her. But be careful. That old woman knows a lot about medicines. When you are going toward her, go with the wind. Don't let the wind come from her. Don't go toward her when the south wind is blowing. Go toward her when the north wind is blowing. Nobody goes directly to her. People talk to her from quite a distance. A person goes to her house only to be put to death. Those persons who guess stand a great way off to do it. When they don't guess right they go to that house and are put to death. She has a large square dish in which she cooks their bodies."

After that the boy went toward the old woman's camp and remained at some distance from her for a very long time, for the south wind was blowing continually. She seemed to know that he was there, and said to her granddaughter, "There is a fellow coming who has been around here for a very long time. He is the one who is going to marry you." The little man had said to the youth he was helping, "Don't tell about me. That old woman has all kinds of dangerous things with which to kill people."

As soon as the north wind began to blow, Little Felon told him to go on, so he approached the old woman unnoticed and stood looking at her for a long time. Finally she looked up, saw him, and said, "Oh! my grandson, from how far away have you come?" He told her, and she invited him in to have something to eat. She gave him all kinds of food. Then, when they were through, she showed him the skin and said, "What kind of skin is this?" He answered, "That is a louse skin, grandma." She looked at him then for some time without speaking. Finally she said, "Where are you wise from, from your father?" "Oh!" he said, "from all around." Then she said "All right, you can marry my granddaughter. But do you see that place over there? A very large devilfish lives there. I want you to kill it."

The youth went back to Little Felon and told him what she had said. "Oh!" he answered, "there is a monster there. That is the way she gets rid of boys, is it " So Little Felon made a hook, went to the place where the devilfish lived, made it small, and pulled it right out. He put the stick over his companion's shoulder and said to him, "Carry it this way." The youth did so and, coming to the old woman's house, he said, "Is this the devilfish you were talking about?" He threw it down, and it grew until it became a monster again that filled the entire house. The old woman felt very badly, and said, "Take it out of this house and lay it down outside." He did so, and the moment he picked it up it grew small again.

Then the old woman said, "Do you see that cliff that goes right down into the water? A monster rat lives there. If you kill it, you shall have my granddaughter." The youth went away again and told Little Felon about it, who said, "I told you so. I knew that she would give you a lot of things to do." So they got their bows and arrows ready, went to the hole of the monster, and looked in. It was asleep. They began shooting it. They blinded it first by shooting into its eyes and then they shot it through the heart. They ran in to it to school, but, as soon as they had wounded it fatally, they rushed out again, and it followed them. It ran right into the ocean, and they could hear it splashing the water about it with its tail. It sounded like thunder. Finally the rat died and drifted ashore.

Then Little Felon told the young man to take it up and carry it to the old woman, and, as soon as he had grasped it, it was very small and light. He carried it in to her and said, "Is this the rat you were talking about?" Then he threw it down, and it filled the house. So she said, "Take it up and put it outside."

Now the old woman spoke again. "Way out there in the middle of the ocean is a sculpin. Go out and fish for it, and you shall get my granddaughter." So he and Little Felon went out there and caught the sculpin, which Little Felon made very small. He threw it into the bottom of the canoe and left it there. When they reached land the youth took it up to the old woman and threw it down inside. Lo! it was an awful monster with great spines.

Now the old woman did not know what to do. She thought, "What kind of boy is this?" Then she said, "Do you see that point? A very large crab lives out there. Go and kill it." When they got out there they saw the crab floating about on its back. It looked very dangerous. Little Felon, however, told the crab to get small, and it did so. He killed it, put it into the canoe, and carried it to the old woman, who exclaimed, "Oh! he has killed everything that belongs to me."

Then the old woman said, "Go far out to sea beyond the

place where you got that sculpin. I dropped my bracelet over-board there. Go and get it." So he and Little Felon set out. But first they dug a quantity of clams and removed the shells. They took these out to that place and threw them around in the water, when all kinds of fish began to come up. Then Little Felon saw a dogfish coming up and said to it, "A bracelet was lost over there. Go and get it for me." He did so, and the youth took it to the old woman.

Then the old woman was very much surprised and said, "Well! that is the last." So she said to her granddaughter, "Come out. Here is your husband. You must have respect for him always." So he married her. After that he went over to Little Felon and asked how much he owed him. "You don't owe me anything" said Little Felon. "You remember that at the time I was suffering so badly you pricked me through the smoke hole." And the youth answered, "Oh! yes, this is the fellow." Little Felon (Kwêqk!ⁿ) is a slender fish that swims close to the beach.

After that the young man and his wife always traveled about together, for he thought a great deal of her. By and by, how-ever, they had a quarrel and he was cruel to her. So she went away and sat down on a point, after which she disappeared and he did not know what had happened to her. He went out on the point and hunted everywhere. He is a lonely beach snipe, called ayʌhīyiya', which is often seen hunting about on the points today, and when they see him the Tlingit say, "There he is looking for his wife."

The Image That Came to Life

A young chief on the Queen Charlotte Islands married, and soon afterward his wife fell ill. Then he sent around everywhere for the very best shamans. If there were a very fine shaman at a certain village he would send a canoe there to bring him. None of them could help her, however, and after she had been sick for a very long time she died.

Now the young chief felt very badly over the loss of his wife. He went from place to place after the best carvers in order to have them carve an image of his wife, but no one could make anything to look like her. All this time there was a carver in his own village who could carve much better than all the others. This man met him one day and said, "You are going from village to village to have wood carved like your wife's face, and you can not find anyone to do it, can you? I have seen your wife a great deal walking along with you. I have never studied her face with the idea that you might want someone to carve it, but I am going to try if you will allow me."

Then the carver went after a piece of red cedar and began working upon it. When he was through, he went to the young chief and said, "Now you can come along and look at it." He had dressed it just as he used to see the young woman dressed. So the chief went with him, and, when he got inside, he saw his dead wife sitting there just as she used to look. This made him very happy, and he took it home. Then he asked the carver, "What do I owe you for making this?" and he replied, "Do as you please about it." The carver had felt sorry to see how this chief was mourning for his wife, so he said, "It is because I felt badly for you that I made that. So don't pay me too much for it." He paid the carver very well, however, both in slaves and in goods.

Now the chief dressed this image in his wife's clothes and her marten-skin robe. He felt that his wife had come back to him and treated the image just like her. One day, while he sat mourning very close to the image, he felt it move. His wife had also been very fond of him. At first he thought that the movement was only his imagination, yet he examined it every day, for he thought that at some time it would come to life. When he ate he always had the image close to him.

After a while the whole village learned that he had this image and all came in to see it. Many could not believe that it was not the woman herself until they had examined it closely.

One day, after the chief had had it for a long, long time, he examined the body and found it just like that of a human being. Still, although it was alive, it could not move or speak. Some time later, however, the image gave forth a sound from its chest like that of crackling wood, and the man knew that it was ill.

When he had someone move it away from the place where it had been sitting they found a small red-cedar tree growing there on top of the flooring. They left it until it grew to be very large, and it is because of this that cedars on the Queen Charlotte Islands are so good. When people up this way look for red cedars and find a good one they say, "This looks like the baby of the chief's wife."

Every day the image of the young woman grew more like a human being, and, when they heard the story, people from villages far and near came in to look at it and at the young cedar tree growing there, at which they were very much astonished. The woman moved around very little and never got to talk, but her husband dreamed what she wanted to tell him. It was through his dreams that he knew she was talking to him.

Nez Perce

There could be few more appropriate conclusions to this section than traditions from the Nez Perce. Because of the oratorical genius of one of its chiefs, Joseph, and the military acumen of several of its war leaders during a heroic but doomed war in 1877, this tribe has come to symbolize the bravery, dignity, and ultimate futility of all North American Indian resistance. The selections assembled here are intended to provide a synoptic view of the history of this tribe from prehuman mythic times, to the origins of the Nez Perce, to the coming of the white man, the inevitable advent of the missionaries, and to the final battle against the United States Army for tribal existence. This is the Nez Perce story, but in a large sense it is the story of all the other tribes whose traditions appear herein.

The Animals Argue about the Length of Day and Night

1. There were people, a great many people. There was no night, no day. It was a problem, should there be named night and day. (2) That is what all the people that were in the land were talking about, they quarreled about it among one another in the land. (3) That is how they were going around, those who were Grizzly, Bear, Cougar, Wolf, Badger, Fisher, Coyote, and all, they were the ones who gathered together. (4) "Now there shall be day, and night. But one night is too long." They all said, "What now supposing it should be one day, and only one night, in darkness?"

2. This is how Bear spoke then. "There shall be five days, and there shall be one darkness. On the fifth day it shall dawn."

From *Hear Me, My Chiefs* by L. V. McWhorter, The Caxton Printers, Ltd.; and *Northwest Sahaptin Texts* by Melville Jacobs (Columbia University Contributions in Anthropology, v. xix, Part 1 [1934]). Reprinted by permission of Columbia University Press.

(2) Grizzly spoke, the older brother of Bear. He said, "It shall be ten years. For ten years there shall be only one darkness, one night." (3) That is how Grizzly spoke. Rattlesnake said, "It shall be five years, and then there shall be only one darkness for five years." (4) His younger brother, named Bull Snake, said, "There shall be three years, one darkness during three years, and then it shall dawn." (5) And that is what the brothers Grizzly and Bear said, and a great many of Rattler's people also.

3. In the very same manner big Toad was there, with a large number of his younger brothers. (2) They said, "By no means shall it be like that, so long a time of years, and then it will be only one darkness. The people (the Indians) coming are already near, it shall never be like that. Rather shall there be only one day, and also only one night." That is what he (Toad) said. (3) Many of them argued about it. Then Frog, the younger brother of big Toad, said, "There shall be only one day, and one night. (Then) it shall dawn."

4. Grizzly became angry, he was a dangerous (powerful) being in this land, all of them feared him. (2) Similarly, Rattler was a dangerous being too, and all of them in the land feared him. (3) They were the ones (Grizzly and Rattler) who became angry. "It shall not be like that!" (4) Those who were also dangerous beings argued about it. "We will argue it out. When darkness comes, then we will argue. Whoever will be so strong (as to talk on) until it dawns, will win. That is how it shall be indeed. (5) The people coming are already near. Never shall there be night for ten years, and only one darkness, never for five years, never for three years." That is what they said.

5. They argued, and when darkness came they talked on. (2) He (Grizzly) said, "Ten years, one darkness." (3) Said Frog, "Only one darkness, only one darkness." Grizzly, "Ten years, ten years." "Only one darkness."

6. When the sun was rising, Grizzly was tired, he was worn out. (2) Frog had the better of him. When the sun rose, Frog had beaten him. Grizzly gave up, he quit. (3) He (Frog) won it from him for good. From then until now there is only one day, and only one darkness. That is how they argued.

Origins of the Nez Perce

1

On the North Fork [of the Clearwater] River a few miles below Bungalow Ranger Station, Idaho, the footprints of a human being are plainly seen, sunken into the basaltic rock formation. The tracks are those of a man running upstream as if in pursuit of something, probably game.

These footprints were made in a soft surface. How long since the change into hard basalt took place nobody knows. That man was older than the stone itself.

On the Snake River there are stony tracks of a woman and child. Also tracks at a bathing place near Fir Bluff, today a solid rock formation. I was told that there is a single human track on a loose rock above Wawawai lower down the Snake River. Of course, all these we naturally regard as of Nez Perce origin.

An old story handed down through many generations tells that there was a flood in earlier days and that Yamustus [Steptoe Butte] stood above the sea and many Indians were there saved from drowning. This probably did occur thousands of years ago for sea deposits are found in many high places.

2

There are two places up Salmon River. Only two spots where the people lived. None were here on the Clearwater; none on Lapwai or Snake rivers; Kakayohneme Creek is one place. The other is about fifteen miles above the mouth of Little Salmon River. It is called Tannish [Cut-Out Trail]. This most wonderful passage among cliffs along Salmon River is not the work of man's hand. It is natural all through. Just as it was before the human race existed on this continent, I suppose. It was there before the white men swarmed over the mountain, taking from us our homes. But no one knows how many centuries back was the beginning.

The first generations of Nez Perces grew up at those two places I have named. I do not know how many snows back of that time. The buffalo was hunted on the head of the Salmon. The people would go there for meat and hides during the

summer moons. Next few snows they go a little farther east.
Following snows they go still farther east, and to the north.
After a time they reach the Yellowstone River. There they
hunt, for the buffaloes are many. Finally they come to [now]
Helena, Montana. There they find people. This tribe proves an
enemy to the Nez Perces. After this they fight. The Bannocks,
the Blackfeet, the Crows, the Cheyennes, the Sioux [Assini-
boins]. All these tribes living in that country became enemies
of the Nez Perces.

3

No Indian knows how or when our people first reached the
Yellowstone River. None know when the first Blackfeet Indians
were met. But Blackfeet is not their proper name, as sign language, interpreted by Nez Perces, denotes. In early days, when
meeting different tribes, in talking by signs at a distance telling
each other to what tribe they belonged, the Blackfeet always
pointed to their leg below their knee, or between the knee and
the foot. Their proper name, therefore, is Blacklegs. These
Indians had another sign name, which is a forward move of the
closed hand above the ear. Their sign for the Nez Perces, as
they knew them, was rubbing the thumb and forefinger together in a peculiar quivering motion, denoting a copper-colored
stain or paint used in decorating buckskin.

But the Nez Perce name for these raiders was Iskoikenic
[Schemers] ! Not only were they enemies of the Nez Perces, but
other tribes were bothered by them. They were the first tribe
to obtain guns from the French, which gave them great advantage in war. They slew many Indians in attacking camps and
villages. They went in large war parties, even stealing horses in
midwinter. They traveled as far as Wyoming and South Dakota
on foot. The Nez Perces had more fights with the Blood and
Piegan Blacklegs than with any other tribe. They would never
keep peace. It was broken by them on several occasions. Only
one minor band of the Blacklegs was friendly to the Nez Perces.
Its members were called the "Small Blankets." All of the same
tribe, they lived in widely scattered districts, some of them
in Canada.

A Legendary Hero Meets the White Man

Red Grizzly Bear was a chief famous among the tribes. His bravery as a warrior was attested by the eighty wounds he carried, received in battles. From these scars, in later years, he was known as Many Wounds. He knew and took part in all the wars of his day. Always a leader, when foraying he went ahead of his band; no one ever traveled in front of him.

Whether night or day, on foot or on horseback (I cannot explain the mystery) some kind of foresight was with him. Even if an enemy were at a distance and invisible, Many Wounds would drop into a trance of prophecy, and while thus sleeping he beheld all enemies passing before him. Everything pertaining to the enemies: the kind to be met, whether the meeting would be that same sun or the next, the number of scalps that would be taken and the kind of horses they would secure. This happened a number of times. Of most wonderful strength, he used principally his right hand and arm in battle. He was known everywhere west of the great mountains [Rockies] even to the big waters [Pacific].

Chief Red Bear first learned of white people through a girl of his band living on Tamonmo. When small she was stolen by the Blacklegs in the buffalo country, who sold her to some tribe farther toward the sunrise. In time she was bought by white people, probably in Canada, where she was well treated. It is a long story; how in time, carrying her little baby, she ran away and after several moons reached the friendly Selish, who cared for her and brought her in a dying condition to her own people at White Bird. Her baby had died on the way. She was called Watkuweis [Returned from a Faraway Country].

She told of the white people, how good they had been to her, and how well she liked them. When the first two white men, Lewis and Clark with their followers, came, Watkuweis said to her people, "These are the people who helped me! Do them no hurt!"

This was why the strange people had been received in friendship. There had been a prophecy about Red Bear and a new people, which was thus fulfilled in 1805. He met the strangers. They first have a smoke. If no smoke, then they must fight. Red

Bear made presents of dressed buckskins, and they gave him
beads and a few other articles. They afterward found the white
man's gifts to be cheap.

The canoes made by Lewis and Clark to descend the Snake
and Columbia rivers were made from five yellow pine trees
given them for the purpose by Chief Walammottinin [Hair or
Forelock Bunched and Tied]. The explorers first met him when
fishing in the Kooskooskie Smaller River, now the Clearwater.
It was in this chieftain's care that they left their horses and
cached goods, all of which they found in the best of condition
upon their return the following year.

After visiting the explorers, Red Bear returned to his home
near the mouth of White Bird Creek, Salmon River. When he
died, he left good council, good instructions for his people. The
whites owe honor to his memory.

My father, Chief Black Eagle, was the son of Chief Red
Bear, Sr., who met Lewis and Clark. I am his grandson. I have
seen one hundred and four snows [1926].

It was during the days of youthful training and development
that Red Bear went on foot to Slate Creek to look for flint
arrowheads where there had been fighting. It was morning and
he stayed until late evening. Starting for home he had gone a
good distance when it grew dark. He lay down by the trail and
slept. In a dream he beheld a great, bloodstained grizzly bear
approaching. Awakening, he sprang to his feet, but no bear
was to be seen. Silently he resumed his buffalo robe and dozed
off, only to be aroused a second time by the same fearful vision,
which vanished as he leaped erect. He again lay down and as he
drowsed the monster bear appeared for the third time. This
time the boy did not awaken entirely, and a voice spoke to him:

"Do not be afraid. You see my body. Blood is all over it.
When you become a man, when you go to war and do fighting,
you shall receive many wounds. Wounds shall cover your body.
Blood like this from my body will course down your limbs.
But you will not die. After these wars, and fights, because of
your wounds and bloodstains people will call you Hohots
Ilppilp [Red Grizzly Bear]."

When this boy had grown to young manhood, and had
received arrow and spear wounds in battle, he told his father

and the people about seeing the blood-reddened grizzly bear, and what it had said to him. From that time he was known as Red Bear, and was made a chief. He was a strong brave warrior.

After taking his name the new chief never used a gun in battle. There were only a few fire-rock [flint-lock] guns, and ammunition was scarce. He had a club made from the hard heavy syringa found growing along the canyon streams. It was nearly arm's length, and entirely unlike the stub-handled, stone-headed war club of the foot warriors. With this tied to his wrist by a thong loop, he would rush into battle. The Bannocks all learned to know and fear him.

At one time when going up Little Salmon, at a place now called Riggins, he discovered a war band of Snake or Bannock Indians coming toward him on the trail. There was a small creek with large rocks intervening. He hid his gun and secreting himself, he waited the advance of the hated enemy. They were out for fighting or stealing horses. When they drew near, Red Bear sprang from hiding and downed the foremost warrior before his presence was fully known. In the confusion he killed others of the startled foe, who, recognizing their unconquerable enemy, swam the Little Salmon to safety.

Advent of the Missionaries

"Injuns sittin' on rocks all around. Injuns sittin' on ground inside rock circle. Lots Injuns! Preacherman Spalding stand about here. Maybe on platform and talk. Spalding call to Injuns. Look up. See Jesus. See Jesus up there!

"One hand pointin' Injuns to Jesus; other hand stealin' Injuns' land! That religion not good for Injun!"

I remember very well when the Spaldings came to the Clearwater. The missionaries brought with them a Good Book which told our people how to live and what to believe, that they might reach the land of a better life after death. A Book that told them what to believe so as to escape the Fire Land of the hereafter. A Book that told all this to the Nez Perces. Changing their lives to a better way of living; a better spirit life.

But the missionary had something behind him which came

with him to the Nez Perces. Behind him was the whisky bottle along with his Good Book. We know what that bottle has done. It would have been better had the Good Book and the whisky bottle been kept from the Nez Perces.

General O. O. Howard Recalls the Fateful Council That Precipitated the Nez Perce War

Too-hul-hul-sote, the cross-grained growler, was again designated as the speaker, and he took up his parable. He was, if possible, crosser and more impudent in his abruptness of manner than before. He had the usual long preliminary discussion about the earth being his mother, that she should not be disturbed by hoe or plow, that men should subsist on what grows of itself, etc. He repeated his ideas concerning "chieftainship," chieftainship of the earth. Chieftainship cannot be sold, cannot be given away. Mr. Monteith and General Howard, he said, must speak the truth about the chieftainship of the earth.

He was answered, "We do not want to interfere with your religion, but you must talk about practicable things. Twenty times over you repeat that the earth is your mother, and about chieftainship of the earth. Let us hear it no more, but come to the business at once."

Chief Joseph's Surrender Speech

"Tell General Howard I know his heart. What he told me before I have in my heart. I am tired of fighting. Our chiefs are killed. Looking Glass is dead. The old men are all killed. It is the young men who say yes or no. He who led the young men is dead. It is cold and we have no blankets. The little children are freezing to death. My people, some of them, have run away to the hills, and have no blankets, no food; no one knows where they are, perhaps freezing to death. I want time to look for my children and see how many of them I can find. Maybe I shall find them among the dead. Hear me, my chiefs. I am tired: my heart is sick and sad. From where the sun now stands, I will fight no more."

II
POETRY
AND ORATORY

I have grouped here two somewhat dissimilar kinds of material, but I have done so with a purpose which was to show how inextricably rooted in *things* Indian thought was, and yet how just this very grounding gave rise to magnificent flights of imagination like birds in liquid loops over a particular landscape. Paul Radin speaks of this marked psychic dualism of the American Indian in *Primitive Man as Philosopher:* on the one hand a very practical realist and startlingly aware of the physical structure of his world, and on the other an abstracter, capable of the furthest ranges of metaphysical departure. Nowhere is this mental tendency more obvious than in these samples of poetry, all of which seem to spring from the earth itself and stretch to the mountains, the sky, and beyond.

The Chippewa (Ojibwa) song of the deer will undoubtedly strike many readers as quintessentially modern with its anticipation of Gertrude Stein in the final line, its imagistic thingness/ineffability. In fact, readers of modern poetry should be getting this odd and ahistorical sense throughout these selections. It is yet another example of how ignorance of one set of traditions (here that of the Indian) leads to extravagant and partially unfounded claims for another (that tradition of modernism founded on Stein and Ezra Pound). It is one of the several special burdens of our time that we must continually discover that many of our "firsts" are not even "seconds" or "thirds," all of which necessitates a rewriting of cultural history and a reshaping of the white Western psyche. Perhaps eventually we will achieve a level of cultural sophistication that permits us to value other and older traditions for what they are while at the same time that we value ours for what they are; at this point it seems necessary to many to denigrate the modernists in order to uphold the Indian.

The speeches are another matter, though, as I say, their metaphors derive from the same mental tradition. These are speeches made to white men, and because they are, they not only function here to show that the Indian was a gifted, often brilliant language craftsman, but they also serve as a bridge to the following section, Culture Contact.

Every white American knows that one part of the *old* Indian stereotype was that he was a grunting, monosyllabic moron. Here again it is necessary to find the buried bit of truth in this: fumbling for expression in an alien tongue he had never been taught, the Indian often appeared to be precisely what his conquerors claimed. But speaking in his own languages he appears altogether different— a speaker whose power must often have secretly shamed those who had to speak against him in formal debates.

There are those who have challenged the authenticity of many of these Indian speeches, and this is only right: what, after all, is our warrant for believing in the absolute accuracy of, say, the Moravian missionary's translation of the speech of the Delaware chief in 1787? Who can say what the precise circumstances of recording were for the celebrated speeches of Logan and Chief Joseph? These are hard and serious questions, and yet I think we can to a certain extent justify the attribution of these speeches to the Indian rather than to white writers with sentimental and poetic bents.

All of these deliveries came out of formal contacts between reds and whites, situations which always called for considerable declaiming on the part of the Indian. Tribal cultures were highly ceremonial and, while there was much in Indian life that was purely spontaneous, there was much more that was strictly governed by ritual and tradition. This often irritated the men of Western civilization, where, by the end of the sixteenth-century at least, ceremony and traditional ways of living had given way to autonomic, free-style individualism: things were done on individual authority, and they were done quickly. Not so within the tribes and least of all on such formal occasions as the meeting of nations. To the often expressible exasperation of the whites, Indian spokesmen consumed whole days reciting tribal history, the history of the whites on this continent, the history of contacts between whites and a particular tribe, and speculations about the future of the world, all or most of which was recorded by official stenographers/interpreters. Indeed, it is a revealing experience to read through the transcripts of treaty meetings as these exist on government microfilms in Washington. The earliest transcripts are scrupulous in the matter of recording the remarks of the Indian speakers, but gradually that culturally induced impatience of which I speak causes the recorder to set down only the principal deliveries and dismiss the others with some such gloss as, "Then six other headmen came forward and gave their speeches." On the basis of my experience with these transcripts I am prepared to vouch for the basic, essential authenticity of speeches attributed to Indian orators herein. In so doing I do not discount the possibility that some fifth-rate white poets could ape the style of Indian orators, though to look at some of their nineteenth-century attempts one must doubt that few outside the poets themselves were fooled. Nor do I mean to brush aside the far likelier possibility that words and phrases may have been occasionally mistranslated, lost, substituted, etc. What I do claim is that both the style and content of these speeches is wholly consistent and that they have the unmistakable resonances of that formal gravity and deep conviction that so marked the behavior of the Indian on such occasions.

POEMS AND SONGS

This Newly Created World

WINNEBAGO

> Pleasant it looked,
> this newly created world.
> Along the entire length and breadth
> of the earth, our grandmother,
> extended the green reflection
> of her covering
> and the escaping odors
> were pleasant to inhale.

Emergence Song

PIMA

Together we emerge with our rattles;
Together we emerge with our rattles,
   Bright-hued feathers in our headdresses.

With our nyñnyïrsa we went down;
With our nyñnyïrsa we went down,
   Wearing Yoku feathers in our headdresses.

From: *In the Trail of the Wind* by John Bierhorst. Copyright © 1971 by John Bierhorst. Reprinted with the permission of Farrar, Straus & Giroux, Inc.

The Magic World, edited by William Brandon, Museum of the American Indian, Heye Foundation.

This is the White Land; we arrive singing,
    Headdresses waving in the breeze.
We have come! We have come!
    The land trembles with our dancing and singing.

On these black mountains all are singing,
    Headdresses waving, headdresses waving.
We all rejoice! We all rejoice!
    Singing, dancing, the mountains trembling.

War Song

SIOUX

        clear the way
        in a sacred manner
        I come
        the earth
        is mine

Two Fragments

DAKOTA

You cannot harm me,
    you cannot harm
        one who has dreamed a dream like mine

OJIBWA

The bush is sitting under a tree and
singing

Song

OJIBWA

        Whence does he spring,
        the deer?
        Whence docs he spring,
        the deer, the deer, the deer?

Magic Formula to Make an Enemy Peaceful

NAVAHO

Put your feet down with pollen.
Put your hands down with pollen.
Put your head down with pollen.
Then your feet are pollen;
Your hands are pollen;
Your body is pollen;
Your mind is pollen;
Your voice is pollen.
The trail is beautiful.
Be still.

Spring Song

OJIBWA

as my eyes
    look over the prairie
        I feel the summer in the spring

Offering

ZUNI

That our earth mother may wrap herself
In a fourfold robe of white meal;
That she may be covered with frost flowers;
That yonder on all the mossy mountains
The forests may huddle together with the cold;
That their arms may be broken by the snow,
In order that the land may be thus,
I have made my prayer sticks into living beings.

Is This Real

PAWNEE

Let us see, is this real,
Let us see, is this real,
This life I am living?
You, Gods, who dwell everywhere,
Let us see, is this real,
This life I am living?

ORATORY

Powhatan

POWHATAN

*Powhatan's Algonquian Confederacy covered tidewater
Virginia from the Potomac south to Albemarle Sound.
John Smith reported his 1609 speech at Werowocomico
(Gloucester County).*

Why will you take by force what you may obtain by love?
Why will you destroy us who supply you with food? What can
you get by war? ... We are unarmed, and willing to give you
what you ask, if you come in a friendly manner....

I am not so simple as not to know it is better to eat good
meat, sleep comfortably, live quietly with my women and
children, laugh and be merry with the English, and being their
friend, trade for their copper and hatchets, than to run away
from them....

Take away your guns and swords, the cause of all our jealousy, or you may die in the same manner.

From Helen Hunt Jackson, *A Century of Dishonor* (New York, 1881),
pp. 32-33; Virginia I. Armstrong, compiler, *I Have Spoken: American;
History Through the Voices of the Indians*, 1971, The Swallow Press,
Chicago; and T. C. McLuhan, *Touch the Earth* (New York, 1971),
pp. 90, 136.

Canassatego

IROQUOIS

Canassatego, in a 1742 treaty negotiation, or renewal, had an exchange with the white leader which poignantly illustrates the basic clash of values, the ironies, and the rationalizations which would plague Indian-white relations while the Earth endureth.

Canassatego: We received from the Proprietors Yesterday, some Goods in consideration of our Release of the Lands on the West-side of Sasquehannah. It is true, we have the full Quantity according to Agreement; but if the Proprietor had been here himself, we think, in Regard of our Numbers and Poverty, he would have made an Addition to them. If the Goods were only to be divided amongst the Indians present, a single Person would have but a small Portion; but if you consider what Numbers are left behind, equally entitled with us to a Share, there will be extremely little. We therefore desire, if you have the Keys of the Proprietor's Chest, you will open it, and take out a little more for us.

We know our Lands are now become more valuable: The white People think we do not know their Value; but we are sensible that the Land is everlasting, and the few Goods we receive for it are soon worn out and gone. . . . Besides, we are not well used with respect to the Lands still unsold by us. Your People daily settle on these Lands, and spoil our Hunting. We must insist on your removing them. . . .

It is customary with us to make a Present of Skins, whenever we renew our Treaties. We are ashamed to offer our Brethren so few, but your Horses and Cows have eaten the Grass our Deer used to feed on. This has made them scarce, and will, we hope, plead in Excuse for our not bringing a larger Quantity. If we could have spared more, we would have given more; but we are really poor; and desire you'll not consider the Quantity, but few as they are, accept them in Testimony of our Regard.

Dragging Canoe

CHEROKEE

Dragging Canoe, Cherokee chief and son of the famous Attakullakulla (the Little Carpenter), was chagrined to learn that his aged father would consider selling land, at The Treaty of Fort Stanwix councils, 1768.

Where now are our grandfathers, the Delawares? We had hoped the white man would not be willing to travel beyond the mountains; now that hope is gone. They have passed the mountains, and have settled on Cherokee lands.... Finally, the whole country, which the Cherokees and their fathers have so long occupied, will be demanded, and the remnant of the *Ani-Yunwiya*, "The Real People," once so great and formidable, will be obliged to seek refuge in some distant wilderness... until they again behold the advancing banners of the same greedy host.... Such treaties may be all right for men who are too old to hunt or fight. As for me, I have my young warriors about me. We will have our lands. *A-Wanin-ki*. I have spoken.

Pachgantschilias

DELAWARE

Pachgantschilias, a Delaware chief, delivered this ringing denunciation of the white man in the hearing of John G. Heckewelder (a Moravian missionary to the Indians) in 1787.

I admit that there are good white men, but they bear no proportion to the bad; the bad must be the strongest, for they rule.

They do what they please. They enslave those who are not of their color, although created by the same Great Spirit who created them. They would make slaves of us if they could; but as they cannot do it, they kill us. There is no faith to be placed in their words. They are not like the Indians, who are only enemies while at war, and are friends in peace. They will say to an Indian, "My friend; my brother!" They will take him by the hand, and, at the same moment, destroy him. And so you [he was addressing himself to the Christian Indians at Gnadenhütten, Pennsylvania] will also be treated by them before long. Remember that this day I have warned you to beware of such friends as these. I know the Long-knives. They are not to be trusted.

Tecumseh

SHAWNEE

Tecumseh in 1810 faced Governor W. H. Harrison to bitterly protest the land sales of 1805-1806. He said they were effected by the use of strong liquor, a breach of the Treaty of Greenville. He refused to enter the Governor's mansion.

Houses are built for you to hold councils in; Indians hold theirs in the open air. I am a Shawnee. My forefathers were warriors. Their son is a warrior. From them I take my only existence. From my tribe I take nothing. I have made myself what I am. And I would that I could make the red people as great as the conceptions of my own mind, when I think of the Great Spirit that rules over us all. . . . I would not then come to Governor Harrison to ask him to tear up the treaty. But I would say to him, "Brother, you have the liberty to return to your own country."

You wish to prevent the Indians from doing as we wish them, to unite and let them consider their lands as the common property of the whole. You take the tribes aside and advise them not to come into this measure. . ... You want by your distinctions of Indian tribes, in allotting to each a particular, to make them war with each other. You never see an Indian endeavor to make the white people do this. You are continually driving the red people, when at last you will drive them onto the great lake, where they can neither stand nor work.

Since my residence at Tippecanoe, we have endeavored to level all distinctions, to destroy village chiefs, by whom all mischiefs are done. It is they who sell the land to the Americans. Brother, this land that was sold, and the goods that was given for it, was only done by a few. . . . In the future we are prepared to punish those who propose to sell land to the Americans. If you continue to purchase them, it will make war among the different tribes, and, at last I do not know what will be the consequences among the white people. Brother, I wish you would take pity on the red people and do as I have requested. If you will not give up the land and do cross the boundary of our present settlement, it will be very hard, and produce great trouble between us.

The way, the only way to stop this evil is for the red men to unite in claiming a common and equal right in the land, as it was at first, and should be now—for it was never divided, but belongs to all. No tribe has the right to sell, even to each other, much less to strangers. . . . *Sell a country! Why not sell the air, the great sea, as well as the earth?* Did not the Great Spirit make them all for the use of his children?

How can we have confidence in the white people?

When Jesus Christ came upon the earth you killed Him and nailed Him to the cross. You thought He was dead, and you were mistaken. You have Shakers among you and you laugh and make light of their worship.

Everything I have told you is the truth. The Great Spirit has inspired me.

Tecumseh, in July 1811, with twenty-four warriors, followed the Wabash River in a second attempt to engage in historic debates to persuade the Indians to unite in a southern confederation. He voiced prophetic warnings.

Where today are the Pequot? Where are the Narragansett, the Mohican, the Pocanet, and other powerful tribes of our people? They have vanished before the avarice and oppression of the white man, as snow before the summer sun.... Will we let ourselves be destroyed in our turn, without making an effort worthy of our race? Shall we, without a struggle, give up our homes, our lands, bequeathed to us by the Great Spirit? The graves of our dead and everything that is dear and sacred to us?... I know you will say with me, Never! Never!...

Sleep not longer, O Choctaws and Chickasaws, in false security and delusive hopes.... Will not the bones of our dead be plowed up, and their graves turned into plowed fields?

Sharitarish

PAWNEE

Sharitarish, Pawnee, visited Washington, D.C., and on February 4, 1882, addressed President James Monroe and Secretary of War John C. Calhoun.

My Great Father: I have traveled a great distance to see you—I have seen you and my heart rejoices. I have heard your words—they have entered one ear and shall not escape the other, and I will carry them to my people as pure as they came from your mouth.

My Great Father: ... If I am here now and have seen your people, your houses, your vessels on the big lake, and a great many wonderful things far beyond my comprehension, which appear to have been made by the Great Spirit and placed in your hands, I am indebted to my Father [Major Benjamin O'Fallon] here, who invited me from home, under whose wings I have been protected ... but there is still another Great Father to whom I am much indebted—it is the Father of us all.... The Great Spirit made us all—he made my skin red, and yours white; he placed us on this earth, and intended that we should live differently from each other.

He made the whites to cultivate the earth, and feed on domestic animals; but he made us, red skins, to rove through the uncultivated woods and plains; to feed on wild animals; and to dress with their skins. He also intended that we should go to war—to take scalps—steal horses from and triumph over our enemies—cultivate peace at home, and promote the happiness of each other.

My Great Father: Some of your good chiefs, as they are called [missionaries], have proposed to send some of their good people among us to change our habits, to make us work and live like the white people. . . . You love your country—you love your people—you love the manner in which they live, and you think your people brave. I am like you, my Great Father, I love my country—I love my people—I love the manner in which we live, and think myself and warriors brave. Spare me then, my Father; let me enjoy my country, and I will trade skins with your people. I have grown up, and lived thus long without work—I am in hopes you will suffer me to die without it. We have plenty of buffalo, beaver, deer, and other wild animals— we have an abundance of horses—we have everything we want—we have plenty of land, if you will keep your people off of it. . . .

There was a time when we did not know the whites—our wants were then fewer than they are now. They were always within our control—we had then seen nothing which we could not get. Before our intercourse with the whites, who have caused such a destruction in our game, we could lie down to sleep, and when we awoke we would find the buffalo feeding around our camp—but now we are killing them for their skins, and feeding the wolves with their flesh, to make our children cry over their bones.

Here, my Great Father, is a pipe which I present you as I am accustomed to present pipes to all the red skins in peace with us. It is filled with such tobacco as we were accustomed to smoke before we knew the white people. It is pleasant, and the spontaneous growth of the most remote parts of our country. I know that the robes, leggings, moccasins, bear claws, etc., are of little value to you, but we wish you to have them deposited and preserved in some conspicuous part of your lodge, so that when we are gone and the sod turned over our bones, if our children should visit this place, as we do now, they may see and recognize with pleasure the deposits of their fathers; and reflect on the times that are past.

Speckled Snake

CREEK

Speckled Snake, aged Creek chief, spoke in 1829 when the Creeks were considering the advice of President Andrew Jackson, who was urging them to move beyond the Mississippi.

Brothers: We have heard the talk of our Great Father; it is very kind. He says he loves his red children....

When the first white man came over the wide waters, he was but a little man ... very little. His legs were cramped by sitting long in his big boat, and he begged for a little land....

When he came to these shores the Indians gave him land, and kindled fires to make him comfortable....

But when the white man had warmed himself at the Indian's fire, and had filled himself with the Indian's hominy, he became very large. He stopped not at the mountain tops, and his foot covered the plains and the valleys. His hands grasped the eastern and western seas. Then he became our Great Father. He loved his red children, but he said: "You must move a little farther, lest by accident I tread on you."

With one foot he pushed the red men across the Oconee, and with the other he trampled down the graves of our fathers....

On another occasion he said, "Get a little farther; go beyond the Oconee and the Ocmulgee [Indian settlements in South Carolina and Georgia]—there is a pleasant country." He also said, "It shall be yours forever."

Now he says, "The land you live upon is not yours. Go beyond the Mississippi; there is game; there you may remain while the grass grows and the rivers run."

Will not our Great Father come there also? He loves his red children, and his tongue is not forked.

Brothers! I have listened to a great many talks from our Great Father. But they always began and ended in this—"Get a little farther; you are too near me." I have spoken.

Senachwine

POTAWATOMI

Senachwine, venerable Potawatomi, spoke at a council fire at Indiantown in Illinois in June 1830, when Black Hawk tried to induce them to join forces to rout the whites. His dissenting speech caused Black Hawk to rise and stalk from the meeting with his band.

For more than seventy years I have hunted in this grove and fished in this stream, and for many years I have worshiped on this ground. Through these groves and over these prairies in pursuit of game our fathers roamed, and by them this land was left unto us as a heritage forever. No one is more attached to his home than myself, and none among you is so grieved to leave it. But the time is near at hand, when the red men of the forest will have to leave the land of their nativity, and find a home toward the setting sun. The white men of the east, whose numbers are like the sands of the sea, will overrun and take possession of this country. They will build wigwams and villages all over the land, and their domain will extend from sea to sea.

In my boyhood days I have chased the buffalo across the prairies, and hunted the elk in the groves; but where are they now? Long since they have left us; the near approach of the white man has frightened them away. The deer and the turkey will go next, and with them the sons of the forest.

Resistance to the aggression of the whites is useless; war is wicked and must result in our ruin. Therefore, let us submit to our fate, return not evil for evil, as this would offend the Great Spirit and bring ruin upon us. The time is near when our race will become extinct, and nothing left to show the world that we ever did exist ... but this I do know, the monitor within my breast has taught me the will of the Great Spirit, and now tells me good Indians will be rewarded, and bad ones punished. My friends, do not listen to the words of Black Hawk for he is trying to lead you astray. Do not imbrue your hands in human blood; for such is the work of the evil one, and will only lead to retribution upon our heads.

Seattle

DWAMISH

Seattle (Seathl), Dwamish chief, spoke to Isaac Stevens, Governor of Washington Territory, in 1854.

Yonder sky that has wept tears of compassion upon my people for centuries untold, and which to us appears changeless and eternal, may change. Today is fair. Tomorrow it may be overcast with clouds. My words are like the stars that never change. Whatever Seattle says the great chief at Washington can rely upon with as much certainty as he can upon the return of the sun or the seasons. The White Chief says that Big Chief at Washington sends us greetings of friendship and goodwill. That is kind of him for we know he has little need of our friendship in return. His people are many. They are like the grass that covers vast prairies. My people are few. They resemble the scattering trees of a storm-swept plain. ... I will not dwell on, nor mourn over, our untimely decay, nor reproach our paleface brothers with hastening it, as we too may have been somewhat to blame. ...

Your God is not our God. Your God loves your people and hates mine. He folds his strong and protecting arms lovingly about the paleface and leads him by the hand as a father leads his infant son—but He has forsaken His red children—if they really are His. Our God, the Great Spirit, seems also to have forsaken us. Your God makes your people strong every day. Soon they will fill the land. Our people are ebbing away like a rapidly receding tide that will never return. The white man's God cannot love our people or He would protect them. They seem to be orphans who can look nowhere for help. How then can we be brothers? ... We are two distinct races with separate origins and separate destinies. There is little in common between us.

To us the ashes of our ancestors are sacred and their resting place is hallowed ground. You wander far from the graves of your ancestors and seemingly without regret. Your religion was written upon tables of stone by the iron finger of your God so that you could not forget. The Red Man could never comprehend nor remember it. Our religion is the traditions of our ancestors—the dreams of our old men, given them in solemn hours of night by the Great Spirit; and the visions of our sachems; and it is written in the hearts of our people.

Your dead cease to love you and the land of their nativity as soon as they pass the portals of the tomb and wander way beyond the stars. They are soon forgotten and never return. Our dead never forget the beautiful world that gave them being.

Day and night cannot dwell together. The Red Man has ever fled the approach of the White Man, as the morning mist flees before the morning sun. However, your proposition seems fair and I think that my people will accept it and will retire to the reservation you offer them. Then we will dwell apart in peace. ... It matters little where we pass the remnant of our days. They will not be many. A few more moons; a few more winters —and not one of the descendants of the mighty hosts that once moved over this broad land or lived in happy homes, protected by the Great Spirit, will remain to mourn over the graves of a people once more powerful and hopeful than yours. But why should I mourn at the untimely fate of my people? Tribe follows tribe, and nation follows nation, like the waves of the sea. It is the order of nature, and regret is useless. Your time of decay may be distant, but it will surely come, for even the White Man whose God walked and talked with him as friend with friend, cannot be exempt from the common destiny. We may be brothers after all. We will see. . . .

Every part of this soil is sacred in the estimation of my people. Every hillside, every valley, every plain and grove, has been hallowed by some sad or happy event in days long vanished. The very dust upon which you now stand responds more lovingly to their footsteps than to yours, because it is rich with the blood of our ancestors and our bare feet are conscious of the sympathetic touch. Even the little children who lived here and rejoiced here for a brief season will love these somber solitudes and at eventide they greet shadowy returning spirits. And when the last Red Man shall have perished, and the memory of my tribe shall have become a myth among the White Men, these shores will swarm with the invisible dead of my tribe, and when your children's children think themselves alone in the field, the store, the shop, upon the highway, or in the silence of the pathless woods, they will not be alone. At night when the streets of your cities and villages are silent and you think them deserted, they will throng with the returning hosts that once filled and still love this beautiful land. The White Man will never be alone.

Let him be just and deal kindly with my people, for the dead are not powerless. Dead, did I say? There is no death, only a change of worlds.

Charlot

FLATHEAD

Charlot, Flathead chief, spoke to his people in 1876 about the white man, when the whites were attempting to oust them from their ancestral home in the Bitterroot Valley of Montana.

Since our forefathers first beheld him, more than seven times ten winters have snowed and melted. . . . We were happy when he first came. We first thought he came from the light, but he comes like the dusk of the evening now, not like the dawn of the morning. He comes like a day that has passed, and night enters our future with him. . . .

To take and to lie should be burned on his forehead, as he burns the sides of my stolen horses with his own name. Had Heaven's Chief burned him with some mark to refuse him, we might have refused him. No; we did not refuse him in his weakness. In his poverty we fed, we cherished him—yes, befriended him, and showed him the fords and defiles of our lands. . . .

He has filled graves with our bones. His horses, his cattle, his sheep, his men, his women have a rot. Does not his breath, his gums stink? His jaws lose their teeth and he stamps them with false ones; yet he is not ashamed. No, no; his course is destruction; he spoils what the spirit who gave us this country made beautiful and clean. . . .

His laws never gave us a blade, nor a tree, nor a duck, nor a grouse, nor a trout. . . . How often does he come? You know he comes as long as he lives, and takes more and more, and dirties what he leaves. . . .

The white man fathers this doom—yes, this curse on us and on the few that may see a few days more. He, the cause of our ruin, is his own snake which he says stole on his mother in her own country to lie to her. He says his story is that man was rejected and cast off. Why did we not reject him forever? He says one of his virgins had a son nailed to death on two cross sticks to save him. Were all of them dead when that young man died, we would all be safe now, and our country our own.

Sitting Bull

SIOUX

Tatanka Yotanka, or Sitting Bull, Sioux warrior, tribal leader of the Hunkpapa Teton division and in later life

From *To Serve the Devil*, Volume I: *Natives and Slaves* by Paul Jacobs and Saul Landau. Copyright © 1971 by Paul Jacobs and Saul Landau. (Random House, Inc.)

a sacred "dreamer," was on the warpath almost contin-
uously from 1869 to 1876. White settlers were pouring
into the land, and even more disastrously for the Indians,
gold had been discovered in the Black Hills country.
Following this discovery, the government in 1875 ordered
the Sioux to leave their Powder River hunting grounds,
land which had been guaranteed to them in the treaty of
1868. The war of 1876 was fought to enforce the govern-
ment's order. At a Powder River council in 1877, Sitting
Bull expressed his great love for his native soil, "a love
wholly mystical," writes a biographer of Sitting Bull.
"He used to say [that] healthy feet can hear the very heart
of Holy Earth. . . . Up always before dawn, he liked to
bathe his bare feet, walking about in the morning dew."

Behold, my brothers, the spring has come; the earth has received the embraces of the sun and we shall soon see the results of that love!

Every seed is awakened and so has all animal life. It is through this mysterious power that we too have our being and we therefore yield to our neighbors, even our animal neighbors, the same right as ourselves, to inhabit this land.

Yet, hear me, people, we have now to deal with another race —small and feeble when our fathers first met them but now great and overbearing. Strangely enough they have a mind to till the soil and the love of possession is a disease with them. These people have made many rules that the rich may break but the poor may not. They take tithes from the poor and weak to support the rich who rule. They claim this mother of ours, the earth, for their own and fence their neighbors away; they deface her with their buildings and their refuse. That nation is like a spring freshet that overruns its banks and destroys all who are in its path.

We cannot dwell side by side. Only seven years ago we made a treaty by which we were assured that the buffalo country should be left to us forever. Now they threaten to take that away from us. My brothers, shall we submit or shall we say to them: "First kill me before you take possession of my Father-land. . . ."

Plenty Coups

CROW

Chief Plenty Coups (Crow) gives a farewell address in 1909 at the Little Bighorn council grounds in Montana.

The Ground on which we stand is sacred ground. It is the dust and blood of our ancestors. On these plains the Great White Father at Washington sent his soldiers armed with long knives and rifles to slay the Indian. Many of them sleep on yonder hill where Pahaska—White Chief of the Long Hair [General Custer]—so bravely fought and fell. A few more passing suns will see us here no more, and our dust and bones will mingle with these same prairies. I see as in a vision the dying spark of our council fires, the ashes cold and white. I see no longer the curling smoke rising from our lodge poles. I hear no longer the songs of the women as they prepare the meal. The antelope have gone; the buffalo wallows are empty. Only the wail of the coyote is heard. The white man's medicine is stronger than ours; his iron horse rushes over the buffalo trail. He talks to us through his "whispering spirit" [the telephone]. We are like birds with a broken wing. My heart is cold within me. My eyes are growing dim—I am old. . . .

III
CULTURE CONTACT

The practical meaning of the term "culture contact" is so well known to Americans that it needs no explanation here. In recent years, however, it has become even clearer to us that in the coming together of a literate, nontraditional, technologically oriented culture with a nonliterate, traditional culture, the former will achieve cultural dominance and whether by design or attrition impose its system on the latter. Whether it is in an isolated valley of New Guinea or on an island in the Philippines, at the first breath of modern civilization, the traditional cultures begin to disintegrate like ancient parchment incautiously exhumed into the common air. This, of course, was so in the Americas, and the process seems fated to continue until every last traditional culture has been "discovered" and "enlightened." It appears to be inevitable that when one people's traditions fail to work as effectively as another's machines that people will reluctantly abandon its traditions and attempt some sort of accommodation with those who in the first crucial moments of contact must seem in important ways stronger. When the first generation of a tribe is forced to seek this kind of accommodation the traditions by which it lives are already doomed: the father's advice to his son, the mother's to her daughter, become qualified with doubts and hesitations; and these children, having become parents themselves in a changed world, remember the old ways more than they live them. The traditions fall away singly and in clusters until even the language itself is like some moth-eaten medicine bundle that nobody opens.

This is an old story for us now, and in these assembled materials—exploration accounts, captivity narratives, Indian autobiographies—it tells itself.

EXPLORATIONS

The Discovery and Conquest of New Spain

Here is an old soldier's laconic account of the first real penetration of the continental land mass of the New World. From 1492 when Columbus made his landfall in the Bahamas until February 1519, when Hernan Cortés sailed on this voyage of conquest, there had been a succession of nibbles at the impenetrable flanks of America: Columbus himself, Cabot, the Cortreals, Cabral, Ponce de Leon, Balboa, the savage and ruthless Pedrarias, who ordered Balboa's execution, and Juan de Grijalva, whose expedition Diaz joined and refers to herein. But it took Cortés, a man of almost superhuman willpower, greed, and historical consciousness, actually to thrust Western civilization's spearhead into the continent's heart. When he landed on the mosquito-infested sands near Vera Cruz, gave his men a lecture on their historical mission, and then turned his face inland, the history of the Indian and the white man in the New World locked into its unalterable position, and the pattern of events recorded herein was to be repeated northward (and southward) until

From Bernal Diaz, *The Discovery and Conquest of New Spain*, translated by A.P. Maudslay (London, 1928), pp. 100-115; 118-29; 265-76.

Indian resistance was no longer a reality but only a fiction. The march to Tenochtitlán which Bernal Diaz del Castillo experienced as one of those under Cortés and then later narrated in his blind old age (it was first published in 1632) is thus one of the primary documents in the history of the Americas, and its artless depiction of the atrocities committed in the "long shadow of the white man" is for North Americans the opening episode of the drama that ends three hundred and seventy-one years later in a frozen gulch at Wounded Knee, South Dakota.

The next morning Cortés ordered Pedro de Alvarado to set out in command of a hundred soldiers, fifteen of them with guns and crossbows, to examine the country inland for a distance of two leagues, and to take Melchorejo the interpreter in his company. When Melchorejo was looked for he could not be found as he had run off with the people of Tabasco, and it appears that the day before he had left the Spanish clothes that had been given to him hung up in the palm grove, and had fled by night in a canoe. Cortés was much annoyed at his flight, fearing that he would tell things to his fellow countrymen to our disadvantage—well, let him go as a bit of bad luck, and let us get back to our story. Cortés also sent the Captain Francisco de Lugo, in another direction, with a hundred soldiers, twelve of them musketeers and crossbowmen, with instructions not to go beyond two leagues and to return to the camp to sleep.

When Francisco de Lugo and his company had marched about a league from camp he came on a great host of Indian archers carrying lances and shields, drums and standards and they made straight for our company of soldiers and surrounded them on all sides. They were so numerous and shot their arrows so deftly that it was impossible to withstand them, and they hurled their fire-hardened darts and cast stones from their slings in such numbers that they fell like hail, and they attacked our men with their two-handed knife-like swords. Stoutly as Francisco de Lugo and his soldiers fought, they could not ward off the enemy, and when this was clear to them, while still keeping a good formation, they began to retreat towards the camp.

A certain Indian, a swift and daring runner, had been sent off to the camp to beg Cortés to come to their assistance; meanwhile Francisco de Lugo by careful management of his musketeers and crossbowmen, some loading while others fired, and by occasional charges, was able to hold his own against all the squadrons attacking him.

Let us leave him in the dangerous situation I have described and return to Captain Pedro de Alvarado, who after marching about a league came on a creek which was very difficult to cross, and it pleased God our Lord so to lead him that he should return by another road in the direction where Francisco de Lugo was fighting. When he heard the reports of the muskets and the great din of drums and trumpets and the shouts and whistles of the Indians, he knew that there must be a battle going on, so with the greatest haste but in good order he ran toward the cries and shots and found Captain Francisco de Lugo and his men fighting with their faces to the enemy, and five of the enemy lying dead. As soon as he joined forces with Francisco de Lugo they turned on the Indians and drove them back, but they were not able to put them to flight, and the Indians followed our men right up to the camp.

In like manner other companies of warriors had attacked us where Cortés was guarding the wounded, but we soon drove them off with our guns, which laid many of them low, and with our good sword play.

When Cortés heard of Francisco de Lugo's peril from the Cuban Indian who came to beg for help, we promptly went to his assistance, and we met the two captains with their companies about half a league from the camp. Two soldiers of Francisco de Lugo's company were killed and eight wounded, and three of Pedro de Alvarado's company were wounded. When we arrived in camp we buried the dead and tended the wounded, and stationed sentinels and kept a strict watch.

In those skirmishes we killed fifteen Indians and captured three, one of whom seemed to be a chief, and through Aguilar, our interpreter, we asked them why they were so mad as to attack us, and that they could see that we should kill them if they attacked us again. Then one of these Indians was sent with some beads to give to the Caciques to bring them to peace, and that messenger told us that the Indian Melchorejo, whom we had brought from Cape Catoche, went to the chiefs the night before and counselled them to fight us day and night, and said that they would conquer us as we were few in number; so it turned out that we had brought an enemy with us instead of a help.

This Indian, whom we dispatched with the message, went off and never returned. From the other two Indian prisoners Aguilar the interpreter learned for certain that by the next day the Caciques from all the neighboring towns of the province would have assembled with all their forces ready to make war on us, and that they would come and surround our camp, for that was Melchorejo's advice to them.

As soon as Cortés knew this for certain, he ordered all the horses to be landed from the ships without delay, and the cross-bowmen and musketeers and all of us soldiers, even those who were wounded, to have our arms ready for use.

When the horses were brought on shore they were very stiff and afraid to move, for they had been many days on board ship, but the next day they moved quite freely.

At that time it happened that six or seven soldiers, young men and otherwise in good health, suffered from pains in their loins, so that they could not stand on their feet and had to be carried on men's backs. We did not know what this sickness came from, some say that they fell ill on account of the [quilted] cotton armor which they never took off, but wore day and night, and because in Cuba they had lived daintily and were not used to hard work, so in the heat they fell ill. Cortés ordered them not to remain on land but to be taken at once on board ship.

The best horses and riders were chosen to form the cavalry, and the horses had little bells attached to their breastplates. The men were ordered not to stop to spear those who were down, but to aim their lances at the faces of the enemy.

Thirteen gentlemen were chosen to go on horseback with Cortés in command of them, and I here record their names : Cortés, Cristóval de Olíd, Pedro de Alvarado, Alonzo Hernández Puertocarrero, Juan de Escalante, Francisco de Montejo, and Alonzo de Ávila to whom was given the horse belonging to Ortiz the musician and Bartolomé García, for neither of these men were good horsemen, Juan Velásquez de Leon, Francisco de Morla, and Lares the good horseman, Gonzalo Domínguez, an excellent horseman, Moron of Bayamo, and Pedro González of Trujillo. Cortés selected all these gentlemen and went himself as their captain.

Cortés ordered Mesa the artilleryman to have his guns ready, and he placed Diego de Ordás in command of us foot soldiers and he also had command of the musketeers and bowmen, for he was no horseman.

Very early the next day which was the day of Nuestra Señora de Marzo [Lady-day, 25th March] after hearing mass, which was said by Fray Bartolomé de Olmedo, we formed in order under our standard bearer, and marched to some large savannas where Francisco de Lugo and Pedro de Alvarado had been attacked, about a league distant from the camp we had left; and that savanna and township was called Cintla, and was subject to Tabasco.

Cortés [and the horsemen] were separated a short distance from us on account of some swamps which could not be crossed by the horses, and as we were marching along we came on the whole force of Indian warriors who were on the way to attack us in our camp. It was near the town of Cintla that we met them on an open plain.

As they approached us their squadrons were so numerous that they covered the whole plain, and they rushed on us like mad dogs completely surrounding us, and they let fly such a cloud of arrows, javelins, and stones that on the first assault they wounded over seventy of us, and fighting hand to hand they did us great damage with their lances, and one soldier fell dead at once from an arrow wound in the ear, and they kept on shooting and wounding us. With our muskets and crossbows and with good sword play we did not fail as stout fighters, and when they came to feel the edge of our swords little by little they fell back, but it was only so as to shoot at us in greater safety. Mesa, our artilleryman, killed many of them with his cannon, for they were formed in great squadrons and they did not open out so that he could fire at them as he pleased, but with all the hurts and wounds which we gave them, we could not drive them off. I said to Diego de Ordás, "It seems to me that we ought to close up and charge them," for in truth they suffered greatly from the strokes and thrusts of our swords, and that was why they fell away from us, both from fear of these swords, and the better to shoot their arrows and hurl their javelins and the hail of stones. Ordás replied that it was not good advice, for there were three hundred Indians to every one of us, and that we could not hold out against such a multitude— so there we stood enduring their attack. However, we did agree to get as near as we could to them, as I had advised Ordás, so as to give them a bad time with our swordsmanship, and they suffered so much from it that they retreated toward a swamp.

During all this time Cortés and his horsemen failed to appear, although we greatly longed for him, and we feared that by chance some disaster had befallen him.

I remember that when we fired shots the Indians gave great shouts and whistles and threw dust and rubbish into the air so that we should not see the damage done to them, and they sounded their trumpets and drums and shouted and whistled and cried "Alala! Alala!"

Just at this time we caught sight of our horsemen, and as the great Indian host was crazed with its attack on us, it did not at once perceive them coming up behind their backs, and as the plain was level ground and the horsemen were good riders, and many of the horses were very handy and fine gallopers, they came quickly on the enemy and speared them as they chose. As soon as we saw the horsemen we fell on the Indians with such energy that with us attacking on one side and the horsemen on the other, they soon turned tail. The Indians thought that the horse and its rider was all one animal, for they had never seen horses up to this time.

The savannas and fields were crowded with Indians running to take refuge in the thick woods near by.

After we had defeated the enemy, Cortés told us that he had not been able to come to us sooner as there was a swamp in the way, and he had to fight his way through another force of warriors before he could reach us, and three horsemen and five horses had been wounded.

As it was Lady-day we gave to the town which was afterwards founded here the name of Santa Maria de la Victoria, on account of this great victory being won on Our Lady's day. This was the first battle that we fought under Cortés in New Spain.

After this we bound up the hurts of the wounded with cloths, for we had nothing else, and we doctored the horses by searing their wounds with the fat from the body of a dead Indian which we cut up to get out the fat, and we went to look at the dead lying on the plain and there were more than eight hundred of them, the greater number killed by thrusts, the others by the cannon, muskets and crossbows, and many were stretched on the ground half dead. Where the horsemen had passed, numbers of them lay dead or groaning from their wounds. The battle lasted over an hour, and the Indians fought all the time like brave warriors, until the horsemen came up.

We took five prisoners, two of them Captains. As it was late and we had had enough of fighting, and we had not eaten anything, we returned to our camp. Then we buried the two soldiers who had been killed, one by a wound in the ear, and the other by a wound in the throat, and we seared the wounds of the others and of the horses with the fat of the Indian, and after posting sentinels and guards, we had supper and rested.

When Aguilar spoke to the prisoners he found out from what they said that they were fit persons to be sent as messengers, and he advised Cortés to free them, so that they might go and talk to the Caciques of the town. These two messengers were given green and blue beads, and Aguilar spoke many pleasant and flattering words to them, telling them that they had nothing to fear as we wished to treat them like brothers, that it was their own fault that they had made war on us, and that now they had better collect together all the Caciques of the different towns as we wished to talk to them, and he gave them much other advice in a gentle way so as to gain their good will. The messengers went off willingly and spoke to the Caciques and chief men, and told them all we wished them to know about our desire for peace.

When our envoys had been listened to, it was settled among them that fifteen Indian slaves, all with stained faces and ragged cloaks and loin cloths, should at once be sent to us with fowls and baked fish and maize cakes. When these men came before Cortés he received them graciously, but Aguilar the interpreter asked them rather angrily why they had come with their faces in that state, that it looked more as though they came to fight than to treat for peace; and he told them to go back to the Caciques and inform them, that if they wished for peace in the way we offered it, chieftains should come and treat for it, as was always the custom, and that they should not send slaves. But even these painted-faced slaves were treated with consideration by us and blue beads were sent by them in sign of peace, and to soothe their feelings.

The next day thirty Indian chieftains, clad in good cloaks, came to visit us, and brought fowls, fish, fruit and maize cakes, and asked leave from Cortés to burn and bury the bodies of the dead who had fallen in the recent battles, so that they should not smell badly or be eaten by lions and tigers. Permission was at once given them and they hastened to bring many people to bury and burn the bodies according to their customs.

Cortés learned from the Caciques that over eight hundred men were missing, not counting those who had been carried off wounded.

They said that they could not tarry with us either to discuss the matter or make peace, for on the morrow the chieftains and leaders of all the towns would have assembled, and that then they would agree about a peace.

As Cortés was very sagacious about everything, he said, laughing, to us soldiers who happened to be in his company, "Do you know, gentlemen, that it seems to me that the Indians are terrified at the horses and may think that they and the cannon alone make war on them. I have thought of something which will confirm this belief, and that is to bring the mare belonging to Juan Sedeño, which foaled the other day on board ship, and tie her up where I am now standing and also to bring the stallion of Ortiz the musician, which is very excitable, near enough to scent the mare, and when he has scented her to lead each of them off separately so that the Caciques who are coming shall not hear the horse neighing as they approach, not until they are standing before me and are talking to me." We did just as Cortés ordered and brought the horse and mare, and the horse soon detected the scent of her in Cortés quarters. In addition to this Cortés ordered the largest cannon that we possessed to be loaded with a large ball and a good charge of powder.

About midday forty Indians arrived, all of them Caciques of good bearing, wearing rich mantles. They saluted Cortés and all of us, and brought incense and fumigated all of us who were present, and they asked pardon for their past behavior, and said that henceforth they would be friendly.

Cortés, through Aguilar the interpreter, answered them in a rather grave manner, as though he were angry, that they well knew how many times he had asked them to maintain peace, that the fault was theirs, and that now they deserved to be put to death, they and all the people of their towns, but that as we were the vassals of a great King and Lord named the Emperor Don Carlos, who had sent us to these countries, and ordered us to help and favor those who would enter his royal service, that if they were now as well disposed as they said they were, that we would take this course, but that if they were not, some of those *Tepustles* would jump out and kill them (they call iron *Tepustle* in their language) for some of the *Tepustles* were still angry because they had made war on us. At this moment the order was secretly given to put a match to the cannon which had been loaded, and it went off with such a thunderclap as was wanted, and the ball went buzzing over the hills, and as it was midday and very still it made a great noise, and the Caciques were terrified on hearing it. As they had never seen anything like it they believed what Cortés had told them was true. Then Cortés told them, through Aguilar, not to be afraid for he had given orders that no harm should be done to them.

Just then the horse that had scented the mare was brought and tied up not far distant from where Cortés was talking to the Caciques, and the horse began to paw the ground and neigh and become wild with excitement, looking all the time toward the Indians and the place whence the scent of the mare had reached him, and the Caciques thought that he was roaring at them and they were terrified. When Cortés observed their state of mind, he rose from his seat and went to the horse and told two orderlies to lead it far away, and said to the Indians that he had told the horse not to be angry as they were friendly and wished to make peace.

While this was going on there arrived more than thirty Indian carriers, who brought a meal of fowls and fish and fruits and other food.

Cortés had a long conversation with these chieftains and Caciques and they told him that they would all come on the next day and would bring a present and would discuss other matters, and then they went away quite contented.

◪

Early the next morning many Caciques and chiefs of Tabasco and the neighboring towns arrived and paid great respect to us all, and they brought a present of gold, consisting of four diadems and some gold lizards, and two [ornaments] like little dogs, and earrings and five ducks, and two masks with Indian faces and two gold soles for sandals, and some other things of little value. I do not remember how much the things were worth; and they brought cloth, such as they make and wear, which was quilted stuff.

This present, however, was worth nothing in comparison with the twenty women that were given us, among them one very excellent woman called Doña Marina, for so she was named when she became a Christian. Cortés received this present with pleasure and went aside with all the Caciques, and with Aguilar, the interpreter, to hold converse, and he told them that he gave them thanks for what they had brought with them, but there was one thing that he must ask of them, namely, that they should reoccupy the town with all their people, women and children, and he wished to see it repeopled within two days, for he would recognize that as a sign of true peace. The Caciques sent at once to summon all the inhabitants with their women and children and within two days they were again settled in the town.

One other thing Cortés asked of the chiefs and that was to give up their idols and sacrifices, and this they said they would do, and, through Auguilar, Cortés told them as well as he was able about matters concerning our holy faith, how we were Christians and worshiped one true and only God, and he showed them an image of Our Lady with her precious Son in her arms and explained to them that we paid the greatest reverence to it as it was the image of the Mother of our Lord God who was in heaven. The Caciques replied that they liked the look of the great Teleciguata (for in their language great ladies are called Teleciguatas) and [begged] that she might be given them to keep in their town, and Cortés said that the image should be given to them, and ordered them to make a well-constructed altar, and this they did at once.

The next morning, Cortés ordered two of our carpenters, named Alonzo Yañez and Alvaro López, to make a very tall cross.

When all this had been settled Cortés asked the Caciques what was their reason for attacking us three times when we had asked them to keep the peace; the chief replied that he had already asked pardon for their acts and had been forgiven, that the Cacique of Champoton, his brother, had advised it, and that he feared to be accused of cowardice, for he had already been reproached and dishonored for not having attacked the other captain who had come with four ships (he must have meant Juan de Grijalva) and he also said that the Indian whom we had brought as an Interpreter, who escaped in the night, had advised them to attack us both by day and night.

Cortés then ordered this man to be brought before him without fail, but they replied that when he saw that the battle was going against them, he had taken to flight, and they knew not where he was although search had been made for him; but we came to know that they had offered him as a sacrifice because his counsel had cost them so dear.

Cortés also asked them where they procured their gold and jewels, and they replied, from the direction of the setting sun, and said "Culua" and "Mexico," and as we did not know what Mexico and Culua meant we paid little attention to it.

Then we brought another interpreter named Francisco, whom we had captured during Grijalva's expedition, who has already been mentioned by me, but he understood nothing of the Tabasco language only that of Culua which is the Mexican tongue. By means of signs he told Cortés that Culua was far ahead, and he repeated "Mexico" which we did not understand.

So the talk ceased until the next day when the sacred image of Our Lady and the Cross were set up on the altar and we all paid reverence to them, and Padre Fray Bartolomé de Olmedo said Mass and all the Caciques and chiefs were present and we gave the name of Santa Maria de la Victoria to the town, and by this name the town of Tabasco is now called. The same friar, with Aguilar as interpreter, preached many good things about our holy faith to the twenty Indian women who had been given us, and immediately afterward they were baptized. One Indian lady who was given to us here was christened Doña Marina, and she was truly a great chieftainess and the daughter of great Caciques and the mistress of vassals, and this her appearance clearly showed. Later on I will relate why it was and in what manner she was brought here.

Cortés allotted one of the women to each of his captains and Doña Marina, as she was good looking and intelligent and without embarrassment, he gave to Alonzo Hernández Puertocarrero. When Puertocarrero went to Spain, Doña Marina lived with Cortés, and bore him a son named Don Martin Cortés.

We remained five days in this town, to look after the wounded and those who were suffering from pain in the loins, from which they all recovered. Furthermore, Cortés drew the Caciques to him by kindly converse, and told them how our master the Emperor, whose vassals we were, had under his orders many great lords, and that it would be well for them also to render him obedience, and that then, whatever they might be in need of, whether it was our protection or any other necessity, if they would make it known to him, no matter where he might be, he would come to their assistance.

The Caciques all thanked him for this, and thereupon all declared themselves the vassals of our great Emperor. These were the first vassals to render submission to His Majesty in New Spain.

Cortés then ordered the Caciques to come with their women and children early the next day, which was Palm Sunday, to the altar, to pay homage to the holy image of Our Lady and to the Cross, and at the same time Cortés ordered them to send six Indian carpenters to accompany our carpenters to the town of

Cintla, there to cut a cross on a great tree called a Ceiba, which grew there, and they did it so that it might last a long time, for as the bark is renewed the cross will show there for ever. When this was done he ordered the Indians to get ready all the canoes that they owned to help us embark, for we wished to set sail on that holy day because the pilots had come to tell Cortés that the ships ran a great risk from a norther, which is a dangerous gale.

The next day, early in the morning, all the Caciques and chiefs came in their canoes with all their women and children and stood in the court where we had placed the church and cross, and many branches of trees had already been cut ready to be carried in the procession. Then the Caciques beheld us all, Cortés, as well as the captains, and every one of us marching together with the greatest reverence in a devout procession, and the Padre de la Merced and the priest Juan Diaz, clad in their vestments, said Mass, and we paid reverence to and kissed the Holy Cross, while the Caciques and Indians stood looking on at us.

When our solemn festival was over the chiefs approached and offered Cortés ten fowls and baked fish and vegetables, and we took leave of them, and Cortés again commended to their care the Holy image and the sacred crosses and told them always to keep the place clean and well swept, and to deck the cross with garlands and to reverence it and then they would enjoy good health and bountiful harvests.

It was growing late when we got on board ship and the next day, Monday, we set sail in the morning and with a fair wind laid our course for San Juan de Ulúa, keeping close in shore all the time.

As we sailed along in the fine weather, we soldiers who knew the coast would say to Cortés, "Señor, over there is la Rambla, which the Indians call Ayagualulco," and soon afterward we arrived off Tonalá which we called San Antonio, and we pointed it out to him. Farther on we showed him the great river of Coatzacoalcos, and he saw the lofty snow capped mountains, and then the Sierra of San Martin, and farther on we pointed out the split rock, which is a great rock standing out in the sea with a mark on the top of it which gives it the appearance of a seat. Again farther on we showed him the Rio de Alvarado, which Pedro de Alvarado entered when we were with Grijalva, and then we came in sight of the Rio de Banderas, where we had gained in barter the sixteen thousand dollars, then we showed him the Isla Blanca, and told him where lay the Isla Verde, and close in shore saw the Isla de Sacrificios, where we found the altars and the Indian victims in Grijalva's time; and at last our good fortune brought us to San Juan de Ulúa soon after midday on Holy Thursday.

On Holy Thursday, in the year 1519, we arrived with all the fleet at the Port of San Juan de Ulúa, and as the Pilot Alaminos knew the place well from having come there with Juan de Grijalva he at once ordered the vessels to drop anchor where they would be safe from the northerly gales. The flagship hoisted her royal standards and pennants, and within half an hour of anchoring, two large canoes came out to us, full of Mexican Indians. Seeing the big ship with the standards flying they knew that it was there they must go to speak with the captain; so they went direct to the flagship and going on board asked who was the Tatuan, which in their language means the chief. Doña Marina, who understood the language well, pointed him out. Then the Indians paid many marks of respect to Cortés, according to their usage, and bade him welcome, and said that their lord, a servant of the great Montezuma, had sent them to ask what kind of men we were, and of what we were in search, and added that if we were in need of anything for ourselves or the ships, that we should tell them and they would supply it. Our Cortés thanked them through the two interpreters, Aguilar and Doña Marina, and ordered food and wine to be given them and some blue beads, and after they had drunk he told them that we came to see them and to trade with them and that our arrival in their country should cause them no uneasiness but be looked on by them as fortunate. The messengers returned on shore well content, and the next day, which was Good Friday, we disembarked with the horses and guns, on some sand hills which rise to a considerable height, for there was no level land, nothing but sand dunes; and the artilleryman Mesa placed the guns in position to the best of his judgment. Then we set up an altar where mass was said and we made huts and shelters for Cortés and the captains, and three hundred of the soldiers brought wood and made huts for themselves and we placed the horses where they would be safe and in this way was Good Friday passed.

The next day, Saturday, Easter Eve, many Indians arrived sent by a chief who was a governor under Montezuma, named Pitalpitoque (whom we afterward called Ovandillo), and they brought axes and dressed wood for the huts of the Captain Cortés and the other ranchos near to it, and covered them with large cloths on account of the strength of the sun, for the heat was very great—and they brought fowls, and maize cakes and plums, which were then in season, and I think that they brought some gold jewels, and they presented all these things to Cortés; and said that the next day a governor would come and would bring more food. Cortés thanked them heartily and ordered them to be given certain articles in exchange with which they went away well content. The next day, Easter Sunday, the governor whom they spoke of arrived. His name was Tendile, a man of affairs, and he brought with him Pitalpitoque who was also a man of importance amongst the natives and there followed them many Indians with presents of fowls and vege-tables. Tendile ordered these people to stand aside on a hillock and with much humility he made three obeisances to Cortés according to their custom, and then to all the soldiers who were standing around. Cortés bade them welcome through our inter-preters and embraced them and asked them to wait, as he wished presently to speak to them. Meanwhile he ordered an altar to be made as well as it could be done in the time, and Fray Bartolomé de Olmedo, who was a fine singer, chanted Mass, and Padre Juan Diaz assisted, and the two governors and the other chiefs who were with them looked on. When Mass was over, Cortés and some of our captains and the two Indian Officers of the great Montezuma dined together. When the tables had been cleared away—Cortés went aside with the two Caciques and our two interpreters and explained to them that we were Christians and vassals of the greatest lord on earth who had many great princes as his vassals and servants, and that it was at his orders that we had come to this country, because for many years he had heard rumors about the country and the great prince who ruled it. That he wished to be friends with this prince and to tell him many things in the name of the Emperor, which things, when he knew and understood them, would please him greatly. Moreover, he wished to trade with their prince and his Indians in good friendship, and he wanted to know where this prince would wish that they should meet so that they might confer together. Tendile replied somewhat proudly, and said, "You have only just now arrived and you already ask to speak with our prince; accept now this present which we give you in his name, and afterward you will tell me what you think fitting." With that he took out a *petaca*—which is a sort of chest, many articles of gold beautifully and richly worked, and ordered ten loads of white cloth made of cotton and feathers to be brought, wonderful things to see, besides quantities of food. Cortés received it all with smiles in a gracious manner and gave in return, beads of twisted glass and other small beads from Spain, and he begged them to send to their towns to ask the people to come and trade with us as he had brought many beads to exchange for gold, and they replied that they would do as he asked. Cortés then ordered his servants to bring an armchair, richly carved and inlaid, and some *margaritas*, stones with many [intricate] designs in them, and a string of twisted glass beads packed in cotton scented with musk and a crimson cap with a golden medal engraved with a figure of St. George on horseback, lance in hand, slaying the dragon, and he told Tendile that he should send the chair to his prince Montezuma, so that he could be seated in it when he, Cortés, came to see and speak with him, and that he should place the cap on his head, and that the stones and all the other things were presents from our lord the King, as a sign of his friendship, for he was aware that Montezuma was a great prince, and Cortés asked that a day and a place might be named where he could go to see Montezuma. Tendile received the present and said that his lord Montezuma was such a great prince that it would please him to know our great King, and that he would carry the present to him at once and bring back a reply.

It appears that Tendile brought with him some clever painters such as they had in Mexico and ordered them to make
pictures true to nature of the face and body of Cortés and all
his captains, and of the soldiers, ships, sails and horses, and
of Doña Marina and Aguilar, even of the two greyhounds, and
the cannon and cannon balls, and all of the army we had
brought with us, and he carried the pictures to his master.
Cortés ordered our gunners to load the lombards with a great
charge of powder so that they should make a great noise when
they were fired off, and he told Pedro de Alvarado that he and
all the horsemen should get ready so that these servants of
Montezuma might see them gallop and told them to attach
little bells to the horses' breastplates. Cortés also mounted his
horse and said, "It would be well if we could gallop on these
sand dunes but they will observe that even when on foot we
get stuck in the sand—let us go out to the beach when the tide
is low and gallop two and two"—and to Pedro de Alvarado,
whose sorrel-colored mare was a great galloper, and very
handy, he gave charge of all the horsemen.

All this was carried out in the presence of the two ambassadors, and so that they should see the cannon fired, Cortés
made as though he wished again to speak to them and a number
of other chieftains, and the lombards were fired off, and as it
was quite still at that moment, the stones went flying through
the forest resounding with a great din, and the two governors
and all the other Indians were frightened by things so new to
them, and ordered the painters to record them so that Montezuma might see. It happened that one of the soldiers had a
helmet half gilt but somewhat rusty, and this Tendile noticed,
for he was the more forward of the two ambassadors, and said
that he wished to see it as it was like one that they possessed
which had been left to them by their ancestors of the race from
which they had sprung, and that it had been placed on the
head of their god—Huichilobos, and that their prince Montezuma would like to see this helmet. So it was given to him, and
Cortés said to them that as he wished to know whether the
gold of this country was the same as that we find in our rivers,
they could return the helmet filled with grains of gold so that
he could send it to our great Emperor. After this, Tendile bade

farewell to Cortés and to all of us and after many expressions of regard from Cortés he took leave of him and said he would return with a reply without delay. After Tendile had departed we found out that besides being an Indian employed in matters of great importance, Tendile was the most active of the servants whom his master, Montezuma, had in his employ, and he went with all haste and narrated everything to his prince, and showed him the pictures which had been painted and the present which Cortés had sent. When the great Montezuma gazed on it he was struck with admiration and received it on his part with satisfaction. When he examined the helmet and that which was on his Huichilobos, he felt convinced that we belonged to the race which, as his forefathers had foretold, would come to rule over that land.

ᨎ

When Tendile departed the other governor, Pitalpitoque, stayed in our camp and occupied some huts a little distance from ours, and they brought Indian women there to make maize bread, and brought fowls and fruit and fish, and supplied Cortés and the captains who fed with him. As for us soldiers, if we did not hunt for shellfish on the beach, or go out fishing, we did not get anything.

About that time, many Indians came from the towns and some of them brought gold and jewels of little value, and fowls to exchange with us for our goods, which consisted of green beads and clear glass beads and other articles, and with this we managed to supply ourselves with food. Almost all the soldiers had brought things for barter, as we learned in Grijalva's time that it was a good thing to bring beads—and in this manner six or seven days passed by.

Then one morning, Tendile arrived with more than one hundred laden Indians, accompanied by a great Mexican Cacique who, in his face, features, and appearance, bore a strong likeness to our Captain Cortés and the great Montezuma had sent him purposely, for it is said that when Tendile brought the portrait of Cortés all the chiefs who were in Montezuma's company said that a great chief named Quintalbor looked exactly like Cortés, and that was the name of the Cacique who now arrived with Tendile; and as he was so like Cortés, we called them in camp "our Cortés" and "the other Cortés." To go back to my story, when these people arrived and came before our Captain they first of all kissed the earth and then fumigated him and all the soldiers who were standing around him, with incense which they brought in braziers of pottery. Cortés received them affectionately and seated them near himself, and that chief who came with the present had been appointed spokesman together with Tendile. After welcoming us to the country and after many courteous speeches had passed he ordered the presents which he had brought to be displayed, and they were placed on mats over which were spread cotton cloths. The first article presented was a wheel like a sun, as big as a cartwheel, with many sorts of pictures on it, the whole of fine gold, and a wonderful thing to behold, which those who afterward weighed it said was worth more than ten thousand dollars. Then another wheel was presented of greater size made of silver of great brilliancy in imitation of the moon with other figures shown on it, and this was of great value as it was very heavy—and the chief brought back the helmet full of fiine grains of gold, just as they are got out of the mines, and this was worth three thousand dollars. This gold in the helmet was worth more to us than if it had contained twenty thousand dollars, because it showed us that there were good mines there. Then were brought twenty golden ducks, beautifully worked and very natural looking, and some [ornaments] like dogs, and many articles of gold worked in the shape of tigers and lions and monkeys, and ten collars beautifully worked and other necklaces; and twelve arrows and a bow with its string, and two rods like staffs of justice, five palms long, all in beautiful hollow work of fine gold. Then there were presented crests of gold and plumes of rich green feathers, and others of silver, and fans of the same materials, and deer copied in hollow gold and many other things that I cannot remember for it all happened so many years ago. And then over thirty loads of beautiful cotton cloth were brought worked with many patterns and decorated with many colored feathers, and so many other things were there that it is useless my trying to describe them for I know not how to do it. When all these things had been presented, this great Cacique Quintalbor and Tendile asked Cortés to accept this present with the same willingness with which his prince had sent it, and divide it among the *teules* and men who accompanied him. Cortés received the present with delight and then the ambassadors told Cortés that they wished to repeat what their prince, Montezuma, had sent them to say. First of all they told him that he was pleased that such valiant men, as he had heard that we were, should come to his country, for he knew all about what we had done at Tabasco, and that he would much like to see our great emperor who was such a mighty prince and whose fame was spread over so many lands, and that he would send him a present of precious stones; and that meanwhile we should stay in that port; that if he could assist us in any way he would do so with the greatest pleasure; but as to the interview, they should not worry about it; that there was no need for it and they (ambassadors) urged many objections. Cortés kept a good countenance, and returned his thanks to them, and with many flattering expressions gave each of the ambassadors two holland shirts and some blue glass beads and other things, and begged them to go back as his ambassadors to Mexico and to tell their prince, the great Montezuma, that as we had come across so many seas and had journeyed from such distant lands solely to see and speak with him in person, that if we should return thus, that our great king and lord would not receive us well, and that wherever their prince Montezuma might be we wished to go and see him and do what he might order us to do. The ambassadors replied that they would go back and give this message to their prince, but as to the question of the desired interview—they considered it superfluous. By these ambassadors Cortés sent what our poverty could afford as a gift to Montezuma; a glass cup of Florentine ware, engraved with trees and hunting scenes and gilt, and three holland shirts and other things, and he charged the messengers to bring a reply. The two governors set out and Pitalpitoque remained in camp; for it seems that the other servants of Montezuma had given him orders to see that food was brought to us from the neighboring towns.

M

As soon as the messengers had been sent off to Mexico, Cortés dispatched two ships to explore the coast farther along, and to seek out a safe harbor, and search for lands where we could settle, for it was clear that we could not settle on those sand dunes, both on account of the mosquitoes and the distance from other towns. They did as they were told and arrived at the Rio Grande, which is close to Panuco. They were not able to proceed any further on account of the strong currents. Seeing how difficult the navigation had become, they turned round and made for San Juan de Ulúa, without having made any further progress.

I must now go back to say that the Indian Pitalpitoque, who remained behind to look after the food, slackened his efforts to such an extent that no provisions reached the camp and we were greatly in need of food, for the cassava turned sour from the damp and rotted and became foul with weevils and if we had not gone hunting for shellfish we should have had nothing to eat. The Indians, who used to come bringing gold and fowls for barter, did not come in such numbers as on our first arrival, and those who did come were very shy and cautious and we began to count the hours that must elapse before the return of the messengers who had gone to Mexico. We were thus waiting when Tendile returned, accompanied by many Indians, and after having paid their respects in the usual manner by fumigating Cortés and the rest of us with incense, he presented ten loads of fine rich feather cloth, and four *chalchihuites*, which are green stones of very great value, and held in the greatest esteem among the Indians, more than emeralds are by us, and certain other gold articles. Not counting the *chalchihuites*, the gold alone was said to be worth three thousand dollars. Then Tendile and Pitalpitoque went aside with Cortés and Doña Marina and Aguilar, and reported that their prince Montezuma had accepted the present and was greatly pleased with it, but as to an interview, that no more should be said about; that these rich stones of *chalchihuite* should be sent to the great Emperor as they were of the highest value, each one being worth more and being esteemed more highly than a great load of gold, and that it was not worth while to send any more messengers to Mexico. Cortés thanked the messengers and gave him presents, but it was certainly a disappointment to him to be told so distinctly that we could not see Montezuma, and he said to some soldiers who happened to be standing near, "Surely this must be a great and rich prince, and some day, please God, we must go and see him"—and the soldiers answered, "We wish that we were already living with him!"

Let us now leave this question of visits and relate that it was now the time of the Ave Maria, and at the sound of a bell which we had in the camp we all fell on our knees before a cross placed on a sand hill and said our prayers of the Ave Maria before the cross. When Tendile and Pitalpitoque saw us thus kneeling, as they were very intelligent, they asked what was the reason that we humbled ourselves before a tree cut in that particular way. As Cortés heard this remark he said to the Padre de la Merced, who was present, "It is a good opportunity, father, as we have good material at hand, to explain through our interpreters matters touching our holy faith." And then he delivered a discourse to the Caciques so fitting to the occasion that no good theologian could have bettered it. Cortés said many things very well expressed, which they thoroughly understood, and they replied that they would report them to their prince Montezuma. Cortés also told them that one of the objects for which our great Emperor had sent us to their countries was to abolish human sacrifices, and the other evil rites which they practiced and to see that they did not rob one another, or worship those curséd images. And Cortés prayed them to set up in their city, in the temples where they kept the idols which they believed to be gods, a cross like the one they saw before them, and to set up in the same place an image of Our Lady, which he would give them, with her precious son in her arms, and they would see how well it would go with them, and what our God would do for them. I recall to mind that on this latest visit many Indians came with Tendile who were wishing to barter articles of gold, which, however, were of no great value. So all the soldiers set about bartering, and the gold which we gained by this barter we gave to the sailors who were out fishing in exchange for their fish so as to get something to eat, for otherwise we often underwent great privations through hunger. Cortés was pleased at this, although he pretended not to see what was going on.

> By this time Cortés has forged an alliance with several hill towns against Montezuma, whose empire has existed on a vast tribute of gold, goods, slaves, and sacrificial victims from these outlying tribes. Montezuma now realizes that he cannot stay the march of these men from the rising sun and so he belatedly "welcomes" them to his capital. This would not be the last time whites would divide before conquering, nor would it be the last time an Indian leader attempted to buy them off.

Just as we were starting on our march to Mexico there came before Cortés four Mexican chiefs sent by Montezuma who brought a present of gold and cloths. After they had made obeisance according to their custom, they said: "Malinche, our Lord the Great Montezuma sends you this present and says that he is greatly concerned for the hardships you have endured in coming from such a distant land in order to see him, and that he has already sent to tell you that he will give you much gold and silver and *chalchihuites* as tribute for your Emperor and for yourself and the other Teules in your company, provided you do not come to Mexico, and now again he begs as a favor, that you will not advance any farther but return whence you have come, and he promises to send you to the port a great quantity of gold and silver and rich stones for that King of yours, and, as for you, he will give you four loads of gold and for each of your brothers one load, but as for going on to Mexico your entrance into it is forbidden, for all his vassals have risen in arms to prevent your entry, and besides this there is no road thither, only a very narrow one, and there is no food for you to eat." And he used many other arguments about the difficulties to the end that we should advance no farther.

Cortés with much show of affection embraced the ambassadors, although the message grieved him, and he accepted the present, and said that he marveled how the Lord Montezuma, having given himself out as our friend, and being such a great Prince, should be so inconstant; that one time he says one thing and another time sends to order the contrary, and regarding what he says about giving gold to our Lord the Emperor and to ourselves, he is grateful to him for it, and what he sends him now he will pay for in good works as time goes on. How can he deem it befitting that being so near to his city, we should think it right to return on our road without carrying through what our Prince has commanded us to do? If the Lord Montezuma had sent his messengers and ambassadors to some great prince such as he is himself, and if, after nearly reaching his house, those messengers whom he sent should turn back without speaking to the Prince about that which they were sent to say, when they came back into his [Montezuma's] presence with such a story, what favor would he show them? He would merely treat them as cowards of little worth; and this is what our Emperor would do with us, so that in one way or another we were determined to enter his city, and from this time forth he must not send any more excuses on the subject, for he [Cortés] was bound to see him, and talk to him and explain the whole purpose for which we had come, and this he must do to him personally. Then after he understood it all, if our presence in the city did not seem good to him, we would return whence we had come. As for what he said about there being little or no food, not enough to support us, we were men who could get along even if we have but little to eat, and we were already on the way to his city, so let him take our coming in good part.

As soon as the messengers had been dispatched, we set out for Mexico, and as the people of Huexotzingo and Chalco had told us that Montezuma had held consultations with his idols and priests, who had said he was to allow us to enter and that then he could kill us, and as we are but human and feared death, we never ceased thinking about it. As that country is very thickly peopled we made short marches, and commended ourselves to God and to Our Lady his blessed Mother, and talked about how and by what means we could enter the City, and it put courage into our hearts to think that as our Lord Jesus

Christ had vouchsafed us protection through past dangers, he would likewise guard us from the power of the Mexicans.

We went to sleep at a town called Iztapalatengo where half the houses are in the water and the other half on dry land, and there they gave us a good supper.

The Great Montezuma, when he heard the reply which Cortés had sent to him, at once determined to send his nephew, named Cacamatzin, the lord of Texcoco, with great pomp to bid welcome to Cortés and to all of us, and one of our scouts came in to tell us that a large crowd of friendly Mexicans was coming along the road clad in rich mantles. It was very early in the morning when this happened, and we were ready to start, and Cortés ordered us to wait in our quarters until he could see what the matter was.

At that moment four chieftains arrived, who made deep obeisance to Cortés and said that close by there was approaching Cacamatzin, the great lord of Texcoco, a nephew of the Great Montezuma, and he begged us to have the goodness to wait until he arrived.

He did not tarry long, for he soon arrived with greater pomp and splendor than we had ever beheld in a Mexican Prince, for he came in a litter richly worked in green feathers, with many silver borderings, and rich stones set in bosses made out of the finest gold. Eight chieftains, who, it was said, were all lords of towns, bore the litter on their shoulders. When they came near to the house where Cortés was quartered, the chieftains assisted Cacamatzin to descend from the litter, and they swept the ground, and removed the straws where he had to pass, and when they came before our Captain they made him a deep reverence, and Cacamatzin said:

"Malinche, here we have come, I and these chieftains, to place ourselves at your service, and to give you all that you may need for yourself and your companions and to place you in your home, which is our city, for so the Great Montezuma our Prince has ordered us to do, and he asks your pardon that he did not come with us himself, but it is on account of ill-health that he did not do so, and not from want of very good will which he bears toward you."

When our Captain and all of us beheld such pomp and

majesty in those chiefs, especially in the nephew of Montezuma, we considered it a matter of the greatest importance, and
said among ourselves, if this Cacique bears himself with such
dignity, what will the Great Montezuma do?

When Cacamatzin had delivered his speech, Cortés embraced him, and gave many caresses to him and all the other
chieftains, and gave him three stones which are called *margaritas*, which have within them many markings of different
colors, and to the other chieftains he gave blue glass beads, and
he told them that he thanked them and when he was able he
would repay the Lord Montezuma for all the favors which
every day he was granting us.

As soon as the speech-making was over, we at once set out,
and as the Caciques whom I have spoken about brought many
followers with them, and as many people came out to see us
from the neighboring towns, all the roads were full of them.

During the morning, we arrived at a broad causeway and
continued our march towards Iztapalapa, and when we saw
so many cities and villages built in the water and other great
towns on dry land and that straight and level causeway going
toward Mexico, we were amazed and said that it was like the
enchantments they tell of in the legend of Amadis, on account
of the great towers and cues and buildings rising from the
water, and all built of masonry. And some of our soldiers even
asked whether the things that we saw were not a dream. It is
not to be wondered at that I here write it down in this
manner, for there is so much to think over that I do not know
how to describe it, seeing things as we did that had never been
heard of or seen before, not even dreamed about.

Thus, we arrived near Iztapalapa, to behold the splendor of
the other Caciques who came out to meet us, who were the
lord of the town named Cuitlahuac, and the lord of Culuacan,
both of them near relations of Montezuma. And then when we
entered the city of Iztapalapa, the appearance of the palaces
in which they lodged us! How spacious and well built they were,
of beautiful stone work and cedar wood, and the wood of other
sweet scented trees, with great rooms and courts, wonderful to
behold, covered with awnings of cotton cloth.

When we had looked well at all of this, we went to the orchard and garden, which was such a wonderful thing to see and walk in that I was never tired of looking at the diversity of the trees, and noting the scent which each one had, and the paths full of roses and flowers, and the many fruit trees and native roses, and the pond of fresh water. There was another thing to observe, that great canoes were able to pass into the garden from the lake through an opening that had been made so that there was no need for their occupants to land. And all was cemented and very splendid with many kinds of stone [monuments] with pictures on them, which gave much to think about. Then the birds of many kinds and breeds which came into the pond. I say again that I stood looking at it and thought that never in the world would there be discovered other lands such as these, for at that time there was no Peru, nor any thought of it. Of all these wonders that I then beheld today all is overthrown and lost, nothing left standing.

Let us go on, and I will relate that the Caciques of that town and of Coyoacan brought us a present of gold, worth more than two thousand pesos.

Early next day we left Iztapalapa with a large escort of those great Caciques whom I have already mentioned. We proceeded along the causeway, which is here eight paces in width and runs so straight to the City of Mexico that it does not seem to me to turn either much or little, but, broad as it is, it was so crowded with people that there was hardly room for them all, some of them going to and others returning from Mexico, besides those who had come out to see us, so that we were hardly able to pass by the crowds of them that came; and the towers and cues were full of people as well as the canoes from all parts of the lake. It was not to be wondered at, for they had never before seen horses or men such as we are.

Gazing on such wonderful sights, we did not know what to say, or whether what appeared before us was real, for on one side, on the land, there were great cities, and in the lake ever so many more, and the lake itself was crowded with canoes, and in the causeway were many bridges at intervals, and in front of us stood the great City of Mexico, and we—we did not even number four hundred soldiers! and we well remembered the words and warnings given us by the people of Huexotzingo and Tlaxcala, and the many other warnings that had been given that we should beware of entering Mexico, where they would kill us, as soon as they had us inside.

Let the curious readers consider whether there is not much to ponder over in this that I am writing. What men have there been in the world who have shown such daring? But let us get on, and march along the causeway. When we arrived where another small causeway branches off [leading to Coyoacan, which is another city] where there were some buildings like towers, which are their oratories, many more chieftains and Caciques approached clad in very rich mantles, the brilliant liveries of one chieftain differing from those of another, and the causeways were crowded with them. The Great Montezuma had sent these great Caciques in advance to receive us, and when they came before Cortés they bade us welcome in their language, and as a sign of peace, they touched their hands against the ground, and kissed the ground with the hand.

There we halted for a good while, and Cacamatzin, the lord of Texcoco, and the lord of Iztapalapa and the lord of Tacuba and the lord of Coyoacan went on in advance to meet the Great Montezuma, who was approaching in a rich litter accompanied by other great lords and Caciques who owned vassals. When we arrived near to Mexico, where there were some other small towers, the Great Montezuma got down from his litter, and those great Caciques supported him with their arms beneath a marvelously rich canopy of green-colored feathers with much gold and silver embroidery and with pearls and *chalchihuites* suspended from a sort of bordering, which was wonderful to look at. The Great Montezuma was richly attired according to his usage, and he was shod with sandals, the soles were of gold and the upper part adorned with precious stones. The four chieftains who supported his arms were also richly clothed according to their usage, in garments which were apparently held ready for them on the road to enable them to accompany their prince, for they did not appear in such attire when they came to receive us. Besides these four chieftains, there were four other great Caciques who supported the canopy over their heads, and many other lords who walked before the Great Montezuma, sweeping the ground where he would tread and spreading cloths on it, so that he should not tread on the earth. Not one of these chieftains dared even to think of looking him in the face, but kept their eyes lowered with great reverence, except those four relations, his nephews, who supported him with their arms.

When Cortés was told that the Great Montezuma was approaching, and he saw him coming, he dismounted from his horse, and when he was near Montezuma, they simultaneously paid great reverence to one another. Montezuma bade him welcome and our Cortés replied through Doña Marina wishing him very good health. And it seems to me that Cortés, through Doña Marina, offered him his right hand, and Montezuma did not wish to take it, but he did give his hand to Cortés and then Cortés brought out a necklace which he had ready at hand, made of glass stones, which I have already said are called *margaritas,* which have within them many patterns of diverse colors; these were strung on a cord of gold and with musk so that it should have a sweet scent, and he placed it round the neck of the Great Montezuma and when he had so placed it he was going to embrace him, and those great Princes who accompanied Montezuma held back Cortés by the arm so that he should not embrace him, for they considered it an indignity.

Then Cortés through the mouth of Doña Marina told him that now his heart rejoiced at having seen such a great prince, and that he took it as a great honor that he had come in person to meet him and had frequently shown him such favor.

Then Montezuma spoke other words of politeness to him, and told two of his nephews who supported his arms, the lord of Texcoco and the lord of Coyoacan, to go with us and show us to our quarters, and Montezuma with his other two relations, the lord of Cuitlahuac and the lord of Tacuba, who accompanied him, returned to the city, and all those grand companies of Caciques and chieftains who had come with him returned in his train. As they turned back after their Prince we stood watching them and observed how they all marched with their eyes fixed on the ground without looking at him, keeping close to the wall, following him with great reverence. Thus space was made for us to enter the streets of Mexico, without being so much crowded. But who could now count the multitude of men and women and boys who were in the streets and on the *azoteas,* and in canoes on the canals, who had come out to see us? It was indeed wonderful, and, now that I am writing about it, it all comes before my eyes as though it had happened but yesterday. Coming to think it over it seems to be a great mercy that our Lord Jesus Christ was pleased to give us grace and courage to dare to enter into such a city; and for the many times He has saved me from danger of death, as will be seen later on, I give Him sincere thanks, and in that He has preserved me to write about it, although I cannot do it as fully as is fitting or the subject needs. Let us make no words about it, for deeds are the best witnesses to what I say here and elsewhere.

Let us return to our entry to Mexico. They took us to lodge in some large houses, where there were apartments for all of us, for they had belonged to the father of the Great Montezuma, who was named Axayaca, and at that time Montezuma kept there the great oratories for his idols, and a secret chamber where he kept bars and jewels of gold, which was the treasure that he had inherited from his father Axayaca, and he never disturbed it. They took us to lodge in that house, because they called us Teules, and took us for such, so that we should be with the idols or Teules which were kept there. However, for one reason or another, it was there they took us, where there were great halls and chambers canopied with the cloth of the country for our Captain, and for every one of us beds of matting with canopies above, and no better bed is given, however great the chief may be, for they are not used. And all these palaces were coated with shining cement and swept and garlanded.

As soon as we arrived and entered into the great court, the Great Montezuma took our Captain by the hand, for he was there awaiting him, and led him to the apartment and saloon where he was to lodge, which was very richly adorned according to their usage, and he had at hand a very rich necklace made of golden crabs, a marvelous piece of work, and Montezuma himself placed it round the neck of our Captain Cortés, and greatly astonished his [own] captains by the great honor

The Expedition of Lewis and Clark

The reader needs little introduction to the expedition of Lewis and Clark, one of the great and successful explorations in the history of the North American continent. Part of its attractiveness lies in the hugeness of the design; the other part in the fact that it was relatively bloodless. The expedition was clearly political and economic in motive: Jefferson wanted to find out what he had bought from Napoleon. Despite this typically utilitarian basis, it is true that these white observers were more acute, less blind than most of their predecessors, and the entries in these journals constitute one of the supremely valuable sources of information on the Plains tribes, those of the Great Basin, and those of the Far West. As we find them here they are living as yet barely contaminated existences, but they are soon to be transformed, in part because of these very white men who saw them, wrote about them, and in so doing (as Henry Nash Smith has said) transformed the West from myth to reality. This excerpt from Chapter 5 picks up the party in November of 1804.

Tuesday 13. We this morning unloaded the boat and stowed away the contents in a storehouse which we have built. At half-past ten ice began to float down the river for the first time: in the course of the morning we were visited by the Black Cat, Poscapsahe, who brought an Assiniboin chief and seven warriors to see us. This man, whose name is Chechawk, is a chief of one out of three bands of Assiniboins who wander over the plains between the Missouri and Assiniboin during the summer, and in the winter carry the spoils of their hunting to the traders on the Assiniboin River, and occasionally come to this place: the whole three bands consist of about eight hundred men. We gave him a twist of tobacco to smoke with his people, and

From John B. McMaster, ed., *History of the Expedition of Lewis and Clark* (New York, 1922), vol. 1, pp. 182-206.

a gold cord for himself: the Sioux also asked for whisky, which we refused to give them. It snowed all day and the air was very cold.

Wednesday 14. The river rose last night half an inch, and is now filled with floating ice. This morning was cloudy with some snow: about seventy lodges of Assiniboins and some Knistenaux are at the Mandan village, and this being the day of adoption and exchange of property between them all, it is accompanied by a dance, which prevents our seeing more than two Indians today: these Knistenaux are a band of Chippeways, whose language they speak; they live on the Assiniboin and Saskashawan rivers, and are about two hundred and forty men. We sent a man down on horseback to see what had become of our hunters, and as we apprehend a failure of provisions we have recourse to our pork this evening. Two Frenchmen who had been below returned with twenty beaver which they had caught in traps.

Thursday 15. The morning again cloudy, and the ice running thicker than yesterday, the wind variable. The man came back with information that our hunters were about thirty miles below, and we immediately sent an order to them to make their way through the floating ice, to assist them in which we sent some tin for the bow of the periogue and a towrope. The ceremony of yesterday seems to continue still, for we were not visited by a single Indian. The swan are still passing to the south.

Friday 16. We had a very hard white frost this morning, the trees are all covered with ice, and the weather cloudy. The men this day moved into the huts, although they are not finished. In the evening some horses were sent down to the woods near us in order to prevent their being stolen by the Assiniboins, with whom some difficulty is now apprehended. An Indian came down with four buffalo robes and some corn, which he offered for a pistol, but was refused.

Saturday, November 17. Last night was very cold, and the ice in the river today is thicker than hitherto. We are totally occupied with our huts, but received visits from several Indians.

Sunday, November 18. Today we had a cold windy morning; the Black Cat came to see us, and occupied us for a long time with questions on the usages of our country. He mentioned that a council had been held yesterday to deliberate on the state of their affairs. It seems that not long ago, a party of Sioux fell in with some horses belonging to the Minnetarees, and carried them off; but in their flight they were met by some Assiniboins, who killed the Sioux and kept the horses: a Frenchman too, who had lived many years among the Mandans, was lately killed on his route to the British factory on the Assiniboin; some smaller differences existed between the two nations, all of which being discussed, the council decided that they would not resent the recent insults from the Assiniboins and Knistenaux, until they had seen whether we had deceived them or not in our promises of furnishing them with arms and ammunition. They had been disappointed in their hopes of receiving them from Mr. Evans and were afraid that we too, like him, might tell them what was not true. We advised them to continue at peace, that supplies of every kind would no doubt arrive for them, but that time was necessary to organize the trade. The fact is that the Assiniboins treat the Mandans as the Sioux do the Ricaras; by their vicinity to the British they get all the supplies, which they withhold or give at pleasure to the remoter Indians: the consequence is, that however badly treated, the Mandans and Ricaras are very slow to retaliate lest they should lose their trade altogether.

Monday 19. The ice continues to float in the river, the wind high from the northwest, and the weather cold. Our hunters arrived from their excursion below, and bring a very fine supply of thirty-two deer, eleven elk, and five buffalo, all of which was hung in a smokehouse.

Tuesday 20. We this day moved into our huts which are now completed. This place, which we call Fort Mandan, is situated in a point of low ground, on the north side of the Missouri, covered with tall and heavy cotton wood. The works consist of two rows of huts or sheds, forming an angle where they joined each other; each row containing four rooms, of fourteen feet square and seven feet high, with plank ceiling, and the roof slanting so as to form a loft above the rooms, the highest part of which is eighteen feet from the ground: the backs of the huts formed a wall of that height, and opposite the angle the place of the wall was supplied by picketing: in the area were two rooms for stores and provisions. The latitude by observation is 47° 21′ 47″, and the computed distance from the mouth of the Missouri sixteen hundred miles.

In the course of the day several Indians came down to partake of our fresh meat; among the rest, three chiefs of the second Mandan village. They inform us that the Sioux on the Missouri above the Chayenne River threaten to attack them this winter; that these Sioux are much irritated at the Ricaras for having made peace through our means with the Mandans, and have lately ill-treated three Ricaras who carried the pipe of peace to them, by beating them and taking away their horses. We gave them assurances that we would protect them from all their enemies.

November 21. The weather was this day fine: the river clear of ice and rising a little: we are now settled in our new winter habitation, and shall wait with much anxiety the first return of spring to continue our journey.

The villages near which we are established are five in number, and are the residence of three distinct nations; the Mandans, the Ahnahaways, and the Minnetarees. The history of the Mandans, as we received it from our interpreters and from the chiefs themselves, and as it is attested by existing monuments, illustrates more than that of any other nation the unsteady movements and the tottering fortunes of the American nations. Within the recollection of living witnesses, the Mandans were settled forty years ago in nine villages, the ruins of which we passed about eighty miles below, and situated seven on the west and two on the east side of the Missouri. The two, finding themselves wasting away before the smallpox and the Sioux, united into one village, and moved up the river opposite to the Ricaras. The same causes reduced the remaining seven to five villages, till at length they emigrated in a body to the Ricara nation, where they formed themselves into two villages, and joined those of their countrymen who had gone before them. In their new residence they were still insecure, and at length the three villages ascended the Missouri to their present position. The two who had emigrated together still settled in the two villages on the northwest side of the Missouri, while the single village took a position on the southeast side.

In this situation they were found by those who visited them in 1796; since which the two villages have united into one. They are now in two villages, one on the southeast of the Missouri, the other on the opposite side, and at the distance of three miles across. The first, in an open plain, contains about forty or fifty lodges, built in the same way as those of the Ricaras: the second, the same number, and both may raise about three hundred and fifty men.

On the same side of the river, and at the distance of four miles from the lower Mandan village, is another called Mahaha. It is situated in a high plain at the mouth of Knife River, and is the residence of the Ahnahaways. This nation, whose name indicates that they were "people whose village is on a hill," formerly resided on the Missouri, about thirty miles below where they now live. The Assiniboins and Sioux forced them to a spot five miles higher, where the greatest part of them were put to death, and the rest emigrated to their present situation, in order to obtain an asylum near the Minnetarees. They are called by the French, Soulier Noir or Shoe Indians; by the Mandans, Wattasoons, and their whole force is about fifty men.

On the south side of the same Knife River, half a mile above the Mahaha and in the same open plain with it, is a village of Minnetarees surnamed Metaharta, who are about one hundred and fifty men in number. On the opposite side of Knife River, and one and a half miles above this village is a second of Minnetarees, who may be considered as the proper Minnetaree nation. It is situated in a beautiful low plain, and contains four hundred and fifty warriors. The accounts which we received of the Minnetarees were contradictory. The Mandans say that this people came out of the water to the east, and settled near them in their former establishment in nine villages; that they were very numerous, and fixed themselves in one village on the southern side of the Missouri. A quarrel about a buffalo divided the nation, of which two bands went into the plains, and were known by the name of Crow and Paunch Indians, and the rest moved to their present establishment. The Minnetarees proper assert, on the contrary, that they grew where they now live, and will never emigrate from the spot; the great spirit having declared that if they moved they would all die. They also say that the Minnetarees Metaharta, that is, Minnetarees of the Willows, whose language with very little variation is their own, came many years ago from the plains and settled near them, and perhaps the two traditions may be reconciled by the natural presumption that these Minnetarees were the tribe known to the Mandans below, and that they ascended the river for the purpose of rejoining the Minnetarees proper. These Minnetarees are part of the great nation called Fall Indians, who occupy the intermediate country between the Missouri and the Saskaskawan, and who are known by the name of Minnetarees of the Missouri, and Minnetarees of Fort de Prairie; that is, residing near or rather frequenting the establishment in the prairie on the Saskaskawan. These Minnetarees indeed told us that they had relations on the Saskaskawan, whom they had never known till they met them in war, and having engaged in the night were astonished at discovering that they were fighting with men who spoke their own language. The name of Grosventres, or Bigbellies, is given to these Minnetarees, as well as to all the Fall Indians. The inhabitants of these five villages, all of which are within the distance of six miles, live in harmony with each other. The Ahnahaways understand in part the language of the Minnetarees: the dialect of the Mandans differs widely from both; but their long residence together has insensibly blended their manners, and occasioned some approximation in language, particularly as to objects of daily occurrence and obvious to the senses.

November 22. The morning was fine, and the day warm. We purchased from the Mandans a quantity of corn of a mixed color, which they dug up in ears from holes made near the front of their lodges, in which it is buried during the winter: this morning the sentinel informed us that an Indian was about to kill his wife near the fort; we went down to the house of our interpreter where we found the parties, and after forbidding any violence, inquired into the cause of his intending to commit such an atrocity. It appeared that some days ago a quarrel had taken place between him and his wife, in consequence of which she had taken refuge in the house where the two squaws of our interpreter lived: by running away she forfeited her life, which might have been lawfully taken by the husband. About two days ago she had returned to the village, but the same evening came back to the fort much beaten and stabbed in three places, and the husband now came for the purpose of completing his revenge. He observed that he had lent her to one of our sergeants for a night, and that if he wanted her he would give her to him altogether: we gave him a few presents and tried to persuade him to take his wife home; the grand chief too happened to arrive at the same moment, and reproached him with his violence, till at length they went off together, but by no means in a state of much apparent love.

November 23. Again we had a fair and warm day, with the wind from the southeast: the river is now at a stand having risen four inches in the whole.

November 25. The wind continued from the same quarter and the weather was warm: we were occupied in finishing our huts and making a large rope of elk-skin to draw our boat on the bank.

Sunday, November 25. The weather is still fine, warm and pleasant, and the river falls one inch and a half. Captain Lewis went on an excursion to the villages accompanied by eight men. A Minnetaree chief, the first who has visited us, came down to the fort: his name was Waukerassa, but as both the interpreters had gone with Captain Lewis we were obliged to confine our civilities to some presents with which he was much pleased: we now completed our huts, and fortunately too, for the next day.

Monday, November 26. Before daylight the wind shifted to the northwest, and blew very hard, with cloudy weather and a keen cold air, which confined us much and prevented us from working: the night continued very cold, and,

Tuesday 27. The weather cloudy, the wind continuing from the northwest and the river crowded with floating ice. Captain Lewis returned with two chiefs, Mahnotah, an Ahnahaway, and Minnessurraree, a Minnetaree, and a third warrior: they explained to us that the reason of their not having come to see us was that the Mandans had told them that we meant to combine with the Sioux and cut them off in the course of the winter: a suspicion increased by the strength of the fort, and the circumstance of our interpreters having been removed there with their families: these reports we did not fail to disprove to their entire satisfaction, and amused them by every attention, particularly by the dancing of the men, which diverted them highly. All the Indians whom Captain Lewis had visited were very well disposed, and received him with great kindness, except a principal chief of one of the upper villages, named Mahpahpaparapassatoo or Horned Weasel, who made use of the civilized indecorum of refusing to be seen, and when Captain Lewis called he was told the chief was not at home. In the course of the day seven of the northwest company's traders arrived from the Assiniboin River, and, one of their interpreters having undertaken to circulate among the Indians unfavorable reports, it became necessary to warn them of the consequences if they did not desist from such proceedings. The river fell two inches today and the weather became very cold.

Wednesday 28. About eight o'clock last evening it began to snow and continued till daybreak, after which it ceased till seven o'clock, but then resumed and continued during the day, the weather being cold and the river full of floating ice: about eight o'clock Poscopsahe came down to visit us, with some warriors; we gave them presents and entertained them with all that might amuse their curiosity, and at parting we told them that we had heard of the British trader, Mr. Laroche, having attempted to distribute medals and flags among them, but that those emblems could not be received from any other than the American nation without incurring the displeasure of their great father the president. They left us much pleased with their treatment. The river fell one inch today.

Thursday 29. The wind is again from the northwest, the weather cold, and the snow which fell yesterday and last night is thirteen inches in depth. The river closed during the night at the village above, and fell two feet; but this afternoon it began to rise a little. Mr. Laroche, the principal of the seven traders, came with one of his men to see us; we told him that we should not permit him to give medals and flags to the Indians; he declared that he had no such intention, and we then suffered him to make use of one of our interpreters, on his stipulating not to touch any subject but that of his traffic with them. An unfortunate accident occurred to Sergeant

Pryor, who in taking down the boat's mast dislocated his shoulder, nor was it till after four trials that we replaced it.

Friday 30. About eight o'clock an Indian came to the opposite bank of the river, calling out that he had something important to communicate, and on sending for him, he told us that five Mandans had been met about eight leagues to the southwest by a party of Sioux, who had killed one of them, wounded two, and taken nine horses; that four of the Wattasoons were missing, and that the Mandans expected an attack. We thought this an excellent opportunity to discountenance the injurious reports against us, and to fix the wavering confidence of the nation. Captain Clark therefore instantly crossed the river with twenty-three men strongly armed, and circling the town approached it from behind. His unexpected appearance surprised and alarmed the chiefs, who came out to meet him, and conducted him to the village. He then told them that having heard of the outrage just committed, he had come to assist his dutiful children; that if they would assemble their warriors and those of the nation, he would lead them against the Sioux and avenge the blood of their countrymen. After some minutes conversation, Oheenaw the Chayenne arose: "We now see," said he, "that what you have told us is true, since as soon as our enemies threaten to attack us you come to protect us and are ready to chastise those who have spilled our blood. We did indeed listen to your good talk, for when you told us that the other nations were inclined to peace with us, we went out carelessly in small parties, and some have been killed by the Sioux and Ricaras. But I knew that the Ricaras were liars, and I told their chief who accompanied you, that his whole nation were liars and bad men; that we had several times made a peace with them which they were the first to break; that whenever we pleased we might shoot them like buffalo, but that we had no wish to kill them; that we would not suffer them to kill us, nor steal our horses; and that although we agreed to make peace with them, because our two fathers desired it, yet we did not believe that they would be faithful long. Such, father, was my language to them in your presence, and you see that instead of listening to your good counsels they have spilled our blood. A few days ago two Ricaras came

here and told us that two of their villages were making moccasins, that the Sioux were stirring them up against us, and
that we ought to take care of our horses; yet these very Ricaras
we sent home as soon as the news reached us today, lest our
people should kill them in the first moment of grief for their
murdered relatives. Four of the Wattasoons whom we expected
back in sixteen days have been absent twenty-four, and we fear
have fallen. But, father, the snow is now deep, the weather cold,
and our horses cannot travel through the plains: the murderers
have gone off: if you will conduct us in the spring, when the
snow has disappeared, we will assemble all the surrounding
warriors and follow you."

Captain Clark replied that we were always willing and able
to defend them; that he was sorry that the snow prevented their
marching to meet the Sioux, since he wished to show them that
the warriors of their great father would chastise the enemies of
his obedient children who opened their ears to his advice; that
if some Ricaras had joined the Sioux, they should remember
that there were bad men in every nation, and that they should
not be offended at the Ricaras till they saw whether these ill-
disposed men were countenanced by the whole tribe; that the
Sioux possessed great influence over the Ricaras, whom they
supplied with military stores, and sometimes led them astray,
because they were afraid to oppose them: but that this should
be the less offensive since the Mandans themselves were under
the same apprehensions from the Assiniboins and Knistenaux,
and that while they were thus dependent, both the Ricaras and
Mandans ought to keep on terms with their powerful
neighbors, whom they may afterward set at defiance, when
we shall supply them with arms, and take them under
our protection.

After two hours' conversation Captain Clark left the village.
The chief repeatedly thanked him for the fatherly protection
he had given them, observing that the whole village had been
weeping all night and day for the brave young man who had
been slain, but now they would wipe their eyes and weep no
more as they saw that their father would protect them. He then
crossed the river on the ice and returned on the north side to

the fort. The day as well as the evening was cold, and the river rose to its former height.

Saturday, December 1. The wind was from the northwest, and the whole party engaged in picketing the fort. About ten o'clock the half-brother of the man who had been killed came to inform us that six Sharhas or Chayenne Indians had arrived, bringing a pipe of peace, and that their nation was three days' march behind them. Three Pawnees had accompanied the Sharhas, and the Mandans, being afraid of the Sharhas on account of their being at peace with the Sioux, wished to put both them and the three Pawnees to death; but the chiefs had forbidden it as it would be contrary to our wishes. We gave him a present of tobacco, and although from his connection with the sufferer, he was more embittered against the Pawnees than any other Mandan, yet he seemed perfectly satisfied with our pacific counsels and advice. The Mandans, we observe, call all the Ricaras by the name of Pawness; the name of Ricaras being that by which the nation distinguishes itself.

In the evening we were visited by a Mr. Henderson, who came from the Hudson Bay Company to trade with the Minnetarees. He had been about eight days on his route in a direction nearly south, and brought with him tobacco, beads, and other merchandise to trade for furs, and a few guns which are to be exchanged for horses.

Sunday, December 2. The latter part of the evening was warm, and a thaw continued till the morning, when the wind shifted to the north. At eleven o'clock the chiefs of the lower village brought down four of the Sharhas. We explained to them our intentions, and advised them to remain at peace with each other: we also gave them a flag, some tobacco, and a speech for their nation. These were accompanied by a letter to Messrs. Tabeau and Gravelines at the Ricara village, requesting them to preserve peace if possible, and to declare the part which we should be forced to take if the Ricaras and Sioux made war on those whom we had adopted. After distributing a few presents to the Sharhas and Mandans, and showing them our curiosities we dismissed them, apparently well pleased at their reception.

Monday, December 3. The morning was fine, but in the afternoon the weather became cold with the wind from the northwest. The father of the Mandan who was killed brought us a present of dried pumpkins and some pemitigon, for which we gave him some small articles. Our offer of assistance to avenge the death of his son seemed to have produced a grateful respect from him, as well as from the brother of the deceased, which pleased us much.

Tuesday 4. The wind continues from the northwest, the weather cloudy and raw, and the river rose one inch. Oscapsahe and two young chiefs pass the day with us. The whole religion of the Mandans consists in the belief of one great spirit presiding over their destinies. This being must be in the nature of a good genius since it is associated with the healing art, and the great spirit is synonymous with great medicine, a name also applied to every thing which they do not comprehend. Each individual selects for himself the particular object of his devotion, which is termed his medicine, and is either some invisible being or more commonly some animal, which thenceforward becomes his protector or his intercessor with the great spirit; to propitiate whom every attention is lavished, and every personal consideration is sacrificed. "I was lately owner of seventeen horses," said a Mandan to us one day, "but I have offered them all up to my medicine and am now poor." He had in reality taken all his wealth, his horses, into the plain, and turning them loose committed them to the care of his medicine and abandoned them forever. The horses, less religious, took care of themselves, and the pious votary traveled home on foot. Their belief in a future state is connected with this tradition of their origin: the whole nation resided in one large village under ground near a subterraneous lake: a grapevine extended its roots down to their habitation and gave them a view of the light: some of the most adventurous climbed up the vine and were delighted with the sight of the earth, which they found covered with buffalo and rich with every kind of fruits: returning with the grapes they had gathered, their countrymen were so pleased with the taste of them that the whole nation resolved to leave their dull residence for the charms of the upper region; men, women, and children ascended by means of the vine; but when about half the nation had reached the surface of the earth, a corpulent women who was clambering up the vine broke it with her weight, and closed upon herself and the rest of the nation the light of the sun. Those who were left on earth made a village below where we saw the nine villages; and when the Mandans die they expect to return to the original seats of their forefathers; the good reaching the ancient village by means of the lake, which the burden of the sins of the wicked will not enable them to cross.

Wednesday 5. The morning was cold and disagreeable, the wind from the southeast accompanied with snow: in the evening there was snow again and the wind shifted to the northeast: we were visited by several Indians with a present of pumpkins, and by two of the traders of the northwest company.

Thursday 6. The wind was violent from the north northwest with some snow, the air keen and cold. At eight o'clock A.M. the thermometer stood at ten degrees above 0, and the river rose an inch and a half in the course of the day.

Friday, December 7. The wind still continued from the northwest and the day is very cold: Shahaka the chief of the lower village came to apprise us that the buffalo were near, and that his people were waiting for us to join them in the chase: Captain Clark with fifteen men went out and found the Indians engaged in killing the buffalo, the hunters mounted on horseback and armed with bows and arrows encircle the herd, and gradually drive them into a plain or an open place fit for the movement of horse; they then ride in among them, and singling out a buffalo, a female being preferred, go as close as possible and wound her with arrows till they think they have given the mortal stroke; when they pursue another till the quiver is exhausted: if, which rarely happens, the wounded buffalo attacks the hunter, he evades his blow by the agility of his horse, which is trained for the combat with great dexterity. When they have killed the requisite number they collect their game, and the squaws and attendants come up from the rear and skin and dress the animals. Captain Clark killed ten buffalo, of which five only were brought to the fort, the rest which could not be conveyed home being seized by the Indians, among whom the custom is that whenever a buffalo is found dead without an arrow or any particular mark, he is the property of the finder; so that often a hunter secures scarcely any of the game he kills if the arrow happens to fall off; whatever is left out at night falls to the share of the wolves, who are the constant and numerous attendants of the buffalo. The river closed opposite the fort last night, an inch and a half in thickness. In the morning the thermometer stood at one degree below 0. Three men were badly frostbitten in consequence of their exposure.

Saturday 8. The thermometer stood at twelve degrees below 0, that is at forty-two degrees below the freezing point: the wind was from the northwest. Captain Lewis with fifteen men went out to hunt the buffalo; great numbers of which darkened the prairies for a considerable distance: they did not return till after dark, having killed eight buffalo and one deer. The hunt was, however, very fatiguing, as they were obliged to make a circuit at the distance of more than seven miles: the cold too was so excessive that the air was filled with icy particles resembling a fog, and the snow generally six or eight inches deep and sometimes eighteen, in consequence of which two of the party were hurt by falls, and several had their feet frostbitten.

Sunday 9. The wind was this day from the east, the thermometer at seven degrees above 0, and the sun shone clear: two chiefs visited us, one in a sleigh drawn by a dog and loaded with meat.

Monday 10. Captain Clark who had gone out yesterday with eighteen men to bring in the meat we had killed the day before, and to continue the hunt, came in at twelve o'clock. After killing nine buffalo and preparing that already dead, he had spent a cold disagreeable night on the snow, with no covering but a small blanket, sheltered by the hides of the buffalo they had killed. We observe large herds of buffalo crossing the river on the ice, the men who were frostbitten are recovering, but the weather is still exceedingly cold, the wind being from the north, and the thermometer at ten and eleven degrees below 0: the rise of the river is one inch and a half

Tuesday 11. The weather became so intensely cold that we sent for all the hunters who had remained out with Captain Clark's party, and they returned in the evening, several of them frostbitten. The wind was from the north and the thermometer at sunrise stood at twenty-one below 0, the ice in the atmosphere being so thick as to render the weather hazy and give the appearance of two suns reflecting each other. The river continued at a stand. Pocapsahe made us a visit today.

Wednesday, December 12. The wind is still from the north, the thermometer being at sunrise thirty-eight degrees below 0. One of the Ahnahaways brought us down the half of an antelope killed near the fort; we had been informed that all these animals return to the Black Mountains, but there are great numbers of them about us at this season which we might easily kill, but are unwilling to venture out before our constitutions are hardened gradually to the climate. We measured the river on the ice, and find it five hundred yards wide immediately opposite the fort.

Thursday 13. Last night was clear and a very heavy frost covered the old snow, the thermometer at sunrise being twenty degrees below 0, and followed by a fine day. The river falls.

Friday 14. The morning was fine, and the weather having moderated so far, that the mercury stood at 0, Captain Lewis went down with a party to hunt; they proceeded about eighteen miles, but the buffalo having left the banks of the river they saw only two, which were so poor as not to be worth killing, and shot two deer. Notwithstanding the snow we were visited by a large number of the Mandans.

Saturday 15. Captain Lewis finding no game returned to the fort hunting on both sides of the river, but with no success. The wind being from the north, the mercury at sunrise eight degrees below 0, and the snow of last night an inch and a half in depth. The Indian chiefs continue to visit us today with presents of meat.

Sunday 16. The morning is clear and cold, the mercury at sunrise 22° below 0. A Mr. Haney, with two other persons from the British establishment on the Assiniboin, arrived in six days with a letter from Mr. Charles Chaubouilles, one of the company, who with much politeness offered to render us any service in his power.

Monday 17. The weather today was colder than any we had yet experienced, the thermometer at sunrise being 45° below 0, and about eight o'clock it fell to 74° below the freezing point

From Mr. Haney, who is a very sensible intelligent man, we obtained much geographical information with regard to the country between the Missouri and Mississippi, and the various tribes of Sioux who inhabit it.

Tuesday 18. The thermometer at sunrise was 32° below 0. The Indians had invited us yesterday to join their chase today, but the seven men whom we sent returned in consequence of the cold, which was so severe last night that we were obliged to have the sentinel relieved every half hour. The northwest traders, however, left us on their return home.

Wednesday 19. The weather moderated, and the river rose a little, so that we were enabled to continue the picketing of the fort. Notwithstanding the extreme cold, we observe the Indians at the village engaged out in the open air at a game which resembled billiards more than any thing we had seen, and which we inclined to suspect may have been acquired by ancient intercourse with the French of Canada. From the first to the second chief's lodge, a distance of about fifty yards, was covered with timber smoothed and joined so as to be as level as the floor of one of our houses, with a battery at the end to stop the rings: these rings were of clay-stone and flat like the chequers for drafts, and the sticks were about four feet long, with two short pieces at one end in the form of a mace, so fixed that the whole will slide along the board. Two men fix themselves at one end, each provided with a stick, and one of them with a ring; they then run along the board, and about half way slide the sticks after the ring.

Thursday 20. The wind was from the N.W., the weather moderate, the thermometer 24° above 0 at sunrise. We availed ourselves of this change to picket the fort near the river.

Friday 21. The day was fine and warm, the wind N.W. by W. The Indian who had been prevented a few days ago from killing his wife came with both his wives to the fort, and was very desirous of reconciling our interpreter, a jealousy against whom, on account of his wife's taking refuge in his house, had been the cause of his animosity. A woman brought her child with an abscess in the lower part of the back, and offered as much corn as she could carry for some medicine; we administered to it, of course, very cheerfully.

Saturday 22. A number of squaws and men dressed like squaws brought corn to trade for small articles with the men. Among other things we procured two horns of the animal called by the French the rock mountain sheep, and known to the Mandans by the name of *ahsahta*. The animal itself is about the size of a small elk or large deer: the horns winding like those of a ram, which they resemble also in texture, though larger and thicker.

Sunday 23. The weather was fine and warm like that of yesterday: we were again visited by crowds of Indians of all descriptions, who came either to trade or from mere curiosity. Among the rest Kogahami, the Little Raven, brought his wife and son loaded with corn, and she then entertained us with a favorite Mandan dish, a mixture of pumpkins, beans, corn, and chokecherries with the stones, all boiled together in a kettle, and forming a composition by no means unpalatable.

Monday 24. The day continued warm and pleasant, and the number of visitors became troublesome. As a present to three of the chiefs, we divided a fillet of sheep-skin which we brought for spunging into three pieces each of two inches in width; they were delighted at the gift, which they deemed of equal value with a fine horse. We this day completed our fort, and the next morning being Christmas.

Tuesday 25. We were awakened before day by a discharge of three platoons from the party. We had told the Indians not to visit us as it was one of our great medicine days; so that the men remained at home and amused themselves in various ways, particularly with dancing, in which they take great pleasure. The American flag was hoisted for the first time in the fort; the best provisions we had were brought out, and this, with a little brandy, enabled them to pass the day in great festivity.

Wednesday 26. The weather is again temperate, but no Indians have come to see us. One of the northwest traders who came down to request the aid of our Minnetaree interpreter informs us that a party of Minnetarees who had gone in pursuit of the Assiniboins who lately stole their horses had just returned. As is their custom, they came back in small detachments, the last of which brought home eight horses which they had captured or stolen from an Assiniboin camp on Mouse River.

Thursday 27. A little fine snow fell this morning and the air was colder than yesterday, with a high northwest wind. We were fortunate enough to have among our men a good black-smith, whom we set to work to make a variety of articles: his operations seemed to surprise the Indians who came to see us, but nothing could equal their astonishment at the bellows, which they considered as a very great medicine. Having here-tofore promised a more particular account of the Sioux, the following may serve as a general outline of their history:

Almost the whole of that vast tract of country comprised between the Mississippi, the Red River of Lake Winnipeg, the Saskaskawan, and the Missouri, is loosely occupied by a great nation whose primitive name is Darcota, but who are called Sioux by the French, Sues by the English. Their original seats were on the Mississippi, but they have gradually spread them-selves abroad and become subdivided into numerous tribes. Of these, what may be considered as the Darcotas are the Minda-warcarton, or Minowakanton, known to the French by the name of the Gens du Lac, or People of the Lake. Their residence is on both sides of the Mississippi near the falls of St. Anthony, and the probable number of their warriors about three hun-dred. Above them, on the River St. Peter's, is the Wahpatone, a smaller band of nearly two hundred men; and still further up the same river below Yellowwood River are the Wahpatootas or Gens de Feuilles, an inferior band of not more than one hundred men; while the sources of the St. Peter's are occupied by the Sisatoones, a band consisting of about two hundred warriors.

These bands rarely if ever approach the Missouri, which is occupied by their kinsmen the Yanktons and the Tetons. The Yanktons are of two tribes, those of the plains, or rather of the north, a wandering race of about five hundred men, who roam over the plains at the heads of the Jacques, the Sioux, and the Red River; and those of the south, who possess the country between the Jacques and Sioux Rivers and the Desmoine. But the bands of Sioux most known on the Missouri are the Tetons. The first who are met on ascending the Missouri is the tribe called by the French the Tetons of the Boise Brule or Burnt-wood, who reside on both sides of the Missouri, about White and Teton Rivers, and number two hundred warriors. Above them on the Missouri are the Teton Okandandas, a band of one hundred and fifty men living below the Chayenne River, between which and the Wetarhoo River is a third band, called Teton Minnakenozzo, of nearly two hundred and fifty men; and below the Warrecoune is the fourth and last tribe of Tetons of about three hundred men, and called Teton Saone. Northward of these, between the Assiniboin and the Missouri, are two bands of Assiniboins, one on Mouse River of about two hundred men, and called Assiniboin Menatopa; the other, residing on both sides of White River, called by the French Gens de Feuilles, and amounting to two hundred and fifty men. Beyond these a band of Assiniboins of four hundred and fifty men, and called the Big Devils, wander on the heads of Milk, Porcupine, and Martha's Rivers; while still farther to the north are seen two bands of the same nation, one of five hundred and the other of two hundred, roving on the Saskaskawan. Those Assiniboins are recognized by a similarity of language, and by tradition as descendants or seceders from the Sioux; though often at war are still acknowledged as relations. The Sioux themselves, though scattered, meet annually on the Jacques, those on the Missouri trading with those on the Mississippi.

CAPTIVITY NARRATIVES

Little more than a century ago "true" first-person accounts of whites captured by Indians were one of the most popular forms of subliterature in America. There were literally hundreds of such documents, ranging from brief pamphlets to those of monograph length, and from wild, lurid, ghost-written romances to sober and often enlightening glimpses into Indian life and customs. And the uses to which such documents were put were almost as various as the contents, styles, and lengths: a captivity narrative, since it always turned out well, could be used as an illustration of God's providence; as a means of whipping up faltering anti-Indian sentiment; or simply as a memorial to one's own life and works.

By far the most popular type of captivity narrative was that written by women. Much ink has been spilled on the status and role of women on the American frontier and in the wilderness, most of it by male writers who have sought to show that women were psychosexually ill equipped for the rigors of a life that most of them quickly came to hate or at best silently endure. There is truth to this idea, but it may be only the truth of a male projection. It is certain at least that the image of the woman as pale (paler somehow than her male counterpart), frail, protected, vulnerable, and above all chaste even in marriage is what furnishes the dramatic tension in the female captivity narrative. Such a figure, spirited away by savage and *half-naked* wild men, supplied the American imagination with that peculiar combination of sex, violence, and wildness that has been its favorite food. Not that the narratives themselves actually describe the rape of the white goddess in the guttering light of campfires; only that in all of them the *possibility* is ever present. Without it the captivity narrative must often turn to a kind of clumsy and racist ethnography—as it often does when written by men.

The two selections reproduced here are intended to suggest the range and variety of this genre. The first, "A Narrative of the Captivity and Restauration of Mrs. Mary Rowlandson," is one of the most famous of all such documents, a perfect gem, and probably, with the narratives of Jemimah Howe and Mary Jemison, the archetypal form. The uses to which it was put will be perfectly clear to the reader, though this is no reason to doubt its essential accuracy. In addition to these, the Rowlandson narrative is a highly valuable if slight glimpse of the Indians during King Philip's War (1675-76). A far different image of this Indian leader emerges in these pages than that current in the war years and just after. Here we find Philip neither devil nor noble philosopher, but instead a harried leader, perhaps not even the principal one at that, in continuous and hopeless retreat before superior and relentless forces, yet still capable of small acts of humanity such as when, near the end of this narrative, he extends a kind word and a helping hand to the faltering woman.

The second example, *John Tanner's Narrative of His Captivity Among the Ottawa and Ojibwa Indians*, remains one of the undiscovered classics of American literature. It was published in 1830 after Tanner dictated it to Dr. Edwin James, and it describes a thirty-years' residence among the tribes of the old Northwest Territory. For Tanner, what began as captivity became choice as the lure of the wild life exerted its huge subterranean strength and ultimately turned the man into a white Indian. The ensuing irony is tragically predictable: when he did emerge from the great woods, Tanner was neither Indian nor white, and he ended his days an outcast and, at last, an accused murderer who vanished back into the woods from which he had come.

The Captivity of Mary Rowlandson

On the tenth of February 1675, Came the Indians with great numbers upon Lancaster: Their first coming was about Sunrising; hearing the noise of some Guns, we looked out; several Houses were burning, and the Smoke ascending to Heaven. There were five persons taken in one house, the Father, and the Mother and a sucking Child, they knockt on the head; the other two they took and carried away alive. Their were two others, who being out of their Garrison upon some occasion were set upon; one was knockt on the head, the other escaped: Another their was who running along was shot and wounded, and fell down; he begged of them his life, promising them Money (as they told me) but they would not hearken to him but knockt him in head, and stript him naked, and split open his Bowels. Another seeing many of the Indians about his Barn, ventured and went out, but was quickly shot down. There were three others belonging to the same Garrison who were killed; the Indians getting up upon the roof of the Barn, had advantage to shoot down upon them over their Fortification. Thus these murtherous wretches went on, burning, and destroying before them.

At length they came and beset our own house, and quickly it was the dolefullest day that ever mine eyes saw. The House stood upon the edg of a hill; some of the Indians got behind the hill, others into the Barn, and others behind any thing that could shelter them; from all which places they shot against the House, so that the Bullets seemed to fly like hail; and quickly they wounded one man among us, then another, and then a third. About two hours (according to my observation, in that amazing time) they had been about the house before they prevailed to fire it (which they did with Flax and Hemp, which they brought out of the Barn, and there being no defence about the House, only two Flankers at two opposite corners and one

"A Narrative of the Captivity and Restauration of Mrs. Mary Rowlandson," *Narratives of the Indian Wars (1675-1699)*, ed. Charles Lincoln (New York, 1913), pp. 118-36.

of them not finished) they fired it once and one ventured out
and quenched it, but they quickly fired it again, and that took.
Now is the dreadfull hour come, that I have often heard of (in
time of War, as it was the case of others) but now mine eyes
see it. Some in our house were fighting for their lives, others
wallowing in their blood, the House on fire over our heads, and
the bloody Heathen ready to knock us on the head, if we stirred
out. Now might we hear Mothers and Children crying out for
themselves, and one another, Lord, What shall we do? Then I
took my children (and one of my sisters, hers) to go forth and
leave the house: but as soon as we came to the dore and appeared, the Indians shot so thick that the bulletts rattled against
the House, as if one had taken an handfull of stones and threw
them, so that we were fain to give back. We had six stout Dogs
belonging to our Garrison, but none of them would stir, though
another time, if any Indian had come to the door, they were
ready to fly upon him and tear him down. The Lord hereby
would make us the more to acknowledge his hand, and to see
that our help is always in him. But out we must go, the fire in-
creasing, and coming along behind us, roaring, and the Indians
gaping before us with their Guns, Spears and Hatchets to devour us. No sooner were we out of the House, but my Brother
in Law (being before wounded, in defending the house, in or
near the throat) fell down dead, wherat the Indians scornfully
shouted, and hallowed, and were presently upon him, stripping
off his cloaths, the bulletts flying thick, one went through my
side, and the same (as would seem) through the bowels and
hand of my dear Child in my arms. One of my elder Sisters
Children, named William, had then his Leg broken, which the
Indians perceiving, they knockt him on head. Thus were we
butchered by those merciless Heathen, standing amazed, with
the blood running down to our heels. My eldest Sister being yet
in the House, and seeing those wofull sights, the Infidels haling
Mothers one way, and Children another, and some wallowing
in their blood: and her elder Son telling her that her Son
William was dead, and my self was wounded, she said, And,
Lord, let me dy with them; which was no sooner said, but she
was struck with a Bullet, and fell down dead over the threshold.

I hope she is reaping the fruit of her good labours, being faithfull to the service of God in her place. In her younger years she lay under much trouble upon spiritual accounts, till it pleased God to make that precious Scripture take hold of her heart, 2 Cor. 12.9. *And he said unto me, my Grace is sufficient for thee.* More then twenty years after I have heard her tell how sweet and comfortable that place was to her. But to return: The Indians laid hold of us, pulling me one way, and the Children another, and said, Come go along with us; I told them they would kill me: they answered, If I were willing to go along with them, they would not hurt me.

Oh the dolefull sight that now was to behold at this House! *Come, behold the works of the Lord, what dissolations he has made in the Earth.* Of thirty seven persons who were in this one House, none escaped either present death, or a bitter captivity, save only one, who might say as he, Job 1.15, *And I only am escaped alone to tell the News.* There were twelve killed, some shot, some stab'd with their Spears, some knock'd down with their Hatchets. When we are in prosperity, Oh the little that we think of such dreadfull sights, and to see our dear Friends, and Relations ly bleeding out their heart-blood upon the ground. There was one who was chopt into the head with a Hatchet, and stript naked, and yet was crawling up and down. It is a solemn sight to see so many Christians lying in their blood, some here, and some there, like a company of Sheep torn by Wolves, All of them stript naked by a company of hell-hounds, roaring, singing, ranting and insulting, as if they would have torn our very hearts out; yet the Lord by his Almighty power preserved a number of us from death, for there were twenty-four of us taken alive and carried Captive.

I had often before this said, that if the Indians should come, I should chuse rather to be killed by them then taken alive but when it came to the tryal my mind changed; their glittering weapons so daunted my spirit, that I chose rather to go along with those (as I may say) ravenous Beasts, then that moment to end my dayes; and that I may the better declare what happened to me during that grievous Captivity, I shall particularly speak of the severall Removes we had up and down the Wilderness.

The First Remove

Now away we must go with those Barbarous Creatures, with our bodies wounded and bleeding, and our hearts no less than our bodies. About a mile we went that night, up upon a hill within sight of the Town, where they intended to lodge. There was hard by a vacant house (deserted by the English before, for fear of the Indians). I asked them whither I might not lodge in the house that night to which they answered, what will you love English men still? this was the dolefullest night that ever my eyes saw. Oh the roaring, and singing and dancing, and yelling of those black creatures in the night, which made the place a lively resemblance of hell. And as miserable was the wast that was there made, of Horses, Cattle, Sheep, Swine, Calves, Lambs, Roasting Pigs, and Fowl (which they had plundered in the Town) some roasting, some lying and burning, and some boyling to feed our merciless Enemies; who were joyful enough though we were disconsolate. To add to the dolefulness of the former day, and the dismalness of the present night: my thoughts ran upon my losses and sad bereaved condition. All was gone, my Husband gone (at least separated from me, he being at the Bay; and to add to my grief, the Indians told me they would kill him as he came homeward) my Children gone, my Relations and Friends gone, our House and home and all our comforts within door, and without, all was gone (except my life) and I knew not but the next moment that might go too. There remained nothing to me but one poor wounded Babe, and it seemed at present worse than death that it was in such a pitiful condition, bespeaking Compassion, and I had no refreshing for it, nor suitable things to revive it. Little do many think what is the savageness and bruitishness of this barbarous Enemy, aye, even those that seem to profess more than others among them, when the English have fallen into their hands.

Those seven that were killed at Lancaster the summer before upon a Sabbath day, and the one that was afterward killed upon a week day, were slain and mangled in a barbarous manner, by one-ey'd John, and Marlborough's Praying Indians, which Capt. Mosely brought to Boston, as the Indians told me.

The Second Remove

But now, the next morning, I must turn my back upon the Town, and travel with them into the vast and desolate Wilderness, I knew not whither. It is not my tongue, or pen can express the sorrows of my heart, and bitterness of my spirit, that I had at this departure: but God was with me, in a wonderfull manner, carrying me along, and bearing up my spirit, that it did not quite fail. One of the Indians carried my poor wounded Babe upon a horse, it went moaning all along, I shall dy, I shall dy. I went on foot after it, with sorrow that cannot be exprest. At length I took it off the horse, and carried it in my armes till my strength failed, and I fell down with it: Then they set me upon a horse with my wounded Child in my lap, and there being no furniture upon the horse back, as we were going down a steep hill, we both fell over the horses head, at which they like inhumane creatures laught, and rejoyced to see it, though I thought we should there have ended our dayes, as overcome with so many difficulties. But the Lord renewed my strength still, and carried me along, that I might see more of his Power; yea, so much that I could never have thought of, had I not experienced it.

After this it quickly began to snow, and when night came on, they stopt: and now down I must sit in the snow, by a little fire, and a few boughs behind me, with my sick Child in my lap; and calling much for water, being now (through the wound) fallen into a violent Fever. My own wound also growing so stiff, that I could scarce sit down or rise up; yet so it must be, that I must sit all this cold winter night upon the cold snowy ground, with my sick Child in my armes, looking that every hour would be the last of its life; and having no Christian friend near me, either to comfort or help me. Oh, I may see the wonderfull power of God, that my Spirit did not utterly sink under my affliction: still the Lord upheld me with his gracious and mercifull Spirit, and we were both alive to see the light of the next morning.

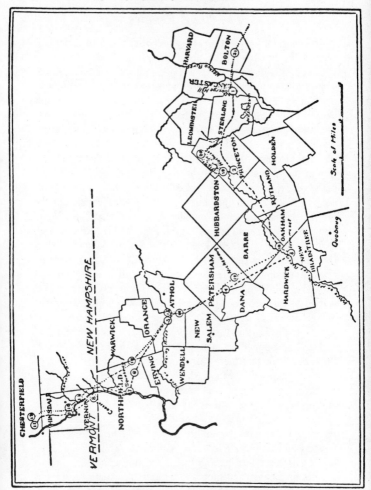

MAP OF MRS. ROWLANDSON'S REMOVES

From Messrs. Nourse and Thayer's edition of the narrative.

The Third Remove

The morning being come, they prepared to go on their way. One of the Indians got up upon a horse, and they set me up behind him, with my poor sick Babe in my lap. A very wearisome and tedious day I had of it; what with my own wound, and my Childs being so exceeding sick, and in a lamentable condition with her wound. It may be easily judged what a poor feeble condition we were in, there being not the least crumb of refreshing that came within either of our mouths, from Wednesday night to Saturday night, except only a little cold water. This day in the afternoon, about an hour by Sun, we came to the place where they intended, *viz.* an Indian Town, called Wenimesset, Norward of Quabaug. When we were come, Oh the number of Pagans (now merciless enemies) that there came about me, that I may say as David, Psal. 27.13, *I had fainted, unless I had believed,* etc. The next day was the Sabbath: I then remembered how careless I had been of Gods holy time, how many Sabbaths I had lost and mispent, and how evily I had walked in Gods sight; which lay so close unto my spirit, that it was easie for me to see how righteous it was with God to cut off the thread of my life, and cast me out of his presence for ever. Yet the Lord still shewed mercy to me, and upheld me; and as he wounded me with one hand, so he healed me with the other. This day there came to me one Robbert Pepper (a man belonging to Roxbury) who was taken in Captain Beers his Fight, and had been now a considerable time with the Indians; and up with them almost as far as Albany, to see king Philip, as he told me, and was now very lately come into these parts. Hearing, I say, that I was in this Indian Town, he obtained leave to come and see me. He told me, he himself was wounded in the leg at Captain Beers his Fight; and was not able some time to go, but as they carried him, and as he took Oaken leaves and laid to his wound, and through the blessing of God he was able to travel again. Then I took Oaken leaves and laid to my side, and with the blessing of God it cured me also; yet before the cure was wrought, I may say, as it is in Psal. 38.5, 6. *My wounds stink and are corrupt, I am troubled, I am bowed down greatly, I go mourning all the day long.* I sat much alone with a poor wounded Child in my lap, which moaned night and day, having nothing to revive the body, or cheer the spirits of her but in stead of that, sometimes one Indian would come and tell me one hour, that your Master will knock your Child in the head, and then a second, and then a third, your Master will quickly knock your Child in the head.

This was the comfort I had from them, miserable comforters are ye all, as he said. Thus nine dayes I sat upon my knees, with my Babe in my lap, till my flesh was raw again; my Child being even ready to depart this sorrowful world, they bade me carry it out to another Wigwam (I suppose because they would not be troubled with such spectacles) Whither I went with a very heavy heart, and down I sat with the picture of death in my lap. About two houres in the night, my sweet Babe like a Lambe departed this life, on Feb. 18, 1675. It being about six years, and five months old. It was nine dayes from the first wounding in this miserable condition, without any refreshing of one nature or other, except a little cold water. I cannot, but take notice, how at another time I could not bear to be in the room where any dead person was, but now the case is changed; I must and could ly down by my dead Babe, side by side all the night after. I have thought since of the wonderfull goodness of God to me, in preserving me in the use of my reason and senses, in that distressed time, that I did not use wicked and violent means to end my own miserable life. In the morning, when they understood that my child was dead they sent for me home to my Masters Wigwam (by my Master in this writing, must be understood Quanopin, who was a Saggamore, and married King Phillips wives Sister; not that he first took me, but I was sold to him by another Narrhaganset Indian, who took me when first I came out of the Garrison). I went to take up my dead child in my arms to carry it with me, but they bid me let it alone: there was no resisting, but goe I must and leave it. When I had been at my masters wigwam, I took the first opportunity I could get, to go look after my dead child: when I came I askt them what they had done with it? then they told me it was upon the hill: then they went and shewed me where it was, where I saw the ground was newly digged, and there they told me they had buried it: There I left that Child in the Wilderness, and must commit it, and my self also in this Wilderness-condition, to him who is above all. God having taken away this dear Child, I went to see my daughter Mary, who was at this same Indian Town, at a Wigwam not very far off, though we had little liberty or opportunity to see one another. She was about ten years old, and taken from the door at first by a Praying Ind and afterward sold for a gun. When I came in sight, she would fall a weeping; at which they were provoked, and would not let me come near her, bade me be gone; which was a heart-cutting word to me. I had one Child dead, another in the Wilderness, I knew not where, the third they would not let me come near to: *Me* (as he said) *have ye bereaved of my Children, Joseph is not, and Simeon is not, and ye will take Benjamin also, all these things are against me.* I could not sit still in this condition, but kept walking from one place to another. And as I was going along, my heart was even overwhelm'd with the thoughts of my condition, and that I should have Children, and a Nation which I knew not ruled over them. Whereupon I earnestly entreated the Lord, that he would consider my low estate, and shew me a token for good, and if it were his blessed will, some sign and hope of some relief. And indeed quickly the Lord answered, in some measure, my poor prayers: for as I was going up and down mourning and lamenting my condition, my Son came to me, and asked me how I did; I had not seen him before, since the destruction of the Town, and I knew not where he was, till I was informed by himself, that he was amongst a smaller percel of Indians, whose place was about six miles off; with tears in his eyes, he asked me whether his Sister Sarah was dead; and told me he had seen his Sister Mary; and prayed me, that I would not be troubled in reference to himself. The occasion of his coming to see me at this time, was this: There was, as I said, about six miles from us, a smal Plantation of Indians, where it seems he had been during his Captivity: and at this time, there were some Forces of the Ind. gathered out of our company, and some also from them (among whom was my Sons master) to go to assault and burn Medfield: In this time of the absence of his master, his dame brought him to see me. I took this to be some gracious answer to my earnest and unfeigned desire. The next day, *viz.*

to this, the Indians returned from Medfield, all the company, for those that belonged to the other smal company, came thorough the Town that now we were at. But before they came to us, Oh! the outragious roaring and hooping that there was: They began their din about a mile before they came to us. By their noise and hooping they signified how many they had destroyed (which was at that time twenty three.) Those that were with us at home, were gathered together as soon as they heard the hooping, and every time that the other went over their number, these at home gave a shout, that the very Earth rung again: And thus they continued till those that had been upon the expedition were come up to the Sagamores Wigwam; and then, Oh, the hideous insulting and triumphing that there was over some Englishmens scalps that they had taken (as their manner is) and brought with them. I cannot but take notice of the wonderful mercy of God to me in those afflictions, in sending me a Bible. One of the Indians that came from Medfield fight, had brought some plunder, came to me, and asked me, if I would have a Bible, he had got one in his Basket. I was glad of it, and asked him, whether he thought the Indians would let me read? he answered, yes: So I took the Bible, and in that melancholy time, it came into my mind to read first the 28. Chap. of Deut., which I did, and when I had read it, my dark heart wrought on this manner, That there was no mercy for me, that the blessings were gone, and the curses come in their room, and that I had lost my opportunity. But the Lord helped me still to go on reading till I came to Chap. 30 the seven first verses, where I found, There was mercy promised again, if we would return to him by repentance; and though we were scatered from one end of the Earth to the other, yet the Lord would gather us together, and turn all those curses upon our Enemies. I do not desire to live to forget this Scripture, and what comfort it was to me.

Now the Ind. began to talk of removing from this place, some one way, and some another. There were now besides my self nine English Captives in this place (all of them Children, except one Woman). I got an opportunity to go and take my leave of them; they being to go one way, and I another, I asked them whether they were earnest with God for deliverance, they told me, they did as they were able, and it was some comfort to me, that the Lord stirred up Children to look to him. The Woman *viz.* Goodwife Joslin told me, she should never see me again, and that she could find in her heart to run away; I wisht her not to run away by any means, for we were near thirty miles from any English Town, and she very big with Child, and had but one week to reckon; and another Child in her Arms, two years old, and bad Rivers there were to go over, and we were feeble, with our poor and course entertainment. I had my Bible with me, I pulled it out, and asked her whether she would read; we opened the Bible and lighted on Psal. 27, in which Psalm we especially took notice of that, *ver. ult., Wait on the Lord, Be of good courage, and he shall strengthen thine Heart, wait I say on the Lord.*

The Fourth Remove

And now I must part with that little Company I had. Here I parted from my Daughter Mary, (whom I never saw again till I saw her in Dorchester, returned from Captivity), and from four little Cousins and Neighbours, some of which I never saw afterward: the Lord only knows the end of them. Amongst them also was that poor Woman before mentioned, who came to a sad end, as some of the company told me in my travel: She having much grief upon her Spirit, about her miserable condition, being so near her time, she would be often asking the Indians to let her go home; they not being willing to that, and yet vexed with her importunity, gathered a great company together about her, and stript her naked, and set her in the midst of them; and when they had sung and danced about her (in their hellish manner) as long as they pleased, they knockt her on head, and the child in her arms with her: when they had done that, they made a fire and put them both into it, and told other Children that were with them, that if they attempted to go home, they would serve them in like manner: The Children said, she did not shed one tear, but prayed all the while. But to return to my own Journey; we travelled about half a day or little more, and came to a desolate place in the Wilderness, where there were no Wigwams or Inhabitants before; we came about the middle of the afternoon to this place, cold and wet, and snowy, and hungry, and weary, and no refreshing, for man, but the cold ground to sit on, and our poor Indian cheer.

Heart-aking thoughts here I had about my poor Children, who were scattered up and down among the wild beasts of the forest: My head was light and dissey (either through hunger or hard lodging, or trouble or altogether) my knees feeble, my body raw by sitting double night and day, that I cannot express to man the affliction that lay upon my Spirit, but the Lord helped me at that time to express it to himself. I opened my Bible to read, and the Lord brought that precious Scripture to me, Jer. 31.16. *Thus saith the Lord, refrain thy voice from weeping, and thine eyes from tears, for thy work shall be rewarded, and they shall come again from the land of the Enemy.* This was a sweet Cordial to me, when I was ready to faint, many and many a time have I sat down, and weept sweetly over this Scripture. At this place we continued about four dayes.

The Fifth Remove

The occasion (as I thought) of their moving at this time, was, the English Army, it being near and following them: For they went, as if they had gone for their lives, for some considerable way, and then they made a stop, and chose some of their stoutest men, and sent them back to hold the English Army in play whilst the rest escaped: And then, like Jehu, they marched on furiously, with their old, and with their young: some carried their old decrepit mothers, some carried one, and some another. Four of them carried a great Indian upon a Bier; but going through a thick Wood with him, they were hindered, and could make no hast; whereupon they took him upon their backs, and carried him, one at a time, till they came to Bacquaug River. Upon a Friday, a little after noon we came to this River. When all the company was come up, and were gathered together, I thought to count the number of them, but they were so many, and being somewhat in motion, it was beyond my skil. In this travel, because of my wound, I was somewhat favored in my load; I carried only my knitting work and two quarts of parched meal: Being very faint I asked my mistriss to give me one spoonfull of the meal, but she would not give me a taste. They quickly fell to cutting dry trees, to make Rafts to carry them over the river: and soon my turn came to go over: By the advantage of some brush which they had laid upon the Raft to sit upon, I did not wet my foot (which many of themselves at the other end were mid-leg deep) which cannot but be acknowledged as a favor of God to my weakned body, it being a very cold time. I was not before acquainted with such kind of doings or dangers. *When thou passeth through the waters I will be with thee, and through the Rivers they shall not overflow thee,* Isai. 43.2. A certain number of us got over the River that night, but it was the night after the Sabbath before all the company was got over. On the Saturday they boyled an old Horses leg which they had got, and so we drank of the broth, as soon as they thought it was ready, and when it was almost all gone, they filled it up again.

The first week of my being among them, I hardly ate any thing; the second week; I found my stomach grow very faint for want of something; and yet it was very hard to get down their filthy trash: but the third week, though I could think how formerly my stomach would turn against this or that, and I could starve and dy before I could eat such things, yet they were sweet and savoury to my taste. I was at this time knitting a pair of white cotton stockins for my mistriss; and had not yet wrought upon a Sabbath day; when the Sabbath came they bade me go to work; I told them it was the Sabbath day, and desired them to let me rest, and told them I would do as much more to morrow; to which they answered me, they would break my face. And here I cannot but take notice of the strange providence of God in preserving the heathen: They were many hundreds, old and young, some sick, and some lame, many had Papooses at their backs, the greatest number at this time with us, were Squaws, and they traveled with all they had, bag and baggage, and yet they got over this River aforesaid; and on Munday they set their Wigwams on fire, and away they went: On that very day came the English Army after them to this River, and saw the smoak of their Wigwams, and yet this River put a stop to them. God did not give them courage or activity to go over after us; we were not ready for so great a mercy as victory and deliverance; if we had been, God would have found out a way for the English to have passed this River, as well as for the Indians with their Squaws and Children, and all their Luggage. *Oh that my people had hearkened to me, and Israel had walked in my ways, I should soon have subdued their Enemies, and turned my hand against their Adversaries,* Psal. 81:13,14.

The Sixth Remove

On Munday (as I said) they set their Wigwams on fire, and went away. It was a cold morning, and before us there was a great Brook with ice on it; some waded through it, up to the knees and higher, but others went till they came to a Beaver-dam, and I amongst them, where through the good providence of God, I did not wet my foot. I went along that day mourning and lamenting, leaving farther my own Country, and travelling into the vast and howling Wilderness, and I understood something of Lot's Wife's Temptation, when she looked back: we came that day to a great Swamp, by the side of which we took up our lodging that night. When I came to the brow of the hil, that looked toward the Swamp, I thought we had been come to a great Indian Town (though there were none but our own Company). The Indians were as thick as the trees: it seemed as if there had been a thousand Hatchets going at once: if one looked before one, there was nothing but Indians, and behind one, nothing but Indians, and so on either hand, I my self in the midst, and no Christian soul near me, and yet how hath the Lord preserved me in safety? Oh the experience that I have had of the goodness of God, to me and mine!

The Seventh Remove

After a restless and hungry night there, we had a wearisome time of it the next day. The Swamp by which we lay, was, as it were, a deep Dungeon, and an exceeding high and steep hill

before it. Before I got to the top of the hill, I thought my heart
and legs, and all would have broken, and failed me. What
through faintness, and soreness of body, it was a grievous day
of travel to me. As we went along, I saw a place where English
Cattle had been: that was comfort to me, such as it was:
quickly after that we came to an English Path, which so took
with me, that I thought I could have freely lyen down and
dyed. That day, a little after noon, we came to Squaukheag,
where the Indians quickly spread themselves over the deserted
English Fields, gleaning what they could find; some pickt up
ears of Wheat that were crickled down, some found ears of
Indian Corn, some found Ground-nuts, and others sheaves of
Wheat that were frozen together in the shock, and went to
threshing of them out. My self got two ears of Indian Corn,
and whilst I did but turn my back, one of them was stolen
from me, which much troubled me. There came an Indian to
them at that time, with a basket of Horse-liver. I asked him
to give me a piece: What, says he, can you eat Horse-liver? I
told him, I would try, if he would give a piece, which he did,
and I laid it on the coals to rost; but before it was half ready
they got half of it away from me, so that I was fain to take
the rest and eat it as it was, with the blood about my mouth,
and yet a savoury bit it was to me: *For to the hungry Soul*
every bitter thing is sweet. A solemn sight methought it was,
to see Fields of wheat and Indian Corn forsaken and spoiled:
and the remainders of them to be food for our merciless
Enemies. That night we had a mess of wheat for our Supper.

The Eighth Remove

On the morrow morning we must go over the River, *i.e.*
Connecticot, to meet with King Philip; two Cannoos full, they
had carried over, the next Turn I my self was to go; but as my
foot was upon the Cannoo to step in, there was a sudden out-cry
among them, and I must step back; and instead of going over
the River, I must go four or five miles up the River farther
Northward. Some of the Indians ran one way, and some
another. The cause of this rout was, as I thought, their espying
some English Scouts, who were thereabout. In this travel up

the River, about noon the Company made a stop, and sate down; some to eat, and others to rest them. As I sate amongst them, musing of things past, my Son Joseph unexpectedly came to me: we asked of each others welfare, bemoaning our dolefull condition, and the change that had come upon uss. We had Husband and Father, and Children, and Sisters, and Friends, and Relations, and House, and Home, and many Comforts of this Life: but now we may say, as Job, *Naked came I out of my Mothers Womb, and naked shall I return: The Lord gave, and the Lord hath taken away, Blessed be the Name of the Lord.* I asked him whither he would read; he told me, he earnestly desired it, I gave him my Bible, and he lighted upon that comfortable Scripture, Psal. 118. 17, 18. *I shall not dy but live, and declare the works of the Lord: the Lord hath chastened me sore, yet he hath not given me over to death.* Look here, Mother (sayes he) did you read this? And here I may take occasion to mention one principall ground of my setting forth these Lines: even as the Psalmist sayes, To declare the Works of the Lord, and his wonderfull Power in carrying us along, preserving us in the Wilderness, while under the Enemies hand, and returning of us in safety again, And His goodness in bringing to my hand so many comfortable and suitable Scriptures in my distress. But to Return, We traveled on till night; and in the morning, we must go over the River to Philip's Crew. When I was in the Cannoo, I could not but be amazed at the numerous crew of Pagans that were on the Bank on the other side. When I came ashore, they gathered all about me, I sitting alone in the midst: I observed they asked one another questions, and laughed, and rejoyced over their Gains and Victories. Then my heart began to fail: and I fell a weeping which was the first time to my remembrance, that I wept before them. Although I had met with so much Affliction, and my heart was many times ready to break, yet could I not shed one tear in their sight: but rather had been all this while in a maze, and like one astonished: but now I may say as, Psal. 137. 1. *By the Rivers of Babylon, there we sate down: yea, we wept when we remembered Zion.* There one of them asked me, why I wept, I could hardly tell what to say: yet I answered, they would kill me: No, said he, none will hurt you. Then came one of them and gave me two spoon-fulls of Meal to comfort me, and another gave me half a pint of Pease; which was more worth than many Bushels at another time. Then I went to see King Philip, he bade me come in and sit down, and asked me whether I woold smoke it (a usual Complement nowadayes amongst Saints and Sinners) but this no way suited me. For though I had formerly used Tobacco, yet I had left it ever since I was first taken. It seems to be a Bait, the Devil layes to make men loose their precious time: I remember with shame, how formerly, when I had taken two or three pipes, I was presently ready for another, such a bewitching thing it is: But I thank God, he has now given me power over it; surely there are many who may be better imployed than to ly sucking a stinking Tobacco-pipe.

Now the Indians gather their Forces to go against North-Hampton: over-night one went about yelling and hooting to give notice of the design. Whereupon they fell to boyling of Ground-nuts, and parching of Corn (as many as had it) for their Provision: and in the morning away they went. During my abode in this place, Philip spake to me to make a shirt for his boy, which I did, for which he gave me a shilling: I offered the mony to my master, but he bade me keep it: and with it I bought a piece of Horse flesh. Afterwards he asked me to make a Cap for his boy, for which he invited me to Dinner. I went, and he gave me a Pancake, about as big as two fingers; it was made of parched wheat, beaten, and fryed in Bears grease, but I thought I never tasted pleasanter meat in my life. There was a Squaw who spake to me to make a shirt for her *Sannup,* for which she gave me a piece of Bear. Another asked me to knit a pair of Stockins, for which she gave me a quart of Pease: I boyled my Pease and Bear together, and invited my master and mistriss to dinner, but the proud Gossip, because I served them both in one Dish, would eat nothing, except one bit that he gave her upon the point of his knife. Hearing that my son was come to this place, I went to see him, and found him lying flat upon the ground: I asked him how he could sleep so? he answered me, That he was not asleep, but at Prayer; and lay so, that they might not observe what he was doing. I pray God he may remember these things now he is returned in safety. At this Place (the Sun now getting higher) what with the beams and heat of the Sun, and the smoak of the Wigwams, I thought I should have been blind. I could scarce discern one Wigwam from another. There was here one Mary Thurston of Medfield, who seeing how it was with me, lent me a Hat to wear: but as soon as I was gone, the Squaw (who owned that Mary Thurston) came running after me, and got it away again. Here was the Squaw that gave me one spoonfull of Meal. I put it in my Pocket to keep it safe: yet notwithstanding some body stole it, but put five Indian Corns in the room of it: which Corns were the greatest Provisions I had in my travel for one day.

The Indians returning from North-Hampton, brought with them some Horses, and Sheep, and other things which they had taken: I desired them, that they would carry me to Albany, upon one of those Horses, and sell me for Powder; for so they had sometimes discoursed. I was utterly hopless of getting home on foot, the way that I came. I could hardly bear to think of the many weary steps I had taken, to come to this place.

The Ninth Remove

But in stead of going either to Albany or homeward, we must go five miles up the River, and then go over it. Here we abode a while. Here lived a sorry Indian, who spoke to me to make him a shirt. When I had done it, he would pay me nothing. But he living by the River side, where I often went to fetch water, I would often be putting of him in mind, and calling for my pay: at last he told me if I would make another shirt, for a Papoos not yet born, he would give me a knife, which he did when I had done it. I carried the knife in, and my master asked me to give it him, and I was not a little glad that I had any thing that they would accept of, and be pleased with. When we were at this place, my Masters maid came home, she had been gone three weeks into the Narrhaganset Country, to fetch Corn, where they had stored up some in the ground: she brought home about a peck and half of Corn. This was about the time that their great Captain, Naananto, was killed in the Narrhaganset Countrey. My Son being now about a mile from me, I asked liberty to go and see him, they bade me go, and away I went: but quickly lost my self, travelling over Hills and thorough Swamps, and could not find the way to him. And I cannot but admire at the wonderfull power and goodness of God to me, in that, though I was gone from home, and met with all sorts of Indians, and those I had no knowledge of, and there being no Christian soul near me; yet not one of them offered the least imaginable miscarriage to me. I turned homeward again, and met with my master, he shewed me the way to my Son: When I came to him I found him not well: and withall he had a boyl on his side, which much troubled him: We bemoaned one another awhile, as the Lord helped us, and then I returned again. When I was returned, I found my self as unsatisfied as I was before, I went up and down mourning and lamenting: and my spirit was ready to sink, with the thoughts of my poor Children: my Son was ill, and I could not but think of his mournfull looks, and no Christian Friend was near him, to do any office of love for him, either for Soul or Body. And my poor Girl, I knew not where she was, nor whither she was sick, or well, or alive, or dead. I repaired under these thoughts to my Bible (my great comfort in that time) and that Scripture came to my hand, *Cast thy burden upon the Lord, and He shall sustain thee,* Psal. 55. 22.

But I was fain to go and look after something to satisfie my hunger, and going among the Wigwams, I went into one, and there found a Squaw who shewed her self very kind to me, and gave me a piece of Bear. I put it into my pocket, and came home, but could not find an opportunity to broil it, for fear they would get it from me, and there it lay all that day and night in my stinking pocket. In the morning I went to the same Squaw, who had a Kettle of Ground nuts boyling; I asked her to let me boyle my piece of Bear in her Kettle, which she did, and gave me some Ground-nuts to eat with it: and I cannot but think how pleasant it was to me. I have sometime seen Bear baked very handsomly among the English, and some like it, but the thoughts that it was Bear, made me tremble; but now that was savoury to me that one would think was enough to turn the stomach of a bruit Creature.

One bitter cold day, I could find no room to sit down before the fire: I went out, and could not tell what to do, but I went in to another Wigwam, where they were also sitting round the fire, but the Squaw laid a skin for me, and bid me sit down, and gave me some Ground-nuts, and bade me come again: and told me they would buy me, if they were able, and yet these were strangers to me that I never saw before.

The Tenth Remove

That day a small part of the Company removed about three quarters of a mile, intending further the next day. When they came to the place where they intended to lodge, and had pitched their wigwams, being hungry I went again back to the place we were before at, to get something to eat: being encouraged by the Squaws kindness, who bade me come again; when I was there, there came an Indian to look after me, who when he had found me, kickt me all along: I went home and found Venison roasting that night, but they would not give me one bit of it. Sometimes I met with favor, and sometimes with nothing but frowns.

The Eleventh Remove

The next day in the morning they took their Travel, intending a dayes journey up the River, I took my load at my back, and quickly we came to wade over the River: and passed over tiresome and wearisome hills. One hill was so steep that I was fain to creep up upon my knees, and to hold by the twiggs and bushes to keep my self from falling backward. My head also was so light, that I usually reeled as I went; but I hope all these wearisome steps that I have taken, are but a forewarning to me of the heavenly rest. *I know, O Lord, that thy Judgements are right, and that thou in faithfulness has afflicted me.* Psal. 119.71.

The Twelfth Remove

It was upon a Sabbath-day-morning, that they prepared for their Travel. This morning I asked my master whither he would sell me to my Husband; he answered me *Nux* [yes], which did much rejoyce my spirit. My mistriss, before we went, was gone to the burial of a Papoos, and returning, she found me sitting and reading in my Bible; she snatched it hastily out of my hand, and threw it out of doors; I ran out and catcht it up, and put it into my pocket, and never let her see it afterward. Then they packed up their things to be gone, and gave me my load: I complained it was too heavy, whereupon she gave me a slap in the face, and bade me go; I lifted up my heart to God, hoping the Redemption was not far off: and the rather because their insolency grew worse and worse.

But the thoughts of my going homeward (for so we bent our course much cheared my Spirit, and made my burden seem light, and almost nothing at all. But (to my amazment and great perplexity) the scale was soon turned: for when we had gone a little way, on a sudden my mistriss gives out, she would go no further, but turn back again, and said, I must go back again with her, and she called her *Sannup,* and would have had him gone back also, but he would not, but said, He would go on, and come to us again in three dayes. My Spirit was upon this, I confess, very impatient, and almost outragious. I thought I could as well have dyed as went back: I cannot declare the trouble that I was in about it; but yet back again I must go. As soon as I had an opportunity, I took my Bible to read, and that quieting Scripture came to my hand, Psal. 46. 10. *Be still, and know that I am God.* Which stilled my spirit for the present: But a sore time or tryal, I concluded, I had to go through, My master being gone, who seemed to me the best friend that I had of an Indian, both in cold and hunger, and quickly so it proved. Down I sat, with my heart as full as it could hold, and yet so hungry that I could not sit neither: but going out to see what I could find, and walking among the Trees, I found six Acorns, and two Ches-nuts, which were some refreshment to me. Towards Night I gathered me some sticks for my own comfort, that I might not ly a-cold: but when we came to ly down they bade me go out, and ly some-where-else, for they had company (they said) come in more than their own: I told them, I could not tell where to go, they bade me go look; I told them, if I went to another Wigwam they would be angry, and send me home again. Then one of the Company drew his sword, and told me he would run me thorough if I did not go presently. Then was I fain to stoop to this rude fellow, and to go out in the night, I knew not whither. Mine eyes have seen that fellow afterwards walking up and down Boston, under the appearance of a Friend-Indian, and severall others of the like Cut. I went to one Wigwam, and they told me they had no room. Then I went to another, and they said the same; at last an old Indian bade me come to him, and his Squaw gave me some Ground-nuts; she gave me also something to lay under my head, and a good fire we had: and through the good providence of God, I had a comfortable lodging that night. In the morning, another Indian bade me come at night, and he would give me six Ground-nuts, which I did. We were at this place and time about two miles from Connecticut River. We went in the morning to gather Ground-nuts, to the River, and went back again that night. I went with a good load at my back (for they when they went, though but a little way, would carry all their trumpery with them) I told them the skin was off my back, but I had no other comforting answer from them than this, That it would be no matter if my head were off too.

The Thirteenth Remove

Instead of going toward the Bay, which was that I desired, I must go with them five or six miles down the River into a mighty Thicket of Brush: where we abode almost a fortnight. Here one asked me to make a shirt for her Papoos, for which she gave me a mess of Broth, which was thickened with meal made of the Bark of a Tree, and to make it the better, she had put into it about a handful of Pease, and a few roasted Ground-nuts. I had not seen my son a pritty while, and here was an Indian of whom I made inquiry after him, and asked him when he saw him: he answered me, that such a time his master roasted him, and that himself did eat a piece of him, as big as his two fingers, and that he was very good meat: But the Lord upheld my Spirit, under this discouragement; and I considered their horrible addictedness to lying, and that there is not one of them that makes the least conscience of speaking of truth. In this place, on a cold night, as I lay by the fire, I removed a stick that kept the heat from me, a Squaw moved it down again, at which I lookt up, and she threw a handful of ashes in mine eyes; I thought I should have been quite blinded, and have never seen more: but lying down, the water run out of my eyes, and carried the dirt with it, that by the morning, I recovered my sight again. Yet upon this, and the like occasions, I hope it is not too much to say with Job, *Have pitty upon me, have pitty upon me, O ye my Friends, for the Hand of the Lord has touched me.* And here I cannot but remember how many times sitting in their Wigwams, and musing on things past, I should suddenly leap up and run out, as if I had been at home, forgetting where I was, and what my condition was: But when I was without, and saw nothing but Wilderness, and Woods, and a company of barbarous heathens, my mind quickly returned to me, which made me think of that, spoken concerning Sampson, who said, *I will go out and shake my self as at other times, but he wist not that the Lord was departed from him.* About this time I began to think that all my hopes of Restoration would come to nothing. I thought of the English Army, and hoped for their coming, and being taken by them, but that failed. I hoped to be carried to Albany, as the Indians had discoursed before, but that failed also. I thought of being sold to my Husband, as my master spake, but in stead of that, my master himself was gone, and I left behind, so that my Spirit was now quite ready to sink. I asked them to let me go out and pick up some sticks, that I might get alone, And poure out my heart unto the Lord. Then also I took my Bible to read, but I found no comfort here neither, which many times I was wont to find: So easie a thing it is with God to dry up the Streames of Scripture-comfort from us. Yet I can say, that in all my sorrows and afflictions, God did not leave me to have my impatience work towards himself, as if his wayes were unrighteous. But I knew that he laid upon me less then I deserved. Afterward, before this dolefull time ended with me,

I was turning the leaves of my Bible, and the Lord brought to me some Scriptures, which did a little revive me, as that Isai. 55.8, *For my thoughts are not your thoughts, neither are your wayes my ways, saith the Lord*. And also that, Psal. 37. 5, *Commit thy way unto the Lord, trust also in him and he shal bring it to pass*. About this time they came yelping from Hadly, where they had killed three English men, and brought one Captive with them, *viz*. Thomas Read. They all gathered about the poor Man, asking him many Questions. I desired also to go and see him; and when I came, he was crying bitterly, supposing they would quickly kill him. Whereupon I asked one of them, whether they intended to kill him; he answered me, they would not: He being a little cheared with that, I asked him about the wel-fare of my Husband, he told me he saw him such a time in the Bay, and he was well, but very melancholly. By which I certainly understood (though I suspected it before) that whatsoever the Indians told me respecting him was vanity and lies. Some of them told me, he was dead, and they had killed him: some said he was Married again, and that the Governour wished him to Marry; and told him he should have his choice, and that all perswaded I was dead. So like were these barbarous creatures to him who was a lyer from the beginning.

As I was sitting once in the Wigwam here, Phillips Maid came in with the Child in her arms, and asked me to give her a piece of my Apron, to make a flap for it, I told her I would not: then my Mistriss bad me give it, but still I said no: the maid told me if I would not give her a piece, she would tear a piece off it: I told her I would tear her Coat then, with that my Mistriss rises up, and takes up a stick big enough to have killed me, and struck at me with it, but I stept out, and she struck the stick into the Mat of the Wigwam. But while she was pulling of it out, I ran to the Maid and gave her all my Apron, and so that storm went over.

Hearing that my Son was come to this place, I went to see him, and told him his Father was well, but very melancholly: he told me he was as much grieved for his Father as for himself; I wondered at his speech, for I thought I had enough upon my spirit in reference to my self, to make me mindless of my Husband and every one else: they being safe among their Friends. He told me also, that a while before, his Master (together with other Indians) where going to the French for Powder; but by the way the Mohawks met with them, and killed four of their Company which made the rest turn back again, for which I desire that my self and he may bless the Lord; for it might have been worse with him, had he been sold to the French, than it proved to be in his remaining with the Indians.

I went to see an English Youth in this place, one John Gilberd of Springfield. I found him lying without dores, upon the ground; I asked him how he did? he told me he was very sick of a flux, with eating so much blood: They had turned him out of the Wigwam, and with him an Indian Papoos, almost dead, (whose Parents had been killed) in a bitter cold day, without fire or clothes: the young man himself had nothing on, but his shirt and wastcoat. This sight was enough to melt a heart of flint. There they lay quivering in the Cold, the youth round like a dog; the Papoos stretcht out, with his eyes and nose and mouth full of dirt, and yet alive, and groaning. I advised John to go and get to some fire: he told me he could not stand, but I perswaded him still, lest he should ly there and die: and with much adoe I got him to a fire, and went my self home. As soon as I was got home, his Masters Daughter came after me, to know what I had done with the English man, I told her I had got him to a fire in such a place. Now had I need to pray Pauls Prayer, 2 Thess. 3. 2. *That we may be delivered from unreasonable and wicked men.* For her satisfaction I went along with her, and brought her to him; but before I got home again, it was noised about, that I was running away and getting the English youth, along with me; that as soon as I came in, they began to rant and domineer: asking me Where I had been, and what I had been doing? and saying they would knock him on the head: I told them, I had been seeing the English Youth, and that I would not run away, they told me I lyed, and taking up a Hatchet, they came to me, and said they would knock me down if I stirred out again; and so confined me to the Wigwam. Now may I say with David, 2 Sam. 24. 14. *I am in a great strait.* If I keep in, I must dy with hunger, and if I go out, I must be knockt in head. This distressed condition held that day, and half the next; And then the Lord remembered me, whose mercyes are great. Then came an Indian to me with a pair of stockings that were too big for him, and he would have me ravel them out, and knit them fit for him. I shewed my self willing, and bid him ask my mistriss if I might go along with him a little way; she said yes, I might, but I was not a little refresht with that news, that I had my liberty again. Then I went along with him and he gave me some roasted Ground-nuts, which did again revive my feeble stomach.

Being got out of her sight, I had time and liberty again to look into my Bible: Which was my Guid by day, and my Pillow by night. Now that comfortable Scripture presented it self to me, Isa.· 54. 7. *For a smal moment have I forsaken thee, but with great mercies will I gather thee.* Thus the Lord carried me along from one time to another, and made good to me this precious promise, and many others. Then my Son came to see me, and I asked his master to let him stay a while with me, that I might comb his head, and look over him, for he was almost overcome with lice. He told me, when I had done, that he was very hungry, but I had nothing to relieve him; but bid him go into the Wigwams as he went along, and see if he could get any thing among them. Which he did, and it seemes tarried a little too long; for his Master was angry with him, and beat him, and then sold him. Then he came running to tell me he had a new Master, and that he had given him some Ground-nuts already. Then I went along with him to his new Master who told me he loved him: and he should not want. So his Master carried him away, and I never saw him afterward, till I saw him at Pascataqua in Portsmouth.

That night they bade me go out of the Wigwam again: my Mistrisses Papoos was sick, and it died that night, and there was one benefit in it, that there was more room. I went to a Wigwam, and they bade me come in, and gave me a skin to ly upon, and a mess of Venson and Ground-nuts, which was a choice Dish among them. On the morrow they buried the Papoos, and afterward, both morning and evening, there came a company to mourn and howle with her: though I confess, I could not much condole with them. Many sorrowfull dayes I had in this place: often getting alone; *like a Crane, or a Swal-*

low, so did I chatter: I did mourn as a Dove, mine eyes ail with looking upward. Oh, Lord, I am oppressed; undertake for me, Isa. 38. 14. I could tell the Lord as Hezeckiah, ver. 3. *Remember now O Lord, I beseech thee, how I have walked before thee in truth.* Now had I time to examine all my wayes: my Conscience did not accuse me of un-righteousness toward one or other yet I saw how in my walk with God, I had been a careless creature. As David said, *Against thee, thee only have I sinned:* and I might say with the poor Publican, *God be merciful unto me a sinner.* On the Sabbath-dayes, I could look upon the Sun and think how People were going to the house of God, to have their Souls refresht; and then home, and their bodies also: but I was destitute of both; and might say as the poor Prodigal, *he would fain have filled his belly with the husks that the Swine did eat, and no man gave unto him,* Luke 15. 16. For I must say with him, *Father I have sinned against Heaven, and in thy sight,* ver. 21. I remembred how on the night before and after the Sabbath, when my Family was about me, and Relations and Neighbours with us, we could pray and sing, and then refresh our bodies with the good creatures of God; and then have a comfortable Bed to ly down on: but in stead of all this, I had only a little Swill for the body, and then like a Swine, must ly down on the ground. I cannot express to man the sorrow that lay upon my Spirit, the Lord knows it. Yet that comfortable Scripture would often come to my mind, *For a small moment have I forsaken thee, but with great mercies will I gather thee.*

The Fourteenth Remove

Now must we pack up and be gone from this Thicket, bending our course toward the Bay-towns, I haveing nothing to eat by the way this day, but a few crumbs of Cake, that an Indian gave my girle the same day we were taken. She gave it me, and I put it in my pocket: there it lay, till it was so mouldly (for want of good baking) that one could not tell what it was made of; it fell all to crumbs, and grew so dry and hard, that it was like little flints; and this refreshed me many times, when I was ready to faint. It was in my thoughts when I put it into my mouth, that if ever I returned, I would tell the World what a blessing the Lord gave to such mean food. As we went along, they killed a Deer, with a young one in her, they gave me a piece of the Fawn, and it was so young and tender, that one might eat the bones as well as the flesh, and yet I thought it very good. When night came on we sate down; it rained, but they quickly got up a Bark Wigwam, where I lay dry that night. I looked out in the morning, and many of them had line in the rain all night, I saw by their Reaking. Thus the Lord dealt mercifully with me many times and I fared better than many of them. In the morning they took the blood of the Deer, and put it into the Paunch, and so boyled it; I could eat nothing of that, though they ate it sweetly. And yet they were so nice in other things, that when I had fetcht water, and had put the Dish I dipt the water with, into the Kettle of water which I brought, they would say, they would knock me down; for they said, it was a sluttish trick.

The Fifteenth Remove

We went on our Travel. I having got one handfull of Ground-nuts, for my support that day, they gave me my load, and I went on cheerfully (with the thoughts of going homeward) haveing my burden more on my back than my spirit: we came to Baquaug River again that day, near which we abode a few dayes. Sometimes one of them would give me a Pipe, another a little Tobacco, another a little Salt: which I would change for a little Victuals. I cannot but think what a Wolvish appetite persons have in a starving condition: for many times when they gave me that which was hot, I was so greedy, that I should burn my mouth, that it would trouble me hours after, and yet I should quickly do the same again. And after I was thoroughly hungry, I was never again satisfied. For though sometimes it fell out, that I got enough, and did eat till I could eat no more, yet I was unsatisfied as I was when I began. And now could I see that Scripture verified (there being many Scriptures which we do not take notice of, or understand till we are afflicted) Mic. 6. 14. *Thou shalt eat and not be satisfied.* Now might I see more than ever before, the miseries that sin hath brought upon us: Many times I should be ready to run out against the

Heathen, but the Scripture would quiet me again, Amos 3.6, *Shal there be evil in the City, and the Lord hath not done it?* The Lord help me to make a right improvement of His Word, and that I might learn that great lesson, Mic. 6. 8, 9. *He hath shewed thee (Oh Man) what is good, and what doth the Lord require of thee, but to do justly, and love mercy, and walk humbly with thy God? Hear ye the rod, and who hath appointed it.*

The Sixteenth Remove

We began this Remove with wading over Baquaug River: the water was up to the knees, and the stream very swift, and so cold that I thought it would have cut me in sunder. I was so weak and feeble, that I reeled as I went along, and thought there I must end my dayes at last, after my bearing and getting thorough so many difficulties; the Indians stood laughing to see me staggering along: but in my distress the Lord gave me experience of the truth, and goodness of that promise, Isai. 43. 2. *When thou passest thorough the Waters, I will be with thee, and through the Rivers, they shall not overflow thee.* Then I sat down to put on my stockins and shoos, with the teares running down mine eyes, and many sorrowful thoughts in any heart, but I gat up to go along with them. Quickly there came up to us an Indian, who informed them, that I must go to Wachusit to my master, for there was a Letter come from the Council to the Saggamores, about redeeming the Captives, and that there would be another in fourteen dayes, and that I must be there ready. My heart was so heavy before that I could scarce speak or go in the path; and yet now so light, that I could run. My strength seemed to come again, and recruit my feeble knees, and aking heart: yet it pleased them to go but one mile that night, and there we stayed two dayes. In that time came a company of Indians to us, near thirty, all on horseback. My heart skipt within me, thinking they had been English-men at the first sight of them, for they were dressed in English Apparel, with Hats, white Neckcloths, and Sashes about their wasts, and Ribbonds upon their shoulders: but when they came near, their was a vast difference between the lovely faces of

Christians, and the foul looks of those Heathens, which much damped my spirit again.

The Seventeenth Remove

A comfortable Remove it was to me, because of my hopes. They gave me a pack, and along we went chearfully; but quickly my will proved more than my strength; having little or no refreshing my strength failed me, and my spirit were almost quite gone. Now may I say with David, Psal. 119. 22, 23, 24. *I am poor and needy, and my heart is wounded within me. I am gone like the shadow when it declineth: I am tossed up and down like the locust; my knees are weak through fasting, and my flesh faileth of fatness.* At night we came to an Indian Town, and the Indians sate down by a Wigwam discoursing, but I was almost spent, and could scarce speak. I laid down my load, and went into the Wigwam, and there sat an Indian boyling of Horses feet (they being wont to eat the flesh first, and when the feet were old and dried, and they had nothing else, they would cut off the feet and use them). I asked him to give me a little of his Broth, or Water they were boiling in; he took a dish, and gave me one spoonful of Samp, and bid me take as much of the Broth as I would. Then I put some of the hot water to the Samp, and drank it up, and my spirit came again. He gave me also a piece of the Ruff or Ridding of the small Guts, and I broiled it on the coals; and now may I say with Jonathan, *See, I pray you, how mine eyes have been enlightened, because I tasted a little of this honey,* 1 Sam. 14. 29. Now is my Spirit revived again; though means be never so inconsiderable, yet if the Lord bestow his blessing upon them, they shall refresh both Soul and Body.

The Eighteenth Remove

We took up our packs and along we went, but a wearisome day I had of it. As we went along I saw an English-man stript naked, and lying dead upon the ground, but knew not who it was. Then we came to another Indian Town, where we stayed all night. In this Town there were four English Children, Captives; and one of them my own Sisters. I went to see how she did, and she was well, considering her Captive-condition. I would have tarried that night with her, but they that owned her would not suffer it. Then I went into another Wigwam, where they were boyling Corn and Beans, which was a lovely sight to see, but I could not get a taste thereof. Then I went to another Wigwam, where there were two of the English Children; the Squaw was boyling Horses feet, then she cut me off a little piece, and gave one of the English Children a piece also. Being very hungry I had quickly eat up mine, but the Child could not bite it, it was so tough and sinewy, but lay sucking, gnawing, chewing and slabbering of it in the mouth and hand, then I took it of the Child, and eat it my self, and savoury it was to my taste. Then I may say as Job, Chap. 6. 7. *The things that my soul refused to touch, are as my sorrowfull meat.* Thus the Lord made that pleasant refreshing, which another time would have been an abomination. Then I went home to my mistresses Wigwam; and they told me I disgraced my master with begging, and if I did so any more, they would knock me in head: I told them, they had as good knock me in head as starve me to death.

The Nineteenth Remove

They said, when we went out, that we must travel to Wachuset this day. But a bitter weary day I had of it, travelling now three days together, without resting any day between. At last, after many weary steps, I saw Wachuset hills, but many miles off. Then we came to a great Swamp, through which we travelled, up to the knees in mud and water, which was heavy going to one tyred before. Being almost spent, I thought I should have sunk down at last, and never gat out; but I may say, as in Psal. 94. 18, *When my foot slipped, thy mercy, O Lord, held me up.* Going along, having indeed my life, but little spirit, Philip, who was in the Company, came up and took me by the hand, and said, Two weeks more and you shal be Mistress again. I asked him, if he spake true? he answered, Yes, and quickly you shal come to your master again; who had been gone from us three weeks. After many weary steps we came to Wachuset, where he was: and glad I was to see him. He asked me, When I washt me? I told him not this month, then he fetcht me some water himself, and bid me wash, and gave me the Glass to see how I lookt; and bid this Squaw give me something to eat: so she gave me a mess of Beans and meat, and a little Ground-nut Cake. I was wonderfully revived with this favour shewed me, Psal. 106. 46, *He made them also to be pittied, of all those that carried them Captives.*

My Master had three Squaws, living sometimes with one, and sometimes with another one, this old Squaw, at whose Wigwam I was, and with whom my Master had been those three weeks. Another was Wattimore, with whom I had lived and served all this while: A severe and proud Dame she was, bestowing every day in dressing her self neat as much time as any of the Gentry of the land: powdering her hair, and painting her face, going with Neck-laces, with Jewels in her ears, and Bracelets upon her hands: When she had dressed her self, her work was to make Girdles of Wampom and Beads. The third Squaw was a younger one, by whom he had two Papooses. By that time I was refresht by the old Squaw, with whom my master was, Wettimores Maid came to call me home, at which I fell a weeping. Then the old Squaw told me, to encourage me, that if I wanted victuals, I should come to her, and that I should ly there in her Wigwam. Then I went with the maid, and quickly came again and lodged there. The Squaw laid a Mat under me, and a good Rugg over me; the first time I had any such kindness shewed me. I understood that Wettimore thought, that if she should let me go and serve with the old Squaw, she would be in danger to loose, not only my service, but the redemption-pay also. And I was not a little glad to hear this; being by it raised in my hopes, that in Gods due time there would be an end of this sorrowfull hour. Then came an Indian, and asked me to knit him three pair of Stockins, for which I had a Hat, and a silk Handkerchief. Then another asked me to make her a shift, for which she gave me an Apron.

Then came Tom and Peter, with the second Letter from the Council, about the Captives. Though they were Indians,

I gat them by the hand, and burst out into tears; my heart was so full that I could not speak to them; but recovering my self, I asked them how my husband did, and all my friends and acquaintance? they said, They are all very well but melancholy. They brought me two Biskets. and a pound of Tobacco. The Tobacco I quickly gave away; when it was all gone, one asked me to give him a pipe of Tobacco, I told him it was all gone; then began he to rant and threaten. I told him when my Husband came I would give him some: Hang him Rogue (sayes he) I will knock out his brains, if he comes here. And then again, in the same breath they would say, That if there should come an hundred without Guns, they would do them no hurt. So unstable and like mad men they were. So that fearing the worst, I durst not send to my Husband, though there were some thoughts of his coming to Redeem and fetch me, not knowing what might follow. For there was little more trust to them then to the master they served. When the Letter was come, the Saggamores met to consult about the Captives, and called me to them to enquire how much my husband would give to redeem me, when I came I sate down among them, as I was wont to do, as their manner is: Then they bade me stand up, and said, they were the General Court. They bid me speak what I thought he would give. Now knowing that all we had was destroyed by the Indians, I was in a great strait: I thought if I should speak of but a little, it would be slighted, and hinder the matter; if of a great sum, I knew not where it would be procured: yet at a venture, I said Twenty pounds, yet desired them to take less; but they would not hear of that, but sent that message to Boston, that for Twenty pounds I should be redeemed. It was a Praying-Indian that wrote their Letter for them. There was another Praying-Indian, who told me, that he had a brother, that would not eat Horse; his conscience was so tender and scrupulous (though as large as hell, for the destruction of poor Christians). Then he said, he read that Scripture to him, 2 Kings, 6. 25. *There was a famine in Samaria, and behold they besieged it, until an Asses head was sold for fourscore pieces of silver, and the fourth part of à Kab of Doves dung, for five pieces of silver.* He expounded this place to his brother, and shewed him that it was lawful to eat that in a Famine which is not at another time. And now, says he, he will eat Horse with any Indian of them all. There was another Praying-Indian, who when he had done all the mischief that he could, betrayed his own Father into the English hands, thereby to purchase his own life. Another Praying-Indian was at Sudbury-fight, though, as he deserved, he was afterward hanged for it. There was another Praying-Indian, so wicked and cruel, as to wear a string about his neck, strung with Christians fingers. Another Praying-Indian, when they went to Sudbury-fight, went with them, and his Squaw also with him, with her Papoos at her back: Before they went to that fight, they got a company together to *Powaw;* the manner was as followeth. There was one that kneeled upon a Deerskin, with the company round him in a ring who kneeled, and striking upon the ground with their hands, and with sticks, and muttering or humming with their mouths; besides him who kneeled in the ring, there also stood one with a Gun in his hand: Then he on the Deerskin made a speech, and all manifested assent to it: and so they did many times together. Then they bade him with the Gun go out of the ring, which he did, but when he was out, they called him in again; but he seemed to make a stand, then they called the more earnestly, till he returned again: They they all sang. Then they gave him two Guns, in either hand one: And so he on the Deerskin began again; and at the end of every sentence in his speaking, they all assented, humming or muttering with their mouthes, and striking upon the ground with their hands. Then they bade him with the two Guns go out of the ring again; which he did, a little way. Then they called him in again, but he made a stand; so they called him with greater earnestness; but he stood reeling and wavering as if he knew not whither he should stand or fall, or which way to go. Then they called him with exceeding great vehemency, all of them, one and another: after a little while he turned in, staggering as he went, with his Armes stretched out, in either hand a Gun. As soon as he came in, they all sang and rejoyced exceedingly a while. And then he upon the Deerskin, made another speech unto which they all assented in a rejoicing manner: and so they ended their business, and forthwith went to Sudbury-fight. To my thinking they went without any scruple, but that they should prosper, and gain the victory. And they went out not so rejoycing, but they came home with as great a Victory. For they said they had killed two Captains, and almost an hundred men. One English-man they brought along with them: and he said, it was too true, for they had made sad work at Sudbury, as indeed it proved. Yet they came home without that rejoycing and triumphing over their victory, which they were wont to shew at other times, but rather like Dogs (as they say) which have lost their ears. Yet I could not perceive that it was for their own loss of men: They said, they had not lost above five or six: and I missed none, except in one Wigwam. When they went, they acted as if the Devil had told them that they should gain the victory: and now they acted, as if the Devil had told them they should have a fall. Whither it were so or no, I cannot tell, but so it proved, for quickly they began to fall, and so held on that Summer, till they came to utter ruine. They came home on a Sabbath day, and the *Powaw* that kneeled upon the Deerskin came home (I may say, without abuse) as black as the Devil. When my master came home, he came to me and bid me make a shirt for his Papoos, of a holland-laced Pillowbeer. About that time there came an Indian to me and bid me come to his Wigwam, at night, and he would give me some Pork and Ground-nuts. Which I did, and as I was eating, another Indian said to me, he seems to be your good Friend, but he killed two Englishmen at Sudbury, and there ly their Cloaths behind you: I looked behind me, and there I saw bloody Cloaths, with Bullet-holes in them; yet the Lord suffered not this wretch to do me any hurt; Yea, instead of that, he many times refresht me: five or six times did he and his Squaw refresh my feeble carcass. If I went to their Wigwam at any time, they would alwayes give me something, and yet they were strangers that I never saw before. Another Squaw gave me a piece of fresh Pork, and a little Salt with it, and lent me her Pan to Fry it in; and I cannot but remember what a sweet, pleasant and delightfull relish that bit had to me, to this day. So little do we prize common mercies when we have them to the full.

The Twentieth Remove

It was their usual manner to remove, when they had done any mischief, lest they should be found out: and so they did at this time. We went about three or four miles, and there they built a great Wigwam, big enough to hold an hundred Indians, which they did in preparation to a great day of Dancing. They would say now amongst themselves, that the Governour would be so angry for his loss at Sudbury, that he would send no more about the Captives, which made me grieve and tremble. My Sister being not far from the place where we now were, and hearing that I was here, desired her master to let her come and see me, and he was willing to it, and would go with her: but she being ready before him, told him she would go before, and was come within a Mile or two of the place; Then he overtook her, and began to rant as if he had been mad; and made her go back again in the Rain; so that I never saw her till I saw her in Charlestown. But the Lord requited many of their ill doings, for this Indian her Master, was hanged afterward at Boston. The Indians now began to come from all quarters, against their merry dancing day. Among some of them came one Goodwife Kettle: I told her my heart was so heavy that it was ready to break: so is mine too said she, but yet said, I hope we shall hear some good news shortly. I could hear how earnestly my Sister desired to see me, and I as earnestly desired to see her: and yet neither of us could get an opportunity. My Daughter was also now about a mile off, and I had not seen her in nine or ten weeks, as I had not seen my Sister since our first taking. I earnestly desired them to let me go and see them: yea, I intreated, begged, and perswaded them, but to let me see my Daughter; and yet so hard hearted were they, that they would not suffer it. They made use of their tyrannical power whilst they had it: but through the Lords wonderfull mercy, their time was now but short.

On a Sabbath day, the Sun being about an hour high in the afternoon, came Mr. John Hoar (the Council permitting him, and his own foreward spirit inclining him) together with the two forementioned Indians, Tom and Peter, with their third Letter from the Council. When they came near, I was abroad:

though I saw them not, they presently called me in, and bade me sit down and not stir. Then they catched up their Guns, and away they ran, as if an Enemy had been at hand; and the Guns went off apace. I manifested some great trouble, and they asked me what was the matter? I told them, I thought they had killed the English-man (for they had in the mean time informed me that an English-man was come) they said, No; They shot over his Horse and under, and before his Horse; and they pusht him this way and that way, at their pleasure: shewing what they could do: Then they let them come to their Wigwams. I begged of them to let me see the English-man, but they would not. But there was I fain to sit their pleasure. When they had talked their fill with him, they suffered me to go to him. We asked each other of our welfare, and how my Husband did, and all my Friends? He told me they were all well, and would be glad to see me. Amongst other things which my Husband sent me, there came a pound of Tobacco: which I sold for nine shillings in Money: for many of the Indians for want of Tobacco, smoaked Hemlock, and Ground-Ivy. It was a great mistake in any, who thought I sent for Tobacco: for through the favour of God, that desire was overcome. I now asked them, whither I should go home with Mr. Hoar? They answered No, one and another of them: and it being night, we lay down with that answer; in the morning, Mr. Hoar invited the Saggamores to Dinner; but when we went to get it ready, we found that they had stollen the greatest part of the Provision Mr. Hoar had brought, out of his Bags, in the night. And we may see the wonderfull power of God, in that one passage, in that when there was such a great number of the Indians together, and so greedy of a little good food; and no English there, but Mr. Hoar and my self: that there they did not knock us in the head, and take what we had: there being not only some Provision, but also Trading-cloth, a part of the twenty pounds agreed upon: But instead of doing us any mischief, they seemed to be ashamed of the fact, and said, it were some Matchit Indian that did it. Oh, that we could believe that there is no thing too hard for God! God shewed his Power over the Heathen in this, as he did over the hungry Lyons when Daniel was cast into the Den. Mr. Hoar called them be-

time to Dinner, but they ate very little, they being so busie in
dressing themselves, and getting ready for their Dance: which
was carried on by eight of them, four Men and four Squaws:
My master and mistress being two. He was dressed in his
Holland shirt, with great Laces sewed at the tail of it, he had
his silver Buttons, his white Stockins, his Garters were hung
round with Shillings, and he had Girdles of Wampom upon
his head and shoulders. She had a Kersey Coat, and covered
with Girdles of Wampom from the Loins upward: her armes
from her elbows to her hands were covered with Bracelets;
there were handfulls of Necklaces about her neck, and severall
sorts of Jewels in her ears. She had fine red Stokins, and
white Shoos, her hair powdered and face painted Red, that
was alwayes before Black. And all the Dancers were after the
same manner. There were two other singing and knocking on
a Kettle for their musick. They keept hopping up and down
one after another, with a Kettle of water in the midst, standing
warm upon some Embers, to drink of when they were dry.
They held on till it was almost night, throwing out Wampom
to the standers by. At night I asked them again, if I should go
home? They all as one said No, except my Husband would
come for me. When we were lain down, my Master went out
of the Wigwam, and by and by sent in an Indian called James
the Printer, who told Mr. Hoar, that my Master would let me
go home to morrow, if he would let him have one pint of
Liquors. Then Mr. Hoar called his own Indians, Tom and
Peter, and bid them go and see whither he would promise it
before them three: and if he would, he should have it; which
he did, and he had it. Then Philip smeling the business cal'd
me to him, and asked me what I would give him, to tell me
some good news, and speak a good word for me. I told him,
I could not tell what to give him, I would any thing I had,
and asked him what he would have? He said, two Coats and
twenty shillings in Mony, and half a bushel of seed Corn, and
some Tobacco. I thanked him for his love: but I knew the
good news as well as the crafty Fox. My Master after he had
had his drink, quickly came ranting into the Wigwam again,
and called for Mr. Hoar, drinking to him, and saying. He was
a good man: and then again he would say, Hang him Rogue:

Being almost drunk, he would drink to him, and yet presently say he should be hanged. Then he called for me. I trembled to hear him, yet I was fain to go to him, and he drank to me, shewing no incivility. He was the first Indian I saw drunk all the while that I was amongst them. At last his Squaw ran out, and he after her, round the Wigwam, with his mony jingling at his knees: But she escaped him: But having an old Squaw he ran to her: and so through the Lords mercy, we were no more troubled that night. Yet I had not a comfortable nights rest: for I think I can say, I did not sleep for three nights together. The night before the Letter came from the Council, I could not rest, I was so full of feares and troubles, God many times leaving us most in the dark, when deliverance is nearest: yea, at this time I could not rest night nor day. The next night I was overjoyed, Mr. Hoar being come, and that with such good tidings. The third night I was even swallowed up with the thoughts of things, *viz.* that ever I should go home again; and that I must go, leaving my Children behind me in the Wilderness; so that sleep was now almost departed from mine eyes.

On Tuesday morning they called their General Court (as they call it) to consult and determine, whether I should go home or no: And they all as one man did seemingly consent to it, that I should go home; except Philip, who would not come among them.

But before I go any further, I would take leave to mention a few remarkable passages of providence, which I took special notice of in my afflicted time.

1. Of the fair opportunity lost in the long March, a little after the Fort-fight, when our English Army was so numerous, and in pursuit of the Enemy, and so near as to take several and destroy them: and the Enemy in such distress for food, that our men might track them by their rooting in the earth for Ground-nuts, whilest they were flying for their lives. I say, that then our Army should want Provision, and be forced to leave their pursuit and return homeward: and the very next week the Enemy came upon our Town, like Bears bereft of their whelps, or so many revenous Wolves, rending us and our Lambs to death. But what shall I say? God seemed to leave

his People to themselves, and order all things for his own holy ends. *Shal there be evil in the City and the Lord hath not done it? They are not grieved for the affliction of Joseph, therefore shal they go Captive, with the first that go Captive.* It is the Lords doing, and it should be marvelous in our eyes.

2. I cannot but remember how the Indians derided the slowness, and dulness of the English Army, in its setting out. For after the desolations at Lancaster and Medfield, as I went along with them, they asked me when I thought the English Army would come after them? I told them I could not tell: It may be they will come in May, said they. Thus did they scoffe at us, as if the English would be a quarter of a year getting ready.

3. Which also I have hinted before, when the English Army with new supplies were sent forth to pursue after the enemy, and they understanding it, fled before them till they came to Baquaug River, where they forthwith went over safely: that that River should be impassable to the English. I can but admire to see the wonderfull providence of God in preserving the heathen for farther affliction to our poor Countrey. They could go in great numbers over, but the English must stop: God had an over-ruling hand in all those things.

4. It was thought, if their Corn were cut down, they would starve and dy with hunger: and all their Corn that could be found, was destroyed, and they driven from that little they had in store, into the Woods in the midst of Winter; and yet how to admiration did the Lord preserve them for his holy ends, and the destruction of many still amongst the English! strangely did the Lord provide for them; that I did not see (all the time I was among them) one Man, Woman, or Child, die with hunger.

Though many times they would eat that, that a Hog or a Dog would hardly touch; yet by that God strengthned them to be a scourge to his People.

The chief and commonest food was Ground-nuts: They eat also Nuts and Acorns, Harty-choaks, Lilly roots, Ground-beans, and several other weeds and roots, that I know not.

They would pick up old bones, and cut them to pieces at the joynts, and if they were full of wormes and magots, they would scald them over the fire to make the vermine come out, and then boile them, and drink up the Liquor, and then beat the great ends of them in a Morter, and so eat them. They would eat Horses guts, and ears, and all sorts of wild Birds which they could catch: also Bear, Vennison, Beaver, Tortois, Frogs, Squirrels, Dogs, Skunks, Rattle-snakes; yea, the very Bark of Trees; besides all sorts of creatures, and provision which they plundered from the English. I can but stand in admiration to see the wonderful power of God, in providing for such a vast number of our Enemies in the Wilderness, where there was nothing to be seen, but from hand to mouth. Many times in a morning, the generality of them would eat up all they had, and yet have some forther supply against they wanted. It is said, Psal. 81. 13, 14. *Oh, that my People had hearkned to me, and Israel had walked in my wayes, I should soon have subdued their Enemies, and turned my hand against their Adversaries.* But now our perverse and evil carriages in the sight of the Lord, have so offended him, that instead of turning his hand against them, the Lord feeds and nourishes them up to be a scourge to the whole Land.

5. Another thing that I would observe is, the strange providence of God, in turning things about when the Indians was at the highest, and the English at the lowest. I was with the Enemy eleven weeks and five dayes, and not one Week passed without the fury of the Enemy, and some desolation by fire and sword upon one place or other. They mourned (with their black faces) for their own losses, yet triumphed and rejoyced in their inhumane, and many times devilish cruelty to the English. They would boast much of their Victories; saying, that in two hours time they had destroyed such a Captain, and his Company at such a place; and such a Captain and his Company in such a place; and such a Captain and his Company in such a place : and boast how many Towns they had destroyed, and then scoffe, and say, They had done them a good turn, to send them to Heaven so soon. Again, they would say, This Summer that they would knock all the Rogues in the head, or drive them into the Sea, or make them flie the Countrey: thinking surely, Agag-like, *The bitterness of Death is past.* Now the Heathen begins to think all is their own, and the poor Christians hopes to fail (as to man) and now their eyes are

more to God, and their hearts sigh heaven-ward: and to say in good earnest, *Help Lord, or we perish:* When the Lord had brought his people to this, that they saw no help in any thing but himself: then he takes the quarrel into his own hand: and though they had made a pit, in their own imaginations, as deep as hell for the Christians that Summer, yet the Lord hurll'd them selves into it. And the Lord had not so many wayes before to preserve them, but now he hath as many to destroy them.

But to return again to my going home, where we may see a remarkable change of Providence: At first they were all against it, except my Husband would come for me; but afterwards they assented to it, and seemed much to rejoyce in it; some askt me to send them some Bread, others some Tobacco, others shaking me by the hand, offering me a Hood and Scarfe to ride in; not one moving hand or tongue against it. Thus hath the Lord answered my poor desire, and the many earnest requests of others put up unto God for me. In my travels an Indian came to me, and told me, if I were willing, he and his Squaw would run away, and go home along with me: I told him No: I was not willing to run away, but desired to wait Gods time, that I might go home quietly, and without fear. And now God hath granted me my desire. O the wonderfull power of God that I have seen, and the experience that I have had: I have been in the midst of those roaring Lyons, and Salvage Bears, that feared neither God, nor Man, nor the Devil, by night and day, alone and in company: sleeping all sorts together, and yet not one of them ever offered me the least abuse of unchastity to me, in word or action. Though some are ready to say, I speak it for my own credit; But I speak it in the presence of God, and to his Glory. Gods Power is as great now, and as sufficient to save, as when he preserved Daniel in the Lions Den; or the three Children in the fiery Furnace. I may well say as his Psal. 107. 12, *Oh give thanks unto the Lord for he is good, for his mercy endureth for ever.* Let the Redeemed of the Lord say so, whom he hath redeemed from the hand of the Enemy, especially that I should come away in the midst of so many hundreds of Enemies quietly and peacably, and not a Dog moving his tongue. So I took my leave of them, and in coming along my heart melted into tears, more then all the while I was with them, and I was almost swallowed up with the thoughts that ever I should go home again. About the Sun going down, Mr. Hoar, and my self, and the two Indians came to Lancaster, and a solemn sight it was to me. There had I lived many comfortable years amongst my Relations and Neighbours, and now not one Christian to be seen, nor one house left standing. We went on to a Farm house that was yet standing, where we lay all night: and a comfortable lodging we had, though nothing but straw to ly on. The Lord preserved us in safety that night, and raised us up again in the morning, and carried us along, that before noon, we came to Concord. Now was I full of joy, and yet not without sorrow: joy to see such a lovely sight, so many Christians together, and some of them my Neighbours: There I met with my Brother, and my Brother in Law, who asked me, if I knew where his Wife was? Poor heart! he had helped to bury her, and knew it not; she being shot down by the house was partly burnt: so that those who were at Boston at the desolation of the Town, and came back afterward, and buried the dead, did not know her. Yet I was not without sorrow, to think how many were looking and longing, and my own Children amongst the rest, to enjoy that deliverance that I had now received, and I did not know whither ever I should see them again. Being recruited with food and raiment we went to Boston that day, where I met with my dear Husband, but the thoughts of our dear Children, one being dead, and the other we could not tell where, abated our comfort each to other. I was not before so much hem'd in with the merciless and cruel Heathen, but now as much with pittiful, tender-hearted and compassionate Christians. In that poor, and destressed, and beggerly condition I was received in, I was kindly entertained in severall Houses: so much love I received from several (some of whom I knew, and others I knew not) that I am not capable to declare it. But the Lord knows them all by name: The Lord reward them seven fold into their bosoms of his spirituals, for their temporals. The twenty pounds the price of my redemption was raised by some Boston Gentlemen, and Mr. Usher, whose bounty and religious charity, I would not forget to make mention of. Then

Mr. Thomas Shepard of Charlstown received us into his House, where we continued eleven weeks; and a Father and Mother they were to us. And many more tenderhearted Friends we met with in that place. We were now in the midst of love, yet not without much and frequent heaviness of heart for our poor Children, and other Relations, who were still in affliction. The week following, after my coming in, the Governour and Council sent forth to the Indians again; and that not without success; for they brought in my Sister, and Good-wife Kettle: Their not knowing where our Children were, was a sore tryal to us still, and yet we were not without secret hopes that we should see them again. That which was dead lay heavier upon my spirit, than those which were alive and amongst the Heathen; thinking how it suffered with its wounds, and I was no way able to relieve it; and how it was buried by the Heathen in the Wilderness from among all Christians. We were hurried up and down in our thoughts, sometime we should hear a report that they were gone this way, and sometimes that; and that they were come in, in this place or that: We kept enquiring and listning to hear concerning them, but no certain news as yet. About this time the Council had ordered a day of publick Thanksgiving: though I thought I had still cause of mourning, and being unsettled in our minds, we thought we would ride toward the Eastward, to see if we could hear any thing concerning our Children. And as we were riding along (God is the wise disposer of all things) between Ipswich and Rowly we met with Mr. William Hubbard, who told us that our Son Joseph was come in to Major Waldrens, and another with him, which was my Sisters Son. I asked him how he knew it? He said, the Major himself told him so. So along we went till we came to Newbury; and their Minister being absent, they desired my Husband to Preach the Thanksgiving for them; but he was not willing to stay there that night, but would go over to Salisbury, to hear further, and come again in the morning; which he did, and Preached there that day. At night, when he had done, one came and told him that his Daughter was come in at Providence: Here was mercy on both hands: Now hath God fulfiled that precious Scripture which was such a comfort to me in my distressed condition. When my heart was ready to sink into the

Earth (my Children being gone I could not tell whither) and my knees trembled under me, And I was walking through the valley of the shadow of Death: Then the Lord brought, and now has fulfilled that reviving word unto me: *Thus saith the Lord, Refrain thy voice from weeping, and thine eyes from tears, for thy Work shall be rewarded, saith the Lord, and they shall come again from the Land of the Enemy.* Now we were between them, the one on the East, and the other on the West: Our Son being nearest, we went to him, first, to Portsmouth, where we met with him, and with the Major also: who told us he had done what he could, but could not redeem him under seven pounds; which the good People thereabouts were pleased to pay. The Lord reward the Major, and all the rest, though unknown to me, for their labour of Love. My Sisters Son was redeemed for four pounds, which the Council gave order for the payment of. Having now received one of our Children, we hastened toward the other; going back through Newbury, my Husband preached there on the Sabbath-day: for which they rewarded him many fold.

On Munday we came to Charlstown, where we heard that the Governour of Road-Island had sent over for our Daughter, to take care of her, being now within his Jurisdiction: which should not pass without our acknowledgments. But she being nearer Rehoboth than Road-Island, Mr. Newman went over, and took care of her, and brought her to his own House. And the goodness of God was admirable to us in our low estate, in that he raised up passionate Friends on every side to us, when we had nothing to recompance any for their love. The Indians were now gone that way, that it was apprehended dangerous to go to her: But the Carts which carried Provision to the English Army, being guarded, brought her with them to Dorchester, where we received her safe: blessed be the Lord for it, For great is his Power, and he can do whatsoever seemeth him good. Her coming in was after this manner: She was travelling one day with the Indians, with her basket at her back; the company of Indians were got before her, and gone out of sight, all except one Squaw; she followed the Squaw till night, and then both of them lay down, having nothing over them but the heavens, and under them but the earth. Thus she travelled three dayes together, not knowing whither she was going: having nothing to eat or drink but water, and green Hirtleberries. At last they came into Providence, where she was kindly entertained by several of that Town. The Indians often said, that I should never have her under twenty pounds: But now the Lord hath brought her in upon free-cost, and given her to me the second time. The Lord make us a blessing indeed, each to others. Now have I seen that Scripture also fulfilled. Deut. 30 : 4, 7. *If any of thine be driven out to the outmost parts of heaven, from thence will the Lord thy God gather thee, and from thence will he fetch thee. And the Lord thy God will put all these curses upon thine enemies, and on them which hate thee, which persecuted thee.* Thus hath the Lord brought me and mine out of that horrible pit, and hath set us in the midst of tender-hearted and compassionate Christians. It is the desire of my soul, that we may walk worthy of the mercies received, and which we are receiving.

Our Family being now gathered together (those of us that were living) the South Church in Boston hired an House for us: Then we removed from Mr. Shepards, those cordial Friends, and went to Boston, where we continued about three quarters of a year: Still the Lord went along with us, and provided graciously for us. I thought it somewhat strange to set up House-keeping with bare walls; but as Solomon sayes, *Mony answers all things;* and that we had through the benevolence of Christian-friends, some in this Town, and some in that, and others: And some from England, that in a little time we might look, and see the House furnished with love. The Lord hath been exceeding good to us in our low estate, in that when we had neither house nor home, nor other necessaries; the Lord so moved the hearts of these and those towards us, that we wanted neither food, nor raiment for our selves or ours, Prov. 18. 24. *There is a Friend which sticketh closer than a Brother.* And how many such Friends have we found, and now living amongst? And truly such a Friend have we found him to be unto us, in whose house we lived, *viz.* Mr. James Whitcomb, a Friend unto us near hand, and afar off.

I can remember the time, when I used to sleep quietly without workings in my thoughts, whole nights together, but now it is other wayes with me. When all are fast about me, and no eye open, but his who ever waketh, my thoughts are upon things past, upon the awfull dispensation of the Lord towards us; upon his wonderfull power and might, in carrying of us through so many difficulties, in returning us in safety, and suffering none to hurt us. I remember in the night season, how the other day I was in the midst of thousands of enemies, and nothing but death before me: It is then hard work to perswade my self, that ever I should be satisfied with bread again. But now we are fed with the finest of the Wheat, and, as I may say, With honey out of the rock: In stead of the Husk, we have the fatted Calf: The thoughts of these things in the particulars of them, and of the love and goodness of God towards us, make it true of me, what David said of himself, Psal 6. 5. *I watered my Couch with my tears.* Oh! the wonderful power of God that mine eyes have seen, affording matter enough for my thoughts to run in, that when others are sleeping mine eyes are weeping.

I have seen the extrem vanity of this World: One hour I have been in health, and wealth, wanting nothing: But the next hour in sickness and wounds, and death, having nothing but sorrow and affliction.

Before I knew what affliction meant, I was ready sometimes to wish for it. When I lived in prosperity, having the comforts of the World about me, my relations by me, my Heart chearful, and taking little care for any thing; and yet seeing many, whom I preferred before my self, under many tryals and afflictions, in sickness, weakness, poverty, losses, crosses, and cares of the World, I should be sometimes jealous least I should have my portion in this life, and that Scripture would come to my mind, Heb. 12. 6. *For whom the Lord loveth he chasteneth, and scourgeth every Son whom he receiveth.* But now I see the Lord had his time to scourge and chasten me. The portion of some is to have their afflictions by drops, now one drop and then another; but the dregs of the Cup, the Wine of astonishment, like a sweeping rain that leaveth no food, did the Lord prepare to be my portion. Affliction I wanted, and affliction I had, full measure (I thought) pressed down and running over; yet I see, when God calls a Person to any thing, and through never so many difficulties, yet he is fully able to carry them through and make them see, and say they have been gainers thereby. And I hope I can say in some measure, As David did, *It is good for me that I have been afflicted*. The Lord hath shewed me the vanity of these outward things. That they are the Vanity of vanities, and vexation of spirit; that they are but a shadow, a blast, a bubble, and things of no continuance. That we must rely on God himself, and our whole dependance must be upon him. If trouble from smaller matters begin to arise in me, I have something at hand to check my self with, and say, why am I troubled? It was but the other day that if I had had the world, I would have given it for my freedom, or to have been a Servant to a Christian. I have learned to look beyond present and smaller troubles, and to be quieted under them, as Moses said, Exod. 14. 13. *Stand still and see the salvation of the Lord*.

Finis.

John Tanner's Narrative
of His Captivity

Chapter One

Recollections of early life—capture—journey from the mouth of the Miami to Sa-gui-na—ceremonies of adoption into the family of my foster parents—harsh treatment—transferred by purchase to the family of Net-no-kwa—removal to Lake Michigan

The earliest event of my life, which I distinctly remember, is the death of my mother. This happened when I was two years old, and many of the attending circumstances made so deep an impression, that they are still fresh in my memory. I cannot recollect the name of the settlement at which we lived, but I have since learned it was on the Kentucky River, at a considerable distance from the Ohio.

My father, whose name was John Tanner, was an emigrant from Virginia, and had been a clergyman. He lived long after I was taken by the Indians, having died only three months after the great earthquake, which destroyed a part of New Madrid, and was felt throughout the country on the Ohio (1811).

Soon after my mother's death, my father removed to a place called Elk Horn. At this place was a cavern—I used to visit it with my brother. We took two candles; one we lighted on entering, and went on till it was burned down; we then lighted the other, and began to return, and we would reach the mouth of the cavern before it was quite burned out.

This settlement at Elk Horn was occasionally visited by hostile parties of Shawneese Indians, who killed some white people, and sometimes killed or drove away cattle and horses. In one instance, my uncle my father's brother, went with a

From Edwin James, ed., *John Tanner's Narrative of His Captivity Among the Ottawa and Ojibwa Indians*, Occasional Papers of the Sutro Branch of California State Library, Reprint Series No. 20, ed. Paul Radin (San Francisco, 1940), pp. 1-13.

few men at night, and fired upon a camp of these Indians; he killed one, whose scalp he brought home; all the rest jumped into the river and escaped.

In the course of our residence at this place, an event occurred, to the influence of which I attributed many of the disasters of my subsequent life. My father, when about to start one morning to a village at some distance, gave, as it appeared, a strict charge to my sisters, Agatha and Lucy, to send me to school; but this they neglected to do until afternoon, and then, as the weather was rainy and unpleasant, I insisted on remaining at home. When my father returned at night, and found that I had been at home all day, he sent me for a parcel of small canes, and flogged me much more severely than I could suppose the offence merited. I was displeased with my sisters for attributing all the blame to me, when they had neglected even to tell me to go to school in the forenoon. From that time, my father's house was less like home to me, and I often thought and said, "I wish I could go and live among the Indians."

I cannot tell how long we remained at Elk Horn; when we moved, we traveled two days with horses and wagons, and came to the Ohio, where my father bought three flat boats; the sides of these boats had bullet holes in them, and there was blood on them, which I understood was that of people who had been killed by the Indians. In one of these boats we put the horses and cattle—in another, beds, furniture, and other property, and in the third were some Negroes. The cattle boat and the family boat were lashed together; the third, with the Negroes, followed behind. We descended the Ohio, and in two or three days came to Cincinnati; here the cattle boat sunk in the middle of the river. When my father saw it sinking, he jumped on board, and cut loose all the cattle, and they swam ashore on the Kentucky side, and were saved. The people from Cincinnati came out in boats to assist us, but father told them the cattle were all safe.

In one day we went from Cincinnati to the mouth of the Big Miami, opposite which we were to settle. Here was some cleared land, and one or two log cabins, but they had been deserted on account of the Indians. My father rebuilt the cabins, and enclosed them with a strong picket. It was early in the spring when we arrived at the mouth of the Big Miami, and we were soon engaged in preparing a field to plant corn. I think it was not more than ten days after our arrival, when my father told us in the morning, that from the actions of the horses, he perceived there were Indians lurking about in the woods, and he said to me, "John, you must not go out of the house today." After giving strict charge to my stepmother to let none of the little children go out, he went to the field with the Negroes, and my elder brother, to drop corn.

Three little children, beside myself, were left in the house with my stepmother. To prevent me from going out, my step-mother required me to take care of the little child, then not more than a few months old; but as I soon became impatient of confinement, I began to pinch my little brother, to make him cry. My mother perceiving his uneasiness, told me to take him in my arms and walk about the house; I did so, but con-tinued to pinch him. My mother at length took him from me to give him suck. I watched my opportunity, and escaped into the yard; thence through a small door in the large gate of the wall into the open field. There was a walnut tree at some distance from the house, and near the side of the field, where I had been in the habit of finding some of the last year's nuts. To gain this tree without being seen by my father, and those in the field, I had to use some precaution. I remember perfectly well having seen my father, as I skulked toward the tree; he stood in the middle of the field, with his gun in his hand, to watch for In-dians, while the others were dropping corn. As I came near the tree, I thought to myself, "I wish I could see these Indians." I had partly filled with nuts a straw hat which I wore, when I heard a crackling noise behind me; I looked round, and saw the Indians; almost at the same instant, I was seized by both hands, and dragged off betwixt two. One of them took my straw hat, emptied the nuts on the ground, and put it on my head. The Indians who seized me were an old man and a young one; these were, as I learned subsequently, Manito-o-geezhik, and his son Kish-kau-ko. Since I returned from Red River, I have been at Detroit while Kish-kau-ko was in prison there; I have also been in Kentucky, and have learned several particulars relative to my capture, which were unknown to me at the time. It appears that the wife of Manito-o-geezhik had recently lost by death her youngest son—that she had complained to her husband, that unless he should bring back her son, she could not live. This was an intimation to bring her a captive whom she might adopt in the place of the son she had lost. Manito-o-geezhik, associating with him his son, and two other men of his band, living at Lake Huron, had proceeded eastward with this sole design. On the upper part of Lake Erie, they had been joined by three other young men, the relations of Manito-o-geezhik, and had proceeded on, now seven in number, to the settlements on the Ohio. They had arrived the night previous to my capture at the mouth of the Big Miami, had crossed the Ohio, and concealed themselves within sight of my father's house. Several times in the course of the morning, old Manito-o-geezhik had been compelled to repress the ardor of his young men, who becoming impatient at seeing no opportunity to steal a boy, were anxious to fire upon the people dropping corn in the field. It must have been about noon when they saw me coming from the house to the walnut tree, which was probably very near the place where one or more of them were concealed.

It was but a few minutes after I left the house, when my father, coming from the field, perceived my absence. My stepmother had not yet noticed that I had gone out. My elder brother ran immediately to the walnut tree, which he knew I was fond of visiting, and seeing the nuts which the Indian had emptied out of my hat, he immediately understood that I had been made captive. Search was instantly made for me, but to no purpose. My father's distress, when he found I was indeed taken away by the Indians, was, I am told, very great.

After I saw myself firmly seized by both wrists by the two Indians, I was not conscious of any thing that passed for a considerable time. I must have fainted, as I did not cry out, and I can remember nothing that happened to me, until they threw me over a large log, which must have been at a considerable distance from the house. The old man I did not now see; I was dragged along between Kish-kau-ko and a very short thick man. I had probably made some resistance, or done something to irritate this last, for he took me a little to one side, and drawing his tomahawk, motioned to me to look up. This I plainly understood, from the expression of his face, and his manner, to be a direction for me to look up for the last time, as he was about to kill me. I did as he directed, but Kish-kau-ko caught his hand as the tomahawk was descending and prevented him from burying it in my brains. Loud talking ensued between the two, Kish-kau-ko presently raised a yell; the old man and the four others answered it by a similar yell; and came running up. I have since understood that Kish-kau-ko complained to his father, that the short man had made an attempt to kill his little brother, as he called me. The old chief, after reproving him, took me by one hand, and Kish-kau-ko by the other, and dragged me betwixt them; the man who had threatened to kill me, and who was now an object of terror, being kept at some distance. I could perceive, as I retarded them somewhat in their retreat, that they were apprehensive of being overtaken; some of them were always at some distance from us.

It was about one mile from my father's house to the place where they threw me into a hickory bark canoe, which was concealed under the bushes, on the bank of the river. Into this they all seven jumped, and immediately crossed the Ohio, landing at the mouth of the Big Miami, and on the south side of that river. Here they abandoned their canoe, and stuck their paddles in the ground, so that they could be seen from the river. At a little distance in the woods, they had some blankets and provisions concealed; they offered me some dry venison and bear's grease, but I could not eat. My father's house was plainly to be seen from the place where we stood; they pointed at it, looked at me, and laughed, but I have never known what they said.

After they had eaten a little, they began to ascend the Miami, dragging me along as before. The shoes I had on when at home, they took off, as they seemed to think I could run better without them. Although I perceived I was closely watched, all hope of escape did not immediately forsake me. As they hurried me along, I endeavored, without their knowledge, to take notice of such objects as would serve as landmarks on my way back. I tried also, where I passed long grass, or soft ground, to leave my tracks. I hoped to be able to escape after they should have fallen asleep at night. When night came, they lay down, placing me between the old man and Kish-kau-ko, so close together, that the same blanket covered all three. I was so fatigued that

I fell asleep immediately, and did not wake until sunrise next morning, when the Indians were up and ready to proceed on their journey. Thus we journeyed for about four days, the Indians hurrying me on, and I continuing to hope that I might escape, but still every night completely overpowered by sleep. As my feet were bare, they were often wounded, and at length much swollen. The old man perceiving my situation, examined my feet one day, and after removing a great many thorns and splinters from them, gave me a pair of moccasins, which afforded me some relief. Most commonly, I traveled between the old man and Kish-kau-ko, and they often made me run until my strength was quite exhausted. For several days I could eat little or nothing. It was, I think, four days after we left the Ohio, that we came to a considerable river, running, as I suppose, into the Miami. This river was wide, and so deep, that I could not wade across it; the old man took me on his shoulders and carried me over; the water was nearly up to his armpits. As he carried me across, I thought I should never be able to pass this river alone, and gave over all hope of immediate escape. When he put me down on the other side, I immediately ran up the bank, and a short distance into the woods, when a turkey flew up a few steps before me. The nest she had left contained a number of eggs; these I put in the bosom of my shirt, and returned towards the river. When the Indians saw me they laughed, and immediately took the eggs from me, and kindling a fire, put them in a small kettle to boil. I was then very hungry, and as I sat watching the kettle, I saw the old man come running from the direction of the ford where we had crossed; he immediately caught up the kettle, threw the eggs and the water on the fire, at the same time saying something in a hurried and low tone to the young men. I inferred we were pursued, and have since understood that such was the case; it is probable some of my friends were at that time on the opposite side of the river searching for me. The Indians hastily gathered up the eggs and dispersed themselves in the woods, two of them still urging me forward to the utmost of my strength.

It was a day or two after this that we met a party of twenty or thirty Indians, on their way toward the settlements. Old

Manito-o-geezhik had much to say to them; subsequently I learned that they were a war party of Shawneese; that they received information from our party, of the whites who were in pursuit of us about the forks of the Miami; that they went in pursuit of them, and that a severe skirmish happened between them, in which numbers were killed on both sides.

Our journey through the woods was tedious and painful: it might have been ten days after we met the war party, when we arrived at the Maumee river. As soon as we came near the river, the Indians were suddenly scattered about the woods examining the trees, yelling and answering each other. They soon selected a hickory tree, which was cut down, and the bark stripped off, to make a canoe. In this canoe we all embarked, and descended till we came to a large Shawnee village, at the mouth of a river which enters the Maumee. As we were landing in this village, great numbers of the Indians came about us, and one young woman came crying directly toward me, and struck me on the head. Some of her friends had been killed by the whites. Many of these Shawneese showed a disposition to kill me, but Kish-kau-ko and the old man interposed, and prevented them. I could perceive that I was often the subject of conversation, but could not as yet understand what was said. Old Manito-o-geezhik could speak a few words of English, which he used occasionally, to direct me to bring water, make a fire, or perform other tasks, which he now began to require of me. We remained two days at the Shawnee village, and then proceeded on our journey in the canoe. It was not very far from the village that we came to a trading house, where were three or four men who could speak English; they talked much with me, and said they wished to have purchased me from the Indians, that I might return to my friends; but as the old man would not consent to part with me, the traders told me I must be content to go with the Indians, and to become the old man's son, in place of one he had lost, promising at the same time that after ten days they would come to the village and release me. They treated me kindly while we stayed, and gave me plenty to eat, which the Indians had neglected to do. When I found I was compelled to leave this house with the Indians, I began to cry, for the first time since I had been taken. I consoled myself, however, with their promise that in ten days they would come for me. Soon after leaving this trading house, we came to the lake; we did not stop at night to encamp, but soon after dark the Indians raised a yell, which was answered from some lights on shore, and presently a canoe came off to us, in which three of our party left us. I have little recollection of any thing that passed from this time until we arrived at Detroit. At first we paddled up in the middle of the river until we came opposite the center of the town; then we ran in near the shore, where I saw a white woman, with whom the Indians held a little conversation, but I could not understand what was said. I also saw several white men standing and walking on shore, and heard them talk, but could not understand them; it is likely they spoke French. After talking a few minutes with the woman, the Indians pushed off, and ran up a good distance above the town.

It was about the middle of the day when we landed in the woods, and drew up the canoe. They presently found a large hollow log, open at one end, into which they put their blankets, their little kettle, and some other articles; they then made me crawl into it, after which they closed up the end at which I had entered. I heard them for a few minutes on the outside, then all was still, and remained so for a long time. If I had not long since relinquished all hope of making my escape, I soon found it would be in vain for me to attempt to release myself from my confinement. After remaining many hours in this situation, I heard them removing the logs with which they had fastened me in, and on coming out, although it was very late in the night, or probably near morning, I could perceive that they had brought three horses. One of these was a large iron-gray mare, the others were two small bay horses. On one of these they placed me, on the others their baggage, and sometimes one, sometimes another of the Indians riding, we traveled rapidly, and in about three days reached Sau-ge-nong, the village to which old Manito-o-geezhik belonged. This village or settlement consisted of several scattered houses. Two of the Indians left us soon after we entered it; Kish-kau-ko and his father only remained, and instead of proceeding immediately home, they left their horses and borrowed a canoe, in which we at last arrived at the old man's house. This was a hut or cabin built of logs, like some of those in Kentucky. As soon as we landed, the old woman came down to us to the shore, and after Manito-o-geezhik had said a few words to her, she commenced crying, at the same time hugging and kissing me, and thus she led me to the house. Next day they took me to the place where the old woman's son had been buried. The grave was enclosed with pickets, in the manner of the Indians, and on each side of it was a smooth open place. Here they all took their seats; the family and friends of Manito-o-geezhik on the one side, and strangers on the other. The friends of the family had come provided with presents; mukkuks of sugar, sacks of corn, beads, strouding, tobacco, and the like. They had not been long assembled, when my party began to dance, dragging me with them about the grave. Their dance was lively and cheerful, after the manner of the scalp dance. From time to time as they danced, they presented me something of the articles they had brought, but as I came round in the dancing to the party on the opposite side of the grave, whatever they had given me was snatched from me: thus they continued a great part of the day, until the presents were exhausted, when they returned home.

It must have been early in the spring when we arrived at Sau-ge-nong, for I can remember that at this time the leaves were small, and the Indians were about planting their corn. They managed to make me assist at their labors, partly by signs, and partly by the few words of English old Manito-o-geezhik could speak. After planting, they all left the village, and went out to hunt and dry meat. When they came to their hunting grounds, they chose a place where many deer resorted, and here they began to build a long screen like a fence; this they made of green boughs and small trees. When they had built a part of it, they showed me how to remove the leaves and dry brush from that side of it to which the Indians were to come to shoot the deer. In this labor I was sometimes assisted by the squaws and children, but at other times I was left alone. It now began to be warm weather, and it happened one day that having been left alone, as I was tired and thirsty, I fell asleep. I cannot tell how long I slept, but when I began to awake, I thought I heard some one crying a great way off. Then I tried to raise up my head, but could not. Being now more awake, I saw my Indian mother and sister standing by me, and perceived that my face and head were wet. The old woman and her daughter were crying bitterly, but it was some time before I perceived that my head was badly cut and bruised. It appears that after I had fallen asleep, Manito-o-geezhik, passing that way, had perceived me, had tomahawked me, and thrown me in the bushes; and that when he came to his camp he had said to his wife, "Old woman, the boy I brought you is good for nothing; I have killed him, and you will find him in such a place." The old woman and her daughter having found me, discovered still some signs of life, and had stood over me a long time, crying, and pouring cold water on my head, when I waked. In a few days I recovered in some measure from this hurt, and was again set to work at the screen, but I was more careful not to fall asleep; I endeavored to assist them at their labors, and to comply in all instances with their directions, but I was notwithstanding treated with great harshness, particularly by the old man, and his two sons She-mung and Kwo-tash-e. While we remained at the hunting camp, one of them put a bridle in my hand, and pointing in a certain direction, motioned me to go. I went accordingly, supposing he wished me to bring a horse; I went and caught the first I could find, and in this way I learned to discharge such services as they required of me.

When we returned from hunting, I carried on my back a large pack of dried meat all the way to the village; but though I was almost starved, I dared not touch a morsel of it. My Indian mother, who seemed to have some compassion for me, would sometimes steal a little food, and hide it for me until the old man was gone away, and then give i me. After we returned to the village, the young men, whenever the weather was pleasant, were engaged in spearing fish, and they used to take me to steer the canoe. As I did not know how to do this very well, they commonly turned upon me, beat me, and often knocked me down with the pole of the spear. By one or the other of them I was beaten almost every day. Other Indians, not of our family, would sometimes seem to pity me, and when they could without being observed by the old man, they would sometimes give me food, and take notice of me.

After the corn was gathered in the fall, and disposed of in the Sun-je-gwun-nun, or Ca-ches, where they hide it for the winter, they went to hunt on the Sau-ge-nong River. I was here, as I had always been, when among them, much distressed with hunger. As I was often with them in the woods, I saw them eating something, and I endeavored to discover what it was, but they carefully concealed it from me. It was some time before I accidentally found some beechnuts, and though I knew not what they were, I was tempted to taste them, and finding them very good, I showed them to the Indians, when they laughed, and let me know these were what they had all along been eating. After the snow had fallen, I was compelled to follow the hunters, and oftentimes to drag home to the lodge a whole deer, though it was with the greatest difficulty I could do so.

At night I had always to lie between the fire and the door of the lodge, and when any one passed out or came in, they commonly gave me a kick; and whenever they went to drink, they made a practice to throw some water on me. The old man constantly treated me with much cruelty, but his ill humor showed itself more on some occasions than others. One morning, he got up, put on his moccasins, and went out; but presently returning, he caught me by the hair of my head, dragged me out, rubbed my face for a long time in a mass of recent excrement, as one would do the nose of a cat, then tossed me by the hair into a snow bank. After this I was afraid to go into the lodge; but at length my mother came out and gave me some water to wash. We were now about to move our camp, and I was as usual made to carry a large pack; but as I had not been able to wash my face clean, when I came among other Indians they perceived the smell, and asked me the cause. By the aid of signs, and some few words I could now speak, I made them comprehend how I had been treated. Some of them appeared to pity me, assisted me to wash myself, and gave me something to eat.

Often when the old man would begin to beat me, my mother, who generally treated me with kindness, would throw her arms about me, and he would beat us both together. Towards the end of winter, we moved again to the sugar grounds. At this time, Kish-kau-ko, who was a young man of about twenty years of age, joined with him four other young men, and went on a war party. The old man, also, as soon as the sugar was finished, returned to the village, collected a few men, and made his preparations to start. I had now been a year among them, and could understand a little of their language. The old man, when about to start, said to me, "Now I am going to kill your father and your brother, and all your relations." Kish-kau-ko returned first, but was badly wounded. He said he had been with his party to the Ohio River; that they had, after watching for some time, fired upon a small boat that was going down, and killed one man, the rest jumping into the water. He (Kish-kau-ko) had wounded himself in his thigh with his own spear, as he was pursuing them. They brought home the scalp of the man they had killed.

Old Manito-o-geezhik returned a few days afterward, bringing an old white hat, which I knew, from a mark in the crown, to be that of my brother. He said he had killed all my father's family, the Negroes, and the horses, and had brought me my brother's hat, that I might see he spoke the truth. I now believed that my friends had all been cut off, and was, on that account, the less anxious to return. This, it appears, had been precisely the object the old man wished to accomplish, by telling me the story, of which but a small part was true. When I came to see Kish-kau-ko, after I returned from Red River, I asked him immediately, "Is it true, that your father has killed all my relations?" He told me it was not; that Manito-o-geezhik, the year after I was taken, at the same season of the year, returned to the same field where he had found me; that, as on the preceding year, he had watched my father and his people planting corn, from morning till noon; that then they all went into the house, except my brother, who was then nineteen years of age; he remained ploughing with a span of horses, having the lines about his neck, when the Indians rushed upon him; the horses started to run; my brother was entangled in the lines, and thrown down, when the Indians caught him. The horses they killed with their bows and arrows, and took my brother away into the woods. They crossed the Ohio before night, and had proceeded a good distance in their way up the Miami. At night they left my brother securely bound, as they thought, to a tree. His hands and arms were tied behind him, and there were cords around his breast and neck; but having bitten off some of the cords, he was able to get a penknife that was in his pocket, with which he cut himself loose, and immediately run toward the Ohio, at which he arrived, and which he crossed by swimming, and reached his father's house about sunrise in the morning. The Indians were roused by the noise he made, and pursued him into the woods; but as the night was very dark, they were not able to overtake him. His hat had been left at the camp, and this they brought, to make me believe they had killed him. Thus I remained for two years in this family, and gradually came to have less and less hope of escape, though I did not forget what the English traders on the Maumee had said, and I wished they might remember and come for me. The men were often drunk, and whenever they were so, they sought to kill me. In these cases, I learned to run and hide myself in the woods, and I dared not return before their drunken frolic was over. During the two years that I remained at Sau-ge-nong, I was constantly suffering from hunger; and though strangers, or those not belonging to the family, sometimes fed me, I had never enough to eat. The old woman they called Ne-keek-wos-ke-cheem e-kwa—"the Otter woman," the other being her *totem*—treated me with kindness, as did her daughters, as well as Kish-kau-ko and Be-nais-sa, the bird, the youngest son, of about my own age. Kish-kau-ko and his father, and the two brothers, Kwo-ta-she and She-mung, were blood-thirsty and cruel, and those who remain of this family, continue, to this time, troublesome to the whites. Be-nais-sa, who came to see me when I was at Detroit, and who always treated me kindly, was a better man, but he is since dead. While I remained with them at Sau-ge-nong, I saw white men but once. Then a small boat passed, and the Indians took me out to it in a canoe, rightly supposing that my wretched appearance would excite the compassion of the traders, or whatever white men they were. These gave me bread, apples, and other presents, all which, except one apple, the Indians took from me. By this family I was named Shaw-shaw-wa ne-ba-se (the Falcon), which name I retained while I remained among the Indians.

I had been about two years at Sau-ge-nong, when a great council was called by the British agents at Mackinac. This council was attended by the Sioux, the Winnebagoes, the Menomonees, and many remote tribes, as well as by the Ojibboways, Ottawwaws, &c. When old Manito-o-geezhik returned from this council, I soon learned that he had met there his kinswoman, Net-no-kwa, who, notwithstanding her sex, was then regarded as principal chief of the Ottawwaws. This woman had lost her son, of about my age, by death; and having heard of me, she wished to purchase me to supply his place. My old Indian mother, the Otter woman, when she heard of this, protested vehemently against it. I heard her say, "My son has been dead once, and has been restored to me; I cannot lose him again." But these remonstrances had little influence, when Net-no-kwa arrived with considerable whisky, and other presents. She brought to the lodge first a ten-gallon keg of whisky, blankets, tobacco, and other articles of great value. She was perfectly acquainted with the dispositions of those with whom she had to negotiate. Objections were made to the exchange until the contents of the keg had circulated for some time; then an additional keg, and a few more presents, completed the bargain, and I was transferred to Net-no-kwa. This woman, who was then advanced in years, was of a more pleasing aspect than my former mother. She took me by the hand, after she had completed the negotiation with my former possessors, and led me to her own lodge, which stood near. Here I soon found I was to be treated more indulgently than I had been. She gave me plenty of food, put good clothes upon me, and told me to go and play with her own sons. We remained but a short time at Sau-ge-nong. She would not stop with me at Mackinac, which we passed in the night, but ran along to Point St. Ignace, where she hired some Indians to take care of me, while she returned to Mackinac by heself. or with one or two of her young men. After finishing her business at Mackinac, she returned, and continuing on our journey, we arrived in a few days at Shab-a-wy-wy-a-gun. The corn was ripe when we reached that place, and after stopping a little while, we went three days up the river, to the place where they intended to pass the winter. We then left our canoes, and traveling over land, camped three times before we came to the place where we set up our lodges for the winter. The husband of Net-no-kwa was an Ojibbeway, of Red River, called Taw-ga-we-ninne, the hunter. He was seventeen years younger than Net-no-kwa, and had turned off a former wife on being married to her. Taw-ga-we-ninne was always indulgent and kind to me, treating me like an equal, rather than as a dependent. When speaking to me, he always called me his son. Indeed, he himself was but of secondary importance in the family, as everything belonged to Net-no-kwa, and she had the direction in all affairs of any moment. She imposed on me, for the first year, some tasks. She made me cut wood, bring home game, bring water, and perform other services not commonly required of the boys of my age; but she treated me invariably with so much kindness, that I was far more happy and content, than I had been in the family of Manito-o-geezhik. She sometimes whipped me, as she did her own children; but I was not so severely and frequently beaten as I had been before.

ACCULTURATION

In the preceding narratives we have had the white view of culture contact, though it would be hard to imagine a less white-influenced account of Indian life than that of John Tanner. Now in these two autobiographies, one of which is reprinted here in full, we discover the immediate meaning of culture contact and its inevitable results. Both of these life histories come out of the same time and place, for they are the histories of a brother and sister living through the disintegration of traditional Winnebago culture. Because of this the experiences recounted herein are in many respects parallel to ones coming to a similar resolution in the Native American Church. But because of the sexual factor there is a radical difference between these narratives, and this as much as anything else prompts their inclusion here.

Most apologists for the Indian prefer to gloss over or skip altogether the relations between men and women within the various tribal cultures. Part of the reason for this is the paucity of available evidence on the subject: many of the earlier gatherers of Indian materials were men who talked to men and wrote about Indian life from that perspective. When they did discuss women it was by way of describing the ancillary roles which women played; or they might admire the fortitude and endurance of the Indian mother who birthed in some thicket, bit off the cord, and rejoined the women's work battalion. Yet there is a deeper reason why Indian women get so little attention from friends of the Indian, and this is because in a majority of tribes women actually did play ancillary roles. True, there were groups which had women leaders, as witness the Tanner document; there were also a great many tribes in which descent was reckoned in the female line; and there were tribes where women were the important and official keepers of ritual as well as the important and unofficial consultants in tribal decision-making (one tribe which officially prohibited women from sitting in council nevertheless allowed them to sit off to one side and comment audibly on the decisions being reached by the men). But by our increasingly liberated standards we would have to conclude that Indian cultures were predominantly "sexist." It was men who were most often the principal actors in the great ceremonies; it was men who sought glory in battle and were subsequently honored among the lodges; it was a man who punished his wife's infidelity by cutting off the end of her nose; and it was a male offspring that brought joy and public rejoicing. It was the male occupations of hunting and warfare that were honorific while other types of labor, no less important, were contemptuously referred to as "women's work." In many tribes no self-respecting male would think of performing the homely tasks of the fireside, and white witnesses to tribal life often commented with incredulity (and, since these were often men, with barely concealed envy) on the studied indolence of Indian men in the presence of their women at heavy manual labor. From the Iroquois in the East to the tribes of the Northwest one of the worst insults that could pass from one man to another was, "You are a woman."

Surely, this is one of the less attractive features of American Indian life, yet for that very reason we need to know more about it and to understand it as well as we can. This is why one is so grateful for Nancy O. Lurie's *Mountain Wolf Woman*. It is one of the very few first-hand histories of Indian women that we have, and it illustrates how in so many central ways women were born into a position of cultural subservience.

It illustrates something else as well, something germane to this section, Culture Contact, and the resultant problems of acculturation. In Margaret Mead's *The Changing Culture of an Indian Tribe* there is an incisive discussion of the role that women play in a culture that has fallen apart. In the traditional culture of this tribe, writes Mead, the men played the dominant social and religious roles while the women played proportionately greater roles in basic and economic activities: child maintenance, preparation and preservation of foods, lodge-keeping, and so forth. Now, however, with the social and religious foundations of the culture largely destroyed (as with the Winnebago), the men of the culture cease to pay much attention to these while at the same time they retain their vestigial contempt for economic pursuits to support the family and their vestigial preference for idleness about the house. The typical situation then finds the man idle, out of work, and the woman providing both support and some semblance of household order. In this way the Indian woman has begun to emerge as at least an equal sharer in the new tribal culture, a privilege which ironically and symbolically came to her in some tribes only with the death of her husband and her own menopause.

All this is here in the reminiscences of Mountain Wolf Woman—as it is in another way in the life history of her brother, "S.B." There are no more poignant accounts, I think, of what it has meant to be born an Indian but to come of age in a white man's world.

The Autobiography of a
Winnebago Indian

1. Early Childhood

Father and mother had four children and after that I was
born, it is said.[1] An uncle of mother's who was named White-
Cloud, said to her, "You are to give birth to a child who will
not be an ordinary person." Thus he spoke to her. It was then
my mother gave birth to me. As soon as I was born and was
being washed—as my neck was being washed—I laughed out
loudly.

I was a good-tempered boy, it is said. At boyhood my father
told me to fast and I obeyed. In the winter every morning I
would crush charcoal and blacken my face with it.[2] I would
arise very early and do it. As soon as the sun rose I would go
outside and sit looking at the sun and I would cry to the spirits.[3]

Thus I acted until I became conscious.[4]

Then there were not as many white people around as there
are now. My father always hunted. Our lodge was covered with
rush mattings and we had reed mattings spread over the floor.
After my father had hunted for a considerable time in one
place we would move away. My father, mother, older sisters,
and older brothers all carried packs on their backs, in which

From Paul Radin, ed. *The Autobiography of a Winnebago Indian*
(New York, 1920, 1963).

[1] He uses the phrase "it is said" for all statements relating to that period
of his life of which he has no clear recollection.

[2] I.e., fast.

[3] I.e., make the ceremonial prayer uttered during the puberty fast.

[4] I.e., from that time on he recollects his childhood. However, the term
conscious is not to be taken in any metaphorical sense. To the Winnebago
mind anything not remembered is grouped together with nonexistent
phenomena. An individual is only conscious of what manifests its existence
to him by means of some inward stirring, be it emotional, intellectual, or
physical. For these things that have happened to him in infancy no such
manifestation exists and he consequently predicates no consciousness for
himself at that period. I do not doubt for a moment that he thinks of
these early years of his life as being identical with any unconscious condition occurring in mature life.

they carried many things. Thus we would pass the time until the spring of the year, and then in the spring we used to move away to live near some stream where father could hunt muskrats, mink, otter, and beaver.

In the summer we would go back to Black River Falls, Wisconsin.

The Indians all returned to that place after they had given their feasts. We then picked berries. When we picked berries my father used to buy me gum, so that I would not eat many berries when I was picking.[5] However, I soon managed to eat berries and chew gum at the same time. After a while I learned to chew tobacco and then I did not eat any berries (while picking them). Later on I got to like tobacco very much and I probably used up more value (in tobacco) than I would have done had I eaten the berries.

In the fall of the year we would pick cranberries and after that, when the hunting season was open, I would begin to fast again.

I did this every year for a number of years.

After a while we got a pony on which we used to pack all our belongings when we moved camp. And in addition about three of us would ride on top of the pack. Sometimes my mother rode and father drove the pony when we moved from one place to another.

After I had grown a little older and taller and was about the size of one of my older brothers, all of us would fast together. My father used repeatedly to urge us to fast. "Do not be afraid of the burned remains of the lodge center-pole,"[6] he would say to us. "Those which are the true possessions of men, the apparel of men,[7] and also the gift of doctoring—these powers that are

---

[5] Cranberry-picking is one of the principal means of support of the Winnebago.

[6] I.e., charcoal with which to blacken one's face while fasting.

[7] I.e., both material and immaterial. He refers mainly to that knowledge which will make a man honored and respected by his fellow men.

"Apparel of men" does not mean clothes, but power and ability; success on the warpath, membership in the Medicine Dance, ability to cure the sick, etc.

"Spread out before you" means "within your power to obtain from the spirits."

spread out before you—do try and obtain one of them," he was accustomed to say to us.

I would then take a piece of charcoal, crush it, and blacken my face, and he would express his gratitude to me.

At first I broke my fast at noon and then, after a while, I fasted all night. From the fall of the year until spring I fasted throughout the day until nightfall, when I would eat.[8] After a while I was able to pass the night without eating and after a while I was able to go through two nights (and days) without eating any food. Then my mother went out in the wilderness and built a small lodge. This, she told me, she built for me to fast in, for my elder brother and myself, whenever we had to fast through the night.

There we used to play around. However, before we were able to spend a night at that particular place, we moved away.

2. Puberty[9]

After a time I passed from this stage of boyhood into another. I began to use a bow and arrow and I spent my time at play, shooting arrows.

Then I found out that my mother had been told, just before I was born, that she would give birth to no ordinary being, and from that time on I felt that I must be an uncommon person.

At about this time my oldest sister married a holy man. My parents gave her in marriage to him. He was a shaman and he thought a great deal of me.

At this stage of life also I secretly got the desire to make myself pleasing to the opposite sex.

Now at that time the Indians all lived in their lodges and the women were always placed in lodges of their own whenever they had their menses. There the young men would court them at night when their parents were asleep. They would then enter

---

[8] No person attempted to fast for twenty-four hours at once without a break.

[9] The physiological and other changes at puberty are definitely noted by the Winnebago and a special word is used to cover the years from approximately twelve to twenty.

these lodges to court them. I used to go along with the men on such occasions for even although I did not enter the lodge but merely accompanied them, I enjoyed it.

At that time my parents greatly feared that I might come in contact with women who were having their menses, so I went out secretly. My parents were even afraid to have me cross the path over which a woman in such a condition had passed.[10] The reason they worried so much about it at that particular time was because I was to fast as soon as autumn came;[11] and it was for that reason they did not wish me to be near menstruating women, for were I to grow up in the midst of such women I would assuredly be weak and of little account. Such was their reason.

After some time I started to fast again throughout the day and night, together with an older brother of mine. It was at the time of the fall moving and there were several lodges of people living with us. There it was that my elder brother and I fasted. Among the people in these lodges there were four girls who always carried the wood. When these girls went out to carry the wood my older brother and I would play around with them a good deal. We did this even although we were fasting at the time. Of course we had to do it in secret. Whenever our parents found out we got a scolding, and the girls likewise got a scolding whenever their parents found out. At home we were carefully kept away from women having their menses, but we ourselves did not keep ourselves away from such. Thus we acted day after day while we were fasting.

After a while some of the lodges moved away and we were left alone. These lodges moved far ahead of us because we ourselves were to move only a short distance at a time. That was the reason the others moved on so far ahead of us. My father and my brother-in-law went out hunting and killed seventy deer between them and in consequence we had plenty of meat.

[10] A very general belief among the Winnebago. Any contact with menstruating women, or even with objects in any way connected with them, will, it is believed, destroy the power of sacred objects or individuals temporarily sacred. Fasting youths were regarded as such.

[11] Fasting always commenced in autumn and never lasted longer than early spring, or until the snakes appeared above ground.

3. Fasting

When the girls with whom I used to play moved away I became very lonesome. In the evenings I used to cry. I longed for them greatly, and they had moved far away!

After a while we got fairly well started on our way back. I fasted all the time. We moved back to a place where all the leaders used to give their feasts. Near the place where we lived there were three lakes and a black-hawk's nest. Right near the tree where the nest was located they built a lodge and the war-bundle that we possessed was placed in the lodge.[12] We were to pass the night there, my older brother and myself. It was said that if anyone fasted at such a place for four nights he would always be blessed with victory and the power to cure the sick. All the spirits would bless him.

"The first night spent there one imagined oneself surrounded by spirits whose whisperings were heard outside of the lodge," they said. The spirits would even whistle. I would be frightened and nervous, and if I remained there I would be molested by large monsters, fearful to look upon. Even (the bravest) might be frightened, I was told. Should I, however, get through that night, I would on the following night be molested by ghosts whom I would hear speaking outside. They would say things that might cause me to run away. Toward morning they would even take my blanket away from me. They would grab hold of me and drive me out of the lodge, and they would not stop until the sun rose. If I was able to endure the third night, on the fourth night I would really be addressed by spirits, it was said, who would bless me, saying, "I bless you. We had turned you over to the (monsters, etc.) and that is why they approached you, but you overcame them and now they will not be able to take you away. Now you may go home, for with victory and long life we bless you and also with the power

[12] Every Winnebago clan has at least one war-bundle; most of them have more. The father of S.B. possessed one, and most of the "power" resident in this particular bundle was supposed to have been bestowed by the thunder-birds and night-spirits. Perhaps that is why a black-hawk's nest was selected for the fasting-lodge, the black-hawk being regarded as a thunder-bird, although my interpreter was uncertain about the matter.

of healing the sick.[13] Nor shall you lack wealth (literally, 'people's possessions'). So go home and eat, for a large war party is soon to fall upon you who, as soon as the sun rises in the morning, will give the war whoop and if you do not go home now, they will kill you."[14]

Thus the spirits would speak to me. However if I did not do the bidding of this particular spirit, then another one would address me and say very much the same sort of thing. So they would speak until the break of day, and just before sunrise a man in warrior's regalia would come and peep in. He would be a scout. Then I would surely think a war party had come upon me, I was told.

Then another spirit would come and say, "Well, grandson, I have taken pity upon you and I bless you with all the good things that the earth holds. Go home now for the war party is about to rush upon you."[15] And if I then went home, as soon as the sun rose the war whoop would be given. The members of the war party would give the war whoop all at the same time. They would rush upon me and capture me and after the fourth one had counted coup, then they would say, "Now then, grandson, this we did to teach you. Thus you shall act. You have completed your fasting." Thus they would talk to me, I was told. This war party was composed entirely of

[13] It was customary for parents, generally grandparents, to tell youths who were fasting what kind of an experience they were to expect, and particularly how they were to recognize the true spirit when he should appear and thus guard against being deceived by an evil spirit. Apparently S.B.'s father told the youth in considerable detail what he was to expect on this particular occasion. The supernatural experience given here is peculiar in a number of respects; first, because it contains many elements distinctly intended to frighten the faster, and secondly, because it contains a well-known motif taken from the origin myth of the Four Nights' Wake. In practically all the fasting experiences I collected among the Winnebago the spirits are pictured simply as offering their blessings and having them refused or accepted by the faster. The test theme so prominent here does not occur at all. Apart from these facts, the experience is a good example of the type one would expect to find among the Winnebago, and perhaps the Woodland-Plains tribes in general.

[14] Practically every Winnebago fasting experience contains an attempt of an evil spirit to deceive the faster.

[15] The foregoing gives an excellent idea of how detailed are the instructions given a faster.

spirits, I was told, spirits from the heavens and from the earth; indeed all the spirits that exist would all be there. These would all bless me. They also told me that it would be a very difficult thing to accomplish this particular fasting.[16]

So there I fasted, at the black-hawk's nest where a lodge had been built for me. The first night I stayed there I wondered when things would happen; but nothing took place. The second night, rather late in the night, my father came and opened the war-bundle and taking a gourd out began to sing. I stood beside him without any clothing on me except the breech-clout, and holding tobacco in each hand I uttered my cry to the spirits as my father sang. He sang war-bundle songs and he wept as he sang. I also wept as I uttered my cry to the spirits. When he was finished he told me some sacred stories, and then went home.

When I found myself alone I began to think that something ought to happen to me soon, yet nothing occurred so I had to pass another day there. On the third night I was still there. My father visited me again and we repeated what we had done the night before. In the morning, just before sunrise, I uttered my cry to the spirits. The fourth night found me still there. Again my father came and we did the same things, but in spite of it all, I experienced nothing unusual.[17] Soon another day dawned upon us. That morning I told my elder brother that I had been blessed by spirits and that I was going home to eat. However, I was not telling the truth. I was hungry and I also knew that on the following night we were going to have a feast and that I would have to utter my cry to the spirits again. I dreaded that. So I went home. When I got there I told my people the story I had told my brother; that I had been blessed and that the spirits had told me to eat. I was not speaking the truth, yet they gave me the food that is carefully prepared for

[16] Some spirits are more difficult to approach than others. The black-hawk, regarded as the chief of the thunder-birds, is one of the most difficult spirits to obtain blessings from. However, blessings from him were quite customary in S.B.'s family.

[17] As we shall see later in connection with S.B.'s conversion to the peyote religion, he expected some definite inward change. Not receiving it he regarded himself as not having been blessed.

those who have been blessed. Just then my older brother came home and they objected to his return for he had not been blessed. However, he took some food and ate it.

That night we gave our feast. There, however, our pride received a fall,[18] for although it was supposedly given in our honor, we were placed on one side (of the main participants). After the kettles of food had been put on twice, it became daylight.[19]

The following spring we moved to the Mississippi in order to trap. I was still fasting and ate only at night. My brothers used to flatter me, telling me I was the cleverest of them all. In consequence I used to continue to fast although I was often very hungry. However (in spite of my desire to fast), I could not resist the temptation to be around girls. I wanted always to be near them and was forever looking for them, although I had been strictly forbidden to go near them, for they were generally in their menstrual lodges when I sought them out. My parents most emphatically did not wish me to go near them, but I did nevertheless.

My parents told me that only those boys who had had no connection with women would be blessed by the spirits. However, all that I desired was to appear great in the sight of the people. To be praised by my fellow-men was all that I desired. And I certainly received all I sought. I stood high in their estimation. That the women might like me was another of the reasons why I wanted to fast. However, as to being blessed, I learned nothing about it, although I went around with the air of one who had received many blessings and talked as such a one would talk.

4. Boyhood Reminiscences

The following spring I stopped fasting. In those days we used to travel in canoes. My father used to spear fish and would always take me along with him, and I enjoyed it very much.

---

[18] It was a common practice for the older people to treat the younger men in this way, in order to train them in humility.

[19] There are two meals served during the war-bundle feast, one at about midnight and one about dawn.

He kept a club in the canoe and after he had speared a fish, I would kill it with the club as it was jumping around in the canoe. Sometimes my mother accompanied us as a third person. She would sit at the rear end and row while father, standing in the prow, speared the fish. I killed all those that were thrown into the canoe with my club.

Sometimes my parents started out without me but I would then cry so bitterly that I always induced them to take me along. Sometimes they would whip me and tell me to go home but I used to follow them so far that they were afraid to let me go back alone and they would let me ride along with them. Indeed I exerted myself greatly in crying for them, and as I cried and ran after them and followed them very far, I was in the end always taken along.

In those days we always lived in the old-fashioned Indian lodges. In winter our fire was placed in the center of the lodge and my father used to keep it burning all night. When he placed a large log in the fire it would burn a long time. This is what we used to do in the winter.

We were three boys, of whom I was the youngest, and at night we used to sleep together. In cold weather we used to fight as to who was to sleep in the middle for whoever got that place was warm, for while those at either end used to pull the cover from each other, the one in the middle was always covered. Even after I grew up I always took the covering away from whomsoever I was sleeping with. I would always fold it under me, for it had become a habit with me to take the cover away from the other person (whenever I slept on the outside).

We always ate out of one dish. Sometimes we did not have enough food on hand and then I would always try to get enough by eating very fast. In this way I always succeeded in depriving the others of their proper portion. Sometimes, on the other hand, I would purposely eat slowly, and then when the others were finished, I would say that I had not been given enough and so I would get some of their food. In this way I developed a habit (that I still have), for I am a fast eater. Even after I grew up, whenever I ate with other people, I always finished sooner than they. (Another habit that I acquired then) was the ability to go without food for a whole day while traveling. I did not mind this in the least for (during my fasting) I had grown accustomed to going without food for long periods of time.

In the summer, at the season when people pick berries, I used to go around visiting, sometimes for a day, sometimes for longer. I would often receive nothing to eat, but I did not mind that. In the summer, when people pick berries, they generally go out in bands and settle here and there. Some were far away from others.

5. *Courting*

It was at this time that I desired to court women and I tried it. However, I did not know the proper thing to say. The young men always went around at night courting. I used to mix with the women in the daytime but when I went to them at night I did not know what to say. A brother of mine, the oldest, seemed to know how to do it. He was a handsome man and he offered to show me how. Then I.went with him at night. We went to a girl who was having her menses at that time. She was a young girl. When girls get their menses they always have to live apart. It was to such a one that we went. We were very cautious about the matter for the girls were always carefully watched as their relatives knew that it was customary to court them at such a time. (One of the precautions they used) was to pile sticks and branches about the lodge so that it would be difficult to enter. If a person tried to enter he was likely to make a noise moving the branches and this would awaken the people living in the larger lodge nearby and they might run out to see what was the matter.

It was to such a place that we went. After working at the obstacles placed near the entrance for some time, my brother entered the lodge. I went as close as possible and lay down to listen. He spoke in an audible whisper so that I might hear him. Sure enough I heard him. However after lying there for some time I fell asleep. When I snored my brother would wake me up. Afterward the girl found out and she sent us both away. Thus we acted every now and then.

After a while I entered the lodges myself. We always had

blankets wrapped around us and we took care to have our heads well covered (on such occasions).

Sometimes a girl was acquainted with quite a large number of men and then these would gather around her lodge at night and annoy her parents a good deal. We would keep them awake all night. Some of these people owned vicious dogs.

There was one old woman who had a daughter and when this daughter had her menses, she stayed in an oblong lodge with just room enough for two persons. She watched her daughter very carefully. Finally she slept with her. We nevertheless bothered her all the time just out of meanness. One night we went there and kept her awake almost all night. However, just about dawn she fell asleep, so we—there were several of us— pulled up the whole lodge, poles and everything, and threw the poles in the thicket. The next morning the two were found sleeping in the open, it was rumored, and the mother was criticized for being over careful.[20]

The reason why some of the (older) people were so careful at that time was because it had been reported that some young men had forced themselves into lodges where they had not been received willingly.

Once I went to see a young girl and arrived there before the people had retired, so I waited near the lodge until they would go to sleep. As I lay there waiting, listening to them, I fell asleep. When I woke up it was morning and as the people got up they found me sleeping there. I felt very much ashamed of myself and they laughed at me. I was not long in getting away.

We always did these things secretly for it was considered a disgrace to be caught or discovered.

On another occasion, in another place, I was crawling into a lodge when someone woke up as I was about halfway in. I immediately stopped and remained quiet and waited for the people to fall asleep again. However, in waiting I, myself, fell asleep. When they woke me up in the morning I was lying half-way inside the lodge, asleep. After waking me up they asked

[20] An excellent example of Winnebago viewpoint. To them it appears as reprehensible to be over careful as it would to be over negligent.

me whether I would not stay for breakfast, but I immediately ran away.

After a while I began going around with some particular girl and I liked it so much that I would never go to sleep at night. My older brothers were very much the same. We used to sleep during the day.

While we were acting in this manner, our parents saw to it that we had food to eat and clothes to wear. We never helped, for we did nothing but court girls. In the fall the Indians used to pick berries after they all came together. We used to help on such occasions. However, we were generally out all night and were not able to do much in the morning. I used to go out courting and be among the lodges all night, and yet, most of the time, I did not succeed in speaking to any of the girls. However, I did not mind that for I was doing it in order to be among the girls and I enjoyed it. I would even go around telling people that I was really keeping company with some of the girls. I used to say this to some of my men associates. In reality, however, I did not get much more than a smile from one or two of the girls, but even that I prized as a great thing.

6. *My Brother-in-Law and His Fasting Experience*[21]

When this was over, we all moved to the hunting grounds and I began to fast (again). I then began to take vapor baths, and also I caused myself to vomit so that I would be purged. My father was a good deer hunter.[22] He was always able to kill many deer and, at times, he also killed some bear.

I had a brother-in-law who thought a good deal of me. He was a holy man and shaman. One day he said to me, "Brother-

[21] This brother-in-law is a very remarkable man. He is one of the few Winnebago living who is supposed to be living his third life on earth. He even claims to be the reincarnated culture hero of the Winnebago, the hare. An account of him is given in "Personal Reminiscences of a Winnebago Indian," *Journal of American Folklore* 26 (1913). The fasting experience given here is apparently only one of the many he had. He seems to have had a remarkable influence on both S. B. and his brother.

[22] Skill in hunting is one of the traits for which S. B.'s family was noted among the Winnebago. S.B. in particular inherited this ability.

in-law, I will bless you. However, you will have to fast for it. I was blessed by four brothers, beings called good giant-cannibals. They said that they had never before blessed anyone. They promised me that if I ever came to any difficulty, they would help me. They blessed me with (long) life. Now I will give this blessing to you.[23] If you fast for four nights (without a break), these (giants) will talk to you." Thus he spoke to me. (Then he continued), "There are four brothers and the oldest one is called *Good-giant;* the second one, *Good-heart;* the third one, *Good-as-he-goes-about,* and the fourth one *Good-where-he-lifts-his-foot-from.* Toward the east, where a promontory is to be found, there they live. Nothing across the large body of water is too difficult for them to accomplish." Thus he spoke.

So when I fasted, I always offered tobacco to them (these spirits) first. Then I would cry to these spirits, but I never fasted overnight.

7. A War-Bundle Feast[24]

When they were through hunting, my father selected ten deer to give a feast with. The attendants[25] then transferred these deer (to the place) where the people always gave their feasts.

I was fasting at that time and ate only in the evenings.[26] Every evening likewise I would go out and appeal to the spirits before I ate.

Five days before the feast we were to give was ready, I began to fast through the night (as well as the day). The fifth night

[23] It was not uncommon for an older man to bestow his blessing upon a younger man. As indicated here, the younger man would in any case have to fast for it. However, it was a foregone conclusion that he would receive it in such a case.

[24] A war-bundle feast consists of two parts, the first part consecrated to the night-spirits (the mythical spirits who are supposed to cause the darkness), and the second part consecrated to the thunder-birds. Both spirits are concerned with the bestowing of war powers. The ceremony consists in the offering of tobacco, buckskins, and eagle-feathers to the various spirits, requesting them to bestow victory in return upon the suppliants.

[25] The attendants are always the male children of the man's sister. Sometimes his brothers help.

[26] I.e., he broke his fast every evening.

we went to the feast, together with an older brother of mine. In the daytime I went out into the wilderness and there I appealed (cried) to the spirits. It was not that I was so hungry as that I was very thirsty, for I don't think that either my mouth or my tongue was even moist.

That night we held aloft the deerskins[27] that were to be offered to the spirits, and thus we stood there crying to the spirits. There we wept and those who gave the feast wept with us as they extended their (holy) compassion to us. Then, at midnight, we stood near the war weapons and again raised our cries to the spirits.

Our feast was given in an eight-fireplace lodge.[28] The host always sits near the last fireplace, at the east end. That is where we stood crying to the spirits. My older brother fell to the ground.[29] We were stark naked except for our breech-clouts as we did this. After doing this, we put on our moccasins. Then they (sat down) to the feast and the kettles were put on (the fireplace). Then it was daybreak. The feasters sang, singing only dance-songs,[30] however. Then we were to pass the deerskin offerings through the roof of the lodge.[31] My older brother took the lead. I followed and the others came behind me. We all had a deerskin apiece. Only those of us who were giving the feast (had the right to hold) one of the ten deerskins. (A person playing) a flute taken from a war-bundle went ahead of us, and following came the people with (incense) of the burning cedar leaves. We marched around the lodge and my brother and I again made our cry to the spirits. At that time

[27] Toward the end of the ceremony the deerskins marked for definite spirits and tied to a stick are held aloft and carried around the lodge in a very dramatic way.

[28] The number of spirits to whom offerings were made varied from feast to feast. An eight-fireplace lodge means that on this particular occasion only eight spirits were propitiated, there always being one fireplace for each spirit.

[29] It was considered a commendable act of piety to fall to the ground exhausted during the performance of a ceremony.

[30] Dance songs were sung at the very end of the ceremony.

[31] This very dramatic rite takes place at the end of the ceremony. The buckskins are thrown through the roof of the lodge and are supposed to be seized by the spirits to whom they are being offered.

we were naked with the exception of the breech-clouts and the moccasins. Four times we made the circuit of the lodge. Then we passed the deerskins up through the roof of the lodge.

Now the feasters were to eat again. A separate kettle had been put on for us (boys) and we were to eat first. They then called upon a man to eat out of our plate.[32] The name of this man was *Blue-sitter*. He was to eat out of our plate first. He was a holy man, a doctor, and a brave man (one who had obtained war honors). Four deer-ribs were dished out to me[33] in a wooden bowl. Then the one who was to eat out of my plate came and sat down near my dish and began to handle my food. He tore it up in small pieces for me. Then he began to tell me of his blessing.

He told me how all the great spirits had blessed him—the Sun, the Moon, the Thunder-birds, the Earth, the Heaven, the Day, and all the spirits that exist in the heavens. All these blessed him, he said. And the spirits who are on the earth, and those under the waters, all these talked to him, he said. (Thinking) of this power (he possessed) did he partake of my food.[34] I was to go through battle unharmed and I was to obtain some war honor. My children, if I had any, were to enjoy a good and happy life. Thus he spoke.

Then he took a piece of my food in his mouth and placed some in my mouth four times. Then I continued eating and the rest of the feasters began to eat. For quite some time I was not able to eat much. Through it all I was not in the least conscious of any dreams or blessings.[35] (All that I was aware of) was that all the people around were taking pity upon me.

I, on the contrary, had my mind fixed on women all the time. (In doing all these things) I imagined that I had accomplished something great and that I had risen greatly in their (women's) estimation. Even though I tried to render myself pitiable in the

[32] This is regarded as a great honor.

[33] I.e., the poorest meat of the deer. Only the warriors received the choice parts.

[34] I.e., he bestowed some of the power with which he had been blessed upon S.B.

[35] Cf. note 17.

sight of the spirits, yet, through it all, my thoughts were centered upon women. I was never lowly at heart and never really desired the blessing of the spirits.[36] All I thought of was that I was a great man and that the women would regard me as a great man.

8. *Wandering and Hunting*

After a while I used to get in the habit of going to town. When I got there, I would look into all the barrels to see if there was any food in them, and if there was I would fill my pockets (with whatever I found). My pockets would be full. I used to steal a great deal.

About springtime we always moved away (from town). We would move to whatever place my father intended to trap in, generally to some farming community where there were few Indians. There my mother used to make baskets[37] and sell them to the farmers. We would also circulate a written petition (asking) for any help people cared to give us. Whenever they went on this kind of a (begging) trip, I always went along with them, for sometimes people would take pity on us and at such times they often gave me old clothes. Sometimes we would even get a good meal at some farmer's house. For these reasons, I was always envious of those who went along on such trips.

Occasionally when we got a lot of provisions I had to carry some of them, but I never minded that. In the spring of the year we would begin to shoot with bows and arrows. When the

[36] It was absolutely essential, in order to obtain a blessing or derive real advantage from participation in a ceremony to be, as S.B. says, lowly at heart, and also to keep one's attention fixed firmly and exclusively on the fast or the ceremony. Your thoughts are not supposed to wander for a moment. S.B. apparently felt that since his thoughts were so frequently deflected in other directions he could not hope to obtain the desired blessing. He is clearly unfair to himself in claiming that he was only interested in being regarded as a great man. He did not receive any blessing and like a good orthodox Winnebago he explained his lack of success as due to his failure to "concentrate" his attention properly.

[37] Basket making, as far as I know, is not a real Winnebago industry. It has probably been recently adopted through the influence of the Ojibwa and Menominee.

birds returned north, father used to make us bows and arrows and we would shoot birds and sometimes kill many of them. We also used to kill squirrels and my grandmother would roast them for us. My older brother used to be a good shot. I was greatly inferior to him. He often killed pheasants.

Whenever (the older people) went to a large town circulating petitions for help, we youngsters always went along with them. We always took our bows and arrows along with us, for the whites wanted to see how well we could shoot and often placed five-cent pieces on some object at a considerable distance and had us shoot at them. We generally hit a number. I would also let my brother shoot at twenty-five-cent pieces that I would hold between my fingers and he never hit my fingers. We would often make as much as five dollars in this manner and we always gave this money to our parents.

In summer the Indians were accustomed to return from the various places (where they had been camping) to Black River Falls. Therefore we also returned to Black River Falls. In summer we would go out shooting with our bows and arrows and we generally stayed away all day. At evening when we got home, of course we always expected to get a scolding so we always had some excuse made up for the occasion. It really would have been better had we returned earlier in the day, but we always enjoyed (the hunting) so much that night would overtake us when we were still a long distance from home. Often we would not eat anything all day, but we were quite accustomed to that. Sometimes we would go fishing down a stream that runs nearby and again we would forget (the time) and not return home until it was very late. We would then get a scolding even if we gave some sort of an excuse.

9. My Grandfather Adopts Me

My father once gave me away. (On my return one day) I found my father talking to my grandfather and after a while (I saw) the old man weep. He had just lost a son, a young man and the last of his children. They had all died. It was this that they were talking about. (I heard) my grandfather say finally that he was tired of living. Then my father, also weeping, called him by his relationship term[38] and said, "I sympathize with you, for you indeed speak the truth. Yet, in spite of it all, I want you to live. Here is my son, my own, and of all my children the one I love best.[39] He is obedient. He is present here and is listening. He shall be your companion and as long as you live he will lead you by the hand." Thus he spoke to him. The old man thanked my father repeatedly.

After that I stayed with him and he thought a great deal of me and I got along very well in every way. He was a great man, a man who doctored and had great knowledge of medicine. This he used to give to the sick. He was also a great medicine man and an old soldier.[40]

Just about this time a school had been built at Tomah, Wisconsin, and I wanted very badly to attend it. My grandfather consented and I went to school there for one winter. In the spring my father came after me and asked the superintendent whether I could go home for two weeks and he consented to let me go.

Then father said to me, "My son, your grandfather is dead and they are going to have a memorial ceremony (in his honor) and this is to take place at a performance of the Medicine Dance. Someone (you know), must take his place (in the ceremony)[41] and they decided that I was to be that one. Now, my son, of all my children I have most control over you. I have never kept anything from you. And you have never willfully disobeyed me. I want you therefore to do me this (favor and take my place). I am getting old and besides I cannot control

[38] I.e., by the term denoting the particular relationship which he bore to the old man. As a rule, among the Winnebago, a man is called by his cardinal name.

[39] This is not so much conceit upon S.B.'s part as a necessary phrase for his father to use, in order to show the old man how deeply he sympathized with him and to what lengths of sacrifice he would go. He would give him the son he loved best!

[40] By medicine man he means here a member of the Medicine Dance. Exactly what is meant by soldier I do not know, but I believe it refers to his having been in the U.S. army, and not to his being an Indian warrior.

[41] Formerly, practically the only way in which a person could join the Medicine Dance was by replacing some deceased member. On such an occasion the ceremony took on the nature of a memorial performance for the departed and a special place was reserved for the group representing the dead man.

my desire for drink any longer and under these conditions I would not be able to live up to the teachings of the lodge. I wish therefore to turn my (right) over to you. Do you take your grandfather's place." Thus my father spoke to me.

10. Initiation into the Medicine Dance[42]

The person who had died and whose place I was to take was an uncle of my father. I was glad of this opportunity for I had always liked the Medicine Dances when I saw them. I had always enjoyed watching from the outside what was going on inside and was always filled with envy. I used to wonder if I would ever be able to be one of them. So, naturally, I was very glad (to join) and anxious as to what (would happen).

We proceeded to the place where the ceremony was to be held, traveling from Tomah to Wittenberg. Sometimes we would have to walk, but I enjoyed it nevertheless. I was very happy.

Finally we arrived at the place and my father explained to the people there that he had turned over his right (to membership) to me and that that was why he had taken me along. They were quite satisfied.

We were to build the lodge immediately, so we went and cut the poles for it, after measuring the length required. Of course we hunted around and got the kind of poles always used for that purpose. Then we made the lodge. We stuck the poles in the earth. We worked together with three old men, brothers of the man who had died. They told me that this ceremony was a holy affair, that it was Earthmaker's play.[43] We always made an offering of tobacco before everything we did. I, of course, thought that it must indeed be a marvelous thing and I was very happy about it. What I was most eager to see was myself killed

---

[42] For a description of the Medicine Dance see my paper "The Ritual and Significance of the Winnebago Medicine Dance," *Journal of American Folklore*, 24, no. 92 (1911).

[43] The Winnebago word means literally "actions, affairs, play," and is the regular ritualistic expression for a ceremony.

and then brought to life again, in the lodge.[44] I also realized that a member of the Medicine Lodge, whether man or woman, was different from a person not belonging to it and I was quite anxious not to be an ordinary person any longer but to be a medicine man.

As soon as we finished building the lodge (the ceremony began) and the first thing the people did was to sing. That first time they kept me up all night and I heard a good deal about sacred affairs. I was not sleepy at any time during the night and I remained this way until morning.[45] I enjoyed it all so much that I did not even go to sleep the next day. The next night they kept me up again, but as before I did not get sleepy. On that night they told me even more things. The third night was the same. Throughout these three nights I did not sleep at all. On the fourth night they sang until morning. On the fifth night they were to have the practice (trial).[46] During the day the people began to come. In the afternoon they went into the sweat lodge. Those (who went in) were all old men. They were the people who had been especially invited with bundles of tobacco. When

[44] The shooting ritual is, dramatically, the most important part of the Medicine Dance. It is the Winnebago counterpart to the Central Algonkin Midewiwin and is naturally the element that attracts most interest from outsiders and children. There seems to be little doubt that the killing and coming to life again in the shooting ritual was always regarded by the older members of the Medicine Dance as symbolical, and that it was merely a dramatic representation of the belief that all members of the society would receive the gift of reincarnation. Nonmembers and children, however, always interpreted this shooting ritual literally and the members of the organization, it must be admitted, did everything in their power to create this impression upon the uninitiated.

[45] He is referring here to the so-called "preparatory nights." There are four of them beginning at sunset and generally lasting until midnight or longer. Each one of the four units (called bands) of which the Medicine Dance is composed has its own four "preparatory nights" at which he is to join.

S.B.'s insistence that he did not in the least become sleepy is not to be interpreted merely as a sign of marked interest but also as an assurance that he was "concentrating his attention" as was demanded.

[46] The Medicine Dance proper consists of two parts; the first, called "trial," lasting from sunset until sunrise, and the second, the "real" performance, lasting from about seven in the morning until sunset. The main difference between the two divisions is that the speeches are shorter in the former and that the initiation rites take place during the day performance.

we came out it was sundown. Then those in the east[47] stopped singing and those especially invited entered.

Then they took me in charge for the whole night and whenever they talked they would say, "In the morning when he for whom we desire life becomes like us."[48] They meant me and that I would be like them in the morning. So I was indeed extremely anxious for the morning to come. They danced most of the night. They were giving their trial performance.

The next morning just before day, even while the dance was still going on, the one (the leader) in the first and second seat and those at the east end, together with some others, took me out in the wilderness.[49] When we got there, we found a place where the ground had been cleared in the outline of the dance lodge. There they preached to me and they told me that the most fearful things imaginable would happen to me if I made public any of this affair. The world would come to an end, they said. Then again they told me to keep everything secret, and that if I told anyone, I would surely die. After that they showed me how to fall down and lie quivering (on the ground) and how to appear dead.[50] I was very much disappointed for I had had a far more exalted idea of it (the shooting). "Why, it amounts to nothing," I thought. "I have been deceived," I thought. "They only do this to make money," I thought. I also thought then that probably many of the sacred things of which they told

[47] The position of honor is given to the band invited first, whose seat is at the eastern end of the lodge. Opposite them, but still regarded as occupying the east, sit the host and his friends. They always enter the lodge first and sing a few songs before the others enter.

[48] The person to be initiated is known as he-for-whom-we-desire-life. The word for life means literally "light," but in rituals it is always used in this symbolic sense. "To become like them" means to have been killed and to have come to life again, i.e., to have been reincarnated.

[49] Everything outside of the cleared ground around the village was called wilderness. In this particular case he refers to the cleared ground some distance away from the ceremonial lodge, where the neophyte is to be initiated into the secrets of the shooting ritual. "Those at the east end" here refers to the members of the host's band.

[50] The person "shot" is supposed to feign death. Those only recently initiated must fall down motionless immediately, but older members have the right to hesitate and to lie on the ground quivering. The right to do this must be bought.

me were not true either.[51] However, I kept on and I did as I was told to do, for I had been taught to deceive in the ceremony in the wilderness. As soon as I was proficient in the act (of feigning death), we started back.

They told me that I would become just like them in body, but I did not have the sensation of any change in me.[52] All that I felt was that I had become a deceiver in one of Earthmaker's creations.[53]

During the day, at the regular meeting, I did as I had been taught to do. We were simply deceiving the spectators. When we were through, those of my band told me that in two years I would be able to imitate the sounds of animals as much as I wanted to, for I had taken the place of a great medicine man.[54] Those who have the privilege of dancing, obtain it by making gifts to the older members and thus get permission. Those who do not buy or get permission, are not allowed to dance. Similarly in shooting[55] they are not privileged to extend their arms when they shoot (unless they buy that privilege), but must hold

[51] Probably the majority of the people initiated are slightly disappointed but few give expression to it, and I doubt whether S.B.'s disappointment was as intense as he claims here. Certainly his deduction that other ceremonies were as untrue as this one is an afterthought due to the influence of the peyote religion. It is, incidentally, the only case I have found where he was influenced by his later beliefs in interpreting his older life.

[52] This is another example of S.B.'s refusal to believe that any change has taken place in him, unless he has some inward sensation of such a change.

[53] The Medicine Dance is, strictly speaking, not the creation of Earthmaker but of the culture hero, Hare. There may be some Christian influence here, for Earthmaker has been generally identified with God. The conservatives have even gone so far at times as to equate Hare with Christ.

[54] By means of whistles, etc., placed inside receptacles made of otter, squirrel, weasel, or other skins, they cause these bags to make noises resembling those made by these animals. It is this spectacular power of the otter-skin bag that greatly impresses the minds of outsiders and children. S.B. does not mean to imply that he is inheriting any of the powers of the man whose place he taking, but that he is expected to emulate him.

[55] Not only is an individual "shot" when he is initiated, but all initiated members indulge in shooting at each other at certain definite periods during the performance of the ceremony. Only members who have purchased the right to shoot enjoy this privilege. Newly initiated people never have this right, or at least they did not have it in former times.

their shooting skins close up to their breasts.[56] The right to drum as well as the right to shake the gourd rattles must be bought before it can be exercised. In fact almost every act is bought before it can be exercised. However I was told that I did not have to do all that, but that I would be a great medicine man immediately.[57] That pleased me. I was given a gray squirrel skin for my medicine bag and they told me that it was alive and that I could make it cry out loud.[58] I had heard them do it and had always envied them in this regard. This was another of the things I was anxious to do. Indeed I wondered greatly how this could be done.

The dance was soon over and my father went away and left me there alone; he left me at the home of the deceased man's wife. I did not go back to school but was asked to stay there and do odd jobs for the old woman. So I stayed there all spring.

I had been told that if a person initiated into the Medicine Dance did not regard the affair as sacred, that this was a sign that he was going to die soon. This frightened me a great deal, for I had been thinking of the whole matter in a light manner and I felt that this was an indication that I was really going to die soon. I therefore did my best to consider it a sacred ceremony but, in spite of it all, I did not succeed.

About this time I left for Tomah. It was about the middle of summer (July fourth). I returned and stayed with my grandfather and from that time on was taught by him (details) of the Medicine Dance. (For instance), when I prepared a sweat bath for him, he would teach me some songs. I therefore did this for

[56] It is believed that the ability to hold the shooting-bag at arm's length is due to the power "shot" into an individual and that therefore a recent member or one recently initiated, who has of course only been "shot" a few times, does not possess this power. Consequently all he can do is to keep the shooting-bag pressed closely to his breast.

[57] If he was told this, it can be explained in only two ways: either the ceremony had greatly degenerated, or the relatives of S.B. had made payments sufficient to cover not only the expenses of initiation but also the right to privileges otherwise enjoyed only by members of some standing. I cannot help thinking that here S.B. has been led astray by his youthful conceit, and that he is not telling the truth. I know that even eight years ago this would not have been permitted among the Nebraska Winnebago, who are the less conservative of the two groups.

[58] This may be true. It must, however, be taken with caution.

him frequently. Whenever I prepared such a bath for him, he would be very grateful to me and that is why I did it.[59] Before long I learned all the songs he knew, so that when I was invited to a Medicine Dance I would do all the singing and he would only have to do the talking. From that time on I said that it was a sacred affair and I took part in the ceremony for the greatness it possessed.[60] (I boasted of its greatness) in the presence of women in order to make a good impression on them.

About this time I went away with a show to dance. I was fond of dancing and now I had a chance to go around and dance all the time and even get paid for it. I had money all the time. The people with whom I went around never saved anything and were always without funds, for they spent all their money on drink. I never drank. After a while I went with these shows every fall, when the fairs start.

11. Marriage

One fall I did not go and instead I stayed with my grandfather. He told me to get married. I was about twenty-three years old then. I had courted women ever since I was old enough. Every time I did anything I always thought of women in connection with it.[61] I tried to court as many women as I could. I wanted badly to be a beau for I considered it a great thing. I wanted to be a ladies' man.

My grandfather had asked me to marry a certain girl, so I went over to the place where she was staying. When I arrived there I tried to meet the girl secretly, which I succeeded in doing. I told her of my intention and asked her to go home

---

[59] S.B.'s utilitarian interpretation of his actions must not be taken too literally as a rule. However, in this particular case it must be remembered that preparing a bath for an older man was merely one of the accepted ways of informing him that you wished to ask him something. Personal regard and affection were shown in other ways. S.B. does not therefore mean, as his words might imply, that he was actuated by purely selfish motives. He was simply doing what custom dictated.

[60] S.B. possessed a very good voice and pronounced musical ability. While the right to sing was considered quite an honor, it often depended largely upon a good voice. S.B. apparently interpreted the privilege as a recognition of his ability and his standing. I doubt whether the others did.

[61] I.e., of the impression he would make on women.

with me. Then she went home for I had met her some distance from her home.

After a while she came back all dressed up and ready. She had on a waist covered with silver buckles and a beautifully colored hair ornament and she wore many strings of beads around her neck, and bracelets around her wrists. Her fingers were covered with rings and she wore a pair of ornamented leggings. She wore a wide-flap ornamented moccasin and in each ear she had about half a dozen ear holes and they were full of small silver pieces made into ear ornaments. She was painted also. She had painted her cheeks red and the parting of her hair red. She was all dressed up.

I went there on horseback. We rode the horse together. We were not going that night to the place from which I had come, because I had previously been asked to sing at a medicine feast by my band (at a place) which was on our way home. I would therefore not go home until the next morning. So on my way there I had the girl hide near the place where we were to have the feast, for we were eloping and that was the custom.[62]

The girl had a red blanket which she was wearing so I had her hide under a small oak bush. It rained all night and the next day. When we were through in the morning, I went to the place (where I had put her) and she was still there, but she was soaked through and through from the rain and her paint was smeared over her face in such a way that one could hardly recognize her. Then we went home. When we arrived home, my grandfather's wife came out to meet us and she helped the girl down from the horse and led her into the lodge. Then we ate. When we were through, the girl took off her clothing and gave it to them and they gave her other clothing to wear.[63] After the girl had stayed there three nights, she had her menses, so she had to camp by herself, and there she had to sleep at night. Then a horse was given to this girl that I had married.

[62] Elopement was one of the accepted methods of marriage. It had none of the connotations that the word has among us, for as S.B. indicated, the union had been arranged by the old man with whom he was staying.

[63] This bridal costume of the girl was intended as a gift to the husband's female residents. As indicated further on, S.B.'s grandparents reciprocated soon after by presenting her with a horse.

After a while my grandfather had a private talk with me, and he said: "Grandson, it is said that this girl you have married is not a maiden but really a widow, and I am not pleased with it, as this is your first marriage and you are a young man. I suppose you know whether it is true or not, whether she is a maiden or not?" "Yes," I answered. "You can stop living with her, if you wish," he said. So I went away on a visit and from there I went away for good. After some time I learned that the woman had gone home. Then I went home. He (my grandfather) was glad that I had not stayed with her. "You can marry another and a better one," said he to me, "one that I shall choose for you, you shall marry." Thus he spoke to me. However, I said to him, "Grandfather, you have begged women for me often enough.[64] Don't ever ask for anyone for me again, as I do not care to marry a woman that is begged for." Thus I spoke to him. He was not at all pleased at this for he said I was not allowing him to command me.

12. Going with Shows

About this time we went to the Sioux country on a visit. There were a number of us. While there I was given a pony. I was made a friend.[65] When I came home, I used to ride my pony about. That same fall a number of people were going out with a show and I went along with them. We went to all the large cities in the country. I was a good dancer.

There were two women with us; they were grass widows. After a while I went with one of them secretly. She used to drink beer. After a while I went with the other one also. They were both accustomed to drink. They would often ask me to drink but I always refused. Finally I married one of the women, but after a while I also lived with the other one. I lived with both of them. We used to live in a tepee. They both drank beer and after a while I also drank beer with them. Finally I

---

[64] This rebellion of S.B. would probably not have occurred in former days. I never heard the phrase "begging for women" used in this connection before.

[65] This is a real term of relationship, and implies a number of definite mutual services.

got to drinking very much and began liking it. However, I did it in secret and told them to keep it secret too. Finally, as I used to drink often, a man friend of mine found out about it and then I began to drink with him. Soon the owner of the show discovered that I was drinking. He thought a great deal of me; he thought that my dancing was better than that of the others and when he learned that I was drinking he said he was going to treat me and the two girls to beer some night. I drank a lot of it and I enjoyed it very much. After this I was not able to keep the fact of my drinking secret. I talked very loudly and I was very happy and would sing out every once in a while. Then I drank some whisky in addition (to the beer) and got drunk. The next morning I said I would never do it again, but afterward I drank beer in secret.

Finally we stopped and went home. We went across Lake Michigan. It was very stormy and we all got sick. Then my friend said, "Say, let us drink so that we may not get sick." Then he took out some whisky. He took out a flask containing two quarts. We drank all night. Very early in the morning we got to Bad Lake (Milwaukee). There we ate our breakfast and again we continued on the train. We were going to Black River Falls and again we drank all day. Then we arrived at Black River Falls. We were still drinking. My relatives saw me and saw that I was drunk. They were very sorry and an older sister of mine wept when she saw me. Then I again made up my mind that I would not do it again. They were paid their annuity money when we got back. After that I did not drink any more (for some time).

After the annuity payment had been (spent), the hunting season was about to open. So I also went to the hunting grounds. I ran away from the women with whom I had been living. I did not continue living with either of them. Then I went to the hunting grounds. There I spent some time hunting. We would start out hunting very early in the morning and would stay out all day and not get home until night. Even if we had run around all day, still we did not take time to have our noon meal. At night, regularly, we would take our sweat baths. We would take them because (they were supposed to act) as charms.[66] I always felt refreshed in the morning after first taking a sweat bath and then bathing in cold water.

13. Dissipation

Once when I returned (to the camp), I found some other people camping near me. In this camp (I found) my grandfather. He had brought along with him one of the women with whom I had been living. I did not like it. He had indeed brought the older of the two. My grandfather asked me to live with her and I lived with her there at these hunting camps. When the hunting season was over, the woman with whom I was living stayed at my house, but I went home with another woman. This woman (my former wife) remained there for some time afterward, but finally when she got tired (of waiting for me) she went away.

(About that time) it was reported that she used some medicine on me, this woman that went away. A medicine feast[67] was made and my scalp was operated upon. It was said that she took one of my hairs and put it in a medicine bundle of hers. It was said that she did this in order that I might not leave her, and that if I left her I would get a headache, and perhaps even die. Thus they said. However, this was discovered, and my scalp was operated upon and the hair she had taken was washed with medicine. Consequently nothing happened to me.

After this I began to try and live with as many women as I could, for I had gotten the notion that I was a lady-killer. So I tried to live with as many women as I could.

14. Brother's Death

Some time after that my older brother was killed. We had grown up together and were hardly ever separated from each other. I felt hearbroken over the matter. I longed to kill the

---

[66] I think he means "as a means of purification" and to insure success on the hunt.

[67] This was a private feast, in no way connected with any important ceremony.

one who had murdered him. I felt that I would be better off if I were dead myself. That is how I felt. After that I began to drink much more. I wanted to die drinking, that is what I used to say, while I was drinking so heavily. Up to this time I had drunk only secretly, but now I drank heavily and openly. After a while I became a confirmed drunkard. I had by this time quite forgotten that I wanted to die, and really enjoyed the drinking very much.

15. Drinking

About this time I got in the habit of giving women whisky and getting them drunk, and when I drank and got a woman drunk, then I would steal anything of value she had (on her person). I used to abuse people a great deal. At one time I got to be very handy with boxing gloves. I was never defeated, and that is why I always acted meanly to people. They were always afraid of me for they knew (of my skill). My father was a strong man and had never been defeated at wrestling and my older brothers likewise had never been defeated. For these reasons I was very arrogant. Besides this, I was very big. I am six feet and two inches tall and I weighed two hundred and fifty-five pounds. As a matter of fact I was not strong but merely acted as though I were, for every time I got drunk, I always found myself bound when I got sober. I never stayed with any woman long. All I did was to wander around visiting and doing nothing but drink.

I had four sisters and it was from them and my parents that I received everything I ever possessed, yet I claimed to be a great man.[68] I then had two women staying with me as my wives, and, at one time I had as many as four, two at my parents' house and two staying with other relatives of mine. I wasn't serious with any of them.[69] I lied all the time and I knew how to tell false-hoods. On one occasion four children were born to me and each one had a different mother. Nevertheless even after that I still courted women and kept on drinking.

    [68] He is not saying this in a sudden burst of remorse, but is simply stating a fact.

    [69] I.e., he was not married to any one of them.

In the spring there was always work that we could do. We would roll logs down the stream, and drink. I always worked at such occupations, because I could drink a good deal at the same time. Whenever I had any money I would spend it on getting some woman drunk.

16. Boasting and Blessings

At the time I began to drink heavily, I began to boast about being a holy man. I claimed that I had been blessed by spirits and I kept on claiming this again and again. I was, of course, not telling the truth, for I had never felt the stirring of anything of that kind within me; I claimed it because I had heard others speak of it. Generally when I was just about drunk and on the verge of getting boisterous, yet still conscious of what I am saying, I would make this claim. Then I would say that I was blessed by a Grizzly-Bear spirit, that it had blessed me with the power of being uncontrollable; that I had been taught certain songs and these I would sing at the top of my voice. I used to imitate a grizzly béar and begin to exert my power. Then the people (around) would (try to) hold me. It generally required a large number of people to control me.[70] Now I thought this (exhibition of mine) an act worthy of praise.

After a while I began to claim that I was blessed by many spiritual beings. Some time after I said that I was one of the

[70] All the details of this blessing are quite correct. He may be lying, as he claims, but I suspect that there was more in it than that. The power of being uncontrollable was the characteristic gift of the grizzly bear.

[71] In the light of this statement, remembering that his brother-in-law had actually turned over to him the blessings he had obtained from these cannibal spirits, it seems reasonable to believe that S.B. is unjust to himself in insisting that he lied about these blessings. It is clear that he did not obtain what he considered the only warrant for their truth, the stirring of something within him, but he doubtless did all that was technically required of him, and therefore his fellow Indians believed him. Theoretically, S.B. was quite right in insisting upon this "thrill," because so the old people taught, but the more practical-minded Winnebago never waited for it. This the older people realized, for in the "teachings" given the children, as S.B.'s father clearly says in Part II of this memoir, provision is made for those who are not able to receive blessings.

giant beings called *Good-Giants*,[71] that I was the second-born one of these and that my name was *Good-Heart;* that I had become reincarnate among human beings, dwelling with them.[72] All this I would claim and they would believe me.

17. The Effect of a Pretended Blessing

Once when I was on a drinking spree, I visited a certain lodge. There I found a girl whom I was accustomed to call "niece" and whom I always used to tease.[73] I used to call her, in jest, "mother," "sister." This particular time (when I came), after I had been offered food and eaten it, I also began to tease the girl sitting there. Then the other women (present) said to me, "My younger brother, your niece is really in a condition to excite your compassion; she is, indeed, practically about to face death, for she is going to be confined, and, on such occasions, she barely manages to escape death." "Ho, very well," said I, "my elder sister, (this time) my niece is not going to suffer. Up above in the heaven there exist four women, sisters, and these blessed me, telling me that if ever I called upon them for help, they would help me. Now to these I will offer tobacco and when she (my niece) is ready (about to be delivered), she must ask them for help." Thus I spoke to her. The woman thanked me then. However, I told a tremendous falsehood. I said all this because I was hungry. Then they gave me enough to appease my hunger. I had nothing else to say.

Some time after this I saw them in town. The woman came over to me (and said), "My younger brother, it is good. Your niece is in the (excellent) condition you claimed she would be; she is very well indeed. She has just given birth to a child. Within three days of her delivery she was able to chop wood. Never before had that happened to her. It is good. As soon as the an-

---

[72] I believe that in making this claim, a rather unusual one, he was probably influenced by his brother-in-law (cf. 21), who claimed to be the reincarnated Hare. Although S.B.'s brother-in-law was a well-known man, his claim was not accepted by most people, and, of course, in the case of S.B. such a claim probably met with no acceptance at all.

[73] I.e., with whom he was on terms of joking relationship. This relationship existed between a man and his maternal uncle, his daughters, and his daughter's daughters ad infinitum.

nuity payment is made you may have the child's share for drink." Thus she spoke.

I was surprised. Perhaps I am really a holy man, I thought.[74]

After (this incident) I boasted even more (of my powers), for now I really thought I possessed sacred power. I therefore talked as those do who have knowledge of all the spiritual beings that exist. I also spoke with the authority of a great medicine man.[75] I used to do the singing for my band, for I had a deep bass voice, and they therefore (liked to have me) do their singing. Sometimes I would be given offerings in kind to make a kettle of food.[76]

I always drank a good deal whenever a Medicine Dance was given and (frequently) I would knock people unconscious, even those in the vicinity of the camp.

18. With a Circus

Once we went out hunting in the fall of the year. We killed some game. We used to sell the hind quarters of the deer we killed. Sometimes we would ship them away to Chicago. We

[74] This interesting experience, to my mind, sheds great light upon the whole question of the relationship of the individual to the spirits and the nature of the efficacy of their power. It seems clear that S.B. had not obtained this particular power either by fasting, or through purchase, or as a gift. Apparently, he had heard about these particular spirits and their functions. That, in part, his desire to appear important and powerful played a role here, there is little question, but that seems to me of minor importance. He wanted to help, and, while strictly speaking he had no right to call upon spirits who had not blessed him, yet every Winnebago had more or less the right to offer tobacco to any spirits he wished. Whether it would be of any avail was I believe a moot question. To the practical minded among them there seems to have been the feeling that if you were to offer tobacco and murmur the proper prayers and be sincere in your desire for help, although even the latter was not absolutely necessary, the spirits would be likely to help you; that, as a matter of fact, they are constrained to help you. All this S.B. did. His success would have been accepted by any Winnebago as a proof that the spirits had hearkened; for some it would have been regarded as a proof that he had been blessed. S.B. with his insistence upon an "inward thrill" was genuinely surprised, and was apparently beginning to realize that power from the spirits could be obtained in another way.

[75] I.e., with the authority of a member of the Medicine Dance.

[76] I.e., to make a feast and offer tobacco to the spirits.

were, of course, only permitted to hunt for thirty days. If any-one hunted longer than that, he would (of course) be arrested (if caught). Such was the law. But in spite of the law we hunted beyond the prescribed time on the theory that the law was only meant for the whites. We shipped some more (deer) away and were detected. We had shipped deer and as a result my elder brother and myself were arrested and taken to court, where we were told that we would have to spend sixty days in jail. We were then put in jail. There we stayed. During our imprisonment I never had my hair cut and from that time on I wore my hair long. I told people that he whom we call Trickster[77] had instructed me to do this and that he had blessed me, and I told my elder brother to do the same thing (i.e., to let his hair grow) and (Trickster) would bless him with (long) life. From that time on I wore long hair.

After a while my hair grew very long. Then I went out among the whites with a show. They (the people) liked me very much because I had long hair and I was well paid. During all that time I drank. After a while I learned to ride a bicycle and I also learned to ride wild horses. I always used to say that I was a cowboy, because I wore my hair long. I used to ride many vicious horses and many times I was thrown off. I did all this because I was wild, not because I (really) was an expert. (At one time) I took part in a bicycle race on a race track. I was in full Indian costume and wore long hair.

This (show) played at St. Paul, Minnesota. I took part in it every summer. Soon I became acquainted with many people and they always asked me to come again. Finally I would not even return to the Indians in winter.

One season someone asked me to get together a number of Indians of whom I was to be in charge. I was told that I would be allowed ten dollars a week for each Indian and that I could

[77] In former times the Indians always wore their hair long and the older conservative Winnebago still do.

The Trickster was not one of the bona fide spirits of the priests' "pantheon" but he was popular with the people, although blessings from him are not common. Offerings were, at times, made to him at the war-bundle feast.

pay them whatever I liked. I was quite satisfied, for I could pay them about five dollars a week and thus make some money, I thought. So I persuaded a number of people to go along with me and we all started. We rode to the place from which (this man) had written. From there we started out and went to the fairs. We never made any money and finally we went bankrupt. The man could not even pay me. We felt angry and went to another show with whose manager I was acquainted. We were to divide the receipts.

We were now about to give our show at a certain place for the last time, for the cold weather was setting in. So it was our last day. (On that day) one of the boys with me told me that someone had struck him. I got angry. I told him to point out to me the offender if he could remember him. Just then the person appeared and I tried to strike him but he ran away so I did not succeed in knocking him down. However I struck him in the face with a drumstick. In the evening it was said that "the man whom one of you struck says that after the show is over this evening, he will kill a certain Indian." "Let him know that perhaps he is also subject to death," I said. "I, also, am anxious to get hold of him." After the show was over, we put on our citizen's clothes and took our handbags. "None of you must go out alone." I said, "for you might get hurt." One of the boys was on horseback, for he wanted to water his horse and was taking it to a trough. But there his pony was taken away from him and he had to return without it. His hat was taken away from him so he returned bareheaded. (As a matter of fact), he barely escaped with his life. "Let us go back," said I. I told the other boys to go on and not to worry about us. I gave them my valise to take along. Then we returned to the place where the boy had been attacked. Before we got there, this same boy was set upon with clubs. We were right in a big crowd of white people. On they went shouting and chasing him. Then they saw me and went at me. I fought them with my bare fists. I just whirled from one side to the other. I was surrounded by them. Whenever anyone got near enough to me, I struck him. They would stand off and strike me with their clubs. Then I started to run and I was hit on the head but not knocked unconscious. Now I was angry and I struck out at all those within my reach. Had I had a weapon I would have killed some of them. Finally several fell upon me. Again I was struck on the head with a club and my head was entirely covered with blood. Then I started for our show tents for they had not been moved yet. Just then the man who had started all the trouble came toward me with a hatchet. I started for him and when I met him and he raised his hatchet, I struck him and knocked him down, for I hit him straight in the mouth.

Just then a policeman came toward us and took me and led me to our show tent. I was covered with blood. The women all wept and told the policeman who I was, that it was not my fault for I had not been drinking. They took me to the jail. Then I told the policeman that we ought not to be locked up, for we had not been the ones who had started all the trouble. Not we but the others should be locked up. It was this other one who had been drinking. Thus I spoke to him. "You are right, I will go and look for your things. But you ought not to be on the street for you have injured many people.[78] You had better stay in jail for a few hours, for they are watching me. Now I'll go for your pony and then you can do whatever you like," he said. Then they put me in jail and there I found the other Indian with whom I had started out. "Well, it is good. I thought they had killed you," he said. "Well, how many did you kill?" he asked me. "I didn't kill anyone," I answered. "It is good, for I thought that they had either killed you or you had killed them," he said.

Then I washed the blood from my head. The policemen returned and brought my pony with them, and also my hat. Then they said, "You are to go right home. It is true that you have been unfairly dealt with, but this is a regular fair town and if any trouble starts in the courts from this affair, it will hurt our fairs in the future. We shall therefore not go to law about it. The man who started this trouble is the owner of a large hotel and one of his men owns a trotting horse. These are the men who started the trouble. Now you have knocked out all the teeth of the hotel-keeper and we do not know wheth-

[78] Whether true or not he naturally would insist that he had hurt a number of people.

er he will live or not; and you have bruised the other person's head badly. So you had better go home," he said.[79]

From there we started for our home. My partner rode a pony and rode through the middle of the town. I went in the same direction. He was afraid to go through the crowd of white people. A policeman took us out to the edge of the town. There we told him that we wanted some whisky. So he went into a saloon and brought us two quarts of whisky. From there we went home. My partner was riding a two-year-old pony and a small one, but nevertheless we both rode on it. Every time a team came up behind us, we were afraid. After we had been drinking, however, then we said that if (the fight) were to occur again, we would (surely) kill someone, for we felt sorry (at its termination). However no one pursued us.

In the neighborhood some Indians lived and we went to them that very night. When I told them about it, they were frightened, for they thought that (these people) might come out there to fight. These people therefore moved away the next morning. The other man and I took up their trail and followed them. We still rode the little pony together. We had plenty of whisky along with us. At night we came upon their camps again. They were really trying to get away from us for they were afraid that someone might still come out and fight with us.

There I found out that my relatives were camping nearby so I went over to them. They felt very sorry for us. They were working there, digging potatoes. There were many Indians working there. I stayed at that place, at a woman's house.

19. Continued Dissipation

As I stayed there, I was one day handed a paper by a woman. She told me she was married at the place where she was staying, but if I came over, she would do whatever I said. I told the woman with whom I was living about it and she said, "Go after her that I may have her as a companion." Her father had a horse and on it I rode over to the woman's house. I went and secretly watched the people digging potatoes, for

[79] In all likelihood this speech is slightly colored in order to motivate S.B.'s willingness to depart and not continue the fight.

their camp was nearby. The man who was living with this woman was also living with another woman.[80] The woman I came for was in the camp. I went over to her secretly. When I got there she began to get ready. Then we rode on the pony and we (happened) to run past the place where the man was working. He chased us, but we got away from him. I (soon) arrived home and the other woman, indeed, received her willingly. They would sleep with me alternately.

When our work was finished there we went to the place from which we had originally come, and just as we reached home, our annuity payment was made. The superintendent of the Wittenberg school made the payment. As soon as we got home, one of the women with whom I was living was taken away from me. She went and lived with another man. When the payment was over, the superintendent went to a place called Yellow-water (Necedah) to pay these people, and then he was to go to Red-Hill. I went along, for I was "chasing up the payment."[81] There I deceived many women and thus I obtained quite a sum of money. Then I started off with a number of other young men. By this time I was spending all my time drinking.

I got on the train at night. At a place called Honsa, we had to change cars. From there we rode on a freight car. When we had gone only a short distance the conductor saw us and put us off. We were all drinking. One of us had lost his hat and was going along bareheaded. We walked into some pasture and there found some dry wood, with which we built a fire. We were going to sleep there. We had all had plenty of whisky. Late at night we became thirsty so we looked around for water. We found pools of water here and there and out of these we drank. Then we went to sleep. The next morning when we woke up we saw a good well near us, but we had drunk out of the water and mud in which the pigs had wallowed.[82]

In the morning when the train arrived, we all boarded it. We got to our destination. There we found many people drink-

[80] Wife stealing is quite common now. It was rare in former times.

[81] This disreputable custom is still in full swing.

[82] He does not relate this incident to point a moral but simply as a fact, and possibly as a humorous occurrence.

ing and a lot of noise. That was what I was looking for. Whenever I saw a person drunk I would steal whatever he had, for that was what I was (a thief). If I saw a woman drunk, I would steal her, for that was what I was (an adulterer).[83] What I was looking around for mainly was to induce a woman to live with me, for in this way I was able to get money from her. If any woman wanted to marry me while staying with me, she would give me all the money she had. This is the kind of work I was doing. I would often, in this way, induce two or three (women) to live with me.

After finishing at Necedah, the superintendent always went to Tomah to make the payment, and when finished there he would proceed to Black River Falls. At Black River Falls the last payment was made, and for that reason, that was always an extremely noisy place. All who liked this kind of life, all who used to chase around for the fun of it (would be there). There marriages would get badly mixed up, the stealing of one another's wives, fighting, robbery of one another's money. Even those married people who had been faithful to each other until then, would become unfaithful on this occasion. Many would be hurt here. And when the last payment was over, all those who had not spent their last cent on drink would begin gambling and the men and women would play poker. Only when our last cent was gone would we stop and settle down. Many of us were generally left without enough money to go home.[84]

20. I Count Coup on a Pottawattomie

I never married any woman permanently. I would live with one woman for a while and then with another. Sometimes while I was living with a woman, I would return after a short absence to find her living with another man. Thus I acted.

My father brought me up and encouraged me to fast that

[83] Here his present religious affiliations have prompted him to call attention to this particular sin, for it is one of the sins the peyote religion specifically condemns.

[84] This saturnalia has developed only in recent times. I know of nothing to suggest that we are here dealing with an old survival.

I might be blessed by the various spirits and (thus) live in comfort. So he said. That I might obtain war honors, that I might not be like one who wears skirts (effeminate), thus my father raised me. For that reason he had me join the Medicine Dance, lest in life I be ridiculed by people. To lead a sober and sane life (my father taught me), and when I lived with my grandfather, he said the same. They encouraged me to give feasts and ask the (spirits) for war honors.[85]

At that time I had a comrade[86] and one day he said to me, "We have been thinking of something (of late, haven't we?). We ought to try and obtain some external emblem of our bravery. Do we not always try to wear feathers at a warrior dance?[87] Well, let us then try to obtain war honors, so that we can wear head ornaments." Thus both of us said. We both liked the idea. We decided to go (in search of war honors). We meant to kill an individual of another tribe, we meant to perform an act of bravery. Finally we started out. There were four of us and we went to a place frequented by other tribes. We took the train, carrying some baggage. We had ropes along, too, for we intended to steal some horses as well as kill a man, if we met one. Horse stealing was regarded as a praiseworthy feat and I had always admired the people who recounted the number of times they had stolen horses, at one of the Brave Dances. That was why I did these things.

We proceeded to a place where horses belonging to men of other tribes used to abound. Just as we got there we saw the owner of these horses and we killed him. My friend killed him. Then we went home and when we got there I told my father about it secretly. I said to him, "Father, you said it was good to be a warrior and you encouraged me to fast, and I did. You encouraged me to give feasts, and I did. Now we have just

[85] Here all the Winnebago ideals are mentioned and the cardinal point of their exhortations to the younger people brought out—"Do all that I tell you lest people ridicule you."

[86] I.e., friend. Cf. note 65. A man had to share every danger with his friend and was not supposed to return from any enterprise on which his friend had been killed. A very similar relationship existed between a man and his maternal uncle.

[87] Indicating that they had been on the warpath and killed an enemy or counted coup.

returned from a trip. We were looking for war honors and the young people (who accompanied me) decided that I should lead them. I told them that it was a difficult thing to lead warriors, my father had always told me; that I had always understood that one led a band of warriors only in consequence of a specific blessing; that I was not conscious of having received such authority." Thus I spoke. "However, they made me an offering of tobacco as they asked me, and I accepted the tobacco saying that I would at least make an offering of tobacco (for them). Then I offered tobacco to the Thunderbirds and asked them for rain, that we might walk in the power (protection) of rain. This offering we made in the morning and it rained all that day. Then we went to the place where we knew we could find horses. When we got there, we met the owner of the horses and spoke to him. We went with him to a carpenter shop nearby and there we killed him. I counted coup first and I announced my name as I gave a war whoop. I shouted, *'Big-Winnebago* has counted coup upon his man.'[88] Then the others counted coup. Then we searched his pockets and found some medicine and money in them. The money we divided among ourselves. After that we cut out his heart, for we had heard that hearts were used for medicine. For that reason we cut out his heart. He had a gun too, and this is it, one of them said. Hide it away, said I to him."

Then my father said to me, "My son, it is good. Your life is no longer an effeminate one. It is this way that our ancestors encouraged us to live. It is the will of those (spirits) in control of war that has led you to do this. On your own initiative you could not possibly have done it."[89] Thus he spoke. "However we had better not have a victory dance. We have the honor nevertheless. We have to be careful about the whites," he said. "In the old time we were at liberty to live in our own way, and

[88] A person always received a new name, which he gave himself, on counting coup for the first time.

[89] I.e., some spirit must have directed you. This would be the religious Winnebago's interpretation of most acts. In this particular case the old man is trying to reassure S.B., who insisted, as we saw a few lines above, that he had received no blessing and was conscious of no authority to lead a war party. To the old man, and he typifies the average Winnebago, two things were of paramount importance: first, that S.B. had succeeded,

when such a deed as yours became known, your sisters would rejoice and dance, it has been said.[90] However, now the law (of the whites) is to be feared. In due time you will get a chance to announce your feat, and then you may wear a head ornament,[91] for you have earned one for yourself," he said.

21. Trip to Nebraska

Soon after this I was to go to Nebraska. I once had a child, a boy, who had died when he was two years old. His mother's father then adopted one in his place. The child was a Menominee. So I went there for I was the (adopted) father of the boy and he was (regarded as) my son, for he had been adopted to fill my dead son's place. At the dance given when a person is adopted to fill a dead person's place, I gave him a horse. The dance was a Sore-Eye Dance.[92] These (people) gave me some

___

and secondly, that S.B. had made an offering of tobacco to the thunder-birds and uttered a prayer asking them for protection. To an old pious Winnebago such as S.B.'s father at this time was, it was clear that the thunder-birds would listen to his son's prayer for, first, the family belonged to the thunder-bird clan, secondly, various members had received blessings from them and, thirdly, the clan war-bundle which they possessed had been bestowed upon an ancestor, not so many generations back, by the thunder-birds. There was, as a matter of fact, a legend current in the family to the effect that this ancestor was the son of a human being and either a thunder-bird or a night-spirit, both of them spirits presiding over the destinies of war. In addition to having his son succeed the thunder-birds had answered by sending rain in response to S.B.'s prayer. S.B. himself probably accepted this as "authority" to proceed.

[90] On the return from a successful war party those who had counted coup were given presents of strings of wampum, and it was customary to give these to one's sisters, who hung them around their necks. The women, especially the sisters wearing their war trophies, also danced around the post where the victory dance was held.

[91] I.e., a feather in your hair. Cf. note 87. These war exploits were always announced at certain dances or at the Four Nights' Wake, but never at the Medicine Dance.

[92] As a rule a special adoption feast was given on such an occasion. Apparently, however, other dances could be substituted.

The Sore-Eye Dance is regarded as one of the oldest of their ceremonies as well as one of the most sacred. Its real name is "the dance of those who have been blessed by the night-spirits," and it is a secret organization. S.B.'s father and brother belonged to it. S.B. does not mention his having joined it and I do not believe he was a member.

beaded bags, two boxes of maple sugar, etc. Just when I was about to start out for Nebraska he came and brought me some things. I was at Wittenberg then. I was living there with a woman. Then I went to Nebraska. The woman let me take many things along with me, so that I might give them to my relatives when I got to Nebraska and get horses in return for them.

When I started I stopped off at Black River Falls. I went to a woman with whom I used to live in order to take her along with me, but she refused. I had gone to her while I was drinking. So I had to go on alone. I had my gun along with me. I arrived in Nebraska in midsummer (celebration time).[93] I arrived very early in the morning and there I met a man whom I had once known. He used to go about with me. There were many people. We sat somewhat away from them and the man and his wife drank with me. Then I told them what I had done and he shook hands with me[94] and said that he (too) had counted coup and that he would wear a head ornament. Then they took me to the place where they lived. They hauled my things for me.

The next morning the Nebraska Winnebago were going to celebrate. They were to come together for a week. They had a large gathering. The people with whom I was staying went out and camped with those at the gathering. Two men arrived there. They recognized me and shook hands with me. They were riding in a buggy and I got in with them. They took me far away. On the road they stopped. We got out of the buggy and took out a jug containing four quarts of (whisky). Then they had me drink with them. After that they brought me back to the gathering and there I met an uncle of mine to whom I presented the gun. He was quite delighted.

It was a large gathering and we danced every day. I got ready

[93] While this celebration has now been merged generally with the Fourth of July festivities, it is really old and was part of a number of festivities that took place at this time, the principal one of which was the feast given by the chief of the tribe to his fellow men. Comparatively little is known of this feast today.

[94] Shaking hands is a custom recently adopted.

also and danced, and there I gave away my things.[95] I received
two ponies and a harness and a top buggy. That much I was
given. After (the celebration) I remained there for a long time.
I even got married there. I kept on drinking all the time. It was
then that a nephew of mine begged me to give him my buggy.[96]
[A nephew has the privilege of asking his uncle for anything
and (the uncle) must give it.[97] In return, the uncle can compel
his nephew to work for him at any time.[98]]

Some time after that I went to visit an uncle of mine.[99] He
said, "Nephew, tomorrow they are going to have a Medicine
Dance. Tonight they are going to have the trial dance. Your
aunt is going to buy provisions for the meal and you may go
along with her." So I went with her. When we got to town we
drank. On the following day it was rumored that the woman
and myself were missing.[100] The buggy we were riding in was
broken up; my hat was gone and my trousers were torn open.
I immediately went back to the place where I had come from,
although the Medicine Dance was taking place. The woman,
it was said, was still missing. Then I returned to the place where
I had been staying and remained there all day. I got very tired.
In the morning I mounted a horse and went to the store. When
I got there I was arrested. They asked me what I was doing
there. "I am not doing anything; I'm merely visiting," I said.

---

[95] I presume he is referring to the *Herucka* dance (the Omaha Grass
Dance) where it was customary to give things away. These dances were
always attended by visitors from other tribes.

[96] Not a nephew in our sense, but one who called S.B. *hide' k'* and
since this relationship is hereditary there were doubtless quite a number
of people to whom he bore this relation.

[97] It might be added that while this right existed theoretically, no properly brought-up nephew would make any impudent demand of his uncle
or vice versa.

[98] This was apparently added for my benefit. As a rule S.B. explained
nothing of his own accord.

[99] Cf. note 96.

[100] The woman was the wife of his uncle *hide 'k'* (his mother's brother)
and may very well have been a young woman. As his *hide 'k'*s wife, any
transgression of this kind would be regarded even now with marked
disfavor, and was probably unthinkable in former times. Any transgression
with his real aunt (from our viewpoint) would be unthinkable even now,
in spite of the complete breakdown of all their moral standards.

Then the one in charge of the law said that I was to pay ten dollars and that if I did not do so he would send me away. So there I sold the horse I had ridden on. It was a good horse and I got twenty-five dollars for it, out of which I paid the ten dollars. Then the lawyer said, "You have committed many crimes and you had better go to the place from which you came. If you stay here any longer we will have to lock you up."

I left that same day. Two old men were going to Wisconsin and I went with them. They did not know how to speak English, so they took me as an interpreter. I left one of my horses there in pasture. These men were very fond of whisky and I bought whisky for them all along our route. After some time we arrived in Wisconsin at the season of cranberry-picking. I was just about drunk when we got there. When we got near our home I said to the men that they should come and visit. This I said and then gave a whoop.

22. *I Have a Quarrel with a Woman*

My father and mother and a woman with whom I was living when I left, met me. They were very glad (to see me). There were many people camping when I got home. The woman fixed a bed for me, gave me some food to eat and told me to lie down. But I, instead, went out and made inquiries about a woman with whom I used to live (and found out that) she was still there. To her (lodge) I went and slept. In the morning the other woman was angry; nevertheless the next night I slept there again. Late that night someone woke me up. "Come out," the voice said. I went out with a blanket around me and there was the other woman (my wife). She it was who had called me. She said, "In the morning the annuity payment is to be made at Necedah. I am going there tonight. I want you to go with me." "I haven't any money," I said to her. "As though you ever had any money of your own, when you did anything!" But I refused to go. She persisted and finally I went back and lay down. After a while she came there and she hit me very hard and she called me names. She kicked me and she pulled my hair. Indeed she did all sorts of things to me. "If I had something with which to kill you, I would kill you," she said. Then I got angry and she stopped bothering me and went away.[101]

23. I Get Delirium Tremens and See Strange Things

During the cranberry-picking season I drank all the time and after that again "chased payments." I continued drinking. Finally all the payments had been made and I went to Black River Falls. I was entirely without money. I was supposed to go back to Wittenberg but I did not have the fare. I went back to the Indians and stayed all night. In the morning I was sick. I was shaking (from head to foot). When I tried to drink coffee, I would spill it. When I lay down I would see big snakes. I would cry out and get up and then when I was about to go to sleep again, I would think that someone had called me. Then I would raise my cover and look around, but there would be nothing. When the wind blew hard (I seemed) to hear singing. These (imaginary people) would spit very loudly. I heard them and I could not sleep. Just as soon as I closed my eyes, I would begin to see things. I saw things that were happening in a distant country.[102]

I saw ghosts on horseback drunk. Five or six of them were on one horse and they were singing. I recognized them, for they were people who had died long ago. I heard the words of their song, as they sang:

"I, even I, must die sometime, so of what value is anything, I think."[103]

Thus they would sing and it made a good song. I myself

---

[101] A man cannot of course strike a woman.

[102] This was usually regarded as a gift greatly to be prized.

[103] Songs are frequently composed in this way. Occasionally a man composes a song quite unconsciously. My interpreter related to me that once while riding from Laredo, Texas, to Kansas City he got drowsy and kept time to the noise of the wheels by humming what he thought was a well-known Winnebago peyote song. On his return to Winnebago he kept on humming and singing it and was asked by his friends where he had picked up that new song. Only then did he realize that he had unconsciously composed a new song. Of course these songs all conform to a certain type; S.B.'s doubtless conforming to the accepted drinking song and my interpreter's to the peyote song.

learned it and later on it became a drinking song and many people learned it. I liked it very much.

The next morning I rode on a train and (after a while) we came to a town. Two days after this I stopped drinking and kept it up through the whole winter, for I was unable to drink. I would vomit every time I drank beer. So all winter I did not drink, and it was not until the following summer that I began again.

24. I Am Arrested and I Confess

Two years elapsed. Then, after some time, it was reported that the men who were responsible for the disappearance of the man of another tribe (the Pottawattomie) had been discovered. So I learned, it was said. One of those involved had been to Nebraska and had announced it in recounting acts of bravery at a Brave Dance. So it was rumored. He had also announced it at a death wake.[104] It was thus that the facts had been learned.

Then after a while, in winter, while I was living in the forest chopping wood, two men came there one night. They were officers. They mentioned a man's name to me and asked me if I knew him. "Yes," I said. "Well, let us go to town and there we want to ask you something," they said. Then they told me to get ready. I got ready and then they had me ride in a wagon they had. Then the men asked, "Did Peter kill this man? Do you know?" "I do not know," I said to them. Then he told me from what source he had learned it, and asked me, "Did you ever hear anything about it?" "No," I answered. "Did you know that this man was missing?" he asked. "I did hear that a man had been missing but as I did not know him, I did not give the matter much thought," I said to him. Then he said, "It has been discovered that Peter did it. Do you think they are right about it?" "I don't believe a word of it," I said.

---

[104] Well-known warriors were always invited to a death wake so that they might recount their war exploits and place at the disposal of the soul whose death is being commemorated, the soul of the people he has killed, in order that they may take care of him and help him safely to his journey's end in spirit-land.

Then he said, "If you continue to say that you do not know anything about this case, I will not let you go home. You shall go wherever Peter goes. We have found out that you were with him and that is why we are doing this. If you do not tell us you will never get out of prison. That is the penalty (for what you have done). If you tell us, you can get away and you will be a witness and can then go home." "I want to get home, and whatever I can do to get home, I will do. But I don't know anything about this matter. You can speak about what you know. (That) I also can do. I do not want to be locked up," I said.

Then we arrived in town. Then he took me into a hotel, and asked me if I knew the murdered man's brother. "Yes," I said to him. Then we went inside and there we found him. The man greeted me and said, "If you know about this affair and confess, we will not lock you up. You will be one of the witnesses. Even if it turns out that you were with him, we will not lock you up (under those conditions). I am not deceiving you. This one here listening to us, is of the same opinion as myself." Then he said, "Sam, I am acquainted with your father. He is a fine old man. Even if you were along with this man (Peter) I will not have you locked up, if you confess. It is merely because Peter is a bad man that I want to know of it." "He must be telling the truth," said I to myself. "I'm going to tell." I thought that they might not take me back with them, in that case. Then I said, "I know of it. I saw him when he killed him." "Good," said they. "How did he do it?" I told it in detail. "Good!" they said. They thanked me. Then the officer took me outside; he took me to jail and he put me in, and saying, "The train will soon be ready," he went out.

(In the jail) I found the man (Peter). "What did they say to you?" he asked. "They did not say anything to me," I said. "They asked me very many questions (Peter said). They asked me if you had done it and they said that if I told them, they would let me go home. I told them however that I did not know anything." Thus I spoke. "They asked me the same things, and I also told them that I did not know anything," I said. "That is good, for without witnesses, they have only hearsay evidence, and they cannot hold us," said he. "Anyhow, the man we killed was crazy and his brothers hated him. They used to ask me to kill him. That's what they once asked me," he said.[105]

Just then the officer came and said, "Boys, the train is due soon. Get ready." When we were ready he took out some handcuffs and tied us together and we went to the station. The white people looked at us in surprise and called out our names and asked what the trouble was. Then the train arrived and we boarded it. We rode all that night and arrived in the morning. Then the officer locked us up in prison. We did not know what to say. After a time I was taken out and brought to the court house. There they again questioned me. A woman was there; a shorthand writer. Then he told me to tell again in detail (what I had told him), and that as soon as the time for the trial arrived he would let me return home. I therefore again told them where we had done the deed and the place; all this I told them in detail. Then when I was through he locked me up again. Then they took the other man to the court. When he returned he had (of course) learned what I had done. He was very quiet. Then I said, "Well, you said you were asked to kill him and you also said that you asked others to kill him. If that is so, you did it because you were asked to do so and you are not to blame.[106] If there are witnesses (to this fact), we will get out," I said. And then again I said this because they had

---

[105] No better proof of S.B.'s honesty in this autobiography could be demanded than this very damaging evidence he gives against himself. His attempt to justify his deed by claiming that the murdered man's brothers hated him and had actually asked him (Peter) to kill him, seems amusing to us. Personally, I feel that something more is involved here than a clumsy attempt at self-justification. To the Winnebago, words have a more definite meaning than to us and if the murdered man's brothers did actually express their hatred openly and ask someone to kill him, if, indeed, only such a wish on their part was known among the people, S.B. is merely giving expression to the normal Winnebago viewpoint, in claiming here and in another passage further on that these brothers shared in the guilt of slaying this man.

[106] He clearly intimates that since he (Peter) was asked to kill this man by the man's own brothers he is free from guilt. The only question, therefore, is to prove it. I do not think that S.B. is merely insisting upon witnesses because such is the white man's procedure. We are dealing here with a war exploit and that was practically the only case where the Winnebago often refused to believe one another unless they took an oath. It is possible that the testimony of witnesses was also accepted.

locked us up alone. I did not like it. The boys were so boisterous; the others ought to be in jail too. That is what I was thinking of when I said it. (Soon) they will bring the boys back and when there are a number of us here, it will not be so lonesome.[107] He was glad of it. After a while the others were brought. There were now four of us. We would make a good deal of noise talking.

25. *The Character of the Murdered Pottawattomie*

About that time it was reported that the man to whom we had done this had been rather crazy. There were three brothers and the one we did this to (killed) was the oldest. Their father had been a chief and they had possessed much land. The others had contributed much money to buy the land. A number of them lived there and they had put in many crops. Then the father of these three men died, and he (the oldest) drove the other people away. When their parent died, he (the oldest) drove these people and his brothers away, it is said. They had many horses and he forcibly kept all these things, it was said. When he heard that any of his brothers were using the horses, he scolded them. When they argued with him, he threatened to shoot them. It was said that he always went around with his gun. For all these reasons his brothers disliked him, it is said, and used to ask Winnebago to kill him. It was also said that all his white neighbors disliked him. He had over a hundred horses and they grew wild in the woods. He did nothing all the time but watch them.[108] He was not able to get near any of them;[109] the only use he ever made of them was to own them.

---

[107] That he dreaded lonesomeness is probably true. The true reason he has given us above, and this was only an excuse invented on the spur of the moment. The statement that Peter was pleased at the idea of having company is unquestionably true.

[108] It is regarded as a sign of stinginess to watch one's possessions all the time.

[109] To be stingy and not even make use of one's possessions personally was regarded as both stupid and inimical to the common good. Horses that were not being used belonged to anyone who cared to use them. A man did not lose the ownership of an object by not using it, but the person who was using it obtained a kind of squatter's right to it. At least such was

Whenever the horses entered a field, they would destroy it completely and if anything was ever said to him he immediately wanted to fight those (who complained). Whenever a person tried to buy one from him, he used to ask an extravagant price,[110] and if one of these (horses) was occasionally taken and he was asked to pay damages, he would threaten to shoot these people. He would go around barefooted with his gun, it was said. For all these reasons his brothers disliked him, and asked the Winnebago to shoot him. They told in what way it was possible to kill him,[111] and then asked someone to kill him, it was said. It was said that he belonged to that class of men whom it was impossible to kill. When he fasted he went without food for a whole winter, until spring, it was said.[112] To kill him one would have to have a wooden knife, paint it red and then stab him with it. Only thus could he be killed, it was said. With all this (evidence) the boys thought we would surely be acquitted.[113]

---

the average Winnebago's view, not always admitted, however, by the owner. The same point came out in connection with the war-bundle of the thunder-bird clan which was the personal property of S.B.'s brother, who had inherited it from his father. When he became a member of the peyote religion he wished to sell it to me, but the people who were at the time using it claimed that he had no right to it any longer because he was not making any use of it and they were. He insisted on his proprietary rights but failed to get the war-bundle because popular opinion, at least, was on the side of those who were using it. My impression was, however, that no one believed that he had permanently lost his proprietary rights in the bundle and that had he returned to the old tribal practices it would have been immediately returned to him without grumbling.

[110] Not only unjustifiable but unfair and unethical.

[111] As indicated further on it was believed that he could only be killed in a certain way. The Pottawattomie were regarded by the Winnebago as possessing uncommon shamanistic powers.

[112] The most powerful blessings were obtained by those who had the strength to fast for so long a period.

[113] I.e., by showing first that he was a wicked man, a nuisance to the community, and that even his own brothers had desired his death. It must also be remembered that S.B. brought Winnebago notions of punishment into this whole question and that while he could see how the whites might regard the killing of a hereditary enemy as murder, yet he probably expected them to demand the same amends that his own tribesman would have demanded namely a payment of some kind to the relatives of the murdered man.

26. Our Prison-Life and the Trial

We were waiting for the spring term of the court. We stayed there all winter. I was very tired of it but I kept that secret, because we used to tease one another.[114] Sometimes I would feel like crying, but I would act as though I did not care at all. I was married at that time and I longed to see my wife and was terrible wrought up, but I told the others that I did not care in the least. The others were also married and some of them showed their lonesomeness markedly. Sometimes one of the women would visit us and the others always said that I was the only one who did not seem to care. (As a matter of fact), I could hardly stand it, but I kept my condition quite secret. I only felt better when I wrote a letter to my wife, and when she wrote to me I felt very happy.

We used to read one another's letters. Whenever our wives wrote to us we would tease one another about the things that were said in these letters.

After a while the spring term of the court arrived and we were happy. However, when the time for the trial came, we were bound over to the fall term. So we stayed there all summer. Then the fall term came and we were bound over until the next spring term. It was enough to cause one to say, O my! (in impatience). During the winter we made bead work. We used to compete to see who could do the best work. We used to make beaded finger rings and they were always purchased

---

[114] There are two reasons why a Winnebago tries not to exhibit his emotions: first, because it is a sign of effeminacy, and secondly, because he thereby lays himself open to ridicule, playful or otherwise, which he dreads. The charge of effeminacy is only associated with the exhibition of suffering in connection with wounds received on the warpath, while being tortured, etc. In the instance cited by S.B. it is not the charge of effeminacy he fears but the possibility of being ridiculed. This apparently wounds a Winnebago's *amour propre* more than anything else and he is apt to remember it for long periods of time. I remember once seeing a chair break under the weight of a Winnebago, the laughter which followed, and the sheepish and angry face of the unfortunate man. Three years after that I happened to meet the same Indian again. He did not at first recognize me but remembered me as soon as I recalled the incident to him. He told me then with glee how he had only recently been revenged on one of those who laughed so heartily at his mishap by playing some practical joke on him.

from us. After a while we had a good deal of money, for we would sell many rings. After a while we made some suspenders. I made thirty of them and we used to sell these for seven dollars a pair. We thus always had plenty of money and we always drank. Some of the people locked up in prison with us, whose terms were almost over, would be allowed to go outside and these would buy us whisky. We also used to gamble with one another. We would play for money.

One day my wife came to visit me. I talked with her through the iron grating. They allowed me to talk to her for a long time. All I could do was to desire her. I wanted her badly. When the wives of the others came they felt just as I did.

Once we had a fight. We had been drinking and were disputing about a game. Afterward we were quite humble about it.

Some time after this, we found out that my wife had married again. I did not feel like eating, but I tried hard to do so, because I thought that the others would notice it.[115] Then I said, "I am glad to hear that it is reported that my wife has married again. When I get out of prison, I will pay the one who has (married her), for he is going to take care of her until I get out. I had been quite uneasy about her for some time, and now I feel quite relieved, for she is going to be taken care of." Thus I said. But the truth of it was that I was about as angry as I could be. I made up my mind that I would take her away from whomsoever she might be living with. Then I thought I would make her feel as sad as I could. I thought that I would disfigure her[116] and leave her; or take her away in the wilderness, whip her soundly, and then leave her there. I could not think of anything else and I did not even know how the food tasted. I often felt like crying. At night I would not be able to sleep, for I could not forget it. I would try to dream of her when I went to sleep at night. Sometimes I would dream of seeing her and then in the morning I would tell the others about

---

[115] Cf. note 114. Realizing that he would not be able to hide his condition, he prefers to tell his companions in a grandiloquent way that a load has been taken off his mind, in order thus to escape the bantering that was bound to take place.

[116] I.e., punish her as an adulteress used to be punished by the Winnebago by cutting off her nose.

it and I would feel better. I never thought of any of my relatives who were really the ones who felt deeply for me.[117] I was not even that (grateful). I only thought of the woman.

The time for the next court term had arrived, and we were taken over to the court. It was the spring term. We were given a trial. When we were taken to the court, they would always handcuff two of us together. We each had a lawyer. At our first hearing, one of us was freed, and three remained in prison. Then the lawyers pleaded our case and two more of us were freed. The one who had actually done the killing was the only one who remained in prison.[118]

27. My Release from Prison

When we got out, we found our relatives waiting for us. My elder brother was there and I went home with him. We began to drink immediately. I was very happy,[119] although when I was in prison I had felt that I would never drink again.

That same day we reached the Winnebago. There I saw a woman whom I married that very night. I had been desiring women for a long time. Then I began to drink again. Then I went on to Black River Falls and when I got there I saw my former wife and I took her back again.

The Indians were celebrating their midsummer ceremony. I went there and took part and I drank all the time. I considered myself a brave man and a medicine man and I also thought myself a holy man, a strong man, and a favorite with women.[120] I regarded myself as being in possession of many courting

[117] Whatever remorse he ever expresses is for his relatives, as is to be expected considering the intensity of the family tie.

[118] This must probably have appeared to S.B. and the Winnebago in general as an amusing indication of the white man's incurable ignorance, for the man who actually kills the enemy is regarded as only second in importance to the four who count coup. That these three should have been acquitted and the other person imprisoned was the height of the ridiculous.

[119] No attempt is ever made to hide the expression of joy except when strangers are around.

[120] The ideal of every Winnebago man.

medicines. I am a great man, I thought, and also a fleet runner. I was a good singer of Brave Dance songs.[121] I was a sport and I wanted whisky every day.

My mother and father had gone to Missouri River (Winnebago reservation in Nebraska) and left me in charge of the two horses they possessed, as well as a vehicle which I was using at the time. Later on, in the fall, when the cranberry season started, I lived with three women. I never did any work, but simply went from one of these women to the other. After a while an annuity payment was made. I went around "chasing the payments" and I sold the horses at that time and spent the money.

28. *My First Acquaintance with the Peyote*

Then my father and mother asked me to come to the Missouri River (Nebraska) but I had been told that my father and mother had eaten peyote[122] and I did not like it. I had been told that these peyote eaters were doing wrong, and therefore I disliked them;[123] I had heard that they were doing everything that was wicked. For these reasons we did not like them. About this time they sent me money for my ticket and since my brothers and sisters told me to go, I went. Just as I was about to start, my youngest sister, the one to whom we always listened most attentively, said to me, "Older brother, do not you indulge in this medicine eating (peyote) of which so much is said." I promised. Then I started out.

As soon as I arrived (in Nebraska) I met some people who

---

[121] Songs sung at the *Herucka* dance.

[122] His conservative relatives were quick to recognize what danger he would run of being converted if he stayed with his parents. Events subsequently proved how correct was their fear.

[123] The feeling against the peyote eaters was very intense, not because they had introduced a new cult or because there were Christian elements in this cult, but because the peyote followers insisted that all the other ceremonies were wrong and must be abandoned and because they destroyed war-bundles, medicine bags, etc., everything dear to the hearts of the conservative Winnebago. S.B. here shows clearly that in spite of the many strictures he makes concerning his religious feeling, he was apparently just as religious as the average Winnebago.

had not joined the peyote eaters[124] and who said to me, "Your relatives are eating the peyote and they sent for you that you also might eat it. Your mother, your father, and your younger sister, they are all eating it." Thus they spoke to me. Then they told me of some of the bad things it was reported that these people had done. I felt ashamed and I wished I had not come in the first place. Then I said that I was going to eat the medicine.[125]

After that I saw my father, mother, and sister. They were glad. Then we all went to where they were staying. My father and I walked (alone). Then he told me about the peyote eating. "It does not amount to anything, all this that they are doing, although they do stop drinking.[126] It is also said that sick people get well. We were told about this and so we joined, and, sure enough, we are practically well, your mother as well as I. It is said that they offer prayers to Earthmaker (God)," he said. He kept on talking. "They are rather foolish. They cry when they feel very happy about anything. They throw away all of the medicines that they possess and know. They give up all the blessings they received while fasting and they give up all the

[124] The drift toward the peyote cult about his time, 1907, was very great in Nebraska and the conservatives were frightened at the inroads the new faith was making even among the members of their most conservative and popular ceremony, the Medicine Dance. Every newcomer was immediately warned against the degrading effects of eating the peyote. The peyote people, on the contrary, carried on no open campaign but resorted to the far more insidious and effective method of winning new people to their cult by treating them with kindness and consideration.

[125] It was clearly foolish of the conservatives and strangers to insist upon the evil effects of peyote while at the same time informing S.B. that his parents and his younger sister belonged to the sect, for family pride was bound to assert itself. Thus I understand S.B.'s sudden declaration that he was going to eat the peyote. It was tantamount to telling them to mind their own business. He had then, of course, no intention of doing anything of the kind.

[126] So completely did all those who joined the peyote cult give up drinking that many Indians and whites were at first inclined to believe that this was a direct effect of the peyote. However, this is an error. The correct explanation is that John Rave, the leader of the cult, gave up drinking when he became a convert and included this renunciation of all liquors in the cult which he so largely molded and dominated. If any additional proof were needed it can be found in the fact that as Rave's personal influence decreased and as the membership increased the number of people who drank liquor and ate peyote at the same time increased.

spirits that blessed them in their fasts. They also stop smoking and chewing tobacco. They stop giving feasts, and they stop making offerings of tobacco. Indeed they burn up their holy things. They burn up their war-bundles. They are bad people. They give up the Medicine Dance. They burn up their medicine bags and even cut up their otter-skin bags. They say they are praying to Earthmaker (God) and they do so standing and crying. They claim that they hold nothing holy except Earthmaker (God). They claim that all the things that they are stopping are those of the bad spirit (the devil), and that the bad spirit (the devil) has deceived them; that there are no spirits who can bless; that there is no other spirit except Earthmaker (God)." Then I said, "Say, they certainly speak foolishly."[127] I felt very angry toward them. "You will hear them for they are going to have a meeting tonight. Their songs are very strange. They use a very small drum," said he. Then I felt a very strong desire to see them.[128]

After a while we arrived. At night they had their ceremony. At first I sat outside and listened to them. I was rather fond of them. I stayed in that country and the young peyote eaters were exceedingly friendly to me. They would give me a little money now and then and they treated me with tender regard. They did everything that they thought would make me feel good, and in consequence I used to speak as though I liked their ceremony. However I was only deceiving them. I only said it, because they were so good to me. I thought they acted in this way because (the peyote) was deceiving them.

Soon after that my parents returned to Wisconsin, but when

[127] This rather remarkable speech of S.B.'s father is of course designed to get his son interested, and in this he succeeds admirably. His frequent declarations that the peyote cult was of no consequence is to be interpreted in two ways: first, in order not to antagonize too much his son, who is after all, still a conservative, and secondly as a survival of what might be called "ritualistic" modesty. In all speeches delivered at ceremonies it was customary to depreciate oneself and one's powers. It is this last tendency which I am inclined to see here, although in his case derogatory remarks are also made about the ceremony itself and other participants in the ceremony, an element entirely absent from the speeches found in the older rituals.

[128] The speech has had the desired effect and the last touch, appealing to every Winnebago's desire for novelty, has been particularly effective.

they left they said they would come back in a little while. So I was left there with my relatives, who were all peyote followers. For that reason they left me there. Whenever I went among the non-peyote people I used to say all sorts of things about the peyote people and when I returned to the peyote people, I used to say all sorts of things about the others.

I had a friend who was a peyote man and he said to me, "My friend, I wish very much that you should eat the peyote." Thus he spoke and I answered him, "My friend, I will do it, but not until I get accustomed to the people of this country.[129] Then I will do it. The only thing that worries me is the fact that they are making fun of you. And in addition, I am not quite used to them." I spoke dishonestly.

I was staying at the place where my sister lived. She had gone to Oklahoma; she was a peyote follower. After a while she returned. I was then living with a number of women. This was the second time (there) and from them I obtained some money. Once I got drunk there and was locked up for six days. After my sister returned she and the others paid more attention than ever to me. Especially was this true of my brother-in-law. They gave me horses and a vehicle. They really treated me very tenderly. I knew that they did all this because they wished me to eat the peyote.[130] I, in my turn, was very kind to them. I thought that I was fooling them and they thought that they were converting me.[131] I told them that I believed in the peyote because they were treating me so nicely.

After a while we moved to a certain place where they were to have a large peyote meeting. I knew they were doing this in

---

[129] There are a number of differences between the Wisconsin and the Nebraska divisions of the tribe, but nothing to justify this statement. While this is merely an excuse, his other declaration as to his being worried about the ridicule to which the peyote people were being subjected is quite truthful, although he claims this too to be merely an excuse.

[130] Their motives were mixed. They seem to have had all the characteristics of the early Christian proselytizers.

[131] He is probably wrong, both in his interpretation of his own motives and of theirs. No Winnebago accepts favors and acts of kindness from others without feeling a sense of obligation. In a way, he is giving us here the interpretation of the conservatives.

order to get me to join.[132] Then I said to my younger sister, "I would be quite willing to eat this peyote (ordinarily), but I don't like the woman with whom I am living just now and I think I will leave her. That is why I do not want to join now, for I understand that when married people eat medicine (peyote) they will always have to stay together. Therefore I will join when I am married to some woman permanently." Then my brother-in-law came and she told him what I had said, and he said to me, "You are right in what you say. The woman with whom you are staying is a married woman and you cannot continue living with her. It is null and void (this marriage) and we know it.[133] You had better join now. It will be the same as if you were single.[134] We will pray for you as though you were single. After you have joined this ceremony, then you can marry any woman whom you have a right to marry (legally). So, do join tonight. It is best. For some time we have been desirous of your joining but we have not said anything to you.[135] It is Earthmaker's (God's) blessing to you that you have been thinking of this,"[136] said he.

---

[132] He is quite right. It is exceedingly interesting to note how insidious the methods of his peyote relatives have been. Not a word have they said to him about the ceremony, with the exception of his father's rather negative speech. But they, his relatives, have piled kindness upon kindness and this too after his release from prison, and after an absence of many months. They have so thoroughly enmeshed him in obligations that they feel they can take the risk of bringing him to a performance of the ceremony, while he, overwhelmed by the sense of obligation, is now concerned merely with putting them off as long as he can, with any pretext he can find.

[133] His rather clever excuse is immediately parried by his brother-in-law with the Christian conception of marriage.

[134] Apparently he considers the opportunity too favorable to let pass. S.B. must join immediately.

[135] Now that S.B. has taken the initiative there is no longer any danger in informing him that they desired him to join the cult.

[136] It is difficult to determine whether this is merely a Christian interpretation or an old Winnebago concept. S.B.'s father very definitely expresses the same viewpoint in connection with S.B.'s war exploit when he says that S.B. could not have thought it (his undertaking against the Pottawattomie) at his own suggestion, but that the spirits had suggested it. Cf. note 89.

29. I Eat Peyote

Therefore I sat inside the meeting-place with them. One man acted as leader. We were to do whatever he ordered. The regalia were placed before him.[137] I wanted to sit in some place on the side, because I thought I might get to crying like the others. I felt ashamed of myself.[138]

Then the leader arose and talked. He said that this was an affair of Earthmaker's (God's), and that he (the leader) could do nothing on his own initiative; that Earthmaker (God) was going to conduct the ceremony. Then he said that the medicine (peyote) was holy and that he would turn us all over to it;[139] that he had turned himself over to it and wished now to turn all of us over to it. He said further, "I am a very pitiable (figure) in this ceremony,[140] so when you pray to Earthmaker, pray also for me. Now let us all rise and pray to Earthmaker (God)." We all rose. Then he prayed. He prayed for the sick, and he prayed for those who did not yet know Earthmaker.[141] He said that they were to be pitied. When he had finished we sat down. Then the peyote was passed around. They gave me five. My brother-in-law said to me, "If you speak to this medicine (peyote), it

[137] Consisting of two peyote, one considered female, one male; a drum, an eagle-wing fan, and a small gourd rattle. These regalia and the custom of placing them in front of the leader, who then passes them on, are ideas taken over directly from the older ceremonies.

[138] After midnight when the effect of the peyote is beginning to manifest itself, it is customary for certain members, any who desire, to go up to the leader and there make a confession of their sins, during which time they cry profusely. This is what he is referring to. Strong remorse, even among the older people, was frequently accompanied by crying.

[139] A phrase borrowed from Christianity, which has become a ritualistic formula, meaning that they were going to enter into communion with Earthmaker through the mediation of the peyote.

[140] Here again the new and the old religious ideas mingle. The phrase itself is a verbatim introduction to the regular speeches delivered at any ceremony, yet, at the same time, he unquestionably wishes to imply that God alone presides over their meeting and the suppliants should offer their prayers directly to him. This is a Christian and an imported notion.

[141] This is of distinctly Christian origin.

will give you whatever you ask of it.[142] Then you must pray to Earthmaker, and then you must eat the medicine." However I ate them (the peyote) immediately for I did not know what to ask for and I did not know what to say in a prayer to Earthmaker (God). So I ate the peyote just as they were.[143] They were very bitter and had a taste difficult to describe. I wondered what would happen to me. After a while I was given five more and I also ate them. They tasted rather bitter. Now I was very quiet. The peyote rather weakened me. Then I listened very attentively to the singing. I liked it very much.[144] I felt as though I were partly asleep. I felt different from (my normal self), but when I (looked around) and examined myself, I saw nothing wrong about myself. However I felt different from (my normal self). Before this I used to dislike the songs. Now I liked the leader's singing very much. I liked to listen to him.

They were all sitting very quietly. They were doing nothing except singing. Each man sang four songs and then passed the regalia to the next one. (Each one) held a stick and an eagle's tail feather in one hand and a small gourd rattle, which they used to shake while singing, in the other. One of (those) present used to do the drumming. Thus objects would pass around until they came back to the leader, who would then sing four songs. When these were finished, he would place the various (things) on the ground,[145] rise, and pray to Earthmaker (God). Then he called upon one or two to speak. They said that Earthmaker (God) was good and that the peyote was good, and that who-

---

[142] This is, of course, good Winnebago doctrine. The peyote was in other words to be treated as a medicinal herb. One of the essential elements of the older culture, namely, the offering of tobacco, is, however, absent.

It might be added that this conception of the peyote and its powers, although it was that of the leader and the older members of the cult, was not shared by the younger adherents who had come into more intimate contact with Christianity and some of whom could read the Bible. At least this was the case in 1908–1909. Since then, however, I understand that the older, original, conception has been adopted by the majority.

[143] The peyote are either eaten in their dried condition or taken in a liquid concoction.

[144] Here again we have S.B. in an expectant mood. He is waiting, as in his former fasts, for some inward change.

[145] This is exactly the procedure in the old pagan ceremonies.

soever ate this medicine (peyote) would be able to free himself from the bad spirit (the devil); for they said that Earthmaker forbids us to commit sins. When this was over they sang again.

After midnight, every once in a while, (I heard) someone cry. In some cases they would go up to the leader and talk with him. He would stand up and pray with them. They told me what they were saying. They said that they were asking (people) to pray for them, as they were sorry for their sins and that they might be prevented from committing them again. That is what they were saying. They cried very loudly. I was rather frightened. (I noticed also that when I closed my eyes and sat still, I began to see strange things.) I did not get sleepy in the least. Thus the light (of morning) came upon me. In the morning, as the sun rose, they stopped.[146] They all got up and prayed to Earthmaker (God) and then they stopped.

During the daytime, I did not get sleepy in the least. My actions were a little different (from my usual ones). Then they said, "Tonight they are going to have another meeting. Let us go over. They say that is the best (thing) to do and thus you can learn it (the ceremony) right away. It is said that their spirits wander over all the earth and the heavens also. All this you will learn and see," they said.[147] "At times they die[148] and remain dead all night and all day. When in this condition they some-

---

[146] Exactly as they stop at this time in the pagan ceremonies.

[147] The notion itself is typical of the Winnebago. Such powers, however, were obtained in former times not by membership in a ceremony but through blessings from spirits. The phraseology is markedly reminiscent of the desciptions of the old Winnebago spirits. It is interesting to note that while in former times this power was desired for some purpose, here all that an individual is to receive is the power itself.

[148] I.e., become unconscious and have visions. The notion itself is old. That is what was expected during fasting except that the semidelirious condition of the faster was never spoken of as dying. This notion probably arose from the observation of a number of cases of complete prostration due to an overdose of peyote; and of cataleptic fits. I think it may even have been due to the cataleptic fits of one of the leaders, A.H., which were well known and frequently commented upon. He himself was in the habit of describing at great length what he saw during these seizures. However, the starting point may also have been the death and resurrection enacted in the Medicine Dance or the holy condition which certain fasters and certain exceptional participants in ceremonies brought upon themselves.

The visions in these cases were always superinduced by the peyote.

times see Earthmaker (God),[149] it is said." One would also be able to see where the bad spirit lived, it was said.

So we went there again. I doubted all this. I thought that what they were saying was untrue.[150] However I went along anyhow. When we got there I had already eaten some peyote, for I had taken three during the day. Now near the peyote meeting an (Indian) feast was being given and I went there instead. When I reached the place, I saw a long lodge. The noise was terrific. They were beating an enormous drum. The sound almost raised me in the air, so (pleasurably) loud did it sound to me.[151] Not so (pleasurable) had things appeared at those affairs (peyote meetings) that I had lately been attending. There I danced all night and I flirted with the women. About day I left and when I got back the peyote meeting was still going on. When I got back they told me to sit down at a certain place. They treated me very kindly. There I again ate peyote. I heard that they were going to have another meeting nearby on the evening of the same day. We continued eating peyote the whole day at the place where we were staying.[152] We were staying at the house of one of my relatives. Some of the boys there taught me a few songs. "Say, when you learn how to sing, you will be the best

[149] The leader mentioned in note 148 claimed to have seen and spoken to God. However, this was an old Winnebago notion. A number of people had tried in their fasting to see Earthmaker, with whom God is now equated. There is, as a matter of fact, a story about one of S.B.'s ancestors who partially succeeded in seeing Earthmaker. This I have published in "The Autobiography of a Winnebago Indian," *Journal of American Folklore*, 26, no. 112 (1913). A.H.'s vision of God was generally known and all new converts tried to emulate him. Visits to Earthmaker and the evil spirit (Herecgu'nina) are frequently mentioned in the old myths.

[150] True to his refusal to believe anything of a religious nature unless he should experience some inward change, he still considers everything that he has so far seen and heard, untrue.

[151] He here voices his delight at getting away from the rather ethical and puritanical atmosphere of the peyote people and again participating in the rites dear to him. The phraseology he uses is the customary one to express the superlative degree of happiness. It is always used to describe the dances indulged in by the ghosts of the departed in spirit-land, who are the happiest of people. This reads almost like a verbatim quotation from the description of the life spirits lead as pictured in the very popular "Origin Myth of the Four Nights' Wake."

[152] It was quite customary to eat peyote during the day in the early days of the peyote cult.

singer, for you are a good singer as it is. You have a good voice," they said to me. I thought so myself.

30. The Effects of the Peyote

That night we went to the place where the peyote meeting was to take place. They gave me a place to sit and treated me very kindly. "Well, he has come," they even said when I got there, "make a place for him." I thought they regarded me as a great man. John Rave,[153] the leader, was to conduct the (ceremony). I ate five peyote. Then my brother-in-law and my sister came and gave themselves up.[154] They asked me to stand there with them. I did not like it, but I did it nevertheless. "Why should I give myself up? I am not in earnest, and I intend to stop this as soon as I get back to Wisconsin. I am only doing this because they have given me presents," I thought. "I might just as well get up, since it doesn't mean anything to me." So I stood up. The leader began to talk and I (suddenly) began to feel sick. It got worse and worse and finally I lost consciousness entirely.[155] When I recovered I was lying flat on my back. Those with whom I had been standing, were still standing there. I had (as a matter of fact) regained consciousness as soon as I fell down. I felt like leaving the place that night, but I did not do it.[156] I was quite tired out. "Why have I done this?" I said to myself. "I promised (my sister) that I would not do it." So I thought and then I tried to leave, but I could not. I suffered

---

[153] A very remarkable man, the leader and directing power of the peyote religion. He became a convert to it in Oklahoma and introduced his version of the cult among the Winnebago. A powerful personality and a wonderful organizer, he molded the cult he had borrowed into something quite new. He possessed the proselytizing zeal to an unusual degree. Through his activity the Winnebago form of the peyote cult has been spread among the Fox, Menominee, Ojibwa, and Dakota.

[154] The actual rite of giving one's self up consisted in standing before the leader, who preached to them and together with them offered up prayers. It was generally a very dramatic moment.

[155] Apparently the effect of the large number of peyote he had eaten.

[156] One of the most marked effects of eating peyote is a feeling of extreme weariness.

intensely.[157] At last daylight came upon me. Now I thought that they regarded me as one who had had a trance and found out something.[158]

Then we went home and they showed me a passage in the Bible where it said that it was a shame for any man to wear long hair.[159] That is what it said, they told me. I looked at the passage. I was not a man learned in books, but I wanted to give the impression that I knew how to read, so I told them to cut my hair, for I wore it long at that time. After my hair was cut I took out a lot of medicine that I happened to have in my pockets. These were courting medicines. There were many small bundles of them. All these, together with my hair, I gave to my brother-in-law. Then I cried and my brother-in-law also cried. Then he thanked me. He told me that I understood and that I had done well.[160] He told me that Earthmaker (God) alone was holy; that all the things (blessings and medicines) that I possessed, were false; that I had been fooled by the bad spirit (devil). He told me that I had now freed myself from much of this (bad influence). My relatives expressed their thanks fervently.

[157] Peyote is supposed to have a very disagreeable effect upon some individuals. This feeling, however, passes away after a while. One of the commonest effects is a feeling of strangulation and general impotence. This suffering, so individuals told me, increases if one struggles against it. Rave, very early after his conversion, interpreted these effects of the peyote as symbolizing the struggle between the peyote and the particular vices of an individual. The increase in the intensity of his suffering when resistance was offered corresponded to his unwillingness to give up the old life.

[158] He is, of course, still unconverted and has come to the same conclusion at which he had arrived during his unsuccessful fasting experiences. Having gone through the ceremony, however, and having actually become unconscious, he was quite willing to let them imagine that he had seen what they had told him he would see. Such had been his procedure throughout life.

[159] This was part of their campaign against the old customs and habits; one of the characteristics introduced by A.H., who knew the Bible fairly well and whose influence was then at its height, especially among the younger people.

[160] He had, externally at least, become a member of the cult. It is extremely interesting to note how they accept his conversion merely because he has permitted his hair to be cut and has given up his *medicines,* for this is simply the old Winnebago attitude. Of course he is almost on the verge of conversion, even from his own standpoint, as is evidenced by his crying.

On the fourth night they had another meeting and I went to it again. There I again ate (peyote). I enjoyed it and I sang along with them. I wanted to be able to sing immediately. Some young men were singing and I enjoyed it, so I prayed to Earthmaker asking him to let me learn to sing right away.[161] That was all I asked for. My brother-in-law was with me all the time. At that meeting all the things I had given my brother-in-law were burned up.

The fact that he (my brother-in-law) told me that I understood, pleased me, and I felt good when daylight came. (As a matter of fact) I had not received any knowledge.[162] However I thought it was the proper way to act, so I did it.

After that I would attend meetings every once in a while and I looked around for a woman whom I might marry permanently. Before long that was the only thing I thought of when I attended the meetings.

31. I Am Converted

On one occasion we were to have a meeting of men and I went to the meeting with a woman, with whom I thought of going around the next day. That was (the only) reason I went with her.[163] When we arrived, the one who was to lead, asked me to sit near him. There he placed me. He urged me to eat a lot of peyote, so I did. The leaders (of the ceremony) always place the regalia in front of themselves; they also had a peyote placed there.[164] The one this leader placed in front of himself this time, was a very small one. "Why does he have a very small one there?" I thought to myself. I did not think much about it.

---

[161] In a former passage when he had been told to pray to God he did not know what to ask for, but now that there is something definite he wishes to possess he finds no difficulty in praying. This he understood; the other, more general prayer, he did not.

[162] I.e., he has not yet experienced the inward change upon which he insists.

[163] Apparently he feels that the motive is wrong now that he is a member of the peyote cult.

[164] The largest and most perfect peyote they happen to possess which they call *huñk'*, chief, as a rule, set aside for this purpose.

It was now late at night and I had eaten a lot of peyote and felt rather tired. I suffered considerably. After a while I looked at the peyote and there stood an eagle with outspread wings. It was as beautiful a sight as one could behold. Each of the feathers seemed to have a mark. The eagle stood looking at me. I looked around thinking that perhaps there was something the matter with my sight. Then I looked again and it was really there. I then looked in a different direction and it disappeared. Only the small peyote remained.[165] I looked around at the other people but they all had their heads bowed and were singing. I was very much surprised.

Some time after this (I saw) a lion lying in the same place (where I had seen the eagle). I watched it very closely. It was alive and looking at me. I looked at it very closely and when I turned my eyes away just the least little bit, it disappeared. "I suppose they all know this and I am just beginning to know of it," I thought. Then I saw a small person (at the same place). He wore blue clothes and a shining brimmed cap. He had on a soldier's uniform.[166] He was sitting on the arm of the person who was drumming, and he looked at every one. He was a little man, perfect (in all proportions). Finally I lost sight of him. I was very much surprised indeed. I sat very quietly. "This is what it is," I thought, "this is what they all probably see and I am just beginning to find out."

Then I prayed to Earthmaker (God): *"This, your ceremony, let me hereafter perform."*[167]

---

[165] He apparently had one of the gorgeous color visions which are frequently induced by eating peyote. Whether we are to interpret the fact that he saw an eagle as connected with blessings from eagle spirits, it is difficult to say.

[166] This is one of the customary visions seen in fasts. Such a spirit appeared to S.B.'s brother when he was fasting. This unquestioned reminiscence of the old fasting experiences suggests that in the two former visions he was also influenced by the old conceptions. We see here the same kind of degeneration as that pointed out in note 140. The figures (spirits) appear, but they have no function; they have become devitalized.

[167] These three visions apparently gave him that sense of an inward change for which he had looked in vain during his early fasts. The italicized sentence is identical with the words used by John Rave in the account of his conversion, and I imagine that his words became a kind of formula used by many people in describing the actual moment of conversion.

32. I See Earthmaker (God) and Have Other Visions

As I looked again, I saw a flag. I looked more carefully and (I saw) the house full of flags. They had the most beautiful marks on them. In the middle (of the room) there was a very large flag and it was a live one; it was moving. In the doorway there was another one not entirely visible. I had never seen anything so beautiful in all my life before.[168]

Then again I prayed to Earthmaker (God). I bowed my head and closed my eyes and began (to speak).[169] I said many things that I would ordinarily never have spoken about.[170] As I prayed, I was aware of something above me and there he was; Earthmaker (God) to whom I was praying, he it was.[171] That which is called the soul, that is it, that is what one calls Earthmaker (God).[172] Now this is what I felt and saw. The one called Earthmaker (God) is a spirit and that is what I felt and saw. All of us sitting there, we had all together one spirit or soul; at least

[168] This, as well as the spread wings of the eagle, is clearly a color vision.

[169] The bowing of the head and the closing of the eyes are old Winnebago customs. It is the fact that the peyote worshipers pray standing that is new.

[170] Apparently both a prayer and a confession. It was the belief of the peyote followers that a new convert would not feel at ease until he had made a complete admission of the error of his former life. Some even believed that the cardinal vices would be symbolically vomited by the new adherent. One individual told me that he felt, at conversion, as though he had vomited a bulldog, which he explained as representing his former pugnacity and stubbornness.

[171] His vision of Earthmaker is more like the old visions of spirits and is quite different from A.H.'s visions of God. The latter's were distinctly Christian in origin and he had them only during a cataleptic fit. S.B. has Earthmaker appear to him in very much the same manner that certain spirits were supposed to manifest themselves to the Winnebago in former times. Certain spirits were never seen but were recognized by the rustling of the wind, leaves, etc., while the presence of others was merely felt as he says here of Earthmaker. Earthmaker, as the apparitions mentioned before, is quite functionless. S.B. merely sees him. Cf. note 166.

[172] This is S.B.'s personal metaphysics and shows how completely he, at least, misunderstood what Rave and A.H. meant by their identification of Earthmaker with God. S.B. probably knew little and bothered himself less about the old concept of Earthmaker for he was not a priest. Knowing little of the older belief he was hard put to it, I imagine, when the new God was defined in terms of the old. Hence arose perhaps this unusual identification of God with soul. In his keyed-up condition of religious expectancy and fervor he apparently identified his sensations with this new God.

that is what I learned. I instantly became the spirit and I was their spirit or soul. Whatever they thought of, I (immediately) knew it.[173] I did not have to speak to them and get an answer to know what their thoughts had been. Then I thought of a certain place, far away, and immediately I was there; I was my thought.[174]

I looked around and noticed how everything seemed about me, and when I opened my eyes I was myself in the body again. From this time on, I thought, thus I shall be. This is the way they are, and I am only just beginning to be that way. "All those that heed Earthmaker (God) must be thus," I thought. I would not need any more food," I thought, "for was I not my spirit? Nor would I have any more use of my body," I felt. "My corporeal affairs are over," I felt.

Then they stopped and left for it was just dawning. Then someone spoke to me. I did not answer for I thought they were just fooling and that they were all like myself, and that (therefore) it was unnecessary for me to talk to them. So when they spoke to me I only answered with a smile. "They are just saying this to me because (they realize) that I have just found out," I thought. That was why I did not answer. I did not speak to anyone until noon. Then I had to leave the house to perform one of nature's duties and someone followed me. It was my friend. He said, "My friend, what troubles you that makes you act as you do?" "Well, there's no need of your saying anything for you know it beforehand," I said.

Then I immediately got over my trance and again got into

[173] This power of knowing beforehand what a person was thinking of is a good Winnebago belief and is one of the gifts promised all those who join the Medicine Dance. There it is considered merely a magical gift resulting from membership in that organization. S.B. very cleverly and acutely has this power flow from his predication of a corporate soul, with which his individual soul is temporarily identified.

[174] The power of transporting one's self at will to a distant place is likewise an old Winnebago conception which members of the Medicine Dance were supposed to possess. In saying that he was his thought he is elaborating his previous identifications of himself with the corporate soul. No unnecessary philosophical implications are to be thought of in this connection. Thought, feeling, etc., were regarded by the Winnebago as objective realities, or, to put it more correctly perhaps, as things that existed just as definitely as what was perceived directly through the senses.

my (normal) condition so that he would have to speak to me before I knew his thoughts. I became like my former self.[175] It became necessary for me to speak to him.

33. Further Consequences of My Conversion

Then I spoke to him and said, "My friend, let us hitch up these horses and then I will go wherever you like, for you wish to speak to me and I also want to go around and talk to you." Thus I spoke to him. "If I were to tell you all that I have learned, I would never be able to stop at all, so much have I learned," I said to him. "However, I would enjoy telling some of it." "Good," said he. He liked it (what I told him) very much. "That is what I am anxious to hear," said he. Then we went after the horses. We caught one of them, but we could not get the other. He got away from us and we could not find him. We hunted everywhere for the horse but could not discover where he had run to. Long afterwards we found it among the whites.[176]

Now since that time (of my conversion) no matter where I am I always think of this religion. I still remember it and I think I will remember it as long as I live. It is the only holy thing that I have been aware of in all my life.

After that whenever I heard of a peyote meeting, I went to it. However my thoughts were always fixed on women. "If I were married (legally) perhaps these thoughts will leave me," I thought. Whenever I went to a meeting now I tried to eat as many peyote as possible, for I was told that it was good to eat them. For that reason I ate them. As I sat there I would always pray to Earthmaker (God). Now these were my thoughts. If I were married, I thought as I sat there, I could then put all my thoughts on this ceremony.[177] I sat with my eyes closed and was very quiet.

Suddenly I saw something. This was tied up. The rope with which this object was tied up was long. The object itself was

[175] He recovered from his trance.

[176] Apparently this unimportant episode had become so definitely associated in his mind with the fundamental changes that were taking place in him that he remembered it in great detail.

[177] This is merely the old Winnebago formula of "religious concentration."

running around and around (in a circle). There was a pathway there in which it ought to go, but it was tied up and unable to get there. The road was an excellent one. Along its edge blue grass grew and on each side there grew many varieties of pretty flowers. Sweet-smelling flowers sprang up all along this road.[178] Far off in the distance appeared a bright light.[179] There a city was visible of a beauty indescribable by tongue. A cross was in full sight.[180] The object that was tied up would always fall just short of reaching the road. It seemed to lack sufficient strength to break loose (of what was holding it). (Near it) lay something which would have given it sufficient strength to break its fastenings, if it were only able to get hold of it.

I looked at what was so inextricably tied up and I saw that it was myself. I was forever thinking of women.[181] "This it is with which I was tied," I thought "Were I married, I would have strength enough to break my fastening and be able to travel in the good road," I thought. Then daylight came upon us and we stopped.

Then I thought of a man I used to know who was an old peyote-man. He always spoke to me very kindly. I went over to see him. I thought I would tell him what had happened to me. When I arrived there he was quite delighted. It was about noon and he fed my horses and asked me to eat with him. Then when we were through eating, I told him what had happened to me. He was very glad and told me that I was speaking of a very good thing. Then (finally) he said, "Now I shall tell you what

[178] These words are taken verbatim from the Winnebago description of the road to spirit-land.

[179] This is of course Christian, but it is clearly an assimilation to the description of Earthmaker's lodge as seen from a distance after one has crossed the four hills as depicted in the myth of the journey to spirit-land in the Medicine Dance; a myth which, of course, S.B. knew very well.

[180] While the idea of the cross here is probably Christian it might be pointed out that two lines crossing at right angles was also the old symbol of Earthmaker and was always painted on the buckskin offered to him at the war-bundle feasts. This symbol is also identified, among the Winnebago, with the four cardinal points.

[181] The metaphor is probably old; its interpretation here, of course, quite new and probably not S.B.'s invention. The peyote people took a number of old Winnebago metaphors, mythical episodes, and mythical characters and gave them specific interpretations.

I think is a good thing (for you to do). You know that if an old horse is balky, you can not break him of (this habit); even if you had bought him and tried to break him (of this habit), you would not succeed. If, indeed, you succeeded, it would only be after very hard work. However, if you had a young horse, you could train it in any way you wished. So it is in everything. If you marry a woman who has been in the habit of getting married frequently, it would be difficult for her to break herself of a habit she loves. You are not the one she loves. If you marry her you will lead a hard life. If you wish to get married, take your time. There are plenty of good women. Many of them are at (government) schools and have never been married. I think you would do best if you waited for some of these before marrying. They will return in the middle of summer. So, don't think of any of these women you see around here, but wait until then and pray to Earthmaker patiently. That would be the best, I think." I liked what he told me and thanked him. I decided to accept his advice, and I did not look around for women after that. I was to wait about three months and (during that time) I paid strict attention to the peyote ceremony.

On one occasion while at a meeting, I suffered (great pain). My eyes were sore and I was thinking of many things. "Now I do nothing but pay attention to this ceremony, for it is good." Then I called the leader over to me and said to him, "My elder brother, hereafter only Earthmaker (God) shall I regard as holy. I will make no more offerings of tobacco. I will not use any more tobacco. I will not smoke and I will not chew tobacco. I have no further interest in these.[182] Earthmaker (God) alone do I desire (to serve). I will not take part in the Medicine Dance again. I give myself up (to you). I intend to give myself up to Earthmaker's (God's) cause." Thus I spoke to him. "It is good, younger brother," he said to me. Then he had me stand up and he prayed to Earthmaker (God). He asked Earthmaker (God) to forgive me my sins.

The next morning I was taken home. My eyes were sore and I could not see. They took me back to a house and there they

---

[182] This completes his severance of all the ties that bound him to his former mode of life.

put a solution of the peyote into my eyes and I got well in a week.[183]

One night, when I was asleep, I dreamed that the world had come to an end. Some people Earthmaker (God) took, while some belonged to the bad spirit (devil). I belonged to the bad spirit (the devil). Although I had given myself up (become a peyote-man) I had not as yet been baptized. That was why Earthmaker (God) did not take me. All those who belonged to Earthmaker (God) were marked, but I was not.[184] I felt very bad about it when I woke up, even although I had only dreamed about it.[185] I felt very bad indeed. I wanted them to hurry and have another peyote meeting soon anywhere. I could hardly wait until I reached the place where the next meeting was to take place. I immediately told the leader (what I wanted) and asked him to baptize me and he baptized me in the morning. After that morning I felt better.

Then I went to work and I worked with a railroad work-gang. I was still working when the time for the midsummer celebration approached. I always went to the peyote meeting on Saturday nights.

The old man was right in what he had told me. The girl students returned in the summer. Shortly (after they returned) a man, a friend of mine who had gone around with me, asked me if I wanted to get married. "Yes, I do," I answered. Then he said, "Listen, I have been thinking of something. What kind of a woman do you wish to marry?" I told him what I had in mind. Then he said, "Come home with me. I have a younger sister. I want her to marry a good man; I would like to have her marry you," he said. Then I went home with him. When

---

[183] The medicinal virtues ascribed to the old herbs were transferred to the peyote, if indeed we can speak here of a transference and not simply an assimilation of the peyote with the medicinal herbs. It was, as might be expected, one of the earliest claims made for the peyote. Cf. my paper mentioned in note 122.

[184] Used metaphorically to mean "baptized." It is commonly used by the pagan Winnebago to refer to clan identification in spirit-land, i.e., the clan affiliations of the ghosts were considered their marks, quite apart from the fact that of course each clan had its specific facial decorations. This is certainly the source from which S.B. derived the idea.

[185] He claims to have lost his faith in dreams, yet he is intensely desirous of having his defect remedied as soon as possible.

we got there (and discussed the matter) the girl gave her consent. The parents also consented.

So there I got married and what I expected has taken place and I have lived with her ever since. On one occasion, after she was used to me, she told me this. (Before she had married, she had determined that) if she ever got married, she would not care to marry a very young man. "I wanted a man who ate peyote and who paid attention to the ceremony."[186] Such a man she desired and such a person was I, she said. She loved me, she said, and she was glad that she had married me. That is what she had asked Earthmaker (God) in prayer. "And, indeed, it has happened as I wished," she said. She believed it was the will of Earthmaker (God) that we had done this, she said. She was therefore glad (that she had married me). Together we gave ourselves up (to the peyote) at a peyote meeting. From that time on we have remained members of the peyote (ceremony).

34. I Have a Strange Experience

Many things are said under the influence of the peyote. The members (would) get into a kind of trance and speak of many things. On one occasion they had a peyote meeting which lasted two nights. I ate a good deal of peyote. The next morning I tried to sleep. I suffered a great deal. I lay down in a very comfortable position. After a while a (nameless) fear arose in me. I could not remain in that place, so I went out into the prairie, but here again I was seized with this fear. Finally I returned to a lodge near the lodge in which the peyote meeting was being held and lay down alone. I feared that I might do something foolish to myself (if I remained there alone), and I hoped that someone would come and talk to me. Then someone did come and talk to me, but I did not feel better, so I thought I would go inside where the meeting was going on. "I am going inside," I said to him. He laughed. "All right, do so," said he. I went in and sat down. It was very hot and I felt

---

[186] Exactly what a conservative Winnebago woman might have said in former times.

as though I were going to die. I was very thirsty but I feared to ask for water. I thought that I was certainly going to die. I began to totter over.

I died, and my body was moved by another life.[187] It began to move about; to move about and make signs. It was not I and I could not see it.[188] At last it stood up. The regalia—eagle feathers and gourds—these were holy, they said. They also had a large book there (Bible).[189] These my body took and what is contained in that (book) my body saw. It was a Bible. The regalia were not holy,[190] but they were good ornaments. My body told them that; and that if any person paid attention to Earthmaker's (God's) ceremony, he would be hearkening to what the Bible said; that likewise my body told them. Earthmaker's son (God's Son) said that he was the only Way. This means that one can only get life from the Word.[191] (My) body spoke of many things and it spoke of what was true. Indeed it spoke of many things. It spoke of all the things that were being done (by the pagan Indians) and which were evil. A long time it spoke. At last it stopped. Not I, but my body standing there, had done the talking. Earthmaker (God) had done his own talking.[192] I would be confessing myself a fool if I were to think that I had said all this, it (my body) told me.

After a while I returned to my normal human condition. Some of those there had been frightened, thinking that I had gone crazy. Others had liked it. It was discussed a good deal. They called it the "shaking" state.[193] It was said that the condition in which I was, was not part of Earthmaker's (God's) religion. I was told that whoever ate a lot of peyote

[187] I.e., he was again his soul.

[188] I.e., he was incorporeal.

[189] To the older members of the cult, including the leader Rave, the Bible was merely one of the regalia. To the younger members it was used for interpretations.

[190] This is a new Christian interpretation. I doubt very much whether Rave would have subscribed to it.

[191] Of biblical origin of course.

[192] As in a previous passage he identifies Earthmaker with his soul.

[193] This condition was regarded as "holy" among the conservative Winnebago likewise.

would, through the peyote, be taught the teachings of Earthmaker (God). Earthmaker's (God's) ways and man's ways are different.[194] Whoever therefore wished to help this religion must give himself up (to it). If you ate a good deal of this peyote and believed that it could teach you something[195] then it assuredly would do so. That at least is the way in which I understand this matter.

Once we had a meeting at the home of a member who was sick. The sick would always get well when a meeting was held in their home, and that is why we did it.[196] At that meeting I got into the "shaking" condition again. My body told (us) how our religion (peyote) was an affair of Earthmaker's (God's), and even if one knew only a portion of it, one could still see (partake of) Earthmaker's (God's) religion.

Thus it went on talking. "Earthmaker (God), His Son (Christ), and His Holiness (the Holy Ghost),[197] these are the three ways of saying it. Even if you know one (of these three), it means all.[198] Everyone of you has the means of opening (the road) to Earthmaker (God). It is given to you. With that (your belief) you can open (the door to God). You cannot open it with knowledge (alone).[199] How many letters are there to the key (the road to God)? Three. What are they?" There were many educated people (there) but none of them said anything. "The first (letter) must be a *K*, so if a person said *K*, that would be the whole of it. But let me look in the book

---

[194] Of biblical origin and quite foreign to Winnebago thought.

[195] It is difficult to determine whether the peyote or the ceremony and its associated beliefs was to teach an individual something. In the former case the notion would be thoroughly Winnebago.

[196] This virtue was also accomplished by a performance of the old pagan rituals and particularly by the Medicine Dance.

[197] This is the peyote translation of the Trinity.

[198] Of Christian origin.

[199] I.e., merely by having read certain things. The inward feeling must accompany the knowledge. This may be in part a criticism of those who could read and quote the Bible glibly and of whose knowledge those members who could not read English were jealous, and whose claims to greater importance they were inclined to resent.

(Bible) and see what that means," said the body. Then it (the body) took the Bible and began to turn the leaves. The body did not know where it was itself, for it was not learned in books.[200] Finally in Matthew, chapter 16, it stopped. There it speaks about it. "Peter did not give himself up" (it says). "For a long time he could not give up his own knowledge. There (in that passage) it says *Key*." That is the work of Earthmaker (God). At least so I understand it. He made use of my body and acted in this manner, in the case of the peyote.

Thus I go about telling (everyone) that this religion is good. Many other people at home said the same thing. Many, likewise, have joined this religion and are getting along nicely.

On one occasion, after I had eaten a good deal of peyote, I learned the following from it; that all I had done in the past, that it had all been evil. This was plainly revealed to me. What I thought was holy, and (by thus thinking) was lost, that I now know was false. (It is false), this giving of (pagan) feasts, of holding (the old) things holy, the Medicine Dance, and all the Indian customs.

35. Finale

I have written of some of these matters and I have spoken out clearly.[201] I talked about this to the older people but they refused to do it.[202] I thought I would write it down so that those who came after me would not be deceived.[203] Then my

---

[200] He wished to show that knowledge of English did not give one complete insight into the Bible and its meaning. He probably used Rev. Stucki's translation of the Bible into the language of the Winnebago, of which there were a few copies in Winnebago, Nebraska.

The theology formulated here is, so far as I know, his own.

[201] He was one of my principal informants and wrote down in the Winnebago syllabary a large amount of valuable information.

[202] I.e., he asked other Winnebago to give me certain information, which they refused to do.

[203] This was the reason I gave for asking him to write these matters down.

brother had us do this work, [204] (aided by) my older brother[205] and my younger brother.[206]

Before (my conversion) I went about in a pitiable condition, but now I am living happily, and my wife has a fine baby.

This is the work that was assigned to me.[207]

This is the end of it.

[204] That is myself.

[205] His older brother, my principal informant, whose knowledge and memory were both remarkable.

[206] My interpreter, Oliver Lamere, who translated practically all the texts I obtained and without whose industry and interest my work would hardly have been successful.

[207] Such was the notion that a number of Winnebago who helped me developed shortly after my coming among them. His brother makes the same statement in my paper mentioned in the Introduction.

Mountain Wolf Woman

Growing Up

At the place where they hunted, father and older brother killed as many deer as they would need for a feast. They set aside ten deer on a high, narrow rack made for storing meat. They cut down crotched poles and set them up in a rectangle with poles across the crotches and other poles forming a platform, similar to the open-sided square shelters used as sun shades, but narrower and higher. They put the deer on it and covered them with the hides.

Once there was a lot of snow on the ground when we went back home. We had come in wagons and when we went back the wagon wheels made a loud noise rolling over the snow. We always returned to our home at Black River Falls where we ordinarily lived. Other Winnebago also did this. They too went away some place, wherever they chose to go to hunt, and then they would give a feast. Father and all the Indians used to give feasts. Father used to hold big feasts, ten fireplaces they said. The row of fireplaces used to stretch off into the distance. Many Indians attended and father used to feed a wigwam full of people. There we would dance all night. Sometimes children were named at feasts. This is what they used to do time and again. Sometimes, those who had been fasting would then eat at the feast.

That is what my older brother Hágaga did, he alone fasted. Hénaga did not have any patience with such things, but brother Hágaga fasted in the woods. My father built a shelter for them to live in and they slept there four nights. But my older brother Hénaga did not do that. Hénaga came home during that time. Mother wept. "Why did you do that? Why did you do that?" she said. "Oh," he said, "I am sick of it so I stopped." But brother Hágaga stayed there. He was trying to remain until

WINNEBAGO LANDS, CESSIONS, AND RESERVATIONS

The Winnebago Indians ceded their homeland in Wisconsin and northern Illinois by treaties in 1829, 1832, and 1837. Between 1846 and 1865 they were prevailed upon by the government to exchange one reservation for another until they were finally settled upon their present reservation in northeastern Nebraska. This reservation, about one hundred thousand acres, was reduced by about two-thirds after 1888, when the Indians were granted patents in fee to individual allotments and could enter into private sales. The questionable practices involved in purchases of Indian lands throughout the nation caused the government to enforce stricter regulations on land sales in 1934. About half of the tribe is presently enrolled on the Nebraska reservation. However, a portion of the tribe claimed that the treaty of 1837 had been fraudulent and therefore refused to be removed from Wisconsin. The last forcible removal of the Wisconsin Winnebago occurred in 1874 and figures in Mountain Wolf Woman's story. After 1875 the Winnebago who wished to remain in Wisconsin were permitted to take up forty-acre homesteads on the public domain, and Mountain Wolf Woman's mother was among those who took up land in Wisconsin. At present, over fifteen hundred Winnebago make their home in their original tribal territory. (Charles Royce and Cyrus Thomas, "Indian Land Cessions," *18th Annual Report, Bureau of American Ethnology,* Washington, 1896-97, Part II.)

feast time. When it was about time for the feast, father and his nephews built the lodge and made all the preparations for it. All these kinsmen that father would invite to the feast he could make work for him. That is what they did. Brother was allowed to return at the time of the feast since at that time one who fasts for a vision may eat.

When he was about to return they went around the lodge with a deer hide. They took a deer hide around the morning he was going to come back. Brother Hágaga must have been a little boy at the time they were taking this white deer hide around. They used it when dancing, taking the deer hide and dancing with it. It seemed to be a very pleasant time. There brother cried to the Thunders. Our aunts and older sisters heard my older brother crying and they cried too, they said. Today they do not do that any more.

My older sister Hińakega and I also used to fast. They used to make us do this. We would blacken our cheeks and would not eat all day. That was at the time of the hunting I have told about, before we returned from hunting. We used to blacken our cheeks with charcoal at the time father left in the morning to go hunting. We used coals from the fire to blacken our cheeks and we did not eat all day. I used to play outside but my older sister used to sit indoors and weave yarn belts. When father returned from hunting in the evening he used to say to us, "Go cry to the Thunders." When father was ready to eat he would give us tobacco and say to us, "Here, go cry to the Thunders." Just as it was getting dark my sister and I used to go off a certain distance and she would say to me, "Go stand by a tree and I am going to go farther on." We used to stand there and look at the stars and cry to the Thunders. This is what we used to sing:

"Oh, Good Spirits
Will they pity me? Here am I, pleading."

We used to sing and scatter tobacco, standing there and watching the stars and the moon. We used to cry because, after all, we were hungry. We used to think we were pitied. We really wanted to mean what we were saying.

When we finished with our song we scattered tobacco at the foot of the tree and returned home. When we got back home father ate and we ate too. We did not eat all day, only at night, and when we had finished eating we put the dishes away. Then father used to say, "All right, prepare your bedding and go to bed and I will tell you some stories." I really enjoyed listening to my father tell stories. Everybody, the entire household, was very quiet and in this atmosphere my father used to tell stories. He used to tell myths, the sacred stories, and that is why I also know some myths. I do not know all of them any more, I just remember parts of stories.

Again we went hunting and returned to Black River Falls and had our feast there. I was a little girl. The people followed the same cycle, winter, spring, summer, and when it was almost fall my oldest brother said, "My little sister should go to school." I was nine years old. He said, "I like to hear women speak English so I would like my little sister to learn how to speak English." They let me go to school at Tomah, Wisconsin, and I attended school there for two years. Then I did not go to school again for a long time. Well, whatever the reason, that is the way with Indians. The Indians do not stay home so that their children can attend school. That is what they have done through the years, but at present they can no longer act in this way.

Then I lived at home and the family went on a short hunting trip. After that they went off to find cranberries and on our return we stopped at the home of grandfather Náqi-Johnga. There it was that mother told me how it is with little girls when they become women. "Some time," she said, "that is going to happen to you. From about the age of thirteen years this happens to girls. When that happens to you, run to the woods and hide some place. You should not look at any one, not even a glance. If you look at a man you will contaminate his blood. Even a glance will cause you to be an evil person. When women are in that condition they are unclean." Once, after our return to grandfather's house, I was in that condition when I awoke in the morning.

Because mother had told me to do so, I ran quite far into the woods where there were some bushes. The snow was still on the ground and the trees were just beginning to bud. In the woods there was a broken tree and I sat down under this fallen tree. I bowed my head with my blanket wrapped over me and there I was, crying and crying. Since they had forbidden me to look around, I sat there with my blanket over my head. I cried. Then, suddenly I heard the sound of voices. My sister Hińakega and my sister-in-law found me. Because I had not come back in the house, they had looked for me. They saw my tracks in the snow, and by my tracks they saw that I ran. They trailed me and found me. "Stay here," they said. "We will go and make a shelter for you," and they went home again. Near the water's edge of a big creek, at the rapids of East Fork River, they built a little wigwam. They covered it with canvas. They built a fire and put straw there for me, and then they came to get me. There I sat in the little wigwam. I was crying. It was far, about a quarter of a mile from home. I was crying and I was frightened. Four times they made me sleep there. I never ate. There they made me fast. That is what they made me do. After the third time that I slept, I dreamed.

There was a big clearing. I came upon it, a big, wide-open field, and I think there was a rise of land there. Somewhat below this rise was the big clearing. There, in the wide meadow, there were all kinds of horses, all colors. I must have been one who dreamed about horses. I believe that is why they always used to give me horses.

Spring arrived, and again deer-hunting time, and winter back at Black River Falls when my father gave feasts, and then it was spring again. Once more we moved to the Mississippi River. When the muskrat season was over we returned to our home. The people engaged in their usual activities, but that time when we returned, after a while, mother and father said that they were not going to put in any garden.—Father must have had word from his uncles, although I did not hear about it. Father's uncles at Wittenberg, Wisconsin, were old men. They lived there at Wittenberg for many years. Father pitied his uncles because they were old and could not help themselves. My parents said that was where we were going to move. My older sister also accompanied us and we moved there. We used big wagons drawn by horses.

North of the town of Marshfield there was a settlement of Indians and we slept there. Some lived in frame houses and some lived in bark-sided gabled cabins with earth-covered roofs. They built these cabins themselves and these were scattered throughout the settlement. They were Potawatomi Indians and mother had relatives there. They were called Chippewa Woman and Hínuga, her daughter. They spoke Winnebago very fluently. Mother knew them and knew that they were living there so we stopped at that place. We must have slept there twice in order to rest the horses. There was a tall frame house where we stayed and the name of the person who lived there was Crotched Tree. He had a wife. It would seem that father was also part Potawatomi because she was his relative. They invited us to eat and so we ate. At that place there was a dance area. It was a sacred place. They invited us to eat there that evening and so we went there to eat.

The wife of Crotched Tree was my father's sister. They gave my parents maple sugar in a hand-woven bag, cakes or hardened syrup which are stored in such bags. In the morning when my mother and father went out I went along. Mother took some things with her when we went to visit the Potawatomi aunt who was my father's sister. Mother brought that woman some necklaces and bracelets and long earrings with coins on the ends. She was very pleased. She was a fine-looking woman. If these people were still living they would be my in-laws because Crotched Tree had daughters of marriageable age and one of them had a son who was the father of my son-in-law. One of my sons-in-law is my nephew.

We left that place and arrived at Wittenberg. We had a grandfather there whose name was High Snake and he lived in a big log cabin. We stopped there and my father went off to get those two dear little old men. They were very old men. It was their son who lived at the place where we stopped. The old men lived at another place and my father went there for them. One was called Good Snake and the other was called Fear the Snake Den. He soon brought them and they began to make preparations at grandfather High Snake's place. They cut trees for lodge poles and hauled them back in a big horse-drawn wagon. There they set up a long lodge. They built a Medicine Lodge. On the east side where the sun rises they completed it and sang upon reaching that end. My older sister White Thunder and my older brother Hénaga were initiated into the lodge and I imagine that is why we went there. Evidently father's uncles told us to come there, and because they were old men we went there.

They had the paraphernalia for a Medicine Dance so the Medicine Dance was held there. They held the Medicine Dance as soon as we arrived. During that time Indians came there to Wittenberg from various places. The Indians were real Indians! Some of them brought wagons and some of them let the horses back-pack their belongings. Some of them arrived riding horseback. There were many Indians and they held a Medicine Dance. We were gathered there in a big group.

When they finished the Medicine Dance somebody said, "About this time they usually peel and dry slippery elm." They used to tie it in a bundle and white people bought it. They paid a good price for slippery elm. "All right," father said, "we can do that. We are a big family and thus we will be able to eat." That is what they did. Mother and her young ones put up a tent next to my grandfather's home and we lived there. Those who were strong went away some place with a wagon and some household goods. Where the trees were very dense they stopped and they asked for the slippery elm from the white people who owned the woods. They called it slippery elm; it is something like the elm tree. They asked, "Could you not give that kind to us so that we can make something to sell?" The white people said, "Help yourself, do whatever it is that you are talking about."

Then they walked about and looked at the trees and wherever they saw a slippery elm they skinned it. They cut the bark from the base of the tree and pulled it loose up to the very top on the tree. Then they slashed it off and it fell down like folding cloth. The trees were easily peeled. Even one tree produced a lot of bark. They measured the bark with their arms and cut it to that length. They made piles big enough for a person to carry on his back and when they had a load for everyone they started back to wherever they were camping. The women peeled off the outer bark with jackknives. They made drying racks and hung up all the bark. They dried a lot of bark and tied it in bundles. In a short time they made many bundles. Only the drying took a long time. They took the bundles to some

town where the white people bought slippery elm. They used
to come and visit those of us who were living at home and
bring us food. Then they went away again to the big forest
where they traveled about gathering slippery elm. Today they
no longer do that. Today the white people who have timber
land keep it for themselves. Years ago it was not that way and
the white people used to say, "Help yourself, do whatever it is
that you are talking about." They looked for slippery elm and
they prepared it to sell. Whatever the situation they always
found something to do and were able to obtain food for themselves by such methods. Whatever the circumstances, the Indian
is always doing something useful.

It must have been fall by that time and my sisters went back
to Black River Falls. Father, mother, my brothers and my
older sister Hiṅakega did not go back. We remained there for a
while. One of my grandfathers who was called Rattlesnake had
land next to the highway and told us that we should live there.
My father made a big round wigwam of bark and there we
lived. That fall I did not go to school at all. We moved to
another place where my father trapped. He was still with my
grandfathers. We went to a place where there is a lake, Green
Lake it is called. My grandfathers were acquainted with some
white people where they used to trap. Father trapped there
along with the grandfathers and they went to some other places
as well. That was during the fall and when the cold weather
was about to set in we went back to Wittenberg. They should
have put me in school that fall. Not until we returned did they
put me in school. I went to the Lutheran Mission School at
Wittenberg. I had attended school at Tomah and finally I went
to school again. I was a teen-age girl and I went to school there
every year.

Once, my older brothers and some other people were going
to go some place to dance. I think it was at Chicago. One time
they sent me a bicycle. Oh, I was proud. Nobody had a bicycle.
I was the first one to have a bicycle, a girl's bicycle. My
brothers did that for me. The girls really thought something
of me. They coaxed me to ride my bicycle and they pampered
me. Bicycles were rare at that time. I suppose I was the first
of the students to have a bicycle.

At the school there was an Oneida woman who was the girls' matron. She was called Nancy Smith. Whenever the Indians were going to have a dance, Nancy Smith and I would ride there on our bicycles. Once when the Indians were going to hold a dance Nancy said, "It would be more fun if we went by horseback." In town they used to have ponies at the place where they sold wagons. They used to be tough. She asked me to hire some of those ponies. There were many horse stalls at the livery stable where I went for the ponies. They put saddles on the horses and I sat on one and went outside. I had a terribly hard time getting on as it was skittish. Leading the other one, I started back. The horse I was riding tried to run, but I held back on the reins. I had to fight that horse all the way, but I finally got back. I used to think horseback riding was a lot of fun. I was like a boy riding horses. When I got back, Nancy also had a hard time getting in the saddle. We started off immediately, letting the horses run. After a while we held the reins in on the horses so they would walk. We continued on our way letting the horses alternately run and walk. We finally arrived where the Indians were dancing. We dismounted and sat and watched the people dance. We sat on a big log, watching them dance. The horses were standing nearby and we were sitting there holding the reins. They had been having a war dance and then they had a "squaw dance." Four Women came over and asked me to dance. Nancy told me to go ahead and dance, and so I did. I was dressed in "citizens clothing," and I really danced! When they used to ask me to dance I would do so. They said that they really liked it for me. When I watched the horse races they used to tell me that they liked it when I enjoyed myself dancing. Whenever something of that sort was taking place I was never embarrassed, no matter the circumstances. I always used to be there. Eventually we started back. We arrived at town and returned the horses. I do not know how much Nancy paid for their hire. When we got to town we walked back to the school.

Nancy Smith was the girls' matron in charge of sewing. Later she was put in charge of the bakery. Whatever she did, she always called upon me to be with her. Eventually she married a workman there at the school.

Marriage

Then I stopped attending school. They took me out of school. Alas, I was enjoying school so much, and they made me stop. They took me back home. They had let me go to school and now they made me quit. It was then that they told me I was going to be married. I cried but it did not do any good. What would my crying avail me? They had already arranged it. As they were telling me about it my mother said, "My little daughter, I prize you highly. You alone are the youngest child. I prize you highly but nothing can be done about this matter. It is your brothers' doing. You must do whatever your brothers say. If you do not do so, you are going to embarrass them. They have been drinking again, but if you do not do this they will be disgraced. They might even experience something unfortunate." Thus mother spoke to me. She rather frightened me.

My father said, "My little daughter, you do not have very many things to wear, but you will go riding on your little pony. You do not have anything, but you will not walk there." I had a little horse, a dapple-gray kind of pony that was about three years old. Father brought it for me and there the pony stood. They dressed me. I wore a ribbon embroidery skirt and I wore one as a shawl. I wore a heavily beaded binding for the braid of hair down my back, and I had on earrings. It looked as if I were going to a dance. That man was sitting nearby. He started out leading the pony and I followed after. When we reached a road that had high banks on the side he mounted the horse and I got on behind him. That is the way he brought me home. We rode together. That is how I became a daughter-in-law.

As a daughter-in-law I arrived. When I arrived he had me go in the wigwam and I went in and sat down. They told me to sit on the bed and I sat there. I took off all the clothing that I was wearing when I got there. I took it all off. I laid down a shawl and whatever I had, all the finery, I put on it; beads, the necklaces, clothing, even the blouse that I was wearing. Finally, the man's mother came in. Outside the wigwam there were canvas-covered wigwams standing here and there. The woman took the things and left. There were women sitting all about outside. They were his female relatives. They divided the things among themselves. As they distributed the things around, everybody contributed something in return. Two or three days from the time of my arrival they took me back with four horses and a double shawl so full of things they could barely tie the corners together. They took me home and later I received two more horses, so they gave me six horses in all. That is how they used to arrange things for young women in the past. They made the girls marry into whatever family they decided upon. They made the arrangements. That is the way they used to do.

At the time that my mother was combing my hair and I was weeping at the prospect of becoming a daughter-in-law she told me, "Daughter, I prize you very much, but this matter cannot be helped. When you are older and know better, you can marry whomever you yourself think that you want to marry." Mother said that to me and I did not forget it!

In the first place, before they made me get married, my older brother had been drinking and was asleep. I guess he slept there all day and when he awoke that man they made me marry, who was not a drinker, was there. He sat there using his hat to fan away the mosquitoes from my brother's face. That is why they made me marry that man. My brother awoke and he surmised, "He is doing this for me because I have sisters. That is what he is thinking to himself." So they made me marry that man. That is what the Indians used to do in the past.

That man was very easily aroused to jealousy of other men. He used to accuse me of being with other men. That made me angry. I hated him. He used to watch me too. So, I said to him one time, "No matter how closely you watch me, if I am going to leave you, I am going to leave you! There are a lot of things right now that I do not like." That is what I did to him. I left him taking the two children with me.

Before that, however, when Hínuga, my oldest daughter, was a little girl, mother and father were going to hold a Medicine Dance. My older brother Hénaga, the second son, had died after he joined the Medicine Lodge and they were going to give a Medicine Dance for him. They were saying that I was to take his place, but I did not even know about it. Likewise, the family that I was living with also asked my father and mother whether they could have me join the lodge. My mother-in-law's mother had been a prominent woman in the Medicine Lodge and they were going to do this for her. They asked my mother and father if they would let me join the lodge. They said that they asked for me and that mother said, "They are saying something good." Mother said, "She is going to earn something for herself. She is going to earn the right to be a lodge member. They are talking about something which is good." So they told them they approved. Thus, I was initiated into the lodge.

My mother-in-law had a big otter-skin medicine bag she prized highly. She would give it to whomever she wanted to have it, and if I were there she would give it to me. That is what she said to mother. That was to be mine, she told her.

Then the time for the Medicine Dance arrived. I did not even know about it when they told me I was going to join the lodge. They even had me sew some things. They made a lodge and it was there that the woman spoke of it to me. They brought everything there and then we ate our evening meal. We ate at the sitting place. She said to me, "We are all going to sit here. Daughter-in-law, this way is a good way. It is a way of life, they say. Daughter-in-law, this is what I am contemplating. As I was planning to replace my mother I wondered who could do this thing. It is a good way that the people have to live, my little granddaughter, and you are going to earn a good life for yourself." This she said to me. As I thought about it, my head felt prickly. They were going to sing medicine songs and they began talking about it. There they made me join the lodge. Then that night when I joined the lodge they held the rehearsal for initiates.

In the morning they went to the woods and when they arrived there they did all the things they still do when they have a Medicine Dance. They even "shot" me. Then that woman asked about for a medicine bag. She did not give me that big otter-skin bag they wanted to give me. She was selfish. She asked about for a medicine bag. Then I was dissatisfied. They finished what they were doing and I looked at my husband and he looked at me. I got up and walked out and we were the first ones to come back. She followed us while we were walking back.

"Well, your mother fooled me," I said to him. "Yes, I heard and saw it too. I did not like it either. Whatever you are thinking, I am thinking the same thing. She said the pouch was yours," he said. I said, "Whenever they ask you to use it, do not use it. Say to her, 'If you want to do so, use it, you prize it so highly, you can use it.'" "Yes," he said, "that is what I am going to say. That is just what I think too." We came away from there in disgust.

We returned to our tent that was near the Medicine Lodge. I washed myself and combed my hair. Those who had gone to the woods returned. That old lady cried and cried. "Daughter-in-law, daughter-in-law, if you would only just do this for us!" That is what she said to me. She asked me very nicely. I thought to myself, "I will do graciously what she asks me to do, but after a while I will do what I want to do." That is what I did. I joined the lodge, but not for long.

But that man was jealous. He used to accuse me of having affairs with other men, even my own male relatives. I hated him. Then when my second daughter was an infant I wanted to go to Black River Falls. They said there was going to be a powwow there. We arrived there in a two-seated buggy I had which belonged to my mother and father. I owned a horse but we left my horse behind and used a horse that belonged to his family. We also used the new harness that his parents owned.—Soon after we arrived, father and mother left for Nebraska. Father was sick and they said he might get better if he went there. So they went to Nebraska.

When the powwow was over and the people from Wittenberg were going home, he said, "Well, are we not going to return?" "No," I said to him, "for my part, I am not going back." "Well," he said, "we have to take back the things that we borrowed. We brought a horse of theirs. After all, it belongs to them."

"And you belong to them too," I said. "Take the horse and

let him carry the harness on his back and ride him and go home," I told him. "Leave the wagon here for me, it belongs to my mother and father." The people were preparing to leave and the ones from Wittenberg went back. He put the harness on the horse and let them take it home.—That man stayed around for a while but I would not go back so he finally left too.

As for myself, I went to my grandmother. We had our own tent. "Grandmother," I said, "I am going to borrow some things." "All right," she said, "I am caring for the baby." I said to her, "When I come back, we are going to move." My sister was also going to move. I went to the mission to my niece, the wife of Bright Feather. I said to her, "Niece, I came to borrow something." "All right," she said, "what did you come to borrow?" "A one-horse harness and buggy hitch." "All right, wherever they are take them. What am I using them for? They are yours," she said. There was a wagon going back to the powwow ground and I asked the people to carry back the harness and the hitch. I rode back with them too. When we got back, the man with the wagon attached the single hitch to the buggy and took our double harness and hitch. He said, "I will take these back to your niece at the mission because I will be going that way. They can probably use them." That is what he did. The only horse I had was a big one and I let him pull the buggy alone. I packed everything and headed for the home of my older sister. Thus I left that man.

I took grandmother with me and moved to where one of my sisters was living at Black River Falls. She was there at a cranberry marsh where picking was in progress. Grandmother and I arrived there in the one-horse buggy. We stayed there for a while and then I moved again to a different marsh where another older sister lived. We used to pick cranberries there every day. Across the marsh they held sore eye dances and my brothers-in-law were the hosts. We would go dancing.

Once they said that they were going to hold a Medicine Dance. My older sister said, "Go if you wish to do so. Then you will be able to set up housekeeping there for the family." I took my tent and grandmother and I went there to the town of Millston. Red Cloud's wife, Little Wíhaŋga she was called, was to be initiated and I helped initiate her into the lodge. We arrived and I put up my tent and we stayed there. It was soon evening, and then night, and immediately the singing began at the entrance of the lodge. Brother Hágaga drank a lot and he did not attend. I thought to myself, "So much the better if he does not come." We had already entered the lodge and were sitting there when we could hear off in the distance, "Ooooooooooooooh! Oʔi, Oʔi, Oʔi!" This war whoop could be heard coming from the direction of the road. Older brother was coming! He was well behaved. Although he was drunk, he was not very drunk. We continued with the Medicine Dance and he came in the lodge too. He had four men for his companions.

A man they called They Bring Him sat in the very first place. They Bring Him was a big medicine man from Wittenberg. "Oh," he said, "this is even better. I thought we were going to be a small group. This is good." It began to rain. The top of the lodge was covered with very heavy canvas and in between the lodge supports the canvas became filled with water as it rained. The hollows were filled with water because the canvas did not leak and the weight of the canvas sagged down the lodge in the center. When they began the singing for the dancing we got up and danced.—We had to bend way down as we danced where the roof sagged. There were puddles here and there. The people left their blankets behind at the sitting places when they got up to dance. The path around the inside of the lodge was full of puddles. My older brother danced really hard, bending way down war-dance style. He danced and splashed mud on the blankets that the people had left at their sitting places. We thought that was so funny that my sister-in-law Four Women and I laughed and laughed. As we were dancing, day overtook us.

They customarily go to the woods then, very early in the morning, and so that is what we did. We left and arrived at the woods. Little Wíhaŋga was a large, heavy woman, and as she watched us perform the shooting rite she was supposed to do whatever we did. When they "shot" us we fell down and trembled. Eventually, we shot at her. She landed with a thud and said, "Ooof!" When she fell she just stayed on the ground.

"Do as they are doing," they would say to her, but she was a big woman and she just could not fall properly. She just could not learn. We continued working with her but finally we came back. There we remained all day at the Medicine Dance.—Next morning we left. Older brother left with his wife and I took down my tent and left with my grandmother.

There was an old lady called White Woman and another woman called Wave who were living at the place where my sister was living. Wave had a small child and had not wanted to go to the Medicine Dance. When we were getting ready to go to the Medicine Dance that old lady had told us, "If you see my nephew Red Horn there, pinch his ear, shake him up, point the direction to him and bring him back."—Wave was Red Horn's wife, and she was my sister. He was walking around there when we had arrived at the Medicine Dance. When we were ready to go home he was sitting in the shade beside a house. I then got down from the buggy and did as they had told me to do. I shook him but I did not take him by the ear. "Go get in the buggy," I said to him, "they said I was supposed to bring you back."

"Ho!" he said. He had a little suitcase that he grabbed and he got in the buggy. He drove. I let him drive the buggy. I brought him back and he laughed and laughed. "Ah, I was having such a good time and then with great cruelty they brought me back!" Then they all laughed at him.

We stayed there and picked cranberries until the end of the season, and then we moved back to my other older sister's place. There my older brother asked for the use of a horse, and there Four Women gave me some things: a blouse decorated with little silver brooches, a very nice one, and necklaces and a hair ornament and earrings. They gave me much finery and again I became a woman to be envied. I remained single and lived at my sister's place all winter long. Whenever there was a feast that winter my niece Queen of Thunder and I used to go to the feast, and we used to dance. There they accused me concerning a man. They gossiped at the winter feast. Alas, I was not even looking at any men. The man that they linked me with began writing letters to me. Well, after all, they were accusing him of it.

Then it became spring and in the spring we camped near Black River Falls where my sister was staying. I went to town to get some things and as I was coming back somebody behind me said, "Sister, sister." I stopped. It was my oldest brother. "Sister," he said, "whoever is saying things to you, I would like it if you did as he says. Little sister, your first husband was not any good. You would never have had any place for yourself and at his home you would have always been doing all the work. But this lad who is now talking to you lives alone. He knows how to care for himself. If you make a home someplace, then I will have someplace to go to visit." That is what my older brother said to me. I did not say anything. And just standing right there was that man, Bad Soldier. I still did not say anything. Then my brother went toward town and the man followed me home. We arrived at the place where my sister was living temporarily near Black River Falls.

After we arrived, the man took the water pail and went after some water. He got the water and brought it back and then later he went into the woods and brought back a lot of firewood. He began working for us, and sister was smiling broadly about it. He said to me, "If you would like it, tomorrow we can go to the courthouse and get our marriage license. If she hears about it, she will give up." He was talking about his wife. He had a wife and I did not want him, but he was persistent in courting me. "We will go to the courthouse and take out a marriage license so that woman cannot bother us," he said. So, that is what we did, we went to the courthouse and took out a marriage license. It was early spring when we did this.

Conversion to Peyote

At the time they built the dam at Hatfield, Wisconsin, we went there to live My husband worked there, taking care of the horses. They used many horses. He used to wake up very early in the morning and be the first one on the job. He fed and harnessed the horses and prepared for whatever the workmen were going to do. Then he would come home to eat and go back again. We were there all summer long and he worked steadily. Then in the fall there was a fair and some of the people said that they were going to go dancing. My husband said, "Suppose we go too?" "All right," I said. So we went dancing with a white man they called Tom Roddy. We went to two or three different towns and then we finally reached Milwaukee where we used to dance. The gathering place where we danced was called Wonderland Park. Now when I ask about it, no one knows about it. That must have been a long time ago.

Eventually we became bored. My husband said, "Shall we go back?" We got together our bedding, blankets, suitcases and clothing and he said, "Now we will go back." Then we stole away. Green Horn was with us. He carried one of our suitcases. There was a high wire-mesh fence and we threw our suitcases on the other side. We threw over the things my husband carried on his back. He rolled up the blankets and we threw that bundle over too. The men climbed up over the fence. My husband said, "Is it going to be all right for you?" "Yes," I said, "it is going to be all right. I am going to come across." —The men began walking on and I tucked my skirt between my legs like trousers and I climbed up the fence and over the top. When we were over on the other side we came upon some train tracks and following the tracks we headed for some woods. We walked along the tracks and reached the town. There we rode in a bus until we came to the depot and then we took the train to Black River Falls.

We did this in the fall and it was in the fall that they gave out money. At that time I said, "I am going to go to Nebraska." I got a bundle and a trunk ready and asked my husband to take me to the depot. They took me there and then I just went off to Nebraska. I arrived at the place where my sister lived. They call it Wakefield, Nebraska. My husband had said, "If it is possible at any time I will come there." He did so later in the fall.

There it was that we ate peyote. My husband never thought much of the Indian customs and whatever there was he mocked. But there he ate peyote and he realized something. Whatever the peyote was, he understood, and from that time we ate peyote. I had two children at that time and I was going to have my third child. When I had children I used to suffer. I used to have a hard time and really suffered until I finally gave birth. There in Nebraska in the wintertime when we were with my sister I was about to give birth. I told her, "I think I am going to be sick." She said, "Little sister, when people are in that condition they use peyote. They have children without much suffering. Perhaps you can do that. You always suffer so much. This way you will have it easily."

"All right, whatever you say, I will do." That was the first time I was to eat peyote. My sister did that for me. She prepared it for me and gave me some and I took it. Then I soon had the baby. I had a boy.

From that time on whenever they held peyote meetings we all attended. Mother, father, we all used to attend the peyote meetings. One time something happened to me. I had three children then and I used to be rather shy. In the evening if I sat in the meeting, that would be all I did. I would just sit there. I would sit there all night. In the morning when they went outside, then I would go out too. It used to be hard for me. Some got up any time and went outside. But I used to think if I stood up, everybody would look at me. I used to respect people. Once when I was eating peyote—I ate quite a bit, perhaps twenty buttons—this is what happened to me.

I was sitting with bowed head. We were all sitting with bowed heads. We were supposed to ponder. We prayed. We were all doing this. We were having our peyote meeting. In the west the sun thundered and made terrible noises. I was hearing this sound. Oh, the sky was very black! I had my head bowed, but this is what I saw. The sky was terribly black. The storm clouds came whirling. When the storm clouds came the sky would become black. Big winds came.—The ground kept caving in. This is the way I saw it. It thundered repeatedly and the sky was dark. The storm was approaching and people came running. The women had shawls about them and they had bundles on their backs. They were carrying something on their backs, and they came running. There was a mighty wind and their clothes were blowing about them. They stumbled and rolled over and over. Then they would get up and run again. And there they came by. It did not seem to me as if it were windy. That is what I was seeing. And I thought to myself, "Where are they fleeing? Nowhere on this earth is there any place to run to. There is not any place for life. Where are they saying that they are fleeting to? Jesus is the only place to flee to." That is what I thought.

Then I saw Jesus standing there. I saw that He had one hand raised high. The right hand, high in the air. I saw that He was standing there. Whatever He was doing, I was to do also. I was to pray, I thought I stood up. Though I was in the midst of all those people my thoughts were not on that. I stood up because I saw Jesus. I will pray to Him, I thought. I stood up and raised my arm. I prayed. I asked for a good life—thanking God who gave me life. This I did. And as the drum was beating, my body shook in time to the beat. I was unaware of it. I was just very contented. I never knew such pleasure as this. There was a sensation of great joyousness. Now I was an angel. That is how I saw myself. Because I had wings I was supposed to fly but I could not quite get my feet off of the ground.—I wanted to fly right away, but I could not because my time is not yet completed.

Then the drummers stopped singing. When they reached the end of the song they stopped. Then I sat down on the ground. I knew when I ate peyote that they were using something holy. That way is directed toward God. Nothing else on earth is holy. If someone speaks about something holy he does not know what he is talking about. But if someone sees something holy at a peyote meeting, that is really true. They are able to understand things concerning God. I understood that this religion is holy. It is directed toward God. I even saw Jesus!

After we had been in Nebraska about a year we lived at the home of my older sister Hińakega and her husband. My husband used to go out husking corn. Then in the spring we went to visit my aunt. Dog Howling she was called. My aunt was also my husband's niece Her husband's name was Sound of Thunder. He said to my husband, "There is something you can do. You are a good worker, you can farm. You can go to the agency and rent some land to farm.—Then I can let you have one of my horses and you can pay me whenever you have the money." That is what he did. He went to the agency there in Nebraska.

Among my relatives there was a man named Little Wolf. He had some land out in the country. The family lived near the town of Winnebago but Little Wolf's land was out toward the town of Emerson. He had eighty acres with a house and a barn. That is what he rented to us. We lived there and they let us charge the cost of horses. We had a lot of little things and the people gave us furniture. There we lived and there my husband farmed. We were going to make a living for ourselves. I planted a vegetable garden. Then we had our oldest boy and he died. Then Hénaga, our second boy was born and he died while he was still small. Then Hínuga, the first daughter was born and then Hágaga, the third son. There we farmed and whenever there was a peyote meeting we attended it.

On one occasion my husband gave me four dozen chickens. He said, "This is from the last of my mother's money that was at the agency. I did this because I thought that you would like it. If my mother were living she would not begrudge you anything she had. That is why I did this. I bought four dozen chickens with this money." He brought chickens for me and so I used to care for a flock of chickens. When they laid eggs I gathered them and in the spring I tended to the nests. We were getting along there quite well. In the fall he would have the huskers come including white men, and he would have them husk corn. There was a lot of corn. There it lay reaped, high like a hill, and after he had it husked they loaded it in a big wagon. He covered it and hauled the wagon to Thurston to sell the corn. He did this several days in a row.

Once I said, "How much are you earning from what we are doing?" He replied, "I paid for what we owed during the year. We owed several hundred dollars." We were paying our bills with all that corn he had been hauling. We had charged mules and even a big wagon and all kinds of big equipment. We must have owed many hundreds of dollars. That is what he was paying.

"Oh," I said, "I have been thinking and have reached this conclusion. Here we get up early in the morning and we farm and we continue doing this until nighttime. Even in the evening we work in this way. But we never see any money. That is what I think. Never any money! If we lived in Wisconsin and picked things as they do there we would have our money. Here we say we are farming and we make money for the white people and we never see any money. I do not like this," I said.

"Well," he said, "we are our own masters. Who is boss over us?" Then he said, "I thought of something we might do." "All right," I said. So, we sold the machinery and bought an automobile. He bought a car there in Nebraska and we went west to where the Sioux lived, near a town called Merriman, South Dakota. There we went to live and we rented a house and we lived there. People trapped there. Once a man named White Thunder and his wife came to us and they lived there too. They used to trap. There were a number of lakes where they used to trap muskrats. Another man named Last to Come came to us and used to trap too. They did fairly well. Muskrat hides were seventy-five cents and soon, in two or three days, they could trap a hundred. So they did quite well.

After we had been there for a while the Sioux adopted me. This was at Martin, South Dakota, where the Sioux lived. Peyotists used to come to us. We used to eat peyote with them. They even used to bring their sick people and we used to have peyote meetings for them. We rented a big house with White Thunder because the peyotists were coming to us. Later my husband rented a house in town and we lived there. He worked for a white man who had a big general store, a grocery store, and butcher shop. My husband worked for him. He took a truck and went to the Indians. The Sioux reservation was quite a distance and he used to go there with groceries to buy cowhides from the Sioux. He used to trade food for hides. It was difficult for the Sioux to get to town. When they came to town with their wagons to buy food they had to sleep there overnight. Therefore my husband would visit the Sioux, trading food for cowhides. The man who employed him bought the cowhides. We must have lived there about two years and he had a good job.

Once he said, "When spring comes they are going to have an election for the position of mailman. They put my name with

the rest. Whoever gets the most votes will be the mailman."
Some time later he said, "I was elected to the position of
mailman. I am going to start with a salary of eighty dollars
a month."

However, I was lonely. I had thought we would return home
and I said, "Stay here and be the mailman!" Then I began
crying. "As for myself, I am going to go home. I have a lot of
relatives. I am lonesome for my relatives, my brothers and
my sisters. I am not going to stay here. Stay here and be
the mailman!"

"Oh," he said, "I thought that you would be pleased. You
have a lot of relatives here." When they adopted me they gave
me four horses, some very fine horses. They thought a lot of
me, those Sioux brothers, sisters and uncles. But I was lonesome. I wept when I said I was going to go back.

"Well then," he said, "it can be that way. Who is our boss?
We can do that. We can go back." He then sold all the household goods at the place where we were living.

White Thunder had become annoyed with us for some reason and that had made me unhappy too. My husband said,
"We are going to go home. I am sending some of the things on
the train this evening. I am sending the trunks back on the
train. We ourselves will take only the good things like the
blankets. I am going to send the things and we will go home
without telling them. They do not like us."

"All right," I said.—We left early the next morning without
telling anybody. Whatever the circumstances, I am always the
one who is spoiling things. If we had stayed there I would have
learned to speak Sioux. We probably both would have learned
to speak Sioux. Instead I thought more of my relatives and so
we came back to Nebraska.

We came back to my sister's place and lived there. Then my
husband said, "Let us go back to Wisconsin." My older brother, Hágaga, then said, "We want to go back to Wisconsin too,
but wait until I do a few things and then it will be time to go."
There they made my older brother a peyote leader. They gave
him the peyote paraphernalia. Then we came back.

We came back to Black River Falls. In Wisconsin they hated
the peyote people. We came back and some people did not

even talk to us. The only people who would talk to us were our closest relatives. People supposedly said that we were not to live any place and not live together. They were going to scatter us. They watched us with harmful intent.

Tom Roddy in town used to like the Indians. The Indians were his friends. He had land below the mission. They called it "Frog Place." "Live there," he said, "nobody is going to say anything to you." So we went there to live. Then Little Thunder, Crosses the Sea and other people who preached to each other came there from Nebraska. Wherever there were peyote people they all came forth. There were quite a few of us. We used to have meetings. Every Saturday night we had a meeting. Every time we had a meeting someone got up and testified. A woman named Walks Through the Village testified and told about what we were going to experience. It was good to hear.

Every Saturday we used to have a peyote meeting. We had a gunny sack full of peyote and that is why we were able to have meetings every Saturday. My husband did not know the songs very well, nor did Young Thunder nor Thunders Suddenly Amongst Us. Only older brother knew them but they sang anyway and older brother was the leader. Black Chief, Young Thunder's son, was a small boy at that time, about four or five years old—so that must have been about 1908.

Eventually it was time to pick blueberries and we moved away to pick blueberries. Then blueberry time was over. Wherever we lived, we peyote people lived together in a group. After all, the others hated us. When the blueberry season ended we moved back to live on land owned by Young Thunder's wife, on top of a hill that used to be called White Brow's land. We made ourselves some big tents. Then we heard that the Nebraskans were coming. At the same time the other people were getting ready to have a powwow. They were saying, "If any of these peyote eaters come we will beat them senseless." They were going to have a powwow and we were going to have a peyote meeting.

At that time the Nebraskans had a lot of money from selling their land and they were enjoying themselves. They filled two train coaches with Indians. They even had their drums and they sang in the train, drumming loudly. They got off at

Black River Falls. We went there with our wagons. Mother and father had a wagon and Young Thunder also had one. Thunders Suddenly Amongst Us had a wagon too. But how many could we bring? There were a lot of them. They used up all the wagons and then they filled a big hay rack. A big group of Nebraska Indians came. Eventually we were going to have a big peyote meeting. They came to us and brought a big tepee. Previously brother and others had cut big poles and trimmed them and covered them over with canvas—so the visitors would have a tent to stay in.

Before we had the peyote meeting someone there foretold that at the beginning of the evening an old bull would visit us. "He is going to come to us," he said, "and then on the second night that we are going to meet, a black mule is going to come to us." They knew this.

Then it was time to put up the tepee. There were all kinds of Winnebago, Nebraskans and a lot of Wisconsin Indians. It was very pleasant. The Medicine Lodge people were at odds with us. We were there in such a pitiful state so that when our relatives came we were very happy. We were cooking all about trying to feed everybody. Industrious women were there too and did a lot of cooking. They even brought their own food.

Then it was evening and time for the bull to come. In the evening before they went inside the tepee, a horse-drawn wagon used for hauling wood arrived, karaŕaš! It was a drunken man —and he just came running with the horses. He was singing and he turned in there. "Get in your children! The children!" they all shouted. The tents were scattered quite a distance around the tepee and he drove around the tepee. He was an old man driving a white horse. The old man had very white hair. He came running the horse. They spoke with him gently for a while and eventually they let him go home unharmed.

Then we held the peyote meeting and the tepee was full. Those that hated us came and saw their relatives who had come from Nebraska. Those who were not peyotists and had talked about beating us came and visited in our midst. They came and visited us to see their relatives.

We held our meeting for two nights and on the second night

the black mule came, Naqiga the son of Light at a Distance.
They used to call him Old Man Naqiga. He came there drunk.
He jeered as soon as he arrived. My husband was a guide.
He said to the drunk, "Grandfather, sit down. Sit down. If
you do not listen to me I am going to tie you up." The drunk
became angry. He was violent. "Well," said my husband, "I
told you, grandfather. I told you in a very polite way, 'I am
going to tie you up,' I said." There was a big tent attached to
the tepee and he let him sit there at the entrance of the tent.
He tied his arms in back of him and tied him to a tent pole.
"All right, sit there. Whatever you are saying does not
matter. You are going to frighten the children running around
here. That is why I am saying this." There he sat and the meeting began.

Later on they asked someone to speak at the meeting.
Squeaking Wing was going to be the one to speak. Then he
stood up and gave thanks. "There is much to be thankful for,"
he was saying. "Our relatives here do not know God. These are
my childhood friends. My nephews, these are my childhood
friends. It is good."—He was thanking them that they brought
peyote to Wisconsin. He said, "They are working for God.
They are doing a good thing here. We came to them and this
evening we are having a very fine meeting. God is doing this.
This religion He started. If I spoke here all night I could never
say all that there is to say about God's word, there is so much
good to tell."

Then the drunk said, "Yes! Yes, that is true! You are bad,
very bad, a big drunk, a fighter, biting off people's noses! Yes,
God made a lot of people! You are never going to bite off all
the people's noses!" Squeaking Wing laughed, "That is my
uncle who is speaking. What he is saying does not matter. He
is just petting me." And we continued through the night until
day came upon us.

In the morning we again began cooking. Then from that
place we were going to go back to Nebraska. Twice we stayed
up until daylight. Peyotists continued to arrive. Some took
peyote there for the first time. The local people, however, never
said anything good about us.

We left Young Thunder and Thunders Suddenly Amongst

Us there. We went to Nebraska when everybody left. Some of the Wisconsin Winnebago went to Nebraska with their relatives. We were in Nebraska for a while and then we returned. My husband and I returned and from that time we ate peyote. Brother also used to eat peyote—but things have changed now.

At first, whoever had been living together had to stay together. The bad men reformed. The women also stopped being bad. They took their marriage vows seriously. They were like that but eventually two or three men left their wives. They did again as they had done long before. They even married other women.—Before that happened, however, they all made a big building in Nebraska for their meeting place and there they used to hold their peyote meetings. They used to preach to one another there. They chose twelve men who were educated and there they used to read. They used to tell what God did when He came to earth. They used to preach in their group.

Later, one of the men who had left his wife built himself a new house. The men who had left their wives and married other women borrowed his old house. There they had their meetings. There they established a peyote meeting place. All they did was sing. That was called the Half Moon rite. They began only with singing. They did not have any preaching along with it.

Over at John Rave's meeting place it was called the Cross Fire rite. That group preached among themselves. The fact that they were preaching to one another touched a sensitive spot and that is why some of them made their own peyote meeting place. Over there at the Half Moon place all they did was sing. That was the beginning of the Half Moon. Yes, the peyote religion was like that. Today the Half Moon is the only rite that is held. Eventually the old men dropped peyote. The young were the ones who continued it.

Only the Half Moon continues today and the peyote leader himself was driven out. They drove him out, they scolded him. That is what they did. "What is he doing for us?" they said. That was my brother, Big Winnebago—the one the white people call Crashing Thunder. However, he said, "There is only one God. I am old. I cannot sit up all night long. It is all right. I do not mind." Today he belongs to the church; "In the church I listen to a little preaching." That is what he does

IV
IMAGE AND ANTI-IMAGE

If white Americans seem to have successfully avoided a knowledge of the continent's first inhabitants, they have not been able to avoid thinking about them—especially so whenever they let their imaginations ramble a bit among the realities of the New World. For whenever the white man thought of the New World—whether he saw it as a garden or as a howling wilderness—he inevitably thought of the Indian. And just as he developed contrasted images of America as another paradise and as a dark place of sorrow and penance, so he developed contrasted images of the Indian as a child of the Golden Age and as blood-red savage. The trouble, of course, was that neither image had much to do with the Indian himself, though they had a great deal to do with the image-makers. Both images were, essentially, deeply derogatory and demonstrate in yet another way the Western habit of looking at the world and its different peoples only in light of their potential *use*. American letters in the belletristic sense of that word reveals this tendency with the utmost fidelity, from its colonial beginnings through its struggles toward nationalism, its brief flowering of romanticism, and on into the realist period. It has only been in the post-realist period that American men and women of letters have begun to learn to look with different eyes at what had until now seemed a wholly familiar object. It has been one of the unique efforts of contemporary American writers to attempt to imagine what a non-ethnocentric literature might be like, and in this effort these writers have tried to see the Indian in a culture-free way. The inclusion here of Berger, Snyder, and Paul Jenkins is thus intended not only as a commentary on this hopeful development in our culture but also as a comment on that ugly ethnocentric past as manifested in Freneau, in Parkman, and in our national folklore. In that past wherein there is so much

485

to shame us all only a few solitary giants such as Herman Melville stand out as writers who attempted to rise above the limitations of vision built into the culture around them.

Luther Standing Bear (Sioux), N. Scott Momaday (Kiowa), Vine Deloria, Jr. (Sioux), James Welch (Blackfeet), Hyemeyohsts Storm (Cheyenne), Ray Young Bear (Sac and Fox), and Simon Ortiz (Pueblo) are distinguished representatives of an Indian renaissance which has forced white writers to re-evaluate the Indian and his part in the American experience. In this they resemble the Black writers whose voices have in recent years forced a rethinking of that aspect of our history. To conclude this collection with the words of these Americans who insist on being remembered and heard instead of ignored and forgotten may be a sign as well as an indication of hope. In addition, it is proof (if any should be needed) that the North American Indian has not vanished but is precisely where he has always been: at the center and heart of American history.

PHILIP FRENEAU

The Indian Convert

An Indian, who lived at Muskingum, remote,
Was teazed by a parson to join his dear flock,
To throw off his blanket and put on a coat,
And of grace and religion to lay in a stock.

The Indian long slighted an offer so fair,
Preferring to preaching his fishing and fowling;
A sermon to him was a heart full of care,
And singing but little superior to howling.

At last by persuasion and constant harassing
Our Indian was brought to consent to be good;
He saw that the malice of Satan was pressing,
And the means to repel him not yet understood.

Of heaven, one day, when the parson was speaking,
And painting the beautiful things of the place,
The convert, who something substantial was seeking,
Rose up, and confessed he had doubts in the case.—

Said he, Master Minister, this place that you talk of,
Of things for the stomach, pray what has it got;
Has it liquors in plenty?—If so I'll soon walk off
And put myself down in the heavenly spot.

You fool (said the preacher) no liquors are there!
The place I'm describing is most like our meeting,
Good people, all singing, with preaching and prayer;
They live upon these without eating or drinking.

From Fred Lewis Pattee, ed., *The Poems of Philip Freneau* (Princeton 1903), vol. 2, pp. 369-73.

But the doors are all locked against folks that are wicked;
And you, I am fearful, will never get there:—
A life of Repentance must purchase the ticket,
And few of you, Indians, can buy it, I fear.

Farewell (said the Indian) I'm none of your mess;
On victuals, so airy, I faintish should feel,
I cannot consent to be lodged in a place
Where's there's nothing to eat and but little to steal.

The Indian Student

Or, Force of Nature

From Susquehanna's farthest springs
Where savage tribes pursue their game,
(His blanket tied with yellow strings,)
A shepherd of the forest came.

Not long before, a wandering priest
Expressed his wish, with visage sad—
"Ah, why (he cried) in Satan's waste,
"Ah, why detain so fine a lad?

"In white-man's land there stands a town
"Where learning may be purchased low—
"Exchange his blanket for a gown.
"And let the lad to college go."—

From long debate the council rose,
And viewing Shalum's tricks with joy
To Cambridge Hall, o'er wastes of snows,
They sent the copper-coloured boy.

One generous chief a bow supplied,
This gave a shaft, and that a skin;
The feathers, in vermillion dyed,
Himself did from a turkey win:

Thus dressed so gay, he took his way
O'er barren hills, alone, alone!
His guide a star, he wandered far,
His pillow every night a stone.

At last he came, with foot so lame,
Where learned men talk heathen Greek,
And Hebrew lore is gabbled o'er,
To please the Muses,—Twice a week.

Awhile he writ, awhile he read,
Awhile he conned their grammar rules—
(An Indian savage so well bred
Great credit promised to the schools.)

Some thought he would in law excel,
Some said in physic he would shine;
And one that knew him, passing well,
Beheld, in him, a sound Divine.

But those of more discerning eye
Even then could other prospects show,
And saw him lay his Virgil by
To wander with his dearer bow.

The tedious hours of study spent,
The heavy-moulded lecture done,
He to the woods a hunting went,
Through lonely wastes he walked, he run.

No mystic wonders fired his mind;
He sought to gain no learned degree,
But only sense enough to find
The squirrel in the hollow tree.

The shady bank, the purling stream,
The woody wild his heart possessed,
The dewy lawn, his morning dream
In fancy's gayest colours dressed.

"And why (he cried) did I forsake
"My native wood for gloomy walls;
"The silver stream, the limpid lake
"For musty books and college halls.

"A little could my wants supply—
"Can wealth and honour give me more;
"Or, will the sylvan god deny
"The humble treat he gave before?

"Let seraphs gain the bright abode,
"And heaven's sublimest mansions see—
"I only bow to Nature's God—
"The land of shades will do for me.

"These dreadful secrets of the sky
"Alarm my soul with chilling fear—
"Do planets in their orbits fly,
"And is the earth, indeed, a sphere?

"Let planets still their course pursue,
"And comets to the centre run—
"In Him my faithful friend I view,
"The image of my God—the Sun.

"Where Nature's ancient forests grow,
"And mingled laurel never fades,
"My heart is fixed;—and I must go
"To die among my native shades."

He spoke, and to the western springs,
(His gown discharged, his money spent,
His blanket tied with yellow strings,)
The shepherd of the forest went.

The Indian Burying Ground

In spite of all the learned have said,
　　I still my old opinion keep;
The posture, that we give the dead,
　　Points out the soul's eternal sleep.

Not so the ancients of these lands—
　　The Indian, when from life released,
Again is seated with his friends,
　　And shares again the joyous feast.[1]

His imaged birds, and painted bowl,
　　And vension, for a journey dressed,
Bespeak the nature.of the soul,
　　Activity, that knows no rest.

His bow, for action ready bent,
　　And arrows, with a head of stone,
Can only mean that life is spent,
　　And not the old ideas gone.

Thou, stranger, that shalt come this way,
　　No fraud upon the dead commit—
Observe the swelling turf, and say
　　They do not lie, but here they sit.

Here sti'l a lofty rock remains,
　　On which the curious eye may trace
(Now wasted, half, by wearing rains)
　　The fancies of a ruder race.

Here still an aged elm aspires,
　　Beneath whose far-projecting shade
(And which the shepherd still admires)
　　The children of the forest played!

[1] The North American Indians bury their dead in a sitting posture; decorating the corpse with wampum, the images of birds, quadrupeds, &c: And (if that of a warrior) with bows, arrows, tomhawks, and other military weapons.—*Freneau's note.*

There oft a restless Indian queen
  (Pale Shebah, with her braided hair)
And many a barbarous form is seen
  To chide the man that lingers there.

By midnight moons, o'er moistening dews;
  In habit for the chase arrayed,
The hunter still the deer pursues,
  The hunter and the deer, a shade!

And long shall timorous fancy see
  The painted chief, and pointed spear,
And Reason's self shall bow the knee
  To shadows and delusions here.

HAROLD W. THOMPSON

Tom Quick

The earliest of the very famous Injun-haters, and the most single-minded of whom legend tells, was the man whose monument at Milford, Pennsylvania, bears the inscription:

Tom Quick, the Indian Slayer;
or
The Avenger of the Delaware

On the north side another inscription tells us that "Thomas Quick, Sr., father of Tom Quick, his oldest child, emigrated from Holland to America, and settled on this spot in 1733." It is likely that this was the same Thomas Quick who took the oath of allegiance in Ulster County, New York, on September 1, 1689, the same person who, on July 20, 1684, bought from an Indian for eight hundred schepels of wheat a piece of land at Mombaccus. Tom's father, therefore, was originally a New Yorker. Certainly many of Tom's exploits were performed in the upper reaches of the Delaware River in New York State, and the antiquary who did more than anyone else to preserve tales about the Indian-slayer was G. E. Quinlan, the historian of Sullivan County, who, in 1851 published at Monticello, New York, a fascinating little book about a man whose deeds are part of our goriest legend.

Tom was born in 1734 in a region long the favorite hunting ground of the Delaware (Leni-Lenape) Indians. The folk say that he cut his teeth on an arrowhead and in childhood chewed lead slugs; that he was one of the first settlers in that section to speak with Indians in their own tongue; that he hunted with the red brothers, learned their woodcraft, and adopted their

From the book *Body, Boots, and Britches* by Harold W. Thompson, Copyright 1939 by Harold W. Thompson. Renewal Copyright © 1967 by Dr. Marian Thompson. Reprinted by permission of J. B. Lippincott Company.

ways of life. When his white brothers were attending school and assisting on the farm, Tom was providing the family with fish and game. He grew to be the tall, gaunt frontiersman of legend, with high cheekbones that resembled an Indian's; his eyes were gray and piercing, his beard was dark, his body was clothed in deerskin.

In his youth began what we still call in New York State the French and Indian wars. While Sir William Johnson was keeping his Mohawks true to the British Crown, the Delawares south of them were restless. They had long hated the Mengwe (Iroquois), who, regarding them as a defeated and subject race, called them "The Women." They needed little prompting from the French to recall that Dutch and British settlers on their river had cheated them abominably in the purchase of land. Before they were pushed back into the sunset, they would strike a blow that would prove them not women. Some of them had eaten the bread of the Quicks, but if there was to be war, it should begin with the family whose mills and farm were best worth looting. After the English General Braddock's defeat, in July of 1755, the Lenape "dug up the hatchet."

One evening Tom, with his father and a brother-in-law, had crossed the Delaware to cut hoop-poles. From ambush a volley was poured from Indian rifles, and the elder Quick fell mortally wounded. The two younger men seized him and attempted to drag him toward the river, but he gallantly and sternly commanded them to leave a dying man, to spread the alarm at Milford. When Tom reached the river, the Indians opened fire again. He fell, tripped by a ball that had struck the heel of his shoe; but directly he was on his feet again, zigzagging across the ice to safety. Then and there he swore eternal vengeance upon the murderers of his father. Too much of an individualist to join the colonial militia, he would bide his time like an Indian; one hatchet would never be buried.

Some two years after the termination of the French and Indian war, Tom entered the Decker tavern on the Neversink —a dark, silent man under a coonskin cap. At the bar an Indian named Muskwink, bold with rum, invited him to drink. For answer Tom returned a curt insult. Muskwink began to recount his exploits in the recent war, soon reaching the story of how he had shot the elder Quick; he grimaced, he imitated the death-agonies of his victim, he exhibited a set of silver buttons. Snatching a French musket from the wall, Tom drove Muskwink out of the door. For a mile the Avenger and his victim marched up the road leading from Wurtsboro to Carpenter's Point. Then Tom spoke, "Indian dog, you'll kill no more white men." A heavy charge of slugs struck the Indian in the back between the shoulders; he pitched onto his face. Putting the silver buttons into his own pouch, Tom dragged the body of Muskwink to an uprooted tree, kicked some dead leaves and dirt upon it, returned the musket to the tavern, and left the neighborhood.

Tom's next exploit was so bloody that he never told it until shortly before his own death, when he confessed to Jacob Quick of Callicoon that once he had carried his vengeance beyond the killing of warriors to the extermination of an entire family. Probably it was not long after the Muskwink affair that he was hunting at Butler's Rift, when, from a hiding place in the reeds he saw a canoe approaching filled with an Indian brave, a woman, and three children. Rising from the reeds, Tom ordered the Indian to shore in a tone so grim and with a gesture so unmistakable that the Delaware cried out, "The hatchet is buried!" Tom remembered that this was one who had eaten at his father's board, one who was thought to have taken part in several outrages upon the frontier. The Avenger's rifle cracked, the Indian leaped from his canoe and "after a few convulsive throes" died in the river. Tom then dispatched the woman and killed the two older children, who, he remembered, "squauked like crows." The third child, an infant, smiled up at him so sweetly that his heart wavered until the memory returned of a ravished frontier, and he dashed out the child's brains. When asked how he could bring himself to such a deed, he answered in a proverb still used in our countryside, "Nits make lice."

Among the folk the favorite tale about Tom concerns the railsplitting. The same story is related about Tim Murphy and other heroes of our frontier; it is even told of Daniel Boone in Kentucky and has claim to being the classic trickster-story of the American frontier. One spring Tom was splitting rails in the Mamakating Valley for a man named Westbrook. Temporarily off guard, he had left his rifle standing against a tree and was driving a wedge into an unusually tough log when he looked up to see seven armed Indians grinning at his predicament. That might have been the end of his railsplitting, but the Indians always made the mistake of wishing to share their fun with an entire village by taking their captive to a place of torture. The secret of Tom's own success was that he was an individualist who hunted redskins alone and shot on sight. In this case, he agreed to go with them quietly if they would help him finish splitting his log. The proposal appealed to two traits which you still find in our Indians—their curiosity and their ironic sense of humor. Dropping their rifles, they ranged themselves as directed, three on one side of the log, four on the other, each with his hands in the split. At Tom's word of command they pulled manfully, but instead of driving the wedge in farther, Tom knocked it out and beheld the pleasing sight of seven enemies caught by the hands in his log. Without wasting powder he swung his ax; he was nearer by seven to his goal of one hundred slain Indians.

Another contribution of the folk to the saga of Tom is the tale of the Buck with Seven Skins. Tom was about to winter at the cabin of a friend who was happy to have so mighty a hunter provide food through the harsh months of snow. An agreement was made between Tom and an Indian who drifted into the neighborhood that they should go hunting together; Tom should have the venison, the Indian should have the skins, which, of course, could be traded for firewater and other coveted goods. Deer were plentiful: at the close of the first afternoon the Indian declared that he was quite satisfied with seven skins, which he proceeded to pack on his back. When Tom returned to the settlements next day with the promised venison plus skins, his friends asked how he happened to come by the hides. "Oh," responded Tom, "I killed a buck with seven skins on his back." Sure enough, there was a single bullet-hole through each of the pelts. The grim reply is matched by another which he made when asked how he managed to keep in such fine condition two guns which he pulled from concealment in a hollow tree: "Every critter, two legged or four, has grease under its hide somewhere." If you are ever trudging through the Shawangunk region and find an old gun or two hidden in a decayed tree-trunk, you can guess who put them there.

Of all the stories which Quinlan gathered about Tom, the most poetical concerns a conversation between Quick and one of his victims who, stopping at Quick's winter quarters, invited him to go hunting next day. Convinced that the Indian meant no good, Tom got up stealthily in the night, unloaded the redskin's rifle, substituted ashes for most of the powder, and put back the ball. Let Quinlan tell the tale—it is his masterpiece of narrative:

The next morning the savage slyly inserted the ramrod in the chamber of the rifle, examined the priming etc., and seemed satisfied that all was right. This and some other circumstances confirmed Tom in the belief that mischief was brewing.

There was considerable snow on the ground, and the hunters found it quite inconvenient to tread through it, and apparently to render the walking easier, the Indian proposed that one of them should go ahead to break the path. To this Tom readily agreed, and the Indian was greatly pleased when Tom made no objection to be the first to go in advance.

After they had proceeded in this way a mile or two, and had come to a very lonely place, Tom heard the Indian's gun snap, and the powder flash in the pan. Tom looked back and asked what the Indian had seen.

"A fine buck," was the reply.

The Indian reprimed his gun, and they went on. Pretty soon Tom heard another snap and flash.

"Well, brother Indian," inquired he, "what did you see this time?"

"An eagle swept over the forest," replied the other as he again primed the gun.

"Brother Indian," said Tom, "the snow is deep. I am tired. You go ahead."

"Brother Yankee speaks well," said the savage gloomily, and took his station in advance.

Tom leveled his rifle.

"Lying Indian dog!" exclaimed he, "what do you see now?"

"The spirit land," was the reply, as the Indian hung his head and drew over it his blanket.

There was that time when two Indians seized him while he was sleeping in a cabin near Port Jervis. One Delaware loaded himself with Tom's deerskins and walked in advance; the other, carrying the two Indians' rifles—one ready cocked—marched in the rear. With his hands bound behind him, Tom was quietly obedient until they reached a dizzy ledge far above the river. The first Indian, laden with the furs, trudged on stolidly; but Tom, pretending to be giddy, advanced only under the compulsion of blows from the man behind him. Finally, at the narrowest place in the path, he backed against the cliff, giving signs of the most craven fear. Taunting him, the second Indian administered a beating and attempted to seize hold of Tom to push him along, when by an "adroit movement" the Indian-slayer put a foot to his captor's stomach and the savage toppled over the brink. Fifty feet below, the brave landed with a broken back in the crotch of a button-ball tree, the guns dropping farther to the river. Tom was away.

At another time, in the autumn of 1788 or 1789, he escaped from a party of Indians because his youthful guard was so inexperienced as to drink a horn of firewater that Tom had managed to secrete under his shirt. But his closest call came when he was a man of fifty, making his headquarters at a lonely cabin on the Lackawaxen. Creeping up in a rainstorm when a heavy fog was on the hills, a party of twenty warriors surprised Tom near nightfall when he was unarmed and unsuspecting the red brothers of the mist. Tired by a long journey and elated by the discovery of a keg of firewater, the Indians decided to remain at the cabin till morning. Tom was bound round and round and taken to the garret or loft; then, as extra precaution, a long piece of deerskin was attached to his bonds and to a rafter. As the evening wore on, he could hear from below the drunken shouts of his captors and the ingenious plans for the torture of their hated foe. By midnight the shouts died down; in the dark above, Tom felt for the first time the poison of despair.

Suddenly he heard the pad of unsteady moccasins on the ladder leading to his loft. A cruel face appeared, lit by a brand of fire; in the Indian's other hand was a knife. One enemy had decided not to wait for the ceremonial torture. There was triumph in his snake-eyes as he whispered, "My knife shall drink the blood of the panther who has slain my kindred." As the Indian lurched forward drunkenly for the death-blow, Tom fell on his face; the knife passed over his head; the Indian lost his balance, fell over Tom's body, struck his brow on a rafter, and lost consciousness. The brand fell to the wet floor, sputtered out. Death was deferred.

Rising to his feet again, Tom listened for signs that the sleeping Indians below had heard the impact of his foe's body. All was still. If only Quick could reach the unconscious Indian—or was he unconscious?—and get that knife. . . . Tom lowered himself and began to crawl softly on his belly. Alas, the Indian had rolled too far away—with a jerk the thong brought up the creeping frontiersman. For a second time that night he felt despair. Death had been deferred that it might be more terrible. As he crawled miserably back to his first position at the wall, his bare foot touched something colder than the floor. It was the knife.

Taking the handle between his teeth, Tom cut the thong that bound him to the rafter and the bonds which held his ankles; but his arms were still pinioned behind him. It seemed ages while he found a crevice in the side of the cabin, and, after attempts which left him bleeding and spent, managed to thrust the knife into a position which permitted him to back up and sever the strips which held his arms. To descend the ladder and pass the sleeping braves was too dangerous. Slowly and quietly he cut a hole in the bark roof, lowered himself, and ran naked through the forest to the settlement of Minisink, where he was clothed and revived.

You might suppose that even a valorous man would have abandoned that cabin. Tom returned a week later. When he found that thirty dollars' worth of skins had been stolen—not to mention the firewater—he was, as a neighbor said, "tearing mad."

The folk like two other tales of escape whose plots I must

give only briefly. There was the evening when an Indian slipped into the pig-pen, where he was pretty well protected by a rampart of logs, and squeezed a pig in the hope of making Tom run out unarmed to investigate. But Tom waited, gun in hand, at a crevice of his door to see what was causing the alarm. Just as Quick opened the crack a little, the unhappy pig bounced up; its rider's head appeared over the topmost log. When the scalplock appeared for a second time, the pig was released from his burden.

A similar stratagem was tried when Tom was living in a cabin near Handsome Eddy. Three Indians, studying his domestic habits, discovered that he always brought home a cow at evening. So they skirmished up a hill behind the cabin, removed the bell, and drove the cow farther away. Tom was on his way to bring home Bossy, when he paused, puzzled. That ringing was too violent, too continuous. (It must be explained that Indians were not cow-keepers; to this day, many Indians will not drink milk.) Tom made a long circle, passing the cow, and slipped from tree to tree till he was behind the Indians. One brave had dropped his rifle and was devoting all his energies to the bell; the other two had their rifles pointed toward the direction from which they hoped to see their foe emerge.

You can realize that the Indian-slayer's position was still one of great danger: there were three armed Indians, and Tom had only one shot. If only he could— A twig snapped under his foot; the Indians came to startled attention, but providentially Bossy appeared, furnishing an explanation for the sound. Providence had done its share; marksmanship must do the rest. At last Tom was in the position which he had sought: two coppery forms were in line. He fired his one shot, bringing down two Indians and slightly wounding the bell-ringer, who abandoned his rifle and sped through the forest.

Once and perhaps only once, Tom spared an Indian who was in his power. Hunting with a cousin one day on the Pennsylvania side of the Delaware, Quick saw an Indian in a canoe and sternly ordered him to land. The cousin, however, had a prejudice against murder. Tom relented, but he was morose all day, murmuring, in the only example of this dialect which

I have found: "Ho could ich, de dunder! out de cano tumbly!" ("By thunder, how I could have tumbled him out of his canoe!")

On his deathbed in 1795 or 1796, Tom grieved to think that he had not fulfilled his ambition to slay one hundred Indians. Quinlan was assured, by a gentleman who was present at Quick's death and his funeral, that Tom died of old age, but the folk have a better story. They say that the Indians, hearing of the demise of their foe, exhumed his body, cut it into pieces, and sent it to several villages. Then Tom had his hundred— for he had died of smallpox. At any rate, when a descendant of Tom—one who helped found the Chicago *Tribune* and reached the honor of being Lieutenant Governor of Illinois— erected in 1889 a monument to the old Indian-slayer, he didn't have a complete skeleton to bury. Says Frederick W. Crumb, who has written the best recent account of Tom:

> Buried under the shaft is a chestnut coffin which contains the few mortal remains of this early American. The coffin contains a glass jar which in turn holds fragments of the original coffin, the tibia of the right leg, a piece of the skull that overhung the socket of the eye, and a phalanx bone from his right hand—perhaps it was his trigger-finger.

THOMAS BANGS THORPE

The Disgraced Scalp Lock

Occasionally may be seen on the Ohio and Mississippi rivers singularly hearty-looking men that puzzle a stranger as to their history and age. Their forms always exhibit a powerful development of muscle and bone; their cheeks are prominent, and you would pronounce them men enjoying perfect health, in middle life, were it not for their heads, which, if not bald, will be sparsely covered with gray hair. Another peculiarity about these people is that they have a singular knowledge of all the places on the river, every bar and bend is spoken of with precision and familiarity—every town is recollected before it was half as large as the present, or no town at all. Innumerable places are marked out, where once was an Indian fight, or a rendezvous of robbers. The manner, the language, and the dress of these individuals are all characteristic of sterling common sense; the manner modest yet full of self-reliance, the language strong and forcible, from superiority of mind rather than from education, the dress studied for comfort rather than fashion; on the whole, you insensibly become attached to them, and court their society. The good humor, the frankness, the practical sense, the reminiscences, the powerful frame, all indicate a character at the present day extinct and anomalous; and such indeed is the case, for your acquaintance will be one of the few remaining people now spoken of as the "last of the flat-boatmen."

Thirty years ago the navigation of the Western waters was confined to this class of men; the obstacles presented to the pursuit in those swift running and wayward waters had to be overcome by physical force alone; the navigator's arm grew strong as he guided his rude craft past the "snag" and "sawyer," or kept off the no-less-dreaded bar. Besides all this, the deep forests that covered the river banks concealed the wily Indian,

From Thomas Bangs Thorpe: *The Spirit of the Times* (1842) 12, 229, 230.

who gloated over the shedding of blood. The qualities of the frontier warrior associated themselves with the boatman, while he would, when at home, drop both these characters in the cultivator of the soil. It is no wonder, then, that they were brave, hardy, and open-handed men; their whole lives were a round of manly excitement, they were hyperbolical in thought and in deed, when most natural, compared with any other class of men. Their bravery and chivalrous deeds were performed without a herald to proclaim them to the world—they were the mere incidents of a border life, considered too common to outlive the time of a passing wonder. Obscurity has obliterated nearly the actions and the men—a few of the latter still exist, as if to justify their wonderful exploits, which now live almost exclusively as traditions.

Among the flat-boatmen, there were none that gained the notoriety of Mike Fink: his name is still remembered along the whole of the Ohio as a man who excelled his fellows in everything, particularly in his rifle shot, which was acknowledged to be unsurpassed. Probably no man ever lived who could compete with Mike Fink in the latter accomplishment; strong as Hercules, free from all nervous excitement, possessed of perfect health, and familiar with his weapon from childhood, he raised the rifle to his eye, and having once taken sight, it was as firmly fixed as if buried in a rock. It was Mike's pride, and he rejoiced on all occasions where he could bring it into use, whether it was turned against the beast of prey or the more savage Indian, and in his day these last named were the common foe with which Mike and his associates had to contend. On the occasion that we would particularly introduce Mike to the reader, he had bound himself for a while to the pursuits of trade, until a voyage from the head waters of the Ohio, and down the Mississippi, could be completed; heretofore, he had kept himself exclusively to the Ohio, but a liberal reward, and some curiosity, prompted him to extend his business character beyond his ordinary habits and inclinations. In accomplishment of this object, he was lolling carelessly over the big "sweep" that guided the "flat" on which he officiated; the current of the river bore the boat swiftly along, and made his labor light; his eye glanced around him, and he broke forth in ecstasies at what he saw and felt. If there is a river in the world that merits the name of beautiful, it is the Ohio, when its channel is "Without o'erflowing, full."

The scenery is everywhere soft—there are no jutting rocks, no steep banks, no high hills, but the clear and swift current laves beautiful and undulating shores, that descend gradually to the water's edge. The foliage is rich and luxuriant, and its outlines in the water are no less distinct than when it is relieved against the sky. Interspersed along its route are islands, as beautiful as ever figured in poetry as the land of fairies; enchanted spots indeed, that seem to sit so lightly on the water, that you almost expect them as you approach to vanish into dreams. So late as when Mike Fink disturbed the solitudes of the Ohio with his rifle, the canoe of the Indian was hidden in the little recesses along the shore; they moved about in their frail barks like spirits, and clung, in spite of the constant encroachments of civilization, to the places which tradition had designated as the happy places of a favored people.

Wild and uncultivated as Mike appeared, he loved nature, and had a soul that sometimes felt, while admiring it, an exalted enthusiasm. The Ohio was his favorite stream; from where it runs no stronger than a gentle rivulet, to where it mixes with the muddy Mississippi, Mike was as familiar as a child could be with the meanderings of a flower garden. He could not help noticing with sorrow the desecrating hand of improvement as he passed along, and half soliloquizing, and half addressing his companions, he broke forth, "I knew these parts afore a squatter's axe had blazed a tree; 'twasn't then pulling a —— sweep to get a living, but pulling the trigger done the business. Those were times, to see; a man might call himself lucky. What's the use of improvements? When did cutting down trees make deer more plenty? Who ever cotched a bar by building a log cabin, or twenty on 'em? Who ever found wild buffalo, or a brave Indian in a city? Where's the fun, the frolicking, the fighting? Gone! gone! The rifle won't make a man a living now —he must turn nigger and work. If forests continue to be used up, I may yet be smothered in a settlement. Boys, this 'ere life won't do—I'll stick to the broad horn 'cordin' to contract, but once done with it, I'm off for a frolic. If the Choctas, or Cherokees, or the Massassip don't give us a brush as we pass along, I shall grow as poor as a strawed wolf in a pitfall. I must, to live peaceably, point my rifle at something more dangerous than varmint. Six months, and no Indian fight, would spile me worse than a dead horse on a prairie." Mike ceased speaking; the then beautiful village of Louisville appeared in sight; the labor of landing the boat occupied his attention—the bustle and confusion that in those days followed such an incident ensued, and Mike was his own master by law until his employers ceased trafficking, and again required his services.

At the time we write of, there were a great many renegade Indians who lived about the settlements, and which is still the case in the extreme Southwest. These Indians generally are the most degraded of the tribe, outcasts, who, for crime or dissipation, are no longer allowed to associate with their people; they live by hunting or stealing, and spend their precarious gains in intoxication. Among the throng that crowded on the flat-boat on its arrival were a number of these unfortunate beings; they were influenced by no other motive than that of loitering round, in idle speculation at what was going on. Mike was attracted towards them at sight, and as he too was in the situation that is deemed most favorable to mischief, it struck him that it was a good opportunity to have a little sport at the Indians' expense. Without ceremony, he gave a terrific war-whoop, and then mixing the language of the aborigines and his own together, he went on savage fashion, and bragged of his triumphs and victories on the warpath, with all the seeming earnestness of a real "brave." Nor were taunting words spared to exasperate the poor creatures, who, perfectly helpless, listened to the tales of their own greatness, and their own shame, until wound up to the highest pitch of impotent exasperation. Mike's companions joined in, thoughtless boys caught the spirit of the affair, and the Indians were goaded until they in turn made battle with their tongues. Then commenced a system of running against them, pulling off their blankets, together with a thousand other indignities; finally they made a precipitate retreat ashore, amidst the hooting and jeering of an unfeeling crowd, who considered them poor devils, destitute of feeling and humanity. Among this crowd of outcasts was a Cherokee who bore the name of Proud Joe; what his real cognomen was no one knew, for he was taciturn, haughty, and in spite of his poverty, and his manner of life, won the name we have mentioned. His face was expressive of talent, but it was furrowed by the most terrible habits of drunkenness; that he was a superior Indian was admitted, and it was also understood that he was banished from his mountainous home, his tribe being then numerous and powerful, for some great crime. He was always looked up to by his companions, and managed, however intoxicated he might be, to sustain a singularly proud bearing, which did not even depart from him while prostrated on the ground. Joe was filthy in his person and habits; in these respects he was behind his fellows; but one ornament of his person was attended to with a care which would have done honor to him if surrounded by his people, and in his native woods. Joe still wore with Indian dignity his scalp lock; he ornamented it with taste, and cherished it, as report said, that some Indian messenger of vengeance might tear it from his head, as expiatory of his numerous crimes. Mike noticed this peculiarity, and reaching out his hand, plucked from it a hawk's feather, which was attached to the scalp lock. The Indian glared horribly on Mike as he consummated the insult, snatched the feather from his hand, then shaking his clenched fist in the air, as if calling on heaven for revenge, retreated with his friends. Mike saw that he had roused the savage's soul, and he marveled wonderfully that so much resentment should be exhibited, and as an earnest to Proud Joe that the wrong he had done him should not rest unrevenged, he swore he would cut the scalp lock off close to his head the first convenient opportunity he got, and then he thought no more of the matter.

The morning following the arrival of the boat at Louisville was occupied in making preparations to pursue the voyage down the river; nearly everything was completed, and Mike had taken his favorite place at the sweep, when looking up the river bank, he beheld at some distance Joe and his companions, and from their gesticulations, they were making him the subject of conversation. Mike thought instantly of several ways in which he could show them all together a fair fight, and then whip them with ease; he also reflected with what extreme satisfaction he would enter into the spirit of the arrangement, and other

matters to him equally pleasing, when all the Indians disappeared, save Joe himself, who stood at times viewing him in moody
silence and then staring round at passing objects. From the
peculiarity of Joe's position to Mike, who was below him, his
head and upper part of his body relieved boldly against the sky,
and in one of his movements he brought his profile face to
view; the prominent scalp lock and its adornments seemed to be
more striking than ever, and it again roused the pugnacity of
Mike Fink; in an instant he raised his rifle, always loaded and
at command, brought it to his eye, and before he could be
prevented, drew sight upon Proud Joe and fired. The rifle ball
whistled loud and shrill, and Joe, springing his whole length
into the air, fell upon the ground. The cold-blooded murder was
noticed by fifty persons at least, and there arose from the
crowd a universal cry of horror and indignation at the bloody
deed. Mike himself seemed to be much astonished, and in an
instant reloaded his rifle, and as a number of white persons
rushed towards the boat, Mike threw aside his coat, and taking
his powder horn between his teeth, leaped, rifle in hand, into the
Ohio, and commenced swimming for the opposite shore. Some
bold spirits present determined Mike should not so easily
escape, and jumping into the only skiff at command, pulled
swiftly after him. Mike watched their movements until they
came within a hundred yards of him, then turning in the water,
he supported himself by his feet alone, and raised deadly rifle to
his eye; the muzzle, if it spoke hostilely, was as certain to send
a messenger of death through one or more of his pursuers as
if it were the lightning, and they knew it; dropping their oars,
and turning pale, they bid Mike not to fire. Mike waved his
hand towards the little village of Louisville, and again pursued
his way to the opposite shore.

The time consumed by the firing of Mike's rifle, the pursuit,
and the abandonment of it, required less time than we have tak-
en to give the details, and in that time to the astonishment of the
gaping crowd around Joe, they saw him rising with a bewildered air; a moment more and he recovered his senses, and
stood up—*at his feet lay his scalp lock*! The ball had cut it clear
from his head; the cord around the root of it, in which were
placed feathers and other ornaments, held it together; the con-

cussion had merely stunned its owner; farther he had escaped all bodily harm! A cry of exultation rose at this last evidence of the skill of Mike Fink; the exhibition of a shot that established his claim, indisputably, to the eminence he ever afterwards held; the unrivaled marksman of all the flat-boatmen of the Western waves. Proud Joe had received many insults, he looked upon himself as a degraded, worthless being, and the ignominy heaped upon him, he never, except by reply, resented; but this last insult was like seizing the lion by the mane, or a Roman senator by the beard—it roused the slumbering demon within, and made him again thirst to resent his wrongs, with an intensity of emotion that can only be felt by an Indian. His eye glared upon the jeering crowd around; like a fiend, his chest swelled and heaved, until it seemed that he must suffocate. No one noticed this emotion, all were intent upon the exploit that had so singularly deprived Joe of his war lock; and smothering his wrath he retreated to his associates, with a consuming fire at his vitals; he was a different man from an hour before, and with that desperate resolution on which a man stakes his all, he swore by the Great Spirit of his forefathers that he would be revenged.

An hour after the disappearance of Joe, both he and Mike Fink were forgotten. The flat-boat, which the latter had deserted, was got under way, and dashing through the rapids in the river opposite Louisville, wended on its course. As is customary when night sets in, the boat was securely fastened in some little bend or bay in the shore, where it remained until early morn. Long before the sun had fairly risen, the boat was pushed again into the stream, and it passed through a valley presenting the greatest possible beauty and freshness of landscape, the mind can conceive. It was spring, and a thousand tints of green developed themselves in the half formed foliage and bursting buds. The beautiful mallard skimmed across the water, ignorant of the danger of the white man's approach; the splendid spoonbill decked the shallow places near the shore, while myriads of singing birds filled the air with their unwritten songs. In the far reaches down the river, there occasionally might be seen a bear, stepping along the ground as if dainty of its feet, and sniffing the intruder on his wild home, he would retreat into the woods.

To enliven all this, and give the picture the look of humanity, there might also be seen, struggling with the floating mists, a column of blue smoke, that came from a fire built on a projecting point of land, around which the current swept rapidly, and carried every thing that floated on the river. The eye of a boatman saw the advantage of the situation which the place rendered to those on shore, to annoy and attack, and as wandering Indians, in those days, did not hesitate to rob, there was much speculation as to what reception the boat would receive from the builders of the fire. The rifles were all loaded, to be prepared for the worst, and the loss of Mike Fink lamented, as a prospect of a fight presented itself, where he could use his terrible rifle. The boat, in the meantime, swept round the point, but instead of an enemy, there lay, in a profound sleep, Mike Fink with his feet toasting at the fire, his pillow was a huge bear that had been shot on the day previous, while at his sides, and scattered in profusion around him, were several deer and wild turkeys. Mike had not been idle; after picking out a place most eligible to notice the passing boat, he had spent his time in hunting, and he was surrounded by trophies of his prowess. The scene that he presented was worthy of the time and the man, and would have thrown Landseer into a delirium of joy, could he have witnessed it. The boat, owing to the swiftness of the current, passed Mike's resting place, although it was pulled strongly to the shore. As Mike's companions came opposite to him, they raised such a shout, half in exultation of meeting him, and half to alarm him with the idea that Joe's friends were upon him. Mike at the sound sprang to his feet, rifle in hand, and as he looked around, he raised it to his eyes, and by the time he discovered the boat, he was ready to fire. "Down with your shooting iron, you wild critter," shouted one of the boatmen. Mike dropped the piece, and gave a loud halloo, that echoed among the solitudes like a piece of artillery. The meeting between Mike and his fellows was characteristic. They joked, and jibed him, with their rough wit, and he parried it off, with a most creditable ingenuity. Mike soon learned the extent of his rifle shot—he seemed perfectly indifferent to the fact that Proud Joe was not dead. The only sentiment he uttered, was regret that he did not fire at the vagabond's head, and if he hadn't hit it, why he made the first bad shot in twenty years. The dead game was carried on board of the boat, the adventure was forgotten, and everything resumed the monotony of floating in a flat-boat down the Ohio.

A month or more elapsed, and Mike had progressed several hundred miles down the Mississippi; his journey had been remarkably free from incident; morning, noon, and night presented the same banks, the same muddy water, and he sighed to see some broken land, some high hills, and he railed, and swore that he should have been such a fool as to desert his favorite Ohio for a river that produced nothing but alligators, and was never at best half-finished. Occasionally, the plentifulness of game put him in spirits, but it did not last long, he wanted more lasting excitement, and declared himself as perfectly miserable, and helpless, as a wild cat without teeth or claws.

In the vicinity of Natchez rises a few, abrupt hills, which tower above the surrounding lowlands of Mississippi like monuments; they are not high, but from their loneliness, and rarity, they create sensations of pleasure and awe. Under the shadow of one of these bluffs, Mike and his associates made the customary preparations to pass the night. Mike's enthusiasm knew no bounds at the sight of land again; he said it was as pleasant as "cold water to a fresh wound"; and, as his spirits rose, he went on making the region round about, according to his notions, an agreeable residence. "The Choctas live in these diggins," said Mike, "and a cursed time they must have of it. Now, if I lived in these parts, I'd declare war on 'em, just to have something to keep me from growing dull; without some such business, I'd be as musty as an old swamp moccasin. I could build a cabin on that ar hill yonder, that could from its location, with my rifle repulse a whole tribe, if they came after me. What a beautiful time I'd have of it. I never was particular, about what's called a fair fight, I just ask a half a chance, and the odds against me; and if I then don't keep clear of snags and sawyers, let me spring a leak, and go to the bottom. Its nature that the big fish should eat the little ones. I've seen trout swallow a perch, and a cat would come along and swallow the trout, and perhaps on the Massissip, the alligators use up the cat, so on until the end of the row. Well, I walk tall into varmint and Indian, it's a way

I've got, and it comes as natural as grinning to a hyena. I'm a regular tornado, tough as a hickory white, long winded as a nor'-wester. I can strike a blow like a falling tree, and every lick makes a gap in the crowd that lets in an acre of sunshine. Whew, boys," shouted Mike, twirling his rifle, like a walking stick around his head, at the ideas suggested in his mind. "Whew, boys! if the Chocta devils in them ar woods, thar, would give us a brush, just as I feel now, I'd call them gentlemen. I must fight something, or I'll catch the dry rot, burnt brandy won't save me." Such were some of the expressions which Mike gave utterance to, and in which his companions heartily joined; but they never presumed to be quite equal to Mike, for his bodily prowess, as well as his rifle, were acknowledged to be unsurpassed. These displays of animal spirits generally ended in boxing, and wrestling matches, in which falls were received, and blows struck without being noticed, that would have destroyed common men. Occasionally angry words and blows were exchanged; but like the summer storm, the cloud that emitted the lightning purified the air, and when the commotion ceased, the combatants immediately made friends, and became more attached to each other than before the cause that interrupted the good feelings occurred. Such were the conversation and amusements of the evening, when the boat was moored under one of the bluffs we have alluded to; as night wore on, one by one of the hardy boatmen fell asleep, some in the confined interior, and others protected by a light covering in the open air. The moon rose in beautiful majesty, her silver light behind the high lands, gave them a powerful and theatrical effect, as it ascended, and as its silver rays grew perpendicular, they finally kissed gently the summit of the hills, and poured down their full light upon the boat, with almost noonday brilliancy. The silence, with which the beautiful changes of darkness and light were produced, made it mysterious. It seemed as if some creative power was at work, bringing form, and life out of darkness. In the midst of the witchery of this quiet scene, there sounded forth the terrible rifle, and the more terrible warwhoop of the Indian. One of the flat-boatmen, asleep on the deck, gave a stifled groan, turned upon his face, and with a quivering motion ceased to live. Not so with his companions—

they in an instant, as men accustomed to danger and sudden
attacks, sprang ready armed to their feet; but before they could
discover their foes, seven sleek, and horribly painted savages,
leaped from the hill into the boat. The firing of the rifle was
useless, and each man singled out a foe, and met him with the
drawn knife. The struggle was quick and fearful, and deadly
blows were given, screams and imprecations rent the air. Yet
the voice of Mike Fink could be heard in encouraging shouts
above the clamor, "Give it to them, boys," he cried, "cut their
hearts out, choke the dogs, here's hell afire, and the river
rising!" then clenching with the most powerful of the assailants,
he rolled with him upon the deck of the boat. Powerful as Mike
was, the Indian seemed nearly a match for him; the two twisted,
and writhed like serpents, now one seeming to have the advantage and then the other. In all this confusion there might
occasionally be seen glancing in the moonlight the blade of a
knife, but at whom the thrusts were made, or who wielded it,
could not be discovered.

The general fight lasted less time than we have taken to describe it. The white men gained the advantage, two of the Indians lay dead upon the boat, and the living, escaping from
their antagonists, leaped ashore, and before the rifle could be
brought to bear, they were out of its reach. While Mike was yet
struggling with his antagonist, one of his companions cut the
boat loose from the shore, and with powerful exertion, managed
to get its bows so far into the current, that it swung round and
floated, but before this was accomplished, and before anyone
interfered with Mike, he was on his feet, covered with blood,
and blowing like a porpoise; by the time he could get his breath,
he commenced talking. "Ain't been so busy in a long time,"
said he, turning over his victim with his foot, "that fellow fou't
beautiful; if he's a specimen of the Chocta, that live in these
parts, they are screamers, the infernal sarpents, the d——d
possums." Talking in this way, he with others took a general
survey of the killed and wounded. Mike himself was a good deal
cut up with the Indian's knife, but he called his wounds mere
blackberry scratches; one of Mike's associates was severely
hurt, the rest escaped comparatively harmless. The sacrifice was
made at the first fire, for beside the dead Indians, there lay one

of the boat's crew, cold and dead, his body perforated with four different balls; that he was the chief object of attack seemed evident, yet no one of his associates knew of his having a single fight with Indians. The soul of Mike was affected, and taking the hand of his deceased friend between his own, he raised his bloody knife towards the bright moon, and swore, that he would desolate "the nation" that claimed the Indians who had made war upon them that night, and turning to his stiffened victim, that, dead as it was, retained the expression of implacable hatred and defiance, he gave it a smile of grim satisfaction, and then joined in the general conversation, which the occurrences of the night would naturally suggest. The master of the "broad horn" was a businessman, and had often been down the Mississippi; this was the first attack he had received, or knew to have been made, from the shores inhabited by the Choctas, except by the white man, and he, among other things, suggested the keeping of the dead Indians, until daylight, that they might have an opportunity to examine their dress and features, and see with certainty who were to blame for the occurrences of the night. The dead boatman was removed with care to a respectful distance, and the living, except the person at the sweep of the boat, were soon buried in profound slumber. Not until after the rude breakfast was partaken of, and the funeral rites of the dead boatman were solemnly performed, did Mike and his companions disturb the corpses of the red men. When both these things had been leisurely, and gently got through with, there was a different spirit among the men. Mike was astir, and went about his business with alacrity; he stripped the bloody blanket from the corpse of the Indian he had killed, as if it enveloped something disgusting, and required no respect; he examined carefully the moccasin on the Indian's feet, pronouncing them at one time Chickasas, at another time Shawnese; he stared at the livid face, but could not recognize the style of the paint that covered it. That the Indians were not strictly national in their adornments was certain, for they were examined by practiced eyes, that could have told the nation of the dead, if such had been the case, as readily as a sailor could distinguish a ship by its flag. Mike was evidently puzzled, and as he was about giving up his task as hopeless,

HERMAN MELVILLE

The Confidence-Man

Chapter XXVI

Containing the Metaphysics of Indian-Hating, According to the Views of One Evidently Not So Prepossessed as Rousseau in Favor of Savages.

"The judge always began in these words: 'The backwoodsman's hatred of the Indian has been a topic for some remark. In the earlier times of the frontier the passion was thought to be readily accounted for. But Indian rapine having mostly ceased through regions where it once prevailed, the philanthropist is surprised that Indian-hating has not in like degree ceased with it. He wonders why the backwoodsman still regards the red man in much the same spirit that a jury does a murderer, or a trapper a wild cat—a creature, in whose behalf mercy were not wisdom; truce is vain; he must be executed.

" 'A curious point,' the judge would continue, 'which perhaps not everybody, even upon explanation, may fully understand; while, in order for any one to approach to an understanding, it is necessary for him to learn, or if he already know, to bear in mind, what manner of man the backwoodsman is; as for what manner of man the Indian is, many know, either from history or experience.

" 'The backwoodsman is a lonely man. He is a thoughtful man. He is a man strong and unsophisticated. Impulsive, he is what some might call unprincipled. At any rate, he is self-willed; being one who less hearkens to what others may say about things, than looks for himself, to see what are things themselves. If in straits, there are few to help; he must depend upon himself; he must continually look to himself. Hence self-reliance, to the degree of standing by his own judgment, though it stand alone. Not that he deems himself infallible; too many

From Herman Melville, *The Confidence-Man*, (New York, 1857), Chapters 26–27.

mistakes in following trails prove the contrary; but he thinks that nature destines such sagacity as she has given him, as she destines it to the 'possum. To these fellow-beings of the wilds their untutored sagacity is their best dependence. If with either it prove faulty, if the 'possum's betray it to the trap, or the backwoodsman's mislead him into ambuscade, there are consequences to be undergone, but no self-blame. As with the 'possum, instincts prevail with the backwoodsman over precepts. Like the 'possum, the backwoodsman presents the spectacle of a creature dwelling exclusively among the works of God, yet these, truth must confess, breed little in him of a godly mind. Small bowing and scraping is his, further than when with bent knee he points his rifle, or picks its flint. With few companions, solitude by necessity his lengthened lot, he stands the trial—no slight one, since, next to dying, solitude, rightly borne, is perhaps of fortitude the most rigorous test. But not merely is the backwoodsman content to be alone, but in no few cases is anxious to be so. The sight of smoke ten miles off is provocation to one more remove from man, one step deeper into nature. Is it that he feels that whatever man may be, man is not the universe? that glory, beauty, kindness, are not all engrossed by him? that as the presence of man frights birds away, so, many bird-like thoughts? Be that how it will, the backwoodsman is not without some fineness to his nature. Hairy Orson as he looks, it may be with him as with the Shetland seal—beneath the bristles lurks the fur.

" 'Though held in a sort a barbarian, the backwoodsman would seem to America what Alexander was to Asia—captain in the vanguard of conquering civilization. Whatever the nation's growing opulence or power, does it not lackey his heels? Pathfinder, provider of security to those who come after him, for himself he asks nothing but hardship. Worthy to be compared with Moses in the Exodus, or the Emperor Julian in Gaul, who on foot, and bare-browed, at the head of covered or mounted legions, marched so through the elements, day after day. The tide of emigration, let it roll as it will, never overwhelms the backwoodsman into itself; he rides upon advance, as the Polynesian upon the comb of the surf.

" 'Thus, though he keep moving on through life, he maintains with respect to nature much the same unaltered relation throughout; with her creatures, too, including panthers and Indians. Hence, it is not unlikely that, accurate as the theory of the Peace Congress may be with respect to those two varieties of beings, among others, yet the backwoodsman might be qualified to throw out some practical suggestions.

" 'As the child born to a backwoodsman must in turn lead his father's life—a life which, as related to humanity, is related mainly to Indians—it is thought best not to mince matters, out of delicacy; but to tell the boy pretty plainly what an Indian is, and what he must expect from him. For however charitable it may be to view Indians as members of the Society of Friends, yet to affirm them such to one ignorant of Indians, whose lonely path lies a long way through their lands, this, in the event, might prove not only injudicious but cruel. At least something of this kind would seem the maxim upon which backwoods' education is based. Accordingly, if in youth the backwoodsman incline to knowledge, as is generally the case, he hears little from his schoolmasters, the old chroniclers of the forest, but histories of Indian lying, Indian theft, Indian double-dealing, Indian fraud and perfidy, Indian want of conscience, Indian blood-thirstiness, Indian diabolism—histories which, though of wild woods, are almost as full of things unangelic as the Newgate Calendar or the Annals of Europe. In these Indian narratives and traditions the lad is thoroughly grounded. "As the twig is bent the tree's inclined." The instinct of antipathy against an Indian grows in the backwoodsman with the sense of good and bad, right and wrong. In one breath he learns that a brother is to be loved, and an Indian to be hated.

" 'Such are the facts,' the judge would say, 'upon which, if one seek to moralize, he must do so with an eye to them. It is terrible that one creature should so regard another, should make it conscience to abhor an entire race. It is terrible; but is it surprising? Surprising, that one should hate a race which he believes to be red from a cause akin to that which makes some tribes of garden insects green? A race whose name is upon the frontier a *memento mori;* painted to him in every evil light; now a horse-thief like those in Moyamensing; now an assassin like a New York rowdy; now a treaty-breaker like an

Austrian; now a Palmer with poisoned arrows; now a judicial murderer and Jeffries, after a fierce farce of trial condemning his victim to bloody death; or a Jew with hospitable speeches cozening some fainting stranger into ambuscade, there to burk him, and account it a deed grateful to Manitou, his god.

" 'Still, all this is less advanced as truths of the Indians than as examples of the backwoodsman's impression of them—in which the charitable may think he does them some injustice. Certain it is, the Indians themselves think so; quite unanimously, too. The Indians, in deed, protest against the backwoodsman's view of them; and some think that one cause of their returning his antipathy so sincerely as they do, is their moral indignation at being so libeled by him, as they really believe and say. But whether, on this or any point, the Indians should be permitted to testify for themselves, to the exclusion of other testimony, is a question that may be left to the Supreme Court. At any rate, it has been observed that when an Indian becomes a genuine proselyte to Christianity (such cases, however, not being very many; though, indeed, entire tribes are sometimes nominally brought to the true light), he will not in that case conceal his enlightened conviction, that his race's portion by nature is total depravity; and, in that way, as much as admits that the backwoodsman's worst idea of it is not very far from true; while, on the other hand, those red men who are the greatest sticklers for the theory of Indian virtue, and Indian loving-kindness, are sometimes the arrantest horse-thieves and tomahawkers among them. So, at least, avers the backwoodsman. And though, knowing the Indian nature, as he thinks he does, he fancies he is not ignorant that an Indian may in some points deceive himself almost as effectually as in bush-tactics he can another, yet his theory and his practice as above contrasted seem to involve an inconsistency so extreme, that the backwoodsman only accounts for it on the supposition that when a tomahawking red-man advances the notion of the benignity of the red race, it it but part and parcel with that subtle strategy which he finds so useful in war, in hunting, and the general conduct of life.'

"In further explanation of that deep abhorrence with which the backwoodsman regards the savage, the judge used to think it might perhaps a little help, to consider what kind of stimulus to it is furnished in those forest histories and traditions before spoken of. In which behalf, he would tell the story of the little colony of Wrights and Weavers, originally seven cousins from Virginia, who, after successive removals with their families, at last established themselves near the southern frontier of the Bloody Ground, Kentucky: 'They were strong, brave men; but, unlike many of the pioneers in those days, theirs was no love of conflict for conflict's sake. Step by step they had been lured to their lonely resting-place by the ever-beckoning seductions of a fertile and virgin land, with a singular exemption, during the march, from Indian molestation. But clearings made and houses built, the bright shield was soon to turn its other side. After repeated persecutions and eventual hostilities, forced on them by a dwindled tribe in their neighborhood— persecutions resulting in loss of crops and cattle; hostilities in which they lost two of their number, illy to be spared, besides others getting painful wounds—the five remaining cousins made, with some serious concessions, a kind of treaty with Mocmohoc, the chief—being to this induced by the harryings of the enemy, leaving them no peace. But they were further prompted, indeed, first incited, by the suddenly changed ways of Mocmohoc, who, though hitherto deemed a savage almost perfidious as Cæsar Borgia, yet now put on a seeming the reverse of this, engaging to bury the hatchet, smoke the pipe, and be friends forever; not friends in the mere sense of renouncing enmity, but in the sense of kindliness, active and familiar.

" 'But what the chief now seemed, did not wholly blind them to what the chief had been; so that, though in no small degree influenced by his change of bearing, they still distrusted him enough to covenant with him, among other articles on their side, that though friendly visits should be exchanged between the wigwams and the cabins, yet the five cousins should never, on any account, be expected to enter the chief's lodge together. The intention was, though they reserved it, that if ever, under the guise of amity, the chief should mean them mischief, and effect it, it should be but partially; so that some of the five might survive, not only for their families' sake, but also for retribution's. Nevertheless, Mocmohoc did, upon a time, with such fine art and pleasing carriage win their confidence, that he brought them all together to a feast of bear's meat, and there, by stratagem, ended them. Years after, over their calcined bones and those of all their families, the chief, reproached for his treachery by a proud hunter whom he had made captive, jeered out, "Treachery? pale face! 'Twas they who broke their covenant first, in coming all together; they that broke it first, in trusting Mocmohoc."

"At this point the judge would pause, and lifting his hand, and rolling his eyes, exclaim in a solemn enough voice, 'Circling wiles and bloody lusts. The acuteness and genius of the chief but make him the more atrocious.'

"After another pause, he would begin an imaginary kind of dialogue between a backwoodsman and a questioner:

" 'But are all Indians like Mocmohoc?—Not all have proved such; but in the least harmful may lie his germ. There is an Indian nature. "Indian blood is in me," is the half-breed's threat.—But are not some Indians kind?—Yes, but kind Indians are mostly lazy, and reputed simple—at all events, are seldom chiefs; chiefs among the red men being taken from the active, and those accounted wise. Hence, with small promotion, kind Indians have but proportionate influence. And kind Indians may be forced to do unkind biddings. So "beware the Indian, kind or unkind," said Daniel Boone, who lost his sons by them.—But, have all you backwoodsmen been some way victimized by Indians?—No.—Well, and in certain cases may not at least some few of you be favored by them?—Yes, but scarce one among us so self-important, or so selfish-minded, as to hold his personal exemption from Indian outrage such a set-off against the contrary experience of so many others, as that he must needs, in a general way, think well of Indians; or, if he do, an arrow in his flank might suggest a pertinent doubt.

" 'In short,' according to the judge, 'if we at all credit the backwoodsman, his feeling against Indians, to be taken aright, must be considered as being not so much on his own account as on others', or jointly on both accounts. True it is, scarce a family he knows but some member of it, or connection, has been by Indians maimed or scalped. What avails, then, that some one Indian, or some two or three, treat a backwoodsman friendly-like? He fears me, he thinks. Take my rifle from me, give him motive, and what will come? Or if not so, how know I what involuntary preparations may be going on in him for things as unbeknown in present time to him as me—a sort of chemical preparation in the soul for malice, as chemical preparation in the body for malady.'

"Not that the backwoodsman ever used those words, you see, but the judge found him expression for his meaning. And this point he would conclude with saying, that, 'what is called a "friendly Indian" is a very rare sort of creature; and well it was so, for no ruthlessness exceeds that of a "friendly Indian" turned enemy. A coward friend, he makes a valiant foe.

" 'But, thus far the passion in question has been viewed in a general way as that of a community. When to his due share of this the backwoodsman adds his private passion, we have then the stock out of which is formed, if formed at all, the Indian-hater *par excellence*.'

"The Indian-hater *par excellence* the judge defined to be one 'who, having with his mother's milk drank in small love for red men, in youth or early manhood, ere the sensibilities become osseous, receives at their hand some signal outrage, or, which in effect is much the same, some of his kin have, or some friend. Now, nature all around him by her solitudes wooing or bidding him muse upon this matter, he accordingly does so, till the thought develops such attraction, that much as straggling vapors troop from all sides to a storm-cloud, so straggling thoughts of other outrages troop to the nucleus thought, assimilate with it, and swell it. At last, taking counsel with the elements, he comes to his resolution. An intenser Hannibal, he makes a vow, the hate of which is a vortex from whose suction scarce the remotest chip of the guilty race may reasonably feel secure. Next, he declares himself and settles his temporal affairs. With the solemnity of a Spaniard turned monk, he takes leave of his kin; or rather, these leave-takings have something of the still more impressive finality of death-bed adieus. Last, he commits himself to the forest primeval; there, so long as life shall be his, to act upon a calm, cloistered scheme of strategical, implacable, and lonesome vengeance. Ever on the noiseless trail;

cool, collected, patient; less seen than felt; snuffing, smelling—a Leather-stocking Nemesis. In the settlements he will not be seen again; in eyes of old companions tears may start at some chance thing that speaks of him; but they never look for him, nor call; they know he will not come. Suns and seasons fleet; the tigerlily blows and falls; babes are born and leap in their mothers' arms; but, the Indian-hater is good as gone to his long home, and "Terror" is his epitaph.'

"Here the judge, not unaffected, would pause again, but presently resume: 'How evident that in strict speech there can be no biography of an Indian-hater *par excellence*, any more than one of a sword-fish, or other deep-sea denizen; or, which is still less imaginable, one of a dead man. The career of the Indian-hater *par excellence* has the impenetrability of the fate of a lost steamer. Doubtless, events, terrible ones, have happened, must have happened; but the powers that be in nature have taken order that they shall never become news.

" 'But, luckily for the curious, there is a species of diluted Indian-hater, one whose heart proves not so steely as his brain. Soft enticements of domestic life too often draw him from the ascetic trail; a monk who apostatizes to the world at times. Like a mariner, too, though much abroad, he may have a wife and family in some green harbor which he does not forget. It is with him as with the Papist converts in Senegal; fasting and mortification prove hard to bear.'

"The judge, with his usual judgment, always thought that the intense solitude to which the Indian-hater consigns himself, has, by its overawing influence, no little to do with relaxing his vow. He would relate instances where, after some months' lonely scoutings, the Indian-hater is suddenly seized with a sort of calenture; hurries openly towards the first smoke, though he knows it is an Indian's, announces himself as a lost hunter, gives the savage his rifle, throws himself upon his charity, embraces him with much affection, imploring the privilege of living a while in his sweet companionship. What is too often the sequel of so distempered a procedure may be best known by those who best know the Indian. Upon the whole, the judge, by two and thirty good and sufficient reasons, would maintain that there was no known vocation whose consistent following calls for such self-containings as that of the Indian-hater *par excellence*. In the highest view, he considered such a soul one peeping out but once an age.

"For the diluted Indian-hater, although the vacations he permits himself impair the keeping of the character, yet, it should not be overlooked that this is the man who, by his very infirmity, enables us to form surmises, however inadequate, of what Indian-hating in its perfection is."

"One moment," gently interrupted the cosmopolitan here, "and let me refill my calumet."

Which being done, the other proceeded:—

Chapter XXVII

Some Account of a Man of Questionable Morality, but Who, Nevertheless, Would Seem Entitled to the Esteem of That Eminent English Moralist Who Said He Liked a Good Hater

"Coming to mention the man to whose story all thus far said was but the introduction, the judge, who, like you, was a great smoker, would insist upon all the company taking cigars, and then lighting a fresh one himself, rise in his place, and, with the solemnest voice, say—'Gentlemen, let us smoke to the memory of Colonel John Moredock'; when, after several whiffs taken standing in deep silence and deeper reverie, he would resume his seat and his discourse, something in these words:

" 'Though Colonel John Moredock was not an Indian-hater *par excellence*, he yet cherished a kind of sentiment towards the red man, and in that degree, and so acted out his sentiment as sufficiently to merit the tribute just rendered to his memory.

" 'John Moredock was the son of a woman married thrice, and thrice widowed by a tomahawk. The three successive husbands of this woman had been pioneers, and with them she had wandered from wilderness to wilderness, always on the frontier. With nine children, she at last found herself at a little clearing, afterwards Vincennes. There she joined a company about to remove to the new country of Illinois. On the eastern side of Illinois there were then no settlements; but on the west side, the shore of the Mississippi, there were, near the mouth of the

Kaskaskia, some old hamlets of French. To the vicinity of those hamlets, very innocent and pleasant places, a new Arcadia, Mrs. Moredock's party was destined; for thereabouts, among the vines, they meant to settle. They embarked upon the Wabash in boats, proposing descending that stream into the Ohio, and the Ohio into the Mississippi, and so, northwards, towards the point to be reached. All went well till they made the rock of the Grand Tower on the Mississippi, where they had to land and drag their boats round a point swept by a strong current. Here a party of Indians, lying in wait, rushed out and murdered nearly all of them. The widow was among the victims with her children, John excepted, who, some fifty miles distant, was following with a second party.

" 'He was just entering upon manhood, when thus left in nature sole survivor of his race. Other youngsters might have turned mourners; he turned avenger. His nerves were electric wires—sensitive, but steel. He was one who, from self-possession, could be made neither to flush nor pale. It is said that when the tidings were brought him, he was ashore sitting beneath a hemlock eating his dinner of venison—and as the tidings were told him, after the first start he kept on eating, but slowly and deliberately, chewing the wild news with the wild meat, as if both together, turned to chyle, together should sinew him to his intent. From that meal he rose an Indian-hater. He rose; got his arms, prevailed upon some comrades to join him, and without delay started to discover who were the actual transgressors. They proved to belong to a band of twenty renegades from various tribes, outlaws even among Indians, and who had formed themselves into a maurauding crew. No opportunity for action being at the time presented, he dismissed his friends; told them to go on, thanking them, and saying he would ask their aid at some future day. For upwards of a year, alone in the wilds, he watched the crew. Once, what he thought a favorable chance having occurred—it being midwinter, and the savages encamped, apparently to remain so—he anew mustered his friends, and marched against them; but, getting wind of his coming, the enemy fled, and in such panic that everything was left behind but their weapons. During the winter, much the same thing happened upon two subsequent occasions. The next year he sought them at the head of a party pledged to serve him for forty days. At last the hour came. It was on the shore of the Mississippi. From their covert, Moredock and his men dimly descried the gang of Cains in the red dusk of evening, paddling over to a jungled island in mid-stream, there the more securely to lodge; for Moredock's retributive spirit in the wilderness spoke ever to their trepidations now, like the voice calling through the garden. Waiting until dead of night, the whites swam the river, towing after them a raft laden with their arms. On landing, Moredock cut the fastenings of the enemy's canoes, and turned them, with his own raft, adrift; resolved that there should be neither escape for the Indians, nor safety, except in victory, for the whites. Victorious the whites were; but three of the Indians saved themselves by taking to the stream. Moredock's band lost not a man.

" 'Three of the murderers survived. He knew their names and persons. In the course of three years each successively fell by his own hand. All were now dead. But this did not suffice. He made no avowal, but to kill Indians had become his passion. As an athlete, he had few equals; as a shot, none; in single combat, not to be beaten. Master of that woodland-cunning enabling the adept to subsist where the tyro would perish, and expert in all those arts by which an enemy is pursued for weeks, perhaps months, without once suspecting it, he kept to the forest. The solitary Indian that met him, died. When a murder was descried, he would either secretly pursue their track for some chance to strike at least one blow; or if, while thus engaged, he himself was discovered, he would elude them by superior skill.

" 'Many years he spent thus; and though after a time he was, in a degree, restored to the ordinary life of the region and period, yet it is believed that John Moredock never let pass an opportunity of quenching an Indian. Sins of commission in that kind may have been his, but none of omission.

" 'It were to err to suppose,' the judge would say, 'that this gentleman was naturally ferocious, or peculiarly possessed of those qualities, which, unhelped by provation of events, tend to withdraw man from social life. On the contrary, Moredock was an example of something apparently self-contradicting, certainly curious, but, at the same time, undeniable: namely. that nearly all Indian-haters have at bottom loving hearts; at any rate, hearts, if anything, more generous than the average. Certain it is, that, to the degree in which he mingled in the life of the settlements, Moredock showed himself not without humane feelings. No cold husband or colder father, he; and, though often and long away from his household, bore its needs in mind, and provided for them. He could be very convivial; told a good story (though never of his more private exploits), and sung a capital song. Hospitable, not backward to help a neighbor; by report, benevolent, as retributive, in secret; while, in a general manner, though sometimes grave—as is not unusual with men of his complexion, a sultry and tragical brown —yet with nobody, Indians excepted, otherwise than courteous in a manly fashion; a moccasined gentleman, admired and loved. In fact, no one more popular, as an incident to follow may prove.

" 'His bravery, whether in Indian fight or any other, was unquestionable. An officer in the ranging service during the war of 1812, he acquitted himself with more than credit. Of his soldierly character, this anecdote is told: Not long after Hull's dubious surrender at Detroit, Moredock with some of his rangers rode up at night to a log-house, there to rest till morning. The horses being attended to, supper over, and sleeping-places assigned the troop, the host showed the colonel his best bed, not on the ground like the rest, but a bed that stood on legs. But out of delicacy, the guest declined to monopolize it, or, indeed, to occupy it at all; when, to increase the inducement, as the host thought, he was told that a general officer had once slept in that bed. "Who, pray?" asked the colonel. "General Hull." "Then you must not take offense," said the colonel, buttoning up his coat, "but, really, no coward's bed, for me, however comfortable." Accordingly he took up with valor's bed—a cold one on the ground.

" 'At one time the colonel was a member of the territorial council of Illinois, and, at the formation of the state government, was pressed to become candidate for governor, but begged to be excused. And, though he declined to give his reasons for declining, yet by those who best knew him the cause was not wholly unsurmised. In his official capacity he might be called upon to enter into friendly treaties with Indian tribes, a thing not to be thought of. And even did no such contingency arise, yet he felt there would be an impropriety in the Governor of Illinois stealing out now and then, during a recess of the legislative bodies, for a few days' shooting at human beings, within the limits of his paternal chief-magistracy. If the governorship offered large honors, from Moredock it demanded larger sacrifices. These were incompatibles. In short, he was not unaware that to be a consistent Indian-hater involves the renunciation of ambition, with its objects—the pomps and glories of the world; and since religion, pronouncing such things vanities, accounts it merit to renounce them, therefore, so far as this goes, Indian-hating, whatever may be thought of it in other respects, may be regarded as not wholly without the efficacy of a devout sentiment.' "

Here the narrator paused. Then, after his long and irksome sitting, started to his feet, and regulating his disordered shirt-frill, and at the same time adjustingly shaking his legs down in his rumpled pantaloons, concluded: "There, I have done; having given you, not my story, mind, or my thoughts, but another's. And now, for your friend Coonskins, I doubt not, that, if the judge were here, he would pronounce him a sort of comprehensive Colonel Moredock, who, too much spreading his passion, shallows it."

FRANCIS PARKMAN

The Conspiracy of Pontiac

Anger of the Indians.—The Conspiracy.

The country was scarcely transferred to the English, when
smothered murmurs of discontent began to be audible among
the Indian tribes. From the head of the Potomac to Lake
Superior, and from the Alleghanies to the Mississippi, in every
wigwam and hamlet of the forest, a deep-rooted hatred of the
English increased with rapid growth. Nor is this to be wondered at. We have seen with what sagacious policy the French
had labored to ingratiate themselves with the Indian; and the
slaughter of the Monongahela, with the horrible devastation of
the western frontier, the outrages perpetrated at Oswego, and
the massacre at Fort William Henry, bore witness to the success
of their efforts. Even the Delawares and Shawanoes, the faithful allies of William Penn, had at length been seduced by
their blandishments; and the Iroquois, the ancient enemies of
Canada, had half forgotten their former hostility, and well-nigh
taken part against the British colonists. The remote nations of
the west had also joined in the war, descending in their canoes
for hundreds of miles, to fight against the enemies of France.
All these tribes entertained towards the English that rancorous
enmity which an Indian always feels against those to whom he
has been opposed in war.

Under these circumstances, it behooved the English to use
the utmost care in their conduct towards the tribes. But
even when the conflict with France was impending, and the
alliance with the Indians was of the last importance, they had
treated them with indifference and neglect. They were not
likely to adopt a different course now that their friendship
seemed a matter of no consequence. In truth, the intentions

From Francis Parkman, *The Conspiracy of Pontiac*, (Boston, 1851)
Chapter 7.

of the English were soon apparent. In the zeal for retrenchment, which prevailed after the close of hostilities, the presents which it had always been customary to give the Indians, at stated intervals, were either withheld altogether, or doled out with a niggardly and reluctant hand; while, to make the matter worse, the agents and officers of government often appropriated the presents to themselves, and afterwards sold them at an exorbitant price to the Indians. When the French had possession of the remote forts, they were accustomed, with a wise liberality, to supply the surrounding Indians with guns, ammunition, and clothing, until the latter had forgotten the weapons and garments of their forefathers, and depended on the white men for support. The sudden withholding of these supplies was, therefore, a grievous calamity. Want, suffering, and death, were the consequences; and this cause alone would have been enough to produce general discontent. But, unhappily, other grievances were superadded.

The English fur-trade had never been well regulated, and it was now in a worse condition than ever. Many of the traders, and those in their employ, were ruffians of the coarsest stamp, who vied with each other in rapacity, violence, and profligacy. They cheated, cursed, and plundered the Indians, and outraged their families; offering, when compared with the French traders, who were under better regulation, a most unfavorable example of the character of their nation.

The officers and soldiers of the garrisons did their full part in exciting the general resentment. Formerly, when the warriors came to the forts, they had been welcomed by the French with attention and respect. The inconvenience which their presence occasioned had been disregarded, and their peculiarities overlooked. But now they were received with cold looks and harsh words from the officers, and with oaths, menaces, and sometimes blows, from the reckless and brutal soldiers. When, after their troublesome and intrusive fashion, they were lounging everywhere about the fort, or lazily reclining in the shadow of the walls, they were met with muttered ejaculations of impatience, or abrupt orders to be gone, enforced, perhaps, by a touch from the butt of a sentinel's musket. These marks of contempt were unspeakably galling to their haughty spirit.

But what most contributed to the growing discontent of the tribes was the intrusion of settlers upon their lands, at all times a fruitful source of Indian hostility. Its effects, it is true, could only be felt by those whose country bordered upon the English settlements; but among these were the most powerful and influential of the tribes. The Delawares and Shawanoes, in particular, had by this time been roused to the highest pitch of exasperation. Their best lands had been invaded, and all remonstrance had been fruitless. They viewed with wrath and fear the steady progress of the white man, whose settlements had passed the Susquehanna, and were fast extending to the Alleghanies, eating away the forest like a spreading canker. The anger of the Delawares was abundantly shared by their ancient conquerors, the Six Nations. The threatened occupation of Wyoming by settlers from Connecticut gave great umbrage to the confederacy. The Senecas were more especially incensed at English intrusion, since, from their position, they were farthest removed from the soothing influence of Sir William Johnson, and most exposed to the seductions of the French; while the Mohawks, another member of the confederacy, were justly alarmed at seeing the better part of their lands patented out without their consent. Some Christian Indians of the Oneida tribe, in the simplicity of their hearts, sent an earnest petition to Sir William Johnson, that the English forts within the limits of the Six Nations might be removed, or as the petition expresses it, *kicked out of the way.*

The discontent of the Indians gave great satisfaction to the French, who saw in it an assurance of safe and bloody vengeance on their conquerors. Canada, it is true, was gone beyond hope of recovery; but they still might hope to revenge its loss. Interest, moreover, as well as passion, prompted them to inflame the resentment of the Indians; for most of the inhabitants of the French settlements upon the lakes and the Mississippi were engaged in the fur-trade, and, fearing the English as formidable rivals, they would gladly have seen them driven out of the country. Traders, *habitans, coureurs de bois,* and all classes of this singular population, accordingly dispersed themselves among the villages of the Indians, or held councils with them in the secret places of the woods, urging them to take up arms against the English. They exhibited the conduct of the latter in its worst light, and spared neither misrepresentation nor falsehood. They told their excited hearers that the English had formed a deliberate scheme to root out the whole Indian race, and, with that design, had already begun to hem them in with settlements on the one hand, and a chain of forts on the other. Among other atrocious plans for their destruction, they had instigated the Cherokees to attack and destroy the tribes of the Ohio valley. These groundless calumnies found ready belief. The French declared, in addition, that the King of France had of late years fallen asleep; that, during his slumbers, the English had seized upon Canada; but that he was now awake again, and that his armies were advancing up the St. Lawrence and the Mississippi, to drive out the intruders from the country of his red children. To these fabrications was added the more substantial encouragement of arms, ammunition, clothing, and provisions, which the French trading companies, if not the officers of the crown, distributed with a liberal hand.

The fierce passions of the Indians, excited by their wrongs, real or imagined, and exasperated by the representations of the French, were yet farther wrought upon by influences of another kind. A prophet rose among the Delawares. This man may serve as a counterpart to the famous Shawanoe prophet, who figured so conspicuously in the Indian outbreak, under Tecumseh, immediately before the war with England in 1812. Many other parallel instances might be shown, as the great susceptibility of the Indians to superstitious impressions renders the advent of a prophet among them no very rare occurrence. In the present instance, the inspired Delaware seems to have been rather an enthusiast than an impostor; or perhaps he combined both characters. The objects of his mission were not wholly political. By means of certain external observances, most of them sufficiently frivolous and absurd, his disciples were to strengthen and purify their natures, and make themselves acceptable to the Great Spirit, whose messenger he proclaimed himself to be. He also enjoined them to lay aside the weapons and clothing which they received from the white men, and return to the primitive life of their ancestors. By so doing, and by strictly observing his other precepts, the tribes would soon be restored to their ancient greatness and power, and be enabled to drive out the white men who infested their territory. The prophet had many followers. Indians came from far and near, and gathered together in large encampments to listen to his exhortations. His fame spread even to the nations of the northern lakes; but though his disciples followed most of his injunctions, flinging away flint and steel, and making copious use of emetics, with other observances equally troublesome, yet the requisition to abandon the use of fire-arms was too inconvenient to be complied with.

With so many causes to irritate their restless and warlike spirit, it could not be supposed that the Indians would long remain quiet. Accordingly, in the summer of the year 1761, Captain Campbell, then commanding at Detroit, received information that a deputation of Senecas had come to the neighboring village of the Wyandots for the purpose of instigating the latter to destroy him and his garrison. On farther inquiry, the plot proved to be general; and Niagara, Fort Pitt, and other posts, were to share the fate of Detroit. Campbell instantly despatched messengers to Sir Jeffrey Amherst, and the commanding officers of the different forts; and, by this timely discovery, the conspiracy was nipped in the bud. During the following summer, 1762, another similar design was detected and suppressed. They proved to be the precursors of a tempest. When, early in 1763, it was announced to the tribes that the King of France had ceded all their country to the King of England without even asking their leave, a ferment of indignation at once became apparent among them; and, within a few weeks, a plot was matured, such as was never, before or since, conceived or executed by a North-American Indian. It was determined to attack all the English forts upon the same day; then, having destroyed their garrisons, to turn upon the defenceless frontier, and ravage and lay waste the settlements, until, as many of the Indians fondly believed, the English should all be driven into the sea, and the country restored to its primitive owners.

It is difficult to determine which tribe was first to raise the cry of war. There were many who might have done so, for all the savages in the backwoods were ripe for an outbreak, and the movement seemed almost simultaneous. The Delawares and Senecas were the most incensed, and Kiashuta, a chief of the latter, was perhaps foremost to apply the torch; but, if this was the case, he touched fire to materials already on the point of igniting. It belonged to a greater chief than he to give method and order to what would else have been a wild burst of fury, and convert desultory attacks into a formidable and protracted War. But for Pontiac, the whole might have ended in a few troublesome inroads upon the frontier, and a little whooping and yelling under the walls of Fort Pitt.

Pontiac, as already mentioned, was principal chief of the Ottawas. The Ottawas, Ojibwas, and Pottawattamies, had long been united in a loose kind of confederacy, of which he was the virtual head. Over those around him his authority was almost despotic, and his power extended far beyond the limits of the three united tribes. His influence was great among all the nations of the Illinois country; while, from the sources of the Ohio to those of the Mississippi, and, indeed, to the farthest boundaries of the wide-spread Algonquin race, his name was known and respected.

The fact that Pontiac was born the son of a chief would in no degree account for the extent of his power; for, among Indians, many a chief's son sinks back into insignificance, while the offspring of a common warrior may succeed to his place. Among all the wild tribes of the continent, personal merit is indispensable to gaining or preserving dignity. Courage, reso-lution, address, and eloquence are sure passports to distinction. With all these Pontiac was pre-eminently endowed, and it was chiefly to them, urged to their highest activity by a vehement ambition, that he owed his greatness. He possessed a command-ing energy and force of mind, and in subtlety and craft could match the best of his wily race. But, though capable of acts of magnanimity, he was a thorough savage, with a wider range of intellect than those around him, but sharing all their passions and prejudices, their fierceness and treachery. His faults were the faults of his race; and they cannot eclipse his nobler quali-ties. His memory is still cherished among the remnants of many Algonquin tribes, and the celebrated Tecumseh adopted him for his model, proving himself no unworthy imitator.

Pontiac was now about fifty years old. Until Major Rogers came into the country, he had been, from motives probably both of interest and inclination, a firm friend of the French. Not long before the French war broke out, he had saved the garrison of Detroit from the imminent peril of an attack from some of the discontented tribes of the north. During the war, he had fought on the side of France. It is said that he commanded the Ottawas at the memorable defeat of Braddock; and it is certain that he was treated with much honor by the French officers, and received especial marks of esteem from the Marquis of Montcalm.

We have seen how, when the tide of affairs changed, the subtle and ambitious chief trimmed his bark to the current, and gave the hand of friendship to the English. That he was disappointed in their treatment of him, and in all the hopes that he had formed from their alliance, is sufficiently evident from one of his speeches. A new light soon began to dawn upon his untaught but powerful mind, and he saw the altered posture of affairs under its true aspect.

It was a momentous and gloomy crisis for the Indian race, for never before had they been exposed to such imminent and pressing danger. With the downfall of Canada, the tribes had sunk at once from their position of importance. Hitherto the two rival European nations had kept each other in check upon the American continent, and the Indians had, in some measure, held the balance of power between them. To conciliate their good will and gain their alliance, to avoid offending them by injustice and encroachment, was the policy both of the French and English. But now the face of affairs was changed. The English had gained an undisputed ascendency, and the Indians, no longer important as allies, were treated as mere barbarians, who might be trampled upon with impunity. Abandoned to their own feeble resources and divided strength, they must fast recede, and dwindle away before the steady progress of the colonial power. Already their best hunting-grounds were invaded, and from the eastern ridges of the Alleghanies they might see, from far and near, the smoke of the settlers' clearings rising in tall columns from the dark-green bosom of the forest. The doom of the race was sealed, and no human power could avert it; but they, in their ignorance, believed otherwise, and vainly thought that, by a desperate effort, they might yet uproot and overthrow the growing strength of their destroyers.

It would be idle to suppose that the great mass of the Indians understood, in its full extent, the danger which threatened their race. With them, the war was a mere outbreak of fury, and they turned against their enemies with as little reason or forecast as a panther when he leaps at the throat of the hunter. Goaded by wrongs and indignities, they struck for revenge, and for relief from the evil of the moment. But the mind of Pontiac could embrace a wider and deeper view. The peril of the times was unfolded in its full extent before him, and he resolved to unite the tribes in one grand effort to avert it. He did not, like many of his people, entertain the absurd idea that the Indians, by their unaided strength, could drive the English into the sea. He adopted the only plan consistent with reason, that of restoring the French ascendency in the west, and once more opposing a check to British encroachment. With views like these, he lent a greedy ear to the plausible falsehoods of the Canadians, who assured him that the armies of King Louis were already advancing to recover Canada, and that the French and their red brethren, fighting side by side, would drive the English dogs back within their own narrow limits.

Revolving these thoughts, and remembering that his own ambitious views might be advanced by the hostilities he meditated, Pontiac no longer hesitated. Revenge, ambition, and patriotism wrought upon him alike, and he resolved on war. At the close of the year 1762, he sent ambassadors to the different nations. They visited the country of the Ohio and its tributaries, passed northward to the region of the upper lakes, and the borders of the River Ottawa; and far southward towards the mouth of the Mississippi. Bearing with them the war-belt of wampum, broad and long, as the importance of the message demanded, and the tomahawk stained red, in token of war, they went from camp to camp, and village to village. Wherever they appeared, the sachems and old men assembled, to hear the words of the great Pontiac. Then the chief of the embassy flung down the tomahawk on the ground before them, and holding the war-belt in his hand, delivered, with vehement gesture, word for word, the speech with which he was charged. It was heard everywhere with approval; the belt was accepted, the hatched snatched up, and the assembled chiefs stood pledged to take part in the war. The blow was to be struck at a certain time in the month of May following, to be indicated by the changes of the moon. The tribes were to rise together, each destroying the English garrison in its neighborhood, and then, with a general rush, the whole were to turn against the settlements of the frontier.

The tribes, thus banded together against the English, comprised, with a few unimportant exceptions, the whole Algonquin stock, to whom were united the Wyandots, the Senecas, and several tribes of the lower Mississippi. The Senecas were the only members of the Iroquois confederacy who joined in the league, the rest being kept quiet by the influence of Sir William Johnson, whose utmost exertions, however, were barely sufficient to allay their irritation.

While thus on the very eve of an outbreak, the Indians concealed their designs with the dissimulation of their race. The warriors still lounged about the forts, with calm, impenetrable faces, begging, as usual, for tobacco, gunpowder, and whiskey. Now and then, some slight intimation of danger would startle the garrisons from their security. An English trader, coming in from the Indian villages, would report that, from their manner and behavior, he suspected them of brooding mischief; or some scoundrel half-breed would be heard boasting in his cups, that before next summer he would have English hair to fringe his hunting-frock. On one occasion, the plot was nearly discovered. Early in March, 1763, Ensign Holmes, commanding at Fort Miami, was told by a friendly Indian that the warriors in the neighboring village had lately received a war-belt, with a message urging them to destroy him and his garrison, and that this they were preparing to do. Holmes called the Indians together, and boldly charged them with their design. They did as Indians on such occasions have often done, confessed their fault with much apparent contrition, laid the blame on a neighboring tribe, and professed eternal friendship to their brethren, the English. Holmes writes to report his discovery to Major Gladwyn, who, in his turn, sends the information to Sir Jeffrey

Amherst, expressing his opinion that there has been a general irritation among the Indians, but that the affair will soon blow over, and that, in the neighborhood of his own post, the savages were perfectly tranquil. Within cannon shot of the deluded officer's palisades, was the village of Pontiac himself, the arch enemy of the English, and prime mover in the plot.

With the approach of spring, the Indians, coming in from their wintering grounds, began to appear in small parties about the various forts; but now they seldom entered them, encamping at a little distance in the woods. They were fast pushing their preparations for the meditated blow, and waiting with stifled eagerness for the appointed hour.

THOMAS BERGER

Little Big Man

In this chapter the hero, Jack Crabb, finds himself once
again with his adopted nation, the Cheyenne. Yet, as the
opening scene makes clear, the initial reception he gets
from a Cheyenne brave is less than cordial. The reason
is that Jack is riding with the cavalry in an action against
his old friends, and as we know, it's hard to tell one white
man from another.

My Indian Wife

"Hold on, Brother," I cried in Cheyenne. "Let us talk."
And then, with my attention so strenuously fixed upon him,
I tripped on that steep slope I was negotiating and plunged
directly toward him, my pistol firing inadvertently as my hands
clenched.

He held up his knife, with his left fingers gripping the right-
hand wrist, so as to give added support for the impact. Which
is to say, I was about to be impaled just below the arch of my
rib-cage. My accidental shot had gone into the air.

Well, I was only falling six feet, but the time consumed by
any type of action is relative, and I recall hanging motionless
there in space like the subject in a photograph or artist's render-
ing. Shadow wore two eagle feathers, aslant one from the other.
There was beads of sweat upon his brown shoulders. He wore
a choker of horizontal porcupine quills divided by vertical
lines of blue beads; and between his left bicep and elbow
cavity, a copper armlet; between his legs a dirty breechclout
of red flannel. The black points of his narrow-lidded eyes was
fixed on the target of my upper belly, and his legs was braced

for the collision. Vermilion was the predominant color of his face paint, with an overlay of yellow bolts of lightning.

Almost at my leisure I floated down upon the point of the knife, and when I struck it and thought sort of lackadaisically that I was sure disemboweled, time speeded up again, and I was tumbling over him at great speed and still unwounded, for without willing it I had somehow altered my style of fall and took the blade in my shirt between arm and ribs. It seemed warm there from the close call, from the threat unsatisfied; had I been cut, I would have felt nothing; that is the peculiarity of knifeplay. Well, roll we did through the sand and scrub brush, and he was a powerful Indian though fifty year old. I had lost my pistol, but he kept his knife. Still I sought to talk, but his thumb was into my throat box so far as almost to break through the floor of my mouth. Being small and limber I kneed him frequent in the lower belly, but his iron ballocks sustained these blows without effect, and I missed my chops at the paralyzing neck-cord below the left ear.

Soon I was pinned between his thighs, like steel pincers from forty years of pony riding, and now I yearned for the knife to plunge and free me from that compression which had caught me on an exhale and my vision was turning black.

He lifted high the blade, a Green River butcher weapon without a guard, and I won't forget its slightest property. And then a little hole sprung beneath his chin, and blood begun to burble out of it. He swallowed twice, like to get rid of a little bone that got stuck in his throat. Only then did I hear the shot. His shoulder jerked as though pushed from behind: another shot. He dropped the knife and leaned towards me, the fluid running from his neck, yet his eyes was still open. Then I pushed him in the chest and back he went all the way, bending like rubber at the waist, for his legs was yet locked about my ribs and killing me, and locking my hands together into a kind of sledge, I smote him at the navel: *spang!* his thigh-grip loosened like a toy when you hit its spring.

Then down leaped that Pawnee Mad Bear from the bank above and putting the muzzle of his Spencer an inch from Shadow's forehead, he gave him a third shot and a middle eye, and shortly ripped away his hair, which parted with a *whap*.

He smirked at me, tore away Shadow's breechclout and wiped
the scalp upon the dead man's private parts, saying something
victorious in Pawnee.

He had saved my life, sure enough, but I reckon I knew how
Younger Bear had felt when I did the same for him them many
years before: I wasn't grateful. Shadow That Comes in Sight had
took me on my first raid, having ever been like an older brother
or uncle. I was right fond of him. What caught me in the heart
now was not that he had been killed, for we all will be sometime. Nor that it had been violent, for as a Human Being he
would not have died another way. Nor even that in an involved
fashion I had been the instrument of his loss. No, the sadness
of it was that Shadow had never known who I was. He had
fought me as an enemy. Well, that's why I was there, wasn't I,
to fight the Cheyenne?

Goddam but he had powerful legs. I still could barely
breathe. I got up and watched Mad Bear climb the bank and
shortly reappear at its brink on his pony, smugly shake his
rifle, and trot away. He hadn't even commented on the loss of
my horse, which had been borrowed from him.

I had not had time to wonder how Shadow happened to be
down in this draw in the first place, but now, moving slow
for I was mighty sore, as I scratched out a shallow grave for
him with his own knife and covered him over, I considered
there might be other Human Beings somewhere below among
the brush and if they wanted to shoot me in the back, they was
welcome to do so. I'd rather that than meet them face to face
and see my old friends and brothers.

But I had just got the tip of his long nose covered over with
sand when I heard a rustling in the bushes down a ways, and it
is queer how my instincts for self-preservation arose without
my conscious will, and I seized my fallen revolver and blowed
and worked the action clean and replaced all the caps. This in
an instant, and then snaked along the bottom of the draw. The
brush was trembling, but whatever it could be was staying
within. I lurked a moment, then parted the twigs and crept
through pistol first, with my face just behind the hammer. I
was looking into a clearing just big enough for one person, and
that person lay upon her back. She was an Indian woman with

her skirt pulled up and her bare legs stretched apart and between them she was giving birth.

The tiny brown head was already emerged, eyes closed and
looking a mite peevish at its entry into reality, and now the little
shoulders squeezed through. There was never a sound except
where that one straining knee was scraping the brush, which
I had heard. She watched what went on and bit from time to
time into a wad of her buckskin collar; maybe her eyes winced
out a drop of moisture, but there was no more commotion than
that. She had been there all the while, and that was the occasion
for Shadow's presence and why he fought so hard.

Cheyenne women at such a time always go off by themselves
into the brush, and when it is done, come out with the infant
and return to work as usual. The only difference here was that
she went into labor in the middle of a battle. But the little fellow
had to come when he was ready.

I was embarrassed for a variety of reasons, giving birth being
an occasion of unusual modesty for a Cheyenne, so much so
that I reckon this woman would take Shadow's death less
heavily than my observation of her. Yet I was fascinated, for
within half a mile from the soles of my upturned feet the firing
had not abated, nor the yells concerning the great day for the
Pawnee. . . . Out of her come the little cleft behind of the infant,
tightly pinched together. She strained some more, and then
the rest of him emerged smooth as a fish onto the blue blanket
spread beneath, and she set up, bit off the cord, tied the baby's
end against his tiny belly, and slapped him into wakefulness,
to which he come like a real Cheyenne: with a little start but
almost no noise. I expected he already knowed a cry would
bring the enemy down on his tribe, so he forbore from loose
utterance, and always would. That was also the first and last
slap he would ever get from his own kind, while moving into
a life that otherwise would know every type of mayhem.

I backed on out of there and went down to the sand heap
under which lay Shadow. In a minute she come out of the
brush, walking strong and vigorous and matter-of-fact, the
child's head a-peeping from the blanket at her bosom. Eying
me, she then went for her belted knife and I reckon might have
been a tough customer with it in spite of her newborn. Only

I put my revolver forward, which would seem brutal did you not understand by now that a Cheyenne, man or woman, has got a terrible thick skull when it comes to hearing white men.

"Now," I says, "I am going to shoot you and your child if you don't listen. Shadow That Comes in Sight was killed by the Pawnee. That was the shot you heard, and then you heard him ride away. If you are related to Shadow then maybe you have heard of Little Big Man, which is what I was called when I lived with Old Lodge Skins's band. I was a friend of the Cheyenne until they stole my wife and son. That is why I am here now. I am going to take you along with me and trade you for them."

She studies me through them dark eyes and says: "All right."

"I don't like to do this," I says, "with your newborn and all, but I have no choice."

"All right," she answers and sets down, opens her dress under the arm, and puts the infant to feed.

"Look," says I, "we had better get to open ground. A Pawnee might come upon us here unawares and kill you before I could explain."

"He must eat first," she tells me quietly and sets solid.

So I kept my watch upon the rim of the draw during the ensuing conversation. I didn't know this woman—girl, rather, too young at the time I lived among them to take my notice, if she had been there. I figured her for Shadow's wife, which accounted for his guarding, but it turned out she was rather one of them young daughters I have mentioned him training, way back, to control her giggle at his funny stories.

"Your husband been rubbed out?"

"By white men," she says without apparent passion. She was a winsome Indian, when I noticed, having a plump face like a berry and large eyes in a slightly Chinee slant and with a sheen across the underlying tear-sacs; fine though short brow beneath the vermilion parting of her hair. Her shining braids was inter-twined with otter-skin, and she wore bright beads, with brass circles in her earlobes.

I started to ask Where, instead of Who, for she probably wouldn't have told his name, when I heard the pounding of at least three riders on the plain above: unshoed horses, signifying

Indians but whether Pawnee or Cheyenne I couldn't say, and so far as that went, I disliked the approach of either in equal measure. Not speaking Pawnee, I might not get time to use the signs afore they had shot down this woman. If it was Cheyenne, well, that is obvious.

I mention this because you might question what I did next: grabbed that girl and hastened her back into the brush, the infant still at her pap, and crouched there with her, holding her still though she made no resistance.

The Pawnee arrived, for so they were as I could tell from their talk, and apparently inspected the ravine bottom from above but did not come down. Shortly they rode off, after I believe, from the sound, one had voided his water right from the saddle down the bank.

Yet me and the girl stayed where we was for some time, and it came to me that sitting on her heels she leaned her firm body back against me, taking support from it, and unwittingly in clutching her I had got through the side-lacings of the nursing dress and that unoccupied left breast of hers, weighty with milk, lay against my hand. Now I gently cupped it, I don't know why, for I surely wasn't lustful in that circumstance. But me and her and the little fellow, who had now went to sleep with his tiny mouth still quavering upon the protruded nipple, we was a kind of family. I had protected them like a father should, and like I had failed to with Olga and little Gus.

She leaned her head back and placed her warm cheek against my forehead. She smelled of suck, that sweet-sourish fragrance, and then of all them Cheyenne things I knowed of old: fire, earth, grease, blood, sweat, and utter savagery.

She says: "Now I believe you. You are Little Big Man, and I will be your wife now to replace the one you lost, and this is your son." She puts him into my arms, and he wakes briefly up and I'll swear, small as he was, grins at me with them beady black eyes. I felt right queer.

She says: "I think we had better be going. They will probably collect at Spring Creek."

"Who?"

"Our people," she answers as if that went without saying. "The Pawnee had great medicine today, but next time we will beat them and cut off their peckers, and their women will sleep alone and weep all night."

I was still holding the baby.

"You have a beautiful son," she says, looking at both of us in admiration, then takes him back. "Do you have any baggage for me to carry?"

I was still sort of stunned and didn't reply, so she fixes the baby inside her bosom, cinches her belt so as to secure his legs, then crawls up the bank to where my dead horse was laying, takes off the blanket from it and the pad saddle and my coat which I had took off and tied behind, and slides back down. She looked disappointed that that was all she had to tote.

"The wolves will eat my father tonight," she says. "We should put him on a burial scaffold, but there is no timber here and it is too far to carry him to where there are trees."

Then she steps back so I can take the lead as a man should. I guess it wasn't until that moment that I gathered her intent.

"We can't go back to the tribe," I says.

"Do you think the white men will let you have a Human Being wife?" she asks. She had a point there, though exaggerated. It wouldn't be a crime, but it would sure seem odd to Frank North were I to come back from that fight with a family I had suddenly acquired from the enemy. I could of course present this woman and child as legitimate captives, only then they'd be let in for considerable abuse from the Pawnee and later be turned over to the Army at some fort, to be held for exchange with whites taken by the Cheyenne. This was what I had had in mind earlier on, with an idea to control the trade and reclaim Olga and Gus. But right now, at a fairly outlandish moment, I got realistic. I had never received one word that my white family was still alive, and I had checked the forts along the Arkansas. And those along the Platte while working on the railroad.

Truth was, I had just about decided they was dead without admitting it.

I says: "In the mood they're in at the moment, the Cheyenne will shoot me on sight."

My woman answered: "I will be with you."

So that is how I rejoined the Human Beings. I didn't have

no regrets, leaving behind only my horse with the blacksmith in Julesburg and my share in our little hauling business. As to my sister Caroline, I ought to say that just before I had went down to Julesburg, she told me Frank Delight, the whoremaster and saloonkeeper, had asked her hand in matrimony, and she was inclined to entertain the proposition favorably.

I won't detail our route down the ravine to an intersecting one and then on, coming out behind a hill that obscured us from the Pawnee, no more of which we encountered. And continued mile upon mile of rise and fall, during which night over took us, and that woman arranged some brush and roofed it with blankets and we slept therein, cheek-by-jowl against the chill you usually get at night upon the prairie, where the wind blows all the time.

The next day we reached Spring Creek and along it found a gathering of the tribe, with remnants like us still coming in. As I expected, I had a close call or two with some of the young Dog Soldiers, but my woman drove them off me like she said she would, for she had a fierce tongue and concentrated purpose.

Old Lodge Skins had got a new tepee since last I seen him, but I recognized his shield hanging before the entranceway.

"Wait here, woman," I says, and she did as told, and I went within.

"Grandfather," I says.

"My son," he greets me, as if I had seen him last two minutes ago. "You want to eat?" He had the most equable temperament I ever knowed in a man.

He looked the same to me when I could make him out, except his eyes stayed closed. I figured he was dreaming, and sure enough he proceeded to paint a verbal picture of the incidents in that ravine.

"I saw you were returning to us," says he. "There was nothing you could have done for Shadow That Comes in Sight. He knew he would die today and told me so. Our medicine was no good against the many-firing rifles. Perhaps we should not have gone again to the iron road, but the young men wished to destroy another fire-wagon if they could catch one. It is very amusing to see the great thing come snorting and

puffing with a spray of sparks as though it would eat up the
world, I am told, then it hits the road which we have bent
into the air and topples off onto its back, still steaming and
blowing, and dies with a big sizzle."

Next to him I took a seat and we smoked then, of course.
And observing that through all this procedure he had not
opened his eyes, I decided at length he could not and had the
bad manners, maybe, to inquire.

"It is true that I am blind," he admits, "though the rifle ball
did not strike my eyes but rather passed through the back of
my neck, cutting the tunnel through which the vision travels
to the heart. Look," he said, opening his lids, "my eyes still
see, but they keep it all within themselves, and it is useless
because my heart does not receive it."

His eyes did look bright enough. I reckon it was the nerve
which had been cut or stunned in some manner.

"Where did that happen, Grandfather?" I handed him back
the long pipe.

He looked some embarrassed, and the smoke stayed inside
him a great time before it come gushing from his mouth and
nose.

"Sand Creek," he finally says.

And I groaned: "Ah, no!"

"I remember your advice," he says, "but we did not go up
to the Powder River, after all. Instead we went to the treaty
council. I shall tell you how it was. Hump had never attended
a conference, and it was one of his needs to own a silver medal
like my own. And then our young men said: 'Why shouldn't
we get presents from the white men for talking to them?
We are always in the north, and these Southern Cheyenne get
everything.' I must admit," Old Lodge Skins goes on, "that I
did not myself mind having a new red blanket.

"So that is why we turned around and came back, and we
touched the pen with the white men sent by their Father, and
Hump received his medal and the young men their new pipe-
hatchets, knives, and looking-glasses, and then we were going
to the Powder River, but the soldier chief said: 'You must stay
in this place. That is what you agreed to do when you touched
the pen.' But I tell you I did not understand that. However,

I know very little about treaties, so I believed the soldier chief was right, and we stayed, though that country was very ugly, with no water and no game. And then the soldiers attacked the village where we were camping with Black Kettle, and they rubbed out a great many of us, and that is where I was hit in the neck and became blind."

Then I feared the worst and asked after Buffalo Wallow Woman.

"She was rubbed out at Sand Creek," says Old Lodge Skins. "And White Cow Woman too. And Burns Red in the Sun and his wife Shooting Star. And Hump and High Wolf and Cut Nose and Bird Bear."

"My brother Burns Red in the Sun."

"Yes, and his wife and children. And many more, whom I will name only if you intend to mourn them, although that was several winters ago and now they will have reached the Other Side where the water is sweet, the buffalo abundant, and where there are no white men."

The latter designation he pronounced nowadays in a special way: not exactly hatefully, for Old Lodge Skins was too much a man to sit about and revile his enemies. That was for a loser, like the Rebs what lost the Civil War. And he wasn't a loser. He wasn't a winner, maybe, but neither was he a failure. You couldn't call the Cheyenne flops unless they had had a railroad engine of their own which never worked as well as the U.P.'s or had invented a gun that didn't shoot straight.

Just to check my impression, I asks him: "Do you hate the Americans?"

"No," he says, closing up his gleaming though dead eyes. "But now I understand them. I no longer believe they are fools or crazy. I know now that they do not drive away the buffalo by mistake or accidentally set fire to the prairie with their fire-wagon or rub out Human Beings because of a misunderstanding. No, they *want* to do these things, and they succeed in doing them. They are a powerful people." He took something from his beaded belt at that point and, stroking it, said: "The Human Beings believe that everything is alive: not only men and animals but also water and earth and stones and also the dead and things from them like this hair. The person from whom this hair came is bald on the Other Side, because I now own this scalp. This is the *way things are.*

"But white men believe that everything is dead: stones, earth, animals, and people, even their own people. And if, in spite of that, things persist in trying to live, white men will rub them out.

"That," he concludes, "is the difference between white men and Human Beings."

Then I looked close at the scalp he stroked, which was of the silkiest blond. For a moment I was sure it come from Olga's dear head, and reckoned also he had little Gus's fine skull-cover someplace among his filthy effects, the stinking old savage, living out his life of murder, rapine, and squalor, and I almost knifed him before I collected myself and realized the hair was honeyer than my Swedish wife's.

I mention this because it shows how a person's passion can reverse on the instant he is reminded of his own loss. I had just been moved by Sand Creek, and the next minute was ready to kill him.

Now, Old Lodge Skins took cognizance of my state though blind.

"Have you," he asks, "a great sorrow or is it only bitterness?"

So I told him, and he never heard of the incident in which Olga and Gus was taken. He could not have lied. I have said that it is amazing what and how Indians know about events far distant from them; but likewise there are things they do not hear. In that era the capturing of white women and children was commonplace. A Cheyenne of one band might not know of those took by another, unless they camped together.

Then Old Lodge Skins said: "Our young men are angry nowadays. Many times they have not the patience to wait to ransom or exchange prisoners, but will become crazy with rage and rub them out. But was that not the voice of Sunshine I just heard outside my tepee? She is the widow of Little Shield, who was killed two moons ago, but now she will be your new wife and give you a new son, so that you have what you had before and better, for of course a woman of the Human Beings is superior to any other kind."

He wasn't being heartless, just making the best of likelihoods, as an Indian had to do in the sort of life he lived. His own two wives was massacred, and so he had mourned them for the proper time and then got himself replacements. These last had come and gone in the tepee while we talked: young women, sisters again, probably fifty year below the chief in age, but by God if they didn't both look pregnant to me.

"All right," I said. "But I tell you this, that if I find my first woman and my son again, I will take them back from whatever man is keeping them. And if they have been rubbed out, I will kill whoever did it."

"Of course," said Old Lodge Skins, for there wasn't nothing an Indian could better understand than revenge, and he would have scorned me only if I had not wanted it.

There couldn't have been a worse era for running with the Cheyenne. They was being chased throughout the whole frontier, and whenever they eluded their pursuers, would commit some new outrage against the whites. So I would be on the one hand a renegade to join them, in danger from the whole of my own race. On the other hand, I was under a constant threat from the Cheyenne themselves, for to many of them the very sight of a white face was the occasion for mayhem. I reckon the only thing that saved me was Old Lodge Skins's band had collected apart from the main force of Chief Turkey Leg, who had commanded the fight at the railroad, so I was most of the time among the group in which I was reared and where the Little Big Man legend still had some power. My woman Sunshine was good protection, and of course Old Lodge Skins too. But there were braves who had growed up since I left the tribe, like young Cut Belly, who one day raided a stage station and come back with a jug of whisky and says to me:

"I want you to go out on the prairie and hide, because though I do not wish to kill you now, I will when I am drunk. I'm sorry for this, because I am told you are a good man, but that is what will happen."

Now the best way to get killed was to let a young fellow like that give you orders, so I says: "I think it is you who had better go out on the prairie for your drinking, because the way I am is that something comes over me when I see a drunk, and

I have to shoot him, even if he is my brother. I can't help it; that's just how I am."

He took my advice in that instance, and I survived other such threats, but can't say I was ever popular, which hurt when I recalled my boyhood up along the Powder River as Little Big Man, but I was grown up now and that always involves disappointments. I was real lucky just in that I had still kept my hair. I lived from day to day, and there is a certain sweetness in that style of life, even when you have a long-range purpose as I did, for I was letting it come to me rather than chase it, and knowing it *would* come, I could live otherwise without apparent point, like an Indian, and eat roast hump when we found buffalo and draw in my slack belly when we didn't, and lay under a cottonwood and watch my woman Sunshine at hard labor with that little fellow sleeping in the cradleboard lashed to her back. His name was Frog Lying on a Hillside, for we had passed such in fleeing that afternoon of the railroad fight and the tiny child seemed to wake up then and nod at it, and both me and Sunshine believed it was right to let a boy pick his own name.

When we had reached the Indian camp, Sunshine had to mourn for her dead father and though she was quite good at that, weeping and wailing with a horrible din, she had to knock it off whenever she was feeding Frog, and she also never felt free to tear her hair or cut herself up with him on her back. So her kin helped out, all through one night and the next as well, for Shadow had been a man of high repute and it was extra terrible that he didn't have a scaffold to protect his carcass from the wolves. So these women howled and moaned until they gasped for air, the way a child does what has cried himself hysteric—I mean a white kid; little Indians don't do that.

Take Frog now, tied up into his cradleboard, with his little head like a brown bean; when he wasn't sleeping or eating, them sharp black eyes was studying everything within short range and never took displeasure. He reminded me frequently of little Gus, for my boy had had the even temperament of his own Ma, but there was a difference no less marked. Gus was ever delighted in my pocket watch, which I'd hang before him to produce its tick, like everybody does with babies and they is fascinated. Not Frog. It didn't make him sorry, for nothing did that, but he just cared nought for it: looked through and listened past it, you might say.

Or maybe what did not interest him was the person holding it. Talk as Sunshine did and Old Lodge Skins too of him being my son, Frog himself was not fooled. He didn't hate me; I was simply to him a kind of device that picked him up on occasion and embraced him, or swung him high into the air and let him down again, and he liked the motion and the contact but acknowledged in it nothing personal.

Then again, maybe the deficiency was mine, for though I liked him, I had had no hand in making him and could see no future for us as boy and Pa, no matter whether I ever found Gus and Olga again or not. The Cheyenne was finished. They knowed it, and I knowed, and little Frog was born into that knowledge. The best I could of done in acting like a father would have been to carry him off to Omaha or Denver and put him in a school. Make him white, bring him up to live in a permanent square house and get up every day and go to work by schedule. But you have seen what he thought of that instrument to measure time.

However, I couldn't have asked for a more ardent wife than Sunshine. That woman was utterly devoted to me, so much so —and I hate to say this, but it was true—that she commenced to bore me. I reckon the circumstances of our meeting had to do with the respective attitudes of us both. She saw it as a peculiarly touching thing that I had showed up in her hour of grievous need—though she exaggerated that: she was tough enough to have had that baby and escaped by herself—whereas to me she had started out as a burden, which while I freely assumed it there in that ravine as an emergency measure, seemed to gain weight as we lived in the camp.

I have to explain, for as you know the Cheyenne male never does what the white world understands as labor. When not hunting I spent most of my time on the flat of my back beneath a tree or, failing that, in the shade of a tepee. I gambled a little with the other braves and occasionally raced my pony which had been given to me by Old Lodge Skins, but was somewhat leery about winning on account of I didn't want trouble with the losers. I did not join no war or raiding parties, for nowadays they was always against white men. You might see mine as an impossible position to maintain, but if so you don't know Indians, whom you can live among on almost any terms but those of outright enmity, and I expect you could even survive the latter situation as long as you had one loyal defender. I had two: the chief and my wife. Sometimes an over-wrought young man would come in with a fresh white scalp and offer to insult me with it, but I'd either handle him like I did Cut Belly or look right through him as if he was glass, depending on the situation and my judgment of his character. Or if Sunshine was around, she'd light into him so rough I'd usually end up secretly on his side, for she had a right sharp tongue and I don't remember as I have said that whereas Cheyenne maidens was shy and soft-spoken, the married women was just the reverse and specialized in themes that in civilization was more common to the saloon than to where ladies gathered. They had license to talk this way, I guess, because in practice they was so respectable. You seldom saw a cut-nosed woman among the Human Beings—did I mention that a Plains Indian clipped off the end of his wife's nose if she dallied with another man?

Well sir, I suppose a bachelor is at a peculiar disadvantage up against a respectable married woman everywhere in the world, and Sunshine would cast reflection on the young fellow's potency and speculate unfavorably on the quality of his endowments, etc., with the other women laughing nearby, maybe including some young girl he had a crush on, and away he'd slink, poor devil, having arrived a hero and departed a buffoon.

Now, as if it wasn't bad enough to be defended by a woman in that style, next Sunshine would get to boasting about me. First it was how I saved her from the Pawnee, and that story growed from what had really happened, us cowering in that bush, to my standing off five or six of them and dropping three. She wasn't a liar: I reckon that somehow that is what she saw through the distorting spectacles of her recollection. Then of course if she could be vocal about another man's sexual abilities of which she knowed nothing, think of what she might do with the man on whom she stood as the local authority: I become a champion stud.

And I tell you it embarrassed me to be so characterized, but you know how it is, a person is sometimes the victim of his own vanity, so I fair killed myself trying to live up to my reputation, during the nights under our buffalo robe. Jesus, there was mornings when I couldn't stand up straight, feeling like I had been kicked by a horse into the small of my back. I guess it ain't right to tell this, for Sunshine was my wife and though a man can talk endlessly of his adulteries and fornications, the subject is in bad taste when it concerns respectable mating, I don't know why.

The only way I finally got off the hook was that Sunshine one day turned up pregnant. That must have been about late March of '68, figuring on the basis of what happened nine months after; otherwise I'd never have had any idea of the time, for by then I had been with the Cheyenne for three seasons and fallen back into the style of dating things by the northward flight of the wild geese, for example, which meant the oncoming of spring, as did the appearance of hair on the unborn calves taken out of buffalo cows we killed.

During all this time we ranged mainly between the Arkansas and the Platte, which is now southern Nebraska and northern Kansas, and there was another railroad building in the latter state: the Kansas Pacific, along the Smoky Hill River, which had been good buffalo country, and so the game grew scarcer and we ate more roots than meat. And the troops was after us, and the Pawnee, but by the superior generalship of Old Lodge Skins, blind though he was, as a village we eluded them all, though our small raiding parties had many a small-scale brush.

Our band continued to live apart from the other Cheyenne, though we'd run into some of them from time to time, and when we would I'd inquire after Olga and Gus. Which was a ticklish business, my being white, and maybe I didn't always hear the truth. Anyway, it availed me nothing except more close calls, for some of these outfits held other white captives and did not want me snooping around their tepees.

Nor was Old Lodge Skins a deal of help in this matter. His blindness cut down his horny behavior—he couldn't eye no more fat wenches—but it had strengthened his intention to go his own way. What happened in the fall of '67 was that the Government signed another treaty with the Southern Cheyenne, Arapaho, Kiowa, and Comanche, by which the Indians agreed to stay down in western Oklahoma, then known as the Nations. A runner found our camp and delivered an invite to Old Lodge Skins, but the chief had had enough of treaties after Sand Creek and wouldn't attend the conference. Nor did he purpose to abide by that agreement.

"I will not live in that bad place," he told me, referring to the western Nations. "The grass is poor there, and the water is bitter. And it is properly the country of the Snake People, who I know are our friends now, but they copulate with horses and that makes them strange to me. Also the People of the Rasp Fiddle"—Apache—"come there, and they are brave but extremely ugly, being short and bowlegged and not at all handsome like the Human Beings. A long time ago when we used to fight them, I captured an Apache woman but it was like lying with a cactus, so I sent her back to her people with some presents, which was a great insult. . . . "

"They tell me Back Kettle attended this conference. I am only too familiar with the kind of treaties to which he touches the pen. I was at Sand Creek with him and lost my family, my friends, and my vision. Without eyes I see more clearly than he."

Now it might have been to my own interest to want to stay down south, and even urge him to join the main body of the Southern Cheyenne, for if my own family was yet alive, that is where they would probably be. But I couldn't, just couldn't. I had a weakness where that old Indian was concerned.

So what I says was: "I can't understand why you don't go up to the Powder River. If you had done that when I first suggested it, you wouldn't have been at Sand Creek."

"I shall tell you why," says Old Lodge Skins. "I prefer it in the Powder River country. I was born there, on the Rosebud Creek. Indeed, my medicine works only half-strength when I come below the Shell River," which is what he called the

Platte. "But the Americans, other than a few trappers, do not care about that country. So long as the Human Beings stay there, they will not be bothered by the white men."

"That is exactly my point," says I, wondering whether the old devil had lost his wits as well as his sight.

"Yes," he said, "and I, chief of the greatest warriors on the face of the earth, I should avoid danger like the rabbit? I should let them drive me from this land where I have killed buffalo and Pawnee for eighty summers? A Human Being has always gone wherever he wished, and if someone tried to stop him, he rubbed them out or was killed by them. If I were so cowardly, my people would never respect me. There are many fine young men in this band, and they no longer have the doubts that our warriors had in the earlier days. They have decided to fight the white men wherever they can find them, and rip up those iron rails and drive away the fire wagons. Once that is done, they will kill all the remaining Americans, so that we can hunt again without being bothered and make war on the Pawnee."

"Grandfather," I says, "do you honestly believe that can be done?"

"My son," says Old Lodge Skins, "if it cannot, then the sun will shine upon a good day to die."

The Beecher Island fight took place, in which five or six hundred Cheyenne cornered fifty white scouts on a sandbar in the middle of the Arickaree Fork and besieged them there for nine days. But the whites was again armed with the Spencer repeaters and held off every charge, killing a good many Indians, among them the great Cheyenne warrior, Roman Nose. Then the cavalry came.

I wasn't there, but our young men were, and they returned to camp full of weariness and defeat. I stayed inside the lodge for a time so as to avoid incidents, but I would not have had to, the way they was feeling. The Cheyenne still didn't have no firearms worth the name, and it must make a man feel pretty bad to have the advantage in number but still be beat by the other fellow on account of his superior armament. I had long since buried that pistol of mine and generally kept the Ballard out of sight: no sense in adding to the ill feeling.

So what them Indians got to doing now was trying to lick the problem from the other end and dream up some medicine to make themselves impervious to bullets. One fellow seemed to have made it, for he had been shot at Beecher's Island through the chest and did some hocus-pocus over the wound and it closed up without unfortunate effect, and he took the name Bullet Proof. So he fixed up several other braves with his medicine and a couple of weeks after the Island fight, they went against the cavalry. Out of seven Human Beings using that medicine, two was immediately rubbed out and Bullet Proof brought them back to camp and tried to raise them from the dead. One twitched his leg a little, stopped, and neither got up. Bullet Proof then admitted his failure.

I reckon it was because of such events that Old Lodge Skins and even his fierce young men had to limit their ambition to mere survival, and after a time we found ourselves with the village of Black Kettle, who the white men in afterdays sometimes called the great Indian statesman, I guess because he was always signing treaties to keep the peace and give away more of the Cheyenne hunting grounds to the railroads and ranchers.

Anyway, that's how I happened to be at the Battle of the Washita. And as usual, on the side that lost.

PAUL JENKINS

Custer's Last Stand

In the cottonwoods below, in the mind's eye,
The kingfisher leaps and dives its magic arc,
Its terrible poise above the circled Sioux.
Rawhide guides its feet, ribbons unfurl
Blood that left the flesh dry years before.
Tomorrow the sun itself will clot. Tonight
A full moon bathes red faces, and the river
Washes it like a clean heat upon herbs.

Unpublished poem by a young West Coast poet currently teaching at the University of Massachusetts at Amherst,

We dream in images of death . . . unspeakable,
Custer recoils. Vultures. Four days' forced march
Breaking troops to discipline—if you come
On a stream shoot the first man in. Water
Bloats a soldier. Stamina, stamina
Is a man's perfection. One hundred fifty-five
Miles in bone-dry hills, skin cracks, and now Montana
Opens before you everywhere. Keep walking.

Feel them below in the dark; they are in the trees,
Scheming to feel your scalp, your luminous skin
Slippery with paint. Indians are eating dogfish,
Faces shining like Mediterraneans.
They make decaying charms of birds
To hypnotize their lust. The Little Big Horn's
High with fever. Make them come north to the
Bare hills. Clear shots. They'll die like flies.

Day dawns on two geographies,
Silence of sagebrush, baked earth, sun,
Above the river's rush through grass and cottonwoods.
Who strikes? Who is more vulnerable?
Sunlight throbs and throbs. The river boils.
The only virtue is skill. My men know
What a straight line's for. I'll level the savages,
Drive them into the sun.

I run downhill. I swim rivers—
Now the grass bends—now I am in your tent—
I am looking your heart in the eye.
Bone-dry valleys raven in red clay.
Indian, Indian, my purpose flows away.
Kill me before my blood runs dry.

GARY SNYDER

Earth House Hold

"It will be a revival, in higher form, of the liberty,
equality, and fraternity of the ancient gentes."

—Lewis Henry Morgan

The Tribe

The celebrated human Be-In in San Francisco, January of
1967, was called "A Gathering of the Tribes." The two posters:
one based on a photograph of a Shaivite sadhu with his long
matted hair, ashes and beard; the other based on an old etching
of a Plains Indian approaching a powwow on his horse—the
carbine that had been cradled in his left arm replaced by a
guitar. The Indians, and the Indian. The tribes were Berkeley,
North Beach, Big Sur, Marin County, Los Angeles, and the
host, Haight-Ashbury. Outriders were present from New York,
London and Amsterdam. Out on the polo field that day the
splendidly clad ab/originals often fell into clusters, with children, a few even under banners. These were the clans.

Large old houses are rented communally by a group, occupied by couples and singles (or whatever combinations) and
their children. In some cases, especially in the rock-and-roll
business and with light-show groups, they are all working together on the same creative job. They might even be a legal
corporation. Some are subsistence farmers out in the country,
some are contractors and carpenters in small coast towns.
One girl can stay home and look after all the children while
the other girls hold jobs. They will all be cooking and eating
together and they may well be brown-rice vegetarians. There
might not be much alcohol or tobacco around the house, but
there will certainly be a stash of marijuana and probably some

LSD. If the group has been together for some time it may be known by some informal name, magical and natural. These house-holds provide centers in the city and also out in the country for loners and rangers; gathering places for the scattered smaller hip families and havens for the questing adolescent children of the neighborhood. The clan sachems will sometimes gather to talk about larger issues—police or sheriff department harassments, busts, anti-Vietnam projects, dances and gatherings.

All this is known fact. The number of committed total tribesmen is not so great, but there is a large population of crypto-members who move through many walks of life undetected and only put on their beads and feathers for special occasions. Some are in the academies, others in the legal or psychiatric professions—very useful friends indeed. The number of people who use marijuana regularly and have experienced LSD is (considering it's all illegal) staggering. The impact of all this on the cultural and imaginative life of the nation—even the politics—is enormous.

And yet, there's nothing very new about it, in spite of young hippies just in from the suburbs for whom the "beat generation" is a kalpa away. For several centuries now Western Man has been ponderously preparing himself for a new look at the inner world and the spiritual realms. Even in the centers of nineteenth-century materialism there were dedicated seekers— some within Christianity, some in the arts, some within the occult circles. Witness William Butler Yeats. My own opinion is that we are now experiencing a surfacing (in a specifically "American" incarnation) of the Great Subculture which goes back as far perhaps as the late Paleolithic.

This subculture of illuminati has been a powerful undercurrent in all higher civilizations. In China it manifested as Taoism, not only Lao-tzu but the later Yellow Turban revolt and medieval Taoist secret societies; and the Zen Buddhists up till early Sung. Within Islam the Sufis; in India the various threads converged to produce Tantrism. In the West it has been represented largely by a string of heresies starting with the Gnostics, and on the folk level by "witchcraft."

Buddhist Tantrism, or Vajrayana as it's also known, is

probably the finest and most modern statement of this ancient shamanistic-yogic-gnostic-socioeconomic view: that mankind's mother is Nature and Nature should be tenderly respected; that man's life and destiny is growth and enlightenment in self-disciplined freedom; that the divine has been made flesh and that flesh is divine; that we not only should but *do* love one another. This view has been harshly suppressed in the past as threatening to both Church and State. Today, on the contrary, these values seem almost biologically essential to the survival of humanity.

The Family

Lewis Henry Morgan (d. 1881) was a New York lawyer. He was asked by his club to reorganize it "after the pattern of the Iroquois confederacy." His research converted him into a defender of tribal rights and started him on his career as an amateur anthropologist. His major contribution was a broad theory of social evolution which is still useful. Morgan's *Ancient Society* inspired Engels to write *Origins of the Family, Private Property and the State* (1884, and still in print in both Russia and China), in which the relations between the rights of women, sexuality and the family, and attitudes toward property and power are tentatively explored. The pivot is the revolutionary implications of the custom of matrilineal descent, which Engels learned from Morgan; the Iroquois are matrilineal.

A schematic history of the family:

Hunters and gatherers—a loose monogamy within communal clans usually reckoning descent in the female line, i.e., matrilineal.

Early agriculturalists—a tendency toward group and polyandrous marriage, continued matrilineal descent and smaller-sized clans.

Pastoral nomads—a tendency toward stricter monogamy and patrilineal descent; but much premarital sexual freedom.

Iron-Age agriculturalists—property begins to accumulate and the family system changes to monogamy or polygyny with patrilineal descent. Concern with the legitimacy of heirs.

Civilization so far has implied a patriarchal, patrilineal family. Any other system allows too much creative sexual energy to be released into channels which are "unproductive." In the West, the clan, or gens, disappeared gradually, and social organization was ultimately replaced by political organization, within which separate male-oriented families compete: the modern state.

Engels' Marxian classic implies that the revolution cannot be completely achieved in merely political terms. Monogamy and patrilineal descent may well be great obstructions to the inner changes required for a people to truly live by "communism." Marxists after Engels let these questions lie. Russia and China today are among the world's stanchest supporters of monogamous, sexually turned-off families. Yet Engels' insights were not entirely ignored. The Anarcho-Syndicalists showed a sense for experimental social reorganization. American anarchists and the I.W.W. lived a kind of communalism, with some lovely stories handed down of free love— their slogan was more than just words: "Forming the new society within the shell of the old." San Francisco poets and gurus were attending meetings of the "Anarchist Circle"—old Italians and Finns—in the 1940s.

The Redskins

In many American Indian cultures it is obligatory for every member to get out of the society, out of the human nexus, and "out of his head," at least once in his life. He returns from his solitary vision quest with a secret name, a protective animal spirit, a secret song. It is his "power." The culture honors the man who has visited other realms.

Peyote, the mushroom, morning-glory seeds, and Jimson-weed are some of the best-known herbal aids used by Indian cultures to assist in the quest. Most tribes apparently achieved these results simply through yogic-type disciplines: including sweat-baths, hours of dancing, fasting, and total isolation. After the decline of the apocalyptic fervor of Wovoka's Ghost Dance religion (a pan-Indian movement of the 1880s and 1890s which believed that if all the Indians would dance the

Ghost Dance with their Ghost shirts on, the Buffalo would rise from the ground, trample the white men to death in their dreams, and all the dead game would return; America would be restored to the Indians), the peyote cult spread and established itself in most of the western American tribes. Although the peyote religion conflicts with pre-existing tribal religions in a few cases (notably with the Pueblo), there is no doubt that the cult has been a positive force, helping the Indians maintain a reverence for their traditions and land through their period of greatest weakness—which is now over. European scholars were investigating peyote in the twenties. It is even rumored that Dr. Carl Jung was experimenting with peyote then. A small band of white peyote users emerged, and peyote was easily available in San Francisco by the late 1940s. In Europe some researchers on these alkaloid compounds were beginning to synthesize them. There is a karmic connection between the peyote cult of the Indians and the discovery of lysergic acid in Switzerland.

Peyote and acid have a curious way of tuning some people in to the local soil. The strains and stresses deep beneath one in the rock, the flow and fabric of wildlife around, the human history of Indians on this continent. Older powers become evident: west of the Rockies, the ancient creator-trickster, Coyote. Jaime de Angulo, a now-legendary departed Spanish shaman and anthropologist, was an authentic Coyote-medium. One of the most relevant poetry magazines in called *Coyote's Journal*. For many, the invisible presence of the Indian, and the heartbreaking beauty of America work without fasting or herbs. We make these contacts simply by walking the Sierra or Mohave, learning the old edibles, singing, and watching.

The Jewel in the Lotus

At the Congress of World Religions in Chicago in the 1890s, two of the most striking figures were Swami Vivekananda (Shri Ramakrishna's disciple) and Shaku Soyen, the Zen Master and Abbot of Engaku-ji, representing Japanese Rinzai Zen. Shaku Soyen's interpreter was a college student named Teitaro Suzuki. The Ramakrishna-Vivekananda line produced scores of books and established Vedanta centers all through the Western world. A small band of Zen monks under Shaku Sokatsu (disciple of Shaku Soyen) was raising strawberries in Hayward, California, in 1907. Shigetsu Sasaki, later to be known as the Zen Master Sokei-an, was roaming the timberlands of the Pacific Northwest just before World War I, and living on a Puget Sound Island with Indians for neighbors. D. T. Suzuki's books are to be found today in the libraries of biochemists and on stone ledges under laurel trees in the open-air camps of Big Sur gypsies.

A Californian named Walter Y. Evans-Wentz, who sensed that the mountains on his family's vast grazing lands really did have spirits in them, went to Oxford to study the Celtic belief in fairies and then to Sikkim to study Vajrayana under a lama. His best-known book is *The Tibetan Book of the Dead*.

Those who do not have the money or time to go to India or Japan, but who think a great deal about the wisdom traditions, have remarkable results when they take LSD. The *Bhagavad-Gita*, the Hindu mythologies, *The Serpent Power*, the *Lankavatara-sūtra*, the *Upanishads*, the *Hevajra-tantra*, the *Mahanirvana-tantra*—to name a few texts—become, they say, finally clear to them. They often feel they must radically reorganize their lives to harmonize with such insights.

In several American cities traditional meditation halls of both Rinzai and Soto Zen are flourishing. Many of the newcomers turned to traditional meditation after initial acid experience. The two types of experience seem to inform each other.

The Heretics

"When Adam delved and Eve span,
Who was then a gentleman?"

The memories of a Golden Age—the Garden of Eden—the Age of the Yellow Ancestor—were genuine expressions of civilization and its discontents. Harking back to societies where women and men were more free with each other; where there was more singing and dancing; where there were no serfs and priests and kings.

Projected into future time in Christian culture, this dream of the Millennium became the soil of many heresies. It is a dream handed down right to our own time—of ecological balance, classless society, social and economic freedom. It is actually one of the possible futures open to us. To those who stubbornly argue "it's against human nature," we can only patiently reply that you must know your own nature before you can say this. Those who have gone into their own natures deeply have, for several thousand years now, been reporting that we have nothing to fear if we are willing to train ourselves, to open up, explore and grow.

One of the most significant medieval heresies was the Brotherhood of the Free Spirit, of which Hieronymus Bosch was probably a member. The Brotherhood believed that God was immanent in everything, and that once one had experienced this God-presence in himself he became a Free Spirit; he was again living in the Garden of Eden. The brothers and sisters held their meetings naked, and practiced much sharing. They "confounded clerics with the subtlety of their arguments." It was complained that "they have no uniform ... sometimes they dress in a costly and dissolute fashion, sometimes most miserably, all according to time and place." The Free Spirits had communal houses in secret all through Germany and the Lowlands, and wandered freely among them. Their main supporters were the well-organized and affluent weavers.

When brought before the Inquisition they were not charged with witchcraft, but with believing that man was divine, and with making love too freely, with orgies. Thousands were burned. There are some who have as much hostility to the adepts of the subculture today. This may be caused not so much by the outlandish clothes and dope, as by the nutty insistence on "love." The West and Christian culture on one level deeply wants love to win—and having decided (after several sad tries) that love can't, people who still say it will are like ghosts from an old dream.

Love begins with the family and its network of erotic and responsible relationships. A slight alteration of family structure will project a different love-and-property outlook through a whole culture...thus the communism and free love of the Christian heresies. This is a real razor's edge. Shall the lion lie down with the lamb? And make love even? The Garden of Eden.

White Indians

The modern American family is the smallest and most barren family that has ever existed. Each newly married couple moves to a new house or apartment—no uncles or grandmothers come to live with them. There are seldom more than two or three children. The children live with their peers and leave home early. Many have never had the least sense of family.

I remember sitting down to Christmas dinner eighteen years ago in a communal house in Portland, Oregon, with about twelve others my own age, all of whom had no place they wished to go home to. That house was my first discovery of harmony and community with fellow beings. This has been the experience of hundreds of thousands of men and women all over America since the end of World War II. Hence the talk about the growth of a "new society." But more; these gatherings have been people spending time with each other— talking, delving, making love. Because of the sheer amount of time "wasted" together (without TV) they know each other better than most Americans know their own family. Add to this the mind-opening and personality-revealing effects of grass and acid, and it becomes possible to predict the emergence of groups who live by mutual illumination—have seen themselves as of one mind and one flesh—the "single eye" of the heretical English Ranters; the meaning of sahajiya, "born together"—the name of the latest flower of the Tantric community tradition in Bengal.

Industrial society indeed appears to be finished. Many of us are, again, hunters and gatherers. Poets, musicians, nomadic engineers and scholars; fact-diggers, searchers and re-searchers scoring in rich foundation territory. Horse-traders in lore and magic. The super hunting-bands of mercenaries like Rand or CIA may in some ways belong to the future, if they can be transformed by the ecological conscience, or acid, to which they are very vulnerable. A few of us are literally hunters and gatherers, playfully studying the old techniques of acorn flour, seaweed-gathering, yucca-fiber, rabbit snaring and bow hunting. The densest Indian population in pre-Columbian America north of Mexico was in Marin, Sonoma and Napa Counties, California.

And finally, to go back to Morgan and Engels, sexual mores and the family are changing in the same direction. Rather than the "breakdown of the family" we should see this as the transition to a new form of family. In the near future, I think it likely that the freedom of women and the tribal spirit will make it possible for us to formalize our marriage relationships in any way we please—as groups, or polygynously or polyandrously, as well as monogamously. I use the word "formalize" only in the sense of make public and open the relationships, and to sacramentalize them; to see family as part of the divine ecology. Because it is simpler, more natural, and breaks up tendencies toward property accumulation by individual families, matrilineal descent seems ultimately indicated. Such families already exist. Their children are different in personality structure and outlook from anybody in the history of Western culture since the destruction of Knossos.

The American Indian is the vengeful ghost lurking in the back of the troubled American mind. Which is why we lash out with such ferocity and passion, so muddied a heart, at the black-haired young peasants and soldiers who are the "Viet Cong." That ghost will claim the next generation as its own. When this has happened, citizens of the USA will at last begin to be Americans, truly at home on the continent, in love with their land. The chorus of a Cheyenne Indian Ghost dance song —"hi-niswa' vita'ki'ni"—"We shall live again."

"Passage to more than India!
Are thy wings plumed indeed for such far flights
O soul, voyagest thou indeed on voyages like those?"

LUTHER STANDING BEAR

Land of the Spotted Eagle

The feathered and blanketed figure of the American Indian has come to symbolize the American continent. He is the man who through centuries has been molded and sculpted by the same hand that shaped its mountains, forests, and plains, and marked the course of its rivers.

The American Indian is of the soil, whether it be the region of forests, plains, pueblos, or mesas. He fits into the landscape, for the hand that fashioned the continent also fashioned the man for his surroundings. He once grew as naturally as the wild sunflowers; he belongs just as the buffalo belonged.

With a physique that fitted, the man developed fitting skills —crafts which today are called American. And the body had a soul, also formed and molded by the same master hand of harmony. Out of the Indian approach to existence there came a great freedom—an intense and absorbing love for nature; a respect for life; enriching faith in a Supreme Power; and principles of truth, honesty, generosity, equity, and brotherhood as a guide to mundane relations.

Becoming possessed of a fitting philosophy and art, it was by them that native man perpetuated his identity; stamped it into the history and soul of this country—made land and man one.

By living—struggling, losing, meditating, imbibing, aspiring, achieving—he wrote himself into ineraceable evidence—an evidence that can be and often has been ignored, but never totally destroyed. Living—and all the intangible forces that constitute that phenomenon—are brought into being by Spirit, that which no man can alter. Only the hand of the Supreme Power can transform man; only Wakan Tanka can transform

From Luther Standing Bear, *Land of the Spotted Eagle* (Boston and New York, 1933), Chapter 9.

the Indian. But of such deep and infinite graces finite man has little comprehension. He has, therefore, no weapons with which to slay the unassailable. He can only foolishly trample.

The white man does not understand the Indian for the reason that he does not understand America. He is too far removed from its formative processes. The roots of the tree of his life have not yet grasped the rock and soil. The white man is still troubled with primitive fears; he still has in his consciousness the perils of this frontier continent, some of its fastnesses not yet having yielded to his questing footsteps and inquiring eyes. He shudders still with the memory of the loss of his forefathers upon its scorching deserts and forbidding mountaintops. The man from Europe is still a foreigner and an alien. And he still hates the man who questioned his path across the continent.

But in the Indian the spirit of the land is still vested; it will be until other men are able to divine and meet its rhythm. Men must be born and reborn to belong. Their bodies must be formed of the dust of their forefathers' bones.

The attempted transformation of the Indian by the white man and the chaos that has resulted are but the fruits of the white man's disobedience of a fundamental and spiritual law. The pressure that has been brought to bear upon the native people, since the cessation of armed conflict, in the attempt to force conformity of custom and habit has caused a reaction more destructive than war, and the injury has not only affected the Indian, but has extended to the white population as well. Tyranny, stupidity, and lack of vision have brought about the situation now alluded to as the "Indian Problem."

There is, I insist, no Indian problem as created by the Indian himself. Every problem that exists today in regard to the native population is due to the white man's cast of mind, which is unable, at least reluctant, to seek understanding and achieve adjustment in a new and a significant environment into which it has so recently come.

The white man excused his presence here by saying that he had been guided by the will of his God; and in so saying absolved himself of all responsibility for his appearance in a land occupied by other men.

Then, too, his law was a written law; his divine decalogue reposed in a book. And what better proof that his advent into this country and his subsequent acts were the result of divine will! He brought the Word! There ensued a blind worship of written history, of books, of the written word, that has denuded the spoken word of its power and sacredness. The written word became established as a criterion of the superior man—a symbol of emotional fineness. The man who could write his name on a piece of paper, whether or not he possessed the spiritual fineness to honor those words in speech, was by some miraculous formula a more highly devoloped and sensitized person than the one who had never had a pen in hand, but whose spoken word was inviolable and whose sense of honor and truth was paramount. With false reasoning was the quality of human character measured by man's ability to make with an implement a mark upon paper. But granting this mode of reasoning be correct and just, then where are to be placed the thousands of illiterate whites who are unable to read and write? Are they, too, "savages"? Is not humanness a matter of heart and mind, and is it not evident in the form of relationship with men? Is not kindness more powerful than arrogance; and truth more powerful than the sword?

True, the white man brought great change. But the varied fruits of his civilization, though highly colored and inviting, are sickening and deadening. And if it be the part of civilization to maim, rob, and thwart, then what is progress?

I am going to venture that the man who sat on the ground in his tepee meditating on life and its meaning, accepting the kinship of all creatures, and acknowledging unity with the universe of things was infusing into his being the true essence of civilization. And when native man left off this form of development, his humanization was retarded in growth.

Another most powerful agent that gave native man promise of developing into a true human was the responsibility accepted by parenthood. Mating among Lakotas was motivated, of course, by the same laws of attraction that motivate all beings; however, considerable thought was given by parents of both boy and girl to the choosing of mates. And a still greater advantage accrued to the race by the law of self-mastery which the young couple voluntarily placed upon themselves as soon as they discovered they were to become parents. Immediately, and for some time after, the sole thought of the parents was in preparing the child for life. And true civilization lies in the dominance of self and not in the dominance of other men.

How far this idea would have gone in carrying my people upward and toward a better plane of existence, or how much of an influence it was in the development of their spiritual being, it is not possible to say. But it had its promises. And it cannot be gainsaid that the man who is rising to a higher estate is the man who is putting into his being the essence of humanism. It is self-effort that develops, and by this token the greatest factory today in dehumanizing races is the manner in which the machine is used—the product of one man's brain doing the work for another. The hand is the tool that has built man's mind; it, too, can refine it.

The Savage

After subjugation, after dispossession, there was cast the last abuse upon the people who so entirely resented their wrongs and punishments, and that was the stamping and the labeling of them as savages. To make this label stick has been the task of the white race and the greatest salve that it has been able to apply to its sore and troubled conscience now hardened through the habitual practice of injustice.

But all the years of calling the Indian a savage has never made him one; all the denial of his virtues has never taken them from him; and the very resistance he has made to save the things inalienably his has been his saving strength—that which will stand him in need when justice does make its belated appearance and he undertakes rehabilitation.

All sorts of feeble excuses are heard for the continued subjection of the Indian. One of the most common is that he is not yet ready to accept the society of the white man—that he is not yet ready to mingle as a social entity.

This, I maintain, is beside the question. The matter is not one of making-over the external Indian into the likeness of the white race—a process detrimental to both races. Who can say that the white man's way is better for the Indian? Where resides the human judgment with the competence to weigh and value Indian ideals and spiritual concepts; or substitute for them other values?

Then, has the white man's social order been so harmonious and ideal as to merit the respect of the Indian, and for that matter the thinking class of the white race? Is it wise to urge upon the Indian a foreign social form? Let none but the Indian answer!

Rather, let the white brother face about and cast his mental eye upon a new angle of vision. Let him look upon the Indian world as a human world; then let him see to it that human rights be accorded to the Indians. And this for the purpose of retaining for his own order of society a measure of humanity.

The Indian School of Thought

I say again that Indians should teach Indians; that Indians should serve Indians, especially on reservations where the older people remain. There is a definite need of the old for the care and sympathy of the young and they are today perishing for the joys that naturally belong to old Indian people. Old Indians are very close to their progeny. It was their delightful duty to care for and instruct the very young, while in turn they looked forward to being cared for by sons and daughters. These were the privileges and blessings of old age.

Many of the grievances of the old Indian, and his disagreements with the young, find root in the far-removed boarding-school which sometimes takes the little ones at a very tender age. More than one tragedy has resulted when a young boy or girl has returned home again almost an utter stranger. I have seen these happenings with my own eyes and I know they can cause naught but suffering. The old Indian cannot, even if he wished, reconcile himself to an institution that alienates his young. And there is something evil in a system that brings about an unnatural reaction to life; when it makes young hearts callous and unheedful of the needs and joys of the old.

The old people do not speak English and they never will

be English-speaking. To place upon such people the burden of understanding and functioning through an office bound up with the routine and red tape of the usual government office is silly and futile, and every week or so I receive letters from the reservation evidencing this fact. The Indian's natural method of settling questions is by council and conference. From time immemorial, for every project affecting their material, social, and spiritual lives, the people have met together to "talk things over."

To the end that young Indians will be able to appreciate both their traditional life and modern life they should be doubly educated. Without forsaking reverence for their ancestral teachings, they can be trained to take up modern duties that relate to tribal and reservation life. And there is no problem of reservation importance but can be solved by the joint efforts of the old and the young Indians.

There certainly can be no doubt in the public mind today as to the capacity of the younger Indians in taking on white modes and manners. For many years, and particularly since the days of General Pratt, the young Indian has been proving his efficiency when entering the fields of white man's endeavor and has done well in copying and acquiring the ways of the white man.

The Indian liked the white man's horse and straightway became an expert horseman; he threw away his age-old weapons, the bow and arrow, and matched the white man's skill with gun and pistol; in the field of sports—games of strength and skill—the Indian enters with no shame in comparison; the white man's beads the Indian woman took, developed a technique and an art distinctly her own with no competitor in design; and in the white man's technique of song and dance the Indian has made himself a creditable exponent.

However, despite the fact that Indian schools have been established over several generations, there is a dearth of Indians in the professions. It is most noticeable on the reservations where the numerous positions of consequence are held by white employees instead of trained Indians. For instance, why are not the stores, post offices, and government office jobs on the Sioux Reservation held by trained Indians? Why cannot Sioux be reservation nurses and doctors; and road-builders too? Much road work goes on every summer, but the complaint is constant that it is always done by white workmen, and in such a manner as to necessitate its being done again in a short time. Were these numerous positions turned over to trained Indians, the white population would soon find reservation life less attractive and less lucrative.

With school facilities already fairly well established and the capability of the Indian unquestioned, every reservation could well be supplied with Indian doctors, nurses, engineers, road- and bridge-builders, draftsmen, architects, dentists, lawyers, teachers, and instructors in tribal lore, legends, orations, song, dance, and ceremonial ritual. The Indian, by the very sense of duty, should become his own historian, giving his account of the race—fairer and fewer accounts of the wars and more of statecraft, legends, languages, oratory, and philosophical conceptions. No longer should the Indian be dehumanized in order to make material for lurid and cheap fiction to embellish street-stands. Rather, a fair and correct history of the native American should be incorporated in the curriculum of the public school.

Caucasian youth is fed, and rightly so, on the feats and exploits of their old-world heroes, their revolutionary forefathers, their adventurous pioneer trail-blazers, and in our Southwest through pageants, fiestas, and holidays the days of the Spanish *conquistador* is kept alive.

But Indian youth! They, too, have fine pages in their past history; they, too, have patriots and heroes. And it is not fair to rob Indian youth of their history, the stories of their patriots, which, if impartially written, would fill them with pride and dignity. Therefore, give back to Indian youth all, everything in their heritage that belongs to them and augment it with the best in the modern schools. I repeat, doubly educate the Indian boy and girl.

What a contrast this would make in comparison with the present unhealthy, demoralized place the reservation is today, where the old are poorly fed, shabbily clothed, divested of pride and incentive; and where the young are unfitted for tribal life and untrained for the world of white man's affairs except to hold an occasional job!

Why not a school of Indian thought, built on the Indian pattern and conducted by Indian instructors? Why not a school of tribal art?

Why should not America be cognizant of itself; aware of its identity? In short, why should not America be preserved?

There were ideals and practices in the life of my ancestors that have not been improved upon by the present-day civilization; there were in our culture elements of benefits; and there were influences that would broaden any life. But that almost an entire public needs to be enlightened as to this fact need not be discouraging. For many centuries the human mind labored under the delusion that the world was flat; and thousands of men have believed that the heavens were supported by the strength of an Atlas. The human mind is not yet free from fallacious reasoning; it is not yet an open mind and its deepest recesses are not yet swept free of errors.

But it is now time for a destructive order to be reversed, and it is well to inform other races that the aboriginal culture of America was not devoid of beauty. Furthermore, in denying the Indian his ancestral rights and heritages the white race is but robbing itself. But America can be revived, rejuvenated, by recognizing a native school of thought. The Indian can save America.

The Living Spirit of the Indian—His Art

The spiritual health and existence of the Indian was maintained by song, magic, ritual, dance, symbolism, oratory (or council), design, handicraft, and folk-story.

Manifestly, to check or thwart this expression is to bring about spiritual decline. And it is in this condition of decline that the Indian people are today. There is but a feeble effort among the Sioux to keep alive their traditional songs and dances, while among other tribes there is but a half-hearted attempt to offset the influence of the government school and at the same time recover from the crushing and stifling regime of the Indian Bureau.

One has but to speak of Indian verse to receive uncomprehending and unbelieving glances. Yet the Indian loved verse and into this mode of expression went his deepest feelings. Only a few ardent and advanced students seem interested; nevertheless, they have given in book form enough Indian translations to set forth the character and quality of Indian verse.

Oratory receives a little better understanding on the part of the white public, owing to the fact that oratorical compilations include those of Indian orators.

Hard as it seemingly is for the white man's ear to sense the differences, Indian songs are as varied as the many emotions which inspire them, for no two of them are alike. For instance, the Song of Victory is spirited and the notes high and remindful of an unrestrained hunter or warrior riding exultantly over the prairies. On the other hand, the song of the *Cano unye* is solemn and full of urge, for it is meant to inspire the young men to deeds of valor.. Then there are the songs of death and the spiritual songs which are connected with the ceremony of initiation. These are full of the spirit of praise and worship, and so strong are some of these invocations that the very air seems as if surcharged with the presence of the Big Holy.

The Indian loved to worship. From birth to death he revered his surroundings. He considered himself born in the luxurious lap of Mother Earth and no place was to him humble. There was nothing between him and the Big Holy. The contact was immediate and personal, and the blessings of Wakan Tanka flowed over the Indian like rain showered from the sky. Wakan Tanka was not aloof, apart, and ever seeking to quell evil forces. He did not punish the animals and the birds, and likewise He did not punish man. He was not a punishing God. For there was never a question as to the supremacy of an evil power over and above the power of Good. There was but one ruling power, and that was *Good*.

Of course, none but an adoring one could dance for days with his face to the sacred sun, and that time is all but done. We cannot have back the days of the buffalo and beaver; we cannot win back our clean blood-stream and superb health, and we can never again expect that beautiful *rapport* we once had with Nature. The springs and lakes have dried and the mountains are bare of forests. The plow has changed the face of the world. Wi-wila is dead! No more may we heal our sick and comfort our dying with a strength founded on faith, for even the animals now fear us, and fear supplants faith.

And the Indian wants to dance! It is his way of expressing devotion, of communing with unseen power, and in keeping his tribal identity. When the Lakota heart was filled with high emotion, he danced. When he felt the benediction of the warming rays of the sun, he danced. When his blood ran hot with success of the hunt or chase, he danced. When his heart was filled with pity for the orphan, the lonely father, or bereaved mother, he danced. All the joys and exaltations of life, all his gratefulness and thankfulness, all his acknowledgments of the mysterious power that guided life, and all his aspirations for a better life, culminated in one great dance—the Sun Dance.

Today we see our young people dancing together the silly jazz—dances that add nothing to the beauty and fineness of our lives and certainly nothing to our history, while the dances that record the life annals of a people die. It is the American Indian who contributes to this country its true folk-dancing, growing, as we did, out of the soil. The dance is far older than his legends, songs, or philosophy.

Did dancing mean much to the white people they would better understand ours. Yet at the same time there is no attraction that brings people from such distances as a certain tribal dance, for the reason that the white mind senses its mystery, for even the white man's inmost feelings are unconsciously stirred by the beat of the tomtom. They are heart-beats, and once all men danced to its rhythm.

When the Indian has forgotten the music of his forefathers, when the sound of the tomtom is no more, when noisy jazz has drowned the melody of the flute, he will be a dead Indian. When the memory of his heroes are no longer told in story, and he forsakes the beautiful white buckskin for factory shoddy, he will be dead. When from him has been taken all that is his, all that he has visioned in nature, all that has come to him from infinite sources, he then, truly, will be a dead Indian. His spirit will be gone, and though he walk crowded streets, he will, in truth, be—*dead!*

But all this must not perish; it must live, to the end that America shall be educated no longer to regard native production of whatever tribe—folk-story, basketry, pottery, dance, song, poetry—as curios, and native artists as curiosities. For who but the man indigenous to the soil could produce its song, story, and folk-tale; who but the man who loved the dust beneath his feet could shape it and put it into undying, ceramic form; who but he who loved the reeds that grew beside still waters, and the damp roots of shrub and tree, could save it from seasonal death, and with almost superhuman patience weave it into enduring objects of beauty—into timeless art!

Regarding the "civilization" that has been thrust upon me since the days of reservation, it has not added one whit to my sense of justice; to my reverence for the rights of life; to my love for truth, honesty, and generosity; nor to my faith in Wakan Tanka—God of the Lakotas. For after all the great religions have been preached and expounded, or have been revealed by brilliant scholars, or have been written in books and embellished in fine language with finer covers, man—all man—is still confronted with the Great Mystery.

So if today I had a young mind to direct, to start on the journey of life, and I was faced with the duty of choosing between the natural way of my forefathers and that of the white man's present way of civilization, I would, for its welfare, unhesitatingly set that child's feet in the path of my forefathers. I would raise him to be an Indian!

N. SCOTT MOMADAY

The Way to Rainy Mountain

Headwaters

Noon in the intermountain plain:
There is scant telling of the marsh—
A log, hollow and weather-stained,
An insect at the mouth, and moss—
Yet waters rise against the roots,
Stand brimming to the stalks. What moves?
What moves on this archaic force
Was wild and welling at the source.

The journey began one day long ago on the edge of the northern Plains. It was carried on over a course of many generations and many hundreds of miles. In the end there were many things to remember, to dwell upon and talk about.

"You know, everything had to begin...." For the Kiowas the beginning was a struggle for existence in the bleak northern mountains. It was there, they say, that they entered the world through a hollow log. The end, too, was a struggle, and it was lost. The young Plains culture of the Kiowas withered and died like grass that is burned in the prairie wind. There came a day like destiny; in every direction, as far as the eye could see, carrion lay out in the land. The buffalo was the animal representation of the sun, the essential and sacrificial victim of the Sun Dance. When the wild herds were destroyed, so too was the will of the Kiowa people; there was nothing to sustain them in spirit. But these are idle recollections, the mean and ordinary agonies of human history. The interim was a time of great adventure and nobility and fulfillment.

Tai-me came to the Kiowas in a vision born of suffering and despair. "Take me with you," Tai-me said, "and I will give you whatever you want." And it was so. The great adventure of the Kiowas was a going forth into the heart of the continent. They began a long migration from the headwaters of the Yellowstone River eastward to the Black Hills and south to the Wichita Mountains. Along the way they acquired horses, the religion of the Plains, a love and possession of the open land. Their nomadic soul was set free. In alliance with the Comanches they held dominion in the southern Plains for a hundred years. In the course of that long migration they had come of age as a people. They had conceived a good idea of themselves; they had dared to imagine and determine who they were.

In one sense, then, the way to Rainy Mountain is pre-eminently the history of an idea, man's idea of himself, and it has old and essential being in language. The verbal tradition by which it has been preserved has suffered a deterioration in time. What remains is fragmentary: mythology, legend, lore, and hearsay—and of course the idea itself, as crucial and complete as it ever was. That is the miracle.

The journey herein recalled continues to be made anew each time the miracle comes to mind, for that is peculiarly the right and responsibility of the imagination. It is a whole journey, intricate with motion and meaning; and it is made with the whole memory, that experience of the mind which is legendary as well as historical, personal as well as cultural. And the journey is an evocation of three things in particular: a landscape that is incomparable, a time that is gone forever, and the human spirit, which endures. The imaginative experience and the historical express equally the traditions of man's reality. Finally, then, the journey recalled is among other things the revelation of one way in which these traditions are conceived, developed, and interfused in the human mind. There are on the way to Rainy Mountain many landmarks, many journeys in the one. From the beginning the migration of the Kiowas was an expression of the human spirit, and that expression is most truly made in terms of wonder and delight: "There were many people, and oh, it was beautiful. That was the beginning of the Sun Dance. It was all for Tai-me, you know, and it was a long time ago."

A single knoll rises out of the plain in Oklahoma, north and west of the Wichita Range. For my people, the Kiowas, it is an old landmark, and they gave it the name Rainy Mountain. The hardest weather in the world is there. Winter brings blizzards, hot tornadic winds arise in the spring, and in summer the prairie is an anvil's edge. The grass turns brittle and brown, and it cracks beneath your feet. There are green belts along the rivers and creeks, linear groves of hickory and pecan, willow and witch hazel. At a distance in July or August the steaming foliage seems almost to writhe in fire. Great green and yellow grasshoppers are everywhere in the tall grass, popping up like corn to sting the flesh, and tortoises crawl about on the red earth, going nowhere in the plenty of time. Loneliness is an aspect of the land. All things in the plain are isolate; there is no confusion of objects in the eye, but one hill or one tree or one man. To look upon that landscape in the early morning, with the sun at your back, is to lose the sense of proportion. Your imagination comes to life, and this, you think, is where Creation was begun.

I returned to Rainy Mountain in July. My grandmother had died in the spring, and I wanted to be at her grave. She had lived to be very old and at last infirm. Her only living daughter was with her when she died, and I was told that in death her face was that of a child.

I like to think of her as a child. When she was born, the Kiowas were living the last great moment of their history. For more than a hundred years they had controlled the open range from the Smoky Hill River to the Red, from the headwaters of the Canadian to the fork of the Arkansas and Cimarron. In alliance with the Comanches, they had ruled the whole of the southern Plains. War was their sacred business, and they were among the finest horsemen the world has ever known. But warfare for the Kiowas was pre-eminently a matter of disposition rather than of survival, and they never understood the grim, unrelenting advance of the U.S. Cavalry. When at last, divided and ill-provisioned, they were driven onto the Staked Plains in the cold rains of autumn, they fell into panic. In Palo Duro Canyon they abandoned their crucial stores to pillage and had nothing then but their lives. In order to save themselves, they surrendered to the soldiers at Fort Sill and were imprisoned in the old stone corral that now stands as a military museum. My grandmother was spared the humiliation of those high gray walls by eight or ten years, but she must have known from birth the affliction of defeat, the dark brooding of old warriors.

Her name was Aho, and she belonged to the last culture to evolve in North America. Her forebears came down from the high country in western Montana nearly three centuries ago. They were a mountain people, a mysterious tribe of hunters whose language has never been positively classified in any major group. In the late seventeenth century they began a long migration to the south and east. It was a journey toward the dawn, and it led to a golden age. Along the way the Kiowas were befriended by the Crows, who gave them the culture and religion of the Plains. They acquired horses, and their ancient nomadic spirit was suddenly free of the ground. They acquired Tai-me, the sacred Sun Dance doll, from that moment the object and symbol of their worship, and so shared in the divinity of the sun. Not least, they acquired the sense of destiny, therefore courage and pride. When they entered upon the southern Plains they had been transformed. No longer were they slaves to the simple necessity of survival; they were a lordly and dangerous society of fighters and thieves, hunters and priests of the sun. According to their origin myth, they entered the world through a hollow log. From one point of view, their migration was the fruit of an old prophecy, for indeed they emerged from a sunless world.

Although my grandmother lived out her long life in the shadow of Rainy Mountain, the immense landscape of the continental interior lay like memory in her blood. She could tell of the Crows, whom she had never seen, and of the Black Hills, where she had never been. I wanted to see in reality what she had seen more perfectly in the mind's eye, and traveled fifteen hundred miles to begin my pilgrimage.

Yellowstone, it seemed to me, was the top of the world, a

region of deep lakes and dark timber, canyons and waterfalls. But, beautiful as it is, one might have the sense of confinement there. The skyline in all directions is close at hand, the high wall of the woods and deep cleavages of shade. There is a perfect freedom in the mountains, but it belongs to the eagle and the elk, the badger and the bear. The Kiowas reckoned their stature by the distance they could see, and they were bent and blind in the wilderness.

Descending eastward, the highland meadows are a stairway to the plain. In July the inland slope of the Rockies is luxuriant with flax and buckwheat, stonecrop and larkspur. The earth unfolds and the limit of the land recedes. Clusters of trees, and animals grazing far in the distance, cause the vision to reach away and wonder to build upon the mind. The sun follows a longer course in the day, and the sky is immense beyond all comparison. The great billowing clouds that sail upon it are shadows that move upon the grain like water, dividing light. Farther down, in the land of the Crows and Blackfeet, the plain is yellow. Sweet clover takes hold of the hills and bends upon itself to cover and seal the soil. There the Kiowas paused on their way; they had come to the place where they must change their lives. The sun is at home on the plains. Precisely there does it have the certain character of a god. When the Kiowas came to the land of the Crows, they could see the dark lees of the hills at dawn across the Bighorn River, the profusion of light on the grain shelves, the oldest deity ranging after the solstices. Not yet would they veer southward to the caldron of the land that lay below; they must wean their blood from the northern winter and hold the mountains a while longer in their view. They bore Tai-me in procession to the east.

A dark mist lay over the Black Hills, and the land was like iron. At the top of a ridge I caught sight of Devil's Tower upthrust against the gray sky as if in the birth of time the core of the earth had broken through its crust and the motion of the world was begun. There are things in nature that engender an awful quiet in the heart of man; Devil's Tower is one of them. Two centuries ago, because they could not do otherwise, the Kiowas made a legend at the base of the rock. My grandmother said:

Eight children were there at play, seven sisters and their brother. Suddenly the boy was struck dumb; he trembled and began to run upon his hands and feet. His fingers became claws, and his body was covered with fur. Directly there was a bear where the boy had been. The sisters were terrified; they ran, and the bear after them. They came to the stump of a great tree, and the tree spoke to them. It bade them climb upon it, and as they did so it began to rise into the air. The bear came to kill them, but they were just beyond its reach. It reared against the tree and scored the bark all around with its claws. The seven sisters were borne into the sky, and they became the stars of the Big Dipper.

From that moment, and so long as the legend lives, the Kiowas have kinsmen in the night sky. Whatever they were in the mountains, they could be no more. However tenuous their well-being, however much they had suffered and would suffer again, they had found a way out of the wilderness.

My grandmother had a reverence for the sun, a holy regard that now is all but gone out of mankind. There was a wariness in her, and an ancient awe. She was a Christian in her later years, but she had come a long way about, and she never forgot her birthright. As a child she had been to the Sun Dances; she had taken part in those annual rites, and by them she had learned the restoration of her people in the presence of Tai-me. She was about seven when the last Kiowa Sun Dance was held in 1887 on the Washita River above Rainy Mountain Creek. The buffalo were gone. In order to consummate the ancient sacrifice—to impale the head of a buffalo bull upon the medicine tree—a delegation of old men journeyed into Texas, there to beg and barter for an animal from the Goodnight herd. She was ten when the Kiowas came together for the last time as a living Sun Dance culture. They could find no buffalo; they had to hang an old hide from the sacred tree. Before the dance could begin, a company of soldiers rode out from Fort Sill under orders to disperse the tribe. Forbidden without cause the essential act of their faith, having seen the wild herds slaughtered and left to rot upon the ground, the Kiowas backed away forever from the medicine tree. That was July 20, 1890, at the great bend of the Washita. My grandmother was there. Without bitterness, and for as long as she lived, she bore a vision of deicide.

Now that I can have her only in memory, I see my grandmother in the several postures that were peculiar to her: standing at the wood stove on a winter morning and turning meat in a great iron skillet; sitting at the south window, bent above her beadwork, and afterward, when her vision failed, looking down for a long time into the fold of her hands; going out upon a cane, very slowly as she did when the weight of age came upon her; praying. I remember her most often at prayer. She made long, rambling prayers out of suffering and hope, having seen many things. I was never sure that I had the right to hear, so exclusive were they of all mere custom and company. The last time I saw her she prayed standing by the side of her bed at night, naked to the waist, the light of a kerosene lamp moving upon her dark skin. Her long, black hair, always drawn and braided in the day, lay upon her shoulders and against her breasts like a shawl. I do not speak Kiowa, and I never understood her prayers, but there was something inherently sad in the sound, some merest hesitation upon the syllables of sorrow. She began in a high and descending pitch, exhausting her breath to silence; then again and again—and always the same intensity of effort, of something that is, and is not, like urgency in the human voice. Transported so in the dancing light among the shadows of her room, she seemed beyond the reach of time. But that was illusion; I think I knew then that I should not see her again.

Houses are like sentinels in the plain, old keepers of the weather watch. There, in a very little while, wood takes on the appearance of great age. All colors wear soon away in the wind and rain, and then the wood is burned gray and the grain appears and the nails turn red with rust. The windowpanes are black and opaque; you imagine there is nothing within and indeed there are many ghosts, bones given up to the land. They stand here and there against the sky, and you approach them for a longer time than you expect. They belong in the distance; it is their domain.

Once there was a lot of sound in my grandmother's house, a lot of coming and going, feasting and talk. The summers there were full of excitement and reunion. The Kiowas are a summer people; they abide the cold and keep to themselves, but when the season turns and the land becomes warm and vital they cannot hold still; an old love of going returns upon them. The aged visitors who came to my grandmother's house when I was a child were made of lean and leather, and they bore themselves upright. They wore great black hats and bright ample shirts that shook in the wind. They rubbed fat upon their hair and wound their braids with strips of colored cloth. Some of them painted their faces and carried the scars of old and cherished enmities. They were an old council of warlords, come to remind and be reminded of who they were. Their wives and daughters served them well. The women might indulge themselves; gossip was at once the mark and compensation of their servitude. They made loud and elaborate talk among themselves, full of jest and gesture, fright and false alarm. They went abroad in fringed and flowered shawls, bright beadwork and German silver. They were at home in the kitchen, and they prepared meals that were banquets.

There were frequent prayer meetings, and great nocturnal feasts. When I was a child I played with my cousins outside, where the lamplight fell upon the ground and the singing of the old people rose up around us and carried away into the darkness. There were a lot of good things to eat, a lot of laughter and surprise. And afterward, when the quiet returned, I lay down with my grandmother and could hear the frogs away by the river and feel the motion of the air.

Now there is a funeral silence in the rooms, the endless wake of some final word. The walls have closed in upon my grandmother's house. When I returned to it in mourning, I saw for the first time in my life how small it was. It was late at night, and there was a white moon, nearly full. I sat for a long time on the stone steps by the kitchen door. From there I could see out across the land; I could see the long row of trees by the creek, the low light upon the rolling plains, and the stars of the Big Dipper. Once I looked at the moon and caught sight of a strange thing. A cricket had perched upon the handrail, only a few inches away from me. My line of vision was such that the creature filled the moon like a fossil. It had gone there, I thought, to live and die, for there, of all places, was its small definition made whole and eternal. A warm wind rose up and purled like the longing within me.

The next morning I awoke at dawn and went out on the dirt road to Rainy Mountain. It was already hot, and the grasshoppers began to fill the air. Still, it was early in the morning, and the birds sang out of the shadows. The long yellow grass on the mountain shone in the bright light, and a scissortail hied above the land. There, where it ought to be, at the end of a long and legendary way, was my grandmother's grave. Here and there on the dark stones were ancestral names. Looking back once, I saw the mountain and came away....

If an arrow is well made, it will have tooth marks upon it. That it how you know. The Kiowas made fine arrows and straightened them in their teeth. Then they drew them to the bow to see if they were straight. Once there was a man and his wife. They were alone at night in their tepee. By the light of the fire the man was making arrows. After a while he caught sight of something. There was a small opening in the tepee where two hides were sewn together. Someone was there on the outside, looking in. The man went on with his work, but he said to his wife: "Someone is standing outside. Do not be afraid. Let us talk easily, as of ordinary things." He took up an arrow and straightened it in his teeth; then, as it was right for him to do, he drew it to the bow and took aim, first in this direction and then in that. And all the while he was talking, as if to his wife. But this is how he spoke: "I know that you are there on the outside, for I can feel your eyes upon me. If you are a Kiowa, you will understand what I am saying, and you will speak your name." But there was no answer, and the man went on in the same way, pointing the arrow all around. At last his aim fell upon the place where his enemy stood, and he let go of the string. The arrow went straight to the enemy's heart.

We Talk, You Listen

One reason that Indian people have not been heard from until recently is that we have been completely covered up by movie Indians. Western movies have been such favorites that they have dominated the public's conception of what Indians are. It is not all bad when one thinks about the handsome Jay Silverheels bailing the Lone Ranger out of a jam, or Ed Ames rescuing Daniel Boone with some clever Indian trick. But the other mythologies that have wafted skyward because of the movies have blocked out any idea that there might be real Indians with real problems.

Other minority groups have fought tenaciously against stereotyping, and generally they have been successful. Italians quickly quashed the image of them as mobsters that television projected in *The Untouchables*. Blacks have been successful in getting a more realistic picture of the black man in a contemporary setting because they have had standout performers like Bill Cosby and Sidney Poitier to represent them.

Since stereotyping was highlighted by motion pictures, it would probably be well to review the images of minority groups projected in the movies in order to understand how the situation looks at present. Perhaps the first aspect of stereotyping was the tendency to exclude people on the basis of their inability to handle the English language. Not only were racial minorities excluded, but immigrants arriving on these shores were soon whipped into shape by ridicule of their English.

Traditional stereotypes pictured the black as a happy watermelon-eating darky whose sole contribution to American society was his indiscriminate substitution of the "d" sound for "th." Thus a black always said "dis" and "dat," as in "lift dat bale." The "d" sound carried over and was used by white gangsters to indicate disfavor with their situation, as in "dis is de end, ya rat." The important thing was to indicate that blacks were like lisping children not yet competent to undertake the rigors of economic opportunities and voting.

Mexicans were generally portrayed as shiftless and padded out for siesta, without any redeeming qualities whatsoever. Where the black had been handicapped by his use of the "d," the Mexican suffered from the use of the double "e." This marked them off as a group worth watching. Mexicans, according to the stereotype, always said "theenk," "peenk," and later "feenk." Many advertisements today still continue this stereotype, thinking that it is cute and cuddly.

These groups were much better off than Indians were. Indians were always devoid of any English whatsoever. They were only allowed to speak when an important message had to be transmitted on the screen. For example, "many pony soldiers die" was meant to indicate that Indians were going to attack the peaceful settlers who happened to have broken their three hundredth treaty moments before. Other than that Indian linguistic ability was limited to "ugh" and "kemo sabe" (which means honky in some obscure Indian language).

The next step was to acknowledge that there was a great American dream to which any child could aspire. (It was almost like the train in the night that Richard Nixon heard as a child anticipating the dream fairy.) The great American dream was projected in the early World War II movies. The last reel was devoted to a stirring proclamation that we were going to win the war and it showed factories producing airplanes, people building ships, and men marching in uniform to the transports. There was a quick pan of a black face before the scene shifted to scenes of orchards, rivers, Mount Rushmore, and the Liberty Bell as we found out what we were fighting for.

The new images expressed a profound inability to understand why minority groups couldn't "make it" when everybody knew what America was all about—freedom and equality. By projecting an image of everyone working hard to win the war, the doctrine was spread that America was just one big happy family and that there really weren't any differences so long as we had to win the war.

It was a rare war movie in the 1940s that actually showed a black or a Mexican as a bona fide fighting man. When they did appear it was in the role of cooks or orderlies serving whites. In most cases this was a fairly accurate statement of their situation, particularly with respect to the Navy.

World War II movies were entirely different for Indians. Each platoon of red-blooded white American boys was equipped with its own set of Indians. When the platoon got into trouble and was surrounded, its communications cut off except for one slender line to regimental headquarters, and that line tapped by myriads of Germans, Japanese, or Italians, the stage was set for the dramatic episode of the Indians.

John Wayne, Randolph Scott, Sonny Tufts, or Tyrone Power would smile broadly as he played his ace, which until this time had been hidden from view. From nowhere, a Navaho, Comanche, Cherokee, or Sioux would appear, take the telephone, and in some short and inscrutable phraseology communicate such a plenitude of knowledge to his fellow tribesman (fortunately situated at the general's right hand) that fighting units thousands of miles away would instantly perceive the situation and rescue the platoon. The Indian would disappear as mysteriously as he had come, only to reappear the next week in a different battle to perform his esoteric rites. Anyone watching war movies during the '40s would have been convinced that without Indian telephone operators the war would have been lost irretrievably, in spite of John Wayne.

Indians were America's secret weapon against the forces of evil. The typing spoke of a primitive gimmick, and it was the strangeness of Indians that made them visible, not their humanity. With the Korean War era and movies made during the middle '50s, other minority groups began to appear and Indians were pushed into the background. This era was the heyday of the "All-American Platoon." It was the ultimate conception of intergroup relations. The "All-American Platoon" was a "one each": one black, one Mexican, one Indian, one farm boy from Iowa, one Southerner who hated blacks, one boy from Brooklyn, one Polish boy from the urban slums of the Midwest, one Jewish intellectual, and one college boy. Every possible stereotype was included and it resulted in a portrayal of Indians as another species of human being for the first time in moving pictures.

The platoon was always commanded by a veteran of grizzled countenance who had been at every battle in which the United States had ever engaged. The whole story consisted in killing off the members of the platoon until only the veteran and the college boy were left. The Southerner and the black would die in each other's arms singing "Dixie." The Jewish intellectual and the Indian formed some kind of attachment and were curiously the last ones killed. When the smoke cleared, the college boy, with a prestige wound in the shoulder, returned to his girl, and the veteran reconciled with his wife and checked out another platoon in anticipation of taking the same hill in the next movie.

While other groups have managed to make great strides since those days, Indians have remained the primitive unknown quantity. Dialogue has reverted back to the monosyllabic grunt and even pictures that attempt to present the Indian side of the story depend upon unintelligible noises to present their message. The only exception to this rule is a line famed for its durability over the years. If you fall asleep during the Late Show and suddenly awaken to the words "go in peace, my son," it is either an Indian chief bidding his son good-bye as the boy heads for college or a Roman Catholic priest forgiving Paul Newman or Steve McQueen for killing a hundred men in the preceding reel.

Anyone raising questions about the image of minority groups as portrayed in television and the movies is automatically suspect as an un-American and subversive influence on the minds of the young. The historical, linguistic, and cultural differences are neatly blocked out by the fad of portraying members of minority groups in roles which formerly were reserved for whites. Thus Burt Reynolds played a Mohawk detective busy solving the crime problem in New York City. Diahann Carroll played a well-to-do black widow with small child in a television series that was obviously patterned after the unique single-headed white family.

In recent years the documentary has arisen to present the story of Indian people and a number of series on Black America have been produced. Indian documentaries are singularly the same. A reporter and television crew hasten to either the Navaho or Pine Ridge reservation, quickly shoot reels on poverty conditions, and return East blithely thinking that they have captured the essence of Indian life. In spite of the best intentions, the eternal yearning to present an exciting story of a strange people overcomes, and the endless cycle of poverty-oriented films continues.

This type of approach continually categorizes the Indian as an incompetent boob who can't seem to get along and who is hopelessly mired in a poverty of his own making. Hidden beneath these documentaries is the message that Indians really *want* to live this way. No one has yet filmed the incredible progress that is being made by the Makah tribe, the Quinaults, Red Lake Chippewas, Gila River Pima-Waricopas, and others. Documentaries project the feeling that reservations should be eliminated because the conditions are so bad. There is no effort to present the bright side of Indian life.

With the rise of ethnic studies programs and courses in minority-group history, the situation has become worse. People who support these programs assume that by communicating the best aspects of a group they have somehow solved the major problems of that group in its relations with the rest of society. By emphasizing that black is beautiful or that Indians have contributed the names of rivers to the road map, many people feel that they have done justice to the group concerned.

One theory of interpretation of Indian history that has arisen in the past several years is that all of the Indian war chiefs were patriots defending their lands. This is the "patriot chief" interpretation of history. Fundamentally it is a good theory in that it places a more equal balance to interpreting certain Indian wars as wars of resistance. It gets away from the tendency, seen earlier in this century, to classify all Indian warriors as renegades. But there is a tendency to overlook the obvious renegades, Indians who were treacherous and would have been renegades had there been no whites to fight. The patriot chiefs interpretation also conveniently overlooks the fact that every significant leader of the previous century was eventually done in by his own people in one way or another. Sitting Bull was killed by Indian police working for the government. Geronimo was captured by an army led by Apache scouts who sided with the United States.

If the weak points of each minority group's history are to be covered over by a sweetness-and-light interpretation based on what we would like to think happened rather than what did happen, we doom ourselves to decades of further racial strife. Most of the study programs today emphasize the goodness that is inherent in the different minority communities, instead of trying to present a balanced story. There are basically two schools of interpretation running through all of these efforts as the demand for black, red, and brown pride dominates the programs.

One theory derives from the "All-American Platoon" concept of a decade ago. Under this theory members of the respective racial minority groups had an important role in the great events of American history. Crispus Attucks, a black, almost single-handedly started the Revolutionary War, while Eli Parker, the Seneca Indian general, won the Civil War and would have concluded it sooner had not there been so many stupid whites abroad in those days. This is the "cameo" theory of history. It takes a basic "manifest destiny" white interpretation of history and lovingly plugs a few feathers, woolly heads, and sombreros into the famous events of American history. No one tries to explain what an Indian is who was helping the whites destroy his own people, since we are now all Americans and have these great events in common.

The absurdity of the cameo school of ethnic pride is self-apparent. Little Mexican children are taught that there were some good Mexicans at the Alamo. They can therefore be happy that Mexicans have been involved in the significant events of Texas history. Little is said about the Mexicans on the other side at the Alamo. The result is a denial of a substantial Mexican heritage by creating the feeling that "we all did it together." If this trend continues I would not be surprised to discover that Columbus had a Cherokee on board when he set sail from Spain in search of the Indies.

The cameo school smothers any differences that existed historically by presenting a history in which all groups have participated through representatives. Regardless of Crispus Attuck's valiant behavior during the Revolution, it is doubtful that he envisioned another century of slavery for blacks as a cause worth defending.

The other basic school of interpretation is a projection backward of the material blessings of the white middle class. It seeks to identify where all the material wealth originated and finds that each minority group *contributed* something. It can therefore be called the contribution school. Under this conception we should all love Indians because they contributed corn, squash, potatoes, tobacco, coffee, rubber, and other agricultural products. In like manner, blacks and Mexicans are credited with Carver's work on the peanut, blood transfusion, and tacos and tamales.

The ludicrous implication of the contribution school visualizes the minority groups clamoring to enter American society, lined up with an abundance of foods and fancies, presenting them to whites in a never-ending stream of generosity. If the different minority groups were given an overriding two-percent royalty on their contributions, the same way whites have managed to give themselves royalties for their inventions, this school would have a more realistic impact on minority groups.

The danger with both of these types of ethnic studies theories is that they present an unrealistic account of the role of minority groups in American history. Certainly there is more to the story of the American Indian than providing cocoa and popcorn for Columbus's landing party. When the clashes of history are smoothed over in favor of a mushy togetherness feeling, then people begin to wonder what has happened in the recent past that has created the conditions of today. It has been the feeling of younger people that contemporary problems have arisen because community leadership has been consistently betraying them. Older statesmen are called Uncle Toms, and the entire fabric of accumulated wisdom and experience of the older generation of minority groups is destroyed.

Rising against the simplistic cameo and contribution schools is the contemporary desire by church leaders to make Christianity relevant to minority groups by transposing the entire Christian myth and archetypes into Indian, black, and Mexican terms. Thus Father Groppi, noted white-black priest, wants to have black churches show a black Christ. This is absurd, because Christ was, as everyone knows, a Presbyterian, and he was a white man. That is to say, for nearly two thousand years he has been a white man. To suddenly show him as black, Mexican, or Indian takes away the whole meaning of the myth.

The Indian counterpart of the black Christ is the Christmas card portraying the Holy Family living in a hogan in Monument Valley on the Navaho reservation. As the shepherds sing and gather their flocks, little groups of Navaho angels announce the birth of the Christchild. The scene is totally patronizing and unrealistic. If the Christchild was born on the Navaho reservation, his chances of surviving the first two years of life would be less than those of the original Jesus with Herod chasing him. (We have not yet reached the point of showing three officials from the Bureau of Indian Affairs coming up the canyon as the Three Wise Men, but someone with a keen sense of relevancy will try it sooner or later.)

This type of religious paternalism overlooks the fact that the original figures of religious myths were designed to communicate doctrines. It satisfies itself by presenting its basic figures as so universalized that anyone can participate at any time in history. Thus the religion that it is trying to communicate becomes ahistorical, as Mickey Mouse and Snow White are ahistorical.

If the attempted renovation of religious imagery is ever combined with the dominant schools of ethnic studies, the result will be the Last Supper as the gathering of the "All-American Platoon" highlighted by the contributions of each group represented. Instead of simple bread and wine the table will be overflowing with pizza, tamales, greens, peanuts, popcorn, German sausage, and hamburgers. Everyone will feel that they have had a part in the creation of the great American Christian social order. Godless Communism will be vanquished.

Under present conceptions of ethnic studies there can be no lasting benefit either to minority groups or to society at large. The pride that can be built into children and youth by acknowledgment of the validity of their group certainly cannot be built by simply transferring symbols and interpretations arising in white culture history into an Indian, black, or Mexican setting. The result will be to make the minority groups bear the white man's burden by using his symbols and stereotypes as if they were their own.

There must be a drive within each minority group to understand its own uniqueness. This can only be done by examining what experiences were relevant to the group, not what experiences of white America the group wishes itself to be represented in. As an example, the discovery of gold in California was a significant event in the experience of white America. The discovery itself was irrelevant to the western Indian tribes, but the migrations caused by the discovery of gold were vitally important. The two histories can dovetail around this topic but ultimately each interpretation must depend upon its orientation to the group involved.

What has been important and continues to be important is the Constitution of the United States and its continual adaptation to contemporary situations. With the Constitution as a framework and reference point, it would appear that a number of conflicting interpretations of the experience of America could be validly given. While they might conflict at every point as each group defines to its own satisfaction what its experience has meant, recognition that within the Constitutional framework we are engaged in a living process of intergroup relationships would mean that no one group could define the meaning of American society to the exclusion of any other.

Self-awareness of each group must define a series of histories about the American experience. Manifest destiny has dominated thinking in the past because it has had an abstract quality that appeared to interpret experiences accurately. Nearly every racial and ethnic group has had to bow down before this con-

ception of history and conform to an understanding of the
world that it did not ultimately believe. Martin Luther King,
Jr., spoke to his people on the basis of self-awareness the
night before he died. He told them that they as a people would
reach the promised land. Without the same sense of destiny,
minority groups will simply be adopting the outmoded forms
of stereotyping by which whites have deluded themselves for
centuries.

We can survive as a society if we reject the conquest-oriented
interpretation of the Constitution. While some Indian nation-
alists want the whole country back, a guarantee of adequate
protection of existing treaty rights would provide a meaningful compromise. The Constitution should provide a sense of
balance between groups as it has between conflicting desires
of individuals.

As each group defines the ideas and doctrines necessary to
maintain its own sense of dignity and identity, similarities in
goals can be drawn that will have relevance beyond immediate
group aspirations. Stereotyping will change radically because
the ideological basis for portraying the members of any group
will depend on that group's values. Plots in books and movies
will have to show life as it is seen from within the group.
Society will become broader and more cosmopolitan as inno-
vative themes are presented to it. The universal sense of
inhumanity will take on an aspect of concreteness. From the
variety of cultural behavior patterns we can devise a new
understanding of humanity.

The problem of stereotyping is not so much a racial problem
as it is problem of limited knowledge and perspective. Even
though minority groups have suffered in the past by ridiculous
characterizations of themselves by white society, they must
not fall into the same trap by simply reversing the process
that has stereotyped them. Minority groups must thrust through
the rhetorical blockade by creating within themselves a sense
of "peoplehood." This ultimately means the creation of a new
history and not mere amendments to the historical interpretations of white America.

JAMES WELCH

Surviving

The day-long cold hard rain drove
like sun through all the cedar sky
we had that late fall. We huddled
close as cows before the bellied stove.
Told stories. Blackbird cleared his mind,
thought of things he'd left behind, spoke:

"Oftentimes, when sun was easy in my bones,
I dreamed of way to make this land."
We envied eagles easy in their range.
"That thin girl, old cook's kid, stripped naked
for a coke or two and cooked her special stew
round back of the mess tent Sundays."
Sparrows skittered through the black brush.

That night the moon slipped a notch, hung
black for just a second, just long enough
for wet black things to sneak away our cache
of meat. To stay alive this way, it's hard....

Christmas Comes to Moccasin Flat

Christmas comes like this: Wise men
unhurried, candles bought on credit (poor price
for calves), warriors face down in wine sleep.
Winds cheat to pull heat from smoke.

Friends sit in chinked cabins, stare out
plastic windows and wait for commodities.
Charlie Blackbird, twenty miles from church
and bar, stabs his fire with flint.

When drunks drain radiators for love
or need, chiefs eat snow and talk of change,
an urge to laugh pounding their ribs.
Elk play games in high country.

Medicine Woman, clay pipe and twist tobacco,
calls each blizzard by name and predicts
five o'clock by spitting at her television.
Children lean into her breath to beg a story:

Something about honor and passion,
warriors back with meat and song,
a peculiar evening star, quick vision of birth.
Blackbird feeds his fire. Outside, a quick 30 below.

In My Lifetime

This day the children of Speakthunder
run the wrong man, a saint unable
to love a weasel way, able only to smile
and drink the wind that makes the others go.
Trees are ancient in his breath.
His bleeding feet tell a story of run
the sacred way, chase the antelope naked
till it drops, the odor of run
quiet in his blood. He watches cactus
jump against the moon. Moon is speaking
woman to the ancient fire. Always woman.

His sins were numerous, this wrong man.
Buttes were good to listen from. With thunder-
hands his father shaped the dust, circled
fire, tumbled up the wind to make a fool.
Now the fool is dead. His bones go back
so scarred in time, the buttes are young to look
for signs that say a man could love his fate,
that winter in the blood is one sad thing.

His sins—I don't explain. Desperate in my song,
I run these woman hills, translate wind
to mean a kind of life, the children of Speakthunder
are never wrong and I am rhythm to strong medicine.

Seven Arrows

As we learn we always change, and so does our perceiving. This changed perception then becomes a new Teacher inside each of us.

Often our first Teacher is our own heart. This Teaching Voice is spoken of by the old Sun Dance Teachers as the Chief. Within the Stories, or Mirrors, this Teacher may be symbolized by the Old Man, the Old Woman, the Little Boy, the Little Girl, the Contrary, the Spirit, or by *Vihio,* the Knowledgeable Fool. These Seven Symbols, or Teaching Arrows, are a tiny portion of the Great Mirror. When you have learned to place these Seven pieces of Mirror together within yourself, you will discover that there are Seven more. Their Reflections will go on and on forever.

Four of these same Seven Arrows are symbolized by the Four Directions. They are the North, South, West, and the East. As you remember, these symbolize Wisdom, Trust and Innocence, Introspection, and Illumination. These are known as the Four Ways. The Mother Earth is the Fifth Mirror. The Sky, with its Moon, Sun, and Stars, is the Sixth Mirror. The Seventh of these Arrows is the Spirit. Among the People, this Spirit is spoken of as the Universal Harmony which holds all things together. All of us, as Perceivers of the Mirrors, are the Eighth Arrow.

Now what we shall do, all of us together, is to Look into another one of these Teaching Mirrors. The Name of this Mirror is the Singing Stone.

The young man you will see in this Mirror is yourself. If you are a woman, then you should change the symbol of the young man to that of a young woman.

From pp. 21-26 in *Seven Arrows* by Hyemeyohsts Storm Copyright © 1972 by Hyemeyohsts Storm. By permission of Harper & Row, Publishers, Inc.

"Sand blows endlessly into the rivers, yet they never fill up," Fire Dog said quietly.

The young man who sat across from him watched their tiny fire and moved uncomfortably.

"Whirlwinds great and small bring the sand. The small ones dance for our eyes, but the great ones are so vast that we can only feel a part of them. We experience them as the prairie wind," Fire Dog went on without looking up. "And so it is with our understanding."

"But why has the Power chosen to Teach us in this Way?" the young man asked. "If the Power is so all knowing, why then does he not just speak to us in a simple way that we can all understand?"

The fire illuminated Fire Dog's white braids. The old man sat quietly and unmoving. The young man watched him intently.

"There is a smile within your eyes, little brother," Fire Dog said softly, "because you think my silence is Trickery from the South."

"You understood my question, did you not?" the young man asked. "I did not wish my question to stake you down, but I have wondered for a long time about this. How is it that we are Taught by the Power in this manner?"

"Place your hand over the fire, Black Elk, and feel of its heat," the old man answered.

The young man placed his hand over the fire. He felt the heat grow within it, until he was forced to pull his hand away again. Then Fire Dog spoke once more.

"All that you feel and see, and the flowers these things open in your mind, are your answers," Fire Dog said, raising his voice. "The fire is life. It is warm, glowing with color, surrounded by the night, yet speaking of the day. It is promising, painful, dangerous, harmonious, visible at this moment, then moving into invisibility, alive, consuming, changing and finally disappearing into death. We ourselves are another fire upon this earth. We are part fire, and part dream. We are the physical mirroring of Miaheyyun, the Total Universe, upon this earth, our Mother. We are here to experience. We are a movement of a hand within millions of seasons, a wink of touching within *millions and millions of sun fires. And we speak with the Mirroring of the Sun."*

"And the whirlwind?" Black Elk asked. "Is this the Teaching Voice? If it is, I have found it silent, for it has taught me nothing."

"The wind is the Spirit of these things," Fire Dog answered, looking up. "The force of the natural things of this world are brought together within the whirlwind. Each tiny grain of sand is separate from the next, but they are all one thing within the whirlwind. Some people bite their own lips in anger when the whirlwind blows sand into their eyes. Others stand in awe or fear of these tiny swirls of wind and sand. Children run among them, and a few learn from them. We too are of this earth, and we too are brought together within these whirlwinds, these turning wheels. These teachers speak loudly to those of us who listen."

"Your Teaching is painted over my eyes," Black Elk said as he added more wood to the fire. "But I am torn with confusion. If these voices speak so loudly, how is it that I cannot hear them?"

"A Shield speaks softly, yet it can reflect for you many of the ways within these whirlwinds that you may hear them sing. Would you have a Shield painted for you?" asked Fire Dog.

"Yes," answered the Youngman. "What is this Story?"

"It is the Story of the Singing Stone," Fire Dog began.

One Day a Youngman of the People Approached his Grandfather and Sat with him.

"Grandfather," the Youngman said, "I Hear that somewhere there Exists a Singing Stone, and that when it is Found, it will Hold great Medicine for its Finder. Is this True?"

"It is True," answered the Grandfather. "Go to the North and you will Find it."

At the Next Sunrise the Youngman Began his Journey to the North. It was his First Day. He had not Gone Far Before he Saw what Appeared to be Smoke in the Distance.

"It is a Fire!" the Youngman thought. "I will be Burned!" He was very Afraid.

But he was Determined to Go On. That Evening he Saw that

the Smoke was the Rainbow Mist of the Sacred Mountains. That Night he Rested.

His Second Day he Walked Among the Pines of the Sacred Mountains until he Came Into a Broad Circle that was Green and Bright with the Sun. The Pines completely Circled this wonderful Place except to the East, which was Left Open. The Youngman Walked with the Sun all that Day to Cross this Place. That Night he Slept.

His Third Day the Youngman Came to a very beautiful Lake. Everything of the World was Mirrored in this Lake. The Flowers, Trees, Beings of the Prairie, Lodges of the People, the Mountains, the Day and Night Sky and the Sun were All Reflected there. This was the Medicine Lake. He Drank the Sweet Water from the Lake and Refreshed himself. Then he Rested.

His Fourth Day the Youngman Saw his Grandfather Sitting Upon a Stone Waiting for him.

"Welcome, Grandson," his Grandfather said.

The Old Man's Hair was White, and his Braids Touched the Ground. The Old Man Fed his Grandson Buffalo Meat, Roots and Berries of the Prairie, and Other wonderful Tasting Food. After the Youngman had Finished his Meal, his Grandfather Offered him a Gift.

"Here are my Braids," the Grandfather said, Cutting his Braids and Offering Them to the Youngman.

But the Youngman could not keep the Braids Upon his Own Head, even when he Tried to Tie Them there.

"Your Braids will not Stay Upon my Head," the Youngman said.

"Then Tie Them to your Waist," the Grandfather answered.

The Youngman did this. Then he said, "I have Come for the Singing Stone."

"The Singing Stone is not to the North" the Grandfather answered. "It is to the South."

The Youngman Returned to his Camp and he Rested. This was the End of his First Day. The Next Morning he Began his Journey South.

His First Day he Met a Mother Fox and her Kit Foxes. They Played with the Youngman and Walked with Him.

"Where are you Going?" the Kit Foxes asked him.

"I am Going to Find the Singing Stone," the Youngman answered. *"Can you Help me?"*

"Yes!" the Kit Foxes answered. *"Follow the River and you will Find the Singing Stone."*

That Night the Youngman Slept.

His Second Day the Youngman Met a Turtle. The Turtle Walked with him All that Day and Sang him Four Songs.

That Night he Rested.

His Third Day the Youngman was Walking Along the River and suddenly Found that he could Go no Further.

"Now what will I Do?" the Youngman asked Himself.

"I will Help you," answered Coyote. *"Just Follow me."*

Now the Youngman could See Coyote, and he Followed him Onto the Prairie. But soon the Trails Coyote Led the Youngman Upon Crossed and Recrossed and Ran Off in Every Direction.

"You have Tricked me!" the Youngman exclaimed.

"No," answered Coyote, *"I have not Tricked you. The River is right Over There."* The Youngman Looked, and he Saw that it was. That Night the Youngman Slept.

His Fourth Day the Youngmen Set Out again. He soon Became Confused and Discouraged.

"Nowhere can I See the Singing Stone!" the Youngman said, *"All that I can See Here are the Mountains, Prairie, Sky, Sun, Trees and Beings of this Place."* He Became very Angry.

Then the Youngman Heard a Voice saying, *"Look at Me!"* It was a beautiful Many Colored Dragonfly. It was Balanced Above the Moving Waters of the River.

And the Youngman Leaned Far Out Over the River to see his beautiful Brother more Closely.

"See how beautiful I am," said the Dragonfly. His Wings Reflected the Sun from Above, and also All that was Upon the Face of the Water.

The Youngman was Held within Wonder at the beauty he Saw Reflected there. Then he Lost his Balance and Fell into the River. He became Afraid and thought he would Drown.

"You have Tricked me!" he cried Angrily.

"No, little Brother," answered Dragonfly. "I have not Tricked you. You have only Fallen into the River. The Singing Stone is not to the South, it is to the West."

The Youngman Returned to the Camp and Rested. This was the End of his Second Day. The Next Day he Began his Journey West.

His First Day Walking West the Youngman Met a She Dog and her Puppies. They Walked with him All that Day. The Youngman Played with the Puppies and Found Comfort with Them. That Night he Rested.

His Second Day he Found a Place of Sweet Grass. It Took him One Full Day to Cross it, and that Night he Slept.

His Third Day he Met a Great Elk with Lightning Painted on his Shoulders and in his Horns. He Walked with the Youngman All that Day, and Sang him Four Songs. That Night the Youngman Rested.

His Fourth Day the Youngman Saw a Mouse, and the Mouse Saw the Youngman. The Mouse Began to Run and the Youngman Chased him All Day. He Chased the Mouse into a Cave. The Cave Became Smaller and Smaller until it was only Big Enough for the Mouse. The Mouse Stopped, Turned Around and spoke to the Youngman.

"Why are you Chasing me?" asked the Mouse.

"I am Seeking the Singing Stone," the Youngman answered.

"This is a Mouse Cave," the Mouse said to the Youngman, "The Singing Stone is not to the West, it is to the East."

This was the End of the Youngman's Third Day and he Went Back to the Camp and Rested. The Next Morning was the Beginning of his Journey East.

His First Day he had not Walked very Far before he Saw a beautiful Lodge in the Distance. And Old Woman met him at that Lodge and Fed him a great Meal which they Ate Together.

"What is this wonderful Lodge, Grandmother?" the Youngman asked.

"This is the Lodge of Gambling, Grandson," answered the Old Woman. He Rested that Night with the Old Woman.

His Second Day after he Left that Lodge he Saw Another Lodge in the Distance. It was even more beautiful than the

First, and it was Glowing Brightly. It was Painted with All the Colors.

Mahko, the Grandfather–Little Boy, Came Out and Greeted the Youngman.

"Welcome my Grandson," Mahko said, Taking the Youngman into his Lodge. "I have been Expecting you. Here, Come Sit with me and Eat this fine Buffalo Meat. It is my Gift to you."

After they had Eaten, the Youngman asked Mahko about the Painted Lodge.

"This is the Lodge of the Painted Arrows, the Sacred Arrows," Mahko answered.

The Youngman Slept there that Night.

His Third Day, the Youngman Came to a very Wide River. He looked Up and Down its Banks for a Place to Cross, but he could Find None. Then he Listened Closely to his Own Heartbeat, and he Felt his Heart say, "There is Always a Place for Children to Cross the River." So he Crossed, and as he Did So the Water never Came Above his Knees. That Night he Rested.

His Fourth Day, the Youngman Sat Upon a Hill. He saw in the Distance a Strange Camp. He Got to his Feet and Walked Toward the Camp. He Became very Afraid because the Paintings and Signs of the Lodges were Strange to him, and he could not Recognize them. The Closer he Came to the Lodges, the more he Felt the Bow of Tension Pulled within him. But he was Determined to Go On.

He Stepped into the Circle of Lodges. Then his Sisters, Mothers, Brothers, Fathers, Grandmothers, Grandfathers, Uncles, Aunts, and all his Relatives Came Out to Greet him, saying, "Welcome to our Counsel Fire, Singing Stone."

"And that cuts it off," Fire Dog said as he reached for his Pipe.

Everything you have just read within this Story, the Singing Stone, is a portion of the Teaching of the Flowering Tree. Now let us listen together, and we shall unfold some of the petals of this Flower.

The young woman in the Story you have just read goes to one of her grandmothers and asks her about the Singing Stone.

This grandmother is a symbol of one of the Six Directions, the North, South, West, East, and the Sky and the Earth. And she is, of course, also a symbol of the Teacher inside the young woman. The young woman begins to speak with this Teacher, which is herself.

"Go to the north," the grandmother tells the young woman in the Story. The Teaching here is that we must first look for those things that we seek within Wisdom.

The Story then speaks of the young woman's sunrise and her First Day. Both of these symbols represent mean new illumination, new beginning, or new questioning.

The fire in the story represents the Spirit of the People. It is also a symbol of the East.

Evening means the time of rest and dreams. It is also the entrance to the Introspective Way of the West.

Rainbows and rainbow mist symbolize the myths that we create here upon the earth.

On the young woman's Second Day, she walks across the place of the pines. This place of the pines, and the broad circle within it, are symbolic of that special place within each of us that is the lodge of all of our feelings, thoughts, fantasies, and dreams.

On her Third Day, the woman comes to a very beautiful lake. This lake is a symbol of the Mirror of Totality, or Wholeness. Some people perceive this Totality to be God, but this is only one of many Reflections within this Mirror.

Even as we unfold some of the Teachings her own Reflection, the grandmother, again. The meal the young woman eats with her Teacher is the food of learning, or information.

The grandmother's braids are symbols of experience. The fact that her braids touch the ground means that her experience touches the Natural Law of the Mother Earth. Her white braids represent experience within Wisdom.

This is the end of the young woman's first day. Within this day there have been four symbolic days representing the Four Great Directions, or the Medicine Wheel. The young woman in this Story has now visited each of these four directions within Wisdom, in order to find Balance within the Way of the North. This understanding can be shown with a simple drawing.

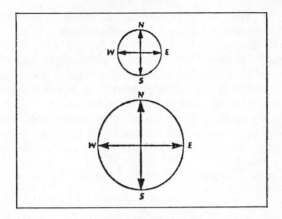

As you can see, above the greater Wheel there is a smaller Wheel to the North, in the Place of Wisdom. This Place of Wisdom is also Balanced within the Four Great Directions.

The young woman in the Story enters the Lodge of Wisdom by first experiencing the Place of the South within Wisdom. That is her First Day, her First Illumination. On her Second Day she visits the West, and on her Third Day she visits the North. On her Fourth and Final Day within Wisdom she visits the East, the Place of Illumination.

She has had full Intercourse with the North and is Illuminated by visiting all of its Four Directions, and experiencing their Balance.

The next morning in the Story is the young woman's Second Day within the Sun Dance Way. The Mother Fox and her Kit Foxes in the Story are symbolic of her peer group.

The Turtle she meets on her Second Day is symbolic of the Traditions of the Earth. The Four Harmonies, or Songs, the Turtle sings to her Reflect the Four Directions, and also Four of the many Harmonies that exist within Tradition. One of these Harmonies is the reality that a man and a woman must come into intercourse with each other in order to have children.

On her Third Day, a Coyote leads her from the river to the prairie. The prairie is a symbol of everyday life, and the river is a symbol of the Spirit of Life

The Coyote, as you have learned, is symbolic of the Gentle
Trickster. He represents all those things that trick us into
learning.

On the young woman's Fourth Day she meets the Dragonfly.
The Dragonfly is symbolic of the many things in our life that
hypnotize us, or cause us to fixate upon something.

Even as we unfold some of the Teachings within this Story,
you may possibly become fixated upon one particular understanding of a symbol that Reflects many meanings. It is for you
to move these symbols within your own experience so that you
may learn.

This is the end of the woman's Second Day. As you can see,

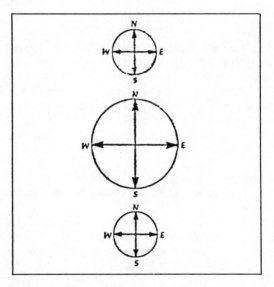

her Second Circle upon the Medicine Mirror Wheel is in the
South. The South, her Place of Trust and Innocence, is also
Balanced now within the Four Great Directions.

On her Third Day the young woman meets a He Dog and
his Puppies. This He Dog and his Puppies are the symbol
of Philosophy. The Dog also represents the servants among
the People.

Sweet Grass is burned for incense. It is the Earth symbol or Mother symbol. Within the Story the Sweet Grass is braided, meaning that these things of the Earth are within our experience.

The Lightning Elk is the symbol of Illumination within Introspection, and also of death and the power of rebirth. The Horns of the Elk symbolize lightning.

The Mouse, as you remember, perceives only whatever is very close to it. The Teaching here is that when we look too closely within our Introspection, we may sit too much within the circle of ourselves to perceive anything clearly. To perceive the Circle òf the West, we must first move outside of it.

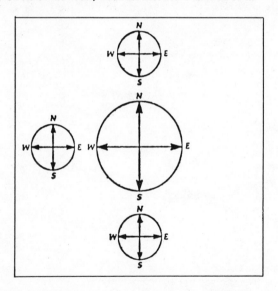

Now, as you can see, the young woman has visited the Third Circle of her Vision Quest. This Circle is within the West, and it is also Balanced within the West, within the Four Directions.

The East is the young woman's Fourth and Final Way. It is the Place of New Questioning, or Illumination. Whenever we experience the Illumination of the East, we will always have new questions.

The Lodge of Gambling represents the many gambles within the realities of our daily lives.

The Lodge of the Sacred Arrows is the Lodge of the Great Mirrors. It is the Heart of the People, and the Song of the Sundance Way Itself. The Lodge of the Sacred Arrows is also the Lodge of the Common Fire of the People.

Within each of our own Separate Lodges, deep within ourselves, there is also part of this same Great Medicine Fire of the People. The question we are always asking ourselves is, "Who am I," or "Who is this living spirit, this fire " The questioning of this mystery is the beginning of our search for Understanding of our Fire of Self, and it is a Circle that always leads us back to the Great Medicine Fire, the Lodge of the Sacred Arrows

RAY YOUNG BEAR

Four Songs of Life

1.) a young man

the blue rain
quiet in feelings
losing
nothing—showing no one
that i am cold
in this
earth
singing different songs
i never heard
from the same people
unable
to
create or remember
their own
songs to keep

The three poems by Ray Young Bear were published in the *South Dakota Review*, 9, no. 2 (Summer 1971).

2.) *an old man alone*

i remember well
my people's
songs.
i will not reveal
to anyone
that i
know these songs.
it was
intended for me
to keep
them in secrecy
for they are now
mine to die with me.

3.) *one who realized*

i sang
to the warm sun
and cold moon
this morning
and offered
myself
to the land
and gods
for them
to
teach
me
the old
hard ways
of living
all over again

4.) *he was approached*

a time
in sadness
within
the night
holding me
and comforting me.
here i am
being
taught
to be
a man
with life
and old sacred
songs to guide
me
and love me forever.

Morning-Talking Mother

... and my love of earth echoes through
the drowned trees inside brown
rivers deep of the winter,
and swelling birth along the woods.
i think of every day when time
grows, bringing the land against
my chest, and birds sing wildly over
my roof, waking the trees into
a sun. i walk over her head
and remember of being told
that no knives must pierce
inside her hair. there are paths
winding over her face and every
step is the same: the feeling of
one who is well known, one who knows
the warmth rising as morning-talking
mother. the preparation by her hands,

sprinkling the snow deeply inside
these valleys where the healing
medicine lifts, seeking birds
to speak of this gift,
where blankets form into hills
inhaling smoke-songs and the help of life.

Through Lifetime

white buffalo runs sleeping through snow and mixes
me into animal bones avoiding to be struck by daylight.

red colored evenings accepted the meat
thrown as offering over this mans old sky shoulders.
it seemed that while he skinned his kill
songs formed from hard life of earthmaker
and he sat with knife eager for his wind
to carry body scent other directions

there are in a house of many years
my shoulders held by fingers of the sun.
a mourning woman who sat in the middle
with rainwater eyes came as mother and wrapped
a red blanket over my ways and edges.

she combed my hair with wings of the seeking owl.
she sang of spring birds and how brown running waters
would be a signal to begin family deaths by witchcraft.
she showed me a handful of ribs shining a land day.

i leaned too close to the sun and felt the warmth of peyote
pumping my blood.
i washed my face with thunder-songs that low
and earth attached a vision of his long followers.
i listened to my sad hunting dogs tremble magically
of two crows chasing spirits away from fasting-ones.
i thought of an intended life and autumn came shyly
bearing songs but no gentle children.

woman of the horses sat in my circles.
she created fire burning only when boars cleaned the skin
of people from their teeth beside dreaming rivers.
the northern lights carried the meaning of life
far past the sufferings of night enemies.
old men inside rainbows offered no messages but whispered
of another existence closer to a prayer than tears

my raining-grandfathers walked speaking in choices
over the black skies.
i stood inside them and released my hand
which held my words gathered into parts of the earth.

SIMON J. ORTIZ

Kaiser and the War

Kaiser got out of the state pen when I was in the fourth grade. I don't know why people called him Kaiser. Some called him Hitler, too, since he was Kaiser, but I don't think he cared at all what they called him. He was probably just glad to get out of the state pen anyway.

Kaiser got into the state pen because he didn't go into the army. That's what my father said anyway, and because he was a crazy nut according to some people, which was probably why he didn't want to go into the army in the first place, which was what my father said also.

The army wanted him anyway, or maybe they didn't know he was crazy or supposed to be. They came for him out at home on the reservation, and he said he wasn't going to go because he didn't speak good English. Kaiser didn't go to school more than just the first or second grade. He said what he said in Indian and his sister said it in English for him. The army men, somebody from the county draft board, said they'd teach him English, don't worry about it, and how to read and write and give him clothes and money when he got out of the army so that he could start regular as any American. Just like anybody else, and they threw in stuff about how it would be good for our tribe and the people of the U.S.A.

Well, Kaiser, who didn't understand that much English anyway, listened quietly to his sister telling him what the army draft-board men were saying. He didn't ask any questions, just once in a while said, "Yes," like he'd been taught to say in the first grade. Maybe some of the interpretation was lost the way his sister was doing it, or maybe he went nuts like some people said he did once in a while because the next thing he did was to bust out the door and start running for Black Mesa.

The draft-board men didn't say anything at first and then

they got pretty mad. Kaiser's sister cried because she didn't want Kaiser to go into the army but she didn't want him running out just like that either. She had gone to the Indian school in Albuquerque, and she learned that stuff about patriotism, duty, honor—even if you were said to be crazy.

At about that time, their grandfather, Faustin, cussed in Indian at the draft-board men. Nobody had noticed when he came into the house, but there he was, fierce-looking as hell as usual, although he wasn't fierce at all. Then he got mad at his granddaughter and the men, asked what they were doing in his house, making the women cry and not even sitting down like friendly people did. Old Faustin and the army confronted each other. The army men were confused and getting more and more nervous. The old man told the girl to go out of the room and he'd talk to the army himself, although he didn't speak a word of English except "goddammey" which didn't sound too much like English but he threw it in once in a while anyway.

Those army men tried to get the girl to come back, but the old man wouldn't let her. He told her to get to grinding corn or something useful. They tried sign language and when Faustin figured out what they were waving their hands around for, he laughed out loud. He wouldn't even take the cigarettes offered him, so the army men didn't say anything more. The last thing they did though was give the old man a paper which they didn't try to explain what it was for. They probably hoped it would get read somehow.

Well, after they left, the paper did get read by the girl, and she told Faustin what it was about. The law was going to come and take Kaiser to jail because he wouldn't go into the army by himself. Grandfather Faustin sat down and talked quietly to himself for a while and then he got up to look for Kaiser.

Kaiser was on his way home by then, and his grandfather told him what was going to happen. They sat down by the side of the road and started to make plans. Kaiser would go hide up on Black Mesa and maybe go up all the way to Brushy Mountain if the law really came to poking around seriously. Faustin would take him food and tell him the news once in a while.

Everybody in the village knew what was going on pretty soon. Some approved, and some didn't. Some thought it was pretty funny. My father, who couldn't go in the army even if he wanted to because there were too many of us kids, laughed about it for days. The people who approved of it and thought it funny were the ones who knew Kaiser was crazy and that the army must be even crazier. The ones who disapproved were mostly those who were scared of him. A lot of them were the parents or brothers of girls who they must have suspected of liking Kaiser. Kaiser was pretty good-looking and funny in the way he talked for a crazy guy. And he was a hard worker. He worked every day out in the fields or up at the sheep camp for his parents while they were alive and for his sister and nephew and grandfather. These people, who were scared of him and said he should have gone into the army perhaps it'll do him good, didn't want him messing around their daughters or sisters which they said he did from time to time. Mostly these people were scared he would do something, and there was one too many nuts around in the village anyway, they said.

My old man didn't care though. He was buddies with Kaiser. When there was a corn dance up at the community hall, they would have a whole lot of fun singing and laughing and joking, and once in a while when someone brought around a bottle or two they would really get going and the officers of the tribe would have to warn them to behave themselves.

Kaiser was okay, though. He came around home quite a lot. His own kinfolks didn't care for him too much because he was crazy, and they didn't go out of their way to invite him to eat or spend the night when he dropped by their homes and it happened to get dark before he left. My mother didn't mind him around. When she served him something to eat, she didn't act like he was nuts, or supposed to be; she just served him and fussed over him like he was a kid which Kaiser acted like a lot of the time. I guess she didn't figure a guy who acted like a kid was crazy.

Right after we finished eating, if it happened to be supper, my own grandfather, who was a medicine man, would talk to him and to all of us kids who were usually paying only half attention. He would tell us advice, about how the world was, how each person, everything, was important. And then he would tell us stories about the olden times. Legends mostly, about the katzina, Spider Woman, where our hano, people, came from. Some of the stories were funny, some sad, and some pretty boring. Kaiser would sit there, not saying anything except "Eheh," which is what you're supposed to say once in a while to show that you're listening to the olden times.

After half of us kids were asleep, grandfather would quit talking, only Kaiser wouldn't want him to quit and he'd ask for more, but grandfather wouldn't tell any more. What Kaiser would do was start telling himself about the olden times. He'd lie on the floor in the dark, or sometimes up on the roof which was where he'd sleep in the summer, talking. And sometimes he'd sing, which is also part of the old times. I would drift off to sleep just listening to him.

Well, he didn't come around home after he went up on Black Mesa. He just went up there and stayed there. The law, which was the county sheriff, an officer, and the Indian agent from the Indian Affairs office in Albuquerque, came out to get him, but nobody would tell them where he was. The law had a general idea where he was, but that didn't get them very far because they didn't know the country around Black Mesa. It's rougher than hell up here, just a couple of sheep camps in a lot of country.

The Indian agent had written a letter to the officers of the tribe that they would come up for Kaiser on a certain day. There were a lot of people waiting for them when they drove up to the community meeting hall. The county sheriff had a bulging belly and he had a six-shooter strapped to his hip. When the men standing outside the community hall saw him step out of the government car, they made jokes. Just like the Long Ranger, someone said. The law didn't know what they were laughing about, and they said, Hello, and paid no attention to what they couldn't understand.

Faustin was among them. But he was silent and he smoked a roll-your-own. The agent stopped before him, and Faustin took a slow drag on his roll-your-own but he didn't look at the man.

"Faustin, my old friend," the agent said. "How are you?"

The old man didn't say anything. He let the tobacco smoke out slowly and looked straight ahead. Someone in the crowd told Faustin what the agent had said, but the old man didn't say anything at all.

The law thought he was praying or that he was a wise man contemplating his answer, the way he was so solemn-like, so they didn't press him. What Faustin was doing was ignoring the law. He didn't want them to talk with him. He turned to a man at his side.

"Tell this man I do not want to talk. I can't understand what they are saying in American anyway. And I don't want anyone to tell me what they say. I'm not interested." He looked at the government then, and he dismissed their presence with his indignation.

"The old man isn't gonna talk to you," someone said.

The agent and sheriff big belly glared at the man. "Who's in charge around here?" the sheriff said.

The Indians laughed. They joked by calling each other big belly. The governor of the tribe and two chiefs soon came. They greeted the law, and then they went into the meeting hall to confer about Kaiser.

"Well, have you brought Kaiser?" the Indian agent asked, although he saw that they hadn't and knew that they wouldn't.

"No," the governor said. And someone interpreted for him. "He will not come."

"Well, why don't you bring him? If he doesn't want to come, why don't you bring him? A bunch of you can bring him," the agent said. He was becoming irritated.

The governor, chiefs and men talked to each other. One old man held the floor a while, until others got tired of him telling about the old times and how it was and how the Americans had said a certain thing and did another and so forth. Someone said, "We can bring him. Kaiser should come by himself anyway. Let's go get him." He was a man who didn't like Kaiser. He looked around carefully when he got through speaking and sat down.

"Tell the Americans that is not the way," one of the chiefs said. "If our son wants to meet these men he will come." And the law was answered with the translation.

"I'll be a son of a bitch," the sheriff said, and the Indians laughed quietly. He glared at them and they stopped. "Let's go get him ourselves," he continued.

The man who had been interpreting said, "He is crazy."

"Who's crazy?" the sheriff yelled, like he was refuting an accusation. "I think you're all crazy."

"Kaiser, I think he is crazy," the interpreter said like he was ashamed of saying so. He stepped back, embarrassed.

Faustin then came to the front. Although he said he didn't want to talk with the law, he shouted, "Go get Kaiser yourself. If he's crazy, I hope he kills you. Go get him."

"Okay," the agent said when the interpreter finished. "We'll go get him ourselves. Where is he?" The agent knew no one would tell him, but he asked it anyway.

Upon that, the Indians assumed the business that the law came to do was over, and that the law had resolved what it came to do in the first place. The Indians began to leave.

"Wait," the agent said. "We need someone to go with us. He's up on Black Mesa, but we need someone to show us where."

The men kept on leaving. "We'll pay you. The government will pay you to go with us. You're deputized," the agent said. "Stop them, Sheriff," he said to the county sheriff, and the sheriff yelled, "Stop, come back here," and put a hand to his six-shooter. When he yelled, some of the Indians looked at him to laugh. He sure looked funny and talked funny. But some of them came back. "All right, you're deputies, you'll get paid," the sheriff said. Some of them knew what that meant, others weren't too sure. Some of them decided they'd come along for the fun of it.

The law and the Indians piled into the government car and a pickup truck which belonged to one of the deputies who was assured that he would get paid more than the others.

Black Mesa is fifteen miles back on the reservation. There are dirt roads up to it, but they aren't very good, nobody uses them except sheep herders and hunters in the fall. Kaiser knew what he was doing when he went up there, and he probably saw them when they were coming. But it wouldn't have made any difference because when the law and the deputies come up to the foot of the mesa, they still weren't getting anywhere. The deputies, who were still Indians too, wouldn't tell or didn't really know where Kaiser was at the moment. So they sat for a couple hours at the foot of the mesa, debating what should be done. The law tried to get the deputies to talk. The sheriff was boiling mad by this time, getting madder too, and he was for persuading one of the deputies into telling where Kaiser was exactly. But he reasoned the deputy wouldn't talk being that he was Indian too, and so he shut up for a while. He had figured out why the Indians laughed so frequently even though it was not as loud as before they were deputized.

Finally, they decided to walk up Black Mesa. It's rough going and when they didn't know which was the best way to go up they found it was even rougher. The real law dropped back one by one to rest on a rock or under a piñon tree until only the deputies were left. They watched the officer from the Indian Affairs office sitting on a fallen log some yards back. He was the last one to keep up so far, and he was unlacing his shoes. The deputies waited patiently for him to start again and for the others to catch up.

"It's sure hot," one of the deputies said.

"Yes, maybe it'll rain soon," another said.

"No, it rained for the last time last month, maybe next year."

"Snow then," another said.

They watched the sheriff and the Indian agent walking toward them half a mile back. One of them limped.

"Maybe the Americans need a rest," someone said. "We walked a long ways."

"Yes, they might be tired," another said. "I'll go tell that one that we're going to stop to rest," he said and walked back to the law sitting on the log. "We gonna stop to rest," he told the law. The law didn't say anything as he massaged his feet. And the deputy walked away to join the others.

They didn't find Kaiser that day or the next day. The deputies said they could walk all over the mesa without finding him for all eternity, but they wouldn't find him. They didn't mind walking, they said. As long as they got paid for their time, their crops were already in, and they'll just hire someone to haul winter wood for them now that they had the money. But they refused to talk. The ones who wanted to tell where Kaiser was, if they knew, didn't say so out loud, but they didn't tell anyway so it didn't make any difference. They were too persuaded by the newly found prosperity of employment.

The sheriff, exhausted by the middle of the second day of walking the mesa, began to sound like he was for going back to Albuquerque. Maybe Kaiser'd come in by himself, he didn't see any sense in looking for some Indian anyway just to get him into the army. Besides, he'd heard the Indian was crazy. When the sheriff had first learned the Indian's name was Kaiser he couldn't believe it, but he was assured that wasn't his real name, just something he was called because he was crazy. But the sheriff didn't feel any better or less tired, and he was getting jumpy about the crazy part.

At the end of the second day, the law decided to leave. Maybe we'll come back, they said; we'll have to talk this over with the Indian Affairs officials, maybe it'll be all right if that Indian didn't have to be in the army after all. And they left. The sheriff, his six-shooter off his hip now, was pretty tired out, and he didn't say anything.

The officials for the Indian Affairs didn't give up though. They sent back some more men. The county sheriff had decided it wasn't worth it, besides he had a whole county to take care of. And the Indians were deputized again. More of them volunteered this time, some had to be turned away. They had figured out how to work it: they wouldn't have to tell, if they knew, where Kaiser was. All they would have to do was walk and say from time to time, "Maybe he's over there by that canyon. Used to be there was some good hiding places back when the Apache and Navaho were raising hell." And some would go over there and some in the other direction, investigating good hiding places. But after camping around Black Mesa for a week this time, the Indian Affairs gave up. They went by Faustin's house the day they left for Albuquerque and left a message: the government would wait and when Kaiser least expected it, they would get him and he would have to go to jail.

Kaiser decided to volunteer for the army. He had decided to after he had watched the law and the deputies walk all over the mesa. Grandfather Faustin had come to visit him up at one of the sheep camps, and the old man gave him all the news at home and then he told Kaiser the message the government had left.

"Okay," Kaiser said. And he was silent for a while and nodded his head slowly like his grandfather did. "I'll join the army."

"No," his grandfather said. "I don't want you to. I will not allow you."

"Grandfather, I do not have to mind you. If you were my grandfather or uncle on my mother's side, I would listen to you and probably obey you, but you are not, and so I will not obey you."

"You are really crazy then," Grandfather Faustin said. "If that's what you want to do, go ahead." He was angry and he was sad, and he got up and put his hand on his grandson's shoulder and blessed him in the people's way. After that the old man left. It was evening when he left the sheep camp, and he walked for a long time away from Black Mesa before he started to sing.

The next day, Kaiser showed up at home. He ate with us, and after we ate we sat in the living room with my grandfather.

"So you've decided to go into the Americans' army," my grandfather said. None of us kids, nor even my parents, had known he was going but my grandfather had known all along. He probably knew as soon as Kaiser had walked into the house. Maybe even before that.

My grandfather blessed him then, just like Faustin had done, and he talked to him of how a man should behave and what he should expect. Just general things, and grandfather turned sternly toward us kids who are playing around as usual. My father and mother talked with him also, and when they were through, my grandfather put cornmeal in Kaiser's hand for him to pray with. Our parents told us kids to tell Kaiser good-bye and good luck and after we did, he left.

The next thing we heard was that Kaiser was in the state pen.

Later on, some people went to visit him up at the state pen. He was okay and getting fat, they said, and he was getting on okay with everybody and the warden told them. And when someone had asked Kaiser if he was okay, he said he was fine and he guessed he would be American pretty soon being that he was around them so much. The people left Kaiser some home-baked bread and dried meat and came home after being assured by the warden that he'd get out pretty soon, maybe right after the war. Kaiser was a model inmate. When the visitors got home to the reservation, they went and told Faustin his grandson was okay, getting fat and happy as any American. Old Faustin didn't have anything to say about that.

Well, the war was over after a while. Faustin died sometime near the end of it. Nobody had heard him mention Kaiser at all. Kaiser's sister and nephew were the only ones left at their home. Sometimes someone would ask about Kaiser, and his sister and nephew would say, "Oh, he's fine. He'll be home pretty soon, right after the war." But after the war was over, they just said he was fine.

My father and a couple of other guys went down to the Indian Affairs office to see what they could find out about Kaiser. They were told that Kaiser was going to stay in the pen longer now because he had tried to kill somebody. Well, he just went crazy one day, and he made a mistake so he'll just have to stay in for a couple more years or so, the Indian Affairs said. That was the first anybody heard of Kaiser trying to kill somebody, and some people said why the hell didn't they put him in the army for that like they wanted to in the first place. So Kaiser remained in the pen long after the war was over and most of the guys who had gone into the army from the tribe had come home. When he was due to get out, the Indian Affairs sent a letter to the governor and several men from the village went to get him.

My father said Kaiser was quiet all the way home on the bus. Some of the guys tried to joke with him, but he just wouldn't laugh or say anything. When they got off the bus at the highway and began to walk home, the guys broke into song, but that didn't bring Kaiser around. He kept walking quiet and reserved in his gray suit. Someone joked that Kaiser probably owned the only suit in the whole tribe.

"You lucky so and so. You look like a rich man," the joker

said. The others looked at him sharply and he quit joking, but Kaiser didn't say anything.

When they reached home, his sister and nephew were very happy to see him. They cried and laughed at the same time, but Kaiser didn't do anything except sit at the kitchen table and look around. My father and the other guys gave him advice and welcomed him home again and left.

After that, Kaiser always wore his gray suit. Every time you saw him, he was wearing it. Out in the fields or at the plaza watching the katzina, he wore the suit. He didn't talk much any more, my father said, and he didn't come around home any more either. The suit was getting all beat-up looking, but he just kept on wearing it so that some people began to say that he was showing off.

"That Kaiser," they said, "he's always wearing this suit, just like he was an American or something. Who does he think he is anyway?" And they'd snicker, looking at Kaiser with a sort of envy. Even when the suit was torn and soiled so that it hardly looked anything like a suit, Kaiser wore it. And some people said, "When he dies, Kaiser is going to be wearing his suit." And they said that like they wished they had gotten a suit like Kaiser's.

Well, Kaiser died, but without his gray suit. He died up at one of his distant relatives' sheep camps one winter. When someone asked about the suit, they were told by Kaiser's sister that it was rolled up in some newspaper at their home. She said that Kaiser had told her, before he went up to the sheep camp, that she was to send it to the government. But, she said, she couldn't figure out what he meant, whether Kaiser had meant the law or somebody, maybe the state pen or the Indian Affairs.

The person who asked about the suit wondered about this Kaiser's instructions. He couldn't figure out why Kaiser wanted to send a beat-up suit back. And then he figured, well, maybe that's the way it was when you either went into the state pen or the army and became an American.

Bibliography

Amos Bad Heart Bull; and Blish, Helen. *A Pictographic History of the Oglala Sioux.* Lincoln, Nebraska, 1968.

Armstrong, Virginia I., ed. *I Have Spoken: American History through the Voices of the Indians.* Chicago, 1971.

Benedict, Ruth. *Patterns of Culture.* Boston, 1934; New York, 1946.

Berger, Thomas. *Little Big Man.* New York, 1964.

Bierhorst, John, ed. *In the Trail of the Wind: American Indian Poems and Ritual Orations.* New York, 1971.

Bourne, Edward G., ed. *Narratives of the Career of Hernando de Soto in the Conquest of Florida, as Told by a Knight of Elvas and in a Relation by Luys Hernandez de Biedma, Factor of the Expedition.* Translated by Buckingham Smith. 2 vols. New York, 1922.

Brandon, William. *The Magic World: American Indian Songs and Poems.* New York, 1971.

Brown, Dee. *Bury My Heart at Wounded Knee.* New York, 1970.

Castaneda, Carlos. *A Separate Reality: Further Conversations with Don Juan.* New York, 1971.

————. *Journey to Ixtlan.* New York, 1972.

————. *The Teachings of Don Juan: A Yaqui Way of Knowledge.* Berkeley, 1968.

Colden, Cadwallader. *The History of the Five Indian Nations.* London, 1727, 1747; Ithaca, New York, 1964.

Converse, Harriet M. "Myths and Legends of the New York State Iroquois." *New York State Museum Bulletin 125,* edited by Arthur C. Parker, Albany, 1908, pp. 5–195.

Curtis, Natalie. *The Indians' Book.* New York, 1923.

DeLaguna, Frederica. *The Story of a Tlingit Community.* Washington, 1960.

Deloria, Vine, Jr. *Custer Died for Your Sins: An Indian Manifesto.* New York, 1969.

————. *We Talk, You Listen: New Tribes, New Turf.* New York, 1970.

Densmore, Frances. *The American Indians and Their Music.* New York, 1926.

Devereux, George. *Reality and Dream: Psychotherapy of a Plains Indian.* Garden City, New York, 1969.

Diaz del Castillo, Bernal. *The Discovery and Conquest of New Spain.* Translated by A. P. Maudslay. London, 1928.

Driver, Harold E. *Indians of North America.* Rev. ed., Chicago, 1969.

Drucker, Philip. *Cultures of the North Pacific Coast.* San Francisco, 1965.

Farb, Peter. *Man's Rise to Civilization as Shown by the Indians of North America from Primeval Times to the Coming of the Industrial State.* New York, 1968.

Forbes, Jack D., ed. *The Indian in America's Past*. Englewood Cliffs, New Jersey, 1964.

Grinnell, George B. *Blackfoot Lodge Tales*. New York, 1920; Lincoln, Nebraska, 1962.

Hagan, William T. *American Indians*. Chicago, 1961.

Hewitt, J. N. B. "Iroquoian Cosmology." *43rd Annual Report of the Bureau of American Ethnology, 1925–26*. Washington, 1928.

Hodge, Frederick W., ed. *Handbook of American Indians North of Mexico*. 2 vols. Washington, 1907, 1910; New York, 1965.

Hyde, George. *Red Cloud's Folk*. Norman, Oklahoma, 1937.

Hyemeyohsts Storm. *Seven Arrows*. New York, 1972.

Jackson, Helen H. *A Century of Dishonor*. New York, 1881.

Jacobs, Melville. *The Content and Style of an Oral Literature: Clackamas Chinook Myths and Texts*. Chicago, 1959.

———. *Northwest Sahaptin Texts*. Columbia University Contributions in Anthropology. Vol. 19, part I. New York, 1934.

James Edwin, ed. *John Tanner's Narrative of His Captivity Among the Ottawa and Ojibwa Indians*, in Paul Radin, ed., Occasional Papers of the Sutro Branch of the California State Library. Reprint Series No. 20. San Francisco, 1940.

Jenkins, Paul. "Custer's Last Stand."

La Farge, Oliver. *Laughing Boy*. Boston, 1929.

———. *A Pictorial History of the American Indian*. New York, 1956.

Lincoln, Charles, ed. "A Narrative of the Captivity and Restauration of Mrs. Mary Rowlandson." *Narratives of the Indian Wars (1675-1699)*. New York, 1913.

Luther Standing Bear. *Land of the Spotted Eagle*. Boston and New York, 1933.

Macgregor, Gordon. *Warriors without Weapons*. Chicago, 1946.

McLuhan, T. C., ed. *Touch the Earth*. New York, 1971.

McMaster, John B., ed. *History of the Expedition of Lewis and Clark*. 2 vols. New York, 1922.

McWhorter, L. V. *Hear Me, My Chiefs! Nez Perce History and Legend*. Caldwell, Idaho, 1952.

Marquis, Thomas, ed. *Wooden Leg: A Warrior Who Fought Custer*. Minneapolis, 1931; Lincoln, Nebraska, 1962.

Mead, Margaret. *The Changing Culture of an Indian Tribe*. New York, 1932, 1966.

———, ed. *Cooperation and Competition among Primitive Peoples*. Rev. ed., Boston, 1961.

Melville, Herman. *The Confidence-Man*. New York, 1857.

Miller, Polly; and Miller, Leon. *Lost Heritage of Alaska*. Cleveland, 1967.

Momaday, N. Scott. *The Way to Rainy Mountain*. Albuquerque, 1969.

Mooney, James. *Myths of the Cherokee. 19th Annual Report of the Bureau of American Ethnology, 1897–98*. Part I. Washington, 1900.

Neihardt, John. *Black Elk Speaks*. New York, 1932; Lincoln, Nebraska, 1961.

O'Bryan, Aileen. *The Díné: Origin Myths of the Navaho Indians. Bureau of American Ethnology, Bulletin 163.* Washington, 1956.

Ortiz, Simon J. "Kaiser and the War." New Mexico Quarterly, 1969.

Pattee, Fred Lewis, ed. *The Poems of Philip Freneau.* 3 vols. Princeton, New Jersey, 1902–1907.

Parkman, Francis. *The Conspiracy of Pontiac.* 2 vols. Boston, 1851.

Pearce, Roy H; and Miller, J. H., eds. *The Savages of America: A Study of the Indian and the Idea of Civilization.* Baltimore, 1965.

Radin, Paul. *The Autobiography of a Winnebago Indian.* New York, 1920, 1963.

———. *Primitive Man as Philosopher.* New York, 1927; rev. ed., New York, 1957.

———. *The Trickster: A Study in American Indian Mythology.* New York, 1956.

Ray Young Bear. "Four Songs of Life," "Morning-Talking Mother," "Through Lifetime." *South Dakota Review* 9 (Summer 1971), 36–40.

Thompson, Harold W. *Body, Boots, and Britches: Folktales, Ballads, and Speech from Country New York.* Philadelphia, 1939; New York, 1967.

Thompson, Laura; and Joseph, Alice. *The Hopi Way.* Chicago, 1944.

Thorpe, Thomas B. "The Disgraced Scalp Lock." *The Spirit of the Times* 12 (1842), 229, 230.

Snyder, Gary. *Earth House Hold.* New York, 1969.

Speck, Frank G. "Penobscot Tales and Religious Beliefs." *Journal of American Folklore* 48 (January–March 1935), 1–107.

———. "Some Micmac Tales from Cape Breton Island." *Journal of American Folklore* 28 (1915), 59–69.

Steiner, Stan. *The New Indians.* New York, 1968.

Stephen, A. M. "Legend of the Snake Order of the Moquis, as Told by Outsiders." *Journal of American Folklore* 1 (April–June, 1888), 109–14.

Swanton, John R. *The Indian Tribes of North America. Bureau of American Ethnology, Bulletin 145.* Washington, 1952.

———. *Tlingit Myths and Texts. Bureau of American Ethnology, Bulletin 39.* Washington, 1909.

Wallace, Anthony F. C. *The Death and Rebirth of the Seneca.* New York, 1970.

Washburn, Wilcomb, ed. *The Indian and the White Man.* Garden City, New York, 1964.

Waters, Frank. *The Book of the Hopi.* New York, 1963.

Welch, James. *Riding the Earthboy 40.* New York and Cleveland, 1971.

Wilkins, Thurman. *Cherokee Tragedy.* New York, 1970.

Wilson, Edmund; and Mitchell, Joseph. *Apologies to the Iroquois; With a Study of the Mohawks in High Steel.* New York, 1959, 1960.